THE HISTORY OF THE INDIAN MOUNTAIN ARTILLERY

Our Trusty and Tireless Servant

THE HISTORY
OF THE
INDIAN
MOUNTAIN ARTILLERY

by

BRIGADIER-GENERAL C. A. L. GRAHAM
D.S.O., O.B.E., D.L., *p.s.c.*

With a Foreword by
FIELD-MARSHAL THE VISCOUNT ALANBROOKE
K.G., G.C.B., O.M., G.C.V.O., D.S.O., D.C.L., LL.D.
Master Gunner, St. James's Park

The Naval & Military Press Ltd

Published by

The Naval & Military Press Ltd
Unit 10 Ridgewood Industrial Park,
Uckfield, East Sussex,
TN22 5QE England

Tel: +44 (0) 1825 749494
Fax: +44 (0) 1825 765701

www.naval-military-press.com
www.nmarchive.com

In reprinting in facsimile from the original, any imperfections are inevitably reproduced and the quality may fall short of modern type and cartographic standards.

DEDICATED

TO OUR FRIENDS

THE INDIAN OFFICERS AND OTHER RANKS

WHO SERVED THE GUNS LOYALLY

FOR NEARLY A HUNDRED YEARS;

NOT FORGETTING OUR TRUSTY AND TIRELESS SERVANT

THE ORDNANCE MULE

Foreword

BY

FIELD-MARSHAL THE VISCOUNT ALANBROOKE
K.G., G.C.B., O.M., G.C.V.O., D.S.O., D.C.L., LL.D.

HAVING NEVER had the privilege of serving in the Indian Mountain Artillery, I feel poorly qualified to write a foreword for this book. I am, however, delighted to accept this honour and in doing so hope I may do justice to this excellent history.

The many and various branches of the Royal Regiment of Artillery have contributed in a multitude of ways to its prestige, traditions and high reputation. Amongst these the Indian Mountain Artillery can certainly claim to have played a prominent part.

With a life of close on 100 years, during which hardly a year passed without taking part in some form of war, punitive expedition or frontier engagement, it is probable that the Indian Mountain Artillery saw as much, if not more, active service than any other branch of the Regiment.

I think it can also claim to have fought in more different theatres than any other component. It is, at any rate, very revealing in the pages of this book to find it, not only continuously distinguishing itself on the North-West Frontier of India, but in addition taking part in hostilities in Afghanistan, Thibet, Burma, Assam, Malaya, Java, Persia, Mesopotamia, Egypt, Palestine, Gallipoli, West Africa, Abyssinia and East Africa.

During its long life, thanks to the exceptional standard of efficiency maintained by highly qualified officers backed by a loyal and soldierly body of native officers and other ranks, it built for itself throughout India, and especially on the North-West Frontier, a reputation second to none.

During the eight years I spent in India, prior to the First World War, I repeatedly came into contact with batteries of the Indian Mountain Artillery on manœuvres, exercises, and ceremonial parades. Those meetings remained clearly engraved in my mind, and left memories of deep admiration combined with a feeling of pride that we all formed part of the same great Regiment.

From the accounts in this history it is clear that the native personnel serving in these batteries took a high pride in their units well worthy of the best traditions of the Regiment. It is therefore a matter of deep regret that with the evacuation of India this very fine branch of the gunners saw the end of its direct connection with the Regiment.

Let us hope, however, that the Indian Mountain Artillery, now partly in India and partly in Pakistan, will continue to exist for many years to come whilst remaining proud of the traditions handed down to them and anxious to preserve them.

Apart from the great loss to the Regiment lies the personal loss of many British Officers and their native friends through the severance of those ties of loyalty and affection that bound them together.

The Royal Regiment of Artillery is indeed fortunate that Brigadier-General C. A. L. Graham has by this book ensured that the history of this very famous part of the Regiment should not become obscured by the passage of time, or even forgotten, but should on the contrary be preserved and for ever find its place in our Regimental History. He is to be congratulated for having given us such an excellent account of the many engagements which the Indian Mountain Artillery took part in, together with a useful background of the military events connected with those engagements. A most readable account has thus been built up for us which brings out the distinction and glory with which the Indian Mountain Artillery covered itself.

We owe him a great debt of gratitude for having undertaken this difficult and painstaking task and for accomplishing it with such success.

November, 1956   ALANBROOKE, F.-M.,
Master Gunner.

Preface

THIS BOOK IS PUBLISHED in the hope of preserving the remembrance of the deeds in peace and war of a little-known branch of Artillery, which for many years formed part of the forces of the Government of India.

Owing to the loss of many units records, this history is far from complete, and in some cases it is difficult to arrive at exact facts. No doubt justice has not been done to the exploits of all units and individuals and it is particularly unfortunate that complete lists of officers, of casualties, and of those awarded decorations are not available.

Frequent changes were made in the designation of batteries, but herein units are generally distinguished by their titles at the time of the Partition of India, at which point this story closes. In many cases their final names are similar to their original ones.

Since 1862 all the British officers of units have belonged to the Royal Artillery, so that it seems unnecessary to designate them as "R.A."

I am much indebted to the Committee of the Royal Artillery Institute for permission to use various articles published by them. Information has been taken from official histories and the *London Gazette*, for which I make due acknowledgment. Statements in units histories and war diaries have throughout been accepted as correct.

I am very grateful to the undermentioned officers, without whose help this book could not have been written:

Lieutenant-General Sir G. MacMunn.
Major-General H. A. Lewis.
Brigadier-General C. De Sausmarez.
Brigadiers: J. H. Birbeck, E. W. Chadwick, A. J. T. Farfan, E. W. Goodman, T. W. R. Hill, B. P. Hughes, J. W. Kaye, R. W. McLeod, A. H. Moberly, L. C. O. Pugh, C. D. Rawson, F. E. Spencer, F. le G. Whitting, J. H. Willans and G. de V. Welchman.
Colonels: R. A. Armstrong, J. F. Barrington, J. English, A. C. Fergusson, C. Reed, J. F. S. Rendall and R. J. Sims.
Lieutenant-Colonels: R. J. Awdry, J. M. Bryant, R. L. Carew, J. B. Chaplin, A. M. Colvile, W. G. Constable, W. J. Cooper, L. M. Davies, J. A. L. Deane, G. V. Dreyer, J. H. Edmond,

E. D. Garnett, L. F. Garratt, H. C. Gould, I. G. Hardie, G. A. Hassels-Yates, M. F. Kemmis-Betty, H. E. Kenyon, R. H. Hill, R. R. Hill, H. A. Kirby, G. L. Hughes, L. H. Landon, M. D. S. Laws, L. R. H. Leach, T. M. Luke, R. N. Lyons, G. P. MacClellan, A. MacGregor, H. H. MacKenzie, G. A. Rowley-Conwy, J. Y. B. Sharpe, H. S. K. Snowdon, M. R. Strover, W. H. Wilberforce and F. H. Lister.

Majors: R. T. Ashby, P. R. Bentley, G. R. Brocklebank, C. J. S. Burne, H. G. Croly, J. C. Edlmann, J. E. L. Furney, H. A. Hardy, J. F. Kenyon, D. Liddell, R. McCaig, W. H. McGowan, W. B. Milne, J. Nettelfield, L. H. Packard, E. L. Sawyer, G. H. Searle, G. L. Sopper, J. H. M. Stevenson, A. E. Tawnay, W. Todd, F. G. S. Thomas and T. M. Witherow.

Captains: P. L. Atkins, G. N. Elsworth and D. A. Warren.

Lieutenant: R. M. Hare.

Also to Lieutenant-Colonels B. C. Barford and C. E. C. Burton for their contributions, and to others who have described operations at which they were present. My thanks are also due to those who have lent photographs.

I very much appreciate the encouragement and assistance given me by Brigadier-General Sir James Edmonds, late R.E., an old friend in the 4th Division of 1914.

Campaigns in the first part of this history are insignificant compared with World War operations, but the energy and fighting spirit expended by all ranks in maintaining efficiency, discipline and fire effect was no less in the early days.

There existed another group of mule batteries which used the same equipment under similar circumstances to those narrated herein—the British Mountain Batteries—which had an official existence from 1889 onwards. Their history must be written elsewhere.

I have received much help from the librarians of the R.A. Institution, the R.U.S. Institution, the War Office, the Bodleian and All Soul's Libraries, for which I am very grateful.

And to Miss D. Sleightholme and Major F. G. S. Thomas for superlative and patient typing and re-typing, I cannot sufficiently express my thanks.

Finally, to Mr. A. L. Kipling, of Messrs. Gale & Polden, whose invaluable advice and great patience made the publication of the History possible, I tender my grateful thanks.

C. A. L. GRAHAM

Contents

		PAGE
FOREWORD	... ...	vii
PREFACE	... ...	ix

CHAPTER

I	THE FIRST NATIVE MOUNTAIN TRAINS	1
II	THE MUTINY TO THE SECOND AFGHAN WAR ...	19
III	THE SECOND AFGHAN AND THIRD BURMESE WARS	41
IV	CHITRAL AND TIRAH, 1895-1897	70
V	THE REARMAMENT PERIOD	100
VI	FIRST WORLD WAR, 1914-18	125
VII	NORTH-WEST FRONTIER, 1920-1935	217
VIII	NORTH-WEST FRONTIER, 1936-1939	244
IX	SECOND WAR	262
X	SECOND WORLD WAR—OVERSEAS OPERATIONS ...	273
XI	PARTITION	422
APPENDICES	... ...	425
GLOSSARY	... ...	451
ABBREVIATIONS	... ...	453
INDEX	... ...	455

List of Illustrations

OUR TRUSTY AND TIRELESS SERVANT	*Frontispiece*
	Facing Page
THE ABBOTTABAD GUN	32
TYPICAL MULE LINES, N.W. FRONTIER	32
THE FIRST MOUNTAIN GUN, 7-PR. R.M.L.	33
ASSEMBLING THE 2.5-INCH—THE SCREW GUN	33
10-PR. B.L. GUN LINE	124
A "KHUD" PARADE	125
CAPTAIN GHULAM MOHAMMED, SIRDAR BAHADUR	260
CAPTAIN KISHEN SINGH, I.D.S.M.	261
3.7-INCH HOWITZER IN ACTION IN BURMA, 1944-45 ...	376
3.7-INCH HOWITZER TOWED BY A JEEP, BURMA, 1945 ...	376
BAHUT-I-TAGRA	377
BIKANIR CAMEL BATTERY	377
HAVILDAR UMRAO SINGH, V.C.	397
IN ACTION WITH FOURTEENTH ARMY, BURMA, 1945 ...	416
3.7-INCH HOWITZER IN ACTION AT GRISSEL, INDONESIA, 1946	416

List of Maps

		Facing Page
1.	GALLIPOLI	134
2.	GERMAN EAST AFRICA	156
3.	PERSIA	184
4.	MESOPOTAMIA	192
5.	ETHIOPIA AND SOMALIA	284
6.	MALAYA	304
7.	BURMA	420
8.	NORTH-WEST FRONTIER, INDIA	424

CHAPTER I

The First Native Mountain Trains

TO MOVE GUNS over country impassable for wheeled vehicles must have been a problem for Gunners ever since the Seven Years War, when mobility on the battlefield became an accepted feature of field artillery. This problem would have been acute in our East Indian possessions.

There is a record of guns being moved by coolie transport as far back as the Bhutan Expedition of 1772, but this method has obvious disadvantages, although it still remains a stand-by for exceptional conditions. Gurkha battalions in Assam kept up coolie transport for 7-prs. of 150 lb. until well into the twentieth century.

The elephant has been a familiar feature in Indian wars from very early days. He carries a heavy load on his back (say 1,000 lb.), is sure-footed but slow-moving, and has been much used in the jungle where the going suits him and where he can easily be given his daily ration of 1,000 lb. of greenstuff. He is delicate and inclined to timidity. Elephants were used during the wars for the expulsion of the French from India and the hill wars against the Mahrattas, and reported on very favourably in Nepal in 1816. In the Bhutan War of 1864-5 all the artillery and ammunition was carried on elephants, and they were mobilized as recently as 1897 as pack animals for guns, but were not used in the field; they were only dispensed with for draught of heavy guns in 1901.

Bullocks were tried for carrying equipment in pack in the Bhutan War of 1864-5, but proved a complete failure, and the same result has attended more recent trials.

That uncongenial pack animal, the camel, has not been overlooked, but he is delicate and fails badly on slippery and rough surfaces. There is a record of a pack camel battery raised in 1819 by Captain I. Frith, Madras Artillery, for use in the Mahratta War. In each sub-division were three camels (one carrying a $4\frac{3}{8}$-inch smooth-bore howitzer on a pack-saddle), three camel drivers, four gun lascars and two European gunners on ponies. This unit was disbanded in 1821.

In 1845 3-pr. guns on camels accompanied Sir Charles Napier's Camel Corps in operations against the Bhugtis, after the conquest of Sind. Sir Charles reported that, in the desert, the camel carried a load of about 250 lb. most satisfactorily, provided he was given a ration above the standard. He also remarked, "An animal more unfitted for military purposes cannot be imagined." The Zambooruk, a very small gun carried in a swivel on a pack-saddle, and fired off the camel's back, can hardly rank as an artillery weapon.

Ponies have been in use for pack artillery work in some countries and have many merits; they are hardy, but are inclined to be fastidious about their rations.

The solution of the problem came from Spain, famous for mules. Their efficiency and endurance, combined with an intelligent and often endearing nature, provided the mountain artillery with a very faithful servant for a century. The mule is sure-footed, and no other animal can compare with him for carrying a load in the rough and precipitous country of the Frontier hills. He is not too particular about his rations, provided that he gets good water. This is not to say that other methods of transport have not been used when circumstances demanded it; sledges, boats, ekkas, mechanical transport, and aeroplanes, all have been used on occasion.

When Wellington's Army reached the Pyrenees at the end of 1813 in pursuit of the French, the need for artillery support from the heights was at once felt, and two half-brigades,* each of three 3-prs., were equipped with pack-saddles on mules and did good service with the Light and 6th Divisions. The gunners were Portuguese and the drivers British, and the unit was raised by Lieutenant W. L. Robe.† This was the first mountain battery in the British Army and, although it disappeared at the end of the war, a committee in London in 1826 advised the Master-General of the Ordnance that the 3-pr. bronze smooth-bore gun was suitable for mountain service. However, on the next occasion demanding mountain artillery, a R.A. battery of volunteers with the British Legion to fight the Carlists in North Spain (1836-1840) was equipped with 4⅜-inch smooth-bore howitzers and rockets. Complete details of mule loads, drill, gunnery, etc., were printed in what was in effect the first Mountain Artillery Drill Book. Coming into action, limbering up, etc., were carried out on the principles of later methods, but lashings were employed instead of straps. The battery acquitted itself well, and was broken up at Woolwich in 1840 after the end of the war.

Serving with this mountain battery in Spain, being at the time on furlough from India, was Lieutenant J. B. Backhouse, Bengal Artillery, whom we next hear of in 1840 in the First Afghan War as a captain of Bengal Horse Artillery. He was ordered to form a Native Mountain Train of six 3-pr. guns for service in Afghanistan

---

* The "brigade" of four or six guns was later termed "battery."
† Died of wounds after Waterloo.

with mule transport, pack and draught, and may well be called the Father of the Indian Mountain Artillery. The Train was in action almost daily after the Ghilzai rising, three guns being brilliantly handled by Captain Backhouse at the Jagdallak Pass and before the retreat to Jalalabad. The other three guns under Lieutenant Green, after the heavy fighting round Kabul, formed part of the Kabul garrison which tried to fight its way out to join our force then besieged in Jalalabad. It was overwhelmed and the guns were lost on the way.

Captain Backhouse and his guns saw the siege through and went on with Sir George Pollock's force to retake Kabul before returning to India. Captain James Abbott, Bengal Artillery, distinguished himself greatly in this campaign and during the siege, and we shall hear of him again. The Train was disbanded in 1843, but its achievements had impressed Bengal Army Headquarters, which assembled a committee at Jutogh in 1844 to report on mountain artillery. In 1853 as a result of this report a Native Mountain Train was ordered to be formed at Peshawar. Whilst these deliberations were going on much had happened.

Maharajah Ranjit Singh, whose frontiers were coterminous with ours along the River Sutlej, had been loyal to us, and after our setback in 1841 the Sikhs allowed us to mobilize our relieving army in Peshawar. Later on the reigning group of Sirdars began a policy of hostility and eventually invaded British India, bringing on the First Sikh War, which cost us very heavy casualties but resulted in a British victory after three months' fighting (1846). Peace in the Punjab was essential for our security in India, and a British Resident was appointed to the Court at Lahore, with a sprinkling of British officers and civilians labelled "Political Officers" put in to administer, and practically rule, large provinces in the name of the Sikh Durbar, as well as to watch the Frontier. In December, 1846, a Frontier Brigade of one light field battery and four infantry battalions and the Guides was ordered to be formed for "Police and General Purposes."

Discontent and anti-British fanaticism were unceasing and culminated in a rising leading to the Second Sikh War in 1849. The Sikhs, after a terrific struggle, were then finally conquered, and the East India Company was forced for its own security to take over the North-West Frontier line, which had never been under control by either Afghans or Sikhs. The line we took over from the Sikhs eventually became our administrative border line. It skirted the six districts of Hazara, Kohat, Peshawar, Bannu, Dera Ismail Khan, and Dera Ghazi Khan. There were about 700 miles of mountainous country to guard, from Hazara to Sind, and the Frontier Brigade was strengthened in May, 1849, to keep order in the Punjab and Trans-Indus provinces, or wherever it might be sent. The new establishment was five regiments of cavalry, five of infantry and three horse light field batteries.

In the interval between the two Sikh Wars, Captain James Abbott, Bengal Artillery, was sent as Commissioner to the Hazara District, and at the beginning of the revolt in 1848 he raised the country against the Sikhs and besieged the fort at Haripur. For this purpose he collected some local men as gunners to strengthen a detachment of artillery* borrowed from the Maharajah of Kashmir, and on the capture of the fort manned the fort guns (one 6-pr. and one 9-pr.) with these local men and some ex-gunners from the Sikh army, one of whom, Sa'at Ali, he appointed Subadar. Two guns from Haripur were present in 1848, on field service at Mangli Ravine, near Abbottabad, in an action against Sirdar Chattar Singh.

In September, 1850, six 3-pr. guns were received and forty-four syces enlisted prior to the entertainment of forty-four mules and two elephants. The Hazara Mountain Train had come into being officially: the first of the Indian mountain batteries and probably the first permanent mountain battery in the world. The establishment consisted of: 2 Native Officers, 3 havildars, 3 naiks, 54 gunners and 2 buglers, 1 darogah and 33 syces. The gun, trail, wheels and two pairs of ammunition boxes per gun were carried on battery mules; other ammunition boxes on hired mules. Each box contained sixteen round shot and four case. Saddles and pads were all made up in the unit, and are reported to have been very heavy.

On 2nd April, 1851, Lieutenant G. G. Pearse, Madras Artillery, was appointed to the charge of the Hazara Mountain Train in addition to his duties as Assistant Commissioner, under the supervision of Major Abbott, the District Commissioner. The unit was under the District Commissioner for all purposes, and remained at Haripur. It was not part of the Frontier Brigade.

The Train's first experience of active service came in December, 1852, when a force was mobilized against the Hassanzais in the Black Mountain, who form a section of the Isazai clan of Yusufzais and reside on both sides of the River Indus. As during the next century several expeditions had to be sent to the Black Mountain, a short description of that tract of country may be useful. This is a long narrow ridge averaging about 8,000 feet above the sea, with higher peaks and deep passes at intervals, about thirty miles long,

---

* See Appendix, page 430, and note at end of this chapter.

east of the Indus between that river and British territory to the north-west of Abbottabad. The whole of the upper portion of the ridge is thickly wooded, deep and narrow glens between large spurs hold the smaller villages; the larger villages are on the banks of the Indus. The Indus valley varies in width from a few hundred yards at Kotkai to nearly two miles at Palosi. There are about a dozen ferries, and the natives are experts at making the crossing on inflated skins. West of the Indus the hills rise gently and are under cultivation to the crest. The winters are severe, with heavy snowfalls.

The weapons of all the Frontier tribes at this time were swords, spears, jezails and matchlocks, without any artillery.

Two British Customs officials were travelling in British territory near the border line in November when they were murdered by some Hassanzais, and, as the tribe refused to hand over the murderers, summary punishment was carried out on the whole tribe. The force under Lieutenant-Colonel Mackeson was divided into three columns —the Hazara Mountain Train (two guns under Subadar Sa'at Ali) was with the Guides and 1st Sikhs in the right column under Lieutenant-Colonel R. Napier (later Lord Napier of Magdala). Major Abbott commanded the centre column of levies, and the left column was mostly comprised of Kashmir troops (Dogras) with Kashmir mountain guns. The reserve consisted of some regular troops which joined up with all the impedimenta for an ordinary march and which Lieutenant-Colonel Mackeson had been forbidden to commit to the mountain-top, so he moved these troops round to the west side between the mountain and the river, in rear of the enemy's position, and sent his three columns to the attack against the enemy manning the heights. Subadar Sa'at Ali handled his guns well in support of the infantry, and when our advanced troops found themselves too far ahead of their supports and had to fall back, the guns were ready to check the enemy's counter-attack.

This is not the last time in the history of the mountain artillery that we find the guns continuing to hold their position in action as a rallying-point for the infantry, and it should be remembered that gun ranges and musket ranges of the day were exceedingly short.

The guns advanced later in support of a second attack which carried the crest, and the force bivouacked in the snow after the other two columns had joined up. Many villages were burnt and the force retired, being closely followed up, but casualties were light.

A few days later the two guns of the Train crossed the river with some infantry to retake the fort of Kotla on the right bank. This was done without opposition, and the fort was handed back to the Khan of Amb, a friendly chief.

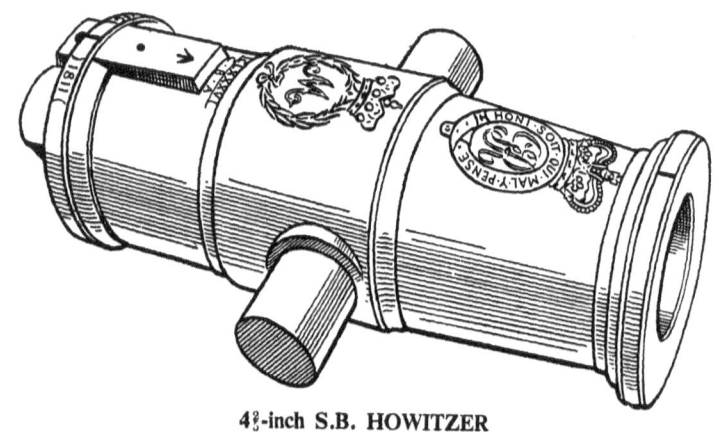

4⅖-inch S.B. HOWITZER

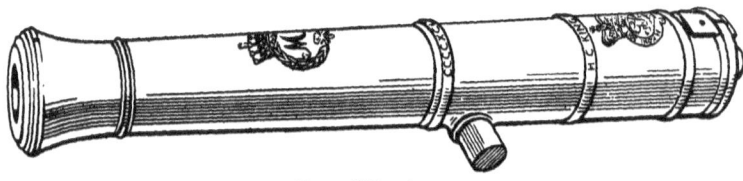

3-pr. S.B. GUN
M was monogram of the Earl of Mulgrave, Master-General of the Ordnance, 1810 to 1818

As already mentioned, the Peshawar Mountain Train was ordered to be formed at Peshawar in 1853, and Captain T. Brougham, Bengal Artillery, was detailed to raise it. His ordnance, four 3-pr. guns and four 4⅖-inch howitzers, arrived in January, and Captain Brougham bought the mules himself in Sind Sagar.

A European field battery of the Bengal Artillery, 2nd Company, 2nd Battalion, manned the Train, the drivers being native; but the following year an irregular company of native gunners was raised to replace the European gunners. The original strength of this company is not known, but it was increased in 1857 to: 1 subadar, 2 jemadars, 8 havildars, 8 naiks (including 1 drill naik), 3 buglers, 104 gunners. Driver establishment: 2 havildars, 2 naiks, 52 drivers first class, 62 drivers second class, 42 syces, 2 mochis, 6 store lascars, 4 cooks.*

---

* Native ranks of the Trains, and afterwards of the mountain batteries, bought their food from the unit bannia, who was controlled by a unit committee.

There is no record of Native Officers in this Train before October, 1854.

The "doing duty" officers, afterwards called 1st and 2nd Subalterns throughout the native mountain artillery, were all from the Bengal Artillery:

Lieutenant S. Stallard (afterwards Major-General).

Lieutenant Tyrwhitt Pulman. (An officer of this name had seen service with the Scinde Mountain Train.)

Lieutenant Bryce.

Lieutenant F. S. Roberts (later Field-Marshal Earl Roberts, V.C.), who was thirteen months in the Train before transferring to horse artillery.

Lieutenants Stallard, Pulman, and Roberts took part in the campaign against the Bori Afridis, 1853, where the Train had its first taste of active service. Before conversion, however, the field battery had a record of a previous campaign in this area in 1850, when it carried 9-prs. on elephants and two 5½-inch howitzers on one elephant.

There was a great deal of raiding and general trouble between Peshawar and Kohat when the road was first opened, and a punitive expedition, which included the Peshawar Mountain Train, was sent out under Colonel Boileau in November, 1853. During one long day's fighting all the Bori villages were set on fire after the inhabitants had been shelled out by the guns, and the latter took a prominent part with the rear-guard, which withdrew with great skill and brought all our troops safely into camp—a stern lesson which prevented trouble on the road for many years.

These new units of a new branch of artillery had no traditions to guide them, so they selected their own standard and chose the highest; a standard that has been maintained to the last. They had the advantage of being officered from the Bengal, Madras and Bombay Artilleries, whose pride was that their standard had always been as high as that of the Royal Regiment of Artillery, to which these Trains were transferred some eighty years later. In the field, their boast from the beginning was that they could take their guns wherever an infantryman could go with his rifle without using his hands and knees.

It is remarkable that native mountain artillery units have never included British non-commissioned officers in their establishments,* as did the Indian Presidency Artilleries and more recent

---

* This applies to combatant ranks. When equipments became more complicated (during the First World War) British fitters were attached to batteries until Indian fitters were trained.

native artillery units organized by the War Office, outside India.
At this time the Trains were armed with 3-pr. smooth-bore bronze guns, weighing 252 lb. (introduced about 1742), and 4⅞-inch smooth-bore bronze howitzers of 280 lb. The latter were first cast in 1728. This howitzer should not be confused with the 12-pr. howitzer, which weighed 3 cwt. and was too heavy for pack transport on mules. Both howitzers fired the same spherical common and diaphragm shrapnel shells, the 4⅞-inch howitzer using a smaller charge. The filled, common, shell weighed 9 lb. and shrapnel 11 lb. They had wooden bottoms riveted on to prevent damage to the bore on firing, and also to ensure that the fuse was on the side away from the charge. The fuses used with common shell were "Fuse, time, wood" (Boxers) and Pettman's L.S. percussion (a metal fuse). The shrapnel was used with the "Fuse, time, wood," and was intended to burst about 50 yards short of the target. The case shot (effective up to 300 yards) had a wooden bottom tacked on to the cylinder and slightly projecting below, the projection being hemispherical. The case shot for the 3-pr. was similar, but had a flat wooden base. The round shot were solid spheres of cast iron.

The gun carriage was made of wood, and the three-foot wheel weighed 66 lb.

Guns were fired by touching off with a port-fire* a quill tube filled with fine powder. Before the tube was inserted the cartridge was pierced with a steel pricker down the vent to aid ignition. The port-fire was lit from a slow match kept burning during action, or when an attack was expected. The copper friction tube was introduced in England in 1853 and taken into use in India a little later. Powder in the tube was ignited by pulling out a friction bar, thus setting fire to the cartridge. As the firing number was kneeling, the friction bar was withdrawn by a smart chop with the edge of the right hand on the stretched lanyard. It must be remembered that a cloud of white smoke accompanied each discharge of the gun and that smokeless powder was not available until the turn of the century. Fire tactics were of the simplest description, and fighting was generally on a small scale. These weapons were presumably not very accurate, but at this period the use of artillery in the hills had a great moral effect on the wild tribes of the Frontier.

Mention has been made of the three horse light field batteries of the Frontier Brigade. In accordance with the Government's policy

---

* The port-fire was carried on the nearside of the gun mules on the march, with the linstock; quick match and slow match were in the ammunition boxes. No. 5 was the firing number, and was responsible for cutting off the match with his knife and sheltering it in bad weather.

they were formed on 18th May, 1849, from personnel lately in the Sikh Artillery: *
No. 1 at Kohat, by Lieutenant W. Hay, Bengal Artillery;
No. 2 at Bannu, by Lieutenant H. Hammond, Bengal Artillery;
No. 3 at Dera Ghazi Khan, by Lieutenant D. McNeil, Bengal Artillery.
The designation "horse" was used for field batteries which were not drawn by bullocks.
No. 1 never became a mountain battery and was reduced in 1870. No. 2 originally consisted of four guns of Hafiz Bakhsh's troop and two guns of Fazal Ali's troop of the Sikh Durbar Horse Artillery, and served at the siege of Multan under Sir H. Edwardes. No. 3 was formed mainly of ex-horse artillery men of the Durbar Army. The batteries had a few European N.C.Os. after the manner of all native units of Bengal Artillery.

These batteries were armed with four 9-pr. guns and two 24-pr. howitzers, all smooth-bores, and they acquired in addition a 3-pr. gun and a mountain howitzer with some mules for pack transport. This ensured their not missing any of the operations that had to be frequently carried out on the Frontier. They came under the Punjab Irregular Force,* as the Frontier Brigade was called after the reorganization by Brigadier J. S. Hodgson, 15th February, 1851.

A system of draught transport as an alternative to pack in mountain artillery seems to have been in vogue from the beginning. Robe's guns certainly had such an arrangement. Apart from the field artillery parentage, to move in draught when and where convenient and thus give relief to the top-load mules seems to be a matter of common sense and was doubtless so regarded by everyone except the purists, who refused to consider any training not carried out in pack on the hillside. No details of the early mode of draught have come down to us, but no doubt light shafts were easily procured and connected the gun with a mule. The War Office produced shafts for the Abyssinian campaign which were very clumsy and never used. Another time a small limber was issued for use in an early South African campaign, but this too was unsatisfactory; another suggestion was the use of a curricle bar, tonga fashion, across a pair of mules. It was a difficult matter to get the weight properly balanced using only a single axle, and this led to undue wear on the pipe-boxes of the wheels, but no steps were taken for many years to produce wheels fit for draught.

The capital of the new province of the Punjab was Lahore, and cantonments as far as the Indus were occupied by units of the

* Hence PIFfer.

Bengal Army. In Peshawar was stationed a brigade of the Bengal Army to hold the main road to Kabul, and to strengthen the Punjab Irregular Force which was distributed at various points in the Frontier districts. This latter force was under the civil government of the Punjab and was used to quell all minor troubles at short notice without calling on the Regular Army. Law and order had to be kept; revenue collected from those who would rather fight than pay; punishment had to be inflicted on the tribesmen from the surrounding hills for frequent raids on our territory and as reprisals for attacks on our posts. The force also defended itself when attacked.

The main aim of these operations was not man-killing so much as collecting malefactors to hand over to the police, though of course there were often casualties on both sides. The smallest of these operations might consist of a battalion or less, marching all night, surrounding a village by dawn, and picking up the wanted men. Many times forces of one or more brigades were organized for larger operations, and the mountain artillery was always in demand for support. Without the perpetual activity of the Punjab Irregular Force in keeping order, the civil authorities would have been unable to carry out their beneficent and expensive public works for the advantage of the inhabitants—roads, railways, canals, etc.—that brought prosperity to a barren land. Furthermore, the army in India lived and trained in security behind the screen of the P.I.F. keeping the Afghans at arm's length. Units of this Force were complete in equipment and transport, and turned out at very short notice when required, and for the first twenty years or so of our rule were more or less continuously engaged. These experiences provided them with the best possible military training and they became the *élite* of the Indian forces and experts in mountain warfare. The life attracted the best type of officer, who learnt his soldiering with picked troops, and the greatest good fellowship existed throughout the Force, which made for practical liaison in the field.

The scene of most of the operations of the Punjab Irregular Force was the territory of the "Independent Tribes," who inhabited the district between the former Sikh frontier and the border of Afghanistan—at this time a vague and indeterminate boundary. The country was mountainous, rocky, and barren except for patches of cultivation to be found infrequently in the valleys. The struggle for existence in such a land produced men of great physical endurance: masterless and warlike, they brooked no control by Afghan, Sikh or, later, the British. They were all Mohammedans and transferred their hatred of the Sikh to the British.

A prominent trait was universal suspicion and distrust which prevented one tribe from combining with another in any but exceptional cases. Loyalty was non-existent, except to a mullah who, on occasion, could work up a following to a high pitch of fanaticism and self-sacrifice. Individual cases of loyalty to British officers by enlisted tribesmen were numerous, as well as loyalty to the Sirkar whose salt they had eaten, but as the years went on it became obvious that their general reliability was weakening.

Of education the tribesmen had none bar the minimum as taught by the village mullah. The Pathan, to give him his usual generic name on the Frontier, would fight to the death to preserve his village and surroundings from any influx of strangers.

He would never make a good neighbour, but his most unforgivable habit was that of raiding and looting villages in British territory, the inhabitants of which had acquired some prosperity by their own labour. Kidnapping rich Hindus he found irresistible, and as he could not keep any agreement and understood no law but force, force had to be used to deter him, though the Government only brought in armed pressure as a last resource.

Most, but not all, of the Pathan tribes had a habit of killing prisoners and wounded and afterwards mutilating them. It was said that the women helped in the latter work. The Afghans had a similar reputation, and it was a point of honour in Frontier warfare never to leave one of our men, dead or alive, on the battlefield.

The majority of the Pathans and the Afghans were of the same blood, and as little heed was given to Afghan laws as to British, but enforcement of penalties by the Afghans was probably more unpleasant, there being little to choose between Pathan and Afghan as regards cruelty and treachery.

From the tactical point of view, an almost insoluble problem was presented by the difficulty of driving home an attack on an enemy who seldom stood to fight, but had only to slip away over the hills to find sanctuary in Afghanistan. The Wazirs and the Mohmands were especially favoured in this respect: the former because their country marched with Afghanistan, and the Mohmands because they inhabited an area part of which was in British India and part in Afghanistan.

An enemy without a base, communications or any kind of permanent organization had complete freedom to appear or disappear as he thought fit, and the seizure of his crops and the destruction of his villages was the only way to obtain submission.

The tribal lashkar was an assembly of armed individuals carrying a few days' food, all fired with a fanatical hatred of the infidel and a fixed intention of leading a life of raiding and looting without interference. As every family had at one time or another a blood feud, the principle of killing without being killed was second nature to the Pathan, and perpetual practice gave him a distinct advantage over the civilized soldier.

The civil district of Peshawar consists of a wide level plain, broken only by deep ravines which intersect it in all directions, and well watered by the Swat and Kabul rivers. The district was never completely under control by the Sikhs and required stern measures by our administrators for some years.

The Mohmands, whose frontier is only about twenty miles from Peshawar, gave more trouble than any other tribe in the district. In August, 1854, a force, which included the newly-formed Peshawar Mountain Train, moved out from Peshawar to join another force at Michni with a view to collecting tribute which was two years overdue. Before returning it was decided to destroy three villages inhabited by hostile Mohmands just across the border, and during this operation "the infantry (1st Sikhs) were ably assisted by a well-directed fire from the mountain guns under Captain T. Brougham."

The Train was on service again six months later with a small force against the Aka Khel Afridis, south of the Bara river, who showed by a series of depredations and murders on our territory their dissatisfaction at having no share in the allowances paid to keep open the Kohat Pass. To put a stop to this the two villages concerned were destroyed, and an attack made on the Afridis who had taken up a strong position on the adjacent hills. About 8 a.m., after forcing the enemy to retire, the Commander commenced his withdrawal by sending back the Mountain Train, and under its protective fire the infantry fell back from crest to crest, followed by the enemy, who kept up a close attack. The Aka Khels were not allowed to resettle in their villages until they had accepted our terms, which included agreements for good behaviour in the future as well as heavy fines.

The Afridis, the Orakzais, the Waziris and the Mahsuds were the most turbulent of our Frontier neighbours. Internecine warfare and the raiding of Cis-Frontier villages featured largely in the lives of these tribesmen.

The Train was on active service with the mountain guns of No. 3 Punjab Light Field Battery in September of the same year against the Rabia Khel Orakzais, who had been very aggressive for some time making raids into the Miranzai Valley and killing British subjects. Operations were undertaken by Brigadier Chamberlain on the recommendation of the Deputy Commissioner, Kohat. Three fortified villages were surrounded at night by three columns, and the mountain guns were with the main body in support. The operation was successful in capturing the enemy's cattle and destroying the villages; and during the retirement, when a piquet was rushed as it was leaving a height, the infantry rallied on the two supporting guns and retook the position. The force returned to Hangu without further incident.

The Miranzai valley was neglected at the annexation, but later became part of the Kohat district at the request of the inhabitants, who nevertheless remained hostile to the Government and unsettled for years, committing raids and refusing to pay revenue. The valley was in fact an asylum for all the robbers and murderers of the district, and in April, 1855, a force moved into Upper Miranzai to fix revenue and show the flag. The force was attacked by some 4,000 ghazis on 29th April, but they were put to flight by a few cavalry and infantry. The force then returned to Kohat, but matters failed to improve as far as raids were concerned, and it was decided in 1856 to send a strong punitive force of 5,000 of all arms. This included detachments of the Peshawar Mountain Train, Nos. 1 and 3 Punjab Light Field Batteries, and five infantry regiments. A particularly refractory village named Torawari was surrounded and surprised, and, after the guns had fired some thirty rounds, the inhabitants surrendered their arms, and the thirteen "wanted" criminals, as well as some hostages to be held as security for a fine. Two sepoys wounded comprised our casualty list. The troops went on to camp in the Kurram valley where the same procedure produced some more "wanted" criminals, and the force returned to Kohat to be broken up after two months' operations, the success of which was largely attributable to the size of the force employed.

At this time, then, there existed the Hazara and Peshawar Mountain Trains at Haripur and Peshawar respectively, and Nos. 1, 2 and 3 Punjab Light Field Batteries, each with a division (later called "section"*) equipped for mountain work, at Dera Ismail Khan, Bannu and Kohat respectively. The two Trains were for local work under the orders of Commissioners of Districts, but the batteries formed part of the Punjab Irregular Force.

In 1856 the Government authorized the transfer of the Hazara Mountain Train to the Punjab Irregular Force, then commanded by Brigadier Chamberlain (later Field-Marshal Sir Neville Chamberlain), and the Peshawar Mountain Train was likewise transferred in 1858. Brigadier Chamberlain commanded this force with distinction for nine years.

---

* This is a sub-unit of a battery, comprising two guns or howitzers with teams and detachments, forming a subaltern's command.

Very few administrative orders have come down to us from the early days. One order (1855) laid down that the composition of the Trains was to be half Mohammedan and half Hindu, and a later one that Pathans were not to be enlisted in the artillery. Up to the time of the First World War batteries carried out their own enlistments, and sent recruiting parties to their favourite recruiting grounds when necessary.

The two elephants were withdrawn from the Hazara Mountain Train in December, 1856, and three of the 3-prs. were exchanged in the following May for three $4\tfrac{2}{8}$-inch howitzers. Equipment was held for six pieces of ordnance, but establishments for four only were kept up. Twenty-five battery baggage mules were added at this time and forty-five muleteers were all that were allowed for these and forty-seven gun mules. This establishment was not as generous as that of the Peshawar Mountain Train.

There is no record of the establishment of the mountain guns of the light field batteries, but it is clear that the gunners required were provided on active service by omitting to man one division of the field battery. On one occasion it took 2 British Officers, 1 Native Officer, 6 non-commissioned officers and 40 gunners to man the mountain guns.

The Hazara Train still had only one British Officer, as had the light field batteries, but "doing duty" officers were posted to the latter batteries from 1856 onwards. The Train and battery commanders were lieutenants, and had to vacate on promotion to captain. They were styled "Commandant" and drew a command allowance of Rs150 a month, which had to include horse and stationery allowance as well as the allowance for repair of arms and accoutrements.

The Native Officers were mostly supplied from those taken over from the Durbar Army at the close of the Sikh War. Some of their records speak for themselves:

Peshawar Mountain Train

 Subadar-Major Jowahir Khan—joined as Jemadar, 1854, after eight years in Sikh Durbar service, finishing by fighting against us at Ferozeshah and Sobraon; then seven campaigns in the Mountain Train; promoted Subadar-Major, January, 1865.

 Jemadar Amir Singh—joined as Jemadar, 1854, after service with the Sikh Army; eight campaigns before transferring to No. 4 or Garrison Company, August, 1870.

 Jemadar Hussein Khan—enlisted in the Bengal Artillery, 1825; eight campaigns before being invalided in 1870.

No. 2 Light Field Battery

Subadar-Major Murdun Ali Shah—promoted Jemadar, 1855; went on pension, May, 1877, with 2nd Class Order of British India (Bahadur).

The Hazara Mountain Train moved to Abbottabad in 1856, where it remained for twenty years except for intervals of active service. The cantonment was built in 1853, and so named in compliment to Major (later Sir James) Abbott, K.C.B.

The Bozdars live in the Suliman Mountains and, unlike most Baluchis of the period, preferred to fight with the matchlock than with the sword. They are very strict Mohammedans, and lived in a perpetual state of feud with their neighbours, in addition to raiding and plundering villages in our territory. After many warnings over six or seven years a punitive expedition was sent against them in March, 1857. Two cavalry regiments, five battalions, No. 1 Punjab Light Field Battery, two mountain guns from each of Nos. 2 and 3 Punjab Light Field Batteries, and a few hundred local levies were assembled at Taunsa.

Baluchistan lies to the south of the River Gomal and to the east of the Afghan and Persian borders all the way to the Arabian Sea. A peculiarity of the hills of the western border from Bannu to Sind is that in many places narrow defiles walled in by precipitous sides cut across the main ranges, and the roads follow these ravines. The pass selected for penetration, the Sangarh, fifty miles west of Dera Ghazi Khan, was fit for wheeled vehicles, but completely commanded for the first few miles where it ran through a narrow defile as far as the Khan Band, after which it opened out and debouched into a wide plain. Fire from a matchlock on one side of the ravine reached the hills on the other side.

The troops started on 7th March, carrying four days' supplies and equipped as lightly as possible, to attack this position, which was held in great strength by the Bozdars. A turning movement by our right flank troops along the Drug Nai was made by the 4th Punjab Infantry, supported by the two mountain guns of No. 2 Punjab Light Field Battery, but this was held up by enemy cross fire from three directions, and reinforcements were called for. With the help of the 2nd Punjab Infantry and the fire of the mountain guns from Nos. 2 and 3 Punjab Light Field Batteries, the enemy's position was attacked and carried with the greatest gallantry, notwithstanding the enemy's strong resistance. Major Coke, commanding the 1st Punjab Infantry, particularly distinguished himself, and was severely wounded. The way was now open to seize the heights on both banks of the Sangarh ravine, this attack being supported by the field guns of No. 1 Punjab Light Field Battery. The Khan Band, being threatened from the rear, was captured with little trouble. The official history states that the hills were too precipitous to admit of the mountain guns being taken up, on rejoining from the right flank.

Resistance was slight once the troops were through the Sangarh defile, and suitable punishment soon brought the Bozdars to sue for terms, which were not severe. Their conduct showed a marked improvement for several years.

The excellent service rendered by the officers and men employed with the mountain guns while supporting Major Coke's attack on the Drug Nai was brought to notice by the Brigadier, and Lieutenants G. Maister and R. Mecham, commanding Nos. 2 and 3 Punjab Light Field Batteries respectively, were mentioned in despatches.

The barren and mountainous country of Baluchistan was never properly controlled by the Sikhs; in fact, when taken over it was in a state of anarchy. The eastern boundary touched Sind and the Punjab province of Derajat, but the frontier was very vague. After the conquest of Sind in 1843 our western frontier was coterminous with Kalat territory, bordering the Baluch tribes on the north and the Brahuis on the west. Captain John Jacob, Bombay Artillery, had served under Napier in Sind and eventually relieved him as the sole political and military authority in Upper Sind. His first work was the pacification of the Sind frontier, which entailed some expeditions against the Baluch tribes. Having made his authority first respected by sheer force, he developed a technique of co-operation with the tribes against all law-breakers which seldom failed during his rule. He realized the danger to India from the Russian advance towards Afghanistan, strengthened the power of the Khan of Kalat, and brought Mekran and Seistan under our influence. He advocated the occupation of Quetta, which our troops first visited in 1854, though it was twenty years before the Government approved his recommendation. He reduced the number of troops on the border and built Jacobabad* as his headquarters, where were located the three regiments of Sind Horse, which maintained order in Sind.

In 1858, just before his death, General Jacob formed two silladar infantry regiments (*i.e.*, the men provided everything from their pay except their arms), Nos. 1 and 2 Jacob's Rifles, which in 1861 were amalgamated as "Jacob's Rifles." Men of these regiments manned from 1858 the guns of the Sind Force Mountain Train at Jacobabad, to which an officer of the Bombay Artillery was attached.

---

* Originally Khangur.

NOTE TO CHAPTER I

Rifled mountain gun, brass, 2-pr. 1849. Calibre 2 inches—length 46 inches—weight 154 lb.

The above gun, No. 2/219 in the catalogue of the Rotunda, Woolwich, is a brass mountain gun designed and manufactured at Abbottabad by Major (afterwards Lieutenant-General) Sir James Abbott, K.C.B. (d. 1896). There is a silver crest (of General Abbott) in front of the vent; the carriage appears to be a makeshift. This is probably the gun which Major Abbott forwarded in December, 1849, through the Punjab Administration to the Government of India with a full report. He received a reply to the effect that "the Governor-General declines to engage in any experiment in this subject, and requests that the Deputy Commissioner may not cast and bore any more guns without asking and obtaining leave."

It appears from the report which accompanied the gun that it had two grooves of plain rifling given a quarter turn only, and fired round shot, as being more effective than any other form of projectile. Major Abbott recommended a double round shot of two 2-lb. balls of hardened lead connected by a neck like a figure of eight; one of the shot to have ridges to engage with the rifling, and the other one plain. He foretold effective fire with this projectile at 800 yards. Shrapnel and grape could also be fired.

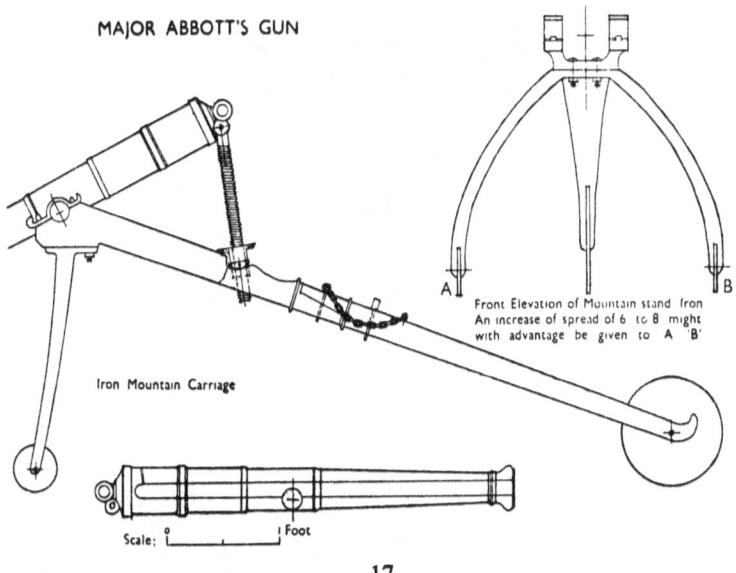

MAJOR ABBOTT'S GUN

Front Elevation of Mountain stand Iron
An increase of spread of 6 to 8 might
with advantage be given to A 'B'

Iron Mountain Carriage

Scale: 0 — 1 Foot

The carriage was recommended to be made similar to that invented by H.H. the Maharajah of Jummoo; with the axle it forms a load for one mule, the gun forming another load. It is best shown by the sketch on page 17.

Arms of the United East India Company

CHAPTER II

The Mutiny to the Second Afghan War

NEWS ARRIVED AT Peshawar on 12th May, 1857, that the Bengal native regiments at Meerut had mutinied on 10th May. This was a case for immediate action: fortunately the Frontier area had been brought under control by civil and military officers of a high standard, and no suggestion of any disloyalty happened in the Punjab Irregular Force. The 55th Native (Bengal) Infantry at Hoti Mardan mutinied, but on the approach of a force sent from Peshawar fled in disorder: 150 were taken prisoner, of whom 40 were executed by being blown away from guns, and 600 or more dispersed into the hills and were hunted down or sold into slavery by the hill-men. Hazara Mountain Train Orders for 17th July, 1857: "The troops will parade this evening at 5.30 p.m. to witness the execution of a body of mutineers of the 55th Native Infantry." Four native battalions in Peshawar were disarmed; one, the 21st, remained loyal. Recruits began to pour into Peshawar, eager to enrol with the British. A movable column of British and Irregular troops was centred on Rawal Pindi, where the Chief Commissioner of the Punjab, Sir John Lawrence, established his headquarters. The Guides (infantry and three squadrons of cavalry) and four infantry regiments of the P.I.F. moved by forced marches to take part in the siege of Delhi, while the remainder of that force held down a large Frontier area which might have been a danger to our armies in India.

The Amir of Afghanistan, Dost Mahomed, resisted the temptation to attack us, and remained our loyal friend.

Practically all the regiments of the Punjab Irregular Force at one time or another took part in the operations at Delhi, the relief of Lucknow or some of the innumerable engagements in Hindustan and the Punjab, increasing their reputation as first-class fighting troops. The two Mountain Trains were busy on the Frontier; Nos. 2 and 3 Light Field Batteries each sent in October, 1858, a division (presumably of 9-prs., but there is no record of the equipment) to Kalpi and Bundelcund, to help the round-up after the mutiny. The Imperial Gazetteer declared afterwards: "The Punjab Irregular Force not only stood firm, but proved itself of the utmost value in the suppression of the mutiny."

In the Ahmednagar Flying Column at this time was No. 1 Company, 4th Battalion Bombay Artillery (with No. 6 Light Field Battery), which had been formed on 28th September, 1827, as the 8th Company, Golandaz Battalion, and had already been awarded the battle honours of "PUNJAUB" and "MULTAN." It carried out many long marches in the operations in pursuit of Tantia Topi, covering 1,300 miles between November, 1858 and March, 1859. It was to become No. 1, later the 5th (Bombay) Mountain Battery (page 37).

An example of a Mountain Train organized for a special purpose and reverted to company work on conclusion of active service is provided by No. 4 Company, 4th Battalion Bombay Artillery (the 4th Battalion was a native one). It supplied a Mountain Train for service in Persia in 1856, which returned to India in 1857, and then went to Satpura Hills, Khandeish, in northern Bombay, with a force against the Bhils, in which expedition an action was fought at Amba Pawnee. This battalion has a record of the formation of several other temporary Mountain Trains—*e.g.*, Malligaum and Aurungabad—but reductions and renumbering left only Nos. 1, 2 and 3 Companies, Bombay Native Artillery, in 1863. At that date No. 1 Company (the original No. 1 Company, 4th Battalion), with the Guzerat Mountain Train, was stationed at Rajcote (Ahmednagar), and No. 3 Company (afterwards renumbered No. 2 Company), with the Jacobabad Mountain Train, was at Jacobabad.

The establishment was: 1 subadar, 1 jemadar, 1 havildar-major, 1 pay and Q.M. havildar, 4 havildars, 4 naiks, 2 buglers, 60 privates, 1 boy and 2 bhisties. The Jacobabad Mountain Train had in addition: 2 driver havildars, 4 driver naiks, 85 drivers, 6 muleteers, 1 farrier. Drivers were not classed as fighting men. The equipment of the Trains was the brass ordnance of the period.

The Sepoy Mutiny was the death-knell of the Honourable East India Company, which had received its charter over 250 years before, and the Queen assumed sovereignty over India on 1st November, 1858. Native cavalry and infantry were in many cases transferred to the service of the crown and reorganized, while the European units of the three artilleries were absorbed by the Royal Regiment of Artillery (1861). It was laid down: "Resolved henceforward, with such few exceptions as may be rendered necessary by local considerations, there shall be no Native Artillery" (G.G.O. 1277 of 1861).

These exceptions were the two Mountain Trains, three Light Field Batteries and the Garrison Battery in the Punjab, two companies Bombay Native Artillery, which afterwards became Nos. 1 and 2 Bombay Mountain Batteries, and, for a long time, four field batteries of the Hyderabad Contingent in Madras.

As there were no other openings for would-be artillerymen, a very fine standard of recruit was always available for the mountain artillery.

The only portion of the Peshawar district in which the tribesmen made trouble during the Mutiny was that part of the northern Yusufzai frontier inhabited by the Hindustani fanatics. This was a colony of Moslem refugees of the Wahabi sect from India originally founded about 1820 by Saiyid Ahmad Shah of Bareilly, who proclaimed a jehad with the object of ejecting the Sikhs from the Punjab. The holy war failed and Ahmad Shah was himself killed by the Sikhs, but his movement survived with the new aim of removing the British.

The fanatics constructed a fort at Mandi near Sitana in Utmanzai territory for their headquarters, whence they carried out their anti-British activities. They were aided by money from traitorous princes and the disaffected in Hindustan and Bengal, and reinforced by outlaws and, at this period, by Mohammedan sepoys who had mutinied. They first came into contact with us in 1853, after they had driven the Khan of Amb, a friendly chief, from his fort of Kotla, but did not oppose our troops who crossed the Indus and restored the village to its owner (page 5).

After the mutiny of the 55th Native Infantry, Mardan had been garrisoned by the 5th Punjab Infantry and two guns of the Peshawar Mountain Train. Major J. L. Vaughan, 5th Punjab Infantry, moved out the two guns and an infantry detachment to drive away a party of tribesmen, mostly Khudu Khels, on trouble bent, who had occupied a near-by village, and had little difficulty in dispersing them. That was on 2nd July, but in a fortnight's time the whole body of fanatics started a jehad and raised the standard of religious war at Narinji, a border village, notorious as an asylum for bad characters. Major Vaughan moved out against Narinji, this time with four guns of the Train, but his force (a party of about 700, including some loyal men of the late 55th Native Infantry) was not strong enough to capture the place, and he had to retire. Reinforcements were sent from Peshawar of 800 native infantry and three parties of British infantry of 50 each from different regiments, together with two 24-pr. howitzers. After a night march, a strong party of infantry was posted to take the enemy in flank and rear, and at sunrise a combined attack on the front and flank speedily dislodged the enemy, killing thirty. On entering the village it was found to be deserted and the towers and houses were destroyed. This punishment had little effect, as within a few weeks a British Assistant Commissioner was attacked, his servants killed and his baggage plundered. A punitive expedition was approved and a force of 5,000 of all arms in two brigades under

Major-General Sir S. J. Cotton set out on 22nd April, 1858, to attack Sitana itself.

The force was divided into three columns before crossing the frontier. A standing camp was formed at Salim Khan, guarded by the third column. With the first column, under the G.O.C., were two guns of the Peshawar Mountain Train and four guns of the Peshawar Light Field Battery, a provisional unit horsed from a disarmed Bengal cavalry regiment. The second column had no guns. The two columns destroyed Chinglai and Panjtar with little trouble and returned to camp on 27th April. On the 28th the first column, with artillery, destroyed Mangal Thana without opposition. There now remained the colony of fanatics at Sitana to be dealt with.

On 3rd May the force camped at Khabal, four miles from Sitana, and an attack was ordered to be carried out the next morning. Major Becher, the Deputy Commissioner of Hazara, had concentrated about 1,000 rifles, two guns of the Peshawar Mountain Train and one gun and two howitzers of the Hazara Mountain Train on the left bank of the Indus, ready to co-operate with General Cotton's force.

Khabal and Sitana with some other villages are in territory belonging to the Utmanzais, who co-operated willingly in order to eject the fanatics. The Khan of Amb, on the right bank of the river, had always been friendly to us, and was also anxious to get rid of them.

On the morning of 4th May, the Hazara force crossed the Indus and attacked the Sitana villages from the east; the Amb forces occupied the hills to the north; and the main column moved against them from the south. The enemy was cornered but fought very bravely, and the fanatics were all either killed or dispersed, being caught between the bayonets of the 6th and 18th Punjab Infantry Regiments. Some of their allies from the Gadun tribe in the neighbourhood fled without a struggle. The troops withdrew to camp on the banks of the Indus and were closely followed up by the enemy, but a few rounds from the $5\frac{1}{2}$-inch mortars of the light field battery kept them in check. British losses were 6 killed and 29 wounded: the enemy lost 60 killed. The Gaduns were forced to make an engagement to expel Saiyids and Hindustanis in future, and the force marched to Nowshera to be broken up. The Peshawar Mountain Train was mentioned in despatches for good service.

This was the first campaign in which the Enfield rifle was used against the tribesmen, and its efficiency made a great impression on them, but hardly a lasting one, as the fanatics reoccupied Sitana without opposition from the Gaduns, and marauding and kidnapping went on as before for several years.

On 5th November, 1859, the Commandant of No. 3 Punjab Light

Field Battery, Captain R. Mecham, Bengal Artillery, was murdered near Latammar on his way from Bannu to Kohat. The murderers fled for refuge to the Kabul Khels, a section of the Darwesh Khel Wazirs, who had frequently given trouble. They refused to hand over the murderers, and it was decided to exact immediate retribution.

A force of 4,000 of all arms, with about 1,000 levies in addition, under Brigadier-General Neville Chamberlain, left Kohat on 15th December, arriving at Thal on 19th. The artillery was composed of four guns of No. 2 Punjab Light Field Battery under Captain G. Maister, Bengal Artillery, two guns of No. 1 Punjab Light Field Battery, four guns of the Peshawar Mountain Train under Captain F. R. de Budé, Bengal Artillery, and three guns of the Hazara Mountain Train under Lieutenant F. R. Butt, Bengal Artillery.

The force crossed the Kurram river and found the enemy in force on the Maidani hills: no information was available about the country, so the Brigadier made a reconnaissance the next day. The enemy's position was on two parallel ranges enclosing a long narrow valley of which the inward slopes were easy going. There were two entrance gorges, one facing the east and the other the south; the former was selected for the advance.

The next morning five battalions and all the mountain guns moved out to attack, marching light. The Guides and 4th Sikhs, supported by the four guns of the Peshawar Train, were ordered to advance along the left-hand ridge, and the 1st and 3rd Punjab Infantry, supported by three guns of the Hazara Train, moved along the right-hand ridge. The 4th Punjab Infantry moved along the ravine in the centre.

The left ridge was protected by breastworks, the right ridge was unprotected and gave little trouble, and the mountain guns on the right enfiladed the breastworks on the left ridge. Despite a brave defence by the enemy, our troops got possession of the position with few casualties, and returned to camp after destroying the enemy's encampments. There was no more fighting and, after showing the flag and mapping the district, the force returned to Kohat. One of the murderers was eventually handed over and hanged.

The Hazara Mountain Train fired 37 round shot (3-pr.) and 13 common and 8 shrapnel ($4\frac{2}{5}$-inch howitzer) in this affair.

Waziristan lies between the districts of Kurram and Zhob (Baluchistan), touching the Afghan frontier on the west and north-west. It is about a third the size of Switzerland, rugged, mountainous and barren, and intersected by ravines running in every direction. The ravines are in places very narrow, and their gorges, or tangis, form natural positions to oppose an enemy. The Tochi valley and the Spin plain, except for small stretches along the water-courses, furnish the only tracts large enough to cultivate. The chief tribes are the Darwesh Khels, the Dawaris, the Bhittannis* and the Mahsuds. "The Mahsuds were celebrated as the earliest, the most inveterate and the most incorrigible of all the robbers of the border" (Extract from official report).

Retribution for a long list of raids and outrages was slow in coming, but was at last provoked by an attack on the town of Tank in March, 1860: the attack was unsuccessful, thanks to the initiative of a Native Officer of the 5th Punjab Cavalry, whose troop, aided by a few levies, accounted for 300 Mahsuds. Brigadier-General Chamberlain was given command of a force of 5,100 all ranks assembled at Tank on 16th April, 1860. The objective of this force was to penetrate to Kaniguram and Makin, the enemy's two chief places, and to impose terms, as they prided themselves that their country had never been entered, and never could be entered.

The artillery of the force consisted of two guns of No. 2 Punjab Light Field Battery under Captain G. Maister, Bengal Artillery; two 24-pr. howitzers of No. 3 Punjab Light Field Battery, with elephants, under Captain T. E. Hughes, Bengal Artillery; the Peshawar Mountain Train of four guns under Captain F. R. de Budé, Bengal Artillery; and the Hazara Mountain Train of three guns under Lieutenant F. R. Butt, Bengal Artillery.

The force moved out from Tank on 17th April, 1860, to Haidari Kach, dropping a strong detachment at Palosin on the line of communication. The 24-pr. howitzers and their elephants were sent back to Palosin when the road through the narrow Tank Zam defile became very bad. No opposition was offered, and, after destroying a fort, the force retired on the 24th.

The camp at Palosin (one cavalry regiment, detachments of Nos. 2 and 3 Light Field Batteries and five infantry battalions) was protected by piquets as usual, and after a quiet night (22nd/23rd) about 3,000 Waziris, who had collected unseen, rushed the camp at dawn, covered by supporting fire. A hand-to-hand conflict ensued—the inlying piquet of the Guides functioned on the enemy's flank and the guns came into action with canister to clear the camp. Subadar Murdun Ali Shah and several gunners were wounded fighting their guns. The enemy was driven out and pursued for three miles, losing at least 140 killed, but our losses were heavy, 63 killed and 166 wounded.

---

* The first two tribes mentioned inhabit North Waziristan, and are generally known as "Wazirs."

The two forces joined and moved to Mandanna Kach, in preparation for a move on Kaniguram. Negotiations were started, and an offer made to the Maliks: a fine of Rs4,300 for cattle stolen, or security for payment, and a free passage for our troops to Kaniguram. These proposals were rejected.

The force advanced, and on 4th May found the enemy in strength holding the Barari Tangi. The sides of this gorge are perpendicular cliffs, forty feet high, above which the mountains rise steeply. Sangars were terraced along the spurs and a cross ravine running into the main one presented further difficulties. The General's plan was to storm the heights on our right, and to send a second column to climb the hills on our left and await an opportunity to attack.

Two howitzers and one gun of the Hazara Train supported the 1st, 2nd, and 3rd Punjab Infantry of the right column, and four guns of the Peshawar Train, the Guides and 6th Punjab Infantry on the left, leaving the light field batteries with the reserve in the centre.

On the right the 3rd Punjab Infantry attacked the front breastworks, but were driven back on to the guns by a rush of the enemy. The guns were thus masked by the infantry retirement, but were loaded with case and the muzzles swung to the right. Lieutenants Arbuckle and Abbott, both of whom had joined since the expedition began, stood in front of the guns, firing their pistols, checking the enemy until the troops were clear and the guns could open fire. The ridge was then carried and the enemy retreated, and Kaniguram was reached the next day. There was little resistance after that; Makin, the centre of the Mahsud iron trade, was left in ruins, Kaniguram was spared on payment of a fine, the surrounding country was surveyed, and the force then marched to Bannu to be broken up.

The Mahsuds were put under blockade until they should come to a settlement, which did not occur until June, 1861.

In this campaign the case shot were filled with leaden bullets instead of iron on the recommendation of Captain de Budé, with excellent results. The Hazara Mountain Train expended 36 round shot and 8 case (3-pr.) and 56 shrapnel and 11 case from the howitzers.

Lieutenant F. R. Butt, commanding the Hazara Mountain Train, who had recommended his officers for mention, received a brevet-majority.

The Madras Artillery manned a Native Mountain Train in the China War of 1860-61, with 12-pr. mountain howitzers and twelve $5\frac{1}{2}$-inch mortars, "with ammunition and harness." Strength on embarkation was 10 officers, 219 other ranks, and 67 horses. The Train does not appear to have taken an active part in the operations.

In this campaign widespread interest was created by the first appearance in war of the Armstrong R.B.L. gun.

From 1st June, 1862, the Peshawar and Hazara Mountain Trains were placed on similar four-gun establishments: until this time the establishment of the former was eight guns, 160 mules, 3 Native Officers and 103 other ranks. That of the Hazara Mountain Train was six guns, with establishment sufficient for four guns: *i.e.*, 2 Native Officers, 72 other ranks, 74 gun and baggage mules. Drivers have not been counted. The Peshawar Train had formerly three British Officers, and the Hazara two: the future establishment was fixed at three.

In the early days, Bengal Artillery officers had to vacate command of Mountain Trains on attaining the rank of Captain, but from 1864 R.A. officers were seconded to batteries for five years. For a short period the designation was changed to "Mountain Train Batteries," and the word "Train" was not officially dropped until 1865.

Major F. R. Butt resigned his appointment as Commandant of the Hazara Mountain Train in June, 1862, and was succeeded by Captain F. R. de Budé, who was transferred from the command of the Peshawar Mountain Train, which he had held for three years.

The Hindustani fanatics had not taken very seriously the terms inflicted on them in 1858, and had in no way changed their rebellious attitude. They had built themselves a new stronghold at Malka and continued to kidnap Hindu traders and generally maraud in our territory.

Their raids increased during 1863 and, a blockade on the line of the Indus having no effect, it was decided to send a strong force under Brigadier-General Sir Neville Chamberlain to stop these offences and prevent any recurrence. The object was to destroy Malka and extirpate the fanatics. Malka was in the territory of the Amazais, a clan of the Yusufzais; the route selected was by the Sarkhawai or Ambela Pass and the Chamla valley.

It was assumed that the operations would be quickly over, and that therefore there would be no danger in starting in October. The transport was hastily and badly organized, and little information was available as to the reception to be expected from the tribes in that region, or as to the practicability of the proposed routes. The north side of the Mahaban mountain was to be occupied to prevent the enemy from falling back into the hills, and on the south side the line of the Indus was to be under blockade; Yusufzai was to be held by a suitable force to keep the tribes quiet and protect the Hazara district.

The top of the pass was occupied with no trouble on the 20th: the

Peshawar and Hazara Mountain Trains, under Captains T. E. Hughes and F. R. de Budé, respectively, were with the advanced column, and half C/19 R.A. with the main body. C/19 transferred the guns to elephants when the track became too bad for wheels, but the road was steep and difficult even for mountain batteries. Most of the main body arrived in camp that night, but the baggage and rearguard were not in until the 22nd.

On that day a cavalry reconnaissance went on to Koga, avoiding Buner country, but had to fight its way back to camp, and was extricated by a detachment of Her Majesty's 71st Regiment and two guns of the Hazara Mountain Train, which Lieutenant W. B. Gillies brought into action eighty yards from the enemy. The enemy attacked the camp until 1 a.m., and during this action Lieutenant Gillies was killed*, one gunner died of wounds, two men were wounded and two mules killed.

It was now clear that the Bunerwals were fighting against us, though it had been hoped they would be neutral, and the fanatics arrived on the 23rd, followed by Swatis and Bajauris. General Chamberlain sent for another infantry regiment to guard his line of communications, and for more ammunition for the Mountain Trains, and sent back sick men, surplus baggage, etc., to Rustam Bazaar. Transport was reduced to a minimum, and other ranks were allowed a poshteen and one blanket only. Extra grain was issued to the mules in lieu of grass.

The position of the force at the head of the pass was in fairly level and open ground sufficient for the bivouac, but with high hills on both flanks that had to be piqueted. The pass widened out in front and the plain of Chamla could be seen. The front and rear were barred with breastworks which held the field guns, while the Mountain Trains reinforced the piquets. In the operations that ensued the British force was to find itself besieged.

On the 26th an attack was being opened on the Eagle's Nest piquet to the north of the camp, and the 71st Regiment and 5th and 6th Punjab Infantry, supported by the Hazara Mountain Train, were sent to reinforce. About 2,000 Bunerwals made two fierce attacks on this and another piquet, and both were repulsed. The native infantry was now armed with the Enfield rifle, which had a superior range to the jezail, and casualties on both sides were heavy. The Train fired shrapnel, common shell and round shot. It remained as part of the garrison of Vaughan's piquet, which covered the left front of the camp, and supported the Eagle's Nest.

---

* Lieutenant Gillies' vacancy was filled by Lieutenant E. J. de Lautour, who was with the battery for sixteen years.

On the 29th two guns of No. 3 Punjab Light Field Battery, under Captain T. H. Salt, joined the camp: this was the right half-battery and consisted of two 24-pr. howitzers. The Crag piquet to the east of the camp was attacked and temporarily held by the fanatics on the 30th, but regained by a counter-attack.

Two British and two native infantry regiments were now ordered from Lahore as reinforcements and more transport collected.

On 6th and 7th November the Peshawar Mountain Train supported a force covering a working party which was attacked when withdrawing. Several attacks were made on the Crag piquet during the night of 12th November, but the Peshawar Mountain Train gave valuable support from their position 250 yards below to the right rear, receiving directions by voice from the piquet. The enemy, however, rushed the piquet in the morning and caused confusion by firing into the camp. The piquet was retaken by the 101st Royal Bengal Fusiliers with the support of the mountain guns.

Attacks were of almost daily occurrence, and duties were very heavy; the nights were very cold and the sick list grew longer.

On the 20th, for the third time, the Crag piquet was rushed. This time the Brigadier turned his guns on to the Crag and then in person led the 71st and 5th Gurkhas to a successful counter-attack. Casualties were very heavy and the brigadier was severely wounded.

Major-General Garvock arrived on the 30th to take over command, and by mid-December his force had increased to 9,000 men. The force was divided into two brigades and the advance was begun.

The first action took place against the enemy holding the "Conical Hill," which had almost perpendicular sides, giving scope to the mountain guns to continue their support of our infantry to almost the last second of the advance. The troops then captured and burnt the village of Lalu, and the next day met the main body of the enemy at Ambela, where a body of 250 ghazis made a furious charge, and were slain to a man. This was the end; the remainder fled, and in order not to give the enemy time to reassemble whilst the troops advanced to Malka, the Bunerwals were ordered to destroy the stronghold there, which was done on 22nd December. The campaign cost 900 casualties.

Captain T. E. Hughes, Peshawar Mountain Train, was awarded a brevet-majority, and Naik Ali Madat and Gunner Ghasita Singh were awarded the Order of Merit for "bringing up ammunition under heavy fire and thus enabling fire to be continued after the capture of the Crag piquet by the enemy." Captain F. R. de Budé, Hazara Mountain Train, was awarded a brevet-majority. Subadar Kaka Singh and Pay Havildar Gurmukh Singh were awarded the Order of

Merit (3rd Class). Havildar Keam Khan was recommended for the Order of Merit for saving the life of Major Hoile, commanding the 6th Punjab Infantry, by a "well-timed round shot."

The attitude of the Gaduns during the campaign was not considered entirely satisfactory, and on 28th December, 1863, the two Mountain Trains formed part of a mixed brigade sent to the Gadun tribes to take guarantees for future behaviour. The tribes were forced to destroy Mandi, an outpost of the fanatics, with their own hands, and this having been completed on the 4th January the troops returned to cantonments.

The Punjab Irregular Force was renamed the Punjab Frontier Force in September, 1865, and several minor administrative changes may be noted. R.A. pattern clothing and gold lace badges for full dress were allowed to the artillery of the Force as a reward for good service. Khaki had been the dress of the Punjab Irregular Force for marching and drill order since 1858. Batta was given to the troops when on furlough; salutris and nalbands ceased to be followers. A bugle major was appointed amongst the batteries; the Punjab Garrison Battery (*vide* Appendix II) was included in this appointment. The Punjab Frontier Force remained directly under the orders of the Punjab Government, with its own Commander and headquarters: it did not come under the control of the Commander-in-Chief in India until many years had passed, actually in 1903.

The new establishment for two 3-pr. S.B. guns and two $4\frac{2}{5}$-inch (now called 12-pr.) howitzers from 1st June, 1862: 1 commandant, 2 "doing duty" officers, 1 subadar, 1 jemadar, 5 havildars, 4 naiks, 2 buglers, 60 gunners. Muleteers: 4 havildars, 4 naiks, 78 muleteers. Followers: 39, including 8 syces and 13 grasscutters. Cattle: 2 yaboos (ponies), 76 gun mules, 24 baggage mules. Twelve Carbines Victoria, smooth-bore, were the only handguns allowed.

Pay and Allowances. British Officers received the same rates of pay as those of native cavalry and infantry units for appointments of a similar responsibility. They had to provide their own horses and saddlery and their pay included an allowance for tentage.

The "doing duty" officer's pay and allowances remained unchanged for many years, except for the addition of horse allowance.

Commandant's pay: Rs435 10 annas, with Rs60 allowance for two horses and Rs30 command allowance. "Doing duty" officers' pay: Rs265 12 annas plus Rs150 allowance.

Contingent, repairs, shoeing and other allowances: Rs350. Shoeing allowance was sufficient for shoeing each mule every month but Ordnance mules were not normally shod.

The subadar received Rs67 and the jemadar Rs30 a month;

havildars and naiks Rs14 and Rs12 respectively; gunners were paid Rs8 and muleteers Rs6 a month.

The muleteers, even those with ordnance mules, were still classed as followers and not yet as fighting men.

After the Ambela campaign the ammunition was redistributed to allow for a reserve in the "Battery* Magazine"; howitzer ammunition being increased at the expense of the 3-pr.

FOR FOUR GUNS AND FOUR HOWITZERS

	12-pr. Howitzer			3-pr.	
	Common shell	Dia-phragm shell	Case	Round shot	Case
Service with guns ..	176	40	40	280	80
Half spare in Battery Magazine	88	20	20	140	40
	264	60	60	420	120

Each 3-pr. to have five pairs of boxes and each howitzer eight pairs.

In 1867 the Home Government decided on sending a punitive expedition to Abyssinia to rescue some British subjects held unjustly in captivity by King Theodore. Throughout the reign of Queen Victoria the Government of the day invariably protected the lives and fortunes of British nationals if their safety was jeopardized by the action of foreign powers, or, failing this, punished the culprits and obtained redress—witness China, Ashanti and other campaigns.

It is not proposed to enter into detail over the Abyssinian campaign, as the only Indian battery present, after being the first artillery unit to arrive in the country with the base troops, was kept at the advanced base at Senafe during the operations. This was Captain Marrett's No. 1 Company, Bombay Native Artillery, with its Mountain Train armed with smooth-bore guns and howitzers, which must have had the experience of seeing three British Mountain Batteries† march to the front with the new 7-pr. rifled gun.

Two of these batteries were equipped on arrival in the country with steel rifled muzzle-loading 7-prs. of 150 lb., for which the pack equipment had been designed at Woolwich. The gun was carried transversely across the mule's back, and a shaft arrangement was

---

* About this time the expression "Train" was replaced by "Battery."
† British Mountain Batteries were R.A. Batteries detailed for a tour of service with mountain artillery equipment. The gunner establishment consisted of British, and the driver establishment of native personnel.

provided which moved two guns and carriages linked together as a four-wheeled vehicle where the going was suitable.

The third battery brought the 7-pr. 224 lb. bronze* R.M.L. converted guns, (3-prs. bored up to 3 inches) which they had used in Bhutan in 1864-5 as a mountain battery. Fighting in Abyssinia was not on a large scale, and the real enemies were the weather, lack of roads, lack of water and forage; the casualties were mostly due to disease. Casualties among the transport animals from overwork and disease were nearly 25 per cent.

The 7-pr. gun was the answer to demands which had been made for several years for a gun with a longer range. A change of tactics had followed the general adoption of rifled small arms which by their longer range prevented the guns from occupying positions in the infantry firing line. The brass smooth-bore pieces had altered little since Tudor days, although experiments with rifled guns had been going on for many years. The 3-pr. S.B. was incapable of breaking up a sangar of loose stones; the $4\frac{2}{5}$-inch howitzer shell had some effect but its range was too short (maximum 1,000 yards), and the alternatives were unsatisfactory. The "converted" 3-pr. was rifled and designed to fire a 7 lb. shell, but the gun was too heavy—224 lb.; the 6-pr. R.B.L. was recommended for mountain service, but was too heavy at 3 cwt.

A 7-pr. R.M.L. made from a solid block of steel was, after several attempts, found satisfactory; the 150 lb. Mark III gun, which had been tried in Abyssinia, being finally replaced by the Mark IV of 200 lb. The latter had a range of 3,100 yards with common shell against the lighter gun's 2,000 yards, though it was inclined to be unsteady on rough ground and had to be carefully "fielded." Its shrapnel was superior to that of the 150 lb. gun, which was ineffective above 600 yards. It was reported that the common shell of the Mark IV stuck uselessly in a mud wall at 450 yards, and would rebound from a stockade to explode on the ground; even the $4\frac{2}{5}$-inch S.B. howitzer common shell gave better results at these targets. Again, although its effect was intensified by filling with sand, the Mark IV common did little damage to a strongly made sangar, and none at all to a stone tower. The need for a howitzer was felt as soon as the new gun came into use, and a double shell to be fired with a reduced charge of 4 oz. was issued. It was not a great success as the low muzzle velocity could not be relied upon to arm the fuze or to ensure that the over-long projectile did not somersault. The calibre was 3 inches, and rotation was effected by means of studs on the body of the shell. The carriage was made of iron.

---

* Bronze and brass were synonymous.

It was reported that the gun could be assembled from mule-back and a round loaded in twenty seconds, or, against time, in twelve seconds.

The normal equipment of a field battery at this period was four guns and two howitzers, and the latter were very much in favour for engaging suitable targets. They were specially useful for mountain batteries in the hills because it was impossible to continue infantry support with a flat trajectory gun right up to the assault except when firing with a large angle of sight. The Frontier towers, too, were better dealt with by a howitzer. It was recommended by higher authority that the 7-pr. carriage should be placed on the ground without wheels and the gun fired therefrom in order to get a howitzer effect. The demand for an efficient howitzer was not satisfied until fifty years later.

The two mountain batteries practised in the Packli valley near Abbottabad in April, 1868, with the 7-pr. rifled gun, but it is not on record that they took these guns on active service in the following August.

The police post of Oghi, in the Agror valley in the Black Mountain area on our side of the Frontier, was attacked by 500 men of the Hassanzai and other tribes on 30th July, 1868: Lieutenant-Colonel Rothney of the 5th Gurkhas moved without delay with 350 of his men and the Peshawar Mountain Battery and reached Oghi by midnight on the 31st, having marched forty-two miles in twenty-five hours. The Khan of Agror objected to the location of the police post at Oghi and had stirred up the tribes to attack it. Lieutenant-Colonel Rothney, even with reinforcements, had some trouble in clearing the Agror valley; twenty-one of our villages had been burnt, and it took some hard fighting to restore order. For these outrages the Government of India decided on the dispatch of a punitive expedition. Major-General Sir A. T. Wylde, K.C.B., commanding the Punjab Frontier Force, was given command of a force of 9,500 all ranks, which included the Peshawar Mountain Battery under Captain Minto Elliot, and the Hazara Mountain Battery under Major de Budé. A telegraph line was laid back from Oghi, an innovation in frontier warfare.

For this campaign tactical instructions were issued as well as meticulous administrative instructions:

"Rules for advancing against the enemy:

"4. Use of Artillery.—The great object to be held in view is to shake the enemy's position with artillery before the Infantry assault. The artillery can be used for this purpose:

The Abbottabad Mountain Gun
See page 17

Typical Mule Lines on the North-West Frontier

The First Mountain Gun, 7-pr. R.M.L.

Assembling the 2.5-inch M.L. Gun: The Screw Gun

(a) When the Infantry have taken up cover and are waiting the final order for the assault.
(b) During the slow but continuous advance of the skirmishers previous to the assault."

The concentration of this force in the Hazara district had a great effect on the tribes. The Swatis, presumably conscience-stricken, attacked the remaining Hindustani fanatics without being asked to take action, and other tribes began to ask for terms. The Khan of Amb remained our friend and gave us every assistance. Kashmir troops also co-operated. The force left Oghi on 3rd October and occupied the Machai peak after an ineffectual resistance by the enemy. The R.H.A. Battery, D/F, took its guns on elephants as far as it could to give covering fire, and the mountain batteries went on to a forward ridge after a very steep and rugged climb, during which two ordnance mules were killed by falling down the khud, but the mountain batteries came into action, alternately covering the infantry by a "most accurate and effective fire." Snow and rain made it a very cold night for the troops bivouacked on top of the mountain.

After twenty days of hard marching, and bivouacking, and showing the flag in the Black Mountain area with little opposition, the force returned to Oghi and eventually arrived at Abbottabad on 3rd November. The tribes had submitted as usual, but the raids began again the following year, and a detachment was maintained in the Agror valley, guns being supplied by the mountain battery at Abbottabad when required. The Agror valley did not settle down for some time and troops from Abbottabad were several times moved out on receipt of alarms.

The smooth-bores became obsolete once the steel 7-pr. of 150 lb. was issued to batteries in 1869. The problem of shafts for draught was not yet settled; a committee in India having reported against their use after the Ambela campaign (1863).

The Orakzais occupy Southern Tirah and the Samana ridge, and found their proximity to British territory provided temptations for raiding.

In 1868 there was trouble with the Bizoti Orakzais at the Ublan Pass over raids and cattle stealing and, as compensation was not forthcoming, the Bizotis were deprived of their share of guarding the pass, and the emoluments thereof. They were also debarred from trade with British territory. On 11th March, 1868, warning was received of a forthcoming raid in strength, but the Deputy Commissioner with some police and levies was on the spot first. A large number of the enemy took up a position on both sides of the pass, troops were called out from Kohat, comprising two mountain guns of No. 2

Punjab Light Field Battery and about 600 cavalry and infantry. The troops followed the enemy up a spur and stormed a breastwork which presented tremendous difficulties, so that the attack failed with some loss to us. More troops and guns were sent for, but the position was impregnable and we lost eleven killed and forty-four wounded. As a result, the pressure of the blockade was increased, but outrages continued, and sanction was received for a sudden raid to be made by us in order to inflict chastisement in the Orakzai homes, which were accounted "inaccessible."

At midnight on 24th February, 1869, a complete cordon was thrown round Kohat, and at 1 a.m. the force of two mountain guns of No. 1 Punjab Light Field Battery with the 1st and 4th Punjab Infantry, under Lieutenant-Colonel C. P. Keyes, C.B., moved to the Ublan Pass, followed by a reserve of the 2nd Punjab Infantry and two 24-pr. howitzers. The plan was to move on Gara, a supposedly friendly village, and if not attacked there, advance to Danakhula, the enemy's headquarters, and destroy it. The force was fired on in Gara, and that village was captured with slight loss. The mountain guns came into action on the crest above the village and hustled the enemy's retirement. When our time came to retire, the mountain guns and howitzers covered a successful retirement down a very steep mountain side and the force returned to Kohat after a twelve hours' absence.

A demonstration was made by troops from Peshawar at the same time, and the Kohat Pass temporarily occupied, and, as a result, by April the Bizotis had paid their fines and made submission.

The Kabul Khel Wazirs broke out again in April, 1869, making a big raid on Thal, which brought out the Kohat troops to demand retaliation. Two guns of 3rd Peshawar Mountain Battery accompanied a force of infantry and levies under Lieutenant-Colonel C. P. Keyes, C.B., and on their arrival at Thal the headmen submitted and paid up the fines imposed.

The issue of the 7-pr. produced a new establishment. Some rates of pay were raised: havildars were now to get Rs16 a month; drivers were classed as fighting men at Rs6, the same pay as the muleteers.

The number of ordnance mules allowed was eighty-five, giving a relief line and four spare mules per gun, with nine ammunition mules. The bugler had become a mounted trumpeter, and four yaboos were allowed instead of two.

Command allowance was raised to Rs150.

Enfield carbines were substituted for the Victoria pattern.

The ammunition allotment for a four-gun battery was:

352 Common shell.   512 Fuzes, time, Boxer, 5-sec. and
 80 Shrapnel.   10-sec.
 80 Case.   793 Friction tubes.
352 Cartridges 3-oz. or for bronze gun 5-oz.
336 Cartridges 6-oz. or for bronze gun 10-oz.
Portfires, slowmatch and priming cartridges were also issued.

In the Hazara Battery the 7-pr. steel guns were replaced by bronze guns of 224 lb. in May, 1870, and the latter were replaced by 200 lb. steel guns in July, 1876.

In March, 1871, Major de Budé was criticizing Kohat as being an unsuitable training ground for a mountain battery. But the cantonments of the P.F.F. were selected on strategic and tactical grounds. Actually Kohat has plenty of hill ground within reasonable access, regularly used by mountain batteries.

Lieutenant-Colonel F. R. de Budé retired in the following year after a long and honourable career, starting in 1848 with the siege of Multan. He had been awarded the Indian Mutiny Medal and the Indian General Service Medal with two clasps for four campaigns. He had been several times mentioned in despatches, and was specially thanked for initiating practical improvements in the "efficient working of a mountain battery."

Captain R. S. Abbott retired shortly afterwards; he had had much service with mountain artillery and seen several campaigns, having commanded both Nos. 2 and 3 Punjab Light Field Batteries. This is the officer who distinguished himself at Barari Tangi a few days after joining the Hazara Mountain Train, and was removed from the Train in the following year for failing to pass the Hindustani test. However, he was back again in the Train six months later.

The Peshawar Mountain Battery soon had to act in a very different terrain. The Lushais live on the Bengal-Burma frontier in a mountainous forest country between the Chin country and the native state of Manipur. There is no level ground and the slopes are cut up by mountain torrents with precipitous banks. As tea-gardens were opened up, so they presented the Lushais with opportunities for raiding and looting, which the Government endured patiently for many years; but negotiations being found to be useless, a punitive expedition had to be sent against them in September, 1871.

Two columns were mobilized, each of about 1,500 native infantry, a company of Sappers and Miners and a half-battery (two guns) of the Peshawar Mountain Battery. The mules and drivers were left in India, and the gunner establishment proceeded by train to Calcutta.

The left column with the left half-battery under 2nd Captain

G. F. Blackwood,* started from Cachar (Silchar) with the objective of the enemy's headquarters in the valley of Cham Pai, reaching there on 17th February and finding it deserted. Several attempts at ambushes had been made and stockades across the track were built and manned, but once the guns came into action, the stockades were abandoned. The enemy, whose weapons were flintlock muskets, spears and dahs, had not been under artillery fire before.

The right half-battery under the Commandant, Brevet Lieutenant-Colonel J. Hills, V.C. (afterwards Lieutenant-General Sir J. Hills-Johnes), had much the same sort of experience, a stronger resistance necessitating some bombardment of the stockades. Two $5\frac{1}{2}$-inch mortars with iron beds had been issued, but transport was so scarce that they were left behind after a week or two, along with some of the heavier battery stores. Infantry detachments were trained to man the mortars; 9-pr. war rockets were tried, but without success. On some of the marches the guns and ammunition were carried on elephants, but Kahars and coolies were mostly used. The coolies were unsatisfactory, and as many Kahars as could be obtained were used instead.

A regular dose of quinine was issued, and the health of the troops was fairly good; rations were of variable quality and not always in full supply. Casualties were very few, and both columns returned to their bases by April. The tribes submitted, giving engagements for good behaviour, and a survey of the country was made.

A small force was ordered to Assam in October, 1875, to compel the release of British subjects held as prisoners by the Duffla tribes. The Hazara Mountain Battery sent the right half-battery (Mohammedans) under the Commandant, Captain de Lautour, with one subaltern and one jemadar. 7-pr. R.M.L. guns (150 lb.) were taken over in Calcutta with bamboo poles fitted for coolie transport. In the jungle the force went in single file; each gun and carriage was carried by eight coolies, a pair of wheels by three, ammunition box by two, but the officers' ponies went everywhere and fed on bamboo leaves. Notwithstanding the very wet weather, the general health of the men was good. The object of the expedition was effected without trouble, and the force was back at the base in two months.

Several changes were now about to take place.

The ammunition allotment was varied to include forty double shell per four-gun battery.

Snider carbines replaced the Enfields.

Slight increases of pay were made to the driver establishment.

---

* Afterwards killed in action at Maiwand.

The allowance for shoeing mules was stopped in 1875, the Government of India remarking that few mules were regularly shod.

Commandants were granted staff pay of Rs250, later increased to Rs300 in addition to staff corps pay of rank, and were required to vacate the appointment on promotion to major.

In 1876 the Peshawar and Hazara Mountain Batteries received the numbers 3 and 4 in addition to their names.

No. 2 and No. 3 Horse Light Field Batteries handed in field artillery equipment and received mountain battery equipment for four-gun batteries—the respective dates of conversion being for No. 2, which became No. 1 Mountain Battery, 8th January, 1877; and for No. 3, which became No. 2 Mountain Battery, 26th December, 1876.* The names "Kohat" and "Derajat" were added three years later.

These field batteries had invariably maintained the highest standard on active service and had had throughout their existence the most favourable reports; one report said: "Although their strong punchy little horses may not be able to gallop through a field day on a parade ground in as dashing a style as larger or more showy horses, on service the guns would always be to the front and fit for any work."

All four P.F.F. Mountain Batteries were on the same establishment.

By General Order 276 of the C.-in-C., Bombay Presidency, dated 10th May, 1876, the following changes in designation were ordered:

> No. 1 Company Native Artillery with Guzerat Mountain Train to be No. 1 Bombay Mountain Battery.
>
> No. 2 Company Native Artillery with Jacobabad Mountain Train to be No. 2 Bombay Mountain Battery.

On becoming No. 1 Bombay Mountain Battery this unit became the oldest unit of all the mountain batteries, having had an unbroken record since 1827. No. 2 Bombay Mountain Battery can only claim to have been a unit since 1862, there having been an unfortunate break in 1857 in the history of the unit usually claimed as the ancestor of this battery. The Jacobabad Mountain Train was formed in 1858, at the same time as Jacob's Rifles. It was generally busy on the Sind frontier, where the Baluchis were sometimes restive, and affairs in Kalat needed attention.

These two batteries, No. 1 Bombay and No. 2 Bombay, were renumbered No. 5 and No. 6 in 1890, when all mountain batteries were numbered consecutively. They became finally 5th (Bombay)

---

* There is no trace of their European N.C.Os.; they may have been transferred to the Royal Regiment of Artillery with the European units of the three Presidency artilleries as from 1st May, 1862.

and 6th (Jacob's) Mountain Batteries and are thus designated herein.

There had always been a contrast between the systems of maintaining law and order in Baluchistan and the North-West Frontier districts. In the latter case the border line ran along the foothills, which provided easy escape for raiders, and the clans or tribes had no recognized chiefs: sections of tribes were mostly at enmity with each other and there was no authority or civil organization with which to deal. The Punjab Government did its best to cultivate friendly relations, but without much success. The establishment of half a dozen dispensaries, which were much used by the tribes, was a very popular move, but it evoked no practical gratitude. The payment of money subsidies was not without disadvantages.

The Baluchi tribesmen had the same proclivities for raids and murder, but the terrain was not so favourable for them. The wide stretch of sandy desert between the foothills and the cultivated districts was easily guarded by the Sind Horse. The Baluchi was accustomed to an oligarchal form of government, so General Jacob had insisted on the Sirdars accepting responsibility for acts committed by members of the tribes owing allegiance to them. Over the Sirdars was the Khan of Kalat, whose power was strengthened by British subsidies and backing, and he was held responsible for the misdeeds of the Sirdars.

Sir Robert Sandeman, on whom the mantle of Jacob had fallen, made a treaty with the Khan in 1876, recognizing the status of the Sirdars and guaranteeing a subsidy to the Khan.* The British Protectorate was distinguished from Independent Baluchistan under the Khan, and the Government of India agreed to arbitrate in case of difficulty. The value of Quetta was recognized and surveys and plans made for roads and railways. This arrangement gave us control as far south as the Persian Gulf, and the occupation of Quetta blocked the road from Kandahar to India by the Bolan Pass. No time was lost in joining Quetta and India with a railway.

On 1st January, 1877, Her Majesty Queen Victoria was proclaimed Empress of India.

In that year the Jowaki Afridis took offence at road improvements we were making in the Kohat Pass, and, as they remained intransigent, an expedition had to be organized to dislodge them. Brigadier-General Keyes, commanding the Punjab Frontier Force, moved out from Kohat with a force timed to work with Brigadier-General Ross's column from Peshawar. General Keyes advanced eastwards

---

* No. 2 Bombay Mountain Battery on several occasions sent a division to strengthen Sandeman's escort.

on 9th November, in two columns from camps east of Kohat. No. 1 Kohat Mountain Battery and two guns of No. 2 Derajat Mountain Battery accompanied these columns, which easily captured Paiah and Ghariba, destroying towers and returning to their bivouacs at night. In the following days Jamu, a cluster of villages, the main stronghold of the Jowakis, was captured and several valleys visited. Very bad weather held up operations and prevented General Ross's column co-operating until 23rd November, when combined operations with General Keyes began. General Ross's force in two columns, including No. 4 Hazara Mountain Battery and two other heavier batteries, advanced from the Sargasha ridge via the Bori ravine and captured the large village of Pastaoni with minor casualties. The Jowakis remaining recalcitrant, the operations dragged on for three months, columns visiting all their valleys, destroying towers and surveying the whole area. We incurred a hundred casualties.

Captain J. A. Kelso, commanding No. 1 Kohat Mountain Battery, was specially commended for the manner in which he took his battery over the very difficult ground traversed by the left attack on Jamu, and for the admirable shooting of his battery on that occasion. It rendered invaluable aid to the infantry at Paiah, Jamu, Ghariba (on two occasions), and the Nara Khula.

The Jowakis had a certain number of Enfield rifles; the British troops were now armed with Martinis, and the native infantry with Sniders.

All six mountain batteries were by this time equipped with four 7-pr. R.M.L. guns of 200 lb.

In March, 1878, the Hazara Mountain Battery went out twice with the Guides, once to Ranizai and once to Utman Khel territory, to surround villages by night, receiving immediate submission at daybreak; the second of these expeditions involved a march of seventy miles in forty-eight hours, during which no man fell out.

These records so far have described the more important campaigns of the mountain batteries, but their battery records show a large number of other activities going on all the time—escorts, manœuvres, practice camps and movable columns—and always marches. Occasionally praise for a subaltern for bringing his mules in without a rub after a very long march may be found. Batteries were justifiably proud of their march discipline, and the maintenance of a pace of four miles an hour. Except on ceremonial parades the men did not march in step. When not marching with other troops, short halts were made to change the top load to the relief mules at intervals of about one and a half hours.

Until now the active service record of the native mountain batteries had embraced only campaigns against Frontier tribesmen—brave hardy foes, good rifle shots and not lacking courage in personal encounters, but not equipped with artillery. They were now to meet in the field equally tough foemen who were able to counter our fire with their artillery, which fortunately turned out to be of a low standard.

CHAPTER III

The Second Afghan and Third Burmese Wars

THE RUSSIANS had been very active in Persia and Central Asia after their attempts to expand through Turkey had been frustrated at the end of the Crimean War. They were predominant in Persia and had taken possession of Khiva in 1873, and, as it was our policy to treat Afghanistan as a buffer state, we could not tolerate any other power exercising a stronger influence on that country than ourselves. Dost Mahomed died in 1867 and his son, Shere Ali, became Amir.

During the Russo-Turkish War of 1877-8 we leased Cyprus from the Turks and sent Indian troops there; fearing intervention by us, the Russians sent an Envoy to the Amir as a counter-measure, whereupon the Amir refused to receive a British Envoy—General Sir Neville Chamberlain—and forcibly barred his passage at Ali Musjid. An ultimatum was sent to the Amir, but as no answer was received, an advance of three columns which were waiting at Jamrud, Kohat and Quetta was ordered on 21st November, 1878.

This was the first occasion on which troops of the Presidencies' armies had been deployed in strength on service since the reorganization after the Mutiny: on the Khyber line was the 1st Division at Jamrud, backed by the 2nd Division at Peshawar, 16,000 men under Lieutenant-General Sir Sam Browne, V.C., K.C.S.I., C.B.; the Kurram valley column consisted of 6,500 under Major-General Frederick Roberts, V.C., C.B.; the Mooltan division, 7,000 under Lieutenant-General Donald Stewart, C.B., was to join the Quetta column of 5,000. The infantry were formed into mixed brigades of one British and three native battalions; the British being armed with Martini-Henry rifles and the native units with Sniders.

Medical arrangements did not go beyond a system of regimental hospitals.

The Khyber column was to advance to Jalalabad; the Kurram column was to clear the country south of the Shutargardan Pass, securing that pass ready to advance on Kabul in the spring; the Quetta column was to establish itself in the Pishin valley, seizing the Khojak Pass, and to await the arrival of the column on its way from Multan. The North-Western Railway ran as far as Jhelum, and another line ran from Karachi to Sukkur: Jhelum and Sukkur were railheads. No transport service existed in India in peace time, so animals had to be requisitioned and obtained in a hurry, many being taken over quite unfit for the work, and the wastage was enormous.

The Khyber column included the Hazara Mountain Battery, P.F.F., under Captain E. J. de Lautour, with Lieutenants C. C. Lindsay and E. C. Wace, which was sent with Brigadier-General Macpherson's brigade to take the fort of Ali Musjid in reverse while two brigades made a frontal attack. Apart from an extremely steep descent to the valley, little trouble was experienced and casualties were light. The garrison evacuated the fort at night,* leaving the troops free to advance, and Jalalabad was reached on 20th December. The battery took part in several small expeditions to punish parties of raiders; once at Shergarh fire was opened at 1,200 yards on a body of men with a red flag, and the second round passed through the flag, killing one man and wounding three. The passage of the Kabul and Kunar rivers had to be made several times, and the battery recorded: "12th January, 1879: Arrived at ferry, 1.30 p.m. Guns etc., across on 'mussack' rafts, 3.5 p.m. Mules arrived from lower ford, 3.20 p.m. Saddled up and left, 3.27 p.m." This battery formed part of a column under Brigadier-General Macpherson sent on 31st March into the Lughman valley to capture a Ghilzai chief, but the force failed in its object. This was the occasion on which a squadron of the 10th Hussars failed to keep to the ford crossing the Kabul river, and one officer and forty-one other ranks were drowned. The battery moved later with a column to Gandamak, arriving 14th April.

The Kurram force met with some opposition. General Roberts's force, the Kurram Valley Field Force, consisted of two infantry brigades and two regiments of cavalry in addition to the artillery, which was commanded by Lieutenant-Colonel A. H. Lindsay and included the 1st (Kohat) and the 2nd (Derajat) Mountain Batteries.† The other batteries were F/A, R.H.A., with 9-prs. on elephants, and G/3 Field Battery. The 1st (Kohat) Battery was commanded by Captain J. A. Kelso, with Lieutenants J. C. Shirres and H. N. Jervois. This battery marched from Kohat to Jamrud in October to join the Khyber Force, but was ordered back to Kohat to join the Kurram Force.

The 2nd (Derajat) Battery was commanded by Captain G. Swinley,‡ with Lieutenants E. A. Smith and C. A. Montanaro.

---

* It was reported that twenty-two Afghan guns were captured as well as a mountain battery complete with guns and mules; the mules had their nosebags on.
† Designated at this time Nos. 1 and 2 Mountain Batteries, P.F.F., respectively.
‡ The last name on the roll of the Bengal Artillery. Commissioned 6th November, 1860.

The force crossed the frontier on 21st November, the advanced troops, which comprised the 12th Bengal Cavalry, 29th Punjab Infantry and 1st (Kohat) Mountain Battery, pushing back the Afghans as far as the Peiwar Kotal, which was reported to be occupied in force.

The depression of the Kotal was commanded on each side by high pine-clad mountains, from which the ascent to the Kotal was completely commanded. Several days were spent in a thorough reconnaissance, and the Major-General decided to turn the enemy's left by the Spingawai Pass, to which the line of approach seemed least difficult. He himself commanded the turning force of five battalions, 1st (Kohat) Mountain Battery and four horse artillery guns on elephants, which left the camp, six miles west of Kurram Fort, at 10 p.m. on 1st December, timed to co-operate with an attack at daybreak on the enemy's front.

The turning force arrived unobserved, and the battle was opened by the 5th Gurkhas and the 72nd Highlanders storming stockades on the ridge. The Afghan guns opened a heavy fire, but did little damage. Two of Captain Kelso's guns were well to the front and came into action in the enemy's left gun position, which had been vacated; but in order to get a better view to enfilade the position, Captain Kelso moved to his right and was immediately shot dead. Lieutenant Shirres took over and his two guns supported the advance of the infantry along the ridge, the other section* of the battery arriving later.

A counter-attack by the enemy was repulsed, and by 6.30 a.m. his line had been turned, at which time the artillery of the frontal attack was in action and the infantry moving forward.

The turning column was very hotly engaged from a strong line in the woods as soon as the Afghans realized that their position had been taken in reverse, and the horse artillery and mountain guns were continuously in action. The latter took up a position which commanded the interior of the Afghan camp in rear of the Peiwar Kotal, and shelled it with such effect that tents were set on fire, and the camp was vacated.

General Roberts then sent four battalions and the artillery of the turning column by a long detour round the enemy's rear, whereupon their guns ceased firing and opposition ended. The Afghans were in full flight, but unfortunately the turning force could not get up in time to cut them off. The enemy's strength was at least 4,000,

---

* To prevent confusion, the sub-unit up to this time called a "division" of a battery is hereafter called a "section," which became its official designation some years later.

the British about 3,000 in all. Our losses were slight: seventeen enemy guns were captured.

The troops spent the winter on the line of communication between Ali Khel, the position of force headquarters, and Thal.

Both mountain batteries went with a flying column under General Roberts to the Khost valley in Afghanistan, the inhabitants of which were showing disaffection, culminating in an attack on our column near Matun, the chief place. This was easily repulsed, and the valley was thoroughly reconnoitred before the troops were withdrawn.

The Quetta Division, under Major-General M. A. S. Biddulph, C.B., advanced on 21st November via Pishin to the Khojak Pass, which was occupied on 9th December, on which date Lieutenant-General Stewart arrived at Quetta to take over command. His division was moving up the Bolan Pass to Quetta, bringing three siege and two heavy batteries which found the going difficult.

The mountain batteries with the Quetta Division were the 3rd (Peshawar) and 6th (Jacob's) Mountain Batteries;* Captain J. Charles commanding the former and Captain R. Wace the latter. Kandahar was occupied without trouble on 8th January.

By way of making a demonstration, General Stewart moved his division to Kalat-i-Ghilzai and back without opposition, and General Biddulph marched a brigade to the Helmand. This latter formation included four guns of the Peshawar Mountain Battery, and the force was occupied in collecting supplies and making a survey. Little happened except brushes with raiders, and early in March the battery with other troops was ordered to return to India via Thal-Chotiali to open up that road, under Major-General Biddulph. This operation will be referred to later (pp. 54, 55).

The political situation had changed in January, 1879, when the Amir left Kabul and shortly afterwards died, being succeeded by his son Yakub Khan, who signed the Treaty of Gandamak in May. This gave the British Government possession of the districts of Kurram, Sidi and Pishin, and Kandahar and control of the Khyber and Michni Passes. The Amir agreed to conduct his relations with foreign states in accordance with the wishes of the British Government, and accepted an annual subsidy of six lakhs. Major Sir Louis Cavagnari, with a small escort of the Queen's Own Corps of Guides, was sent to Kabul as British Envoy. Arrangements were made immediately for the withdrawal and breaking up of the armies.

The Hazara Mountain Battery was part of the force left to garrison

---

* At this date designated Peshawar Mountain Battery, P.F.F., and No. 2 Bombay Mountain Battery, respectively.

Landi Kotal. Captain de Lautour resigned the command and Captain A. Broadfoot was appointed Commandant. The former officer on his departure received a brevet-majority and high praise in a complimentary order issued by the Brigadier-General Commanding the Punjab Frontier Force. The 1st (Kohat) Battery remained at Kurram and the 2nd (Derajat) Battery at Ali Khel. All batteries were increased to six-gun strength in June and the establishment raised accordingly.

The 3rd Class Order of Merit was presented on a parade of the troops to Havildar Sapooran Singh and Naik Gul by General Roberts, who complimented the Kohat Mountain Battery on the gallant service it had rendered at the Peiwar Kotal.

The transport of the army had been demobilized and troops were settling into peace stations when it became known that the Envoy and his staff and escort had been massacred by Afghan troops on 3rd September. Cavagnari and the escort had fought magnificently a whole day before they were overwhelmed. Their epitaph is written on their memorial at Mardan: "The annals of no army and no regiment can show a brighter record of devoted bravery than has been achieved by this small band of Guides."

General Roberts's force moved towards Kabul at the end of September over the Shutargardan Pass, leaving two battalions and the Kohat Mountain Battery, now commanded by Captain H. R. L. Morgan, to hold the pass behind him. This force was heavily attacked by Ghilzais on 2nd and 14th October and the mountain battery was busily engaged. The second attack was continued until the 18th, when the position, which was held by the 3rd Sikhs and the 21st Punjab Infantry, was surrounded by 10,000 of the enemy, and there was some very hard fighting. The battery had four guns in the camp, which were moved about to defend threatened points and to break up enemy sangars, firing from behind breastworks of atta bags, which saved many casualties. Ammunition, however, could not be replenished and there was no water for the mules. On the morning of the 19th a relieving force arrived, which included four guns of the Derajat Mountain Battery, and the enemy was driven off under heavy shell fire. The front was afterwards withdrawn to the Peiwar Kotal, and the Shutargardan given up as it was no longer of importance, the line of communication having been transferred to the Khyber. Colonel G. N. Money, commanding the troops at Shutargardan, reported: "It is impossible to speak too highly of the admirable way in which both Captain Morgan and Lieutenant Shirres have handled their guns on every occasion they have been engaged with the enemy. On the 2nd and 14th October our success was in a great measure due to the crushing fire of their guns." Of the action of the 18th and 19th he wrote: "I have never before seen such perfect artillery practice."

General Sir F. Roberts later, at a parade of the battery and the 3rd Sikhs (the 21st Punjab Infantry being elsewhere), said, after compliments: "The safety of my right flank and rear depended mainly on the safety of the Shutargardan, for if the latter had fallen, the tribes would have attempted to hinder my march. . . . Repeated attacks were made on the position you were holding, and so confident were the Ghilzais of their success, that I hear they brought down their women to witness your discomfiture. . . . You have set a good example to the whole force by showing what a few men can do when properly led. . . . I am aware that the Viceroy has sent you a special message thanking you for your bravery."

The main force concentrated at Kushi for the advance on Kabul, but did not arrive there without a fight. On reaching Charasia, eleven miles from Kabul, where the road ran through a defile, masses of Afghans were seen to be lining the heights on both sides of the road, and several batteries were in position. Immediate action was necessary as the rear-guard could not move until transport was sent back from the main column after the latter had arrived at its destination, and to prevent disaster the rear-guard had to be in the new camp before dark.

This time the Major-General turned the enemy's right, and Brigadier-General Baker was sent off for this purpose with three battalions, supported by the centre section of the Derajat Mountain Battery under Lieutenant F. E. Allsopp, and two Gatlings. Major G. White,* 92nd Highlanders, commanded the frontal attack, and was ordered to push his cavalry through the pass as soon as the turning movement had thoroughly developed.

The enemy had twenty guns on the heights, and the flank attack had to capture a succession of strongly held hilltops along the ridge; but the dash and gallantry of the 72nd Highlanders, 5th Gurkhas and 5th Punjab Infantry proved irresistible, and by 4 p.m. the enemy was in flight and Major White's column advanced and held the heights on both sides of the defile.

The section of the Derajat Mountain Battery fired 104 rounds and had one mule wounded.

Little further opposition was met, and the troops marched through Kabul city on 10th October, camping in the Bala Hissar a day later.

---

* Afterwards Field-Marshal Sir George White, V.C., G.C.B., G.C.S.I., G.C.I.E.. G.C.V.O.

In November the troops moved into cantonments at Sherpur, a mile north-east of Kabul city, where the British troops were accommodated in buildings and the native troops made temporary hutments. The Amir, Yakub Khan, surrendered and was banished to India, and General Roberts became administrator of the country pending the installation of a new Amir. Sir Frederick Roberts was promoted to Lieutenant-General, to command the two divisions in eastern Afghanistan; the 2nd Division, being that of General Bright, was strung out down the line of communication to Jamrud.

The mountain batteries were busy during December* escorting convoys and carrying out punitive measures in the district, which was becoming very restless, and risings on a large scale were threatened from Kohistan and Maidan, headed by Mullah Mahomed Jan.

On 5th December the right section of the Kohat Battery went with a force under Brigadier-General Tytler, V.C., C.B., into the Zaimukht country, and did not return to the Kabul force until 16th January, 1880, when it reached Landi Kotal. Its doings will be related later (pp. 52, 53).

The other four guns were with Brigadier-General Macpherson's column, sent westwards to Arghandi with a view to forcing an enemy column on to Baker's brigade which was blocking the Ghazni road near Beni Badam. An initial success was followed by a setback in which three squadrons of cavalry and a horse artillery battery were overwhelmed by masses of Kohistanis on unsuitable ground, but later on the day was retrieved by the infantry supported by Captain Morgan's two guns.

Brigadier-General Baker's force, which included two sections of the Derajat Mountain Battery under Captain Swinley, when moving northwards to make connection with General Macpherson's force, found it was opposed by the whole mass of Kohistanis who had attacked Macpherson the day before, and had to fight its way back to Sherpur.

---

* Excerpts from Major Swinley's letters:
"The R.A. officers at Kabul bought the Peshawar Vale hounds and hunted the jackal round Kabul.

"Office work on active service was ten times as great as in peace time; it was quite intolerable.

"Promotion examinations were held on active service as in peace time.

"Dress: in Nov. 1878 native ranks wore Khaki, pagris as well. In Feb. 1879 the khaki pagri had a red and blue fringe. In Spring 1880 they wore blue norfolk coats, blue serge knickerbockers, and blue puttees.

"Range cards were made out at Kabul, ranges being taken by officers using sextants."

More counter-attacks were made in the next few days, and large hordes kept closing in with a view to overwhelming the British forces: meantime the forward movement of troops up the line through the Khyber Pass was proceeding steadily.

On 14th December Baker's brigade, to which were attached Captain Swinley's four guns, was ordered to drive the enemy off the Asmai heights. The heights were captured and the enemy driven off, but the Kohistanis in vastly superior numbers returned and swept our troops off the hill, and two mountain guns had to be temporarily abandoned. Lieutenant C. A. Montanaro brought the other two guns out of action, all the gun detachments having behaved in a gallant fashion. Surgeon J. Duke was specially mentioned for his attention to the wounded under heavy fire. The failure on this day led the Lieutenant-General to decide to defend the Sherpur cantonment, pending the arrival of the 2nd Division.

In a sortie on the 19th sent to destroy a fortified village close to our lines, Lieutenant Montanaro was mortally wounded in the act of laying one of his guns.

An attempt to take Sherpur by storm was made on the 23rd by a force estimated at 20,000, but every time the enemy reached the trenches they were beaten back. Attacks were mounted almost continuously from before daylight until noon, when a counterstroke was made by a cavalry regiment and a field battery, which moved out to take the attackers in flank. This broke up the main attack and General Roberts sent out his cavalry in pursuit. The enemy scattered and the next day none were to be seen.

The two mountain batteries took a share in the defence. Brigadier-General H. Gough, C.B., reported of the 1st (Kohat) Battery: "The two guns under the command of Lieutenant Shirres attached to the force under my command at the defence of Bemaru on the 23rd December, were exposed to very heavy and continuous musketry fire for some hours. The behaviour of the men was most excellent, and I was much struck with the coolness and steadiness with which the guns were worked."

The Centre Section joined in the pursuit. The 2nd (Derajat) Battery had a section in action in a bastion alongside the 72nd Highlanders.

The ensuing weeks were spent in strengthening the defences of Sherpur and Kabul, making roads and bridges, and preparing for the arrival of the Khyber force. In March the Kabul Field Force under Sir F. Roberts was reorganized in two divisions; the 1st under Sir F. Roberts, and the 2nd under Brigadier-General Ross;

Brigadier-General Bright became Inspector-General of Communications and G.O.C., Khyber Line Force.

The posts were strengthened along the route to Jamrud, and the 4th (Hazara) Mountain Battery was divided, leaving eventually two guns on the line of communications; battery headquarters and four guns joining the 2nd Division at Kabul. Here Surgeon G. S. Robertson, who met the battery again when he was Assistant Political Officer in Gilgit, took over medical charge. The battery was united in April and took part in several minor operations destroying villages of recalcitrant tribesmen.

On 25th April four guns of the 2nd (Derajat) Battery went at short notice with a force to relieve Colonel Jenkins's detachment at Charasia, where it had gone to break up a rising which turned out to be on a larger scale than could be dealt with without assistance. The reinforced column had no difficulty in disposing of the enemy, and the battery returned to Sherpur the same night.

At Besud in May a section of the 1st (Kohat) Mountain Battery under Lieutenant F. R. Thackeray engaged a tower which contained some ghazis, and cut it down to within a few feet from the ground at a range of thirty-five yards. The mules had to swim the Kabul river, and the section was highly complimented by Brigadier-General Doran for good shooting, gallantry and displaying the attributes of good soldiers.

Sardar Abdur Rahman Khan, a grandson of Dost Mahomed, had been selected by the Government of India as the future Amir, and arrangements having been satisfactorily concluded, the Kabul Field Force, now named Northern Afghanistan Field Force, 1st and 2nd Divisions, prepared to evacuate the country, starting on 11th August, 1880.

At the time when the British Envoy in Kabul was murdered (September, 1879), the Kandahar Field Force had been in process of withdrawal, but Sir Donald Stewart was still in Kandahar, and immediate orders had been given for the force to reassemble. It consisted now of a cavalry brigade, two infantry brigades and some artillery. One brigade was sent to make a demonstration towards Kabul, and marched to Kalat-i-Ghilzai (eighty-seven miles). It advanced a few miles farther and had a brush with the Ghilzais at Shahjui, returning to Kandahar in November, having left a small force at Kalat-i-Ghilzai. At the same time another brigade executed a "reconnaissance in force" to the Helmund river, and occupied the fort of Girishk. Four guns of the Peshawar Mountain Battery accompanied this force. A clash with some Afghans occurred on 26th February, and the division returned to Kandahar on 2nd March.

At the end of March, 1880, a Bengal division, composed of British and Bengal troops under Lieutenant-General Sir D. Stewart, started to march to Kabul via Ghazni, in view of the unsettled state of the area round Kabul.

General Stewart took two months' rations for British troops and seven days' for natives. A column under General Ross was to be sent from Kabul to meet him at Saidabad with more rations. Among the artillery was a British mountain battery, 11/11 R.A., with six 7-prs.

The movement was unimpeded until 19th April, when the force was opposed by a large party of Afghans (8,000 to 10,000) at Ahmad Khel, just short of Ghazni. This was a stiff fight, but the enemy's fanatical onslaught was stopped by steady infantry and artillery fire, the guns firing case and reversed shrapnel at short ranges. From Ghazni communication was established by heliograph with General Ross's force, and, except for a brush at Arzu where a reconnaissance party was attacked, the march to Kabul ended on 2nd May, and Sir Donald Stewart took over command of all the troops in Afghanistan, of which the Bengal Division became the 3rd Division.

Trouble had been brewing in southern Afghanistan, fostered by Ayub Khan, a brother of the deposed Amir, who intended to make a bid for the possession of Kandahar, and proclaimed a jehad at Herat, from which place he started on 4th June with about 7,000 men. This number increased rapidly, and the countryside was in a state of unrest as far back as Chaman, which was usually in a disturbed state. The 6th (Jacob's) Mountain Battery had a section on the line of communication at Chaman under Captain E. C. Wace, Commandant, and a small force including the section had to be sent to capture the ringleader of a party which destroyed a post in April.

A mixed brigade including E/B. R.H.A. was sent from Kandahar to support the Wali of Kandahar at Girishk, but the commander found himself in an untenable position and withdrew to a position covering Kandahar. He moved to Maiwand on 27th July to attack Ayub Khan's force, and the story of that action is too well known to need repeating. The survivors of this disaster withdrew to Kandahar Fort, which then came under siege, communication having ceased on the morning of the 28th.

The Government realized that the quickest method of relieving Kandahar was the dispatch of a force from Kabul, and a mixed division was immediately prepared to proceed as a flying column, there being no base or line of communication available. A cavalry brigade and three infantry brigades were detailed, along with three mountain batteries, it having been decided to take no wheeled transport in case it might be necessary to move across country. This "Kabul-Kandahar Field Force" was commanded by Sir Frederick Roberts; Colonel A. Johnson commanded the Artillery; 6/8 R.A., later to become No. 3 Light Battery, was armed with six 2.5-inch R.M.L. guns, and the other British battery, 11/9 R.A., and 2nd (Derajat) Mountain Battery with six 7-prs. each; 190 rounds per gun were taken, of which 30 were in the field park. The total of fighting men in the force was just under 10,000 with nearly 9,000 animals. The force began its 300-mile march on 8th August.

Each day's march began at 2.30 a.m. and the troops found the heat very trying; long stretches of desert were without water for the animals; nevertheless they arrived at Kandahar in excellent order. It is noteworthy that the conditions of this war produced two other movements of large columns without any line of communication: General Roberts's march from the Shutargardan to Kabul on the renewal of operations in November, 1879, and General Stewart's march from Kandahar to Kabul.

The force arrived at Kandahar on 31st August, and the General made an immediate reconnaissance for the attack on the following day. Ayub Khan's troops were entrenching the hills covering Kandahar, from which their artillery was shelling the camp, and the plan of attack for the next day was to threaten the enemy's left while the main attack turned his right. The plan worked successfully and, driven out of his first position, the enemy took up a second, but refused to face British bayonets, and the day was ours. The enemy numbered about 12,000, with 1,200 killed; our casualties were 35 killed.

The troops from Kabul were sent to India on the breaking up of the force: the Derajat battery marched to Sibi, whence it was railed to Rawalpindi, taking four days. Its destination was Kohat. This was its first experience of moving by rail. Kandahar was evacuated on 21st April, 1881. The 6th (Jacob's) Mountain Battery, already mentioned as being on the lines of communication, had been very busy protecting convoys and had moved towards Kandahar with a relief force under General Phayre, but too late to take part in the battle of Kandahar. This battery had only just raised another section to complete six guns, and as suitable native gunners were not available, British gunners were lent for a time by the Garrison battery at Quetta, and mules obtained from the Commissariat. This scratch section acquitted itself well in action at the Khojak Pass on its way to join the battery at Chaman.

Later on, the 5th (Bombay) Mountain Battery, now at Rajkote, furnished some men to replace others of poor physique, and the whole of the equipment was renewed to bring it up to the standard of the Punjab batteries. The 6th Battery contained many Mahrattas, who had stood the hardships of the campaign very well.

In commemoration of their gallant conduct during the campaign, Her Majesty the Queen Empress permitted words to be borne on the colours or appointments of Batteries as follows:

No. 1 (Kohat): "PEIWAR KOTAL"; "KABUL, 1879"; "AFGHANISTAN, 1878-80".

No. 2 (Derajat): "CHARASIA"; "KABUL, 1879"; "KANDAHAR"; "AFGHANISTAN, 1878-80".

No. 3 (Peshawar): "AFGHANISTAN, 1878-79".

No. 4 (Hazara): "ALI MUSJID"; "KABUL, 1879"; "AFGHANISTAN, 1878-80".

No. 2 (Bombay*): "AFGHANISTAN, 1878-80".

To individuals present during the campaign a silver medal was awarded, on the reverse of which was an elephant bearing a gun under the word "Afghanistan" and above the dates "1878-79-80". Bars inscribed "Ali Musjid", "Peiwar Kotal", "Charasia", "Kabul", "Ahmed Khel" and "Kandahar" were also granted. For the march of General Roberts from Kabul to Kandahar a bronze star was given, made from guns captured at Kabul, and showing the inscription "Kabul to Kandahar", with the date 1880.

At the end of the campaign Captain H. R. L. Morgan was promoted to brevet-major, and in recognition of their services, horse artillery jackets were given to Lieutenants F. R. Thackeray, C. A. Anderson and Captain A. Broadfoot. Lieutenant J. C. Shirres was specially selected for a jacket, but preferred to remain in his mountain battery with the prospect of obtaining command.

Captain G. Swinley, who had already received a brevet-majority, now received a brevet-lieutenant-colonelcy.

The punitive expedition against the Zaimukhts already mentioned was a reprisal for numerous raids on our convoys, both on the Kohat–Thal road and in Kurram. The tribe had given no trouble for a few years until they murdered a British officer riding along the road, whereupon a force was sent into their country. The artillery consisted of four guns of 1/8 R.A., a British Mountain Battery, and a section of No. 1 (Kohat) Mountain Battery. Only slight opposition was met with, but it is noteworthy that this was the first occasion

---

* Later 6th (Jacob's).

of the use on service of the 2.5-inch R.M.L. screw-gun,* with which 1/8 R.A. was armed; this was to be the mountain artillery weapon for the next twenty-five years.

The roads were extremely bad, and some fighting took place for the capture of Zawo, but the results of the expedition were satisfactory and fines were paid up. The Kohat-Thal road was free from outrage for many years afterwards.

The tribesmen were very restless for some years after the conclusion of the war, no doubt because the Afghans resented the peace terms forced upon them. These were less onerous than the terms agreed at Gandamak, in that Kandahar was returned to the Afghans and the British representative at Kabul was to be a Mohammedan.

Trouble amongst the Waziristan tribes was being stirred up by the followers of a Mullah who was ejected from Khost by our troops in January, 1879, and the Bhittannis of Jandola had given passage through their territory to a large number of Wazirs on mischief bent, without informing us. This was contrary to our pact of friendship, and a small force was sent to destroy Jandola. Three guns of the 3rd (Peshawar) Mountain Battery took part in this operation, which went off peacefully once the battery had opened fire.

The Mahsuds and Wazirs had taken part in numerous acts of hostility while our troops were engaged in Afghanistan, and as they refused to abstain from raids and make submission, a force consisting of Punjab Frontier Force troops, with some Sappers and Miners and Pioneers added, assembled at Tank in April, 1881.

The usual orders had been given by the Government of India that fortified places were to be destroyed, the property of ringleaders confiscated, and armed resistance punished by the seizure of cattle and crops.

There was little opposition to this powerful force (seven battalions and three batteries) until it was one day's march short of Kaniguram, when great numbers of the enemy suddenly charged the 1st Sikhs, who were halted in the open. The battalion, supported by the fire of the 3rd (Peshawar) Mountain Battery, easily stopped the attack. The force arrived at Makin via the Tank Zam and found the Bannu column (in which the 1st Kohat Mountain Battery was included), which had advanced by the Khaisora route, waiting at Razmak to co-operate. This force had little to chronicle, and returned to Bannu without trouble, taking with it the 2nd (Derajat) and 4th (Hazara) Mountain Batteries, 1st Kohat Mountain Battery transferring to the Tank column.

Fines were levied and submission made; the blockade which had

---

* This was the first portable screw-gun on record.

lasted three years was lifted, and hostages were taken before the main force retired to be broken up. Brigadier-General Kennedy, C.B., commanding the expedition and the Punjab Frontier Force, expressed his satisfaction with the discipline of the batteries and the work they had done.

The want of a direct route from the Punjab to Quetta had been apparent during the Second Afghan War, and in 1879 the Thal-Chotiali Field Force was formed to reconnoitre the old trade route from Pishin to the Derajat. The strategical importance of Baluchistan was enhanced by our occupation of Quetta and the Bolan Pass, whereby the flank of Afghanistan was turned, but our position could not be considered secure until Zhob and Mekran had been brought under our control. It was desirable to forestall any possible advance by the Afghans in that area, as they were feeling sore about the districts of which they were being deprived in accordance with the peace terms, but the Baluchistan district had to be retained to protect our communications with Quetta and the railway now being made via Harnai.

The Field Force left Pishin in March, 1879, in three columns, only one of which—that containing 6th (Jacob's) Mountain Battery—met with much resistance. That column, under Major Keene, of four companies of the 1st Punjab Infantry and two squadrons of cavalry, was opposed without warning at Baghao by a body of 3,000 tribesmen of the Zhob and Bori valleys. The enemy was halted by fire from the battery and put to flight by the attack of our small force. After getting through to Thal-Chotiali without further trouble, two of the guns were left there as part of a small garrison, while the Field Force went on to Dera Ghazi Khan and was broken up. Much useful survey work had been accomplished.

For the action at Baghao, Lieutenant R. W. Robertson and Captain R. Wace were mentioned in despatches, the latter receiving a brevet-majority.

When the news of the disaster at Maiwand spread, the Baluchistan tribes became very unsettled and started raiding on a large scale, especially the Marris who had been working on the new railway. Two guns of 6th (Jacob's) Mountain Battery were with one of the columns which arrived at Thal after very trying marching but no fighting, and was left in garrison there for some months. The Marris submitted and agreed to our terms that all roads should be open to traffic (1880).

The Thal-Chotiali district remained full of unrest, being in the next valley to the Boris, who were particularly truculent and made no attempt to give up their disorderly habits. In April, 1884, the

Government of India decided to send a force into the Zhob valley to enforce the authority of the British Raj. In the Zhob valley expedition were 9/1 Northern Division, R.A., with screw-guns, and 1st (Kohat) Mountain Battery. The expedition left Thal-Chotiali on 5th October, 1884, and went into standing camp at Dulai in the Bori country. Little opposition was met with until the column reached the Zhob valley, where it was engaged at Ali Khel by a number of tribesmen who were soon routed. The force then carried out a survey of the Zhob valley and surroundings as far east as Mina and received the submission of the tribes, being withdrawn in November.

A reconnaissance and survey was also made of the Takht-i-Suleiman mountain in November, 1883 with a strong escort of 1,500 bayonets, 100 sabres, and the 4th (Hazara) Mountain Battery, all these troops belonging to the Punjab Frontier Force. The force moved from Dera Ismail Khan round the north of the range and came in from the western side. No opposition was met until the force arrived at Pezai Springs, where the kotal over which the road lay was held by the Khidarzais, a disaffected tribe. Their main position was almost inaccessible, but was turned by the 1st Sikhs after a difficult climb, and the enemy dispersed. The battery was commanded by Captain W. M. Campbell; it fired only six rounds. The survey was carried out successfully. The mountain was found to be a gigantic mass of limestone consisting of two parallel ridges, of which the highest point was 11,300 feet, with a waterless maidan in between, about 9,000 feet. All water had to be brought up from the springs where the camp was fixed in bitter weather.

Loralai was later decided on as a permanent cantonment dominating the Thal-Chotiali area, but the Zhob valley remained a battleground for the local tribes for some years.

Sir Robert Sandeman toured the region with an escort which included the 3rd (Peshawar) Mountain Battery, setting out from Loralai in December, 1889, where this battery had recently relieved the 2nd (Derajat) Battery. The Peshawar Battery was now armed with six 2.5-inch R.M.L. guns, but had little opportunity for using them during the marches on escort duty. The force camped at Apozai, which was selected as the future headquarters of the Political Agent, Zhob, and was given the name of Fort Sandeman. The tour proceeded as far as Kajuri Kach and most of the Zhob valley tribes gave the agreements required. The battery marched on to its new station, Kohat, via Dera Ismail Khan.

Notwithstanding Sir Robert Sandeman's efforts to make the Zhob tribes keep the peace, owing to the importance of that area from a military point of view and its proximity to the Ghazni caravan route, the tribes refused to give up their quarrels and raids, and the Government decided to occupy the country and at the same time to open up the Gomal route to the Derajat. In October, 1890, the Zhob Field Force under Major-General Sir George White, V.C., K.C.B., was formed for these purposes, about a brigade in all, and marched by three routes from the western side to concentrate at Fort Sandeman. This went off smoothly and the tribes, except the Khidarzais and other sections of the Shirannis, accepted the British protection offered.

As part of the Shirannis were under the Punjab Government and part under the Baluchistan Agency in the Bombay Presidency, some Punjab troops were sent to join Sir George White's force, now about to traverse Shiranni country. Included in this column, which was commanded by Colonel A. G. Ross, C.B., 1st Sikhs, were a section of 7th (Bengal) Mountain Battery* and 1st (Kohat) Mountain Battery less one section. The Right Section of the latter battery was in garrison at Fort Sandeman. Two small forces were placed as stops at the eastern exits of Khidarzai country, and the main advance made by Sir George White from the west.

The tracks were appallingly bad, for many miles impassable even for mules, but after a few days road making troops were able to reach the two principal villages in the mountainous country just south of the Takht-i-Suleiman.

The Khidarzais surrendered, but during the next few days the troops were fired on and some villages had to be burnt as reprisals. By mid-November all our terms had been accepted.

Sir George White took this opportunity to climb the Takht with fifty rifles of the King's Own Yorkshire Light Infantry and fifty of the 2nd Baluch Regiment, fully accoutred. The path up the eastern face, the most difficult one, was selected for the ascent, and although in places the troops climbed on their hands and knees they reached the summit of the kotal, though not the shrine at 11,000 feet. The nights were extremely cold and water was short, and it impressed the Shirannis as a great feat of endurance.

Eventually the surrender was complete, and few outrages took place in the Zhob area for a number of years.

The 1st (Kohat) Mountain Battery returned to Dera Ismail Khan, less one section which formed part of Sir Robert Sandeman's escort to Mekran later in the year and one section at Fort Sandeman.

A detachment of this battery had had a short campaign on the North-East Frontier, in conditions very unlike those prevailing on the North-West Frontier.

---
* The first appearance of this battery on the N.W. Frontier.

On 31st December, 1883, a detachment of the 1st (Kohat) Mountain Battery under Captain J. C. Shirres, who was now Commandant, left Kohat for Tezpore in Assam, where it joined the force under Brigadier-General R. S. Hill, C.B., proceeding against the Aka tribe. At Tezpore two 7-prs. of 150 lb. complete with coolies were taken over, and after some jungle marches the enemy's main position was attacked. His weapons were bows and poisoned arrows. A clearing had to be cut to get a position for the guns from which the enemy's breastwork was commanded, and the infantry advance was supported to the first obstacle, the guns then shooting after the enemy in flight in the jungle. One of the 7-pr. carriages broke but otherwise no hitch occurred and the enemy submitted. Brigadier-General Hill issued an order thanking the troops for their endurance and cheerfulness in combating the great natural obstacles of the Assam forest country, and thanked the battery for its support and assistance. The detachment was back in Kohat in six weeks.

The armament of mountain batteries was reduced from six to four guns in 1882, with a corresponding reduction in establishment, but the battery baggage establishment was increased by twenty-four mules. An extra follower—a munshi—was now allowed in each battery.

In 1885 a collision between Russian and Afghan troops at Panjdeh on their frontier led to great tension between Russia and Great Britain, and preparations* were made in India against the possibility of war. The situation quietened down once the British showed firmness, but the effect on mountain artillery was an increase to six-gun batteries. In the same year it was ordered that batteries were to consist of four 2.5-inch R.M.L. (jointed) guns and two 7-prs.; the latter to be used as howitzers. In 1888 or 1889 the 7-prs. were taken away and batteries made up to six 2.5-inch R.M.L. guns.

It was a good gun, the best mountain gun of any nation at that time. But its adoption was not bringing any nearer the advent of the mountain howitzer, so long looked-for for work on the Frontier. A 20-pr. jointed R.M.L. howitzer† in three parts was in the experimental stage in England, but it failed to pass the tests, though not before a handbook was printed. Possibly the Home authorities, in producing the 2.5-inch gun with a flat trajectory, had been influenced by the prominence obtained by mountain guns in the Russian and Balkan armies, where they shared the role of the field artillery.

---

* The princes of India seized this opportunity to show their loyalty by offering help which developed into the organization of Imperial Service Troops for the service of the Empire.
† See note at end of chapter.

Originally called "the 7-pr. R.M.L. jointed steel gun of 400 lb.," it became "the 2.5-inch R.M.L.," perhaps to prevent the Ordnance Department from confusing the two kinds of 7-pr. shell. This new gun, with a charge of 1 lb. 8 oz., fired a 7 lb. 6 oz. shell, having a muzzle velocity of 1,440 f.s.; range, 4,000 yards (common or ring* shell) or 3,300 yards (shrapnel).

Rotation was effected by a copper driving band spun on to the shell.

The carriage was made of steel, and was fitted to carry the dismounting hammer on the outside of the left bracket and the worm wadhook and rammer on the outside of the right bracket. The combined sponge and rammer was in two pieces connected by a screw-joint.

A very comprehensive "Manual of Mountain Artillery," published in India in 1882, gave all that a mountain artilleryman should know from first joining to his "funeral party." It gave details of both guns, drill movements, gun drill, harness and march routine, but scanty mention of work in the field. Drill movements of a battery with camel and elephant pack transport were shown with diagrams.

To limber up, the gun was lifted out of the trunnion-holes to a vertical position with the cascable in a dismounting block on the trail, and a metal trunnion guard having been placed on the left trunnion, No. 2 struck it with a 7 lb. sledge hammer to loosen the junction nut. The trunnion ring having become loose, it was turned until the parts of the gun were separated, and the breech and muzzle parts were then loaded on to their mules. A similar performance was gone through in reverse to join the gun up when coming into action.

The next war was not a favourable occasion to test a gun of this type, as it took place in Burma, where the 2.5-inch shell made a neat hole in a stockade and disappeared into the jungle behind. The two native mountain batteries detailed—4th (Hazara) and 5th (Bombay)—were armed with 7-prs., which were more likely to burst their shell on the stockades.

---

* Ring shell were made of rings welded together, each ring breaking up into small segments on explosion.

The Third Burmese War (1885-1891)

Thebaw, King of Burma, refused to receive a British representative at Mandalay, and as he had for some years broken trade agreements and plundered British traders without redress, it was found necessary by the Government to send an expedition to bring him to book.

Burma is a country ill-suited for military operations; the whole transport system of the country was confined to the great rivers, which all ran from north to south. Between the valleys was a series of parallel mountain ranges, forest-covered and roadless, penetrable only by very small bodies of troops. The Irrawaddy river was the main highway of commerce, being navigable for 1,000 miles from its mouth (as far as Bhamo) and providing irrigation over a large dry zone north and south of Mandalay. The Chindwin is a tributary joining the main river below Mandalay. The Sittang and the Salween rivers run parallel, the latter entering the sea at Moulmein. The great port of Rangoon at the mouth of the Irrawaddy was included in the province of Pegu, which had been annexed in 1852 after an expedition had been sent from India. Acts of aggression and interference with traders by the Burmese had been of frequent occurrence for many years, and after a former expedition in 1826 the East India Company had annexed Arakan and part of the coast-line.

Assam was sealed off from the Irrawaddy valley by a vast mountain barrier, which, except for a few tracks in the north, was pierced only by an ungraded road from Tamu to Imphal, six feet wide.

In addition to these physical drawbacks, for six months of the year the rainfall varied from 200 to 100 inches.

The Burma Field Force under Major-General H. Prendergast, V.C., comprised three brigades and a siege train of twenty-eight pieces for the reduction of forts and redoubts. The artillery was carried in river steamers and in flats towed by the steamers, from which they fired. The 4th (Hazara) Battery, Commandant Captain E. C. Wace, was attending a camp of exercise at Ambala in October, 1885, when it received an order to send all mules and drivers to Abbottabad and proceed immediately to Burma without them. A similar order reached 5th (Bombay) Battery, and both batteries arrived in Burma on 10th November. There were no coolies ready for them, and the guns were arranged two in the bow of a steamer and two in the outer bow of each flat.

What afterwards became No. 5 Mountain Battery, R.G.A., but was called by the C.R.A., Colonel W. Carey, in his account the "European Mule Battery," armed with 2.5-inch R.M.L. guns, brought its mules, but was also transferred to the flats. The force started off from Thayetmyo up the Irrawaddy on 14th November, accompanied by a Naval Brigade, and easily reduced several forts, which were then garrisoned by British and native infantry and guns of 5th (Bombay) Mountain Battery.

Myingyan fort was silenced and garrisoned by similar detachments and, higher up the river, Ava surrendered after a demonstration on 27th November. The Burmese army then took to the jungle with its weapons and operated as dacoits. The 4th (Hazara) Battery, after joining the guard of the Palace at Mandalay, went on upstream on 19th December with the 3rd Brigade, which was detailed to capture Bhamo. The battery was now given 450 coolies for transport, but after several attempts at movement, coolie carriage proved a failure and mules and drivers were telegraphed for. Bhamo was captured without a fight and the cantonment marked out.

On some of the marches the guns, ammunition, etc., were carried on elephants, but Kahars and coolies were generally used. As many of the coolies as possible were exchanged for Kahars, who were more satisfactory for the carriage of the guns.

The right section was issued with $2\frac{1}{2}$-inch mortars with iron beds, manned by sepoys, but transport was so difficult that they were left behind after a week or two, along with some of the heavier battery stores.

A kukri was issued to each of the rank and file for jungle work, the useful mountain battery sword having been superseded by an infantry bayonet. The sword was reintroduced shortly afterwards.

The next twelve months were spent by the batteries in fighting the Kachins and chasing dacoits, as, although the Viceroy announced the annexation of Upper Burma to the British Empire from 1st January, 1886, it was long before the country settled down. The Hazara Battery received its mules from India in April, but it took some time to harden them after their long journey, and men began to fall sick from malaria and dysentery.

A small column under Captain Wace was in action against Kachins on the Yunnan frontier, in the course of which he himself, one gunner and one driver were wounded. Captain Wace being invalided Lieutenant W. J. Honner, First Subaltern, was promoted captain and posted as Commandant. In a second expedition against Kachins in May, in which 500 rifles, Royal Welsh Fusiliers, and the 26th Punjab Infantry with four guns of 4th (Hazara) Battery took part, many stockades were turned and the enemy retreated, but no practical result was attained. Small engagements with some sharp fighting went on almost incessantly, and when the rains set in the battery was laid up: only two guns could turn out in marching order;

twelve men died and at one time the number in hospital was 104. The 5th (Bombay) Battery quartered at Myingyan with a section at Nyaungoo was in a similar state under similar conditions.

The mules at this time were doing well, and escaped an outbreak of surra. They were fed on a ration made up of 2 lb. each of gram, bran, and paddy.

In September the batteries were inspected by the Commander-in-Chief, Sir Frederick Roberts, who was pleased with the general turn-out and the condition of the mules.

Bhamo was rushed by a body of Chinese, Shans, and Kachins one night in November, but they were quickly expelled. All through the dry weather the dacoits were pursued with varying success, and the work took a heavy toll of the troops. Single-fly tents were issued for the first time.

A new order became effective that men enlisted for one battery would be held liable to serve in any of the other batteries of the Punjab Frontier Force, and might be transferred in time of war. Men from Nos. 1, 2, 3, and 5 (Garrison) Batteries actually joined in Bhamo to replace casualties.

While at Bhamo, Battery Standing Orders of the 4th (Hazara) Battery were compiled; Hindustani words of command were to be discontinued, and English names used in dealing with ammunition.

In March, 1886, the Upper Burma Field Force under Brigadier-General G. S. White was divided into two brigades, with headquarters at Mandalay and Bhamo. Faced with the task of settling 100,000 square miles of jungle overrun by armed bands, the Force garrisoned posts and sent out swift-moving columns of about 200 rifles, to which artillery was sometimes attached. The moral effect of artillery fire was great, and generally scattered the enemy groups, but this prevented the infantry from engaging at close quarters. The solution of the problem lay in an unrelenting pursuit of the dacoit chiefs and in harrassing the armed bands which were perpetually breaking out from the jungle to devastate villages and ambush our convoys.

In 1886 more than a hundred small engagements were chronicled inside four months; apart from casualties, sickness and disease took their toll.

The Burma Military Police, recruited from the Punjab and North-West Provinces, reached a total of 6,500, and the number of troops in Upper Burma was about 23,000, including reinforcements of British and Indian troops. For the winter campaign General Sir Frederick Roberts, Commander-in-Chief in India, transferred his headquarters to Mandalay. Six brigades were formed and, as a result of strenuous operations during the winter, many leaders were captured and dacoit gangs rounded up and destroyed.

There was a great deal of similarity in these operations of small columns, sometimes acting singly, sometimes two or three converging on the objective; but a great improvement in the situation was noticeable by the time Major-General Sir George White took over in 1887, and the system of patrolling and sending out small flying columns led to satisfactory progress in the work of pacification. The Military Police, now increased to 13,000, were becoming very efficient, which permitted a reduction of troops. Forty-eight N.C.Os. and men of the Hazara Mountain Battery transferred to the Military Police.

Two new Bengal mountain batteries, No. 1 Bengal and No. 2 Bengal, had been raised in October, 1886, by Captains C. P. Triscott and E. A. Smith, at Rawalpindi and Mian Mir* respectively. Each battery was armed with six 7-pr. guns of 200 lb. on the same establishment as the Frontier Force batteries, which assisted by supplying drafts. After four years they were renumbered No. 7 Bengal and No. 8 Bengal Mountain Batteries respectively†.

In March, 1887, the Hazara Battery was relieved by No. 1 Bengal Mountain Battery, mules and equipment being left at the station for exchange.‡ The 5th (Bombay) Mountain Battery was similarly relieved by No. 2 Bengal Mountain Battery. Captain E. C. Wace was awarded the D.S.O., mentioned in despatches, and recommended for promotion; Lieutenant A. H. C. Birch was mentioned and recommended for promotion; Captain W. J. Honner was mentioned.

Two Native Officers of the 2nd (Derajat) Mountain Battery, P.F.F., were appointed to No. 2 Bengal Mountain Battery and one other Native Officer, Jemadar Sher Singh, was directly commissioned.

There now opened up the problem of shielding the new Burmese subjects of the Crown from the depredations of tribes on the border, who were unlikely to give up their marauding habits until compelled. These were the Chins in the Chin Hills and the Kachins in the area north of Myitkyina.

The 7th (Bengal) Mountain Battery provided a section with the column under Captain C. P. Triscott which established British authority in January, 1888, in the northern area in the vicinity of Mogaung, near the jade mines.

---

* Lahore Cantonment.

† After several changes they became 7th (Bengal) and 8th (Lahore) Mountain Batteries, respectively.

‡ This is the first recorded instance of a battery being ordered to hand over all its mules to another—a very unpopular exigency of the service.

An expedition to Wuntho took place in 1890; this territory was classed as a Shan State though practically a part of Burma, and was the resort of all the bad characters from Burma. A rebellion broke out suddenly in February and two flying columns, each with a section of 6th (Jacob's) Mountain Battery, the whole force under Brigadier-General G. B. Wolseley, C.B., restored order in a very short time, the actual rebellion having been suppressed in a few days by the defeat of a large enemy force by Mounted Military Police and a detachment of the Devonshire Regiment.

Fifty miles east of the Irrawaddy at Mogok were the famous ruby mines; a British mountain battery supplied the section with the column responsible for taking Mogok, but the native batteries took their turn in supplying two guns from time to time for the garrison.

The Chin country lies to the west of the Chindwin river and consists of a contorted mass of mountains intersected by deep valleys. The steep spurs are covered with dense jungle, but the higher hills are bare and dotted with villages and patches of cultivation. The tribes' arms at this time were flint-locks, spears, and dahs. They were adepts at guerilla warfare in the jungle, firing from ambush and cutting up stragglers from our columns, which consisted generally of about 200 men with the same number of coolies, forced to march in single file through thick jungle. The Chin would hide below the track, fire his gun at very close range into his victim's back and scuttle down the khud out of sight.

Occasional drives were made in 1887-8 to disperse dacoit gangs, but raiding and kidnapping continued, and in December, 1889, the Chin Field Force started operations on the Chin border. Two guns of the 7th (Bengal) Mountain Battery joined this force, which after several actions began in March to advance into the hills from Tokhlaing (afterwards named Fort White). Tiddim, Tartan, and several other villages were burnt and the headmen began to come in. Tartan was very strongly defended and had to be cleared with the bayonet. After that, peace was soon made and captives were given up.

The Lushais, who lived in the country between the Chin Hills and the Indian frontier, like the Chins, were perpetually raiding and enslaving Burmans in our new territory, and giving shelter and assistance to the Burmese guerillas. It was decided to punish them and pacify the area, for which purpose a column of 1,000 infantry was formed, based on Demagiri. The Right Section of 6th (Jacob's) Mountain Battery under Lieutenant C. de C. Hamilton was sent from Poona in January, 1889, to join this force. The section took 7-prs.

of 200 lb. with mules and was railed to Madras, thence by sea to Calcutta and Chittagong. The force had first to make a road to the Kaladan river, whence a flying column of 250 infantry and police with one gun of the section was sent ahead to the village of the chief offenders, who had massacred a survey party headed by a British officer. On arrival it was found that the enemy had decamped into the jungle, and the force returned after building a fort which was handed over to the police. The section had some severe marches and the men suffered from malaria; it returned to Poona to rejoin the battery in April. In October the whole battery entrained to Bombay, went by sea to Rangoon, by train thence to Mandalay and by river steamer to Bhamo for a tour of duty.

The last expedition not having produced satisfactory results, the Chin-Lushai Expedition was decided on, to enter the country simultaneously from the Indian and Chin borders, the whole force being commanded by Brigadier-General W. P. Symons. His orders were to punish tribes who had offended and not made submission, to explore the unknown parts of the country, and to establish posts where necessary. There were two columns from the Burma side; to the southern column were attached two guns of the 7th (Bengal) Battery. The operations started in November, 1889: the column from Chittagong punished certain villages, but was mainly concerned in making a road from Demagiri to Haka before the main operations could take place. Several police posts were established, some of which were given sub-units of Gurkha regiments to stiffen the garrisons.

The Burma columns were also occupied in making a road to Haka, through the Chin country. The Myittha river between Kan and Kalewa became part of the line of communications, but the road-making took much longer than was expected. This delay, however, gave the disaffected tribes an opportunity for submission of which they took advantage. The Chittagong and Burma columns did not meet at Tao until 26th February, but the reactions of the inhabitants were satisfactory and the road to Bengal was completed. The troops during this expedition suffered almost universally from malaria.

The 7th (Bengal) Mountain Battery returned to India in 1889 and was rearmed with the 2.5-inch R.M.L. gun in 1890. Captain E. A. Smith was promoted brevet-major and mentioned in despatches.

The 6th (Jacob's) Battery arrived at Bhamo on 28th October, 1889, in relief of the 8th (Lahore) Battery. The Right Section went with a column in December which joined a small force operating from the ruby mines with orders to expel certain dacoit chiefs and to punish the Kachins of Tonhon for harbouring them. There was some stockade fighting and a not very protracted resistance, and the troops were back in Bhamo in April, the dacoit leaders being still free. A good feat of marching was done by Lieutenant J. G. Baldwin with two mule-loads of common shell which were sent up to Tonhon: the party marched eighty miles over bad jungle roads in forty-eight hours and were back at Bhamo on the fifth day.

The Kachins did not settle down very quickly and further expeditions on a small scale took place. There was one in 1891-2 to which a section of the 6th (Jacob's) Battery was sent from Bhamo. Jemadar Sukoji Rao commanded the section until a British officer arrived. On 30th December, 1891, the column arrived at Sadon, a hostile village near Myitkyina about a hundred miles north of Bhamo and about twelve miles from the Chinese frontier. The column was fired on very often and had to fight to capture Sadon, and, once there, set to work to build a police post. The local Kachins were very friendly until the main body of the column departed on 5th February, leaving behind a small garrison, when they took the offensive and tried to capture the post with its garrison of 200 rifles.

At this time Lieutenant G. F. MacMunn* was on his way from Loralai to join his section of 6th (Jacob's) Battery, and left Myitkyina on 7th February, intending to join at Sadon. He picked up a small party of mounted infantry and some transport mules, and met no opposition until the third morning out when his party was fired on by Kachins from a line of trenches on the flank. These trenches were outflanked and the enemy expelled, but farther on the road was blocked by trees, and a running fight was carried on for several miles, until the party was stopped by a stockade blocking the way about six miles from Sadon. This was attacked from the front and cleared; but the mounted infantry jemadar was wounded, and more stockades had to be dealt with. The enemy, too, kept up an inaccurate fire all the way, even in Sadon village which was not far from the fort. It was now dark, and the mules and ponies stampeded, but Lieutenant MacMunn and the remains of his party reached the fort at last. He himself, the jemadar, and two men were wounded, and in the stampede several kegs of rum were lost. The fort was then besieged for ten days under musketry fire until relieved, during which time Lieutenant MacMunn made a gun of bamboo and wire which fired bamboo projectiles. The garrison lost 8 killed and 27 wounded; Kachin losses were probably 60. With the relieving column was the

---

* Afterwards Lieutenant-General Sir George MacMunn, K.C.B., K.C.S.I., D.S.O.

section which Lieutenant MacMunn had been posted to command. He was awarded the D.S.O. for his gallantry on the march to Sadon.

The section stayed at Sadon until relieved by a section of 5th (Bombay) Battery in November, 1892. The 6th (Jacob's) Battery, less one section at Bhamo, returned to Poona in January, 1893; the detachment returned four months later.

The North-East Frontier was also in a restless state. The Chief Commissioner of Assam proceeded to Manipur in March, 1890, on business connected with a revolution in that state, and was murdered with several other Europeans, notwithstanding the presence of a Gurkha escort. A punitive expedition was organized at once to proceed in three columns converging on Imphal from Tamu, Silchar and Kohima. The 8th (Lahore) Mountain Battery was hastily mobilized at Dehra Dun, where it was busy rearming after its tour in Burma, and marched without completing harness-fitting; two guns were posted to the Silchar column and four to the Kohima column, but one gun had to be left behind at the latter place. These two columns were all-native, with Assam Military Police attached.

The Silchar column met with slight opposition, but the three columns met at Imphal and in a few days the Rajah submitted and the murderers were punished. Cholera then broke out among the men of one section and glanders among the mules of another, causing the deaths of many mules, as did an outbreak of surra. The men suffered from malaria and intestinal diseases. Captain Birch, Commandant, and Lieutenant H. W. Iles were mentioned in despatches.

As the battery was preparing to return to India, it was diverted to the Chin Hills. Several months of severe marching, with men and mules out of condition, were completed before the battery embarked at Rangoon in May, 1892, for Dehra Dun.

The Third Burmese War is considered as having been brought to a close at the end of the Wuntho expedition in April, 1891, and bars to the India General Service Medal of 1854 were awarded to those present by Her Majesty the Queen Empress, as follows: "Burma 1885-87", "Burma, 1887-89", "Burma, 1889-92", "Lushai, 1889-92", "Chin-Lushai, 1889-90", "N.E. Frontier, 1891", "Chin Hills, 1892-93", "Kachin Hills, 1892-93".

Similar medals and bars in bronze were given to all recognized government followers who accompanied the troops.

The privilege of adding "BURMA 1885-87" to their colours or appointments was granted to the following mountain batteries: 4th (Hazara), 5th (Bombay), 7th (Bengal), 8th (Lahore).

Several batteries acquired a brass gun as a trophy of this campaign.

At the end of hostilities a native mountain battery was quartered in Burma as part of the garrison.

There are few administrative changes to record: a third Native Officer was allowed in 1885 when batteries were increased to six guns; the expressions "first," "second," and "third" for subaltern officers ceased to be used; Nos. 1 and 2 Bombay Mountain Batteries were renumbered Nos. 5 and 6 respectively; good conduct pay was granted to N.C.Os.; the expression "division" for a sub-unit of two guns was changed to "section," but "sub-division" remained in use to denote a single gun, gun-detachment and team for some years longer. The Martini-Henry carbine replaced the Snider about this time.

The Punjab Frontier Force came under the orders of the Commander-in-Chief in India from 1st August, 1886.

In 1887 the subject of the Prize Essay for a gold medal offered by the Royal Artillery Institution was "Mountain Artillery, its organization, equipment, and tactics." This gave rise to a flow of articles during the next few years, mostly by senior mountain artillery officers of great experience, giving all the possible points of view on controversial matters: the advantages and disadvantages of draught; of dundersticks;* of picketing methods; of guns designed for mountain service when used in "countries not hilly"; of gun shields; of harness; of establishments—in fact of everything that had a bearing on the efficiency of a mountain battery.

It was even urged that the stamp of ordnance mule was deteriorating, with little other evidence than that, as the old brass 3-pr. weighed 252 lb., the mule that carried it was superior to one which carried any one of the top-loads of the new screw-gun weighing 50 lb. less. There was general agreement that the ideal ordnance mule for a top-load was 13.3 to 14 hands with a girth of 63 to 67 inches and a shank measuring $7\frac{1}{2}$ inches. A straight back and a short step in walking were essential.

In those days a first-class country-bred mule cost Rs200, though the Bombay Government used to pay Rs300 for the mules they bought in Persia. Mules of lighter build were used for ammunition carrying. Up to Rs250 was given for a government pony.

Lieutenant-Colonel G. Swinley was sent by the War Office to St. Louis, Mo., to buy mules for service in Egypt in 1882, and had no difficulty in procuring mules of "stamina and substance," height 13.3 to 14 hands, between five and eight years old.

In 1889, mountain artillery became a separate branch of the Royal Regiment of Artillery, and officers of mountain artillery were held

---

* Later called headsticks.

on a separate list for posting. Ten batteries formed a permanent British mountain branch, and reversion to fortress work after eight years as mountain batteries ceased to be the normal procedure. Officers generally left their mountain batteries on promotion.

NOTE ON EXPERIMENTAL 4-INCH R.M.L. JOINTED HOWITZER (1890)

The howitzer was in three parts, the trunnion portion joining the breech and muzzle together with a gas ring at each joint; the parts were arranged vertically in the same way as the 2.5-inch R.M.L. and the junction nuts set home with a hammer.

The carriage was also in three parts, to form three loads.

Total weight was 600 lb. Common, shrapnel, and star shell was carried as well as case shot.

The 6 lb. R.F.G. 2 cartridge was to be used singly, doubled, or trebled to produce M.Vs. of 452, 702 and 835 f.s. respectively. Angles of descent at 1,500 yards: $43° 10'$, $13° 57'$, and $7° 51'$ respectively. Maximum range: 4,000 yards.

The detachment consisted of eleven numbers; seven mules formed the first line plus one ammunition mule: 102 rounds per howitzer were carried.

N.B.—This gun was never issued.

NOTE ON R.M.L. MOUNTAIN GUNS

Immediately the gun was fired, No. 2 from his position kneeling on the right of the muzzle inserted the sponge, already wet, into the bore and forced it to the end of the bore, giving it a twist of two half-turns, then withdrawing it. It was particularly forbidden to rest the sponge head on the ground lest it collect sand or dirt which could be pushed down the bore, with possible damage to the gun and injury to the detachment. While No. 2 was sponging out, No. 4 "served" the vent by putting his left thumb on it, elbow raised, to keep the air from coming through the vent in case any smouldering debris remained in the bore from the round just fired.* By reversing the sponge, the rammer head was ready to ram home the cartridge placed in the bore by No. 3. No. 2 then rammed home in one motion and No. 4 pushed a steel pricker down the vent into the cartridge when the shell was rammed home, after which No. 2 withdrew the rammer and the gun was ready to be laid and fired.

---

* There was a tradition handed down from the early days that No. 2 was entitled to hit with the rammer the number whose duty it was to serve the vent, if the latter failed in his duty.

The pricker was marked in divisions of 6/10th of an inch, and was also used to measure difference of level of wheels; the number of divisions multiplied by the number of degrees of elevation gave the number of minutes of deflection to be given on the side of the higher wheel. A reciprocating sight, for mountain guns only, avoided this calculation by the setting of a level on a separate bracket which fitted into the sight socket.

CHAPTER IV

Chitral and Tirah (1895-1897)

THE NORTH-WEST FRONTIER had little peace during the nineties. Before referring to Chitral some minor affairs require mention.

Many outrages had been committed by the Black Mountain tribes in the Agror valley, one of which involved casualties to troops sent to restore order. The Hassanzai and Akazai were involved amongst others, and a punitive expedition, the Hazara Field Force, was formed under Brigadier-General J. W. McQueen, C.B., and concentrated at Oghi and Darband by 1st October, 1888.

Its orders were to coerce into submission the Akazais and Khan Khel Hassanzais, and the G.O.C. was given a free hand to deal with developments. Two brigades were formed and a C.R.A. and staff appointed. The artillery consisted of two British Mountain Batteries, two guns of the Derajat Mountain Battery, and the Hazara Mountain Battery. Kashmir infantry and artillery and a detachment of Khyber Rifles under Major Mahomed Aslam Khan joined this force. The British batteries were equipped with the 2.5-inch R.M.L., and the native batteries with their 7-prs. played only a small part.

Extract from the report of C.R.A., Hazara Field Force, to I.G. Artillery, India:

"5. The guns principally used were the 2.5-inch R.M.L. as the effect of the 7-pr. of 200 lb. was apparently very slight, and in many cases the objective was out of their range. Finally, the 7-prs. were left to keep open the communications, and the 2.5-inch guns kept to the front.

* * * * *

"8. No. of rounds expended:

	Shrapnel	Common	Case	Double
2/1 So. Div., R.A. ... ... (Afterwards No. 1 Mountain Battery)	55	80	3	—
3/1 S. I. Div., R.A. ... (Afterwards No. 6 Mountain Battery)	129	132	—	—
No. 2 Derajat M. B. ...	9	24	2	—
No. 4 Hazara M. B. ...	23	20	—	3

"11. Having had on this expedition a part of No. 2 Derajat Mountain Battery and No. 4 Hazara Mountain Battery, both part of the Punjab Frontier Force, I consider it right to inform you that they have very fine mules, which are in very good condition; but it seems to me they require periodical inspections by a senior artillery officer to enforce regulations being adhered to."

The object of the expedition was achieved with few casualties, and our troops marched all over the Black Mountain country and again destroyed the settlement fort of Hindustani fanatics at Maidan, killed many, and dispersed the survivors. Agreements were reached for opening up the country by making roads and for carrying out a survey. However, the tribesmen did not fulfil their side of the agreement, and attacked a body of our troops marching over the Black Mountain. This called for further operations in 1891. In March, 1891, an expedition was sent under Major-General E. R. Elles, C.B.,* to enforce the submission of the Hassanzai and Akazai clans. Headquarters and the left half-battery 2nd (Derajat) Mountain Battery, joined the River (or Left) Column at Darband, while the right half-battery joined the reserve at Oghi. With the Right Column was No. 9 British Mountain Battery. General Elles's plan was to occupy the Hassanzai country on both banks of the Indus, and to move the Right Column along the middle levels of the mountain to the north of the Akazai country. This plan had to be changed owing to lack of forage, the Right Column being drawn in towards the Indus. Some forts were blown up, but little resistance was met with, and the tribes agreed to the road-making deemed necessary. The Derajat Battery had little to do and the left half-battery returned to Abbottabad in June; the right half-battery marched and entrained to Kohat to join the Miranzai Field Force (p. 74).

The Isazai Field Force under Major-General Sir William Lockhart was formed to punish Hassanzai villages which harboured an outlaw in breach of agreement in 1892. No resistance was offered to the two brigades and four batteries (one of which was the 1st (Kohat) Mountain Battery) which marched through the disaffected area and destroyed some towers, but without capturing Hashim Ali, the outlaw chieftain. A new invention, the maxim gun, was first seen on active service on the Frontier.

British paramountcy extended as far north as the Hindu Kush and Mustagh mountain ranges which divide Kashmir territory and dependencies from China, Russia, and Afghanistan, and since 1889 the British Agent in Gilgit had represented the Indian Government's interests in the border states facing the Hindu Kush.

* Later General Sir Edmond Elles, K.C.B., Military Member of Council.

Communications to the north were poor and unsuitable for the passage of large bodies of troops, but, the area being within the British sphere, Russian emissaries sought from time to time to tamper with the loyalties of the mountain chieftains whose interests were bound up with those of the loyal Maharajah of Kashmir and the British Government. The district was garrisoned by Kashmir troops supervised by British Inspecting Officers. This part of the world is famous as being the original home of polo—polo of a very rough-and-ready kind before rules were introduced by the British.

The chiefs of Hunza and Nagar were in receipt of subsidies, in return for which they signed agreements allowing us to make roads through their territories towards the passes on to the Pamirs. Both these states broke their agreements and combined against us in order to keep us out of the country.

It was therefore decided to send a small force consisting of the Left Section of the 4th (Hazara) Mountain Battery under Lieutenant R. St. G. Gorton (two 7-pr. guns) and 200 rifles of the 5th Gurkhas to enforce existing agreements with the chiefs.

The section started from Bannu in September, 1891, in intense heat. Captain Honner's march routine for his battery in hot weather, when not with other troops, consisted of a start in the cool before sunset, and at the end of the march on arrival in camp, after watering and feeding the animals, the men slept where they liked until early stables, when tents were pitched.

After leaving Bandipur, the section had to undergo some very severe marches on the way to Gilgit at opposite extremes of temperature. Two passes, the Tragbal, 11,500 feet, and the Burzil, 13,000 feet, had to be crossed, the track being already covered with three feet of snow, and although it was by no means late for travelling, a caravan had already been overwhelmed by a blizzard on the Tragbal Pass. A convoy of 1,000 mules with rations and treasure had to be escorted, and by the time the Burzil Pass was reached the snow was six feet deep. The rear detachment of the column suffered nearly a hundred casualties from frost-bite, which the section had avoided by wearing grass shoes instead of boots. Snow goggles were improvised by the mistri.

Extreme heat was met on descending to the Indus at Hatu Pir, a 6,000-foot drop in six miles, after which the Indus had to be crossed at Bunji. The current was strong and the waves considerable, but the crossing was successfully made by means of Captain Aylmer's* flying bridge. About ten mules were put on board at a time, and a

---

*Afterwards Lieutenant-General Sir F. J. Aylmer, V.C., K.C.B.

rope passed round their quarters made fast to the bow and stern of the boat. As soon as the boat was well in the current, the rope was cast off and the mules made for the opposite shore on their own. Only three mules were drowned during the crossing.

Gilgit was reached on 21st November, and two battalions of Kashmir Imperial Service Infantry, some details of Bengal Sappers and Miners and 20th Punjab Infantry, along with 200 Punial Levies, were awaiting the arrival of the Gurkhas and guns, the whole force being under the command of Lieutenant-Colonel A. G. Durand, the British Agent. Lieutenant-Colonel Durand, after inspecting the section, reported to the Commander-in-Chief that, notwithstanding a march of 540 miles from Bannu and the crossing of two snow passes, the section had arrived without a single mule being galled. The reply received was that "Sir Frederick Roberts was much pleased with this further proof of the efficiency of the artillery of the Punjab Frontier Force."

The mountains of the Hindu Kush rise so sheer that flat spaces on the banks of the rivers are rare and of small area. The narrowness of the valleys may be judged by the fact that the sun is only visible from the bottom for an hour or so a day in many places.

The road, or rather track, to Nagar ran in a narrow ravine and was blocked by a stone fort with walls eight feet thick, on which the 7-prs. had no effect even at 250 yards. This (Nilt) fort was, therefore, captured by blowing in the gate under a heavy fire and fighting hand-to-hand inside. The troops showed the utmost bravery and coolness in this operation, gallantly led by Captain Aylmer, R.E., and Lieutenant Boisragon, 5th Gurkhas, both of whom received the Victoria Cross; Lieutenant Badcock, 5th Gurkhas, received the D.S.O., and six other ranks the Indian Order of Merit.

The track to Nagar continued up a deep ravine, on both sides of which were precipitous hills running up to the snowline, 1,500 feet above the river. Enemy sangars were sited very high up, and a heavy fire was opened every time troops tried to use the track. The force was delayed some days whilst a way up to the enemy's position on the right bank was found and positions for the guns were prepared high up on our (left) bank from which the enemy's sangars could be kept under fire during an attack. Eventually a track was found which enabled a storming party of 100 rifles under Lieutenant Manners-Smith, Assistant Political Officer, to climb the precipitous hill and attack the sangars, supported by covering fire from the two 7-prs., now under Lieutenant Molony* (Lieutenant Gorton having been

---

* Lieutenant C. A. Molony had brought two guns of No. 1 Kashmir Mountain Battery, which did not come into action during this operation.

wounded), and a covering party of infantry in the vicinity. This attack met with complete success, Lieutenant Manners-Smith being awarded the Victoria Cross for gallantry in the attack. A hundred of the enemy were killed and 118 captured as against our loss of two wounded. Both tribes now capitulated, and among the terms imposed was the cessation of the slave trade which was practised in this region.

There were disturbances in Chilas in 1893 over this same matter of road-making, and in August Lieutenant A. W. Money marched the left section of the 1st (Kohat) Mountain Battery to Chilas to overcome the objection of the inhabitants to the making of a road in their country. The marches were long and exhausting, but there was no fighting.

Before returning to this area of the Frontier, trouble elsewhere must be related. Some sections of the Orakzais had for years shown defiance by raiding the Kohat–Thal road and villages in the vicinity. British territory went as far north as the Samana Ridge; lawlessness was encouraged by the Khan of Hangu, who received an allowance for controlling certain tribes implicated. As no settlement seemed possible, the Miranzai Field Force was organized, based on Hangu. Brigadier-General Sir William Lockhart, K.C.B., commanding the Punjab Frontier Force, commanded the force of seven battalions, with the 3rd (Peshawar) and 4th (Hazara) Mountain Batteries, which in January, 1891, marched up the Khanki valley without opposition. The jirgahs came in and accepted the terms imposed, which included the building of posts on the Samana Ridge. After this the force was broken up.

On 4th April a treacherous attack was made on a party of the 29th Bengal Infantry working on the road, by some Pathans who had accepted work as road-makers. A large force had collected under cover and attacked the few troops we had on the spot, causing the temporary abandonment of the Samana range. Troops were hastily collected for the 2nd Miranzai Field Force under Sir William Lockhart; No.1 Column at Hangu included No. 3 British Mountain Battery; No. 2 Column at Darband, 3rd (Peshawar) Mountain Battery; and No. 3 Column at Darband, three guns of 2nd (Derajat) Mountain Battery—a force of 7,000 in all.

The 2nd (Derajat) detachment received a telegram of congratulation from H.E. the Commander-in-Chief on the "rapid march of three guns Derajat Battery to Kohat" (from the Hazara Field Force). The Peshawar Battery was commanded by Captain F. H. J. Birch, with Lieutenants L. C. Gordon, C. G. Watson, G. R. Lamb, and the Derajat (three 7-prs.) by Lieutenant J. L. Parker, with Lieutenant

L. W. P. East. The Punjab Garrison Battery brought from Kohat four 12-pr. R.B.L. guns drawn by bullocks, but it took little part in the operations. The C.R.A. was Lieutenant-Colonel E. J. de Lautour.

The mountain batteries covered the advances of the columns along the Samana ridge, meeting little opposition and keeping the tribesmen on the move with a few rounds of shrapnel. Care was taken to avoid disturbing the Afridis, and hostilities were confined to the Orakzais, mostly in the Chagru and Khanki valleys, where many towers were destroyed. There was an attempt at a pitched battle for Saragarhi, but the artillery was responsible for heavy losses among the enemy, who fled and are reported to have said, "We do not mind the rifles but cannot stand against shrapnel fire."

The Mishti clan on the left bank of the Khanki, who had been very prominent in lawlessness, were awarded a special punishment of having their towers blown up in the presence of their own jirgah: and the Mamuzais, who had boasted that their district at the head of the Khanki valley was inaccessible, were obliged to endure the sight of troops marching through it. Formal submission having been made, the force left a garrison on the Samana and the remainder went to Kohat to be dispersed.

Agreement had been made for the delimitation of the new international boundary by British and Afghan commissioners, and as the attitude of the Wazirs was uncertain, an escort of about a brigade for the British Commissioner, Sir Mortimer Durand, was mobilized, backed by a reserve brigade at Dera Ismail Khan.

On 25th October, 1894, the escort, which included the 3rd (Peshawar) Mountain Battery, was encamped at Wana under Brigadier-General A. H. Turner.

A new mischief-maker had arisen in the Mullah Powindah, a Mahsud with a bad character who did his best to embroil the maliks with the Government. Reports came in that he intended to attack the camp with a large following, but the Political Officers did not believe them. The camping-ground was not selected for military reasons, and was surrounded by a circle of piquets who had been ordered to withdraw to camp on being attacked.

The night of 2nd November passed quietly until 5.30 a.m., when the part of the perimeter held by the 1st Gurkhas was rushed by a large body of ghazis who had crawled up a ravine close to the camp and were inside before the troops could get out of their tents. Another party broke into the horse-lines. The Gurkha inlying piquet blocked the main street and was at once engaged in a hand-to-hand fight, supported by the 3rd Sikhs and the 20th Punjab Infantry, who cleared their way through the camp with the bayonet.

The Mountain Battery had no information or orders, so fired a couple of star shell over the Gurkhas' front, followed by two more. The view was restricted and the battery commander thought all the star shell burst too short, but reports afterwards testified that they were of the greatest value to the infantry. He noted down a suggestion that reports should be sent to the battery by the infantry concerned on such occasions as to the efficacy of the star shell.

The stout resistance put up in the camp caused the Mahsuds to withdraw, but not before they had killed two British and two Native Officers, 18 rank and file and 24 followers; their own loss was put at 800. A hundred animals were killed and a large number of rifles carried off.

As the reparations demanded were not agreed to, the Waziristan Field Force of three brigades was constituted on 2nd December under Sir William Lockhart, now Lieutenant-General. The escort became the 1st Brigade, the 2nd Brigade at Jandola included the 8th (Lahore) Mountain Battery, and the 3rd Brigade at Mirian (near Bannu) included the 1st (Kohat) Mountain Battery.

The brigades were set in motion on 16th December; their objectives being Kaniguram, Makin via the Tank Zam, and Razmak respectively. They arrived at their destinations on the 21st. The weather had become bitterly cold and snow fell, so that on the 23rd several Indian rank and file died of pneumonia. Many towers were destroyed and the country overrun, but little opposition was met, and the next month was spent in flying-column marches. The jirgahs all came in early in March and our terms were complied with. Except for the boundary escort, the troops were withdrawn less a small force left to hold the Tochi valley, which was now taken over.

Captain F. H. J. Birch, Commandant, 3rd (Peshawar) Mountain Battery, received a brevet-majority at the end of the campaign.

To return now to the Gilgit Agency. Chitral, the capital of the state of that name, is about 250 miles west of Gilgit. It had come into prominence during the Russian scare in 1885, when its importance as the back door to India was first recognized. A British Mission formed cordial relations with the Mehtar, the ruling chief, and a British subsidy was added to the allowance being paid by Kashmir.

At the Mehtar's death in 1892, civil war raged whilst the succession was being decided by the usual oriental method of liquidation of heirs; but by January, 1895, Amir-ul-Mulk had settled himself in power by murdering his uncle and was acknowledged by the Indian

Government. Chitral was part of the Gilgit Agency under Surgeon-Major G. S. Robertson, C.S.I., who had had a brilliant career on that part of the Frontier, and an Assistant Political Officer was stationed in Chitral with a small escort.

There remained a claimant to the Mehtarship, one Sher Afzul, who had reigned for a few months, but had withdrawn to avoid assassination, and now collected his adherents to make another bid for power. He had as ally Umra Khan, freebooter, murderer, and outlaw, who held sway over Bajaur and various tribes of Yaghistan and now looked forward to a profitable adventure in Chitral.

These two conspirators captured Kila Drosh and demanded the withdrawal of the British Mission from Chitral. Major Robertson moved to Chitral with reinforcements and, after an engagement in which our casualties were very heavy, Chitral Fort was surrounded and the historic siege which was to last forty-six days began on 4th March.

As soon as communication was cut off, a relief expedition of three brigades under Major-General Sir R. C. Low, K.C.B., was assembled at Nowshera. Sir Robert Low was an officer of great experience, having served at the sieges of Delhi and Lucknow, in the Second Afghan War, and in Burma.

The divisional troops included the 2nd (Derajat) Mountain Battery, less one section in the Kurram valley under Lieutenant H. E. J. Brake, two British Mountain Batteries (Nos. 3 and 8), and the 15th Field Battery. The Derajat Battery was commanded by Captain J. L. Parker. The 4th (Hazara) Mountain Battery was part of the line of communication troops, having been discarded by Brigadier-General W. F. Gatacre, D.S.O., Commanding the 3rd Brigade, because it was armed with the 7-pr. It remained at Dargai during these operations. Colonel W. W. Murdoch was C.R.A.

Insolent replies having been received from Sher Afzul and Umra Khan, and news having arrived that a party of the 14th Sikhs had been overwhelmed near Mastuj and Captain Ross and forty-six Sikhs killed, the Chitral Relief Expedition, now at Hoti Mardan, advanced on 1st April, 1895.

On 3rd April the 2nd Brigade, supported by the mountain artillery, stormed the Malakand Kotal, where the 1st Brigade spent the night. This brigade moved on down to Khar in the Swat valley next day.

During the attack on the Malakand Kotal, the batteries, which had opened a not very effective fire on the enemy sangars at 4,000 yards, closed forward as the infantry advanced and supported the final assault by keeping the sangars under a heavy fire of time shrapnel close over the heads of the infantry climbing up the hill.

Major J. Dacres-Cunningham controlled by voice the three mountain batteries as a brigade, and, once the sangars were captured after a very stubborn resistance, concentrated fire on the village. The range of the 2.5-inch gun permitted the exercise of such fire tactics, here recorded for the first time. The Derajat Battery fired 30 ring and 140 shrapnel during the day. The Lee-Metford rifle was used by the British infantry for the first time; wounds inflicted by it appeared slight in comparison with those of the Martini-Henry used by the native infantry. Major Cunningham noted that the shrapnel shell, Mark III, often failed to break up, the bullets remaining solid in their resinous matrix. Major Shirres, who commanded the other British Mountain Battery, had distinguished himself in the Second Afghan War with the 1st (Kohat) Mountain Battery and was awarded the D.S.O. after the campaign under notice.

By now the shortage of transport, which was always a problem of any sizeable Frontier campaign, had begun to make itself felt, and rations were not coming up as they should.

The advanced guard pushed on to Sado without opposition, the Derajat Battery losing a carriage mule on a bad road near Sado; it sank in thirty feet of water in the adjoining river, but was washed up, load and all, some distance downstream next day.

On the 13th the Derajat Battery was ordered to cover the Guides Infantry who were isolated on the right bank of the Panjkora river by a sudden flood. The infantry were heavily attacked and, after covering their retirement, the battery fired star shell at intervals during the night.

On 9th April Chitral Fort was relieved by Colonel Kelly with the 32nd Pioneers, some Kashmir Infantry, Engineers, and two guns of No. 1 Kashmir Mountain Battery after a hazardous march from Gilgit. See Appendix I, page 425.

The 2nd (Derajat) Battery went ahead with the Buffs and the 4th Gurkhas as a flying column while the Sappers and Miners put in some hard work on the road over the Lowarai Pass, which was still under snow.

After a reconnaissance on 25th April by Brigadier-General Gatacre and Captain J. L. Parker, the brigade commander ordered the advance over the pass to be undertaken next day. The track was appallingly bad and the loads were taken off the transport mules and slid down by hand.

On 15th May Gatacre's force reached Chitral Fort with the troops of the 3rd Brigade mentioned above.

After a long wait at Dargai, the Hazara Mountain Battery moved forward to the Swat valley, where it found the Khan of Aladand very friendly. He tried to borrow a 7-pr. for his annual fight with the Khan of Thana, and offered the battery front seats to see the fun.

Sher Afzul was brought in and banished to Dharmsala, where the ex-Mehtar, Amir-ul-Mulk, was also sent. Umra Khan was last heard of in an Afghan prison.

Two battalions (later reduced to one) and the Centre Section of the 4th (Hazara) Mountain Battery were left as garrison in Chitral and Kila Drosh, with the prospect of annual relief. Substantial forts were built at Drosh, Chakdara and the Malakand, and garrisoned. The existence of the permanent headquarters of the Corps of Guides at Hoti Mardan, about a hundred miles from Chitral, was valuable as constituting the rear link in the line of communications. The Corps, comprising three squadrons of cavalry and an infantry battalion, contained sub-units of every fighting race in the north of India, and was famous for providing men from every part of the North-West Frontier when required for special service.

For a time there was a lull on the Frontier and the only matter worthy of note was a conference of mullahs held by the Amir, Abdur Rahman, which was an unusual affair and was looked upon with suspicion by the Government of India. These mullahs were notorious for spreading hostility to the British Raj and stirring up the tribes for a religious war. However, the Amir's explanation was accepted, and peace continued until, in June, 1897, an isolated outbreak occurred in the Tochi valley.

On the 10th of that month, Mr. Gee, a Political Officer, arranged to meet the Madda Khel maliks at the village of Maizar over the matter of an unpaid fine, and to fix the site of a levy post. Lieutenant-Colonel Bunny of the 1st Sikhs was in command of the escort, consisting of 200 rifles of his own regiment, 100 rifles of the 1st Punjab Infantry (Coke's Rifles), 12 sabres of the 1st Punjab Cavalry and a section of the 6th (Jacob's) Mountain Battery* under Captain J. F. Browne and Lieutenant H. A. Cruickshank.

The escort camped near the village with proper military precautions, while Mr. Gee met the maliks and carried out the business which was the cause of the visit.

The maliks pointed out the camping ground and brought food for the Mohammedan sepoys, and no hint of unfriendliness was given; the question of the fine was settled amicably. At about 2 p.m., while the pipers were playing, a signal shot was fired and a fusilade opened on the British officers, who were grouped together, and the Sikhs of the escort. Colonel Bunny and Captain Browne were

---

* At this time designated No. 6 (Bombay) Mountain Battery.

mortally wounded and Lieutenant Cruickshank shot down. The guns opened fire at once at 100 yards with case and did great execution among a party of men who tried to rush them.

Lieutenant Cruickshank behaved with the utmost courage, getting up and continuing to fight his guns until he was killed by another bullet.

The guns then continued to fire under the orders of Nos. 1 until their ammunition was expended. The carriage mule of No. 3 gun was wounded, so Havildar Nihal Singh and a naik and a gunner carried the load to the relief line, 170 yards away. No. 4 gun somersaulted twice, but was picked up and went on firing; two lanyards also broke at this gun, but the detachment under Naik Sharaf Ali carried on. When limbering up, the gun mule was wounded and bolted; then the gun was carried to the relief line by Havildar-Major Mahomet Ismail and two gunners. Salutri Kewal dressed Captain Browne's wounds under fire, and the drivers all behaved admirably, even loading up the greatcoats on the relief line mules.

With no less conspicuous bravery did the infantry behave, covering the withdrawal of the guns by successive retirements deliberately and in an orderly way under their native officers after the British officers were all wounded and unable to carry on. Many infantrymen gave their lives to secure the withdrawal of their comrades and the wounded: great heroism was shown by Subadar Sundar Singh, 1st Punjab Infantry, who took charge at the first withdrawal.

The Wazirs were increasing in numbers and enveloping the flanks while the retirement from ridge to ridge eventually found a good position three miles in rear, and it was 5.30 p.m. before reinforcements came in sight. They had covered the nine miles from Datta Khel in less than an hour and a half, under Lieutenant H. S. de Brett of the battery, and consisted of two companies of the 1st Sikhs with some 7-pr. ammunition. The heights and the village of Sheranna were shelled (the latter at 1,400 yards) and an unmolested withdrawal to camp then took place.

Casualties in the battery, in addition to the two British officers, were one havildar and one driver killed, and three wounded. Several mules were killed and wounded. Infantry casualties were twenty killed and twenty-four wounded. At least a hundred of the enemy were killed.

Lieutenant de Brett had been unable to bring more guns because all the gun and carriage saddles of the battery were with the two guns at Maizar. He found one serviceable gun when he joined the retiring troops, but there was no sponge with it; this meant there was no rammer as these two stores were on the same stave in the 7-pr.

equipment. At great risk he loaded the first few rounds himself, ramming home the charge with a rifle, and reloading without sponging. This dangerous operation was later obviated by using a sowar's lance with a pagri wrapped round the end. Fire from the gun caused the dispersion of the attackers, and the safe withdrawal of the force was attributable to Lieutenant de Brett's courageous act. For his gallantry he was awarded the Distinguished Service Order.

The following awards were made for gallantry and devotion to duty at Maizar:

Order of Merit, 3rd Class: Havildar-Major Muhammad Ismail, Havildar Nihal Singh, Naik Sharaf Ali, Sulutri Kewal, Driver-Havildar Rur Singh, Gunner Jawala Singh, Gunner Diwan Singh, 2357 Naik Utam Chand, Gunner Dulla Khan.

The widows of Havildar Umardin and 2432 Lance-Naik Utam Chand were granted the pensions of the Order of Merit which would have been awarded to their husbands if they had survived.

This treacherous attack was not followed by a rising and was accepted as a purely local outburst, but it was obviously planned beforehand and it transgressed the laws of hospitality in a way seldom heard of on the Frontier.

The Government acted without delay and within a week the Tochi Valley Punitive Force of two brigades was formed under Major-General G. C. Bird, C.B. With the first brigade was the 3rd (Peshawar) Mountain Battery. This force met with no opposition and its greatest enemy was the excessive heat in the Tochi valley, which accounted for a number of casualties. A lot of sniping went on at night, but the enemy seems to have been cowed by the size of the force and the destruction of some of his villages.

A few weeks after Maizar, trouble came in the north. In the evening of 26th July Major Deane, Political Agent at the Malakand informed Colonel W. H. Meiklejohn, commanding the troops, that groups of tribesmen were on the move from the Swat valley towards the Malakand. There had been no interference with the polo at Khar that afternoon, and the only hint of trouble had been rumours of the presence of a "Mad Faqir" at Landakai.

The Malakand position included the kotal on the road running almost due north from railhead at Nowshera to our detached post at Chitral; at this time it was held by a force consisting of a squadron of cavalry, a company of Madras Sappers and Miners, the 24th and 31st Punjab Infantry, 45th Sikhs, less two companies, and the 8th (Lahore) Mountain Battery* under Lieutenant F. A. Wynter. The

---

* At this time designated No. 8 Bengal Mountain Battery.

other officers of the battery were the Commandant, Captain A. H. Č. Birch, who rejoined on the 30th, and Lieutenant F. A. Twiss (attached).

At Chakdara, eight miles to the north, guarding the bridge over the River Swat, stood a strong recently-built fort holding two companies of the 45th Sikhs—small companies of eighty or ninety rank and file, each commanded by a native officer, the double company system not having been adopted at this time.

At Malakand the infantry held the perimeter; the hospital, various enclosures and a small fort were on level ground inside, but the whole camp was surrounded by higher ground and lay, as it were, at the bottom of a saucer. The battery camped with the 31st Punjab Infantry at North Malakand, a piece of high ground a few hundred yards west of the kotal.

Arrangements were being made to meet the customary dawn attack, but about 10 p.m. an unexpected rush was made by several hundred Pathans on the 45th Sikhs' front which straddled the Buddhist road. The enemy were driven out, but kept up an incessant fire all night at fifty yards range. The centre of the camp was soon overrun by masses of tribesmen, the bazaar was looted, and the Sappers and Miners' quarter-guard was overcome. Hand-to-hand fighting went on until about 3.30 a.m., when the enemy withdrew to the heights round the camp, from which the range was about 800 yards. This early withdrawal was contrary to the enemy's custom, but sniping went on, although with little effect.

The Guides Cavalry (three squadrons in all) was called up from Mardan and made the journey in eight hours, notwithstanding the intense heat. The next day was spent in clearing up and concentrating all troops on the kotal. A column consisting of the 31st Punjab Infantry with the 8th (Lahore) Mountain Battery, less one section, was sent to get through to Chakdara, but failed and had to return.

A piquet of the 24th Punjab Infantry to the west of the camp was attacked about 5 p.m. and forced to retire, but the hill was retaken by the regiment at once with the support of a section of the mountain battery.

The enemy returned at night in largely increased numbers, apparently from the Utman Khel country, and the attack was renewed with increased vigour. A counter-attack was made on the west side by the 24th Punjab Infantry, and a section of the battery under Subadar Sher Singh provided effective support. Many of the enemy fled to Jalalkot and the guns shelled the village with good effect. Two gunners were wounded.

The next day, the 28th, was occupied in repairing and strengthening defences, putting out more wire, and building sangars for the Guides Infantry who were expected to arrive in the evening. They did so at 7 p.m. after a very rapid march, all the tum-tums and ekkas in the district having been requisitioned to carry ammunition, etc. They marched through the great heat of the day without casualties, thirty-six miles in sixteen hours, arriving fit and ready to go into action, and impressed all beholders by their smartness in returning the salutes of the guards which had turned out to them. They went straight on to the perimeter without rest or food alongside the 45th Sikhs, and fought off many attacks during the night, losing two men killed and ten wounded; the gunners were very active firing into parties charging down the hillside, and lost two more gunners wounded. The next day was Jumarat* and the biggest attack of all was expected. It started at 5.30 p.m. and in places stormed into our sangars, but a sortie by the 24th Punjab Infantry on to a high spur poured a reverse fire into a large party and caused many casualties.

Attacks went on all night, but the enemy retired just before dawn. This day reinforcements in the shape of the 35th Sikhs and the 38th Dogras arrived. The 35th Sikhs from Nowshera had lost twenty-one men from heat and apoplexy. On the 30th news came in that enemy losses had been very heavy during the night and that the "Mad Faqir" had been wounded. On the nights 30th/31st and 31st July/1st August, similar attacks were pressed, causing us more casualties. On 1st August the cavalry moved out at 3 p.m. for the relief of Chakdara, eight miles to the north, but the enemy were working round them in large numbers and they had to be withdrawn, but not before they had brought off a charge which left about a hundred enemy bodies on the field.

The garrison of Chakdara which guarded the bridge over the River Swat comprised about 300 rifles, with two Maxims and a 9-pr. R.M.L. gun, the latter manned by the infantry. A steep spur on the west held a signal tower for communication with the Malakand heliograph manned by Sikh signallers, but part of the fort was open to enemy fire from the high ground. It was attacked at the same time as the Malakand and in a similar manner. The tribesmen tried to climb the walls of the fort with ladders, but were repulsed. The 9-pr. gun had a very good effect and was fired on night lines.

The telegraph was cut at an early stage and the garrison depended on the signallers for communication, which could be carried out only by the exposure of a signaller. Water was sent up to the tower

---
* The eve of the Moslem Sabbath.

under covering fire from the Maxims, but this was not possible after the 31st, as the enemy occupied a strong position between the tower and the fort. The last signal received was on the 1st of August—"Help us!"

On this day a vast force of tribesmen assembled, estimated at 10,000, and at daybreak on the 2nd an assault was pressed with the utmost determination. About 9 a.m., when the situation was becoming critical, the cavalry of the relieving column appeared on the Malakand road, and the garrison at once made a sortie and caught and killed a large party of the enemy who were now beginning to withdraw. Another sortie cleared Signal Tower, and the cavalry came into action in the plain with telling effect. Over 2,000 bodies were counted outside the fort, a loss only approached by the Afghans at Ahmed Khel, where 1,200 killed were counted. The 9-pr. was of the utmost value in the defence; one discharge fired at a group leaving an enclosure killed a number of them.

The relieving column, with which was the 8th (Lahore) Mountain Battery less one section, moved at daybreak and met with a stubborn but short resistance from the heights on the east of the road. This position was cleared with the bayonet at great loss to the enemy, and another stand at Amandarra met the same fate. The battery had three gunners and eight mules wounded, and one mule killed.

There was now no doubt that a rising on a large scale had to be dealt with, and without delay the Malakand Field Force of two brigades with divisional cavalry and artillery, commanded by Major-General Sir Bindon Blood, K.C.B., was mobilized with a reserve brigade in support. Lieutenant-Colonel W. Aitken, C.B., was appointed C.R.A., with Captain H. D. Grier as his adjutant; and the artillery consisted of 10th Field Battery, Nos. 1 and 7 British Mountain Batteries and the 8th (Lahore) Mountain Battery. The mountain batteries all had six 2.5-inch R.M.L. guns.

The reserve brigade was commanded by Brigadier-General J. H. Wodehouse, C.B., C.M.G.,* an artillery officer.

The enemy's numbers were estimated at about 10,000 from the Swat valley and neighbouring districts, and swift action was necessary lest his numbers be increased by additions from the Utman Khels and Bunerwals.

The inhabitants of Lower Swat surrendered unconditionally at once, but the Upper Swatis refused to come in. The Bunerwals, who are Yusufzais inhabiting the Buner valley, were a doubtful problem, but it was known that several sections of them were out against us.

---

* Later General Sir J. H. Wodehouse, G.C.B., C.M.G.

On 16th August Sir Bindon Blood moved a brigade to Thana,* with which were 10th Field, No. 7 British Mountain, and the 8th (Lahore) Mountain Batteries, with the object of clearing Upper Swat, where many hundreds of the tribesmen were still assembled, particularly on the Jalala spur. The next day the main attack was developed on the right and was by three battalions supported by the Lahore Mountain Battery, which joined the firing line and came into action at 500 yards. The enemy did not wait for the assault and left us in possession of the ridge—their retirement being hastened by our artillery fire.

The Guides Cavalry went on in pursuit, which was impeded by the rough going, and here at Landakai occurred the celebrated incident in which two officers were killed who were well ahead of the leading squadrons, and two officers were awarded the V.C. for great gallantry in charging into a great mass of the enemy in an attempt at rescue. The 8th (Lahore) Mountain Battery and some infantry hurried to the scene and the tribesmen withdrew. That closed the operation for the day, and in fact in the Swat valley altogether, as the troops had a peaceful walk-over there.

The next step was to open up the road to Chitral; the bridges were found intact, and no opposition was experienced in this direction.

Meanwhile, trouble had broken out elsewhere. On Saturday, 7th August, about four o'clock in the afternoon, a fierce and unexpected attack was made on Shabkadar, only eighteen miles from Peshawar, by 4,000 or 5,000 Mohmands. The bazaar was looted and burnt, and the occupants took refuge in the fort which was gallantly held by a few Border Police. This raid was traceable to the Hadda Mullah, a priest of great influence and strong anti-British tendencies.

In 1893 the Mohmand country had been divided between the Amir and the Government of India, but tribesmen from both districts joined whole-heartedly in any attack on the British.

Brigadier-General E. R. Elles, commanding at Peshawar, sent out at once a force of infantry with a field battery, and the morning found the raiders in position on the high ground a mile and a half from the fort, with their numbers rapidly increasing. Two squadrons of cavalry arrived from Peshawar and skirmished with little effect owing to the broken nature of the terrain. The next day the whole force advanced to drive the enemy out of their position, but there were 6,000 of the tribesmen, and our small force would have been surrounded but for a brilliant charge by the 13th Bengal Lancers. The infantry again attacked and the enemy fled to the hills.

* Near Chakdara.

Two more reserve brigades were mobilized at Rawalpindi: this item was shown in the Government Gazette under the heading of "Disturbances." The 3rd Field Battery and No. 3 British Mountain Battery were posted to these new formations. A brigade about 2,000 strong was left at Shabkadar watching the Mohmands, and the Peshawar garrison was strengthened.

The Mohmand Field Force of two brigades under Brigadier-General, now Major-General, E. R. Elles was formed to move into the Mohmand country and co-operate with two brigades of the Malakand Field Force under Sir Bindon Blood acting from the east, while the third brigade held the line of communications through Chakdara. In the Mohmand Field Force were No. 3 British and 5th (Bombay) Mountain Batteries, the C.R.A. being Lieutenant-Colonel A. E. Duthy.

The most serious events were now happening on another part of the Frontier; a return to the Mohmand campaign will be made later.

Since the treaty of Gandamak (p. 44) the British Government had allowed the Afridis, whose lands fringed the Khyber Pass, to be responsible for the security of the Pass, in return for a guarantee of independence and a subsidy. This was carried out loyally by a corps of Jezailchis (afterwards the Khyber Rifles) under British supervision.

In the beginning of August rumours of a joint Orakzai and Afridi rising were rife in Peshawar, and the troops in Peshawar were increased to a total of 11,000 men. On the 21st a definite report came in that the Afridis had risen and were marching on the Khyber. Whatever steps were taken to oppose this move had no effect, as on the 23rd the Afridis rushed up the Pass in great force and made a clean sweep of the forts and their garrisons. Many of the Khyber Rifles, themselves Afridis, remained loyal and marched into Jamrud with their rifles. Our policy of masterly inactivity had lost us the Khyber.

This rising was put down to the Aka Khel Mullah, a prominent fanatic, and troops were hastily pushed up to Kohat to combat any action by the Orakzais, who fortunately failed to synchronize their efforts with those of the Afridis. The Kurram valley contains another of the main roads to Kabul, and part of the road is commanded by the Samana range, half-way between Kohat and Thal. This range was in the hands of the Orakzais, but forts had been erected and garrisoned by us after exemplary punishment had been carried out on that tribe in return for a treacherous outbreak in 1891.

At this time at Parachinar was a section of the 2nd (Derajat) Mountain Battery with infantry amounting to a battalion, and at

Kohat the Samana movable column of one squadron of cavalry, the 5th Punjab Infantry, and 2nd (Derajat) Battery (less one section) under Captain J. L. Parker was ready at very short notice. The movable column went to Hangu on 22nd of August and stayed there for a few days. The Kurram Militia (armed with Sniders) held the levy posts with great reliability.

On the 27th a force including the 2nd Punjab Infantry and No. 9 Field Battery moved from Kohat to restore the situation at the Ublan Pass, which was reported to have been occupied. It was extremely hot weather and, after clearing the kotal, our retirement was followed up in strength, and heat casualties were added to the battle casualties. The pass was quiet the next day, but the Orakzais rose in force on the 30th and destroyed two levy posts. Two other levy posts were relieved by the movable column on 27th after a march of twenty-two miles in fifteen hours.

The Samana forts were held by half a battalion of the 36th Sikhs, and a strong force from Hangu convoying rations and ammunition for the Samana garrison met with no opposition on 7th September.

By the 10th the situation had altered. Thousands of Afridis from the Peshawar side joined the Orakzais with a view to making one of the biggest raids known. Then began the siege of the Samana forts, celebrated for the heroic defence of Saraghari, a signal link held by twenty-one men of the 36th Sikhs, whose small fort was surrounded by thousands of tribesmen and the garrison killed to a man. Faithful to their salt, they remained at their post.

The enemy then returned their attention to the other forts, which were built on a larger scale and had bigger garrisons. These held off the enemy for fifty-two hours, being relieved in the afternoon of the 14th. The enemy's numbers were estimated at 8,000. Captain Parker's Derajat Mountain Battery made splendid practice, dispersing groups of the tribesmen, who did not wait to meet the infantry of the relieving force.

The lashkars made a last effort by attacking the post at Sadda, which commands a defile leading from the Kurram river towards the Afridi country; reinforcements and two guns of the 2nd (Derajat) Battery arrived just before the enemy attacked, and except for a great deal of sniping, the situation was saved. The Kurram line was now intact and the enemy withdrew. The Khyber Pass was still closed, but retribution was being prepared against the time that the frontier districts north of the Kabul river had been brought to book.

Never before had risings on such a grand scale occurred, all demanding immediate action which could not be undertaken at once owing to transport difficulties; the most important matter was obviously the protection of our line of communication to Chitral through Dir territory, and at the same time the punishment of the Mohmands.

On 8th September, General Blood's division crossed the Panjkora river, leaving the 1st Brigade to hold the communications back to Chakdara. On the 14th, Divisional Headquarters and the 3rd Brigade, reinforced by two battalions from the 2nd Brigade and the 8th (Lahore) Mountain Battery, were at Nawagai, a position of great strategical importance, and also one of some danger. General Elles was nearly fifty miles away, moving up the Gandab defile from the south, and a big lashkar was holding the Bedmanai Pass, between the two forces. To the north of Nawagai was a Mamund lashkar waiting for the opportunity to attack.

The Mohmands made a night attack in force on the 20th/21st, bringing their baggage animals to remove the loot, but in the end they were not required. Under cover of musketry fire, thousands of swordsmen attacked two faces of the camp in the most courageous way for five and a half hours; the mountain guns fired star shell and case, and the infantry fired volleys very steadily and effectively. When the enemy withdrew it was found that we had one man killed and twenty-eight wounded; the enemy losses were put down at 300; and the Mohmands went back to the Bedmanai Pass, which was about to be forced by General Elles's troops.

General Elles left Shabkadar on the 15th and crossed the Nahakki Pass without opposition, where a brigade was left to guard the flank, while the main force was to attack the Bedmanai Pass on the 25th. The 20th Punjab Infantry led the 1st Brigade on a turning movement on our left, supported by Maxim guns, and cleared the first ridge before the mountain guns opened fire. With little opposition the frontal attack worked up the valley, supported by four guns of the 5th (Bombay) Mountain Battery, one section of which had been left at Nahakki. The Pass was captured with a loss of two killed and three wounded, the brigade encamping for the night in Bedmanai village.

General Elles met Sir Bindon Blood this day and was informed by the latter that the Mamunds had risen, and that he was himself taking a brigade to assist Brigadier-General Jeffreys, whose 2nd Brigade had been attacked in the northern area. General Blood's 3rd Brigade was transferred to the Mohmand Field Force, and after taking part in some of General Elles's operations, left on 26th September to join the Tirah Expeditionary Force.

General Elles's first objective was the fort of Jarobi in the Jarobi valley, where the source of all the unrest lived—the Mad Mullah's home, never yet seen by a European. It was situated in a picturesque and fertile valley approached by a narrow gorge, where an attempt was made to ambush our column. The fort was destroyed, as were others during the next few days when the force, sniped at all day, moved from one valley to another to compel submission and to collect the rifles to be handed over as part of the peace terms. The 5th (Bombay) Mountain Battery had a great deal of marching and occasional opportunities for action, and moved to Kohat in October to join the Tirah Expeditionary Force.

In the meantime a setback had occurred in the Mamund country, where Brigadier-General Jeffreys had been sent with a brigade to exact retribution for an attack on his camp at Inayat Kila. He advanced on 16th September in three columns up the Watelai valley to carry out a programme of destroying forts: No. 1 Column included the 8th (Lahore) Mountain Battery less one section (left in camp) and detachments of the Buffs and the 36th Sikhs and No. 4 Company, Bengal Sappers and Miners. This column, afterwards joined by No. 3 column, carried out a part of its task against a great deal of opposition, and was roughly handled during its withdrawal to camp, losing twenty-two rifles and having forty-two casualties. The Brigadier-General now took charge and, darkness having fallen, most of the infantry lost touch and returned to camp, but the battery and Sappers and Miners and a few of the Buffs were ordered to halt for the night just outside the village of Bilot, three and a half miles from camp. A small enclosure was made for protection—fortunately the relief line of mules had been sent back early—but the party was under heavy fire from tribesmen in the village. Several sallies were made but without effect and a great number of casualties occurred among men and animals in a very cramped space. The mules and drivers were in the middle and the saddles were used for protection from bullets. About midnight the party was relieved by a detachment of the 35th Sikhs and the tribesmen decamped. Battery casualties: killed, Lieutenant A. T. Crawford, 6 N.C.Os. and men, 1 follower, and 23 mules; wounded, Lieutenant F. A. Wynter, 1 Native Officer, 21 N.C.Os. and men, 1 follower, and 5 mules. Lieutenant Wynter was severely wounded through both thighs, having only just rejoined on recovering from a wound received in the attack on the Malakand. He behaved with great gallantry, as did all the officers, two R.E. officers being awarded the V.C., which Corporal Smith of the Buffs also received.

On Sir Bindon Blood's arrival, fresh infantry were sent up and the force reorganized in two brigades, but the threat was enough for the Mamunds and they capitulated. The Salarzais had also been implicated in the rising, but proved quite amenable when the troops moved into their valley.

There was nothing left for the Malakand Field Force to do but to ensure the security of the road to Chitral by establishing a movable column with headquarters at Khar, and the Field Force was demobilized in January, 1898.

The 8th (Lahore) Mountain Battery, having experienced a very strenuous three months, arrived at the Malakand on 29th October to refit. The Battery's prominence during this time may be judged from the list of awards:

> Captain A. H. C. Birch (Commandant), brevet-majority.
> Lieutenant F. A. Wynter, D.S.O.
> Subadar Sher Singh and Jemadar Nawab, 2nd Class Order of British India with title of Bahadur.
> Admitted to Order of Merit, 3rd Class—
>> For conspicuous gallantry at Bilot on 16th September, 1897, Jemadar Isher Singh, Jemadar Nawab, Gunners Magh Singh, Nur Mohammed, Fateh Ali, Driver Nihala, Trumpeter Jiwan.
>> For conspicuous gallantry at Malakand on 27th July, 1897, Naik Hussain Muhammad, Gunners Gul Ahmad, Imam Din, Hospital Assistant Kashi Ram } for killing charging tribesmen with their swords.
> Mentioned in despatches: Captain A. H. C. Birch (three times), Lieutenant F. A. Wynter, Jemadar Nawab, Trumpeter Jiwan.

The 8th (Lahore) Mountain Battery had been in North Malakand refitting during November until the 22nd, when it marched with the Utman Khel Force under Colonel Reid to Agrah, arriving there on the 29th. The Utman Khels had taken part in the attack on the Malakand in July, but realized that the long arm of the Sirkar had reached them at last, and made haste to hand in their quota of rifles and to accept our terms.

The Battery casualties during the strenuous campaign had been temporarily filled by gunners from the Hyderabad Contingent, who were now sent back. The battery then joined the Buner Field Force.

The Bunerwals had not made submission nor complied with the punitive terms imposed on them for their participation in the attack at Malakand and Chakdara. The Malakand Field Force became the Buner Field Force under Sir Bindon Blood for the operations which began in January, 1898. Buner lies north-east of Mardan between the Indus and Swat rivers, and the concentration took place at Sanghao (twenty-one miles north of Mardan) of the two brigades and two regiments of cavalry, the latter under Lieutenant-Colonel R. B. Adams, V.C., of the Guides.

A frontal attack on the enemy holding the Tangao Pass was supported by the fire of a field battery and two mountain batteries, while the 20th Punjab Infantry scaled the hills on the left of the Pass and appeared from a covered position immediately behind the enemy's line as the frontal attack was closing in. The enemy fled and were followed up into the plain below by the Royal West Kent. Colonel Adam's column, having crossed by another pass, arrived on the plain the next day and the fighting was over. The Bunerwal's armament was of a low standard: they had a few rifles among their matchlocks and tried to check the advance by rolling stones down the hillside. After accepting complete submission, the Buner Field Force returned to Mardan by another pass and was broken up. The 8th (Lahore) Mountain Battery went to Burma at the end of the year, and took over 7-prs.

The Khyber Pass had not yet been reopened to traffic, but we had recovered our prestige north of the Kabul river; a great deal had to be done, however, before the weather became too severe to exact retribution from the Afridis and Orakzais for unprovoked aggression, attacks on frontier posts and damage to life and property.

Under Sir William Lockhart, a force of two divisions, each of two mixed infantry brigades, was mobilized as a striking force; as well as a brigade for line of communications defence from the striking force to Kohat, movable columns at Peshawar and Kurram, and a reserve brigade at Rawalpindi. The whole force totalled over 50,000, including 20,000 followers.

The mixed brigades of the force consisted of two British and two native infantry battalions each. The native mountain batteries were:

> 1st Division—1st (Kohat) and 2nd (Derajat) C.R.A., Lieutenant-Colonel A. E. Duthy.
>
> 2nd Division—5th (Bombay) C.R.A., Lieutenant-Colonel R. Purdy.

Three British mountain batteries were also included. Lines of Communication Troops—No. 1 Kashmir Mountain Battery. C.R.A. at Force Headquarters—Brigadier-General C. H. Spragge.

Railhead was at Khushalgarh, with only one siding and with an immediate bottleneck at the bridge of boats across the Indus; but by dint of tremendous efforts by the "Q" staff the move began on 17th October.

The plan of campaign was a simple one: to march the striking force from the southern side of Afridi and Orakzai territory to the northern, returning to India by the Bara river. The Kurram and Peshawar Columns were to assist by giving such support as circumstances required. Terms were to be dictated to the enemy at Maidan, a stronghold in the plain between the Waran and Bara rivers. This place was only thirty miles from Shinawari, our advanced base, which was about forty-five miles from Kohat. The country to be traversed was mountainous and extremely difficult, but it was hoped to find the enemy in force in one of two strong defensive positions in order to punish him severely.

The road of the advance was dominated by the Dargai heights, which were carried by the 2nd Division with few casualties on 18th October, the 5th (Bombay) Mountain Battery being with the main attack. This position was, however, evacuated the same day.

The main body began to advance on the 20th and, finding the Dargai heights reoccupied by the enemy, proceeded to eject him again, the possession of the heights being essential for movement along the roads.

The 2nd Division, reinforced by the 1st (Kohat) Mountain Battery and two battalions from the 1st Division, moved from Shinawari early on the 20th with orders to advance to Karappa via Chagru Kotal, clearing the Dargai heights which commanded the road. General Lockhart considered that the enemy would probably retire from Dargai as soon as the troops pushed on, but in fact the heights had to be cleared first. In front were 12,000 Orakzais and Afridis in a fortified position 300 feet above a narrow neck—the only approach—at a range of some 500 yards. No. 9 British Mountain Battery was to co-operate from the Samana ridge, our right flank, and the main artillery support was provided by the 1st (Kohat) and the two batteries of the 2nd Division in action at Chagru Kotal; Lieutenant-Colonel R. Purdy was in command of the batteries. No. 9 Battery's range was about 3,300 yards; the range of the other batteries, about 1,800 yards.

After an accurate and steady fire from the guns, the 1/2nd Gurkhas dashed across the open space under the concentrated fire of hundreds of marksmen at short range. The survivors found cover at the foot of the cliff which was lined by the enemy sangars. These sangars, about two feet high, were breastworks of heavy stone on the edge of the cliff, and quite impervious to any shelling by 2.5-inch guns. The position on the Chagru Kotal was 700 feet below the sangars, and no better support could be given than to fire time shrapnel and try to smother the target. The battery on the Samana alone was able to apply a useful angle of descent, being more or less on the same level, and was probably responsible for most of the damage inflicted.

Further attempts after similar preparation were made by the Dorsets and Derbyshires, with the result that the casualties were very heavy; it seems that the guns stopped firing as soon as the infantry began to advance. This was certainly the case in the final and successful assault made by the Gordon Highlanders, followed by the 3rd Sikhs. The artillery opened a rapid concentrated fire for three minutes, on the conclusion of which Lieutenant-Colonel Mathias gave his men the word to advance over the open space and led them on up the track in single file—which was the only way of approaching the summit. The four batteries fired some 1,300 rounds during the day, nearly all shrapnel. Our total casualties were 5 officers killed and 13 wounded, 182 other ranks killed and wounded.

The division crossed the Khanki river the next day and the whole force encamped at Kharappa. A great deal of sniping was endured every night until the neighbouring heights were piqueted.

During a foraging expedition, a gun of the 1st (Kohat) Mountain Battery burst just in front of the junction nut and could not be unscrewed.

The road to the Tirah led over the Sampagha Pass, which was captured on 29th October. The six mountain batteries supported this attack, firing on sangars before the infantry assaulted. On the occasion of a move forward to a new position, Captain F. R. McC. De Butts, 5th (Bombay) Mountain Battery, was killed by a bullet while bringing his battery into action; the battery command then devolved on Lieutenant E. E. Edlmann. The pass was taken with few casualties, and a move was made to the Arhanga Pass, which was captured on the 31st, and the troops found themselves in the summer home of the Afridis, till then unvisited by Europeans.

The Force, less one brigade in the Mastura valley, encamped at Maidan, in Zakka Khel country.

The next three weeks were spent in visiting nearly every part of the Tirah, collecting forage and destroying the towers of the tribesmen who had attacked us. The camp was constantly sniped at night, and the enemy, who were well armed and past-masters in the art of guerilla warfare, did all they could to obstruct, and gained several successes on a small scale, cutting up reconnoitring and foraging parties. One or more of the mountain batteries took part in all these expeditions.

Negotiations were opened with the tribes, and the Orakzais, who seemed to have little fight left, accepted our terms on 12th November; the Zakka Khel and Aka Khel were still irreconcilable.

On the 9th a column which included No. 8 British, commanded by Major J. C. Shirres, D.S.O., and the 5th (Bombay) Mountain Batteries made a reconnaissance of Saran Sar, a pass leading into the Bara valley, about 2,500 feet above Maidan camp. As usual, all went well until our troops started to retire to camp, when the rear company of the rear-guard was heavily attacked from a wooded spur of the hill on their right, and afterwards, when extricated, moved towards camp along a deep nullah without putting out flankers on the top edges. One small party lost its way and never got back, the retirement having started so late that the rear-guard arrived in camp after dark. The movement to Saran Sar was repeated two days later with very few casualties.

A force including the same batteries went on 13th November to the Waran valley, where they stayed until the 16th with no trouble bar night sniping; but on their return journey to Maidan the rear-guard was attacked to such effect from a wooded spur on the flank that Lieutenant-Colonel Houghton and the 36th Sikhs went back to extricate it. After a tough fight, darkness closed in, but having captured some houses at the point of the bayonet, the troops spent the night in them under cover.

The whole force (less the 1st Brigade in the Mastura valley) moved on the 18th to Bagh, a sacred place to the Afridi. Its arrival was unexpected, but nevertheless it had to undergo several hours of musketry fire from the hills round the camp. The batteries did their best, but it took an infantry charge to clear the heights. Captain J. L. Parker was shot through his breeches, and Lieutenant H. S. de Brett had a portion of an ear carried away. Reconnaissance and punitive expeditions, supported by the mountain batteries, continued to be sent out.

Administrative arrangements were now begun for the evacuation of Tirah down the Bara valley, and during this period General Lockhart went with Gaselee's brigade, which was accompanied by 1st (Kohat) and 2nd (Derajat) Mountain Batteries, from Bagh to join the Kurram movable column in the Massozai country. The Mamuzais, who also belonged to the Orakzai tribe, and the Chamkannis had refused to accept our terms, and remained defiant.

The Durbi Khel Pass (8,700 feet) had to be crossed, the path being extremely steep and rocky, after a running fight all the way from Bagh, and the resistance stiffened on the pass, which was flanked by a forest affording plenty of cover to the tribesmen. Both batteries were firing at 1,000 (sometimes 500) yards, and after crossing the pass and reaching Dargai (in Mamuzai country) had to clear the surrounding hills under heavy rifle fire before the camping ground could be occupied. Batteries fired about 120 rounds each. Lieutenant Wyatt and a driver of the 2nd (Derajat) Battery were wounded and several mules killed and wounded.

The Massozai jirgahs came in on the 29th, and part of the column paid a visit to Thabi, headquarters of the Chamkannis; but owing to the precipitous nature of the ground, the village could not be destroyed in one day and a second visit had to be paid in the face of a very obstinate resistance. The Gurkha Scouts under Captain F. G. Lucas distinguished themselves here by clearing sangars with some tough bayonet fighting. This highly trained body of specially selected Gurkhas was the prototype of the "commandos" and did magnificent work throughout the campaign.

No further opposition was met with, and the G.O.C. accepted the submission of all concerned except the Chamkannis. Their severe punishment did not, however, prevent them from misbehaving again in 1899, killing villagers and stealing cattle. In that year a surprise raid in force had so great an effect that they paid up the fines owing, handed in the rifles demanded, and gave no trouble for at least ten years.

The withdrawal of the expedition was a military operation of extreme difficulty. A tremendous number (8,000 or more) of baggage animals had to move in single file under escort over a very rough and slippery countryside with many defiles: it was in fact one long rear-guard action for both columns. The 1st Division moved via the Mastura valley, the 2nd Division down the Bara valley, the force joining at Bara Fort. The Peshawar Column was to move to Bara Fort and prepare for the arrival of the Tirah Force.

Except for a diversion to destroy some forts in the Aka Khel valley, which was carried out with few casualties, the 1st Division had no incidents and met the Peshawar Column at Fort Bara on 17th December. The 2nd Division had some heavy rear-guard fighting on its way down the valley.

Its first march to Dwatoi was very rough going and the baggage was left out all night. The camp was heavily sniped. The weather had turned very cold and a chilling rain made the going more difficult than ever. The transport animals were soon overtired and many loads were lost. Throughout the march the long column was shot at and sniped, and so was the camp at night, notwithstanding the piquets. The mountain batteries were called on to dislodge parties of the enemy and long-range snipers.

Thanks to the superb spirit of the troops and followers, the 2nd

Division got through, though with nearly 200 casualties in the ten days' march. A very welcome rest was given the troops at Fort Bara. The Zakka Khels were next dealt with in their own valleys. This duty fell to the 1st Division and the Peshawar Column. The Peshawar Column marched to Jamrud on 23rd December and on to Landi Kotal without interference, finding at the latter place that the fort had been gutted and the water supply damaged. The pass was piqueted for the passage of convoys, and the village defences of those concerned in the original outbreak were destroyed with very few casualties. By March the pass was reopened for the Tuesday and Friday convoys in the regular way. On 25th December the 1st Division started to move into the Bazar valley in two columns, No. 2 (Derajat) Mountain Battery with the left column and No. 1 (Kohat) with the right.

Little opposition was met, though the weather was appallingly bad, and after destroying the villages of those implicated in the attacks in the Bara valley, China and Bara, the 1st Division and the Peshawar Column were reorganized into three brigades as the Khyber Force. This force was reduced from time to time and finally recalled in 1900 when the Khyber Rifles took over their former responsibilities for the pass.

The final settlement with the Afridis did not take place for some months, but eventually they surrendered unconditionally.

Before the demobilization of the 2nd Division, one final affair must be chronicled in which the 5th (Bombay) Mountain Battery took part. On 29th January, 1898, an attempt was made to round up a large number of cattle grazing on the Kajurai Plain, which lies between the Bara and Bazar valleys, in order to exert pressure on the tribesmen. This was made a combined movement of the 1st and 2nd Divisions; the former sending two columns from the Khyber line to block all exits from the plain to the Bazar valley, and the 2nd Division sending one column to block the Shinkamar Pass, and a column from the 3rd Brigade at Bara to operate against the tribesmen on the plain and seize their cattle.

The column of the 4th Brigade, consisting of the K.O.Y.L.I. and the 36th Sikhs, with two guns 5th (Bombay) Mountain Battery, on starting to return to camp without having found any of the enemy, prematurely withdrew a piquet on a hill commanding the road over the kotal. This hill was immediately seized by the enemy, who now showed themselves and poured a heavy fire into our column. The hill had to be retaken before our move could continue, causing us considerable losses, and even greater losses were incurred before the troops got clear, by the help of a reinforcement of 300 rifles and two more guns of the 5th (Bombay) Mountain Battery. Among our losses were five British officers and twenty-six British other ranks killed. An expedition had to be made on the following day to recover the bodies. Very few cattle were captured that day, and it was thought that the enemy were aware of our plan.

While waiting for the enemy to accept our terms, the 2nd Division was put on to road-making. It was demobilized in April, 1898.

After these strenuous months, the Frontier had a year or two of peace. On the conclusion of these operations batteries were given permission to bear on their colours and appointments:

"CHITRAL": 2nd (Derajat), 4th (Hazara) Mountain Batteries.
"PUNJAB FRONTIER, TIRAH": 1st (Kohat), 2nd (Derajat), 5th (Bombay) Mountain Batteries.
"PUNJAB FRONTIER, MALAKAND": 8th (Lahore) Mountain Battery.

By 1895 the India General Service Medal of 1854 had been issued with twenty-three different bars, and a new India General Service Medal was issued for the Chitral Expedition and the campaigns that followed. Personnel who had taken part in the various expeditions were given the new medal with the corresponding bars: "Relief of Chitral 1895", "Punjab Frontier 1897-98", "Malakand 1897", "Samana 1897", "Tirah 1897-98". Followers were granted similar medals and bars in bronze.

In May, 1896, the 5th (Bombay) Mountain Battery mobilized with the Suakin Force of one cavalry regiment and two infantry battalions under Brigadier-General C. C. Egerton, C.B., D.S.O.* These Indian troops were sent to Suakin to relieve the garrison of Egyptian troops ordered to join the Dongola Expeditionary Force. The battery was made up to war strength by drafts of men and mules from the 6th (Jacob's) Battery. The Indian contingent returned to India after the capture of Dongola in September, 1896.

Personnel of the Suakin Force were awarded the Sudan Medal, 1896-7.

In March, 1899, a new mountain battery, No. 9 (Native) Mountain Battery, was raised at Rawalpindi by Captain L. W. P. East.

The pay of a salutri, which was 21 rupees a month in 1895, was in that year raised by two rupees, as was the pay of all N.C.Os. and men. The following year driver havildars and naiks were granted a further increase of one rupee.

Football was being played by officers and men in the nineties, to

---

* Later Field-Marshal Sir Charles Egerton, K.C.B., D.S.O.

be superseded in the following decade by hockey, at which some batteries became very proficient.

"Mountain Artillery Drill, 1897," was published in Calcutta in October of that year by order of the Inspector-General of Artillery in India. It was a very complete manual of a convenient size, referring to the 2.5-inch R.M.L. steel jointed gun, with establishments for British and native batteries. It devoted 28 pages to the tactical employment of mountain artillery in the field. Except in purely mountain warfare three batteries were to be organized as a "brigade division."* The range table gave the slope of descent as 1 in 10 at 2,000 yards, 1 in 5 at 3,000, and 1 in 3 at 4,000. The rangefinder described was the mekometer. It was laid down that on coming into action two pairs of ammunition boxes, with the case shot and small store box, were to be unloaded and placed conveniently for the service of the gun. During an operation the relegation of a number of ammunition mules from batteries to form an ammunition column in rear was encouraged. It was also decreed that cavalry drill was to be used in officers' sword exercise, instruction on foot, and movement by fours. There was a special drill for the mountain artillery sword. The foot-drill was elaborated in an appendix published in 1901.

Army Order 96 of June, 1899, was of great importance to officers of mountain artillery. In 1891 the formation of a bifurcated list of lieutenants had been ordered for the purpose of separating the mounted and dismounted branches of the Artillery. The results were not satisfactory and a complete bifurcation became necessary. By Army Order 96 the Royal Regiment of Artillery was divided into two Corps, the Royal Horse and Royal Field Artillery, and the Royal Garrison Artillery. It was laid down that all appointments to British and Native Mountain Artillery should be made from the latter Corps.

In 1901, owing to the addition of a fourth subaltern to every battery and an increase in the number of batteries, subalterns could be appointed to native mountain batteries without the necessary language qualification, but were required to pass the Higher Standard Urdu within twelve months. Qualified officers were preferred. The new regulation cancelled an earlier one which required a candidate to have completed two years' service before presenting himself, thus opening the appointment to second-lieutenants. In the early days of mountain artillery officers' names were not considered for posting until they had completed three years' service.

---

* This expression did not last long, but was soon changed to "brigade," and eventually to "Regiment."

Promotion to captain became very slow a few years later and lieutenants automatically became captains after thirteen years' service; it will be noticed that many battery subalterns held the higher rank in 1914.

After service in India, R.A. and R.E. officers received an increment to the normal pension, the minimum being an extra £50 p.a. after thirteen years in the country.

CHAPTER V

The Rearmament Period

THE LONG-OVERDUE rearmament of the mountain artillery was forced on the Government of India by the fiasco of the South African War, when 2.5-inch batteries caused consternation to our troops by firing black powder giving clouds of smoke on battlefields occupied by guns and rifles using smokeless powder.

There are several events to chronicle in the last stages of the 2.5-inch R.M.L. gun.

A new mountain battery was raised in Abbottabad in 1900 by Captain E. E. Edlmann with drafts from the older batteries. It was named 10th (Native) Mountain Battery.

Designations of all batteries were changed in 1901 by dropping all numbers: 5th, 6th, 7th, and 8th Batteries were named Quetta, Jullundur, Gujrat, and Lahore respectively. The 9th and 10th became Murree and Abbottabad Mountain Batteries. This lasted about two years, and batteries were, in 1903, known by numbers only; except the four Frontier Force batteries which kept in addition their original names and their distinction "(Frontier Force)" and the "Jullundur," for which the name "Jacob's" was substituted. These names were not shown in brackets, which came into use in 1921. The numbers were obtained by adding 20 to the original numbers, and it was understood at the time that this was done to prevent confusion with British mountain batteries. It was with these designations that batteries entered the First World War.

Lord Kitchener came to India in 1902 as Commander-in-Chief and made great changes. The three Presidency Armies were amalgamated into the Indian Army, divided into Northern and Southern Armies, and amongst other changes the Punjab Frontier Force ceased to exist as a separate body on 31st March, 1903, after fifty-four years of distinguished service. Its regiments were treated as of equal value with other Indian regiments and several were sent down-country. The frontier districts of the Punjab, with the frontier agencies, had been formed into the North-West Frontier Province in 1901 under the direct control of the Governor-General in Council; its capital was Peshawar, which remained the headquarters of the military district.

Lord Curzon was Viceroy from 1899 to 1905, and there were no major expeditions during his term of office. He extended the policy of replacing regular troops on the Frontier by irregular militias recruited from local tribes, after the manner of the Khyber Rifles, in most of the trans-border territories, *e.g.*, Kurram, Tochi, Wana. The Khar movable column was broken up and the battery quartered in Nowshera, which became a mountain battery station.

A policy of opening up the Frontier with railways for commercial as well as strategical purposes was now in force; the 2 ft. 6 in. line from Nowshera to Dargai (Malakand) was taking traffic in 1901 and the Khushalgarh-Kohat in 1902, though with only a bridge of boats over the Indus.

A contingent of Native officers and men under Captain E. E. Edlmann represented the Native Mountain Artillery at the Coronation in 1902, camping at Hampton Court.

On 1st January, 1903, a Durbar was held at Delhi on the most lavish oriental scale to celebrate the accession of His Majesty King Edward VII, who was represented by His Royal Highness the Duke of Connaught. At the Royal review the Mountain Artillery were represented by two brigade divisions, one British and one Native, under Lieutenant-Colonel E. Gunner. The Native unit was commanded by Lieutenant-Colonel A. Keene, D.S.O., and consisted of the 3rd (Peshawar), 5th (Bombay), and No. 1 Kashmir Mountain Batteries; the latter was commanded by H.H. The Maharajah in person.

The description "Native" for units and personnel was changed to "Indian" in 1904.

A number of Indian mountain batteries were among the troops reviewed by His Royal Highness the Prince of Wales at Rawalpindi in November, 1905.

The drawbacks of the 2.5-inch R.M.L. gun had long been known in India, but its failure in South Africa led to a hasty rearmament of all mountain batteries. A 10-pr. jointed B.L. gun was in the experimental stage and its trials were hurried on so that all batteries were rearmed by the end of 1903; but, although far superior to the 2.5-inch gun, it was still behind the times. By this time field artillery carriages had a top cradle to take up the recoil so that the carriage remained steady when the gun was fired; the 10-pr. carriage differed little from that of the 2.5-inch and the recoil was controlled by a similar "check rope" round the trail. The two portions of the gun could be united without noise with a wrench. The breech portion was wire wound.

Weights, etc., of the 10-pr. gun: Weight, 404 lb.; calibre, 2.75 in.;

length, 6 ft. 4½ in.; grooves, 16; wheel track, 2 ft. 10 in.; maximum elevation, 25 degrees; maximum depression, 15 degrees; muzzle velocity, 1,289 f.s.; charge, 6 oz. 14 drs. cordite; ammunition mules, 6 per gun; Range, 6,000 yards, but sights engraved to 4,200 yards only.

The gun was provided with shrapnel and star shell; case shot was originally issued but soon withdrawn; the use of cordite and the breech-loading system made for a more rapid rate of fire than could be got out of the R.M.L. gun, and the range was half as long again. Common shell was provided later.

The issue of the new gun was a great tonic to the mountain artillery, and its appearance on active service quickly restored confidence which had been weakened by the old equipment, but much had to be learnt to get the best from the new equipment in order to give the infantry maximum support.

Training became more complicated as firing from behind cover became habitual; the application of fire, its direction from covered positions, and control of dispersed batteries, all had to be mastered, and in addition a fresh system of ranging a battery had to be learnt nearly every year. Pending the issue of instruments, improvised ones were made up which the Indian gunners mastered with amazing efficiency. Lines were laid out parallel, more or less, by a complicated system of "laying cords." The gun-arc, a stick with holes half a degree apart to receive a movable foresight, gave little trouble once the layer had grasped that an order for 3 degrees right meant the insertion of the movable foresight at 3 degrees left. Dial sights were not issued for several years. The field clinometer had been in batteries for years; in some units it was suitably called the "digri." Some batteries used traditional names which died hard: in one, a case shot was provided with the greatest rapidity on the word "grupp," although grape-shot fell out of use in the days of brass guns. Directors were made up with wooden base-plates and alidades.

Signalling had become a feature of fire tactics, but batteries had to be content with flags for some years, sending messages in "Roman Urdu." Only five paid signallers were allowed for each battery. Pending the issue of telephones some enthusiastic batteries bought their own telephones.

The rangefinder in use was the mekometer, a two-man instrument.

In a year or two a demand arose for a long-recoil carriage, and trials were begun which eventually resulted in an up-to-date carriage with buffer and running-out springs under the name of 2.75-inch B.L.

The old cry for a mountain howitzer was revived without results;

after some experience, battery commanders improvised with a half-charge or a star shell cartridge.

The question of movement in draught was raised again and was officially approved, but no gear was issued.

Practice camps were held annually, generally of two or three batteries which could conveniently concentrate; at Hatti, in 1906, a combined camp was held for British and Indian batteries, nine being present. Marks were given for tactics and fire discipline and for fire effect, the results being shown by the award of badges of different classes to be worn by the rank and file for twelve months. Elementary practice was carried out beforehand. The number of rounds allotted for practice was increased from 376 to 600 in 1913.

Lieutenant-General L. W. Parsons, Inspector-General of Artillery in India from 1903 to 1906, took a great interest in mountain artillery and was responsible for the rapid advance in efficiency made by the batteries. He insisted on mountain batteries attending practice camps with field artillery in the plains as an alternative to the usual practice camp in rough country, and although the occasional purist regretted having to "fire off a ploughed field," the results were of great benefit. Several batteries always attended Army or Command manœuvres, temporarily brigaded, and were thereby trained for civilized as against frontier warfare.

The Russo-Japanese War of 1904-5 brought mountain artillery into prominence, and by a correction dated May, 1907, to "Combined Training," mountain artillery was acknowledged as part of the field army artillery. In Manchuria the close support which had to be provided for the infantry was given by sending forward mountain batteries, which were less conspicuous. The use of artillery in mountain warfare had been referred to in "Frontier Warfare, 1901."

Another innovation due to this war was the sending forward of an artillery officer with a telephone with advancing infantry to send back information. This developed into the Forward Observing Officer, who sent back information over the telephone and directed the fire of the battery when required.

Batteries had become majors' commands about 1908 owing to the size and importance of six-gun batteries, and a captain* and three subalterns were posted instead of four subalterns. Captains in permanent command were not superseded, but were allowed to complete their tour until promoted regimentally. For fifty years the commandant of an Indian mountain battery had been a captain—an independent command and a much-sought-after position of responsi-

* Majors and captains were allowed horse allowance for a second charger.

bility and prestige, successfully filled by officers of high quality and great promise. His status had been that of a battalion commander, but within a few years the majors whose batteries were brigaded found themselves in the position of a company commander of infantry.

Two more batteries were raised at Dehra Dun in 1907: the 31st by Major J. L. Parker and the 32nd by Major O. C. Williamson-Oswald; these were the first majors appointed commandants. Each battery was armed with six 10-pr. guns, and the personnel were half Jat Sikhs and half Punjabi Mohammedans. Nuclei were drawn from existing batteries, thereby providing promotion which had become rather stagnant. Both these batteries were fortunate in seeing active service a short time after their formation.

The next step was to form batteries into artillery brigades under lieutenant-colonels, but this was not brought about until 1911, when three Indian Mountain Artillery Brigades were formed (of two batteries each), two at Abbottabad and one at Dehra Dun. An extra captain had been allowed for Abbottabad since 1908.

Other changes were brought in at this period. The pay and quartermaster havildar became quartermaster havildar, and the munshi was replaced by a pay havildar, who was allowed an assistant. The battery baggage establishment was replaced by 6 drivers, 1 nalband, and 51 ordnance mules; these animals carried reserve ammunition and baggage and constituted a reserve for animals in the first line. The baggage mules and muleteers were transferred to the Supply and Transport Corps. The salutri was mounted; the tindal and mutsuddy were discharged.

Reductions took place in 1914, bringing the number of mules from 174 to 164, and the different portions of the battery were ordered to be called "Firing Battery, First Line, Second Line Transport" instead of "First Line, Second Line, Baggage."

The increase in the number of batteries entailed a large increase in the number of mules. The Punjab Government owned a stud which produced country-breds, but not in sufficient numbers, and ordnance mules were collected from many parts of the world—Italy, China, Persia, South and North America; a first-class mule of the last-named breed cost about Rs900 landed in Bombay. In 1906 the official standards of height and girth for ordnance and baggage mules was published; the former to measure 14.1 to 13.2 hands; the latter, 13.2 to 12.3.

More accommodation had to be provided now that the number of batteries was increased; there were two new lines in Abbottabad, and one battery was quartered in the camp at Kakul originally built to hold Boer prisoners of war. For a time Indian units were ordered to build their own lines; the 4th (Hazara) Battery did this in Nowshera in 1902.

The following batteries had sent a section to form part of the garrison of Chitral at least once since 1900: 2nd (Derajat) (F.F.), 3rd (Peshawar) (F.F.), 4th (Hazara) (F.F.), 5th (Bombay), 10th (Abbottabad).

The reliefs were not interrupted during the period under consideration, but the 1914 relief was cancelled.

The battery stationed at Nowshera usually performed this duty. This detachment was of the greatest value to a subaltern from a professional point of view; the battery commander being inaccessible, the young officer had to depend on himself for twelve months. Big game shooting more or less unlimited and chikor drives on the hillsides provided sport with the minimum of expense; the local allowance of Rs150 a month was much appreciated.

Socially—*i.e.*, existence in cantonments and in the mess—things had changed little from the previous decade. The tempo was still geared to the pace of the horse, the internal combustion engine not yet having established itself on the Frontier. The first Mountain Artillery Mess was opened at Abbottabad in 1903*; becoming eventually an R.A. Station Mess. In the early days, batteries had lived in battery messes, or more usually in Frontier Force messes (as honorary members in the case of non-Piffer batteries) or in messes of other units.

Batteries owned a mess tonga, a very strong two-wheeled vehicle generally made at Roorkee and capable of going almost anywhere when pulled by a pair of ordnance mules. Officers going shooting would lay out relays beforehand and cover the journey with surprising speed.

There was generally some shooting within reach of cantonments, and a trip to Kashmir or Ladakh for big game was within the means of most officers. Every officer was granted two months' privilege leave annually, and this could be saved up for two years, permitting a period of three months' leave thereby. In some stations far from the railway—*e.g.*, Bannu and Dera Ismail Khan—three months was the normal period, but after the arrival of the railway this concession was withdrawn.

Improved facilities for spending leave in England were changing the outlook of the Indian Army officer whose interests had formerly

---

* This was made the occasion for the presentation to the 5th Gurkhas of silver breech and chase mules with drivers in gratitude for their hospitality over many years to the Mountain Gunners stationed there.

been concentrated on life with his unit, punctuated by his year's leave out of India every four or five years. It was now possible to return to England at shorter intervals, and although R.A. officers seconded to Indian mountain batteries were little affected, an all-round tendency to loosen regimental ties was noticeable.

Furlough rules were the same as for Indian Army officers. Until about 1895 two years' furlough could be taken, but after that time a year's furlough at a reduced rate of pay could be had after every four or five years' service, if the officer could be spared.

Polo was ceasing to be the inexpensive game it had been for many years: the price of ponies was increasing rapidly, and the standard of the game improved. However, station polo was always available and battery ponies were generally suitable for training.

Gunner and driver N.C.Os. and men had from the earliest days been armed with swords, with brown leather shoulder and waist belts. The curved sword had a brass hilt; the shoulder belt had a frog and was originally called the "Hazara Mountain Battery" pattern. These swords were taken away in 1902, but reissued to driver personnel in 1904. Gunner N.C.Os. and men were rearmed with "carbines, M.E. Artillery," carried slung with 70 rounds in a bandolier: 125 carbines replaced the 18 carbines formerly issued; this was a legacy from the South African War, and swords were taken away from the Royal Horse Artillery about the same time. Batteries kept the five buckshot rifles issued for sentry duty. In 1912 the carbines were exchanged for the "Rifle M.L.E. short," and in 1913 the number in a battery was reduced to 71. Indian officers and trumpeters carried Webley pistols.

British officers at this period wore a khaki drill jacket hooked at the neck with a turn-down collar, R.A. ball buttons, Bedford cord breeches, brown leather gaiters M.B. (loose round the ankles, fastening with leather loops at the side and strap at the top), ankle boots and "spurs, M.B. hunting." Badges of rank were worn on shoulder-straps with brass R.A. "numerals." The "coat, warm, British" was officially permitted. A khaki "Cawnpore" topee was often worn in marching order instead of a khaki helmet. British and Indian officers alike wore brown Sam Browne belts carrying the revolver, and the sword was attached to the saddle.

Full dress was Royal Artillery full dress with brown leather gaiters and ankle boots, and as head-dress a white cork helmet with white pagri.

Indian other ranks wore a khaki drill jacket and knickerbockers, putties and ankle boots. On shoulder-straps was worn an abbreviated battery title; *e.g.*, D.M.B. Until about 1905 all Indian ranks drew a free issue of blue for full dress, which was worn with a red pagri. This free issue was discontinued and an annual allowance was drawn of Rs10/8 a year for gunners and drivers in addition to a sum of Rs40, kit money on enlistment. In 1908 this was increased to Rs60 plus an extra Rs5 per annum boot money. Khaki drill was brought in bulk and made up in the battery.

Monthly pay was increased from 1st January, 1909, to:

	Rs
Subadar	100
Jemadar	50
Gunner Havildar	20
Gunner Naik	16
Gunner and Trumpeter	12
Driver Havildar	20
Driver Naik	18
Driver	11

all with a free issue of firewood.

Reservists were maintained under battery arrangements, and generally came up for training a few at a time. Before 1900 the establishment was 14, but in that year it was fixed at 22 gunners and 34 drivers; further increases were made until in 1908 it stood at 30 gunners and 49 drivers. A battery going on active service left behind at its station a small depot for which the personnel was extra to the battery establishment. The concentration of these depots, first at Abbottabad and then at Ambala, led to the formation of the Mountain Artillery Training Centre.

A number of senior Indian officers retired about this time, many with honorary rank. The names include:

Honorary Captains:
   Subadar-Major Bhanga Singh, Sirdar Bahadur.
   Subadar-Major Ghulam Muhammed, Sirdar Bahadur.
   Subadar-Major Akbar Ali, Sirdar Bahadur.
   Subadar-Major Sher Singh.
   Subadar Kharak Singh, Bahadur (joined his battery in 1865 and saw eight campaigns with it).
   Subadar-Major Harditt Singh, Sirdar Bahadur.*
   Subadar-Major Nur Alam, Sirdar Bahadur.
   Subadar-Major Jowahir Khan, Sirdar Bahadur.

---

* Subadar-Major Harditt Singh was invested with the insignia of the Order of the British Empire by His Majesty King George V on the occasion of the Delhi Durbar, 1911.

Honorary Lieutenants:
Subadar-Major Chanda, I.O.M., Sirdar Bahadur.
Subadar-Major Santa Singh, Bahadur, I.D.S.M.

Several Native officers of the Punjab Frontier Force batteries received a special mention in farewell orders on the breaking up of that Force:
Subadar-Major Ali Madat, Sirdar Bahadur.
Subadar-Major Nazar Khan.
Subadar-Major Sadulla Khan, Bahadur.
Subadar-Major Murdun Ali Shah, Bahadur.
Subadar-Major Imam Din, Bahadur.
Subadar Fattoo, Bahadur.
Subadar Sheikh Himmat.

Subadar-Major Rattan Singh, Sirdar Bahadur, must not be forgotten. He had over forty years' service in his battery after serving three and a half years in the Police. He held the Indian Mutiny medal, two India G.S. 1854 medals with clasps, Afghanistan medal 1878-80 with clasp, and the India G.S. 1895 medal with clasp. He went on pension in 1898.

These senior officers of twenty to forty years' service, in addition to very many others, had always been entirely loyal to, and trusted friends of, the British officers of the batteries.

In April, 1909, the establishment of subadar-majors was raised to three, and of trumpet-majors to four; all to be on one roster.

In June, 1907, the Indian Distinguished Service Medal was instituted to reward commissioned and non-commissioned officers and men who distinguished themselves in peace or on active service. In 1917 the grant was extended to non-combatants on field service.

The followers of Indian units formed a distinctly agreeable feature of army life. Those in Indian batteries in nearly every case showed as much *esprit de corps* as the fighting men whose status, both army and social, was so much higher. Humble men they were, doing humble work, but proudly maintaining a high standard of their work. Most of them seem to have no civil background; they were probably descendants of followers from the days of John Company, and for generations followed the flag—within India and outside, wherever sent. In 5th (Bombay) Battery in 1900 was serving a smith who claimed to have been in the battery for fifty years—a Poona man.

In the early days, drivers, salutris and shoeing-smiths were graded as followers, as were the muleteers with the battery baggage mules until their reduction in 1908. There was a jemadar of muleteers in charge and a duffadar to each section; each man was allotted three mules, their loads being: hospital and veterinary boxes, cooking pots, treasure chest, half-wroughts containing various stores and kits (one mule carried the kits of six fighting men or eight followers).

Some followers were attested as combatants, some as non-combatants, and others only enrolled.

ESTABLISHMENT

Six-gun 7-pr. bty. (1878)	Six-gun 10-pr. bty. (1908)
1 tindal	1 tindal
3 store lascars	6 cooks
6 langris	3 syces
4 syces	1 head smith
40 grass cutters*	3 smiths
1 head smith	1 head carpenter
2 file men	2 carpenters
1 head carpenter	1 head saddler
2 carpenters	4 saddlers
2 hammer men	1 munshi
2 firemen	3 pakhalis †
2 mochis	3 sweepers
3 pakhalis	1 mutsuddy
1 sweeper	1 bhisti
1 mutsuddy	

A sufficient hospital establishment had always been provided for batteries: the earliest one comprised a native doctor at Rs25, a dresser at Rs6, one cook, one bhisti, one sweeper, and six Kahars for the dhoolis. The native doctor was later replaced by a trained Hospital Assistant, and before the First World War Kahars became very scarce and were replaced by personnel of the Army Bearer Corps.

In the ensuing years during the First World War batteries were rearmed, as occasion permitted, with the 2.75-inch B.L. gun. This was the 10-pr. without trunnions, recoiling through a cradle, after firing, to the extent allowed by the piston of a hydraulic buffer, and forced back to the firing position by the energy of springs compressed during the recoil. This equipment was called 2.75-inch converted, Mark I. A later pattern was called 2.75-inch B.L. Mark I: this had a breech ring.

A long trail which made two loads for transport was provided, and a reversible axle which could be used in "high" or "low" position. A steel shield made in four parts hinged together protected the detachment; it weighed 78 lb. and was carried on the

---

* Fewer in the Bombay batteries where the supply was made partly by the Commissariat.
† The pakhali was replaced by a hand bhisti in 1913.

same mule as the rear end of the trail. The gun itself was a few pounds lighter than the 10-pr. Other differences were:
- Wheel track, 3 feet.
- Maximum range, 5,500 yards. Full charge, 7 oz. 12 dr. ballistite, M.V. 1,300 f.s.; Half charge, M.V., 775 f.s.
- Height of axis of gun:
- High position, $43\frac{1}{2}$ inches elevation 22°, depression 8°.
- Low position, $32\frac{1}{2}$ inches elevation 15°, depression 15°.

Sighting was up to date, *i.e.*, independent line of sight and a No. 7 dialsight were provided.

Projectiles: Shrapnel, weight $12\frac{1}{4}$ lb.; H.E., weight $12\frac{1}{2}$ lb.; Star, weight $12\frac{1}{2}$ lb.

This equipment was approved for issue in 1911, but Indian batteries did not receive it until several years later. Its transport took an extra mule and relief mule, *i.e.*,

| Wheel and axle | Trail, front part | Breech |
| Recoil cradle | Trail, rear part | Chase |

Each ammunition box weighed 25 lb. more than the 10-pr. box, and the battery carried 714 shrapnel, 42 H.E. and 24 star shell.

The equipment for draught weighed 75 lb. The two-man mekometer was still issued. A fuze indicator was provided with a corrector scale. Fuze T. and P. No. 80 was issued for shrapnel and D.A. No. 44 for H.E. The shrapnel was exceptionally powerful and won good opinions everywhere. There was little difference in the rate of fire compared with the 10-pr. as a single motion breech mechanism was not provided, but this gun had the great merit of not overturning when fired from bad ground.

The handbook was published in 1914.

OPERATIONS DURING THIS PERIOD
NORTH-WEST FRONTIER

There had been in 1898 a recrudescence of outrages in Southern Waziristan* for which the Mulla Powindah appeared to be responsible, and raids and acts of hostility continued for the next few years. In October, 1900, the Border Military Police post at Nasran, north of Tank, was surprised, two sepoys killed, and rifles and ammunition stolen. As the Mahsuds refused to settle our claims, a blockade of their territory was decided upon and came into operation on 1st December, 1900. A cordon was instituted, the roads were blocked and traffic stopped, but raids and offences continued, and by

---

* An attempt had been made during the nineties to introduce the "Sandeman" system (p.38) on the North-West Frontier, but it proved unsuccessful.

the following April less than half the fine had been paid. The blockade having failed, the Government decided on active retaliation. A section each of the 2nd (Derajat) and the 7th (Bengal) Batteries went with the first column of 900 rifles, which did a five-day march destroying defences and capturing prisoners and cattle, finally destroying most of Makin and returning via Razmak. Other columns went out, generally with a section of guns, and were very slightly opposed, owing to the strict secrecy of the arrangements. Strong measures brought the Mahsuds to submission, anyhow for a time. A bar to the 1895 medal, "Waziristan 1901-2", was awarded for the operations carried out between November, 1901 and February, 1902.

The Kabul Khel Wazirs continued their career of defiance of authority, plunder and outrages. A small column from Bannu surrounded Gumatti in February, 1899, to bring in some outlaws, but they took refuge in a masonry tower, which defied the attempts of the mountain guns to breach it.

The state of affairs became worse, and in November, 1902, four small columns under Major-General Egerton set out from Thal, Idak, Barganatu and Bannu, more or less simultaneously. Gumatti was again attacked and the guns again failed to make a breach at 400 yards: Colonel Tonnochy and Captain White, of the 3rd Sikhs, were killed in this affair, which resulted in the death of all the outlaws concerned. The other columns harassed the enemy in their districts and the short campaign resulted in the destruction of sixty-six towers and the capture of thirty prisoners. The 1st Kohat, 2nd Derajat (one section) and 7th Bengal (two sections) Mountain Batteries were allotted to these columns.

Money earned in road-making over the next few years went some way towards keeping these tribes quiet, but they never ceased to be restless. Lieutenant J. A. D. Langhorne, 3rd (Peshawar) Battery, was attacked by a ghazi in April, 1903, and although both shot and stabbed, he secured his man, who was afterwards hanged.

The introduction of the 10-pr. gun came as a great shock to the frontier tribesmen. For some years they had been having a good laugh at the smoke of discharge of the 2.5-inch gun and then taken cover before the arrival of the shell. It was a great change to have the first indication of artillery fire from the actual burst of the shell very close up. This is what happened when the Bazar Valley Field Force, under Major-General Sir James Willcocks, K.C.M.G., C.B., D.S.O., moved out in February, 1908, to punish the Zakka Khels for continued marauding and raids into British Territory. The security of life and property in the Kohat and Peshawar districts had been seriously menaced. Colonel A. W. Money, late R.A., was

A.A. and Q.M.G. of the force, and Lieutenant A. P. Y. Langhorne, 4th Hazara Mountain Battery was one of General Willcocks's A.D.Cs. The Zakka Khels are adepts at hill warfare and were at this date largely armed with Lee-Metfords and Martinis. Their leaders had recently returned from a visit to Kabul, where they had no doubt received encouragement to continue raiding British territory, and this culminated in a raid on Peshawar city, where property worth a lakh of rupees was looted. Punitive measures were approved and were executed without delay.

Four guns of 2nd (Derajat) Mountain Battery (F.F.) under Captain C. De Sausmarez, with Lieutenants N. Robertson-Glasgow and S. Carwithen (the other section being on detachment at Chitral), joined on 12th February the 1st Brigade of the Field Force, commanded by Brigadier-General C. A. Anderson, C.B.,* a gunner who had at one time served in an Indian mountain battery. No time was wasted, and on 15th the 1st Brigade reached Chora, and the 2nd Brigade, Walai, where it was joined by a column from Landi Kotal, to the north. This rapid concentration in the heart of their country bewildered the enemy and deprived him of the initiative. The battery marched to Walai and joined two guns of No. 3 Mountain Battery, R.G.A., in the support of an attack by the Seaforth Highlanders and 45th Sikhs of a hill held by the enemy. Fire was kept up until our infantry were sixty feet below the crest, at a range of 1,500 yards. Fifty shrapnel were fired.

During the next few days several villages were destroyed, but the battery had few targets. On one occasion a snap shot at a walled enclosure broke up a funeral party at 3,600 yards, killing some mourners. On the 21st the battery was supporting the attack of the 1st Brigade at Halwai when Driver Mangal Singh of the Centre Section was hit at limbering up, but bravely hung on to his very restive mule. He was awarded the I.D.S.M. for bravery in action, and was mustered gunner, much to his delight. The brigade retirement was covered by alternate sections successfully, and altogether 176 shrapnel were fired. Except for sniping at night there was little resistance by the enemy, and the tribe not only sued for peace but its good conduct was guaranteed by several other Afridi tribes. The object of the expedition having been attained, the force was back in Peshawar on 2nd March; the rapidity with which the operations were carried out was due to the excellent training of the infantry.

The battery was delighted with the new gun—it proved very accurate and encouraged shooting at fleeting opportunities, which

---

* Later Lieut.-General Sir Charles Anderson, K.C.B., who commanded the Indian Army Corps in France in 1914-5

often occurred in that type of fighting. Captain De Sausmarez was mentioned in despatches and awarded a brevet-majority.

While operations were in progress against the Zakka Khels, the Mohmands, spurred on by Afghan intrigue and the preaching of hostile mullahs, collected lashkars of their trans-border tribes with other Afghan subjects with the intention of attacking us in the rear. The Zakka Khel operations, however, were concluded more rapidly than was expected, before the Mohmands were ready to do more than make demonstrations on the Peshawar border.

The situation quickly became more serious as the lashkars increased to about 17,000 men, half being from Afghan territory. Villages in British territory were raided and our frontier posts attacked. Troops were rushed from Peshawar, and the Centre Section of 2nd (Derajat) Mountain Battery stationed at Nowshera marched to Peshawar under Lieutenant N. Robertson-Glasgow on the night of 20th/21st April, moving thence to Shabkadar with 18th Battery, R.F.A. The section was out on a reconnaissance with Major-General Willcocks and fired 67 shrapnel, but the enemy were not inclined to undertake major aggressions, and the section returned to Nowshera on the 29th.

Offensive operations on our part were indicated, and the Mohmand Field Force of three brigades was mobilized as from 24th April under Major-General Sir James Willcocks.

In the Divisional Troops were No. 8 Mountain Battery, R.G.A., 3rd (Peshawar)* and 8th (Lahore)† Mountain Batteries; the Peshawar Battery was commanded by Captain G. G. W. Corrie and the Lahore Battery by Major (Brevet Lieutenant-Colonel) R. W. Fuller.

It is noticeable that, as in the Bazar Valley Field Force, no officer was appointed as C.R.A., and in the event the batteries were used singly or by separate sections. By the end of the month the force was nearly complete, and the 2nd Brigade Headquarters had moved to Shabkadar with 3rd (Peshawar) Mountain Battery when a diversion occurred in the Khyber. An Afghan army appeared before Landi Kotal and the Political Agent asked for the dispatch of regular troops. General Willcocks went to Jamrud himself, and moved the 3rd Brigade, including 8th (Lahore) Mountain Battery, to that place, and 2nd Brigade, with 3rd (Peshawar) Mountain Battery, to Peshawar *en route* for Ali Musjid. The enemy were estimated at 13,000 or more, but they were disheartened by General Willcocks's prompt measures and confined themselves to sniping. On 4th May the enemy were attacked at Khargali, but made little resistance, and even allowed our withdrawal to camp to be

---
* At this date designated 23rd Peshawar Mountain Battery (F.F.).
† At this date designated 28th Mountain Battery.

carried out peacefully. The 8th (Lahore) Battery fired 151 shrapnel. The Left Section of this battery remained at Landi Kotal, while the remainder of the force returned to the Mohmand border by 10th May, where orders for an advance were issued. Cholera broke out in certain regiments, necessitating several reliefs, and it was the 13th before an advance was made. It was decided to punish the Balzai and Khwaizai tribes who had been foremost in aggressive action; the route to be followed being that taken by General Elles's force in 1897, up the Gandao valley to its junction with the Bohai Dag. At this date the tribesmen had a far greater number of breech-loading rifles than in the previous expedition. 8th (Lahore) Battery headquarters and Right and Centre Sections moved with the 1st Brigade to Dand, and on 15th the Centre Section went on with the advance guard to Nahakki. The road over the Nahakki Pass showed no signs of the work done on it in 1897. On the 16th the 1st Brigade moved into camp at Kasai, three miles to the north, and the 2nd Brigade took over the camp at Nahakki. The next day was spent in the destruction of villages within reach of the two camps. Four guns of 3rd (Peshawar) Mountain Battery were with one column of the 2nd Brigade which met with little opposition; the other section of the battery had no trouble in dislodging a few groups of tribesmen near Kwaja Kuhai and Chingai.

On the 18th the 2nd Brigade, supported by both Indian mountain batteries, moved up the Bohai Dag nullah and both batteries were in action during the advance, which culminated in the Brigade halting for the night at Ata Jor. Meantime the 1st Brigade camped at Nahakki.

The next day the force destroyed Kung, the largest of the Khwaizai villages, and the day after the village of Mazrina, and the column was then withdrawn safely to Kasai. The 1st Brigade was sent to tour the valleys to the north, inhabited by the Dawezai and Utmanzai tribes. With this force went the Right Section of 8th (Lahore) Mountain Battery, as well as No. 8 British Mountain Battery. Some opposition was offered at Yakh Dand in very broken ground, and here the guns came into play; various villages were destroyed on this and the following day, the force camping at Lakarai on 22nd. The section of 8th (Lahore) Mountain Battery covered the destruction of some more villages and shared in the engagement of a large body of 300 of the enemy caught lying in ambush. Gumbatai was destroyed and the force camped at Mullakalai, having its first undisturbed night for about ten days; a feature of this expedition was the incessant nightly sniping by the enemy. The section was ordered to proceed with a force to Yakh Dand, which had not complied with an ultimatum, but agreement was reached without fighting.

All the tribes had now submitted, or been punished, except the Koda Khel Balzai. The 2nd Brigade with 3rd (Peshawar) Mountain Battery and two guns of 8th (Lahore) moved on Koda Khel up the Bohai Dag on the 29th: the Seaforths, covered by four guns of 3rd (Peshawar) Battery, occupied the ridge to the east of the village, and the Guides Infantry held the other flank supported by the two guns of 8th (Lahore) Battery. The inhabitants evacuated the village and retired to the Afghan frontier on the crest behind. The enemy afterwards followed up our withdrawal, but without success. The force then marched to Galanai, where the Centre Section, 8th (Lahore) Battery had been since 15th May. The objects of the expedition having been accomplished, the Field Force was withdrawn and dispersed. Ammunition expended: 3rd (Peshawar) Battery 580 rounds; 8th (Lahore) Battery 488 rounds; these totals include 3 and 24 star shell respectively. The 3rd (Peshawar) Battery had one gunner wounded. Jemadar Fata of this battery was awarded the 2nd Class of the Order of British India, with the title of Bahadur. A new India General Service medal was issued for the operations just described; the last issued during the reign of King Edward VII. A bar "North-West Frontier 1908" was granted.

The Frontier remained comparatively peaceful for the next few years, except for occasional raids which were promptly dealt with. A couple of examples will suffice to show the state of constant readiness maintained by batteries.

In October, 1911, a gun was required at short notice at Tank in connection with a raid. Lieutenant F. R. Phillips of the 1st (Kohat) Battery took No. 2 gun with detachment and ammunition in two tongas from Dera Ismail Khan, afterwards making a night march of nineteen miles across country in draught. The G.O.C., Derajat Brigade, wrote that he was "very pleased with the celerity with which the gun reached its destination."

The 8th (Lahore) Mountain Battery was out with the movable column from Bannu in April, 1913, rounding up outlaws and relieving Spina Khaisora post. On one occasion "E" Sub-section moved in five tum-tums, mounted drivers leading seven gun mules. It covered twenty-nine and a half miles in six hours.

Tibet

Tibet, in the heart of Asia, surrounded by mountain ranges so high and vast as to be almost inaccessible, separates China from India and various states under British protection. China had always claimed suzerainty of a vague kind, and had almost a monopoly of what trade there was; but trading facilities with India had been in force for some years until, at the beginning of the century, the Russians began to take an interest in Tibetan affairs and were freely received by the rulers. Although the nearest Russian territory was more than 300 miles from Tibet, the Government of India in 1903 decided that the time had come to regularize matters. Accordingly, a diplomatic mission was prepared and the Chinese Amban and Tibetan officials agreed to meet the British Commissioners, one of whom was Colonel F. E. Younghusband, to discuss frontier matters.

The Tibetans had always excluded Europeans from their country, and distrusted and hated them: a policy no doubt laid down by the priesthood, which had entire control of the country.

The conference failed to achieve any result owing to the refusal of the Tibetans to receive any communications, and the Government of India ordered the Commissioners to resume negotiations at Gyantse in Tibet, and backed them with a military escort of 3,000 men under Major-General J. R. Macdonald, C.B. The matters at issue were breaches of treaty obligations, refusal to receive communications, seizure of British subjects, and the military preparations of Tibet.

The troops detailed were the 8th Gurkhas, two battalions of Sikh Pioneers, a company of Sappers and Miners, along with a section of No. 7 British Mountain Battery, R.G.A., under Captain F. A. Easton, and a section of 7-pr. guns of 200-lb. under Captain T. M. Luke, manned by Gurkhas. The British section were armed with 10-pr. B.L. guns with shrapnel only; the 7-pr. guns had double common shell, which was effective on the few occasions in which it was used.

This 7-pr. section was maintained by the 8th Gurkhas at Shillong, and was trained by a British Mountain Artillery sergeant in peace time. The guns were carried by porters.

The Chumbi valley along which the advance was first directed is about 9,000 feet above sea-level, but the theatre of operations lay at an average height of 14,000 feet, and 50 degrees of frost in winter was not unusual. Special warm clothing and snow goggles were issued to all ranks.

The whole countryside was barren and sterile; the roads were only tracks until improved after great exertions, and the chief difficulty of the expedition lay in the transport and supply organization, as every item, large and small, had to be brought from India. Even firewood had to be brought all the way because there was none in the country, and the supply of ammunition had to be restricted.

The way lay over the Jalap La, a difficult pass of 14,000 feet, forming a bottleneck which had to be kept open whatever the weather lest the troops starved. Chumbi was reached on 15th December, and a small column pushed on to Phari Jong in five marches, traversing a road with several narrow rocky gorges which were fortunately not contested. At Chumbi a halt of three months was made to get up supplies. Three companies of mounted infantry which were formed proved invaluable.

Yaks were tried as transport animals; they could find some sort of sustenance from moss under the snow, but were liable to fatal diseases. Ekkas were dismantled and brought up by coolies from railhead, but the mainstay of the transport was our old friend the mule. The commissariat mule played the game under all conditions of climate and overwork; in one case, after twelve hours up to his neck in a frozen lake, the victim was full of activity when pulled out. Their casualties by the end of the campaign were extraordinarily few.

The oil on the mechanism of the Maxim machine guns and rifles froze in the very low temperatures, and the Maxim jackets were filled with a mixture of water, rum, and kerosene to prevent freezing.

Gyantse was at the end of a barren tract 100 miles ahead, and the main body advanced from Chumbi on 24th March. The Tibetans offered some slight opposition on the way, and a more serious clash occurred at the Lamdang Gorge where the Gurkhas climbed the hills to turn the enemy's flanks, after which the advance continued, supported by the guns. The enemy had many casualties, and the mounted infantry carried on the pursuit.

The Commissioner settled in at Chunglu, close to Gyantse Jong, in a walled enclosure, with a small escort, whilst the main body returned to Chumbi in spite of very bad weather as it could not be maintained at the front.

The Mission was now in a precarious situation, but, thanks to the splendid leadership of Colonel Sir Francis Younghusband and his astute method of countering oriental diplomacy, the next three months were passed with the force in the same position.

The Tibetans attacked the Mission post while a column had gone out to attack a force on the Karo La, an action fought at 16,000 feet in a cutting wind. The attack on the post was beaten off, after which several small operations took place in order to improve the position.

Reinforcements were sent forward and the Tibetans informed that if their representatives did not arrive at Gyantse by 25th June, the force would proceed to Lhasa.

By this time the Tibetans had mustered some 16,000 men, mostly rifle and matchlock men, with about 800 breechloading rifles.

Swords and bows and arrows were also used. Some thirty jingals*
and other small cannon were in action at various times.

Reinforcement of the Royal Fusiliers and 40th Pathans arrived
in May from India, and at the same time Battery Headquarters and
two sections of No. 7 Mountain Battery, R.G.A., under Major
R. W. Fuller, and a section of 10th (Abbottabad) Mountain Battery†,
armed with 10-prs., with Lieutenants C. C. Marindin and H. G.
Boone, came up. Some common shell were sent up for the 10-prs.,
the shrapnel having proved ineffective against monasteries. The
common shell proved very effective and the guns played a great part
in an action at Niani where the enemy tried to hold up the force,
which nevertheless reached Gyantse the same day, 26th June.

The next move was to Lhasa, but first the Gyantse district had to
be cleared of the enemy, about 6,000 strong, who occupied a monastery and the Jong. On 28th June the Tsechen monastery on an
isolated hill to the north of Gyantse was attacked and carried by the
infantry with the support of the 10-pr. guns, and on 5th July the
attack on Gyantse Jong began. The place was strongly fortified,
but the Gurkhas and Royal Fusiliers stormed a breach made by the
10-prs. and captured the Jong. During the night the monastery was
evacuated and the advance on Lhasa began on 10th July.

The column consisted of 200 mounted infantry, 1,900 infantry
and sappers, the 10-prs. (eight guns in all), six Maxims, 2,000
followers, and 3,900 animals.

Some opposition was met at the Karo La Pass (16,600 feet), and
the troops had to fight at 18,000 feet, but the advance to the Sangpo
(Brahmaputra) continued over the Khomba La Pass (16,400 feet).
The river was 200 yards wide and the crossing took place without
opposition on ferry boats hauled along a wire. A section of 7th
(Bengal) Mountain Battery‡ had been sent to Chumbi to strengthen
the line of communications. The officers with it were Lieutenants
K. D. Field and W. M. Turner.

The Military Mission encamped before Lhasa on 3rd August, but
were now short of rations, which were not forthcoming, the crops not
yet being ripe. A demonstration outside a large monastery produced
the supplies on requisition and there was no shortage afterwards.

The Dalai Lama had departed before the Mission arrived, but a
treaty was signed by the Regent and the Chinese Amban, and the
object of the Mission achieved. The casualties of the campaign
amounted to 35 killed, all ranks, and 187 wounded. The force left

---

* Leather-barrelled cannon.
† At this period designated 30th Mountain Battery.
‡ At this time designated 27th Mountain Battery.

Lhasa on 23rd September, only just in time to reach India before the passes were blocked by snow, and after some very cold nights returned to their peace stations.

The G.O.C. reported in his despatches that "The Artillery co-operated with the Infantry in a manner which did credit to their training, and I attribute the comparatively small losses we sustained in several of the more important actions to the thorough artillery support afforded to the assaulting infantry."

Extreme cold, high altitudes, bad weather—every kind of physical hardship, in fact—were the keynote of this campaign, unique in its successful challenge to nature.

A medal, Tibet 1903-4, was awarded to those serving in this campaign at or beyond Siliguri, with a bar inscribed "Gyantse" for those qualified to receive it.

Mekran

Mekran, the coastal province of Baluchistan, had been in a state of turmoil for some time owing to the disaffection of the sirdars, who demanded the expulsion of the Khan of Khalat's Diwan. Open rebellion broke out in January, 1898; the Diwan was shut up in his fort, and a survey camp under a R.E. officer was attacked and looted. Prompt measures were taken and a double company of the 30th Baluchis was sent off at once from Karachi by sea, followed by troops to protect the telegraph offices on the coast. More infantry followed and a section of the 4th (Hazara) Mountain Battery (F.F.) under Lieutenant J. H. Paine was rushed to Karachi to join the force at Pasni, under the command of Lieutenant-Colonel Mayne, 30th Baluchis. A squadron of the 6th Bombay Cavalry (Jacob's Horse) and Sappers and Miners and administrative details arrived a few days later at Pasni, which was chosen as the base of operations, and a column set out on the 27th January, 1898, to relieve the Wazir, who was imprisoned by the rebels in a fort at Kalatak. The column was opposed near Turbat and found the enemy in position at the defile of Gokh-Prusht.

The guns and infantry opened fire from a hill on the left of the road and turning movements were made on both flanks. As the action developed, the guns advanced and opened oblique fire with very good effect, and, as the infantry advanced, fire was switched on to the entrance to the defile, causing the enemy great loss. The guns finished up in the infantry firing line using case shot at 300 yards.

The enemy fled in disorder; many sirdars were amongst the 250 killed. The section's casualties were one killed and one wounded, out of four killed and twelve wounded in the force.

Turbat fort and several others were demolished; the surviving rebels were fined and the loyal sirdars rewarded in the name of the Khan of Khalat. Lieutenant J. H. Paine was awarded the D.S.O., and as no medal was awarded for this expedition, although it counted as war service, the D.S.O. ribbon was the only one worn for several years by this officer. The guns returned to India via Quetta, where they formed part of an escort to the political agent, the Khan's troops being left to police the country.

Peace did not last long and the sirdars started fighting and raiding as usual. This time the Nazim appealed for help to the political agent, who went with a strong escort to the centre of the disturbances. This escort was commanded by Major Tighe, D.S.O., 27th Baluchis, and included a section of the 9th (Murree) Mountain Battery under Lieutenant E. G. Hart. In December, 1901, the section marched fifty-nine miles in twenty-six hours direct to the battlefield and went into action after a rest of an hour and a half. The object was the capture of Nodiz fort, which held some of the insurgents and was being invested by the Nazim.

The targets for the guns were:

(1) The loopholed tops of the west flank towers.
(2) The top of the main tower.

The change from 1 to 2 was to be signalled by the "Battery Call" on the trumpet.

The guns were 600 yards from the fort and under rifle fire all the time, the mules being sheltered in a nullah. The targets were engaged and the guns ceased fire on the "Charge" being sounded. The guns then advanced and blew in the top of the western redoubt, and the garrison surrendered.

The Khan's troops, having been proved unfit to keep order, were relieved by the Mekran Levy Corps commanded by the assistant political agent.

Persian Gulf

During this period gun-running in the Persian Gulf was assuming serious proportions, and a landing force was organized to raid the depots in which the rifles were collected and stored after being landed in small numbers. The Mekran coast was a favourite place for these depots, being practically desert, but approachable from the landward side to kafilas from Afghanistan, the destination of most of the weapons. The mountain gun was ideal for rapid embarkation or disembarkation in boats on an open beach, and 11th (Dehra Dun)* Mountain Battery was ordered in January, 1910, to

---

* At this time named 31st Mountain Battery.

send a section with a small force for land work, which included a section of Sappers and Miners and four companies, 123rd Outram's Rifles.

The total strength of the section was two British officers (Captain L. S. Bayley and Lieutenant H. E. Kenyon), 1 Indian officer, 41 gunners, 44 drivers, 8 followers, and 36 mules, and it embarked in the R.I.M.S. *Hardinge* on 21st January. On arrival at Khorlash, close to Jask, on the evening of the 25th, the section with other troops was ordered to land in order to capture an arms depot fifteen to twenty miles inland.

The *Hardinge* had to lie two miles off, and disembarkation was carried out in the dark without previous practice, using the only boats available, which were steel lifeboats.

The arms depot was found after a nineteen-mile march; the guns fired 18 rounds; several Afghans were killed and 760 M.H. rifles captured. These were destroyed and the force re-embarked next day from Jask.

Several landings were made but no more arms depots were found, and many days had perforce to be spent on board. Swimming mules ashore was not a success.

The section returned to Bombay in April, and after a wait at Kirkee rejoined the battery at Dehra Dun in July.

The Centre Section of the 12th (Poonch)* Mountain Battery under Major O. C. Williamson-Oswald, along with two infantry battalions, was sent to the Persian Gulf for similar operations in May, 1911. It returned to Dehra Dun after five weeks, having made no captures and had no casualties.

ADEN

There was trouble over the delimitation of the Aden–Turkish Frontier in 1903 owing to obstruction by the Turks. In March a small force was sent to clear up the situation: this included the 10th (Abbottabad) Mountain Battery† and two 7-pr. guns drawn by camels and manned by R.G.A. from Aden. Later No. 6 British Mountain Battery (six 10-pr. guns) under Major G. C. Dowell joined the column. No action occurred until a convoy was attacked in May. A small column under Major G. C. Dowell, R.G.A., was sent to destroy the towers of the village of Chali which harboured the attackers. This was the first occasion the 10-pr. gun was used on active service. No further hostilities occurred and 10th (Abbottabad) Mountain Battery returned to India in June.

---

* At this time named 32nd Mountain Battery.
† At this time named 30th Mountain Battery.

SOMALILAND

British Somaliland, on the African shore of the Gulf of Aden, is a waterless country with a little trade in gums and cattle. It had been a big game resort for troops stationed at Aden for some years before 1900.

In that year a restless young Somali named Hassan took to raiding, and after some successes collected a large force and attacked villages in both British and Abyssinian Somaliland. He acquired the nickname of the "Mad Mullah." After a couple of years these raids became such a nuisance that stern measures became necessary and the War Office took the affair in hand, sending Brigadier-General W. H. Manning to command the troops collected at Berbera and Obbia. The Centre Section, 28th Mountain Battery, disembarked in January, 1903, by permission of the Italian Government, on an open beach at Obbia, the animals swimming three-quarters of a mile to the shore. With the section were Lieutenants H. E. Henderson and J. F. Barrington. Five hundred rounds per gun were taken. Except for the officers' revolvers, the section had no personal weapons, this being in the interregnum between the withdrawal of swords and the issue of rifles.

The plan was for the Obbia forces to sweep north-eastwards and join up with the Berbera force, shifting the base from Obbia to Berbera by sea. The Abyssinian army was to co-operate from the west. The plan did not come off, as the necessary transport could not be obtained. Also the Abyssinians failed to co-operate. General Manning advanced from Obbia on 22nd February, 1903. He divided his force into two columns because of the scarcity of transport and water. On arrival at Galkayu, 160 miles from Obbia, news was received that a reconnaissance column under the command of Colonel A. W. V. Plunkett, K.A.R., had met the main body of the Somalis on 15th April at Gumburu. After a desperate fight it had been exterminated. Nine British officers and 250 O.R. of the 2nd Sikhs and K.A. Rifles were killed. After this reverse, General Manning collected his force at Bohotle.

In July, Major-General Sir C. C. Egerton, K.C.B., D.S.O., took over command with more troops and reorganized the force into a mounted brigade and two infantry brigades.

The section arrived at Upper Sheikh, some 6,000 feet up, in August and went on to Berbera to exchange the 2.5-inch equipment for 7-pr. guns, taking over 23 camels and 23 Somali drivers who were most unsatisfactory. Equipment for draught had to be improvised in the battery. As the feeding and watering of the mules presented great difficulties, the battery drivers and mules were sent back to India in October except for seven mules which were retained to take the guns into action in draught with a pair of ammunition boxes for each gun.

The Mad Mullah's force was still very elusive, but on 10th January, 1904, it was located at Jidballi. The main body, with which marched the section of the 28th (Lahore) Battery inside the square, attacked from the west side while the mounted brigade worked round the enemy's flank. The Somalis also attacked, but after two desperate charges broke and fled. The section came into action outside the square and fired 60 rounds, but owing to the thick bush and limited view there was little scope for artillery. The section had one gunner killed and two drivers wounded.

The Mullah went off into Italian territory and in May, 1904, the campaign concluded with a formal surrender.

The section rejoined at Dera Ismail Khan on 3rd June, 1904. Strength: one British and one Native Officer, 39 other ranks, 5 mules, 4 ponies (one with foal).

The Africa General Service Medal was awarded to the troops taking part in the above operations, with bars inscribed "Somaliland, 1902-04" and "Jidballi".

JUBALAND

In 1900 the Ogaden tribes on the Somaliland frontier revolted and murdered Mr. Jenner, the Sub-Commissioner. As they refused a pacific settlement, a punitive expedition assembled at Kismayu in January, 1901, by permission of the Italian Government. It consisted of about 1,500 East African Rifles, Somali Police, etc., to which was added a section of 9th (Murree) Mountain Battery* under Lieutenant K. G. Campbell from Abbottabad. After a few brushes with the tribesmen, the force was concentrated at Afmadu on 10th February, notwithstanding a great shortage of water and the difficulty of movement in the jungle. A flying column, to which one gun was attached, moved to Samasa, about fifty-seven miles northwest of Afmadu, where a surprise attack was launched on the column while it was engaged in making a zeriba in the bush. This was beaten off with casualties to the enemy, and the force moved back to Afmadu on the Juba river, fighting off several small-scale attacks on the way. After the rains set in in April, several mules died from the bite of the tsetse fly and the section moved back to Kismayu. The Sultan surrendered and the expedition was broken up, the section embarking for India on 12th June.

---

* At this date designated 29th Mountain Battery.

The section received the sincere thanks of the O.C. Field Force for its good work.

The Africa General Service medal was awarded to troops taking part in this expedition, with a bar inscribed "Jubaland".

The day was about to arrive when mountain batteries would be tested in war by standards far more severe than had ever been imagined, and would acquit themselves as well as the best.

The distribution of the Indian Mountain Artillery in August, 1914, was as follows:

	Mountain Battery, Designation 1914	Batteries, Final Designations
1st Indian Mountain Artillery Brigade: Lieut.-Col. H. D. Grier. Abbottabad.	27th 30th	7th (Bengal) 10th (Abbottabad)
5th Indian Mountain Artillery Brigade: Lieut.-Col. O. C. Williamson-Oswald. Abbottabad.	23rd (Peshawar) (F.F.) 28th	3rd (Peshawar) (F.F.) 8th (Lahore)
7th Indian Mountain Artillery Brigade: Lieut.-Col. J. L. Parker. Dehra Dun.	21st (Kohat) (F.F.) 26th Jacob's	1st Royal (Kohat) (F.F.) 6th (Jacob's)
Mountain Artillery, Burma: Lieut.-Col. H. de T. Phillips. Maymyo.	22nd (Derajat) (F.F.)	2nd (Derajat) (F.F.)

Unbrigaded:

Hong Kong	24th (Hazara) (F.F.)	4th (Hazara) (F.F.)
Nowshera	25th	5th (Bombay)
Bannu	29th	9th (Murree)
Kohat	31st	11th (Dehra Dun)
Dera Ismail Khan	32nd	12th (Poonch)

Note: All the above were six-gun 10-pr. batteries.

10-pr. B.L. Gun Line

Face page 124

A "Khud" Parade

CHAPTER VI

First World War, 1914-18

A. FORMATION OF NEW UNITS

AMONGST the enormous increases to the Indian Army, seventeen new Indian mountain batteries were raised in the latter part of the war. Ten of them were reduced or amalgamated within a few years after the conclusion of operations.

	Date Raised	Final Designation or Disposal
33RD (RESERVE), raised by Major J. A. H. B. Somerville at Abbottabad from personnel of Indian Mountain Artillery Depot.	5th March, 1917	13th (Dardoni)
34TH (RESERVE), raised by Major E. R. C. Wilson, M.C., at Abbottabad from 3rd (Peshawar), 5th (Bombay), 8th (Lahore), and 9th (Murree) Mountain Batteries. (Authority: Government of India Army Department, No. 11235 of 29/7/17).	8th July, 1917	14th (Rajputana)
35TH (RESERVE), raised by Major R. M. L. Dutton, M.C., at Abbottabad from drafts from various batteries.	23rd July, 1917	15th (Jhelum)
36TH (RESERVE), raised by Captain C. R. Willis, M.C., at Bandar Abbas from one section of 3rd (Peshawar) and two of 33rd (Reserve) (Authority: Government of India Army Department, No. 65469 of 18/5/18).	30th March, 1918	16th (Zhob)
37TH (RESERVE), raised by Major G. V. Dreyer at Sohan Camp (Authority; 01571 A. G. in India, 14/5/18).	13th May, 1918	117th (Rawalpindi), 1921. Reduced April, 1923
38TH (RESERVE), raised by Major J. H. Hayes-Sadler at Sohan Camp from 3rd (Peshawar), 8th (Lahore), Mountain Batteries and Indian Artillery Depot. Half Jat Sikhs, half Punjabi Mohammedans (Authority: 01571 A.G. in India, 14/5/18).	1st June, 1918	18th (Sohan)
39TH (RESERVE), raised by Major W. D. Lindsay at Maymyo from the Ahir and Punjabi Mohammedan section of 32nd Mountain Battery as 2/32nd Mountain Battery; became 39th (Reserve) 3rd June, 1918.	19th April, 1918	19th (Maymyo)

	Date Raised	Final Designation or Disposal
40TH (RESERVE), raised from personnel of 3rd (Peshawar) Mountain Battery and Indian Mountain. Artillery Depot at Dehra Dun by Brevet Lieutenant-Colonel A. C. R. Greene.	August, 1918 (Served in Iraq)	Reduced April, 1922
41ST (RESERVE), raised by Brevet Lieutenant-Colonel A. J. T. Farfan, D.S.O., at Abbottabad, and in October, 1921, amalgamated with 44th (Reserve) to form 41st Pack Battery.	1918 (Saw service in Palestine Served in Burma)	Reduced as 41st Pack Battery in January, 1922
42ND (RESERVE), raised at Kohat by Lieutenant R. E. M. Brady from details of 8th (Lahore) and 10th (Abbottabad) Mountain Batteries. Designated 120th (Ambala) Pack Battery, July, 1920. Amalgamated with 121st (Nowshera) Battery and renumbered 117th (Nowshera), Pack Battery, April, 1925.	April, 1919 (Saw service in Iraq)	17th (Nowshera)
43RD (RESERVE), raised at Dehra Dun by Major G. N. Buckland, D.S.O. Renamed 121st (Nowshera), July, 1922; 117th (Nowshera), 1925; amalgamated with 120th (Ambala) as above.	May, 1919	
44TH (RESERVE), raised at Rawalpindi by Captain K. G. Campbell. Amalgamated with 41st (Reserve) to form 41st Pack Battery, October, 1921.	1918	
45TH (RESERVE), raised at Ambala by Captain R. A. Armstrong.	1919 Saw service in Mesopotamia	Reduced October, 1921
46TH (RESERVE), raised at Abbottabad by Major H. S. K. Snowdon from one section each of 1st (Kohat) and 3rd (Peshawar) Batteries.	May, 1920	Reduced August, 1921
47TH (RESERVE), raised at Rawalpindi.	June, 1920	Reduced June, 1921
49TH (RESERVE), formed at Basra by Major H. H. Mackenzie on reduction of No. 14 British Mountain Battery, Euphrates L. of C.	1st February, 1919	Reduced at Roorkee, October, 1921
50TH (RESERVE), raised at Basra 1917 as B. Battery L. of C. by Major G. A. Hassells-Yates and reformed at Kut by Major E. C. Harrington on reduction of No. 15 British Mountain Battery, Tigris L. of C.	1st February, 1919	Reduced at Ambala, May, 1921

Notes 1. There is no trace of the formation of 48th (Reserve) Mountain Battery.
2. The composition of all these batteries was half Punjabi Mohammedans and half Sikhs, except where otherwise stated.
3. The expression (Reserve) was dropped from mountain battery designations by I.A.O. 319 of 1920.
4. By I.A.O. 592 of 1920 the word "Pack" was substituted for "Mountain" in battery designations.
5. In November, 1921, 80 was added to the number of all batteries up to 41 inclusive. (I.A.O. 1279 of 1921).

B. GALLIPOLI

By August, 1914, when mobilization was ordered, all batteries were trained to a high pitch of efficiency in so far as their equipment permitted, and all were eager for the coming test of a world war against the Germans and their allies. It turned out that mobilization equipment was not available as rapidly as was expected according to mobilization schemes.

Some Indian units complained that mobilization notices were held up by post-masters, and cases were reported of a fee being collected for delivery. There was no lack of enthusiasm amongst the men, and many who were on furlough paid their fares in order to get back to their units without delay.

The 7th I.M.A. Brigade under Lieutenant-Colonel J. L. Parker, comprising 1st (Kohat) Mountain Battery (F.F.) and 6th (Jacob's) Mountain Battery* was the first to move to an embarkation port, sailing on 17th September from Karachi after a few days' delay there. The Brigade was landed at Suez and spent the next six months in the Canal line defences at Kantara and Ismailia. During this period shields for the 10-pr. guns were made up in the workshops of the Suez Canal Company, and proved a very satisfactory addition to the equipment.

Early in November the Turks declared war, and the question of the attitude of the Punjabi Mohammedans arose. At a brigade durbar the latter expressed their willingness to fight the Turks or anyone else, and they kept their word loyally. Later, when the Brigade moved to Gallipoli, these men were the only Mussulman fighting men on the Peninsula on the Allies' side. Only one gunner, acting as assistant moulvi, reported sick and was sent away.

Various alarms and excursions took place on the Canal line and batteries were in action several times, helping to repel one major and several minor Turkish attacks, supporting whatever division was holding the Canal at the time.

---

* At this time these batteries were designated: 21st Kohat Mountain Battery (F.F.), 26th Jacob's Mountain Battery.

In the early months of 1915 it was realized that the Western Front was at a deadlock: the Russians were not doing well in the Caucasus, and the Germans were strengthening the situation of Turkey in the Near East with a view to German predominance, the ultimate object being an outlet for Germany in the Persian Gulf. Russia was calling for a diversion which would draw the Turks from the Caucasus, and the capture of Constantinople by us would effect this.

An unsupported naval attack on the Dardanelles passage on 18th March failed, and it was decided, after delay, to send an expeditionary force under General Sir Ian Hamilton with the primary object of assisting the fleet to force the Dardanelles. Landings were to be made on the Gallipoli peninsula on the European side of the Straits with a view to an advance on Constantinople once the Turkish defending army had been defeated and the fleet had got through.

The 7th I.M.A. Brigade embarked at Alexandria on 4th April, 1915, and joined the Australian and New Zealand Army Corps under Lieutenant-General Sir W. Birdwood,* K.C.S.I., at Mudros, the rendezvous forty miles from the peninsula. The Brigade was a complete formation with ammunition column, field ambulance section under Captain T. J. Carey Evans, I.M.S., ordnance field park, supply section and post office.

During the wait at Mudros, disembarkation was practised and a strong *entente* grew up between the Indian ranks and the Anzacs, blossoming into a mutual admiration society which endured for the campaign—and after.

Several changes of officers had taken place since mobilization, but the battery commanders remained unchanged, Major A. C. Fergusson commanding 1st (Kohat) and Major J. E. L. Bruce 6th (Jacob's) Battery.

The Australian and New Zealand Army Corps was allotted the landing at Ari Burnu—or Anzac Beach as it will be called for ever in honour of the finest fighters who ever fought for the British Empire. It was to be landed on an unknown shore without reconnaissance and with a minimum of information about the terrain and the enemy's defences, to cut off the retreat of the Turks opposing the troops to be landed at Cape Helles, the southern end of the peninsula.

The most prominent feature was a massif about three miles north-east of the beach. Possession of this high ground would bring into view the Narrows, about five miles away, and command most of the movement in the peninsula. The highest point was

---

* Afterwards Field-Marshal The Lord Birdwood, G.C.B., G.C.S.I., G.C.M.G., G.C.V.O., C.I.E., D.S.O.

Hill 971; the ridge Chunuk Bair ran south from it, and the whole hill-mass was called by us Sari Bair.

The Mountain Artillery Brigade, with fifty-six mules only from each battery, was ordered to land close on the heels of the covering force and to come under its orders. The C.O., adjutant, and one subaltern of each battery landed with the leading infantry at 3.15 a.m., 25th April. In the event, the covering force was put ashore in the wrong place, away from the allotted beach, the troops were mixed up and confusion reigned. Hence the leading battery, 6th (Jacob's), was rushed into a position to cover some infantry and, though it gave them much encouragement by its presence, attracted a great deal of fire to itself. It suffered seventeen casualties and was withdrawn about 2.30 p.m. Lieutenant P. C. Chapman was mortally wounded and another section commander, Jemadar Dulla Khan, seriously wounded. Captain H. A. Kirby was also wounded, but escaped from the hospital ship and returned to the beach.

After withdrawal, the battery moved over to the left and was split up—the Left Section in sandbagged emplacements about 200 yards behind our front trenches, and the other section on a small plateau some distance to the right. The third section was temporarily out of the line. The section on the right was commanded for some time by a fine old Sikh officer, Subadar Jowala Singh, who was twice wounded. The first time he said nothing about it, having his wound dressed daily by the Indian Assistant Surgeon. Later, he was hit in the foot by a machine-gun bullet and was taken to the field ambulance, where he had to divulge that he had been wounded before. This section was later taken over by Lieutenant F. N. C. Rossiter, who brought reinforcements.

The guns of the left section (Captain H. A. Kirby) were in a very exposed position. It was an almost daily occurrence for the emplacements to be knocked down by enemy gun fire and built up again at night, the only damage to equipment being to wheels which were easily replaced.

The terrain was covered with scrub and cut up by deep ravines; maintaining direction and keeping communication were matters of extreme difficulty, and reinforcements of men and guns were not immediately available. The covering force was held up by Turkish fire which increased hourly, and the line the force had been detailed to make good was never reached during the campaign.

The 1st (Kohat) Battery landed about 6.30 p.m. on a beach covered with wounded and under constant fire. The situation was saved by H.M.S. *Bacchante* standing close in and smothering a Turkish battery at Gaba Tepe which was enfilading the beach at

600 yards range. After the Kohat Battery got clear without casualty the Centre Section was detached; during the next day the battery carried on the close support of the infantry on its own initiative, also neutralizing guns on Battleship Hill. It fired 648 rounds. On this day, the 6th (Jacob's) Battery had four guns in action and the divisional field artillery were not firing.

Despite attempts to advance on our part and counter-attacks by the Turks during the next few weeks, the line was advanced only about 200 yards at the cost of very heavy casualties. The reckless daring and enthusiasm of the Anzacs made up for lack of training and they quickly acquired war experience.

The guns were distributed in sections or singly, causing heavy work for the officers, of whom many were wounded or sick. A state of trench warfare set in with fierce attacks and counter-attacks kept up with great vigour. The farthest point inland reached by our trenches was less than a mile from the sea, and the perimeter through this point was about two miles long from beach to beach. The Turkish battery at Gaba Tepe, known as "Beachy Bill," which later enfiladed our front line as well as the beach was never finally silenced, and its neutralization occupied one of Captain Rawson's guns more or less permanently. One day a shell off the line burst over one of our mule dug-outs, killing twenty mules and wounding twenty; it also killed the salutri and wounded eight drivers.

Many acts of gallantry were performed. For instance; on 19th May, while Captain Rawson's section of the Kohat Battery was being heavily shelled, Lance-Naik Karm Singh was detailed to pass fire orders from the O.P. It was noticed that he was covering his eyes with his hand, though at no time was there any delay or interruption in the transmission of orders. Later, during a lull, it was found that a bullet had passed behind both eyes and he was quite blind. Karm Singh stuck to his duty until forcibly removed. For his bravery, he was awarded the Indian Order of Merit.

The same award was made to Naik Jan Mahommed in Captain Thom's section for maintaining fire as ordered at enemy embrasures after his emplacement had been blown in by a high-explosive shell which knocked out Captain Thom. He fired seventeen rounds and knocked out two guns. Driver Naryan Singh of the same battery was awarded the I.D.S.M. for many instances of bravery while mending telephone lines under fire.

The batteries were under rifle, machine-gun and artillery fire by day and often by night during the whole period the Brigade was in the peninsula; fortunately the Turks had to be as careful of their ammunition expenditure as we had. Gun positions were very difficult to find, and eventually a section of 1st (Kohat) Battery on the right (firing south, east, or north) was the only support the mountain guns could give to the 1st Australian Division; the other ten guns covered the front of the New Zealand and Australian Division, in addition to the divisional artillery. Captain Rawson's section was detached on the right, Captain Thom and Captain Trenchard being with the remainder of the battery. As time went on and officers became casualties, Major R. Hoskyn was borrowed from 6th (Jacob's), and several junior officers joined as reinforcements. Subadar Mit Singh proved a capable section commander. The adjutant often acted as relief section commander; and at No. 2 Post, where Captain Trenchard's anti-machine-gun activities took place, almost anybody carried on when a fresh machine-gun was spotted. This gun claims to have knocked out fourteen machine-guns, firing through a tunnel with direct laying.

The drivers behaved splendidly throughout and never failed to bring up ammunition from the beach where it was stored.

The shrapnel broke up badly, the resin being too hard, and recourse was had to boiling the shell before use, which produced the desired effect. The 10-pr. was ill-adapted for the work required, the configuration of the ground and short ranges demanding the use of a howitzer, and so the cartridge was cut in two to make half-charges, which were used on many occasions until it was found that the star shell cartridge could be used instead. Improvised range tables were used.

The Anzac Corps, of course, had its own artillery, but the mountain batteries continued support without relief. Major J. E. L. Bruce, commanding 6th (Jacob's) Battery, was killed on 29th May, and Major K. G. Campbell took over his battery. The shortage of officers continued. Provision of water was an ever-present problem and it was found necessary to resort to very strict rationing. On this account the majority of the mules were sent back to Mudros.

In August the Commander-in-Chief ordered an attack from the Anzac front eastward with the object of capturing Sari Bair. An enveloping movement was staged from the north-west, involving a surprise landing at Suvla Bay. Major-General Godley, with the New Zealand and Australian Division, 13th Division, and attached troops, ordered the attack on the Sari Bair ridge to be made in two columns. The Right Column, which included 6th (Jacob's) Battery less one section, had Chunuk Bair as objective; the Left Column, with 1st (Kohat) Battery less one section, was to capture Hill 971 and Hill Q. No animals other than artillery mules were to accompany the assaulting columns.

During the advance on the night of the 6/7th August, part of the Left Column lost its way and fell behind time. The artillery support of the Right Column ceased too early and, notwithstanding the utmost bravery on the part of the assaulting troops, the operation was a failure. After several months of continual hardship, the tasks set the troops were beyond their physical capacity. By the next day the Turks were ready in strength to repel attacks.

The flank landing by IX Corps in Suvla Bay was not pressed sufficiently owing to the confusion of units, excessive heat, and lack of water—and judgment; the whole offensive was thus brought to a halt. In the unsuccessful attack after this landing, the 6th (Jacob's) Battery moved up in close support of the infantry and finally came into action on a spur below Chunuk Bair. Its task was now to knock out machine-gun posts, etc.; for this purpose a single gun was brought into action by night on the parapet of a trench and the target engaged as soon as it could be seen over the sights. This was carried out many times at short range and was much appreciated by the infantry.

After the repulse of Turkish counter-attacks, the front was stabilized while the British and French governments made up their minds what course to pursue. The troops proceeded to make themselves as comfortable as possible before the cold weather came on. In September, Lieutenant-Colonel J. L. Parker was appointed B.G.R.A. of a division at Suvla, Major A. C. Fergusson replacing him. Major R. Hoskyn took over 1st (Kohat) Battery.

Brigade Headquarters organized a hot bath for every man once a week and provided clean clothes every three weeks. Improvised drying rooms saved much sickness and the health of the batteries remained good. A spell of particularly severe weather arrived at the beginning of December.

Evacuation was decided on. It was carried out by a masterpiece of organization, without casualties and without the Turks suspecting on 18th and 19th December. The 6th (Jacob's) Battery prides itself on being the last artillery unit to leave Anzac, and both batteries are proud to have fought alongside such grand troops as the Anzac Corps.

CASUALTIES

Killed: Major J. E. L. Bruce, commanding 6th (Jacob's) Battery.
Died of wounds: Lieutenant P. C. Chapman, 6th (Jacob's) Battery.
Wounded: Captain J. H. Thom } 1st (Kohat)
Captain C. D. Rawson } Mountain
Captain G. B. B. Trenchard } Battery (F.F.)

Wounded: Captain H. A. Kirby } 6th (Jacob's)
Captain E. C. Harrington } Mountain Battery

Total casualties: 1st (Kohat) Mountain Battery—killed 11, wounded 134.
6th (Jacob's) Mountain Battery—killed 12, wounded 144.

Mule casualties: 1st (Kohat) Mountain Battery—killed 35, wounded 119.
6th (Jacob's) Mountain Battery—killed 27, wounded 93.

AMMUNITION EXPENDED

1st (Kohat) Mountain Battery: 12,248 rounds.
6th (Jacob's) Mountain Battery; 9,135 rounds.

HONOURS AND AWARDS

7th Indian Mountain Brigade Headquarters

Lieutenant-Colonel J. L. Parker	C.M.G., mention in despatches.
Captain H. E. Kenyon	Mention in despatches.
Captain T. J. Carey-Evans, I.M.S.	M.C., twice mentioned.

1st (Kohat) Mountain Battery (F.F.)

Major A. C. Fergusson	Brevet Lieutenant-Colonel, three times mentioned.
Major K. G. Campbell	D.S.O., twice mentioned.
Major R. Hoskyn	Mention.
Captain J. H. Thom	D.S.O., mention.
Captain C. D. Rawson	D.S.O., twice mentioned.
Captain G. B. B. Trenchard	Mention.
Subadar Mit Singh	Order of British India (2nd class), twice mentioned.
Subadar Chanda	Indian Order of Merit, twice mentioned.
Three other awards of *	Indian Order of Merit.
Five awards of	Indian Distinguished Service Medal.
Driver Naik Ali Ahmed	Twice mentioned in despatches.
Eight Indian other ranks	Mentioned in despatches.
S. A. S. Daulat Singh	I.S.M.D., Indian Order of Merit and mention.

* Includes Pay-Havildar Mahomed Baksh, for bravery and resource when a transport was sunk by a submarine.

6th (*Jacob's*) *Mountain Battery*

Major J. E. L. Bruce ...	Mention in despatches. Killed in action.
Captain E. Le G. Whitting ...	M.C., twice mentioned.
Captain H. A. Kirby ...	M.C. and mention.
Lieutenant F. C. Rossiter	M.C. and mention.
Subadar Jowala Singh	Indian Order of Merit and twice mentioned.
Subadar Hem Singh ...	I.D.S.M. and mention.
Jemadar Mahomed Baksh ...	Indian Order of Merit and mention
Havildar Gurditt Singh	Indian Order of Merit and mention
Driver Havildar Inder Singh ...	Indian Order of Merit and mention
Gunner Fazl Ilahi ...	Indian Order of Merit and mention
Shoeing-Smith Sahib Singh ...	Mention in despatches.
Seven Indian other ranks	Mention in despatches ⎫
Two other awards of ...	Indian Order of Merit ⎬ Indian Other Ranks
Three other awards of ...	I.D.S.M. ⎭

Officer Reinforcements

The following joined during the operations:

Captain H. C. J. Salvin	Lieutenant R. A. Armstrong
Lieutenant L. B. Tyler	Lieutenant Draper
Lieutenant Armitage	Lieutenant O'Leary.

General Birdwood frequently visited the batteries and was beloved and admired by all ranks. His farewell message reads:

To O.C., 7th Indian Mountain Brigade

27th January, 1916.

" ... I want, however, to thank you, both your batteries, and all your officers and men for the really magnificent work they have done for us during the months when, I am glad to say, we were all together at Anzac. I think you will all have realized what a very high regard the Australian troops have for your two batteries, and I am so delighted that this is the case, for they have thoroughly deserved their high reputation ...

(*Sd.*) W. B. BIRDWOOD."

The Gallipoli episode may have been a military failure, but the Indian Mountain Artillery took advantage of this their first campaign against well-trained, well-led, and well-armed forces to prove that their courage and loyalty were as good as the best. During these

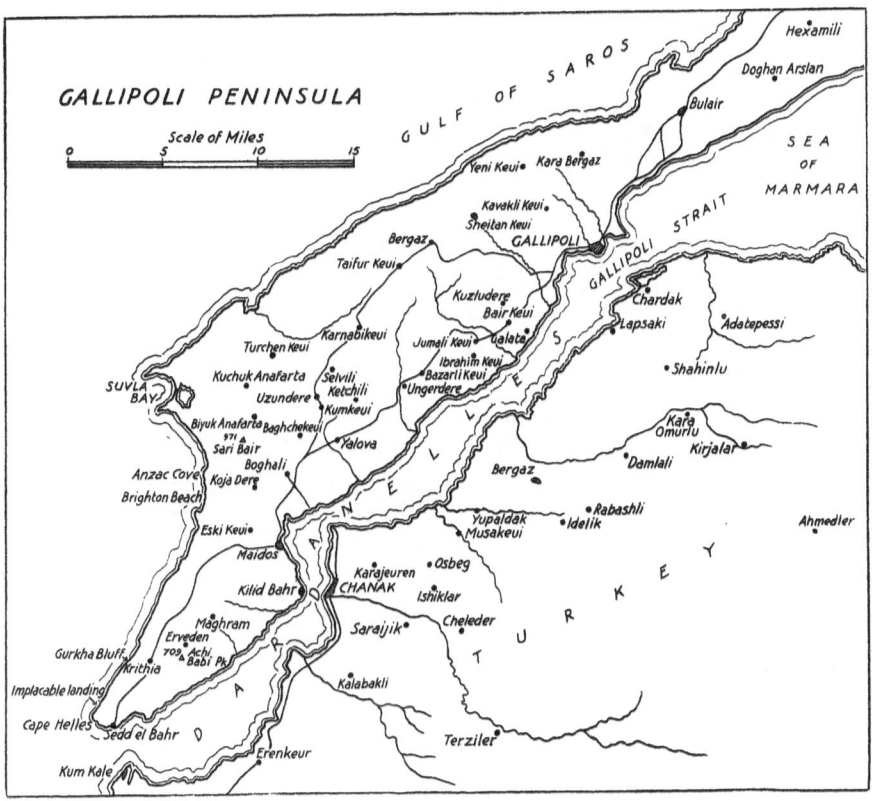

months in action without rest, they surpassed the high standard fixed by Mountain Artillery from its inception.

Gallipoli Day, 25th April, is celebrated annually, and greetings are exchanged between the batteries and the Australian and New Zealand forces.

The 1st (Kohat) Mountain Battery (F.F.) and 6th (Jacob's) Mountain Battery were granted permission to bear on their colours and appointments the words:

The Great War.—"ANZAC", "LANDING AT ANZAC", "DEFENCE OF ANZAC", "SUVLA", "SARI BAIR", "GALLIPOLI, 1915", "SUEZ CANAL", "EGYPT, 1915-1916".

C. EAST AFRICA

German East Africa was a country as large as British East Africa and Uganda combined, and held about an equal native African population. It was bounded on the east by the Indian Ocean, on the south by Portuguese East Africa and Nyasaland, on the west by Lake Tanganyika and the Belgian Congo, and on the north by the two British Protectorates mentioned above.

Dar-es-Salaam and Tanga were potential hostile naval bases, and it was essential to prevent the Germans from basing commerce raiders on these ports and to maintain our prestige among the Africans by preventing an invasion of our territories, which were practically defenceless.

Indian Expeditionary Force "C," of three battalions of infantry, was promptly sent from India in August, 1914, and with it sailed the 7th (Bengal) Mountain Battery,* commanded by Major O. K. Tancock, armed with six 10-pr. guns. With him were Captains F. W. Richey, L. M. Davies, A. J. T. Farfan and Lieutenant D. D. Haskard. These troops were sent to reinforce the defence troops in British East Africa, which consisted of two and a half battalions of King's African Rifles widely scattered. Immediately afterwards India was asked to supply a second Expeditionary Force "B" to capture and hold Dar-es-Salaam.

The theatre of war takes in most of the great plateau of Central Africa east of Lake Tanganyika, stretching over 800 miles south of the Equator. Between the sea and this plateau, which has an average height of 3,000 feet, runs a low-lying coastal belt, narrow at Mombasa but widening to the south where it stretches far inland. This is an area of great heat and humidity, with an unhealthy malarial climate,

---

* Designation at this time 27th Mountain Battery. It was incorrectly described by the Official Historian as belonging to the Royal Artillery.

wherein the white man finds it impossible to keep fit. Farther inland on higher ground the nights are cool and the climate moderate in temperature, but alternating between heavy rains and seasons of drought. Mosquitoes, ticks, "jiggers," etc., make life anything but pleasant for human beings, while tsetse and germs producing "horse-sickness" are deadly for animals.

Along the former Anglo-German border are the temperate highlands from which rise the snow-capped mountain Kilimanjaro (19,710 feet); several lesser ranges border the plateau, notably the Pare and Usambara mountains running from Kilimanjaro southeast to the coast.

The wide variation of climate and the insect pests affected detrimentally all troops as well as the native carriers on whom nearly all movement away from the railways depended, the tsetse fly making the use of horses and mules impossible in the lower country.

Cultivation existed only in the neighbourhood of towns and villages: the "bush" varied from open parkland to dense forests and waterless deserts. In the southern areas were vast swamps, flooded in the rainy season, and steep ranges only passable by narrow valleys; in fact it would be difficult to find a terrain less suitable for military operations.

It was indeed a war of human endurance.

The roads were for the most part mere tracks, and apart from them the only communication was the Uganda Railway, running across British East Africa north-west from the sea at Mombasa to Kisumu on Lake Victoria (587 miles) more or less parallel to the Anglo-German frontier, and in places only 100 miles or so from it.

The Germans had a railway from the seaport of Tanga to Moshi in the Kilimanjaro district (218 miles), and their Central Railway ran from Dar-es-Salaam 787 miles in a westerly direction to Kigoma on Lake Tanganyika via Morogoro and Tabora.

The German forces consisted at first of about 260 Germans and 2,500 Askaris, formed into fourteen independent companies. Each company had a ration strength of about 400, including carriers. The carrier organization was thorough and efficient, and the Askaris had been well trained in bush warfare. The German commander was Colonel von Lettow-Vorbeck, a brilliant trainer of troops and a great leader in war, with a reputation as an expert in machine-gun warfare. Neither side had made any preparations for war, and the British East African authorities had not collected any information which might have been of military importance or made good maps. The most useful map of the Kilimanjaro area was a German one. The first few weeks were taken up with minor frontier brushes, and the main body of the German forces was concentrated in the vicinity of Mount Kilimanjaro, the slopes of which were high-lying and healthy.

Expeditionary Force "B," under Major-General A. E. Aitken, arrived off Mombasa on 30th October. The infantry, excepting the one British battalion, 2nd Battalion Loyal North Lancashire Regiment, were a mixed lot who had done no training together, and had many changes of officers at the last moment. The best Indian troops had been sent to France, and those in Force "B" were not only of a lower grade but their efficiency was much reduced by a fortnight's uncomfortable sea voyage.

The only artillery in the force was the 8th (Lahore) Mountain Battery,* armed with six 10-pr. guns, commanded by Major C. E. Forestier-Walker. The other officers were Captain A. M. Colville, Lieutenants R. P. Landon, E. R. C. Wilson and R. M. L. Dutton. In addition were three Indian officers and 277 other ranks, 31 followers and 164 mules. This unit was in the transport *Bharata*.

The expedition was under the joint control of the Colonial and Indian offices, and was dispatched without consultation with the General Staff at the War Office. The G.O.C.'s instructions were: "To secure the safety of British East Africa by occupying the country between Tanga and Kilimanjaro." To attain this end it was suggested that he should first occupy Tanga.

There was no accurate information as to the enemy occupation of Tanga, and local reproductions of rough sketches were the only maps available. Mine-sweeping was carried out in the harbour, delaying the disembarkation from 7 a.m. until dark; being thus forewarned, Lettow-Vorbeck entrained his troops at Moshi at 10 a.m. and rushed them to Tanga.

The landing was made by two Indian battalions under Brigadier-General M. J. Tighe, C.B., on the far side of a bush-covered peninsula four miles south of Tanga, during the night of 2/3rd November against a minimum of opposition, but the advance into Tanga in the early morning was stopped by machine-gun fire. The only artillery support available was provided by the 6-inch and 4.7-inch guns of H.M.S. *Fox* and the 10-pr. guns of the mountain battery, the latter having been ordered to remain on board and to fire off the deck, for which purpose the ship closed the shore at about 1,000 yards. There was a visual signal station on the shore, but communication from it to the forward troops was erratic. The battery commander

---

* At this time designated 28th Mountain Battery. It was incorrectly described by the Official Historian as belonging to the Royal Artillery.

tried to observe from the masthead without success owing to the dense vegetation.

The rest of the infantry were landed for the capture of the town, the advance beginning at 12 noon, and covered "as far as possible" by the guns of H.M.S. *Fox* and the mountain battery. The Germans by this time were present in strength and held up our advance, which suffered heavy casualties. The German Askaris had been thoroughly trained in bush fighting, and our tired-out infantry fighting in unfamiliar surroundings had no chance of success.

The battery fired about 150 rounds, mostly unaimed, directed towards the sound of the firing in the town. On the ship's iron decks the guns, though partially anchored by coal bags, recoiled unsteadily, and little but the water-front could be seen even from the mast-head. As time went on the *Bharata* swung with the tide and the guns ceased to bear on the target. The battery commander's request to send an officer ashore was negatived, and the only information available was that brought in by a boat's crew.

Some of the infantry fought magnificently, but by dark the covering party were badly shaken and the remainder had suffered many casualties. The G.O.C. decided to withdraw, and this was done in daylight, finishing at 3 p.m. with little molestation from the Germans. The expedition then returned to Mombasa, and the battery at once entrained for Nairobi, detaching the centre section to Uganda.

The 7th (Bengal) Mountain Battery on arrival in the country in September, thanks to the initiative of Captain Farfan, was provided with gun shields, made in Nairobi, one for the gun carriage and one on each side of it, and one to fit the lid of an ammunition box. These were very effective, saving many casualties, and the shields were copied by the 8th (Lahore) Mountain Battery on arrival from Tanga. A few months later the original shields were replaced by a lighter pattern, made also in Nairobi, of special steel.

The protection of the frontier which covered the vital Uganda railway was the most pressing need, and what troops were available were distributed along it at important posts. The 7th (Bengal) Battery, less one section, formed part of a mixed force detailed to make a "reconnaissance in force" of the enemy's position at Longido, in order to divert his attention during the Tanga operation. This attack failed and the force withdrew with some casualties, including one officer and two other ranks of the battery wounded.

The general situation in East Africa was now not encouraging, and the best that could be done was to keep the Germans out of our territory. Their prestige had been enormously increased by their success at Tanga, and ours had correspondingly deteriorated.

Actually a situation of stalemate existed for the next twelve months as no reinforcements were available for this theatre, and the German Commanders seized every opportunity during this period to enrol and train more Askaris. The Germans made much better use of their white settlers than we did of ours; for they trained theirs as junior officers, as N.C.Os., or as machine gunners, the less important work being done by Askaris; while we collected our settlers into white units (E.A.M.R., Belfield's Scouts, etc.), making highly intelligent white men merely act in the ranks. So the German forces expanded as our local ones did not; and in most actions we lost white men when the Germans only lost Askaris.

The frontier was divided into two zones, and a complete reorganization was undertaken during which frequent minor operations took place. Administrative arrangements required much hard work to make them efficient; transport was non-existent, and thousands of porters had to be enrolled. Indian troops and King's African Rifles were differently equipped, rationed and maintained. The Indian mountain batteries had to deal with paymasters in Great Britain, India, East Africa and, later, South Africa.

The 7th (Bengal) Mountain Battery was divided between the Magadi and Voi-Tsavo areas and spent the next few months countering enemy raids on the railway. Lieutenant-Colonel Tancock acted as C.R.A. from March, 1915 until January, 1916, when Brigadier-General J. H. V. Crowe arrived.

In July, 1915, a section went out from Maktau with a column to attack Mbuyuni, whence systematic raiding parties hindered the extension of our railway by derailing trains between Voi and Maktau. This expedition was unsuccessful, and the enemy raiders became even more aggressive.

The sections of 8th (Lahore) Battery spent the first three months of 1915 on different operations. The Left Section went with a small force without drivers or mules to support the garrison of Jasin, just across the border on the coast, but Lettow-Vorbeck collected nine companies and made a strong attack on the post on 18th January. The section engaged German machine guns at 300 yards and put four out of action, and then repulsed an infantry attack with "shrapnel, zero"; it fired forty rounds in five minutes and claimed 100 enemy dead. Our small garrison of 150 infantry fought all day, but ammunition ran out and they had to surrender. However, the enemy evacuated the place shortly afterwards.

The Centre Section arrived at Kisumu, railhead on Lake Victoria, on 23rd November, 1914. Porters were allotted to carry rations, and it joined "D" Company, 4th King's African Rifles, and fought two engagements. The section moved to high ground owing to horse-sickness and was not fit to move again until 14th February.

The Right Section embarked at Kisumu on 7th January, and firing from on board ship covered an infantry landing at Shirati. A very successful engagement took place on German territory on 9th March, when two companies of King's African Rifles with the Right Section ran into a big German raiding party, which they were looking for, at Mwaika. A brisk action ensued, during which Major A. M. Colville man-handled one of his guns to within 200 yards of a German machine gun, and knocked it out. The Germans withdrew at nightfall, and the honours were with our side.

In June the Left Section went with a column to capture Bukoba, a German stronghold on Lake Victoria. A German field gun which was holding up the advance was forced to move and later knocked out, as was a machine gun; the section then supported the assault on the fort, which was completely successful. The fort was destroyed and the German gun captured. In July Gunner Mehr Khan was awarded the I.D.S.M. and Subadar-Major Nur Alam was promoted to the first class of the Order of British India. The battery moved to Matrau in August.

The troops were greatly cheered in July by the destruction in her "hide" in an estuary of the Rufiji river of the German cruiser *Konigsberg*, the only German warship to put in an appearance in East African waters. Her guns had been salved by the Germans and were a great acquisition to their land forces.

A change of policy also helped to improve matters, as reinforcements were promised from India and England, and a South African Expeditionary Force was known to be in preparation. Mechanical transport began to arrive in driblets.

The whole of 1915 was occupied in jungle warfare and preparing for an advance. Casualties amongst the mules from the tsetse fly were heavy, and one section of each mountain battery was experimentally equipped with porters instead of mules for a short time. Attempts were made to utilize oxen as pack animals without success. The mules of 7th (Bengal) Battery were regularly treated with cattle-dip for a period during 1915 in an endeavour to extend their usefulness.

Malaria and shortage of rations were weakening the troops all this time.

Practical co-operation was started with Belgian troops from the Congo and with Colonial troops from Rhodesia and Nyasaland. Our Indian troops found they had much to learn from the King's African Rifles as regards jungle fighting.

On 1st December a brigade headquarters was formed at Maktau for the two mountain batteries; it was designated the 4th Indian Mountain Artillery Brigade, under Lieutenant-Colonel C. E. Forestier-Walker, who was replaced in 8th (Lahore) Mountain Battery by Major A. M. Colville. These two batteries never fought as an artillery brigade, and the new headquarters was used as a group headquarters to command various artillery units from time to time. Major (local Lieutenant-Colonel) L. M. Davies took over the 4th I.M.A. Brigade on 8th February, 1916, being replaced in command of 7th (Bengal) Mountain Battery by Major A. J. T. Farfan.

In February, 1916, Lieutenant-General J. C. Smuts, the famous South African leader, became Commander-in-Chief of the forces in East Africa. A South African Expeditionary Force had arrived; artillery and many ancillary units had been sent from England and India or formed in the country, and two divisions were now in being; the total strength available was 27,000 with 71 guns. Half these men were new to the country and not acclimatized. Eight aeroplanes of the South African Squadron, R.F.C., brought a great moral and physical advantage to the force.

Minor operations continued, culminating in an attack on the German position at Salaita, ten miles east of Taveta, supported by the Lahore Mountain Battery and various guns and howitzers of field and medium calibres, and two 4-inch naval guns off H.M.S. *Pegasus*. One section of the mountain battery brought its guns into the firing line, and all the batteries used for the first time a F.O.O. with the infantry, but notwithstanding this support, the attack failed owing to the width of open space in front of the enemy's trenches. The artillery covered the retirement with skill.

General Smuts' first consideration was to clear the Germans out of the Kilimanjaro area before the rainy season set in.

The enemy's strength was now about 1,000 Europeans, 5,000 Askari and 13,000 porters: the Askari knew every trick of jungle fighting and could almost maintain themselves, and were of course thoroughly acclimatized. Many of the porters were trained as Askaris.

General Smuts ordered the 2nd Division with the mounted troops to start from Serengeti in British territory, to move west and to force the gap at Taveta, which provided the only road from east to west, south of the Kilimanjaro massif. The 1st Division, starting at Longido on the international boundary, were to move south, leaving the massif on their left, and cut off the Germans by making for Moshi, the terminus of the railway from Tanga. The 7th (Bengal)

Mountain Battery was with the 1st Division, but after a difficult march through the jungle, this column was late so that the pincer movement failed and the Germans slipped through the gap.

The sections of the 8th (Lahore) Battery were temporarily detached for short periods between September, 1915 and January, 1916, with forces on minor operations preparatory for the advance. The Right Section under Captain R. M. L. Dutton moved out on 8th January with a column of 300 rifles of the Loyal North Lancashire Regiment and a company of the Royal Fusiliers, the guns in draught and ammunition carried by porters, to attack a force at Ngurugani. The column was ambushed in dense bush and the escort and porters bolted, but the guns fired point-blank into the bush, fuze $1\frac{1}{2}$, with good effect. The guns were towed back by the infantry, and the detachments carried the ammunition.

In an action at Salaita on 12th February the enemy were occupying trenches in front of the high ground, and were not located. The Left Section under Lieutenant A. R. Cope came into action at a range of 350 yards to engage two German machine guns, which were put out of action. The infantry took no advantage of this support, and the force retired, the battery losing two men and seven ordnance mules wounded.

In February, 14 Cape Boys, 13 Army Transport carts and 30 mules were attached to the battery. At the same time the reserve ammunition mules with drivers and saddlery were returned to a transport unit.

On 7th March Lieutenant-Colonel L. M. Davies took over command of the battery for the forthcoming offensive. The infantry had received little training for jungle warfare, but forced the enemy to evacuate Chala, opening up the Taveta gap.

The Longido column had joined up on 14th March at Moshi, and the next objective for the whole force was the line of the Ruwu river, for which purpose the key position of Kahe had first to be seized.

A sharp action occurred at Rast Haus on 19th March, during which 348 shrapnel were fired, and Lieutenant Eden and three other ranks wounded. The fire of the battery, directed by Lieutenant Eden, saved the 12th South African Infantry from being surrounded and suffering very heavy casualties. Eden carried out his duties coolly and efficiently under heavy rifle and machine-gun fire.

Brigadier-General S. H. Sheppard, D.S.O., with a force nearly the strength of a division, which included the 7th (Bengal) Mountain Battery, made for the river while a strong force under Major-General J. L. Van Deventer attacked the Kahe position. Owing to the dense bush there was no communication between these two forces, but the operation was successful, and left us in possession of all the country to the north of the Ruwu river. The artillery officers had to climb trees and even then could see little of their target. The work of the 7th (Bengal) Battery evoked high praise for being in action in the infantry firing line throughout the day, coming out with its shields covered with bullet marks.

It was now a race to make as much ground as possible in order to settle the troops in healthy quarters before the rains came. The force was reorganized into three divisions, of which the first comprised all non-South African troops under Major-General A. R. Hoskins. The two mountain batteries were sent where they could be best used; the 7th (Bengal) Battery went into camp on high ground above Old Moshi, near General Headquarters, and the 8th (Lahore) Battery was sent farther west to Aruscha.

General Smuts' forceful methods pushed the 2nd Division, under General Van Deventer, through the rains to capture Kondoa Irangi to forestall the enemy's capture of this important road centre.

During this advance from Aruscha to Kumbulun the 8th (Lahore) Mountain Battery, after a very trying march of eighty-five miles on half rations through a countryside which had become a marsh, with the 10th South African Infantry Regiment, fought an action to capture the fort of Mbulu.

Guns and stores had to be floated across sixty yards of water on improvised rafts, and the ravages of the tsetse fly permitted the employment of two sections only. Lieutenant-Colonel Davies was ordered to make a frontal attack up the Inaku Pass with 100 infantry and two machine guns supported by a section of 10-prs., while the commander of the force took most of the remaining effective troops round the southern flank of the position. The frontal attack was held up until a gun was placed in action on high ground from which the enemy firing line could be seen at less than 1,000 yards range, and hostile infantry were engaged by the guns whenever visible. The enemy then evacuated his position, but the steepness of the pass and obstructions prevented a pursuit. The turning column arrived exhausted six hours later, having seen no enemy.

The battery moved to Kondoa Irangi to join the force there, 48 ordnance mules having died of horse sickness during May.

Our positions were under daily bombardment by the guns salvaged from the *Konigsberg* and sustained occasional attack during the next few weeks; Lieutenant-Colonel Davies having charge of the north-eastern half of the artillery front. Our guns were generally sited behind hills, to defend the fronts of other hills, as the German

4.1-inch and 3.5-inch guns outranged them. They were also sited to fire over nullahs, which prevented dust from blast giving their positions away. This arrangement proved effective.

Early in June two sections supported an attack on an enemy position and helped to beat off a counter-attack, firing 435 shrapnel. Enemy shelling ceased on 24th June and it was found that the enemy had evacuated his main forces. While preparations were being made for an advance a draft of 31 gunners and 37 drivers arrived from India.

The Germans had concentrated some 4,000 men against Kondoa Irangi by withdrawing troops from the eastern wing, leaving the Usambara range and the valley of the Pangani river lightly held. Handeni was the key-point of this piece of country leading to the Central Railway, which was General Smuts' next bound. His supply situation was eased by railway extension beyond Taveta to join the Tanga railway, which was not yet fit for anything heavier than trolley traffic. In front of railhead, unit transport was mainly motor-lorries, except for the South African Infantry which was equipped with mule wagons.

With Handeni as objective, three columns were moved south; the main column along the left bank of the Pandani river, a small column down the Tanga railway, and a third down the Usambara Ridge; the two latter were to join up at the Same Gap. The 7th Mountain Battery (less one section) moved with the main column on 22nd May and the section was with the Usambara column.

Apart from an attack on the enemy's rear-guard on 30th May, during which the mountain battery had a good climb with a turning force without much resistance, the enemy had been manœuvred out of several strong positions, and General Smuts' two columns were on the line Bwiko–Mkomazi by 1st June.

The left column, to which was attached a section of 7th Mountain Battery, was directed on Mombo on the Tanga railway, whence a trolley line, gauge 1 foot 11½ inches, ran to Handeni. Short of Mombo the section of the mountain battery knocked out a machine-gun with a direct hit, and after another minor action at the River Mlesa the enemy withdrew under our strong pressure, leaving us to enter Handeni on 18th June.

By this time rations were short and bad, transport worn out, and the troops reduced by sickness, but the moral effect of chasing an enemy who could not stand up to them carried the troops over every physical hardship. Besides, the situation was improving in the west, where the Belgian and Nyasaland-Rhodesia Field Force under Brigadier-General Northey were advancing. General Van

Deventer's force at Kondoa Irangi was awaiting the order to advance; more aircraft had arrived, and Tanga had fallen to us without opposition.

After leaving Handeni on 20th June our advance was opposed with vigour; every day or two the enemy made a stand and put up a rear-guard action in the most skilful way. Once, in the affair at the Lukigura river, the 7th (Bengal) Mountain Battery, which was in the infantry firing line, limbered up vainly looking for targets in the thick bush, charged with the Royal Fusiliers and the 2nd Kashmir Rifles, who for once in a way had found an opportunity for a bayonet charge—Norman Ramsay's troop could not have done better.

But by now this force had marched and fought to a standstill, and a standing camp was opened at the River Msiha, eighty miles from the Central Railway. Supplies were still short, soap and tobacco were unknown, a tin of jam was looked upon as a miracle, and there was no attempt at, or opportunity for, any kind of welfare or amenity among the troops. As the History of the Royal Army Service Corps put it "there were too many troops for the transport at the disposal of the Army."

Major-General Van Deventer's 2nd Division, reinforced and rested, moved out on 14th July with the objective of the Central Railway in his front.

The Lahore Mountain Battery was split up for this operation, the Centre Section moving with Colonel Kirkpatrick's column to the west, to cut the railway at Saranda, about seventy miles west of Dodoma, the objective of the main body. In an action on the 25th at Kwa Tevero, the guns had to change position hastily, being worried by wild bees. A few shells in the right place got the enemy on the move, and the force arrived at Saranda on the 30th, and the section continued to march parallel with the railway to rejoin the battery. Headquarters and remainder of the battery moved to Dodoma with little opposition, arriving 31st July. Lack of water was the greatest trouble. During the month of July the battery lost 29 mules from disease.

The main body of the 2nd Division then moved east in order to be able to support General Smuts' column if required; but met with some opposition, having to fight a series of actions.

The main column at Msiha Camp very soon found itself undergoing day and night bombardment by high-explosive shell with a time fuze and dug-outs became popular; no retaliation was possible except by bombing from the air. A move against Morogoro on the railway was indicated, but this was by no means easy. The road to that place was commanded by the Uluguru and Kanga mountains, where very strong opposition was to be expected as the enemy forces from Dodoma had retired in that direction.

It was found that the mountains were unsuitable for movement of wheeled traffic, and the mountain guns of the 7th (Bengal) Battery were invaluable at the action of Matomondo on 10th August. The action went on all day and the Germans withdrew during the night. The natural difficulties of the Uluguru mountains had proved too formidable for General Smuts' proposed flank attack, and the Germans withdrew practically unmolested.

The crossing of the Wami river gave an opportunity for a gun of the 7th (Bengal) Battery, skilfully brought into the front line by Captain D. D. Haskard, R.A., to silence three German machine guns while in close support.

By the time the troops arrived in Morogoro (27th August) the Germans had evacuated the town and slipped away.

The enemy not having been brought to bay as General Smuts had hoped, the pursuit was continued with the worn-out men and animals. The Uluguru mountains, running south from Morogoro, were ideal for rear-guard actions, and General Smuts attempted to cut off the enemy's retreat by sending the 1st Division round the eastern side of the range, while blocking the southern exit at Kisaki.

A succession of actions took place on the eastern line, in which the 7th (Bengal) Mountain Battery proved invaluable, but the enemy never stood to fight for any length of time, and the 1st Division continued the pursuit to the Mgeta river.

The 57th Wilde's Rifles were supported by a section of the 7th (Bengal) Battery on a flanking movement on the 10th, on which occasion the battery destroyed a German gun with a direct hit, but the German retirement continued, and by the 13th September they were in position along the Mgeta river.

The mounted troops, of whom about 60 per cent. had no horses, occupied Kisaki at the same time, unfortunately too late to catch the enemy. A force under Lieutenant-Colonel Burne, from the 2nd Division, was pushed forward from Uleia to outflank the Mgeta position, but met with strong opposition and was held up. It was presently reinforced by Lieutenant-Colonel Davies, in command of the 12th South African Infantry, and his 8th (Lahore) Mountain Battery. Davies then took his command across the Luhembe river and, managing to get well forward, captured the eastern slopes of the Bismarckberg Range. This forced the Germans to withdraw, whereupon both Burne's and Davies' detachment occupied Kidodi, fifty miles west of Kisaki, on 10th September. The supply question had become more and more difficult as the force advanced, and a halt was indicated.

General Smuts in his despatch wrote:

"The plain tale of the achievements of the troops bears the most convincing testimony to the spirit, determination and prodigious efforts of all ranks. Their work has been done under tropical conditions which not only produce bodily weariness and unfitness, but which create mental languor and depression, and finally appal the stoutest hearts. To march day by day, and week by week, through the African jungle of high grass, in which vision is limited to a few yards, in which danger always lurks near but seldom becomes visible even when experienced, supplies a test to human nature often in the long run beyond the limits of human endurance."

The coast-line now received attention and Dar-es-Salaam fell without opposition; the Navy then made good half a dozen other ports to the south, including Kilwa Kivinge (commonly Kilwa), where a column was landed for operations. The Central Railway was restored as far as Dodoma for motor tractors (300 miles), and the sea base was transferred to Dar-es-Salaam. By the end of December 12,000 white troops were evacuated and replaced by the Gold Coast Regiment and new battalions of the King's African Rifles.

The 8th (Lahore) Mountain Battery was less affected than its associated South African Infantry and mounted units by the privations and excessive work common to all, owing to its superior discipline and sanitary observance (common to all Indian mountain batteries). The men were badly in need of clothing and boots, and were anæmic from under-feeding. The mules were in a very bad state, no grain having been issued since the battery left Kondoa Irangi, while the losses of animals from "fly" and horse-sickness were terrific. A draft of 101 mules and 17 horses arrived in October. These were fine big animals; but the best animals were the least able to survive: 76 mules and 10 horses died during October.

Tabora was occupied by the Belgians on 19th September, and in a few weeks' time the whole of the Central Railway had passed into Allied hands. Brigadier-General Northey's Nyasaland-Rhodesia Field Force was directed on Iringa, where the enemy was expected to make a stand after being driven off the Central Railway. This place was reached on 29th August, and General Van Deventer made it his headquarters. Some minor operations became necessary to clear the way for the operations due to begin in January, 1917.

The Centre Section of the 8th (Lahore) Mountain Battery was

involved in a sharp action at Mahansi on 20th October/1st November when out with a small column sent to relieve a beleaguered post. Enemy details crept through the bush and occupied some high ground close to the guns, which was kept under fire with shrapnel at fuzes varying from 1 to 4. Captain Wilson being severely wounded, Lieutenant Eden took command. Ammunition and stores had to be carried across an open space under fire, and the gunners performed this work with great courage, beating off attacks until dark, firing 95 shrapnel. Ammunition had to be husbanded for the expected attack, which came next morning and was continued all day. The enemy withdrew the following night. One gunner was killed and six wounded, and Jemadar Sher Ali and twelve other ranks were recommended for awards for gallantry in action. Three of these were awarded the I.D.S.M.

On 5th November the 4th Indian Mountain Artillery Brigade ceased to exist, and Lieutenant-Colonel Dayies resumed his permanent rank of Major. A composite section moved to Iringa, leaving details at Kilossa, and joined the centre section.

An attempt was made by General Van Deventer to round up an enemy column reported at Lukegeta. A column with a section of mountain guns was ordered to cross the mountains by an unreconnoitred track to cut the road in the German rear, starting on 24th December. Major Davies made up a section of which the transport consisted of 63 ordnance mules, all in poor condition, and 140 porters. The column, under Colonel Taylor, advanced up the steepest possible slopes during heavy rain all day. Nine mules fell over the khud and had to be shot; two porters also fell and were killed. Many loads were lost and rations came up in short supply.

The column advanced on Christmas Day and the following day with all the troops exhausted, the gunners on occasion carrying the gun loads and behaving in magnificent fashion, helped by a company of King's African Rifles. The enemy slipped away through the bush in small parties during the night. These operations caused the greatest suffering to all those in Colonel Taylor's column; the men and animals were so reduced by fever and starvation that the forcing of a path through country unfit for any form of pack transport was a very severe strain, and the battery commander reported that the subsequent reduced state of the battery was largely due to the sufferings of this march, coming after all the privations already suffered. During December 96 mules and 3 ponies died from casualties, "fly" and debility, and 109 mules were received; 66 mules died in January.

The 8th (Lahore) Mountain Battery had worn itself out; half the men were unfit for any duty and the remainder weak and anæmic. It was sent to India to re-form and refit; a great-hearted battery which fought for over two years in unfamiliar surroundings, in extremes of climate, with few of the thrills of victory, half-starved and rotten with fever, but which produced with half-trained men and mules all the support demanded by the infantry.*

Two fresh mountain batteries had already arrived from India; No. 1 Kashmir Mountain Battery disembarked at Dar-es-Salaam on 5th December, 1916, and the 2nd (Derajat) Mountain Battery (F.F.)† at Kilwa on the 18th. Major A. F. Cole was with the Kashmir Battery as Special Service Officer, with Captain Gray and Lieutenant Jones as assistants. The battery was commanded by Major Dharam Singh, Bahadur, with Subadar Alaf Khan as second-in-command. With the Derajat Mountain Battery were Major S. Perry (Commandant) and Lieutenant J. P. Doyle, I.A.R.O., Second-Lieutenants A. Baston and W. Hawes, both R.A. (S.R.).

General Smuts' plan was, first to seize a crossing of the Rufiji river, and then, with three brigades under his own hand, to attack the Mgeta front and by joining up with General Hoskins' 1st Division in the Kilwa area to envelop the enemy on the Rufiji. General Van Deventer was in charge at Iringa, to the west.

The Kashmir Mountain Battery (which started with 198 rank and file and 172 mules) went with Brigadier-General Beves' 2nd South African Infantry Brigade, which was directed to cross the Rufiji and move on Mkalinso; the crossing was done without opposition, and the battery swam the mules across on 4th January, 1917, supporting a successful attack on Mkalinso on 9th February. By this time it was obvious that the enemy had slipped away again, the gap not being closed, and his main forces were moving south-east.

General Smuts handed over the command on 20th January; Lieutenant-General A. R. Hoskins, C.M.G., D.S.O., commanded until 30th May, 1917, when General Van Deventer took over.

This turned out to be the wettest rainy season for many years, but training and reorganization went on in the force, and every effort was made to harass the enemy.

In February, the 1st Kashmir Battery joined Brigadier-General

---

* Major Davies was afterwards awarded the French Croix de Guerre and Major E. R. C. Wilson the Military Cross and the Italian Silver Medal. The honorary rank of Captain was conferred on Subadar-Major Nur Alam, Sirdar Bahadur.

† At this time designated 22nd Derajat Mountain Battery (F.F.)

Sheppard's* eastern column: the Right Section was complimented for its behaviour in support of an attack on Mkindu on 16th February and the Left Section was in action at Nyakisiku. The battery then moved to Dodoma.

The 2nd (Derajat) Mountain Battery was reorganized as a four-gun unit and took over two guns and shields from 7th (Bengal) Mountain Battery. Captain R. P. Landon of the latter battery took over command in February of the Derajat battery, which was already running short of mules and experienced the usual shortage of rations and forage. By the end of March the battery was without a mule at all and relying on porters. Captain J. H. M. Stevenson arrived from India and took over command of the battery with the rank of Acting Major.

The pursuit of the enemy prevented the force from occupying healthy, high ground as it had done in the 1916 rainy season, and the troops were drawn into flooded, sodden country which caused much malaria and horse-sickness.

The battery was split up, sending single guns with small columns, but by the end of April was concentrated at Rumbo, with 445 porters as transport and only 16 rounds of shrapnel per gun. It remained for some weeks in a perimeter camp a mile and a half from the enemy. During June the battery was engaged in training 251 remount mules which had been sent from South Africa.

At this time the column consisted of the 40th Pathans, 2/2nd King's African Rifles, and the Gold Coast Regiment. The latter had two 2.95-inch mountain guns carried by porters, and the mountain gunners became very friendly and used to visit each other's gun-park. The porters of the Gold Coast Battery are reported to have beaten off an attack on their guns by charging the enemy with machetes and putting them to flight.

On 23rd June Major G. V. Dreyer joined the battery and assumed command; with him came Lieutenant J. C. Bowering, R.A. (S.R.), and Lieutenant R. W. Carrigan, M.C.

The roads by now had dried up and light motor lorries were working. The enemy was retiring slowly southwards, and our forces were closing in from the west.

The 4th (Hazara) Mountain Battery (F.F.),† which had left Nowshera for East Africa in March, 1917, disembarked at Dar-es-Salaam on 26th April. It left by train on 6th May for Morogoro,

---

* Brigadier-General S. H. Sheppard had served in East Africa from the start of the campaign, then being G.S.O.1.
† At this time named 24th Hazara Mountain Battery (F.F.)

but the train ran off the line while crossing a bridge, killing or drowning sixteen men, including the salutri. Eventually the battery arrived at Dodoma on 10th May and took over guns and mules from 8th (Lahore) Mountain Battery, and also 156 remounts. Battery officers were Major C. R. Crowdy, Captain F. C. Rossiter, M.C., Second-Lieutenants Ellis and Potter, Subadar Gurditt Singh and Jemadar Ghulam Mahomed. The battery then marched to Iringa, ready for the advance ordered for the end of June.

When General Van Deventer assumed command of the Forces in East Africa the Germans were in two bodies. One, commanded by Oberst Tafel, was based on Mahenge, consisting of 2,000 to 3,000 men, with a strong detachment at Likuju. The stronger force, 4,000 to 5,000 was in the coastal area, facing our troops at Kilwa and Lindi. This was commanded by Lettow-Vorbeck himself. A large raiding party of 600 men under Naumann had crossed the Central Railway, east of Tabora, and was moving northwards.

General Van Deventer decided to make his main advance from Kilwa and Lindi, to operate against the Mahenge force from Dodoma and Kilossa, and to use General Northey's force from Songea to assist in the Mahenge operations.

The Kilwa force under Brigadier-General Beves was in two columns: the 2nd (Derajat) Battery was with one, and the 7th (Bengal) Battery with the second.

The advance of the Kilwa force began on 5th July, and the enemy withdrew slowly, but was found to be holding Narungombe in force. A concerted attack by the two columns took place on 19th and a sharp action ensued, lasting all day. The O.P. party (Major Stevenson) was left in the air after a counter-attack on the South African infantry and had to retire, wiping out a machine-gun detachment with rifle fire as they moved back. Major Stevenson established a line with a few infantry and engaged his target with the guns, shelling the enemy in retreat. The O.P. party was very steady during this action, and Lance-Naik Painda Khan received the I.D.S.M. for his behaviour. Major Stevenson was awarded the Military Cross.

July was a very bad month from the supply point of view: the 2nd (Derajat) Mountain Battery recorded that the personnel had nothing but what they stood up in, and the animals nothing but what they could pick up on the road. Hence there was a heavy sick roll and 70 mules died during the month.

A section of this battery was in action under Major G. V. Dreyer at Nanyati on 5th August, supporting an infantry attack from an O.P. 170 yards from the enemy. When the enemy had overrun the battalion headquarters in the left rear, Major Dreyer took charge and brought the infantry out of action, but all reserves having been used up, our column had to retire.

The battery used a home-made corrector scale in the shape of a ring of 6-inch diameter, worn by No. 4 as an armlet. At the end of August, the battery received four 2.75-inch guns to replace the 10-prs.

The Lindi force advanced with little opposition to Mayani and prepared for a further movement in August. In the meantime the Songea column had driven the enemy towards Mahenge and the Iringa column forced him to the line of the Ruaha river. General Northey's forces had driven an enemy column out of Portuguese East Africa, and the German line was now river Idete–Mpondas. Naumann's raid was giving a lot of trouble and drawing off troops required elsewhere. Eventually, after a very remarkable performance, the raiding force was obliged to surrender on Liuta Hill on 1st October, Belgian columns having blocked its passage westwards.

There were now no strategical objectives left—the country held by the enemy was wild and inhospitable, and communications were non-existent. The campaign had developed into a pursuit of scattered enemy forces through the bush.

By mid-September reinforcements had arrived, and the main advance began, southwards by the Kilwa column and south-westwards by the force from Lindi. The 1st Kashmir Mountain Battery was from now on attached to the column under Brigadier-General O'Grady.

The enemy retired slowly southwards, offering strong opposition. The capture of their position at Nahungu, 26/27th September, caused a little delay, but the enemy evacuated as usual after two days' fighting. The 7th (Bengal) Mountain Battery distinguished itself by making a direct hit on a German gun, and the 2nd (Derajat) Mountain Battery (Right Section) was in action at 1,700 yards until the guns were nearly surrounded. Jemadar Jagat Singh was wounded and the guns had to retire, No. 2 gun having been out of action for some time.

The 1st Kashmir Mountain Battery gave "effective support" to a column on 25th September in an action for which Jemadars Sarup Singh and Khushal Khan were awarded the Indian Order of Merit for gallantry, but no details of this are available.

September was again a bad month for mules. Those of 2nd (Derajat) Mountain Battery were on one occasion in such a pitiable state after sixty-seven hours without water that the infantry (127th Baluchis and 3rd King's African Rifles) gave up their reserve water to the animals.

The mules did not refuse bully beef when offered.

On 16th, 17th and 18th October, took place one of the most severe actions of the campaign. A strong stand was made by the German main force at Nyangao, attack and counter-attack continuing without cessation, with heavy losses on both sides. The two mountain batteries, 7th (Bengal) and 1st Kashmir, were kept hard at work on bombardments and supporting fire, using a great deal of ammunition. On the 19th the enemy evacuated their position.

One section of the 7th (Bengal) Mountain Battery, under Captain R. P. Landon, was with O'Grady's column from August onwards. The battery was rearmed with the 2.75-inch gun in August.

General Northey's force from Songea advanced, driving the enemy down the Luwegu River. The Belgians had advanced slowly and occupied Mahenge on 9th October, causing the German commander (Oberst Tafel) to withdraw southwards.

The 4th (Hazara) Mountain Battery had taken part in several actions with the column based on Iringa, and later had joined the Belgians, returning to Iringa on 9th September. At Dodoma on 2nd October, it took over four 2.75-inch guns with a proportion of H.E. shell, and the battery arrived at Lindi on 2nd November.

The Allies' lines of communication were now unduly extended, but they rushed forward with what troops they could feed.

The Kilwa and Lindi forces continued the pursuit on 6th November in a succession of rear-guard fights, and the two forces joined up at the strong natural position of Chiwata. This was not defended and our objective was now to prevent the two German forces from joining up. The speed of our movements prevented the junction; Lettow-Vorbeck escaped across the Portuguese border, unhindered by the Portuguese, with about 300 Europeans and 1,500 Askaris; Oberst Tafel, after being chased to the Rovuma river, surrendered unconditionally on 28th November.

The last German colony was now cleared after a heroic and skilful resistance by meagre forces who never lost their morale, and who extended our troops to the utmost, being only crushed in the end by the determined gallantry and endurance of the Allies.

The war was not yet over. Lettow-Vorbeck was loose in Portuguese East Africa, a vast country as large as France and as difficult as German East Africa for carrying on a campaign. The capture of several Portuguese posts provided him with ammunition and food and improved the morale of his troops. No maps were available and the natives were generally unfriendly to us.

The 1st Kashmir battery took its share of the pursuit in Portuguese

East Africa until February, when it went to Dar-es-Salaam to embark for India.

Extract from the Battery history:

"During the time the battery was in Africa, owing to malaria and other sickness, a very large proportion of the personnel had to be replaced from India, most coming from No. 2 Kashmir Mountain Battery. Of the animals taken out by the battery only one survived to the end of 1917, all the rest having succumbed to the tsetse fly and horse-sickness."

In addition to the awards already mentioned, Major Dharam Singh was awarded the Order of British India (1st Class), with the title of Sardar Bahadur, and Subadar Alaf Khan the 2nd Class of that Order, with the title of Bahadur. Naik Kamal Singh was awarded the I.D.S.M. and seven other ranks the M.S.M. Twelve men were mentioned in despatches.

The battery had 24 casualties, all except three being deaths from sickness.

The 7th (Bengal) Mountain Battery had already embarked for India on 2nd January, 1918.

The G.O.C.'s intention was to form a barrier to the north of the Rovuma, and to close in on the enemy from east and west simultaneously. The line taken up was Songda-Turnduru-Ngomano.

The Right Section of 2nd (Derajat) Mountain Battery under Major Stevenson joined Colonel Rose's column at Port Amelia in January, 1918.

The column pushed slowly inland, halting at Ankuabe for some weeks, where two 3.7-inch howitzers were issued in exchange for 2.75-inch B.L. guns. It was said that they had been landed by mistake, being intended for Egypt; but Major Stevenson rushed to the base and secured them, no doubt by devious ways. The howitzers were in action for the first time at the capture of Medo fort, 11th April, where they gave intense satisfaction to everybody except perhaps the tenants of the fort. Major Stevenson controlled the fire of the battery from a stretcher, Lieutenant O. G. Davies was in an O.P. forward, and Subadar Santa Singh in the battery. Lieutenant C. A. Kestin was severely wounded when forward with the infantry. The enemy was shelled out of the fort, which was then occupied. Lieutenant O. G. Davies was awarded the Military Cross for his share in the day's work.

One night a stampede of porters was stopped by the mules, who handled very roughly the porters who fled amongst them. For many days the pursuit of the Germans continued through the jungle, the force moving on a single track and being held up several times a day by machine guns in ambush. The usual procedure was for the O.P. party to go on with the vanguard, laying a cable as they went, which was later reeled in by the battery. When resistance was met, a gun was brought into action and fired at a range calculated from the amount of wire run out, and on the line of the firing in front. There was always a competition to get a round off before the Stokes mortars with the vanguard opened fire.

After a shoot on an enemy headquarters at Koronji on 1st May, the section was heavily attacked whilst moving through bamboo jungle so thick that the guns could not fire. The gunners defended themselves by rifle fire, and the drivers were very steady. Seven men of the rear section were killed in this ambush and seven wounded; eleven mules were killed and eight wounded. A breech mule bolted and was killed, but the breech was retrieved by Staff-Sergeant Fitter E. Mason, assisted by Naik Naraya Singh and Gunner Majhi Khan. The Staff-Sergeant was awarded the Distinguished Conduct Medal for gallantry. Several awards for gallantry and devotion to duty were made to this battery: Subadar Santa Singh, Order of British India, Second Class; Havildar-Major Ghazan Khan, Lance-Naik Auranzeb, Gunner Santok Singh, Indian Distinguished Service Medal, which was also awarded to Sub-Assistant-Surgeon Mehdi Hassan Khan.

The enemy continued to retire slowly westwards along the Koronji–Nanungu road, being closely followed up by Colonel Rose's column from the east, General Northey's troops meanwhile closing in from the west, down the Lujenda river. After one or two engagements Lettow-Vorbeck, who still had some 240 Europeans and 1,300 Askari, but little food or ammunition, moved south of the Lurio river, near Malema, where the country was more dense and difficult than ever. Moving with great speed, he went south to Alto Molocue and Ille, where stores and supplies were replenished by capture from the Portuguese. His farthest advance south was to Nhamacurra, fifty miles north of Quelimane, where three columns were sent to hem him in, but without success.

At this time the fittest men in the battery were formed into the Centre Section with 3.7-inch howitzers under Lieutenant J. C. Bowering, and the remainder sent to Dar-es-Salaam to refit. When it was found that the Germans had slipped away to the north-east by Murrua, the 3.7-inch howitzer section was sent with a force to the River Lurio to cut them off. They, however, had gone north-west and later turned due east on meeting General Northey's force. By August the enemy had settled down in the rich country round Ligonha, where a converging movement was made on them, but they retreated south-west to Ille, closely followed up. On 30th August they were at Lioma, where they attacked one of our columns and were repulsed with considerable loss, but by moving northwards they kept out of touch for a month.

The 2nd (Derajat) and the 4th (Hazara) Mountain Batteries were sent back to India in November. Lettow-Vorbeck continued moving northwards towards Songea after crossing the Rovuma, and averaged eighteen miles a day on his last flight, but after wheeling left to attack Fife on 2nd November his force was repulsed by Northern Rhodesian Police. He was informed of the Armistice of 11th November on the 13th, and surrendered to General Edwards on instructions from Berlin. His strength was 30 German officers, 125 German other ranks, 1,168 Askaris and 1,522 carriers. He and his officers were allowed to keep their swords, and the European rank and file retained their arms as far as Dar-es-Salaam. The German Commander had undertaken to tie up in East Africa the greatest possible number of Allied troops, and carried out his undertakings very well and very economically.

The casualties in the mountain batteries amongst the men were mostly due to disease, and it should be recorded that in two years 2nd (Derajat) Mountain Battery lost 948 mules by disease and 11 killed in action.

Batteries were permitted to bear on their colours and appointments the following honours:

The Great War.—2nd (Derajat) (F.F.), "EAST AFRICA 1916-18"— "NARUNGOMBE". 4th (Hazara) (F.F.), "EAST AFRICA 1917-18". 7th (Bengal), "EAST AFRICA 1914-18"—"KILIMANJARO", "NARUNGOMBE", "NYANGAO". 8th (Lahore), "EAST AFRICA, 1914-17"— "KILIMANJARO". No. 1 Kashmir, "EAST AFRICA, 1916-18".

None of the actions in this campaign were officially recognized as "battles."

D. MESOPOTAMIA, PERSIA AND IRAQ

Mesopotamia includes all the territory between the Rivers Tigris and Euphrates as well as a great tract of country surrounding them. These two rivers dominated the campaign, as they had dominated the country since the Flood. They provided the means of transport as well as irrigation for the rich soil. Four hundred years of Turkish misrule and corruption had caused the irrigation to be neglected, and the lands of many Arab tribes—which were encouraged by the Turks to remain in a state of conflict—became desolate. Out of

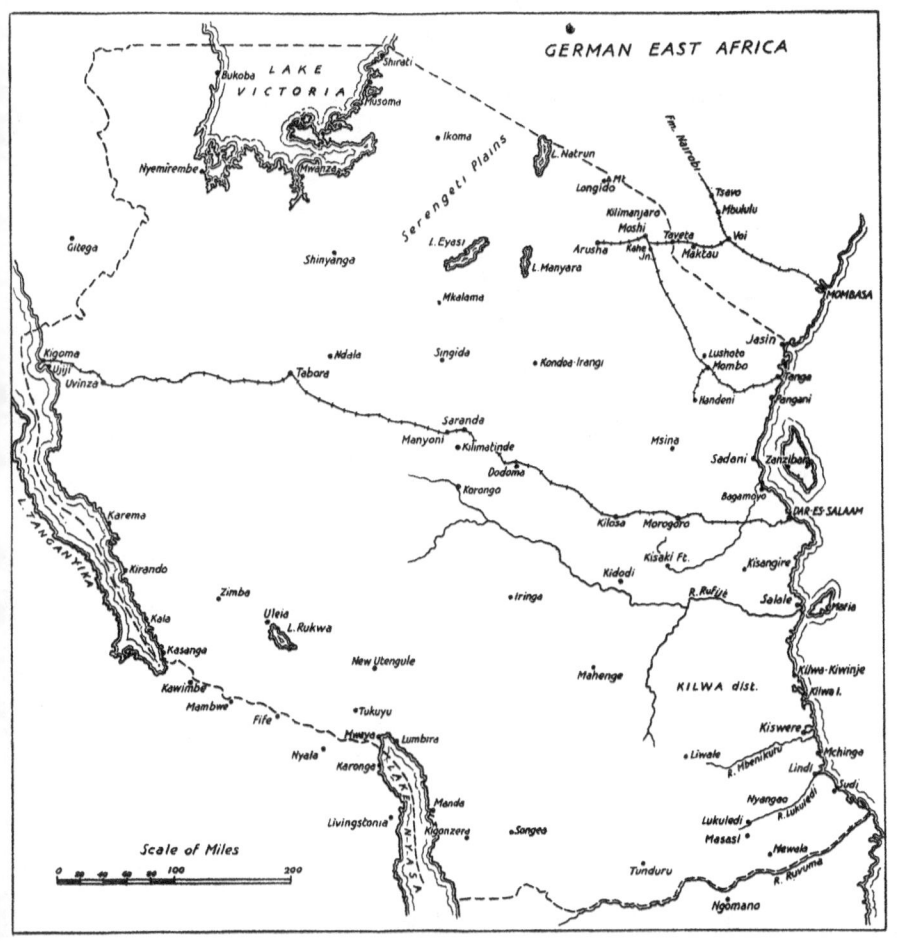

an area of 27,000 square miles, less than one-ninth was under cultivation in 1914.

The country is a plain with many swamps, and except for the caravan route from Kut al Amara to Baghdad it is road-less. Rain and floods turn the soil into impassable quagmires, although wheeled traffic is practicable in the dry season except where hindered by ditches and watercuts which require bridging.

In the hot season, great heat and lack of water try the stamina of men and animals: severe dust storms are frequent, preventing co-operation between the arms in battle. Mirages are common occurrences, and they render artillery work almost impossible. On the other hand, the climate from November to March is pleasant and healthy.

Many diseases were prevalent, such as plague, smallpox, cholera, dysentery and typhus, making Mesopotamia an undesirable country in which to wage a war. Baghdad, the capital, is nearly 600 miles by river from the sea. A channel known as the Shatt-al-Arab (one and a half miles wide at the mouth) connects the town of Basra with the sea some seventy miles away. The depth of water at Basra was about twenty feet, and the depth gradually lessened until at Al Qurna, the junction of the Tigris and Euphrates, a distance of forty-six miles upstream, there were only eight feet of water in the dry season and twelve feet in the floods. Two hundred and ten miles below Baghdad there were only three and a half feet in the dry season.

The broad-gauge railway from Constantinople to Baghdad which was in process of being built with German capital had not been completed in 1914; some of the gaps were filled during the war, but there remained to the end a 300-mile gap north of Tikrit.

The local garrisons in Mesopotamia were mostly formed of Arabs, who were hoping that the invading British Army would bring them freedom from their Turkish oppressors, and so fought only half-heartedly against us at first; but in time our army met trained Turkish troops who checked our advance and altered the situation.

Great Britain and France declared war on Turkey on 5th November, 1914, and we proceeded to protect our vital interest in the Southern Mesopotamia oil-field. A great oil-field in the Upper Karun valley had been opened up under British auspices, a pipe-line 150 miles long laid to Abadan* island in the Shatt-al-Arab and refineries installed there by 1912. The Admiralty attached the utmost importance to the maintenance of this supply, and military protection had to be provided.

The army in India had not been organized with a view to throwing

* Abadan and the Karun river are in Persian territory.

off overseas expeditions on a large scale, but it soon found itself compelled to send troops to France, Gallipoli, and East Africa as well as Mesopotamia.

In October, 1914, four battalions of the 16th (Poona) Infantry Brigade with 1st Indian Mountain Artillery Brigade (Lieutenant-Colonel H. D. Grier, with Captain H. C. L. Cock as adjutant), comprising 3rd (Peshawar) Mountain Battery (F.F.)* under Major E. E. Edlmann and 10th (Abbottabad) Mountain Battery† under Major H. J. Cotter, arrived off Bahrein Island on 23rd October. The strength of each battery was 302 other ranks, 17 public and 6 private followers, 7 chargers, 6 ponies, 164 ordnance mules, and its armament was six 10-pr. B.L. guns, with 735 rounds shrapnel per gun. The force was commanded by Brigadier-General W. S. Delamain, and designated Indian Expeditionary Force "D."

Orders were received for the force to co-operate with the Navy in an immediate attack on Fao to clear the Turks out of the Shatt and its vicinity as far as an island five miles above Mohammerah, and then to await the arrival of reinforcements from India. The attack on Fao was made on 6th November: H.M. Sloop *Odin* with six 4-inch guns silenced the guns of the fort, and the centre section of 10th (Abbottabad) Mountain Battery landed with the infantry covering force. It had no difficulty in landing the mules from the ship's boats. The Peshawar Mountain Battery made ready to fire their guns off the saloon deck. Next day the force was re-embarked, and by 10th November Brigadier-General Delamain had landed his force at Sanniya, opposite the oil refinery, without interference by the enemy. An enemy attack was made at dawn on the 11th, but beaten off by an Indian battalion, supported by the 3rd (Peshawar) Mountain Battery which expended 115 shrapnel. Having no news of reinforcements, the force halted until 14th November, when Lieutenant-General Sir A. A. Barrett, commanding 6th (Poona) Division, arrived with two cavalry regiments and an infantry brigade. On the 19th the remainder of the Division arrived, and Force "D" was correspondingly enlarged and reorganized as a Division.

On the 15th Brigadier-General Delamain had moved out to attack a force at Saihan, two miles west, with two battalions, supported by 10th (Abbottabad) Mountain Battery, and drove it away to the north, where it was found in position on the 17th. The attack was supported by the two mountain batteries and eight 18-prs., and in two or three hours the fort was captured and the enemy were with-

---

* At this time designated 23rd Peshawar Mountain Battery (F.F.).
† At this time designated 30th Mountain Battery.

drawing rapidly. His numbers were estimated at 3,500 regulars and 1,000 Arabs with twelve guns. Mohammerah and the mouth of the Karun river, the end of the pipe-line and the refinery were now secured and three river steamers became available.

On the 21st news came in that the enemy had evacuated Basra and withdrawn a further 140 miles to Amara. Major-General C. I. Fry was sent on at once with two battalions and a section of the 10th (Abbottabad) Mountain Battery in two river steamers, while three of H.M. sloops negotiated the blocked river channel and steamed ahead, arriving at Basra that evening.

The troops had been delayed by embarkation difficulties, but took over the shore duties on arrival early on the 22nd. General Barrett's main column marched to Basra, arriving about noon on 22nd after a trying march of twenty-nine miles.

At this time Basra had few port facilities. Ocean-going ships could not come alongside, but discharged into native craft which were allowed to drift into shallow water, whence they could be poled in to the bank.

The rapid success of Force "D" whetted the appetite of those in authority for a further advance, for which preparations were ordered. Without the co-operation of the loyal Arabs, the prospects for an advance were not good; and the political authorities had neglected to make the right approach before our invasion. As the Arabs were disaffected equally to the Persian and the Turkish Governments, and placed no reliance on our promises to protect them from eventual reprisals, any assistance they did render could never be depended upon.

Qurna is on the right bank of the Tigris at its junction with the old channel of the Euphrates. General Barrett decided to capture this place, which was of strategical importance; and as the small force sent at first was unsuccessful, General Fry was sent with reinforcements which included the 10th (Abbottabad) Mountain Battery. The attack was launched at 7 a.m. on the 7th December, supported by ten 18-prs. and six 10-prs., and the enemy was driven out by 4 p.m. By the next day a section of 10th (Abbottabad) Mountain Battery and two battalions had been put across to the right bank, by a flying bridge, and the Turks capitulated.

The chief enemy forces were now reported to be at Amara (90 miles north of Qurna) and at Nasiriya (100 miles NNW. of Basra). By the end of the year nothing had happened to indicate the strength of the opposition which might be encountered.

The 10th (Abbottabad) Mountain Battery formed part of a force which made a "strong demonstration" on the Turkish position on a line of sandhills about six miles north of Qurna on 20th January; but, after the position had been captured, the country beyond was found to be almost impassable, and the British force was withdrawn.

On 26th January, 1915, a threat to Ahwaz on the Karun developed, and in February the Arabs reached the oil-field, looted the stores and cut the pipe-line. On 11th February Brigadier-General C. T. Robinson, C.R.A., 6th (Poona) Division, was ordered to take some cavalry, three battalions and the centre section of 3rd (Peshawar) Mountain Battery (Captains W. M. Hunt and R. M. N. Forbes) to reinforce the battalions at Ahwaz and check the Turkish advance. Small garrisons were to be placed on Abadan island and on the Karun above Mohammerah. At this time a flood had come down and Qurna had to be evacuated, and two cavalry regiments with "S" Battery, R.H.A., which had gone out with General Delamain to create a diversion, fought a very brisk action, losing seven British officers, before they got clear of an Arab encircling movement.

On 3rd March Brigadier-General Robinson's force fought a sharply contested action in the Karun valley. He moved out to attack the enemy position ten miles north-west of Ahwaz. Captain W. M. Hunt, commanding the section of 23rd (Peshawar) Mountain Battery (F.F.), greatly distinguished himself in this action. The infantry he was covering broke, leaving the guns to be temporarily overwhelmed by Turks and tribesmen. He ordered Captain R. M. N. Forbes to withdraw the guns, covering their retirement single-handed with an infantryman's rifle. He shot down several of the enemy at short range, until severely wounded in the shoulder. A few other ranks of the Dorset Regiment gallantly tried to rally the broken infantry. A timely charge by a troop of the 33rd Cavalry saved a serious situation, in which the drivers were leading their mules with one hand and slashing with their swords with the other. Captain Forbes found Captain Hunt wounded and brought him in. He then made up one gun and, aided by an 18-pr. of the 82nd Battery, R.F.A., they covered each other's retirement till the situation was restored by the arrival of fresh infantry and the guns of a ship on the Karun river. One 18-pr. and one chase and one breech of a 10-pr. were lost. Our casualties included four British officers killed and seven wounded. Enemy casualties were heavy.

In May a much larger force under Major-General Gorringe cleared out the enemy and secured the pipe-line, and by 13th June oil was reaching Abadan again.

More troops were sent from India, and Lieutenant-General Sir

J. E. Nixon was sent to command Force "D," now to be reorganized as a Corps, and entitled II Indian Corps from 1st April, 1915.

There was a deplorable shortage of field artillery in the force, the 10th Field Brigade (eighteen 18-prs.) having to supply support for two divisions. Two 60-pr. batteries, some 15-prs. manned by Calcutta volunteers and a Hampshire Territorial Howitzer Battery with 5-inch howitzers were all the artillery available over and above the field and mountain batteries.

General Nixon's primary task was to retain complete control of Lower Mesopotamia. Shaiba (five miles north of Zubair) had been occupied, like Qurna, as an outpost essential for the protection of Basra. An attack on Shaiba appeared imminent, and actually took place on 12th April, the enemy's strength being estimated at 25,000 Turks and Arabs, with twenty-four guns. The 3rd (Peshawar) Mountain Battery was behind the centre, with a field battery in rear of the right flank and a field battery and "S" Battery, R.H.A. in rear of the left. The 10th (Abbottabad) Mountain Battery was ordered to move to the battlefield from Basra, but did not complete the journey owing to delay in river transport arrangements.

This attack on the 12th was beaten off, and on the next day General Delamain with three battalions, supported by the fire of all the artillery, attacked a strong force of Arabs who were holding a mound to the north of the camp, and drove them off. More attacks at various points of the three-and-a-half-mile perimeter were made by the enemy, but all were beaten off. A strong counter-attack was made with five battalions and a cavalry brigade in the afternoon, which met with great success, causing severe loss to the enemy. Two of their mountain guns were captured.

The next day Major-General Melliss, commanding the 30th Infantry Brigade, left two battalions in camp and attacked with the rest of his force. As the force advanced it became clear that the enemy's main body was entrenched in front of a wood about two miles to the westward, the line of trenches being about three miles long; and on each flank were large masses of Arabs. The attack began about 11.30 a.m. covered by the 63rd and 76th Batteries, R.F.A., and the 10-prs. of 3rd (Peshawar) Mountain Battery. The trenches were sited behind a low ridge, and our leading battalions were engaged as soon as they topped the ridge; fortunately the enemy's artillery fire had little effect.

The 63rd Battery, R.F.A., and 3rd (Peshawar) Mountain Battery moved up in close support of the infantry and suffered heavy casualties. The C.R.A. was wounded and was relieved by Major

E. E. Edlmann, commanding 3rd (Peshawar) Battery. This officer was severely wounded ten minutes later and died of his wounds two days afterwards. Captain Forbes was wounded as well.

Our infantry were only 400 yards from the enemy trenches, when they were halted until a general advance was ordered about 3.30 p.m. They responded magnificently; the front line was taken, and the white flag was shown before our troops reached the second line. Shortage of ammunition, fatigue and the extreme heat prevented a pursuit, but it transpired that the Arabs turned on the Turks who escaped from the trenches and slaughtered them mercilessly. Our losses had been severe: casualties were about 1,000, including 160 killed. The mountain battery had fired 711 rounds.

So ended the battle of Shaiba, a victory with decisive results. It restored the initiative to the British and cleared the approaches to Basra.

The 3rd (Peshawar) Mountain Battery went into camp at Zubair and the 10th (Abbottabad) was quartered in Basra. The province of Basra, the occupation of which covered General Nixon's orders to control Lower Mesopotamia, was included in the triangle Basra-Nasiriya-Amara, and his next move was to occupy Amara, an operation carried out by the 17th Infantry Brigade under Major-General Townshend, with the 10th (Abbottabad) Mountain Battery in support.

General Townshend issued orders for a frontal attack from boats on the river, movement on land being impossible owing to floods and marshes; battalions had been training "bellum" parties for some time. Each bellum (native boat) carried ten men, a day's rations, ammunition, etc., and a proportion of them were fitted with shields. The 10-prs. were allotted to rafts from which they were to fire. A turning attack, to which one section of the mountain battery was allotted, was to be made on the east side of the Tigris, and the main attack carried out by 17th Infantry Brigade and Sirmoor Sappers with 10th (Abbottabad) Mountain Battery less one section, preceded by a bombardment from naval guns and heavy guns in barges. Reserve troops were waiting to be brought up the river in transports.

The turning attack started at 1 a.m., but after going a short way the water became too shallow for further progress, and as the gunners were unable to get the rafts along by pushing them, the section returned to Qurna.

With the main attack, the mountain battery opened fire at 2,700 yards against the first objective (Norfolk Hill) and the battery advanced by alternate sections in close support of the infantry, who went forward without a check. Under cover of the fire of the guns at 1,750 yards, the leading company of 1st Oxfordshire and Buckinghamshire Light Infantry rowed to within a hundred yards of its objective and splashed through the water to the final successful assault.

The infantry then re-embarked and two more objectives were captured in the same way under covering fire from the battery, completing the day's success. The heat was extreme and the glare off the water very trying, but arrangements were made by the 17th Brigade and the battery for a similar advance next day. The Turks withdrew early and the retirement became a rout. This success was a brilliant display of naval and military co-operation: our casualties were 25, while the Turkish loss was 100 with 1,700 taken prisoner, as well as seventeen guns and a number of river craft. The next two days were occupied by a combined naval and military pursuit, Amara being entered on 4th June. The mountain battery was halted at Abu Aran, afterwards returning to Qurna.

In these actions aeroplanes assisted Force "D" for the first time, and from now on the assistance of aircraft was always available.

The next objective was Nasiriya, on the Euphrates. This attack was to be carried out in a somewhat similar way to the capture of Amara: the 10th (Abbottabad) Battery's mountain guns on rafts; 18-prs. of 63rd Battery, R.F.A., to fire from steamers, 4.7-inch guns from barges, and a naval flotilla in support. The 30th Infantry Brigade, now reduced by sickness to 2,000 was detailed for the operation. The enemy was found to be entrenched astride the river some seven miles from Nasiriya, and the force disembarked to make an attack on both sides of the river.

As a preliminary, on 5th July an advanced Turkish position was attacked by the 24th and 76th Punjabis, supported by two sections of the mountain battery firing from rafts; the third section pushed forward with the infantry. Fire was handicapped by date palms and delayed by arranging for indirect fire with forward observing officers, but the position was carried and two guns and 91 prisoners were captured.

All the troops except 63rd Battery, R.F.A., were landed and provided with tents, owing to the great heat.

Reconnaissances found the enemy in strength covering Nasiriya, and on the 10th he opened heavy gun-fire, mostly directed on the section of the mountain battery in the forward line, where its commander was killed.

On 14th July an attack was mounted on both banks of the river, 10th (Abbottabad) Mountain Battery, less one section, on the right bank and the third section on the left. The attack on the right bank failed, and the one on the left bank was cancelled; the 18th Infantry Brigade was sent for, and some more heavy guns. A fresh attack was mounted on 24th with an infantry brigade on each bank of the river, the mountain battery being in support of the 12th Infantry Brigade on the left. The brigade, led by the Royal West Kent Regiment, made a dashing and gallant attack over the open ground, cleared the trenches which were their objective and, after re-forming, continued the advance northwards.

The right attack found some difficulty in advancing through high grass, but wading waist deep through water channels, under cover of the fire of heavy guns, with great courage and dash the 30th Infantry Brigade pushed back the Turks, and by 6 p.m. the two brigades were level on both banks, the Turks were fleeing in disorder across the marshes, and white flags were flying in Nasiriya.

Turkish casualties were estimated at 2,000, the British 533; and 15 guns were captured by the victors.

General Nixon's despatch praised very highly the gallantry and devotion of the troops in trying heat and unhealthy marshes; British vied with Indians to display gallantry and devotion to duty worthy of the highest tradition. His Majesty the King's message ran: "The splendid achievement of General Gorringe's column in spite of many hardships and intense heat fills me with admiration."

The Basra vilaiyat was now secure, and the oil-field and refinery covered and protected.

These victories produced a wave of optimism among the powers that be, anxious for a success in the Middle East to make up for our lack of success in Gallipoli, and a dash to capture Baghdad was seriously considered. This would entail reinforcing Force "D," and India could ill spare any troops. The internal situation there was deteriorating, and the frontier tribes had been giving trouble. In Waziristan and in Mohmand country big raids had taken place and efforts were being made to start a jehad; the trans-frontier Pathans in the Indian Army were not eager to fight the Turks, and a state of unrest was growing in the Punjab, where efforts were being made to tamper with Indian troops and a general rising had to be guarded against. The early arrest of the conspirators had a very good effect.

Shields were made up in the ordnance workshops at Basra for the 10-prs., but they were found to be not bullet-proof at 600 yards and their use was discontinued. Observation ladders were issued in July, 1915, giving a command of ten feet, which was generally enough to overcome the mirage. The frames were telescopic, and the whole contraption could be carried on one mule.

The mountain batteries did not take part in General Townshend's advance to Ctesiphon and withdrawal to Kut al Amara. The headquarters of the 1st Indian Mountain Artillery Brigade went with the 6th (Poona) Division as far as Ctesiphon; strength, one British officer and seven Indian other ranks. Captain Cock, the Adjutant, was wounded at that place and eventually died of wounds. Brigadier-General H. D. Grier, C.B., was wounded in Kut while acting as C.R.A.

The 6th (Poona) Division received reinforcements, but still remained short of field artillery, and was supported by a river flotilla and reconnaissance aeroplanes in its advance in the early part of September; it fought its way up the Tigris for nearly 500 miles until it was halted at Ctesiphon by strong Turkish forces.

River transport was found insufficient for the work; and land transport was of a very mixed nature; the going, too, was very rough and cut up by nullahs, and the Division found itself up against trained Turkish troops instead of, as heretofore, Arab forces stiffened by Turks. Nothing but the high quality of the endurance and bravery of British and Indian soldiers could have taken the Division so far. There was nothing to be done but withdraw, with numbers much reduced by sickness and casualties, and the troops, mostly young soldiers, responded to the extra call on their endurance and discipline in a truly magnificent way.

The garrison of the entrenched camp at Kut, which included one section of the 3rd (Peshawar) Mountain Battery, was withdrawn, and General Townshend's force marched in on 3rd December, 1915, being beleaguered by five or six Turkish divisions immediately afterwards. The camp was on a peninsula about two miles by one mile, and thus surrounded on three sides by water. General Townshend's ration strength was about 9,000.

Immediate steps were taken by General Nixon to prepare a relieving force, but reinforcements had to be awaited.

Infantry brigades were sent from India and the two divisions of the 1st Indian Corps in France, which were now available, were embarked piecemeal at Marseilles. The force was now an Army, of which the Tigris Corps was commanded by Lieutenant-General F. J. Aylmer, V.C.

In order not to break into the Tigris Operations for the relief of Kut, a digression is here made to describe an operation on the Euphrates line in which the 10th (Abbottabad) Mountain Battery took part. Large enemy forces had been reported near Butaniya, about twelve miles north of Nasiriya, to deal with which General Gorringe was ordered to move a column up the Shatt al Hai. On

14th January, 1916, a force of one battalion and a section of the mountain battery moved out of Butaniya and ran into a large force of Arabs, who at once tried to surround the small column. A rearguard action was begun and two battalions and two more mountain guns were hurried to the scene to extricate the force, which returned to camp, but not before it had suffered forty casualties.

To return to the Tigris: it seemed to General Nixon that it was imperative to relieve Kut before the Turks who had been released from Gallipoli by our withdrawal should have reinforced the investing army, and General Aylmer was ordered to move to Kut with all the troops available. The first attempt at relief falls into three operations, none of which was successful. The 3rd (Peshawar) Battery (four guns) was on the Tigris line at Amara until the relief force was collected, when it joined Corps troops at Ali Gharbi.

The Turks had entrenched a force at Shaikh Saad, some miles below Kut: General Younghusband with 7th (Meerut) Division and details was ordered to advance to Shaikh Saad and no farther. He advanced on 4th January, 1916, with a brigade on each bank, and found the Turks in front of Shaikh Saad in much greater strength than he expected. The Turkish trenches outflanked our front on both sides of the river. Storms and rain made the going bad. The four guns of the 3rd (Peshawar) Mountain Battery were part of the reserve brought up from Ali Gharbi by General Aylmer on 6th January. On the 7th one section of the mountain battery marched with the 21st Infantry Brigade along the right bank, and the other section with the 9th Infantry Brigade along the left bank to reinforce the 7th (Meerut) Division.

The attack was put in at noon: Major-General Kemball on the right bank had the 28th Infantry Brigade, one field battery and the mountain battery; Major-General Younghusband on the left bank had three infantry brigades supported by four field batteries.

The Turkish trenches were well sited, and the left bank column, advancing with difficulty to within 300 or 400 yards of the trenches, dug themselves in. The mud and the rain, added to desultory fire, provided a most unpleasant night, and there were many casualties. The right bank column met with more success—the fire of the field battery directed by a Forward Observing Officer among the infantry was very effective, and the mountain battery, firing at 2,500 yards, kept down the fire from the trenches flanking the advance. Two lines of trenches were taken by assault, but a further advance could not be made and the force bivouacked on the spot. Here also casualties were very numerous; the 51st and 53rd Sikhs and 56th

Rifles each lost over 200 officers and men. The Turkish force was about 12,000 rifles and 30 guns.

The next day no advance was made on the left bank, and a very short one by General Kemball on the right bank. The rain and the mud prevented movement, the troops were exhausted, and the medical arrangements quite inadequate. The next day the force advanced to Shaikh Saad, which had been evacuated by the Turks, and the force halted and was reorganized. Casualties were about 4,000 on both sides.

The Turks then occupied a position some eight miles to the northwest, behind the River Wadi, which runs into the Tigris at right angles on the left bank. Entrenchments were thrown up on the right bank and some watercuts covering their extreme left flank were also entrenched. By this time Field-Marshal von der Goltz, a German of great reputation, had arrived and taken over command of the Turkish armies in Southern Mesopotamia.

General Aylmer ordered the 7th (Meerut) Division to cross the Wadi about four miles from its junction with the Tigris, starting from a position of assembly in the desert, to which the Division would move in the hours of darkness. The 9th Brigade, R.F.A., 1/1 Sussex Battery, R.F.A., and the 3rd (Peshawar) Mountain Battery (four guns) comprised the divisional artillery for this operation. The 28th Infantry Brigade was to cross by the bridge from the right bank and hold the enemy in front, while the 7th (Meerut) Division and Cavalry Brigade were to envelop the position by a wide turning movement.

The 7th (Meerut) Division was held up by fire from a line of trenches covering the Turks' left flank, and the Wadi proved to be a very difficult obstacle. The 3rd (Peshawar) Mountain Battery moved forward between the 19th and 35th Infantry Brigades to give close support, and the Turkish trenches were penetrated, but our troops were afterwards driven out. The 28th Infantry Brigade attacked prematurely with the greatest determination over open country, but were unable to cross the Wadi and suffered very heavy casualties. The Turks slipped away during the night to their next position, the Hanna defile. They had again been beaten, and again the weather changed for the worse, making movement impossible. The countryside was now a sea of mud.

The 10-prs. expended 400 shrapnel at the actions of Shaikh Saad and the Wadi.

The 3rd (Lahore) Division under Major-General H. D'U. Keary was now concentrating at the front, and the 3rd (Peshawar) Mountain Battery joined the 3rd Divisional Artillery; C.R.A., Colonel

F. S. Stallard. The bridge over the Tigris having been destroyed by a storm, the section of the battery which was ordered to the right bank had to be ferried over, and the other followed the next day.

It was now 17th January and General Townshend had only twenty-one days' rations left in Kut. At this time General Nixon's health broke down and on 19th he was relieved by Lieutenant-General Sir P. H. Lake as commander in Mesopotamia.

The Turks had thoroughly fortified the new position and erected wire entanglements by the time the weather cleared to permit of an attack. The position stretched between the Tigris and a marsh, with an equally strong line in rear at Sannaiyat, the other end of the defile. A frontal attack was to be put in after a ten-minute bombardment, when the guns were to lift on to the second line. On the right bank the 7th Infantry Brigade was supported by the 3rd Divisional Artillery, which was almost enfilading the Turkish front trenches.

The 35th Infantry Brigade advanced with the utmost gallantry and, where the wire was cut, penetration was made; but this was only on a length of 150 yards and, as no supporting troops arrived, the British were forced to retire when counter-attacked.

The weather became extremely bad and the troops were numbed with cold and soaked, and the force was withdrawn from contact. The casualties had again been very heavy—2,700, including 78 British officers; an indication of the gallantry and determination with which the attack was pushed home.

The effect of the fire from the right bank appears to have been small. During this attack the 10-prs. fired 955 shrapnel and the 18-prs. 8,000 shrapnel, no H.E. or smoke shell having yet been issued. The 60-prs. of the force were in Kut and the only batteries, other than field and mountain, available for these attacks in January were armed with eight 5-inch howitzers and two 4-inch guns. The gunboats which took part had 4-inch guns and 12-prs. This armament proved too light for the support of an attack on a strongly entrenched position.

No further attempt could be made to relieve Kut without a reorganization and some fresh troops. The month of February was occupied with these preparations and occasional shoots by the mountain guns at aeroplanes. This was carried out by dropping the trail into a hole, and the gun was traversed by pivoting the carriage round the trail. Laying was over open sights, and fuzes were guessed. It was noted that Major Hunt found time to shoot a certain number of sand grouse. The 3rd (Peshawar) Mountain Battery (four guns) remained in the 3rd Divisional Artillery during the second and third attempts to relieve Kut.

By the beginning of March General Aylmer's Corps had been increased to 24,000 rifles and 92 guns, and he decided to attack the enemy position on the right bank at Es Sinn, some eight miles up-river from Sannaiyat, on 8th March. A strong-point, the Dujaila redoubt in the Dujaila depression (a former bed of the Tigris of varying depth) on the Turkish right, had first to be captured. The beleaguered garrison was to co-operate.

The plan was to surprise the Turks after a night march across the desert, which for the artillery was about six miles, with a total force of 18,000 rifles, 68 guns and a cavalry brigade. The strength of the Turks was thought to be about 11,000.

Two columns under Major-General Kemball were responsible for the attack; Major-General Keary's force consisted of three infantry brigades and the divisional artillery (36 pieces). The latter had orders to be in action by 6.15 a.m. about 3,500 yards from the enemy's position covering the line from Suin Abtar redoubt to Dujaila redoubt. Once in action, it was to be under the hand of the Corps Commander. The infantry of the 3rd (Lahore) Division were to support by fire General Kemball's flank attack.

Nine aeroplanes (rather the worse for wear) were available, but were not mentioned in the Operation Order.

The night march met with delays, and General Kemball's force was late arriving at the depression in which he placed his troops under cover whilst reconnaissance was made for the attack.

The Turks were surprised, but had time to reinforce their right before the British advance began at 9.35 a.m. It was found that the redoubt was much farther off than it seemed, and a long advance had to be made in open country before the infantry came up against the wire and trenches in front of the redoubt, which had been neglected by the artillery, owing to F.O.O. having been killed.

The 37th Infantry Brigade, which was under Corps Headquarters, had been put into the fight and was occupying a trench 400 yards south-east of the redoubt; the other attacking brigades were at a much greater distance from the redoubt, held up by fire from the Turkish trenches. After midday the 8th Infantry Brigade and the 3rd (Peshawar) Mountain Battery were moved to a position from which they could support the 37th Infantry Brigade.

An assault was made at 4.30 p.m. by the 8th Infantry Brigade with two battalions of the 37th Infantry Brigade, supported by a heavy bombardment. The 8th Brigade had 3,000 yards to go before the actual assault could begin, but the advance progressed steadily and, dashing through heavy machine-gun and rifle fire, companies of the 1st Manchesters, backed by an accurate artillery barrage, were first into the redoubt, followed by portions of other units. Unfortunately they could not stay there: grenades ran short and a strong counter-attack drove them out, their withdrawal splendidly covered by the 47th Sikhs.

This was practically the end: it was getting dark and the troops were exhausted. The Turks made no counter-offensive, and the British drew off next day without molestation except for a few shells, and went back to camp at Wadi.

British casualties amounted to 3,474; several battalions losing over 30 per cent. of their strength. The situation never became sufficiently favourable to allow of General Townshend's force co-operating.

The artillery had again proved insufficient in numbers and inadequate in fire power to support the storming of a strongly entrenched position. More artillery was on its way to the front, as well as a more powerful gunboat for the Navy, mounting two 6-inch and two 12-pr. guns.

On 11th March, Lieutenant-General Gorringe took over command from Lieutenant-General Aylmer.

By April the force included eight 60-prs., 102 18-prs., with high-explosive shell for both these types, but was still short of howitzers, there being only twelve 4.5-inch and twenty-four 5-inch in the country. On 8th March the 7th Indian Mountain Artillery Brigade, comprising 1st (Kohat) and 6th (Jacob's) Mountain Batteries,* arrived at Basra, having been refitted in Egypt after the Gallipoli operations and rearmed with the 2.75-inch gun. For a short time it acted as divisional artillery to the new 15th (Indian) Division, but was later transferred to the line of communication. It included the 10th (Abbottabad) Mountain Battery until the latter departed for East Africa in October, 1916. Major H. J. Cotter had been posted to the Indian Mountain Artillery Depot at Abbottabad in June, and Captain F. O. Wyatt now commanded this battery. The 1st I.M.A. Brigade Headquarters was absorbed into the batteries in February, 1917.

The administration of the army was in a confused state owing to the inadequacy of Basra as a base port, and to the difference between British and Indian establishments. Brigadier-General G. F. MacMunn, D.S.O., formerly in the mountain artillery, became Inspector-General of Communications on 16th April.

Regular floods were to be expected in April, and General Townshend's troops were very near the end of their rations—so speed was imperative for an early relief of Kut. The maximum number of

---

* At this time named 21st Kohat and 26th Jacob's Mountain Batteries.

troops which could be maintained up the river was collected, and an advance on the Hanna position was prepared for 5th April.

The 13th, an all-British Division, commanded by Major-General F. S. Maude, had recently arrived from Egypt, having been re-equipped after the evacuation from Suvla, and was entrusted with the attack, supported by the 7th (Lahore) Division. The artillery bombardment was to start three minutes after the commencement of the infantry advance and the guns on the right bank, which formed the majority of the artillery, were to maintain a barrage in front of the infantry, taking the trenches in enfilade.

The Turkish trenches were found to be unoccupied and General Maude's infantry advanced without delay to keep contact, finding the Turks occupying a position four miles in rear. The 13th Division with the utmost bravery assaulted this position, and carried it after meeting with strong resistance. During the day's work the division suffered 1,868 casualties out of 1,885 for the whole force.

It was a further three miles to the main Turkish position at Sannaiyat, and orders were issued for attack next day at dawn by the 7th (Meerut) Division. The 3rd (Lahore) Division during 5th April had advanced on the right bank, meeting with little resistance, and by night was holding a line about four miles long at right angles to the river from opposite Sannaiyat.

There had not been time for much reconnaissance and the floods were now pronounced, especially on the right bank, where the 3rd (Lahore) Division had to be supplied from boats. The attack went in and was stopped about 400 yards in front of the trenches. Another attack the next morning by the 13th Division failed, with 1,800 casualties in the division, which was now much under strength; in this action the Oxfordshire and Buckinghamshire Light Infantry (Provisional Battalion) started with 13 officers and 266 other ranks, and all the officers and 220 other ranks were either killed or wounded.

The floods had now become inundations; the weather was very hot, and plagues of sandflies afflicted both animals and men.

General Lake decided that the next attempt should be made on the right bank of the Tigris.

On 10th April the forward line of the 3rd (Lahore) Division extended southwards from the river about three miles at Abu Rumman. It was almost surrounded by floods, but there was a fairly dry tract to the south-west and General Keary proposed to move his division from that direction to attack the Turkish position at Bait Isa. For the last few days the troops had been called on to throw up embankments in order to make any kind of movement possible, and torrents of rain fell, making the ground waterlogged.

Notwithstanding the difficulties, the division advanced, most of the time under fire, about 2,500 yards nearer Bait Isa, and established a line of trenches. The 3rd (Peshawar) Mountain Battery was held in readiness at Abu Rumman to act as required.

The Turks, aided by a north-easterly gale, managed to increase the discomfort by making the inundations deeper, and some of the trenches had to be evacuated. The floods were bad all the way back to Amara, preventing land movements and necessitating river transport for all movement on the line of communications.

On 15th April an attack by the 7th and 9th Infantry Brigades captured some Turkish trenches nearer Bait Isa, and the 3rd (Peshawar) Battery and 14th Brigade, R.F.A., were brought forward to Rohdes Piquet. On the 16th preparations were made for the attack of Bait Isa, 600 to 900 yards from our front line. On this occasion the 7th and 9th Infantry Brigades dashed into their first objective before the bombardment stopped. They went on and completed their programme and consolidated with a view to handing over to the 13th Division at night.

At 7.30 p.m. the Turks counter-attacked in overwhelming numbers and broke through our right. Isolated detachments stood fast and fought on, and the arrival of the 13th Division mended matters. On our left the Turks encircled the 8th Infantry Brigade, but men of the Manchesters, 47th Sikhs and 59th Rifles, supported effectively by the four guns of the 3rd (Peshawar) Mountain Battery behind them, beat off all attacks with grim determination.

Three more counter-attacks were put in by the Turks during the night, but they failed to break the stout defence of the 8th Infantry Brigade, and, of the supporting artillery, the 3rd (Peshawar) Mountain Battery under Major Hunt was reported as having rendered especially effective assistance.

The 3rd Indian Army Corps' Order of the Day, dated 29th April, 1916, stated " . . . During this stand, the following units especially distinguished themselves: 23rd Mountain Battery . . ." (followed by the names of seven other units).

The Official History, Vol. II, page 420, states: "The main honours of the fighting during the night lay with the Connaught Rangers, No. 2 Company, Manchesters, 27th Punjabis, 47th Sikhs, 59th Rifles, and the 14th and 66th Field and 23rd (Peshawar) Mountain Batteries."

Undeterred, with his effective fighting strength reduced to half its original numbers, General Gorringe decided to make a final attempt to capture Sannaiyat by direct assault. The 3rd (Lahore) and 13th Divisions were to remain on the right bank and support with machine-gun and artillery fire.

The 7th (Meerut) Division made a most gallant attack and captured part of the Turkish first line; the attackers were up to their knees in water, some even up to their waists, but they were not in sufficient strength to withstand counter-attacks. Their gallantry and pluck were superb, but they had reached their limit. On 22nd April it was decided to abandon the relief, and Kut surrendered on the 29th. Notwithstanding the stupendous efforts of the troops, they had failed in their object, but they were defeated by the weather more than by the enemy.

In the course of four months' operations the Tigris Corps had lost over 23,000 officers and men.

General Maude shortly afterwards took over the Tigris Corps from General Gorringe, a few days after Halil Bey had taken over command of the Turkish Armies in Mesopotamia on the death of Field-Marshal von der Goltz.

In July the War Office took over control of the campaign, and in the following month Lieutenant-General F. S. Maude was appointed Commander-in-Chief. The remainder of the year was free from large-scale operations while preparations for an advance were in hand.

After the fall of Kut the 3rd (Peshawar) Battery, less one section, was sent down-river to South Persia to join the force protecting the oil-fields and pipe-line. Sections were frequently out with movable columns. Many changes of officers took place; Major Hunt, who left in April to command a field battery, had distinguished himself at Ahwaz and Bait Isa.

The right section under Captain R. S. Rothwell, which had been left at Basra when the battery went up-river, was sent to Bushire in May, 1916, and struck off the strength of the battery; it was replaced in the following September by a new section raised for the purpose in India. The battery soon afterwards returned to India, arriving at Burhan Camp in December, 1916.

In September, 1916, while on the line of communication, the 1st (Kohat) and 6th (Jacob's) Batteries took part in a minor operation to punish some Arabs at As Sahilan (five miles north-east of Nasiriya) for attacking a small mixed detachment. Part of our force destroyed the fortifications of the village, whilst the remainder protected the communications. After the withdrawal of the first column, the advancing Arabs became engaged with the second column and a very brisk fight ensued. The 1st (Kohat) Battery fired 438 rounds and had three gunners wounded. The Arabs had about 1,000 casualties compared with our 200. The moral effect of this success was enormous and peace reigned in that district for many months.

Batteries practised crossing rivers, and reported that any mule-load complete with saddle, wrapped in a pawlin, would float; also that a gun turned upside down, wrapped in a large pawlin with log-line tied to form the framework of a boat, would not only float but carry two men as well.

The 6th (Jacob's) Battery was employed on the Tigris L. of C. until it was sent forward in December, 1917, for the third action of the Jabal Hamrin.

The 1st (Kohat) Battery was divided between Ahwaz and Basra from November, 1916 until May, 1918, when it reassembled at Baghdad, Major R. C. Garrett being in command.

It was relieved by the 31st Mountain Battery [later to be renamed the 11th (Dehra Dun) Mountain Battery] under Major S. Perry. Captain H. H. Mackenzie left the Kohat Battery in December, 1917, to command No. 14 British Mountain Battery, R.G.A. This battery had been formed at Basra for L. of C. defences in October, 1917, and had an establishment for draught only: two mules per gun and one for ammunition, minimum detachments, no battery staff, four officers, and one horse. Major G. A. Hassells-Yates, R.G.A., raised this battery at Basra as well as No. 15 Mountain Battery, R.G.A., on the same date and on similar lines. Many of the gunners came from field artillery, and the native drivers were sent from India. The batteries were armed with six 2.75-inch guns, and in November, 1917, were moved, No. 14 to the Euphrates L. of C. and No. 15 (Captain C. Flowers, R.F.A.) to the Tigris line, relieving at Bughaila the 6th (Jacob's) Mountain Battery. These two British batteries became the 49th and 50th Indian Mountain Batteries respectively in February, 1919, on the normal establishment, and fought during the Arab rebellion (1920).

No mountain batteries took part in General Maude's operations which led to the occupation of Baghdad on 11th March, 1917, after the rout of the Turkish Army.

After the capture of Baghdad neither troops nor transport were available to complete the pursuit of the Turkish armies, and General Maude had to be content with room for manœuvre. The Turkish line stabilized for a time about Tikrit on the Tigris and Hit on the Euphrates; but the Turks actively supported the Kurds in Kurdistan and North-West Persia, who were carrying out raids and harassing our flanks as much as possible. The Russians were guarding the flank at Qizil Rabat; but their assistance faded out as the results of the Russian Revolution of March became known, and they withdrew northwards. As the probability of Russian help receded, so the actual danger on the Persian border increased. German and Turkish emissaries financed by Germany were overrunning Persia and fostering anti-British activities which, it was thought, might penetrate to Afghanistan.

By September, 1917, the Turks, though incapable of a large offensive, began to send small bodies of troops into Persia, and occupied the western slopes of Jabal Hamrin. Possession of this range would screen off the Turks from Persia, and General Marshall was sent with III Corps to capture and hold it. His plan was to secure Deli Abbas, then hold the Turks in front and roll up their left.

With the Right Group (Major-General Egerton) of one cavalry and two infantry brigades, a section of 6th (Jacob's) Mountain Battery was included in the artillery, which consisted of six 13-prs., twenty-two 18-prs. and ten 4.5-inch howitzers. The Centre and Left Groups were equally well provided with artillery.

The Right Group moved to a point twelve miles east of Shahraban while the other groups drove the Turks back on to the hills. On 19th October General Marshall sent the cavalry brigade to cut the Khanigin road, whereupon the Turks withdrew and the infantry moved along the crest in a north-westerly direction. The Centre Group was not opposed, but the Left Group found itself facing a strongly entrenched position. Early on the 20th the Turks withdrew, and our mounted troops rode into Qizil Rabat. Our total casualties were less than forty.

To the great regret of the whole army, General Maude died of cholera at Baghdad on 18th November, 1917, in the same house in which Field-Marshal von der Goltz had died. Lieutenant-General W. R. Marshall, III Corps Commander, was appointed Commander-in-Chief in his place.

In December, 1917, the Russians made an armistice with the Turks, and the problem confronting General Marshall became more serious. A British mission was sent to the Caucasus in January, 1918, under Brigadier-General L. C. Dunsterville ("Dunsterforce"), with instructions to raise effective local forces on the Caucasus front and to counter Bolshevik propaganda in Persia, where, in face of a strong anti-British element, what Persian army existed was incapable of keeping order.

The only practicable line of communication ran via Khanigin, Kermanshah and Hamadan to Enzeli on the Caspian, about 600 miles, and the occupation of this line also covered the right flank of the Expeditionary Force. Its extent swallowed up more transport than the army could readily spare, and major operations had to be restricted.

With a few cars General Dunsterville left Kermanshah on 4th February, and found the roads almost impassable. The attitude of the tribes along the route and of the Persians was unfriendly and the whole area was devastated and famine-stricken. The column was greatly delayed by snow, and on reaching Enzeli found the Bolsheviks in control; it then withdrew to Hamadan. While waiting here for the remainder of the mission and for roads to become passable, famine relief work and the raising of levies were undertaken.

Dunsterville's orders were varied in May to advance to Baku and cover the oil-fields, in which direction Turkish forces were known to be advancing. The Turks were collecting an army in the Caucasus with a view to paying off some old scores against the Russians, incidentally overrunning Armenia, whereupon hundreds of thousands of Armenians overflowed into Persia as refugees. The line of communication to Hamadan had caused some concern, the result being that a small force under Lieutenant-Colonel Matthews, consisting of his 1/4th Hampshire, one section of 6th (Jacob's) Battery, and ancillary troops, advanced from Pai Taq to Kermanshah in March, and by the end of the month the whole line from Qasr-i-Shirin to Hamadan was occupied, under command of the 36th Infantry Brigade Group.

In April the 13th Division moved north from the Diyala, and after an engagement at Tuz Khurmatli occupied Kirkuk, the centre of an oil-producing district. The divisional artillery included 6th (Jacob's) Mountain Battery (less one section at Surkadiza), which had thirteen casualties. Troops of I Corps advanced on the left at the same time, but on the capture of Kirkuk fell back to Samarra. The force at Kirkuk withdrew south-east to Tuz Khurmatli in May.

The Turks in Transcaucasia were now very active, and German troops were moving towards Baku, which was in the hands of the Bolsheviks, who were at this time an unknown quantity. In June "Dunsterforce," strength about 400 of the mission, with in addition a mobile column of two companies each of 1/4th Hampshire and 1/2nd Gurkhas, a squadron of 14th Hussars, a section of 1st (Kohat) Mountain Battery, six armoured cars and 500 Ford vans, was at Kazvin and Hamadan. A flight of aircraft was now at Hamadan. The section of 6th (Jacob's) Battery was at Kermanshah.

In pursuance of his new orders, General Dunsterville was getting ready to advance to Baku—control of its oil-fields would indirectly give command of the Caspian sea and its shipping. The 39th Infantry Brigade (two weak battalions plus details) and the 8th Field Brigade, R.A., pushed ahead along the line of communication. In June the Right Section of the 1st (Kohat) Battery (Captain R. E. Ross and Lieutenant M. R. W. Johnston, I.A.R.O.), leaving their mules behind, joined Colonel Matthews' mobile column with their guns in Ford vans (these were the original Model T and were inclined to be temperamental). The column opened the road via Kasvin to Resht, and were followed by the troops destined for Baku. Before their arrival an attack was launched on Resht on 20th July by Jangali troops. These were irregulars from the province of Gilan (which included Resht), but they had been organized and trained by German and Austrian officers. The attack was beaten off, but the section lost Lieutenant Johnston, who was ambushed and murdered. For gallantry and resource in this operation, Havildar Jaggat Singh and Gunner Kishen Singh were awarded the I.D.S.M.

The section was sent to Zenjan in August, where it was rejoined by its mules, and went on to Turkmachai to support some troops withdrawing from Tabriz, afterwards returning to Zenjan. The section rejoined battery headquarters in May, 1919.

The Centre Section under Lieutenant Armitage was based on Kermanshah during most of 1918, occupied in pursuing Kurd raiders.

Much marching in rocky country brought to the fore the question of shoeing. It was ordered by G.H.Q. in 1918 that all mules were to be shod, but it seems that section commanders used their discretion. One section could only obtain Persian shoes, a light plate covering the whole foot. Another section had to shoe five mules; the third section none at all. Care in looking after the feet was essential. It is interesting that very many of the marches were carried out in draught.

Captain A. L. Pemberton, M.C., assumed command of the 1st Kohat Battery in August, 1918, and took it to Hamadan, where it spent the next twelve months, until the battery concentrated at Kasvin in September, 1919, before returning to India. It arrived at Abbottabad on 19th December after over five years overseas, and, as the Commandant recorded, throughout the First World War it did not once come into action as a whole battery.

The force which captured Baku in July had to withdraw owing to lack of support and Bolshevik hostility, and was back at Enzeli in September, at which time "Dunsterforce" was renamed North Persia Force, under Major-General W. M. Thomson, with headquarters at Hamadan.

Persia had been in a state of chaos throughout the war owing to the depredations of independent feudal leaders, and the presence of British and Indian troops was essential to implement our policy of keeping the country neutral. The War Office, Foreign Office and the Government of India assumed control of our interests in different parts of the country.

The Commander-in-Chief, Mesopotamia, was responsible for the North Persia Force, which in September, 1918, was increased to two brigades with attached troops spread out from Hamadan to Enzeli. Two and a half flights of aeroplanes and ample wireless communication were provided.

The Government of India controlled the Transcaspian Force of the 44th Battery, R.F.A., and one battalion, which were under the orders of Major-General Malleson, in charge of the Mission at Meshed. A section of this battery distinguished itself at Kaakha, near Krasnovodsk, in September by beating off a strong Bolshevik attack by its own fire unsupported by other troops. The possession of Krasnovodsk was necessary in order to carry out General Marshall's instructions to secure control of the Caspian Sea.

There seemed at this time to be little to fear from the Turks, who were now not on the best of terms with the Germans.

A British consul had been stationed at Nasratabad, on the border of Afghanistan and Persia, before the outbreak of war, and a line of communication to that place from railhead at Nushki was very lightly held by a few Indian troops and levies.

In order to prevent the infiltration of German agents through Persia into Afghanistan and the tribal districts of the North-West Frontier of India, and to stop gun-running to those areas, the East Persian Cordon was formed by the Government of India. Its line ran from Askabad in the north through Meshed and Birjand to Robat, and thence to Nushki; the section north of Meshed was in Russian hands until the Bolsheviks came into power, whereupon we took it over. In addition to being a supply depot for troops and levies on the Cordon, Meshed became a centre for relief of refugees from Armenia, and as the line ran over a waterless desert for 900 miles from railhead at Nushki, the only means of transport was by camel. To make up for a shortage of camels the railway was extended, and eventually reached Duzdab,* 250 miles from Nushki, in February, 1919.

In November, 1915, the 5th (Bombay) Mountain Battery† was railed to Quetta, and detached from there a section of 10-prs. under

---
* Later, called Zahidan.
† At this time, 25th Mountain Battery.

Lieutenant W. H. McGowan and J. English which marched 250 miles from Nushki to Robat in twenty-five marching days over heavy sand. Robat was the headquarters of a force of about a hundred infantry and a troop of cavalry, commanded by Brigadier-General R. E. H. Dyer.

The tribes of this district, the Sarhad, well armed with Mauser rifles, had no other occupation than raiding and looting the military convoys sent out to our posts. Brigadier-General Dyer in brilliant fashion, with his tiny force, a great deal of bluff, and a great deal of hard marching in extreme heat in a dry and waterless country, defeated the three most important tribes one by one. They were not familiar with artillery and were impressed with the 10-pr. shooting, so that in a few months the Sarhad was at peace, and raiding ceased for the time being.

In Seistan another section of the 5th (Bombay) Battery with two battalions was doing similar protective work, and our line was continued southwards to the Persian Gulf, there being a Mekran Mission escort at Chahbaz.

The battery at this time had its headquarters and one section at Quetta, the above two detached sections and a fourth section in Chitral.

Work continued in the Cordon with no important disruptions, and the section returned to India in March, 1917. However, as Bolshevik pressure from Merv went on increasing, an extra battalion was sent to the Cordon from India, along with No. 1 Kashmir Mountain Battery (see page 425) in February, 1919. The Cordon was closed down in October, 1920, and the troops returned to India.

The section of the 3rd (Peshawar) Mountain Battery which was sent to Bushire found itself in a very disaffected district, owing to the skilful way in which the German ex-consul Wassmuss organized anti-British elements from the local outlaws and brigands. Bushire itself, which is on a peninsula, was cut off from the mainland for a time and had to be relieved; and the important trade route to Shiraz, 200 miles inland, was completely blocked for several months. The latter place was the headquarters of a Mission under Sir Percy Sykes, for which the Foreign Office was responsible, whereas Bushire was under the Mesopotamian Expeditionary Force.

On the arrival of the section, a relieving force was sent to Shiraz via Kermanshah; the direct road from Bushire, though several hundred miles shorter, crossed a high pass amid some difficult country which could not be attempted with the force available.

The section under Major R. S. Rothwell was in Shiraz for a time, whilst the South Persia Rifles was being formed. This was a force of all arms of 10,000 levies, including two mountain batteries, each with two British and five Persian officers and three British N.C.O. instructors.

The section was very busy on convoy work in addition to several minor actions against the outlaws. There was a brisk affair when an attempt was made to force a passage along the main trade route to Shiraz, and Major Rothwell was in command of a small mixed force which carried out a successful punitive operation at Khwaja Jamali.

Shiraz was again besieged in 1918, and the situation was not properly in hand until more troops arrived from India and the Bushire Field Force was formed. The 35th (Reserve) Mountain Battery—later the 15th (Jhelum)—under Major R. M. L. Dutton was among the reinforcements; the Centre Section under Captain J. S. Heaton-Ellis was landed at Bunder Abbas on the way, and the battery, on arrival at Bushire on 27th July, was made up to six guns by the attachment of the section of the 3rd (Peshawar) Battery already at that place, which had remained independent. This did not take place until 30th November; the battery, however, had been in action several times with four guns.

There was an affair in the hills above Borazjun during which the F.O.O. and party moving with the flank guard were surrounded by the enemy, whereupon Signaller Sirdar Khan broke through the enemy to bring information, and the party was extricated. At Ahram fort the battery appropriated a 7-cm. bronze Krupp gun as a souvenir.

On 20th December the battery supported the 55th Coke's Rifles at the capture of the Kamarij Pass, one section going forward in close support while the remainder covered the advance. The commander, Brigadier-General Elsmie, thanked the battery "for the accuracy and judgment of its covering fire," and all ranks of Coke's Rifles sent thanks for the "able support which saved many casualties." This success finally opened up the road to Shiraz, though many outlaws remained at large. The battery remained for some months at Kazerun, where the Centre Section rejoined from Saidabad, 120 miles north of Bunder Abbas, where it had spent seven months. The Field Force was absorbed into the garrison in May, 1919, and the battery was ordered back to India.

It had one last operation while waiting at Bushire to embark, being sent off with a punitive force against some outlaws, when it marched fifty miles in twenty hours in great heat. It arrived back in India in May, and was warned for service in the Tochi at once.

In March, 1918, Major Rothwell's section of the 3rd (Peshawar) Mountain Battery was ordered to Shiraz, there to be combined with two sections of the 33rd (Reserve) Mountain Battery which had been sent for the purpose from India, landing at Bandar Abbas on the 30th. The three sections joined in May and were called locally "I.M.A. Shiraz" for a short time until Captain C. R. Willis formed them into the 36th (Reserve) Mountain Battery, later to be known as the 16th (Zhob) Mountain Battery. A draft of Jemadar Sher Khan and fifty-two men from the 2nd (Derajat) Battery was sent to complete the battery.

The fort of Khan-i-Zinian, thirty miles west of Shiraz, was garrisoned by a detachment of South Persia Rifles, and on information being received that it was surrounded by great numbers of hostile Qashqais,* a relief column set out on 24th May under Colonel E. F. Orton. In the column were 3/124th Baluchis, Burma Mounted Rifles and 16th (Zhob) Mountain Battery less one section. At Deh Shaikh on the way the tribesmen were found in force and were at once attacked, the fight lasting all day. The sections of the battery, commanded by Captain Willis and Lieutenant O. R. Pender-Smith, supported different units and fired 500 rounds between them before the enemy was completely dispersed. It was learnt that some of the garrison had mutinied, and the South Persia Rifles were found to be unreliable, so the column returned to Shiraz on the 27th and organized a defensive position there.

This position ran through a number of Persian gardens (baghs) adjoining one another, about a quarter of a mile outside the city; four gun positions were prepared, two of which were occupied by day and the guns withdrawn at night. The strength of the garrison was about 1,700 with the six 10-prs. and one field gun (manned by British N.C.O. instructors).

The first attack was made on 8th June by about 5,000 tribesmen, and the Left Section fired 25 rounds to support the Baluchis, who drove off the enemy. On the 10th a piquet of the 16th Rajputs was attacked all night, but held out and was relieved on the 11th by a column with four 10-prs. There was some resistance and the battery fired 500 rounds.

An attack was expected on the 16th, and Colonel Orton took out his column as soon as the light permitted and drove off the enemy. All six mountain guns were present and gave splendid support covering the withdrawal to the Shiraz lines at the end of the day. The Left Section when nearly cut off had occasion to fire 17 rounds

---

* Pastoral nomads, who paid no taxes.

"magazine fire" at fuze O. The battery fired about 700 rounds this day.

An attack seemed probable for the 27th, so a column moved out to anticipate it, and it faded away. A column engaged the enemy again on 8th July, but met with little resistance.

On 10th July the Left Section went with a small column of Burma Mounted Rifles and Baluchis to relieve Abadeh Fort, about 180 miles north, on the road to Isfahan, where the small garrison of British and Indian troops had been beleaguered since the 28th June by Qashqais and mutineer levies. Lieutenant-Colonel Fraser had held out against enormous odds, and the fort was relieved on 17th July by the column, which made a forced march of 180 miles in seven days in intense heat.

Shiraz was now free from siege, and convoys were running through; with the first one (5th August) came Major R. S. Rothwell, the new commandant of the battery. For services during the siege Captain C. R. Willis was awarded the Military Cross; Subadar Karam Singh, the Indian Order of Merit; Jemadar Sher Khan, Havildar-Major Munsha Singh, and Havildar Habib Khan, the I.D.S.M., and several other ranks were mentioned in despatches.

There was a small operation in October, but two sections which were out on a column to protect a friendly khan were caught by the influenza epidemic which created havoc in our armies in 1918. They were in bivouac, and lost 64 men out of 192 from pneumonia and influenza. The Right Section in Shiraz lost 13 men.

The Indian troops were much impressed with the transport mules of South Persia; standing 15 hands high, they carried a weight half as much again as the Indian mules—240 lb. instead of 160.

From April, 1919, until it was withdrawn to India with the remaining Indian troops in April, 1920, the battery remained at Shiraz, with one section on detachment at Kazerun.

The 11th (Dehra Dun)* Battery was very busy at Ahwaz and on the Karun protecting the pipe-line, and one section was mentioned in a despatch by the Commander-in-Chief for having covered a distance of 395 miles in twenty-eight marching days during the hottest period of the year, "returning with men and animals in most excellent condition."

In November, 1919, the battery was with the North Persia force, at this time reduced to six battalions. It was in excellent company, the only other artillery unit being the Chestnut Troop. In October, 1920, Major-General Sir Edmund Ironside, K.C.B., D.S.O. (after-

---

* At this time, 31st Mountain Battery.

wards Field-Marshal Lord Ironside of Archangel), a Royal Artillery officer, took over command of the "Norper Force" and remained in command until injured in an aeroplane accident in the following March. The force was soon afterwards withdrawn, and the Indian troops sent back to India.

To return to the main operations in Mesopotamia.

The 7th (Indian) Division was replaced by a new 17th Division in December, 1917, and the 3rd (Indian) by the 18th Division in March, 1918. The infantry of the new divisions was formed in brigades consisting of one British and three Indian battalions, as were all the other brigades in the force except those of the 13th Division, which remained all British throughout. Operations were now being carried out in divisional or brigade groups.

The Turks were placed in a position of great difficulty by the British victories in Palestine, and General Marshall was ordered to advance towards Mosul in order to keep them on the move and to hinder any fostering of anti-British feeling amongst the local populations.

The advance up the Tigris was made in two groups, the 18th Division Group operating on the left bank, and the 17th Division Group on the right bank. Good air support was available. The enemy was occupying a strongly entrenched position at the Fat-ha gorge; on either side the Jabal Makhul and the Jabal Hamrin rose abruptly 1,000 feet. Steep and rocky slopes made movement difficult.

Support by mountain guns was given by 2nd I.M.A. Brigade, consisting of the 5th (Bombay) and 14th (Rajputana)* Mountain Batteries which had recently arrived in the country. The latter battery (Major E. R. C. Wilson), less one section, was with the 17th Division Group, and the remainder of the brigade was with Brigadier-General Nightingale's 54th Infantry Brigade of the 18th Division on the Jabal Hamrin.

The advance began on 23rd October and, as contact was not made at once, both groups started a pursuit. On the left bank the Jabal Makhul afforded reasonably good going, but the Jabal Hamrin was precipitous and in many places impossible to climb. The 14th (Rajputana) Battery was later sent across the river with a column and engaged the artillery of the Turkish rear-guard. The fighting was not severe, but the troops were exhausted and the mules had to climb down a steep cliff and go several miles to water. On the 27th the centre section under Lieutenant B. W. P. Dodds rejoined the battery which was sent in support of the 34th Infantry Brigade, and the

---

* At this time, 34th Mountain Battery.

pursuit was continued, an enemy position being successfully carried.

On the 29th the 2nd I.M.A. Brigade took part in the battle of Sharqat, supporting the 51st Infantry Brigade which was held up by a strong enemy position. On the arrival of the divisional artillery an eight-minute barrage was fired, with a 300-yard lift for the next three minutes. Lieutenant Dodds as F.O.O. engaged infantry and machine-gun targets under heavy artillery fire, and the position was carried.

Lieutenant Dodds was awarded the Military Cross for coolness and gallantry in the action of 29th October, and two other ranks of his F.O.O. party were awarded the I.D.S.M. Lieutenant F. McF. Walker and Subadar Haidar Khan were mentioned in despatches.

On the 30th the advance was continued, but came to a sudden end at 7.15 a.m., at which hour the Turks surrendered and news of the armistice was published.

The total British and Indian casualties during the campaign in Mesopotamia were 14,000 killed, 12,000 died of disease, and 13,000 prisoners or missing.

The armistice with the Turks included a clause whereby we occupied Mosul and the Mosul vilayet which included Kurdistan. The Kurds were brave and warlike highlanders who lived by raiding and brigandry in much the same way as the North-West Frontier Pathans—in fact their modes of life were similar. They were not ill-disposed to us at this time, but seldom resisted an opportunity to cut up a poorly-guarded convoy. Early in the war they had been promised independence, but the promise was not kept and they became bitterly hostile. They had little in common with the Arabs of the plains, who were always rebellious but less warlike; fortunately incompatibility of temperament and interests of the two races prevented their combining even against a common enemy.

Steps were at once taken to reduce the troops in the country to the number thought necessary for an army of occupation. This was fixed, as regards fighting troops, at two divisions, and the 17th and 18th Divisions were detailed. Lieutenant-General MacMunn was appointed Commander-in-Chief in January, 1919.

Operations in Kurdistan

It had been generally believed that the British would continue to maintain an effective control of Mesopotamia after the war; but a decision was so long delayed and so few troops were left in the country that the tribesmen, who, as a result of the war, were very well armed, began to take to their old habits of brigandage.

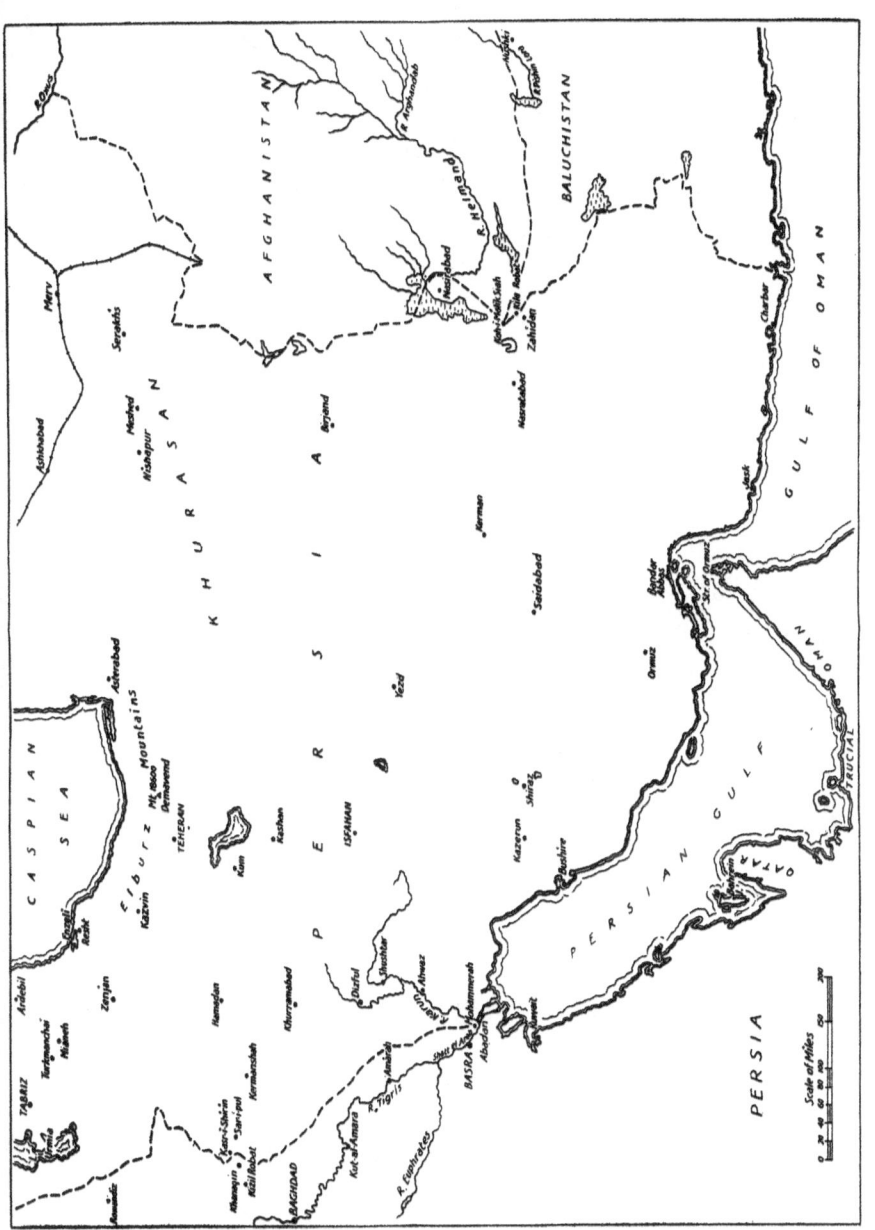

The Turks and Syrians had done their best from the time of the armistice to incite the Kurds to revolt, and the first sign of rebellion came in May, 1919. One Shaikh Mahmud collected some followers and started a rebellion at Sulamaniya. Reinforcements were sent from Kirkuk and actions took place at the Bazyan Pass, and later at Qara Dagh. On the latter occasion the Kurds were disheartened at finding troops of the 55th Infantry Brigade above them on the hillside and gave way. Sulamaniya was occupied by us the next day, and Shaikh Mahmud was deported. The 5th (Bombay) Battery and one gun of 6th (Jacob's) Battery took part in this affair, and one section of 50th Mountain Battery was on the line of communication.

An outbreak of much greater importance took place in Central Kurdistan in July which led to three months' arduous campaigning. A British Political Officer was murdered at Amadia, about eighty miles north of Mosul, at the end of July. Without delay the 18th Division formed two groups for punitive operations; one under Brigadier-General R. W. Nightingale to assemble at Suwara, fifteen miles from Amadia (Night Col), and one at Zakho under Colonel Wooldridge (Lumb Col). Night Col contained two and a half battalions and the 14th (Rajputana) Mountain Battery less one section: Lumb Col of about the same strength contained the 49th Mountain Battery less one section left on the line of communication. Lumb Col advanced against the Goyan and Guli tribes in a thorough fashion, marching through all the valleys and demolishing strongholds. It reported that the country in which it had to work combined the jungles of the North-East Frontier of India with the rocky mountainous terrain of the North-West Frontier.

Night Col left Suwara on 31st July and occupied several villages, destroying the chiefs' towers, and meeting little opposition. The continuation of the advance led over the formidable ridge of Ser Amadia, which rises sheer out of the valley to a height of 2,000 feet. The track was a very rough and steep stone stairway strewn with enormous boulders, a narrow cutting through almost perpendicular rocks, called the Mazurka gorge. On 8th August a reconnoitring party of one company of the 1/52nd Sikhs and the Centre Section of the 14th (Rajputana) Battery (Captain R. J. Sims and Lieutenant B. W. P. Dodds, M.C.) was sent up the gorge to report on its practicability for pack animals and the prospects of finding water on the high ground.

As political information was to the affect that no Kurds were in the vicinity, the column was sent up into the gorge without first piqueting the heights on either side.

At about 0700 hours, when the column was halted for the rear to close up, large numbers of Kurds appeared above and on both flanks and poured in a heavy fire, killing Lieutenant Dodds and two other British officers in the column. Surprise was complete, and the gorge was suddenly crowded with Kurds from the caves with which the heights were honeycombed. The guns could not be brought into action as many of the men and mules were shot down, and when a position for action was reached outside the gorge various parts of the guns were missing. Great gallantry was shown by several N.C.Os. and men who tried to carry gun cradles across the open under heavy fire, until further efforts were forbidden owing to the number of casualties incurred. About 1000 hours a relief column arrived with another section of the battery, and the high ground on one side of the gorge was made good, but the caves were full of Kurds, and a party headed by Captain Sims which was sent into the gorge to recover equipment was unable to get out again before dark. The Kurds withdrew during the night, and all equipment was subsequently found. The reconnaissance party lost three British and one Indian officer killed, with 34 Indian other ranks: 11 mules killed and 10 wounded.

The Centre Section of the battery withdrew to Suwara to refit, and found itself in another action on 14th August when Suwara was heavily attacked by about 1,000 Kurds, mostly Gulis and Goyans. Only one gun was available and it came into action at once, commanded with great gallantry by Jemadar Harnam Singh. It was in the open and several gunners were hit immediately, so some protection was hastily made and the gun pulled in behind cover after Gunner Natha Singh had gallantly fixed drag-ropes in the open. Air support was sought and given, and after a long day's fight in a very hot sun, the enemy withdrew. The camp had been under fire all day at very short range and zero shrapnel had been found very effective.

Night Col detached a party with a section of 14th (Rajputana) Mountain Battery to make a combined attack with Lumb Col on Benuna, the home of the Gulis, and the village was destroyed without opposition. Many other villages were so treated and the valley thoroughly searched, in which operations many rifles were found and confiscated.

The two columns combined for an attack on Karoar as a final effort, and apart from a considerable attack at Qavrak which gave trouble at first, the Kurds were driven from ridge to ridge after a bayonet attack, and "their retirement was much influenced by the accurate shooting of the 14th (Rajputana) Battery at ranges of 4,200-4,500 yards."

A force of 850 rifles and four guns captured Karoar and burnt it on 4th October, and the campaign was over. Lumb Col returned to Zakho and Night Col was broken up. The 14th (Rajputana) Battery was divided between Suwara and Zakho.

Raids by no means ceased, and the battery records many marches during the next few months without any actions of importance. The 6th (Jacob's) Battery was in action at the end of the year, as was the left section of 14th (Rajputana) Battery under Captain Sims, both with columns co-operating against Aqra. The 6th (Jacob's) Battery was relieved by 40th Mountain Battery in January, 1920.

On the whole our prestige was restored and peace reigned in Kurdistan for the next year or two. The operations described above were counted as very successful, and they at any rate took the heart out of the Kurd. It turned out that he had not the tenacity of the Frontier Pathan and gave in more easily. The Kurd casualties were about 500, but he never stood up to a strong attack. He seemed unable to make the most of the natural strength of his country, which is precipitous and wooded and ideal for surprise and defensive tactics. He was quick on the hills and good at taking cover, but did not press an attack, preferring to fire at long ranges. He does not kill prisoners.

The following awards were granted to the 14th (Rajputana) Battery for gallantry and devotion in the actions in August, 1919:

M.C.	Captain R. J. Sims.
I.D.S.M.	Jemadar Harnam Singh.
	Gunner Natha Singh.
	Naik Nadir Ali.
	Naik Fazal Dad.
M.S.M.	Naik Jagat Singh.
Mentioned in Despatches	Major E. R. C. Wilson, M.C.
	Subadar Haidar Khan.
	Jemadar Nizam Din, M.S.M.
	Trumpeter Chanan Singh.

On Lieutenant-General MacMunn's appointment as Q.M.G. in India, the Mesopotamian Command was taken over by Lieutenant-General Sir Aylmer Haldane (March, 1920). The country was still unsettled, and as our evacuation progressed matters in this respect deteriorated. Our mistake, in the interests of economy, in leaving too few troops to control a large country was obvious, and Turks and Arabs combined to make our position as difficult as possible. The Mosul district was especially disaffected, but a rebellious

attitude spread all the way down the Euphrates to Nasiriyeh.
The 17th and 18th Divisions were still the only fighting formations, the divisional artillery now consisting of one R.F.A. brigade and one I.M.A. brigade. The 13th British Mountain Battery was with 45th and 49th Indian Mountain Batteries in the 17th Division as the 13th Indian Mountain Artillery Brigade; 5th (Bombay), 14th (Rajputana), 40th and 50th Indian Batteries served in the 18th Division as the 2nd Indian Mountain Artillery Brigade.

It is to be noted that in June, 1920, all mountain batteries were reduced to a four-gun establishment.

A slight disturbance occurred at Aqra in April when a convoy was attacked; a small column with 500 rifles with the left section of 14th (Rajputana) Battery was sent to deal with this and had a brush with Kurds. Afterwards the guns were used singly with a few infantry to reduce some villages harbouring men known to be brigands. There was also a section at Zacho which was often out against raiders.

THE ARAB REBELLION

Our supremacy was greatly weakened by the withdrawal of troops, and the Arabs of the Mid-Euphrates districts became the prey of anti-British agitators who held out great hopes of loot; this provoked a restlessness which culminated in open rebellion in July, 1920. The scene of the outbreak was Rumaithah, twenty-eight miles above Samawah, where the Indian infantry garrison was besieged for over a fortnight. One section of the 45th Mountain Battery was part of a relief force which was unable to get through on 7th July, and the whole battery was with a larger force of six battalions which relieved the garrison on the 20th after a sharp action.

This was probably the first time a mountain battery had carried out an operation marching alongside a railway train to its objective. The train was used for supplies, water, and medical arrangements, and on reaching a place where the line was cut the entire force had to wait while it was repaired. The total casualties in the whole affair, including the investment, were 148 all ranks.

Political Officers were inclined to call for small detachments of troops to be sent to centres of unrest, operations which might lead to unwarrantable risks from a military point of view, and in which failure would encourage the rebels and spread the rebellion. Yet the risks were taken, with the result that other places with small garrisons were besieged.

At the end of July the rebels numbered 85,000, of whom half were armed with modern small-bore rifles, and a division plus ten extra battalions were asked for as reinforcements. These were promptly sent from India.

The withdrawal of the garrison of Diwaniyeh to Hillah began badly and could not be completed until a force of five battalions and three batteries (of which the 45th Mountain Battery was one) was sent to cover the movement. This was carried out using two railway trains, and occupied eleven days. The artillery support in attack was strengthened by bombing from the air.

The railway from Hillah to Baghdad had to be repaired and guarded, and Musayib, the place from which the Hindiyah Barrage was controlled, was captured and strengthened. The heat during these operations was very great. A jehad was proclaimed from the holy city of Karbala on 6th August, a few days after water was cut off from the Barrage. There was no doubt that Turkish gold and propaganda were the driving force behind the rebellion, aided by Arab nationalists in Syria whose finances were provided by the British Government.

Fortunately, the Kurds disliked the Arabs and did not join the rebels when the trouble spread to the north of Baghdad, where the first sign was the cutting of the railway line at Baqubah. A small column (which included a section of mountain guns), sent to deal with insurgents near Baqubah, while marching at night ran into some raiders who were out for loot and fired on the troops; this stampeded the mules of the section and upset the column of march. The one 2.75-inch gun which remained after this incident did good work. The section of the Chestnut Troop, R.H.A., which was also in the column, had to dismount their detachments to replace missing draught horses.

Fresh troops from India were arriving, but the disturbances spread and the Persian line of communication was now affected. The 45th Mountain Battery was with the column sent to Shahraban, where some British officers had been murdered, but met with little resistance, and the battery was left with a small force to keep the area in order.

The 45th Mountain Battery took part in the relief of Kufah on the Euphrates after it had been besieged for eighty-nine days, and this led to the submission of Karbala, a hotbed of sedition. By this time it was mid-October.

Samawah, about seventy miles west by north of Nasiriya, another place in which a garrison had been locked up, was relieved on 14th October after a siege of eight weeks. This was the end of the main operations, and it was now necessary to collect the rifles which were to be handed in by the rebels. After many weeks of traversing the whole country by every conceivable means of transport, by the end of January, 1921, 52,000 had been collected.

North of Baghdad the situation had been unsatisfactory, but never critical. The railway line was cut and the tribesmen gave some trouble at Kifri, but did not stay to fight it out with a relieving column.

The 49th Mountain Battery (Major W. J. Stanbridge) was divided between the Bazyan Pass and Kirkuk, where the troops were kept employed maintaining a line of posts to Kingarban, the railhead. This was some seventy miles away and about six miles from Kifri, which was surrounded and became an opportunity for a sharp action. Another time the section went north seventy miles nearly to Rowanduz, a place of strategical importance on the Persian border in the north-west corner of Kurdistan, and yet another day marched thirty miles at speed trying to keep up with the 32nd Lancers. The Bazyan Pass, which lies between Kirkuk and Sulamaniya, was little affected by the rebellion. The climate is good, sport was plentiful as regards partridge, duck, and snipe, and snow leopards were reported to have been seen. Not only was there polo, but jackal-hunting was carried out with polo sticks.

Operations were officially ended in February, 1921, and the inhabitants were then able to expend their energies on internal politics, pending the accession of King Feisul in August.

The mountain batteries with the higher numbers were sent to India for reduction, leaving at the end of the year the 5th (Bombay) and the 14th (Rajputana) Batteries; the latter left for India in January, 1922.

Note.—All "Mountain" batteries were designated "Pack" batteries from October, 1920, but as names were changed again to "Mountain" in 1927, the latter designation has been retained to avoid confusion.

OPERATIONS IN IRAQ*

Iraq has always been an expensive country to run. Even in the days of Turkish sovereignty it absorbed a large number of troops to keep order. In the interests of economy, command was transferred from the Army to the R.A.F. from 1st October, 1922, and the number of troops was considerably reduced. The new garrison consisted of four battalions, one mountain battery, eight squadrons R.A.F., four armoured car companies, and 15,000 irregulars.

---

* In 1922 Mesopotamia became officially Iraq.

By this time the prestige of the Turks had greatly increased owing to their victory over the Greeks, and they were making preparations to retake Mosul, having more than a year before occupied Rowunduz without being ejected by our troops.

The only Indian mountain battery in Iraq at this time was the 17th (Nowshera) (four 3.7-inch howitzers), then designated the 120th (Ambala) Pack Battery, at Mosul (Major and Brevet Lieutenant-Colonel G. P. MacClellan, D.S.O.) A section of this battery with a company of the 15th Sikhs and some Levy cavalry went to Rania to deal with a raid by Shaikh Mahmud; but when withdrawing, either through treachery of a guide or lack of reconnaissance, plunged into a bog and lost a number of ordnance and transport mules and their loads, which included one breech portion, one chase portion and, unluckily, both recuperators.

Shaikh Mahmud had from the beginning been responsible for most of our trouble in this area. He had been deported as an undesirable in 1919 after a futile revolt, and, incredible though it seems, had been brought back and installed as Governor of Sulamaniya in 1922.

Backed by the Turks, he organized another rebellion and was again ejected; he returned in triumph to Sulamaniya in 1924 and was bombed out by the R.A.F. He was allowed back in 1927 under promises of good behaviour, which he did not keep, and mounted in 1930 a rebellion on a large scale which took Iraqi troops and R.A.F. several months to break up. This was his last.

Early in 1923 the Air Officer Commanding in Iraq, Sir John Salmond, decided to clear up the situation in Kurdistan and to eject the Turks from Mosul vilayet. The R.A.F. first bombed the Turks out of Koisanjak, a place seventy miles within our border, and they were replaced there by Iraqi police. In February, 1923, Shaikh Mahmud threatened an attack on Kirkuk as a preliminary to a general insurrection; so in March a column of three battalions, the 17th (Nowshera) Mountain Battery and a company of Madras Sappers and Miners moved on Rania, which was retaken and the missing parts of the guns lost the previous year were recovered in good order. A Levy column co-operated, and Rowanduz was reoccupied on 22nd April, the Levies being left in garrison there.

The main column under Colonel-Commandant* Berkeley Vincent was then directed on Sulamaniya, having an affair on the way with some Turks with machine guns who were brushed aside at the

---

* The rank of Brigadier-General had been abolished in January, 1921, and the rank of Colonel-Commandant, which replaced it, was in use until 1928. From that time, such officers held the rank of Brigadier.

expense of 68 rounds from the supporting guns. Dysentery and malaria now had hold of the British troops, and they were exchanged for Indian battalions pending the advance on Sulamaniya, which was occupied without resistance on 17th May. Shaikh Mahmud disappeared for the time being and operations ceased.

As had happened before, the difficulties of the terrain were greater than the opposition of the enemy, in addition to great heat and often very heavy rain. This was the first operation of importance directly controlled by the R.A.F., whose planes were of great use in engaging enemy ground targets, in dropping messages and urgent stores, such as boots. The sick were evacuated by aircraft, but the technique of dropping stores by parachute had not yet been perfected, and rations were pushed up the line of communications as usual. The E.F. canteen arrangements broke down, but the old-fashioned unit hawker kept up with the troops.

The following honours were awarded in connection with the campaign:

O.B.E. and Mention	Brevet Lieutenant-Colonel G. P. MacClellan, D.S.O.
Mention	Captain R. V. Garry.
I.D.S.M. and Mention	Subadar Bara Singh
	Fitter-Havildar Manawar Khan.

As already stated, the battery returned to India in the following year.

Batteries which took part in the above-mentioned campaigns were granted the distinction of bearing on their Colours and appointments:

The Great War

1st (Kohat) F.F. ...	"MESOPOTAMIA 1916-18", "PERSIA 1918".
3rd (Peshawar) F.F. ...	"BASRA", "SHAIBA", "TIGRIS 1916", "MESOPOTAMIA 1914-16".
5th (Bombay)	"SHARQAT", "MESOPOTAMIA 1918".
6th (Jacob's)	"MESOPOTAMIA 1916-18", "PERSIA 1918".
10th (Abbottabad) ...	"BASRA", "SHAIBA", "MESOPOTAMIA 1914-16".
11th (Dehra Dun) ...	"MESOPOTAMIA 1918", "PERSIA 1918".
14th (Rajputana) ...	"SHARQAT", "MESOPOTAMIA 1918".
15th (Jhelum)	"PERSIA 1918".
16th (Zhob)	"PERSIA 1918".

In addition to the medals granted for service in the Great War

To face p. 192.

(page 215), the General Service Medal was awarded to individuals who qualified by service in Iraq, Kurdistan, South Persia, North-West Persia, with the appropriate bars.

E. PALESTINE

After their abortive attack on the Canal Line in February, 1915, the Turks withdrew northwards and contact was confined to patrol encounters whilst operations were being carried out in Gallipoli.

On 14th November, 1915, the Sultan of Turkey proclaimed a jehad on all those making war on Turkey or her allies, but this did not bring about the expected results except in the Western Desert which was Egyptian territory as far as a line drawn south from Sollum. This desert country contained a number of oases in the hands of the powerful Senussi tribe, a sect of strict Mohammedans who were easily induced by German and Turkish propaganda to undertake active hostilities against the infidel British.

No Indian mountain batteries were involved in this area, but it is worthy of mention that, attached to the Camel Corps in the ensuing operations, was the Hong Kong–Singapore Mountain Battery armed with six 10-pr. B.L. guns on pack camels.* It was a R.G.A. unit of which all the personnel were men of the Punjab under British officers with a few British N.C.Os. In December, 1916, the Camel Corps (now "Imperial"), consisting of three battalions and the battery, was transferred to the Egyptian Expeditionary Force now beginning its advance against the Turks.

The advance was dependent on the speed with which the railway and a 12-inch water pipe were pushed forward, and it continued until, on 19th April, 1917, the army was checked on the line Beersheba–Gaza, and reinforcements became necessary.

By June, 1917, when General Sir Edmund Allenby took over command of the Egyptian Expeditionary Force, it had grown to three cavalry and four infantry divisions, with two more infantry divisions in process of forming. Our own and the enemy troops were facing each other in trenches at Gaza, and Allenby's instructions were to drive the Turks out of Palestine.

For his advance Allenby demanded one more infantry division to make seven, and very strong reinforcements of artillery of all natures, especially 60-prs. (in those days called "Heavy" artillery) and 6-inch howitzers (called "Siege"). He was woefully short of field howitzers, but was promised sixteen 3.7-inch mountain howitzers to make up.

---

* In each section were 3 horses, 73 riding and 47 pack camels.

He had VIII and IX British Mountain Artillery Brigades and the Hong Kong-Singapore Battery,* but all these batteries were not yet rearmed with the 3.7-inch howitzer.

Beersheba, Jaffa, Jerusalem and Jericho fell to Allenby's victorious army by the spring of 1918, when our set-back on the Western Front led to the weakening of the E.E.F. by the withdrawal of reinforcements for France. In exchange the 3rd (Lahore) and 7th (Meerut) Divisions came over from Mesopotamia, and India sent the 10th I.M.A. Brigade (Lieutenant-Colonel A. M. Colvile), consisting of the 9th (Murree), 12th (Poonch) and 19th (Maymyo) Mountain Batteries.† The Brigade concentrated in June, 1918, at Kantara, where it drew its armament—four 2.75-inch B.L. guns for each battery—and mules, good but untrained.

The 9th (Murree) Battery came from Bannu, the others from Maymyo. Battery commanders were Majors J. A. H. B. Somerville, F. C. A. Troup and W. D. Lindsay, respectively.

The 32nd Mountain Battery mobilized at Maymyo in April, 1918, as two four-gun 2.75-inch batteries, 1/32nd and 2/32nd, later renamed 12th (Poonch) and 19th (Maymyo) Batteries. The 32nd was the first to enlist Ahirs as Jat Sikhs had been scarce since 1916, and the Ahirs formed the Right Section of the 19th (Maymyo) Battery.

The 9th (Murree) Battery was mobilized at the strength of: 6 British officers, 4 Indian officers, 99 gunners, 16 drivers, 23 public followers and 3 private followers.

After some hectic weeks of training, the Brigade [less 19th (Maymyo) Battery, which entrained for Ludd] marched to the bivouac area near Jericho, arriving in August ready for the autumn offensive.

Between the central Palestine ridge (the Mountains of Samaria) and the Mediterranean Sea stretches the Plain of Sharon, seven or eight miles wide, where the Turkish right lay strongly entrenched. This sector was to be attacked by XXI Corps of five divisions with strong artillery support, and, as soon as the objective was gained, the Desert Mounted Corps was to pass round to the left and make for Beisan–El Afule to cut the enemy's communications and block his retreat. XXI Corps was then to wheel to the east, seize the high ground east of the railway, and pursue the enemy in the direction of Jenin. XX Corps (10th and 53rd Divisions) was ordered to gain a line south of Nablus from which it could co-operate with XXI

---

* At this time a mule pack battery.
† At this time designated 29th, 32nd and 39th Mountain Batteries respectively.

Corps with a view to making good the high ground north of Nablus. On the extreme right, with its flank on the Dead Sea, was a formation called Chaytor's Force, the pivot of the whole movement, which was ordered to be ready to move forward when required. The Turkish line ran in front of Nablus to Es Salt and Amman.

Water arrangements were detailed in orders, and 1,000 rounds per gun were provided at, and in front of, railhead.

To follow first the operations of the 19th (Maymyo) Mountain Battery, which was directly under the orders of the 53rd (Welsh) Division, supporting the 160th Infantry Brigade : In this Division the confusing numbers of the Indian battalions, which had been recently changed, were abandoned, and units were named after their commanding officers—e.g., Kidd's Battalion. On 18th/19th September, the night before Z day, the 53rd Division brought up its right flank, a minor operation entailing a scramble up a very difficult track and drawing some fire from the Turks. The task of this Division in the forthcoming battle of Nablus was to move up on the east side of the Jerusalem–Nablus road, driving the Turkish rearguard into the cavalry which were moving round to the line Jenin-Beisan, north of Nablus, to prevent the Turks getting away.

The 160th Brigade deployed for several rear-guard actions, supported by the 19th (Maymyo) Battery, which fired 236 rounds the first day of the advance. Water was some distance away, so that only a few mules could be sent to it at one time, and the going was very bad indeed until troops were put on to make a road for wheeled vehicles.

The battery claims to have been the first battery in action across the Turkish lines in the final advance of the Expeditionary Force. Some counter-attacks had to be dealt with, but on 21st September it was found that the Turks had gone, leaving their guns behind them.

The Division pushed forward to cut off a Turkish retreat to the east—e.g., from Nablus to the Jordan; but the battery was pulled out and hastily rearmed with 3.7-inch howitzers, for which a gun-drill had to be improvised. It was equipped for service in Salonica and got as far as parading at Kantara to entrain for embarkation, but its movement was cancelled. It spent the next two years in the army of occupation, part of the time in Jerusalem. During this period detachments of Mohammedan troops were sent at the expense of the Government to make the pilgrimage to Mecca.

Lieutenant D. H. Shaw, R.A. (T.), was awarded the Military Cross, Major W. D. Lindsay a mention in despatches and Subadar-Major Mohammed Ismail, Sirdar Bahadur, the Indian Order of

Merit, as well as a mention. Later, grants of land were given to the Subadar-Major and the Q.M. Havildar Abdul Latif.

Major-General S. F. Mott, commanding the 53rd Division, expressed his thanks for the splendid support given to the infantry, and Field-Marshal Lord Allenby wrote: "Please express to all ranks my high appreciation of the services they have rendered, and their admirable spirit and conduct in all circumstances. Your battery has worthily maintained the high standard of efficiency of the Regiment."

By 25th March, 1921, the battery was in Dehra Dun, re-equipping with four 2.75-inch guns.

Brigade Headquarters with the 9th (Murree) and 12th (Poonch) Batteries joined General Chaytor's mounted force which was guarding the right flank pivot of the operation. Both batteries were in the right sector covering the bridgehead at the Wadi Aujah up to Z day, and carried out harassing fire. On 21st September the 9th (Murree) Battery moved at night with the New Zealand Mounted Brigade to Damiye to cut off an enemy column retreating from Nablus, and the British column bumped into a considerable Turkish column in the dark. The situation was not adjusted until daylight, when the 1st Light Horse Brigade arrived and a number of Turks were captured. The battery fired 121 rounds that morning, and the next day received orders to march to Es Salt with the New Zealand Mounted Brigade. Chaytor's Force was now in hot pursuit with four columns in the hills on a fifteen-mile front. Es Salt was outflanked and surrendered that afternoon with 500 prisoners.

During the night (23rd/24th September) General Chaytor received orders to continue the pressure and to cut off the enemy's retreat from Amman. There was a delay owing to the non-arrival of rations, but at 6 a.m. on the 25th two columns, each of a brigade of the Australian and New Zealand Mounted Division, supported by an Indian mountain battery, advanced on Amman. The Turks put up a fight at first, but the result was that the prisoners numbered 2,500 and ten guns were captured. A number of enemy troops had evacuated by train, but the Arabs were making breaches in the railway farther north, so they must have been forced to detrain in haste. The 12th (Poonch) Battery had some shooting on trenches from a covered position, and the F.O.O. knocked out some machine guns, but the affair was soon over.

This was the end of the campaign for the mountain batteries: three cavalry divisions of the Desert Mounted Corps were pursuing the Turks through Damascus to Aleppo as fast as their horses could go, and there was no employment for the pack guns.

There had been some sickness among the men, and, some of the mules having sore feet, marches were to a great extent carried out in draught. The new saddles were not entirely satisfactory, requiring frequent refitting.

Brigadier-General G. Ryrie, 2nd Australian Light Horse Brigade, sent the 12th (Poonch) Battery his thanks and congratulations for its good work: it had had some very strenuous marches, and the mules had remained saddled at one time for fifty-six hours except for one or two short intervals.

Jemadar Kifayat Ullah and Lance-Naik Sham Singh were awarded the Indian Distinguished Service Medal.

The 12th (Poonch) Mountain Battery remained in Palestine until December, 1920, when it was sent to Jutogh.

The 9th (Murree) Mountain Battery returned to Dehra Dun in January, 1922.

The three batteries, 9th (Murree), 12th (Poonch), and 19th (Maymyo), were granted the right to bear on their Colours and appointments:

The Great War.—"PALESTINE 1918", "MEGIDDO", "NABLUS".

The 41st Mountain Battery did a tour of duty in the Army of Occupation, arriving at Nazareth in December, 1920, and detaching sections to Roshpina and Samakh. It went to Roorkee for reduction in July, 1921.

The 38th and 42nd Batteries also did a tour in Egypt and Palestine.

F. NORTH-WEST FRONTIER OF INDIA

India freely gave her men and material for the defence of the Empire. Formations were sent without delay to France, Egypt, Mesopotamia, and East Africa, and prompt steps were taken to recruit men to replace casualties and to form new units. The Princes and landowners set a splendid example of loyal service.

The men of the Punjab (which furnished half the Indian Army in peace time) were responsible for more than half the enlistments during the war; of these, half again were Mohammedans who remained loyal notwithstanding the fact that many of them might be called upon to fight the Turks, their co-religionists.

As many men as the Army wanted came forward: all volunteers and almost exclusively rural—the urban intelligentsia and student classes were seldom seen in fighting units. Local recruiting boards were formed during the war for the better distribution of recruits.

The Indian mountain batteries which remained in India were

occupied in the routine work of guarding the Frontier and, until the establishment of the Mountain Artillery Depot, in enlisting and training drafts for batteries overseas.

At this time the 1st Division had its headquarters at Peshawar, the 2nd Division at Rawalpindi, and the 4th at Quetta. Each of the three frontier brigades was allotted an Indian mountain battery, at Kohat, Bannu and Dera Ismail Khan.

North of the Kabul river comparative peace reigned until August, 1915, when the Haji of Turangzai, a religious zealot who had recently come into prominence, raised an army of some 4,000 Bunerwals, including a party of Hindustani fanatics, at Ambela. This lashkar was attacked and dispersed as soon as it invaded British territory. The Malakand Movable Column was engaged in September, and the following month defeated a force of Bajauris advancing to attack Chakdarra.

The Haji moved on to the Mohmands and collected a force of about 10,000 at Hafiz Kor in September, which was dispersed by troops from Peshawar, armoured cars being employed on the Frontier for the first time in this operation and proving extremely useful. A similar threat which was made in October met the same fate.

During the cold weather of 1914-15 operations in the Tochi needed the presence of extra troops to support the Bannu Movable Column and the North Waziristan Militia against Khostwals from across the Durand Line. The 9th (Murree) Mountain Battery* took part in an attack on a large force in position near Miranshah on 26th March, 1915, the success of which was largely due to an encircling night march made by the Militia with a section of the battery. After the enemy's repulse on this occasion no outbreaks occurred for a couple of years, but local raiding showed no signs of ceasing, and on all sections of the Frontier the tribesmen were rearming themselves with high-velocity small-bore rifles.

Mechanical transport for supplies was used for the first time on the Frontier in these operations and proved invaluable, as without it the forces could not have been maintained in the field. The day of the two-wheeled army transport cart was passing; it was adjustable for two mules or two bullocks as required, and the load was 10 maunds or 800 lb. The mules' saddles could be used for either pack or draught. Using lorries, granted reasonable roads, the usual supply troubles were over, or anyhow much diminished.

Raids of Mohmands into the Peshawar area kept increasing and

---

* At this date, 29th Mountain Battery.

a blockade was established along their border, a chain of blockhouses connected with a wire fence being constructed and manned. A lashkar of 6,000 threatened Shabkadar in November, 1916, but was attacked and driven off. The occasion is noteworthy for the working of the 1st (Peshawar) Divisional Artillery with air observation.

By the beginning of 1917 the Frontier was alive with propaganda stories of Turkish and German victories spread through Afghan channels, and an irreconcilable mullah, Fazl Din, son of the Mullah Powindah, thought the time had come for a rising. The Mahsuds wanted no encouragement as their plundering bands were abroad attacking our posts and convoys as usual. Punitive operations were decided on, and the Khaisora valley was selected for the operation of punishing the sections responsible for the outrages. Two brigades of the 16th (Indian) Division under Major-General W. G. L. Beynon were to concentrate at Wana for a march through the valley. The 3rd (Peshawar) Battery* was detailed to the 45th Infantry Brigade and the 10th (Abbottabad) Battery† (less one section at Sarwekai) to the 43rd Infantry Brigade.

On 16th May a section of 10th (Abbottabad) Battery was with a convoy escort which was ambushed near Khajuri Kach, but on the arrival of reinforcements the Mahsuds disappeared; it was reported that harvesting had begun.

The Gomal river being in flood, the orders for the striking force were varied: the concentration was to be at Jandola, and the advance to Wana was to be made by way of the Shahur Tangi. From Tank to Jandola and onwards only pack transport was possible.

The concentration of the South Waziristan Field Force was completed on 10th June in very severe heat; meanwhile the 10th (Abbottabad) Battery went with a force to ration all the posts in advance, and the R.A.F. had been making photographic reconnaissances and produced a serviceable representation of the area of operations.

Tut Narai post in Northern Waziristan, garrisoned by Militia, was captured by an unusual coup on 31st May: some Mahsuds arrived accompanied by two girls, and whilst the sentry's attention was distracted slipped inside the barbed wire. Six Militia men were killed and fifty-nine rifles stolen, and the two girls turned out to be ex-Militia men in disguise. The post was regarrisoned the next day by the Tochi Force, which included 9th (Murree) Battery, and the

* At this time, 23rd Peshawar Mountain Battery (F.F.).
† At this time, 30th Mountain Battery.

area remained quiet afterwards. The battery stayed in the Tochi until it went to Palestine in 1918.

The advance from Jandola began on 12th June, and the Shahur Tangi was cleared without opposition and selected villages were destroyed. On the 19th the enemy made a stand at Barwand, and 3rd (Peshawar) Battery fired 105 rounds supporting the withdrawal of piquets. Fierce attacks were made during the night on a piquet of the 54th Sikhs which was covered by gun fire directed by lamps from the piquet. The post was held, but only three rounds a rifle remained at daybreak; four men were killed.

On 21st June an operation was undertaken to capture the village of Nanu (two miles north of Ispana Raghza), which was protected by a large enemy force in well-sited sangars on rocky heights covering the village. The 3rd (Peshawar) and 10th (Abbottabad) Batteries and a section of No. 1 British Mountain Battery supported the advanced piquets, which were under a heavy fire until the heights were carried.

The advance continued daily over difficult country and against opposition of varying strength. On 24th June, during the retirement after the destruction of a village, two sections of 3rd (Peshawar) Battery found themselves in danger of being cut off by Mahsuds coming through broken ground and had to be withdrawn at a smart pace. The next day the 10th (Abbottabad) Battery had a similar experience during the withdrawal to Ispana Raghza, where the force halted for some days.

The R.A.F. were now experienced in reconnaissance in this difficult country and in bombing raids. It was reported that Mullah Fazl Din's house received a direct hit; but in any case the Mahsuds were getting disheartened and a jirgah applied for peace. One of the Government's terms was a settlement of Major Dodd's murder case; this officer, in April, 1914, when Political Agent at Tank, was shot by his Pathan orderly, who at the same time shot and killed Lieutenant Hickie of the 12th (Poonch) Battery. Peace was announced on 10th August, and the troops due for demobilization returned to India.

During these operations a temporary ammunition column for the mountain batteries was formed with pack camels. Batteries reported that the men's boots gave trouble as they were never dry and lasted for a very short time. A large number of mules went lame owing to the hard going and had to be shod, but the ordnance had an inadequate supply of shoes of the right sizes.

As the war developed, more mountain batteries were required and the existing ones were combed of officers and men to form them.

The shortage of trained officers was very great and vacancies had to be filled by any officers available. In all, seven six-gun batteries and eight four-gun batteries were raised as well as two batteries and a section of an ammunition column for internal security.

The system of brigading batteries had not brought about any tactical improvements, and batteries were in almost every case fought singly; separate sections were often used, establishments having been laid down with that end in view. Brigade headquarters, when they existed were, however, valuable for administrative purposes.

Of the original I.M.A. brigade headquarters:

1st saw service in Mesopotamia and was reduced in Kut, December, 1915.

Nos. 2, 3 and 13 were formed in Mesopotamia and reduced there.

In India, 3rd was formed in the Kohat Kurram Force, June, 1919, and the name changed to 9th Pack Artillery Brigade, 1920.

4th had a short existence as an artillery group command in East Africa, December, 1915 to November, 1916.

5th remained in India, becoming 11th Pack Artillery Brigade at the reorganization in October, 1920.

6th remained in India.

7th saw service in Egypt, Gallipoli and Mesopotamia and was re-formed at Abbottabad in May, 1920, as 7th Mountain, later 7th Pack Artillery Brigade.

No. 10 was formed for service in Palestine in July, 1918, and became 5th Pack Artillery Brigade in 1920.

At the reorganization in 1920, when "Mountain" was altered to "Pack," six pack artillery brigades were formed in India, 6th to 11th inclusive, each consisting of one British pack battery armed with four 3.7-inch howitzers and three 4-gun 2.75-inch Indian pack batteries: 6th at Jutogh, 7th at Abbottabad, 8th at Peshawar, 9th at Parachinar, 10th at Quetta, 11th at Dera Ismail Khan.

There were three other brigades at this time: 3rd, which was No. 2 renumbered (in Mesopotamia); 4th, which was No. 13 renumbered (in Mesopotamia); 5th, originally No. 10 (in Palestine). These three were shortly afterwards reduced.

Artillery schools had been formed in Commands, and these existed until April, 1923, when the School of Artillery, India, was opened at Kakul: Lieutenant-Colonel A. H. Moberly, D.S.O., a mountain gunner, was the first Commandant (page 226).

The School of Mountain Warfare was started in Abbottabad in March, 1920, under Lieutenant-Colonel J. P. Villiers-Stuart, 5th Gurkhas. A mountain battery was attached for demonstrations.

The 3rd (Peshawar) Battery, under Major E. G. Campbell, joined the Marri Field Force on 9th March, 1918, at Dera Ghazi Khan. The centre section under Captain T. F. Hennessey, with 55th Coke's Rifles, marched to the vicinity of Fort Munro and encamped on the 13th. Early on the 15th the camp was attacked by 3,000 Marris and Khetrans, mostly armed with swords, having very few rifles. The tribesmen occupied some bungalows at Fort Munro and a near-by hill, and the section supported the attack of two companies of the 55th to clear the enemy out. The range was 1,700 yards, and the enemy began to retire from Fort Munro before the infantry reached them. The hill was retaken without trouble, and after the guns had expended thirty-two rounds the enemy retired in disorder. The tribesmen had believed the story spread by mullahs all down the Frontier that the Sirkar had no troops left in India.

The whole force, amounting to nearly a brigade, moved to Vitakri (fifty miles) and met no opposition, returning to Dera Ghazi Khan on 20th April, where it crossed by the ferry steamer as the bridge of boats had been taken up.

The Marris put up little opposition against the Baluchistan Field Force advancing from Quetta.

In the abnormal conditions due to the war, seditious propaganda was increasingly active on the Frontier. Bengal was the home of revolutionary conspiracies, aided by German money, the anti-British agitators found little difficulty in spreading their doctrines throughout the Punjab and over the border to the trans-Frontier tribesmen, who, rather surprisingly, fell easy victims to the arguments. After 1917 trans-Indus and trans-Frontier Pathans were not sent to the Mesopotamian Expeditionary Force.

Emissaries came to Amir Habibullah from across his western boundaries with bribes from Germans and Turks, but these were treated with the same scorn as the vapourings of Hindu politicals; the Amir Habibullah remained our loyal ally in the face of strong temptation to declare against us.

The situation changed suddenly in February, 1919, when he was murdered. His third son, Amanullah, who seized the throne, decided that the time was ripe for the conquest of India, and after a few weeks began to move his troops to the Frontier. His chief spy, the Afghan postmaster of Peshawar, had reported that the

Indian Government had not sufficient troops in India; nevertheless, two mixed divisions and three frontier brigades were waiting opposite the north-western border, backed by a division in reserve, with another division at Quetta. There were also three cavalry brigades and a mounted brigade. The infantry brigades consisted of one British and three Indian battalions, and the divisional artillery of a field artillery brigade and a British mountain artillery brigade, except in the 16th Division in reserve, where the British brigade was replaced by the 1st I.M.A. Brigade consisting of the 4th (Hazara)* and 10th (Abbottabad) Batteries.

The other Indian mountain batteries mobilized for this campaign were:

15th† (Jhelum) and 37th (Reserve) M.Bs. with G.H.Q. troops.
2nd (then 22nd) Derajat M.B. in the Peshawar area.
3rd (Peshawar) M.B. (less one section in Chitral) and 8th (Lahore) then 28th M.B. in the Kohat area.
13th (Dardoni) (then 3rd Reserve) M.B. in the Bannu area.
7th (Bengal) (then 27th) M.B. at Tank in the Derajat area.

The 18th (Sohan) M.B. (then the 38th) was mobilized at Quetta, and the Frontier Garrison Artillery was waiting at its various posts on the Frontier.

The majority of the mountain batteries were armed with the 10-pr. B.L. gun.

The usual shortage of transport was accentuated by the carriage of ammunition of all kinds on a more lavish scale than formerly, and the higher standard of welfare for the troops which had become customary.

The troops on the North-West Frontier formed the N.W. Frontier Force under General Sir A. A. Barrett, G.C.B., K.C.S.I., K.C.V.O., A.D.C.;‡ this command included the troops on the Khyber front, the Malakand and Chitral garrisons, and the three independent brigades. The front covered ran from Chitral to the Zhob.

To describe the operations, commencing on the right: the garrison of Chitral consisted of a section of mountain artillery,§ a battalion of Rajputs (not at full strength), a section of Sappers and Miners, 1,000 Chitral Scouts, and the Mehtar's bodyguard armed

---
* At this time 24th Hazara Mountain Battery (F.F.).
† At this time numbered 35th (Reserve) Indian Mountain Battery.
‡ Later Field-Marshal Sir A. A. Barrett, G.C.B., K.C.S.I., K.C.V.O.
§ This section had originally been part of the 5th (Bombay) Mountain Battery and had so remained until taken over by 3rd (Peshawar) Battery in September, 1918.

with muzzle-loaders and matchlocks, except 150 who had Martini-Henry rifles.

Snow on the passes prevented an attack from the north and the Afghan troops moved up the Kunar valley; their force comprised eight battalions and twelve guns, and it crossed the border on 12th May. After a sharp encounter with Chitrali irregulars north of Arnawai, the Afghans took up a strong position at that place. This was attacked by four columns on 23rd May, the main column with the guns moving down the left bank of the Kunar river. The guns came into action to cover the Rajputs' attack, and except for nests of snipers the enemy force withdrew to Asmar in Afghan territory.

An armistice was signed with the Amir on 3rd June, but was ignored by the Afghan commander in this area who, now that the passes were clear, attempted to invade Chitral from the west and north. Nothing came of the threat from the north, but the Afghans reoccupied Arnawai and a small force from the west occupied Bumboret, ten miles north-west of Kila Drosh, in July. It was driven out by some Chitral Scouts and withdrew to hold the passes along thirty miles of the Afghan frontier. Operations ceased on 8th August.

This campaign is interesting in that local troops with a backing of regulars defeated the Afghan troops and behaved throughout with great loyalty and courage, notwithstanding that the scene of operations was completely isolated and reinforcements were out of the question. It also proved the accuracy of the original estimate of a suitable garrison.

The Mohmands, who had been shut off from India in 1916 by a barbed wire fence between Abazai and Michni with a live wire curtain in front, after having given a great deal of trouble, had been behaving well; the live wire had been removed in 1917, and the Mohmand Militia was raised to relieve regular troops. They became restive after the arrival of two Afghan battalions in their territory on 14th May, and about 4,000 gathered together with a view to invading British territory. Columns were sent to Shabkadar and Michni, but about the 24th the tribesmen withdrew, their provisions having run out, and our columns were withdrawn to Peshawar.

On the Khyber front the Afghans, eight battalions with several large bodies of tribesmen, attacked our post at Landi Kotal, which was promptly reinforced to the strength of an infantry brigade, the 1st. The 2nd Infantry Brigade followed as a striking force to attack the main Afghan position at Bagh. Two battalions of the 2nd Brigade were detrained at Peshawar on their way to the front in order to arrest certain revolutionaries; twenty-three were collected, including the Afghan postmaster, without trouble.

The assault on Bagh was carried out under the covering fire of twenty-two machine guns, a field battery, and a British mountain battery with an additional section of 3.7 howitzers. Afghan resistance was weak and the position was taken with a loss of eight killed against a hundred Afghan dead. The artillery and machine guns had maintained a very accurate fire, and the dash and energy of the infantry, who kept up close to the supporting fire, was very marked.

On 13th May the 1st Cavalry Brigade went through to Dakka, which was consolidated at once, and although the line of communication through the Khyber was obstructed and sniped, all was ready for an advance on Jalalabad on 26th May. This did not take place as negotiations were in hand, and on 31st May an armistice was asked for by the Amir; this was granted on 3rd June.

There had been no Indian artillery in these operations in the Khyber, but the 3rd (Peshawar) and 8th (Lahore) Batteries took part in events in the Kurram about to be described, the former temporarily commanded by Captain E. G. Campbell, the latter by Captain S. St. B. Collins.

The Kurram salient was surrounded by Afghan territory on the north, west, and south sides and was very vulnerable to attack, but as we had not enough troops to take the initiative we were compelled to remain on the defensive. The Afghan commander, Nadir Khan, moved his force to Matun, whence he could attack the Kurram district and was equally well placed to move on the Tochi valley, which was thinly held and where he could rely on the Wazirs joining him. When he moved, which was not until 23rd May, he marched with some 3,000 infantry and nine guns down the Kaitu river to Spinwam, a militia post. This place was twenty miles from Idak, Bannu, and Thal, and his objective was unknown. The Militia were withdrawn from Spinwam, and a small column, which included a section of 13th (Dardoni) Battery, moved out from Bannu to cover that place. Hordes of Wazirs joined the Afghans as soon as they crossed the border; the Upper Tochi posts were evacuated, and many Wazirs of the North Waziristan Militia went over to the enemy, including a subadar who had been awarded the I.O.M. and other decorations for distinguished service in the field while in the Indian Army. The Tochi Relief Column restored the situation without difficulty and the garrison of Miranshah was strengthened by a regular detachment.

The Afghans brought no practical assistance to the Tochi Wazirs, but took every opportunity of inciting their hostility; and when the

Amir sued for peace, Nadir Khan promised that a general amnesty for the tribesmen would be included in the terms. Hence raids and attacks continued without ceasing and many minor actions took place.

Notwithstanding the assurance of a local mullah that he could cast a spell over any aeroplane and destroy it, when the Wazirs attacked the aerodrome at Bannu, they were driven off with many casualties. Between May and November, 1919, fifty raids and offensives, resulting in the deaths of thirty-two officers and men and enormous losses of cattle and stores, were committed by the Tochi Wazirs; and as similar activities went on to an even greater extent in Southern Waziristan, the Government sanctioned the carrying out of punitive operations in November. These will be referred to later (see page 210).

To return to the Kurram: the friendly tribes who inhabited the valley had to be protected, so the garrisons of Thal and Parachinar were strengthened and the defences improved. Nadir Khan made a dash for Thal, fifty-five miles west of Kohat (at the end of the 2 ft. 6 in. railway), and invested it on 27th May. Major-General F. J. Eustace, commanding the Kohat Brigade, commanded the Thal garrison of a squadron of cavalry, a company of Sappers and Miners, four Indian battalions, and one section each of 3rd (Peshawar) and 8th (Lahore) Batteries. These two sections and two 15-pr. guns of the F.G.A. were under Lieutenant R. E. M. Brady, 8th (Lahore) Battery. The troops who had to occupy the fort and hornwork were in rather cramped quarters, and had it not been for the poor quality of the Afghan ammunition, of which about 80 per cent. was ineffective, casualties would have been very heavy. Our guns could not reach the Afghan guns, which were firing at ranges of 4,000-5,000 yards from two directions, setting fire to one of the ration dumps and the petrol dump, and the enemy's 10-cm. howitzers had a great deal of their own way. Our guns, however, did good work against an attack on the 28th, firing with fuze $\frac{1}{2}$ and fuze 1. On the night 29th/30th an attack was made on an infantry piquet on a spur south of the fort and the section of the 8th (Lahore) Battery produced some effective results using star shell in one gun and shrapnel in the other. Our aeroplanes had been bombing the Afghan guns during the day, but that did not prevent the fort having to undergo a heavy fire the following day.*

The aeroplanes continued their support, but there was little enemy activity on the 31st owing to the approach of a relief column. As

---

* Lieutenant R. E. M. Brady was awarded the Military Cross.

soon as the siege began a mobile column had been formed at Hangu, twenty-six miles west of Kohat, from the troops available—a field battery, a section of the 3rd (Peshawar) Battery and the equivalent of a battalion and a half—and this column came under Brigadier-General R. F. H. Dyer, C.B.,* when he arrived with his 45th Infantry Brigade to form the Thal Relief Force on 30th May. He picked up some more 15-prs. in Kohat and towed them along by lorries. The Force marched through fierce heat to Darsamand, nine miles short of Thal, and on 1st June met a large force of tribesmen from Khost with a stiffening of Afghan regulars and four guns on the east bank of the Kurram river. Accurate artillery fire and an infantry attack pushed home with vigour dispersed the tribesmen, and the next day another attack was launched on a two-battalion front on the Afghans, who forthwith retired with speed, harassed by aeroplanes and armoured cars, thus ending the siege.

News of the armistice on 3rd June prevented exploitation of this success. The sections had fired about 500 rounds each during the siege. Artillery casualties were remarkably few.

While Thal was undergoing its siege, Parachinar, fifty miles farther west along the salient, was engaged in a different kind of warfare. On 26th May the Afghans began demonstrating with four large groups on a front of twenty-nine miles just inside tribal territory. The garrison of Parachinar, having a sufficient reserve, was excellently placed for dealing with these detachments with the advantage of interior lines. The 8th (Lahore) Battery, less one section, formed part of the garrison, and one section took part in the last and most successful of these operations near Karlachi on 2nd June, killing sixty Afghans and burning the headquarters of the Afghan general. Peiwar was another of these disputed points, defended by a party of Kurram Militia with a section of guns, and a section of the 8th (Lahore) Battery was kept with two companies of infantry on the Peiwar Kotal for several weeks afterwards as the Afghans continued to make raids. About this time, 7th or 8th June, the troops in the area were reorganized as the Kohat-Kurram Force under Major-General A. Skeen, and at the same time the 3rd (Peshawar) and 8th (Lahore) Batteries were formed into the 3rd I.M.A. Brigade under Lieutenant-Colonel T. M. Luke, D.S.O., relieved later in the year by Lieutenant-Colonel A. C. Fergusson, C.M.G., D.S.O. Both batteries were rearmed with 2.75-inch equipment in December, ammunition being H.E. and shrapnel in equal proportions.

The Brigade was in the Kohat-Kurram area until 1923, and its

---

* Brigadier-General Dyer had recently quelled a riot at Amritsar.

units had many small affairs with adjacent Wazirs during the intervening years.

To continue along the front: the South Waziristan Militia posts were hurriedly withdrawn into the Zhob district on 26th May after the evacuation of the Upper Tochi posts for the same reason—*i.e.*, in the event of an Afghan invasion reinforced by tribesmen the posts could not be supported. The South Waziristan Militia headquarters at Wana was overrun by Wazirs before it started withdrawing, and a running fight began which lasted for sixty miles. Three hundred of the Militia remained loyal and followed Major G. H. Russel, the Commandant, for three days and nights of nightmare marching and fighting, during which five British officers were killed. Over 1,000 Militia men deserted with their rifles, and the tribesmen looted the evacuated posts. Later, a small Afghan force occupied Wana temporarily.

The Zhob Militia were 1,000 strong and the majority showed great loyalty and courage throughout. They stopped the onrush of Wazirs who were pursuing the party from Wana, but the excitement spread to the Shirannis and Kakars and in a few days the whole of the Zhob Valley was "up."

Communications with Fort Sandeman were cut and every convoy coming from Loralai had to fight its way through; and although a number of Militia posts had to be evacuated, some were reinforced and held, and from 1st June the Waziristan Force ceased to form part of the N.W.F. Force and came directly under the Commander-in-Chief, India.

The Baluchistan Force was not attacked though there were considerable Afghan forces at Kandahar, and attempts to raise the tribes against the British were unsuccessful. Major-General R. Wapshare, commanding the 4th Division, with two brigades and two batteries of field artillery, carried out a surprise attack on the Afghan fort of Spin Baldak on 27th May with complete success. The armistice left the British in possession.

As already mentioned, the armistice with Afghanistan was signed on 3rd June, but its terms were not carried out by the Afghans. Peace was not signed until 8th August, and this period of delay led to much trouble with the tribesmen, especially as British prestige had fallen very low all the length of the Frontier owing to the evacuation of the Tochi and South Waziristan posts.

Our troops were inactive during this period, but the Amir continued to incite the tribesmen to hostilities everywhere. They gave a great deal of trouble in the Khyber and interfered with convoys until permanent piquets were established and day piqueting discontinued.

The Afridis from the Bazar valley staged an attack in July on piquets near Fort Maude. One was captured by a detachment of ex-Khyber Rifles in splendid style, though with considerable loss. As a punishment, an attack was made on Chora Khandao after careful reconnaissance and some road-making. This took place on 13th September and use was made of 6-inch howitzers. The fort was levelled to the ground. A column also went out to the Khajuri plain to round up more Afridis. None of these forces contained Indian mountain batteries as the country was suitable for field artillery.

Trouble continued in the Zhob valley, for which the Shirannis were principally responsible. The 18th (Sohan) Battery, from Quetta, under Major F. N. C. Rossiter, M.C., provided a section for convoy duty on the Fort Sandeman–Loralai road. Second-Lieutenant V. J. Gilbert was on this duty with his section on 6th July; two miles west of Kapip or six miles east of Fort Sandeman, where the road enters a defile, about 600 Shirannis attacked the convoy and had to be dislodged from the heights. During the action Second-Lieutenant Gilbert ran forward a gun and opened an accurate fire on a party which was holding up our infantry and the advance continued. The Jemadar of the battery and three I.O.Rs. were wounded in this affair.

On the 15th the convoy was held up at Babar post, the next post to Kapip and about nine miles south, and a relieving column was sent out from Fort Sandeman to meet it and bring it in. This force consisted of two companies 3/1st Gurkhas and 75 Zhob Militia, with the section of 18th (Sohan) Battery, and when it arrived at Babar after opposition the garrison was found to have suffered many casualties. The next day, the road being reported clear, the relieving column, convoy, and the remains of the garrison started off for Fort Sandeman. On arrival at the Kapip defile it was found to be strongly held by an enemy force, afterwards ascertained to consist of 2,000 Wazirs and Shirannis. The infantry were unable to capture the heights, and the four infantry officers were killed, leaving Second-Lieutenant Gilbert in command. To advance was impossible, and after a burst of rapid fire the tribesmen attacked and seized the convoy, sweeping away the escort by sheer numbers. The guns were captured, but not before the gunners had put them out of action. The rear-guard of Zhob Militia inflicted casualties with a Lewis gun as the enemy made off with their loot, and Second-Lieutenant Gilbert brought in the rear-guard at 0900 hours the next day. Casualties in the section were one I.O.R. killed and seven wounded, amongst whom was Second-Lieutenant Gilbert. He was awarded the Military Cross for distinguished service; two havildars received the I.D.S.M. and nine I.O.Rs. were mentioned in despatches.

The tribesmen collected at Kapip again, expecting another convoy, but as none arrived they started to besiege Fort Sandeman. Their numbers increased to 4,000, but they began to disperse after being bombed from the air, and the fort was relieved on 19th August.

It was, however, a long time before conditions in the Zhob became peaceful.

The peace celebrations which took place in England in the summer of this year were attended by a detachment of the Indian Army, which contained a representative body of Mountain Artillery men.

The undermentioned operations were linked to the First World War, being undertaken to punish the tribes of Waziristan for hostile action during the Afghan operations and for numerous wanton outrages since the last patching up of terms in 1917.

The Tochi Column under Major-General A. Skeen, including 13th (Dardoni) and 15th (Jhelum) Batteries, concentrated at Miranshah on 8th November, proceeded to Datta Khel, and having received the submission of the Tochi Wazirs, was back at Dardoni on 26th. The outlying sub-tribes gave in after a few bombs had been dropped on them.

The column was renamed the Derajat Column and marched to Tank via Bannu and Pezu (140 miles), joining the troops of Derajat District. The 7th (Bengal) Battery was with the latter formation and the 50th (Jhelum) Battery was on the line of communication.

Apart from units of the R.A.F., No. 6 British Mountain Battery, armed with 3.7-inch howitzers, was the only British unit in the forthcoming campaign. A divisional ammunition column formed part of the force.

It was sixty years since the first punitive expedition had entered the country of the Mahsuds: during that time their nature had not altered, but their fighting capacity and armament had undergone enormous improvement. Still no white man dared penetrate their country alone, and there was still no prospect of any sectional or tribal form of organization for control. The establishment of boys' schools in certain places in the N.W.F.P. was a distinct civilizing influence, however.

The presence of 2,000 ex-Militia men and ex-soldiers amongst the enemy was responsible for several noteworthy examples of combined fire and shock tactics carried out with the utmost determination and courage. About 50 per cent. of the Mahsuds (about 3,500) were armed with small-bore rifles, and these were generally concentrated for an action, the owners of rifles firing a non-smokeless powder, being kept out of the firing-line and not being allowed to discharge their weapons by day.

The lines of communication from Dera Ismail Khan, where Headquarters L. of C. were established, consisted of a metalled road, part of which was taken up by a Decauville railway, to Tank; forward of this place was a metalled road to Khirgi, used by Ford vans; beyond this was a double camel track running up the Tank Zam; forward of Piaza Raghza the Column operated with its own mule and camel transport. Posts were connected up by telephone.

It had been the custom for many years to carry out the maintenance of a column by a system of daily convoys protected by an escort, from which troops for piqueting were taken as required. This system was expensive in manpower and became less efficient as the tribesmen acquired more rifles of an up-to-date type. Permanent piquets were now established in sangared and wired posts on commanding ground on each side of the route used. The construction of these works took time, and gave opportunity to the enemy to fight first for the ground to be used and then to attack the working party and covering force.

Air operations were first carried out on a large scale for a month, but without bringing about the submission of the Mahsuds. Derajat Column Headquarters arrived at Jandola on 17th December, and a fierce and sudden attack was made that afternoon on the covering party of a permanent piquet in the making, causing thirty-four casualties.

The main column, 67th Infantry Brigade with attached troops, moved the next day to Palosina (three miles). While here, both mountain batteries were occupied in covering working parties: in some cases several days were needed to complete the establishment of a piquet. The infantry were young and their training was not up to the standard required for fighting Mahsuds, but, thanks to good leading, a rapid improvement was made.

The next bound was to Sorarogha, through the Ahnai Tangi, a gorge only eighty yards long and thirty yards wide with precipitous sides of 150 feet. An attempt to establish strong-points beforehand had been prevented by the enemy, and General Skeen decided on a night march* in order to secure the difficult ground before the enemy had time to organize an attack. This operation was successful and

---

* The night march was a feature of this campaign, and though seldom more than about two miles in length, often achieved a distinct surprise by an arrival at daybreak. For many years it had been the custom for troops to stay inside a perimeter camp at night. A notable exception was provided by the activities of the Gurkha Scouts in the Tirah campaign.

both banks of the gorge were in our hands when the main body advanced on 14th January, 1920.

One section of the 7th (Bengal) Mountain Battery was with the advanced guard; with the main body another section and No. 6 British Mountain Battery less one section; one section of each battery covered the move of the transport in rear of the Column. Two companies of 2/5th Gurkhas formed a flank guard.

The far end of the Tangi was found to be very strongly held, and this day's action turned out to be the most stubbornly fought of the whole campaign. The enemy held the high ground on each side of the river in great strength, and until they were driven off the main column could not advance through the Tangi. The advanced guard got through, thanks to its guns, and the flank guard was ordered forward to capture the enemy position on the right. The Gurkhas had been heavily engaged and were short of ammunition; so the C.O., Lieutenant-Colonel J. D. Crowdy, tried to carry out his orders by leading a bayonet charge, in which he was killed[*]; and although the Gurkhas were reinforced, the enemy was not driven out after a whole day's fighting. The Column, therefore, had to halt for the night where it stood in the bed of the Tank Zam in a very unfavourable position. Nine British officers had been killed in this action and six wounded. Piquets were established in time for an advance on the 18th which met with little opposition. The camping ground at Sorarogha was found to have room for an aerodrome.

The next bound to Piazha Raghza led through the Barari Tangi, where the Hazara Mountain Battery had distinguished itself in 1860. This was 900 yards long, flanked at the exit by bluffs which made natural firing positions for stopping the Column's advance. The first forward piquet was established in one day, and Brigadier-General F. G. Lucas'[†] 67th Infantry Brigade, starting by night, moved through the Tangi on 28th January with air assistance from the Sorarogha aerodrome. On arrival some Afghans with two mountain guns were encountered, but fortunately very few of their shell burst, and casualties this day were slight.

The next march was through very difficult broken country; but a good start was made in the dark, and the Mahsuds received a surprise attack from which they did not recover for several days. The mountain batteries had many good targets, including the Afghan guns, which were silenced by a couple of rounds.

---

[*] Lieutenant-Colonel Crowdy had been in the R.A. before joining the Indian Army.
[†] Brigadier-General F. G. Lucas commanded the Gurkha Scouts in the Tirah Campaign, 1897.

The 15th (Jhelum) Battery had been pushed up the line of communication, and was used on convoy work or with the striking force as required.

Very severe cold was now experienced and heavy falls of snow made conditions very unpleasant for the troops, though an issue of "jerkins, leather" somewhat alleviated the discomfort. The force remained for some days at Piaza Raghza, but as the enemy gave no sign of accepting our terms and did not believe that we intended to carry out our promise to destroy Makin if the rifles to be forfeited were not forthcoming, preparations were made for an advance.

The towers and walls of Makin were destroyed on the 20th February, not without casualties, as a large number of troops had to be employed to keep the tribesmen at a distance, thus giving many opportunities to snipers. The next day, Marobi, the village of Mullah Fazl Din, was razed to the ground, the mosque only being spared. Makin was evacuated on 1st March with little loss, and the Sappers and Miners exercised their ingenuity in setting booby traps.

The force arrived at Kaniguram, the chief—in fact, the only—town, on 6th March. Its sole products were, as might be expected, rifles and knives. Resistance had now practically ceased, but the quota of rifles to be handed over was not forthcoming, and orders were received that a garrison was to be left in the country. A permanent camp to hold an infantry brigade, a battery, and a field company was therefore constructed at Ladha. The 15th (Jhelum) Battery remained at Piazha Raghza.

During the occupation the number of permanent piquets was reduced, and the larger posts were ordered to send out patrols for convoy work.

Up to 8th April, casualties had been 366 killed all ranks, 237 missing and 1,683 wounded.

Unrest was not confined to Waziristan, and in the northern part of the Border the Black Mountain tribes were, as usual, ripe for armed rebellion, owing to the spread of rumours that the authorities were likely to give way to the clamour of irreconcilables. As an example, in August the Abbottabad movable column under Lieutenant-Colonel A. C. Fergusson, which included a section of the Kohat Mountain Battery, after arresting a troublesome agitator at Mansehra, was sent to Oghi, always a hot-bed of trouble-makers, and by its presence prevented a rising. The camp was sniped nightly, but no offensive operations were carried out. The Nawab (formerly the Khan) of Amb was very loyal and helpful, as he had never failed to be on previous similar occasions.

The supply of mules was kept up throughout the war, but they were not all of a very high standard; for instance, 188 which were brought from China in May, 1919, were all found unfit by November and replaced by American mules.

Many administrative changes were made with a view to the improvement of the sepoy's condition and the encouragement of recruiting. A messing allowance was paid and free rations became a normal issue; formerly, on active service, if sanctioned by Government, free rations were issued and batta paid, batta being generally 50 per cent. of the pay. There had been also a lower rate of batta (Rs1.8) for service over the Frontier, which was now increased to Rs5 for fighting men, followers receiving a smaller amount.

In 1920 the rate of exchange was fixed at Rs10 to the pound, having been Rs15 for the previous twenty years.

It had been customary for many years inside British India to pay all Indian ranks and followers an allowance as "compensation for dearness of provisions" when the monthly cost of a standard daily ration exceeded a figure fixed by Government; this allowance was now increased where applicable. Rates of pay were increased by 10 to 20 per cent. The new rates of pay were (Rupees per mensem):

Commandant	...	950+300 staff pay+30 for 2 horses			
Captain	...	750+200 staff pay+15 for 1 horse			
Subaltern	...	475+150 staff pay+15 for 1 horse			
Subadar	...	... 150	Jemadar	...	... 80
Gunner Havildar	...	27	Driver Havildar		... 25
Gunner Naik	...	22	Driver Naik		... 22
Gunner	...	... 17	Driver	...	... 16

The "other ranks" with Good Conduct pay in addition. Various allowances were granted to individuals: *e.g.*, havildar-major, signallers, layers, etc.

A bonus of Rs50 was given to recruits on enlistment and an additional Rs15 on completion of training. From 1st June, 1918, a bonus was given after every six months' service; this was afterwards incorporated in a man's pay. The qualifying period for pension was reduced from eighteen to fifteen years, and family and widow's allowances were increased. Kit money, which had replaced the original half-mounting allowance (abolished in 1917), was replaced by free issues of clothing and boots. The allowances formerly paid for extra wear and tear on the Frontier were discontinued.

Mule transport drivers received all the above concessions on a lower scale.

Some jagirs were granted to Indian officers for good service as hereditary assignments, in addition to other awards.

Over 300 Honorary King's Commissions were awarded during the war, and ten cadetships a year to the R.M.C. Sandhurst were allotted to the Indian Army.

Amongst many others, the following senior Indian officers received honorary rank:

    Subadar-Major Fateh Din, Sirdar Bahadur, to be Honorary Captain;

    Subadar-Major Nur Alam, Sirdar Bahadur, to be Honorary Captain;

    Subadar-Major Lal Din to be Honorary Lieutenant;

    Subadar-Major Sher Ali to be Honorary Lieutenant.

Bars for "Afghanistan N.W.F. 1919", "Waziristan, 1919-21", "Mahsud 1919-20", to the India General Service Medal, 1908, were awarded for the above campaigns and the medal itself to individuals not already in possession of it. Followers received silver medals now instead of bronze.

Batteries were authorized to bear on their Colours and appointments:

    3rd (Peshawar) F.F.: *The Great War.*—"NORTH-WEST FRONTIER OF INDIA 1917", "BALUCHISTAN 1918".

    3rd (Peshawar) F.F.: "AFGHANISTAN 1919".

    5th (Bombay): *The Great War.*—"NORTH-WEST FRONTIER OF INDIA 1915".

    7th (Bengal): *The Great War.*—"AFGHANISTAN 1919".

    8th (Lahore): *The Great War.*—"AFGHANISTAN 1919".

    9th (Murree): *The Great War.*—"NORTH-WEST FRONTIER OF INDIA 1914-15, 17".

    10th (Abbottabad): *The Great War.*—"NORTH-WEST FRONTIER OF INDIA 1917".

    15th (Jhelum): "AFGHANISTAN 1919".

Many issues of the Meritorious Service Medal, with and without gratuity, were made. Medals for the war of 1914-18 were granted to individual personnel as under:

1914-15 Star — To those who were on the strength of a unit before 31st December, 1915 in
    (*a*) Gallipoli
    (*b*) Egyptian theatre.
    (*c*) British East Africa and German South-West Africa.
    (*d*) Mesopotamia.
    (*e*) Various operations on North-West Frontier.

British War Medal (silver)   To those who entered a theatre of war on duty, or who left places of residence for approved service overseas.

Victory Medal (bronze)   To those on the establishment of a unit in a theatre of military operations.

(The final date for the two latter awards in India was 8th August, 1919.)

A bronze oak leaf was worn on the ribbon of the Victory Medal to denote one or more "mentions in despatches."

At the end of the war, "In recognition of the distinguished services and gallantry of the Indian Artillery prior to and during the Great War," His Majesty the King Emperor was graciously pleased "to confer the title 'Royal' on the 21st (now 101st) Kohat Pack Battery (Frontier Force)." (I.A.O. 59 of 1922.)* This great honour, as General Birdwood pointed out in his letter of congratulation to the battery, had never been conferred on any battery of artillery.

---

* Two other units of the former Punjab Frontier Force, the 59th Scinde Rifles (originally the 6th Punjab Infantry) and the 5th Gurkha Rifles, were also granted the title "Royal." The Bombay Sappers and Miners were given the honour as well.

CHAPTER VII

North-West Frontier, 1920-1935

DURING 1920 THE SITUATION in Waziristan continued to deteriorate, and the striking force (one brigade) at Ladha required three more brigades to hold the line of communication via Jandola. The Afghan nuisance party remained at Wana, causing as much trouble as possible, so it was decided to occupy that place, for which purpose two fresh infantry brigades were allotted. With them were No. 6 British and 15th (Jhelum) Mountain (now Pack) Batteries, the former armed with 3.7 howitzers and the latter with 2.75-inch guns.

The column left Jandola on 12th November, the two batteries being formed into two composite batteries, each comprising a section of howitzers and a section of guns, under Major G. S. Low and Captain H. S. Lickman respectively. A squadron of Bristol fighters with wireless communication accompanied the force. On 16th December it reached Dargai Oba, meeting with strong resistance which gave way under the fire of the batteries; the 15th Battery fired 228 rounds that day. Opposition stiffened during the advance to Karab Kot on the 19th, and as the left section (2.75-inch guns) of the 15th Battery was coming into action it was swept by the fire of a party of several hundred Mahsuds at a distance of a few hundred yards. This was one of those short sudden attacks out of the apparently empty hills which illustrated once again the improved fire discipline of the Mahsuds after the Great War, and the efficacy of shrapnel, fuze $\frac{1}{2}$. The combined fire of the one gun it was found possible to bring into action on a knife-edge ridge and of the Lewis guns (issued to the section a day or two before) proved too much for the enemy. Casualties were sustained by the 4/3rd Gurkhas, who had just taken over advanced guard duties from the 1st Norfolks.

Lieutenant F. G. S. Thomas was awarded the Military Cross and Havildar Alam Khan the I.D.S.M. for initiative and gallantry in this brisk action (immediate awards).

The column reached Wana on 22nd December without further opposition, and the Afghans withdrew.

During the next twelve months convoys were raided incessantly, and as there seemed to be no prospect of a peaceful outcome, instructions were given that Wana was to be evacuated in December,

1921, the post and roads to be taken over by Khassadars. These were well-intentioned Mahsuds, organized in small companies under their own N.C.Os., for the protection of the roads and security of convoys. This system proved a success and was introduced into the Gomal as well as North and South Waziristan; within a year 4,000 men had been enlisted in the two latter districts.

In order to consolidate the occupation of Mahsud country, it was decided to construct a metalled road up the Tank Zam from Jandola to Ladha with Mahsud labour, and at the same time to punish the irreconcilables. For the latter purpose two 6-inch howitzers were sent to Ladha in June, 1921; these weapons threw a 100-lb. shell over 10,000 yards, and so, with air observation, could reach out to the enemy in inaccessible places. (Before firing, warning notices were sent out so that women and children could be evacuated.) Their employment caused a change in the attitude of the local tribesmen; raids and convoy molestation became less frequent and men came forward to work on the new road.

During 1921 the 25th I.M.A. Brigade (then the 11th) was pushed up the Tank L. of C., two batteries being at Ladha, one and a half at Piaza Raghza, one section at Kotkai and one battery at Jandola. The 1st Royal (Kohat) Battery formed composite batteries with No. 6 British Mountain Battery, which had the 3.7 howitzers. During the withdrawal of the Wana Column in December through the Shahur Tangi a mule slipped on a buried Stokes mortar shell* which detonated, killing three mules and severely wounding three drivers.

A great deal of hard work was done protecting convoys, and punitive columns were often out between Jandola and Ladha, but opportunity was found to hold a horse show at the latter place in August, 1922, at which the 1st Royal (Kohat) Battery won the prize for the best mule in the show and two equal firsts for the best saddled mule.

In the spring of 1922 it was decided that the main garrison should be located at Razmak instead of Ladha; the former is on a high plateau and healthier. It is on the boundary of the tribal areas, Mahsud and Wazir, and in a central position. It has access from the Tochi over the Razmak Narai and from the south via the Tank Zam, and the making of a circular road would give communication with two railheads. At this time the proposal of the Government of India for the permanent occupation of Waziristan was accepted by

---

* The Stokes mortar was welcomed on the Frontier as invaluable, but the authorities withdrew it from the infantry equipment after a few years.

the British Government. Such a policy could not have been contemplated before the days of motors and motor roads, and it was hoped to bring about the civilization of these savage tribesmen by opening up their country and providing work.

The occupation troops were to be based on Bannu and their advance was to be regulated by the progress of the new road which left the Tochi valley near Idak by way of Damdil and Razani. The Razmak Force, under Major-General A. le G. Jacob, consisted of three Indian infantry brigades (containing amongst them only one British battalion) with a section of field howitzers, and the 23rd Indian Mountain Artillery Brigade comprising No. 11 British 8th (Lahore)* and 17th (Nowshera) Indian Batteries. Some Sappers and Miners and Pioneers were with the force for road-making at difficult places.

Little opposition was met, and the 7th Indian Infantry Brigade, with the 17th (Nowshera) Battery, occupied the Razmak plateau in heavy snow on 23rd January, 1923. The 8th (Lahore) Battery was left at Asad Khel, moving up to Razmak on 29th.

An extra battery, 14th (Rajputana) under Major E. R. C. Wilson, M.C., was sent from Quetta, arriving at Jandola† on 25th January, 1923, to reinforce the artillery required for an operation against Makin to be carried out by troops from Ladha and Razmak as the Makin Column. This battery was on the L. of C. at Piazha Raghza during the Makin operation.

Makin is an area containing a number of villages, both friendly and hostile; from the west side a river runs through a deep gorge in a steep and almost inaccessible mountain system containing a particularly hostile village called Mandech.

On 4th February, 1923, the 7th Infantry Brigade moved from Razmak to Tauda China, where it was joined by the 9th Infantry Brigade, forming the Makin Column. The 12th British Pack Battery and the 1st Royal Kohat under Major H. S. K. Snowdon made up two composite batteries for the operation; the 6th (Jacob's) under Lieutenant-Colonel A. E. C. Burney was also with this column.

The force moved out on the 6th, one brigade to the north of the Makin area and the other to the south. Selected villages were destroyed, little opposition being met with until the withdrawal began, when artillery and machine-gun fire had to be used to keep

---
* At this time named 108th (Lahore) and 121st (Nowshera) Pack Batteries.
† The extension of the light railway from Tank to Khirgi where the battery detrained had recently been opened.

the enemy from closing in. A heavy snow-storm delayed the completion of the operation, but similar action took place until the hostile villages were destroyed.

Mandech was shelled by 6-inch howitzers (brought up from Piazha Raghza with some difficulty) with aeroplane spotting. Nos. 27 and 28 Squadrons, R.A.F., in addition to their artillery observation and bombing roles, providing assistance to the infantry in reconnaissance and direct support.

The mountain batteries gave protection to the demolition parties and shelled hostile villages, and on the 12th the three mountain batteries and the 6-inch howitzers carried out a concentrated bombardment on the villages in the river gorge. One of the battery commanders noted that "It was a fine spectacular performance, but not very successful."

The weather now became very bad, and as the Mahsuds did not wish the operations to be continued they accepted the Government's terms.

The glare off the snow was fierce and, pending the provision of snow glasses, the troops improvised gauze veils from their first field dressings.

The North Waziristan (Tochi) and South Waziristan Scouts had been reorganized on the lines of the former Militia with fewer British officers, and they had replaced the Khassadars at Wana, but the Government decided to garrison this post with Khassadars again, and a strong column containing two pack batteries covered this operation in April, 1923, establishing scout posts at Sarwekai, Haidari Kach, and Chagmalai on the return journey. Touch was kept weekly with Wana by an aerial patrol, and this system lasted for the next six years. Road-making was continued, and the South Waziristan Scouts took over the protection of the road from Jandola to Razmak. Several thousand Khassadars were organized to police the whole of Waziristan as the beginning of a system of tribal responsibility, the establishment of which was so much desired. So far the only sign of tribal organization had been a definite cleavage in the village between elements hostile to the Government and those well disposed.

In April, 1924, Waziristan was made a military district under Northern Command, and troops serving therein ceased to be considered on active service, losing accordingly certain privileges of pay and furlough.* The district, with headquarters at Dera Ismail Khan, included the troops from that place to Bannu con-

---

* These privileges were restored in 1926.

nected by the circular road. One mountain (now Pack) artillery brigade at Razmak, having a detached battery at Manzai, was allotted to the force, and many of the posts contained "post guns" manned by the Frontier Brigade, there being eight 15-prs. and four 4.5-inch howitzers in the posts between Bannu and Razmak. A section of 6-in. howitzers of the 13th Medium Battery, R.A., was stationed at Razmak.

Infantry brigade headquarters were at Bannu, Razmak, and Manzai, and except for one British battalion in Razmak the infantry were all Indian.

The number of raids into British territory dropped from 129 in 1921 to 25 in 1924, and in the case of a recalcitrant section of one tribe, three months of continuous air action produced complete surrender; this success led to an examination by the authorities of a suggestion that the air arm should take over control of the tribal area, a proposal which did not fructify.

The troops who had been present were awarded the India G.S. Medal, 1908, with bar "Waziristan 1921-24" unless they were already in possession of the medal, in which case they received the bar only.

The cessation of operations provided an opportunity for the Mahsuds and Wazirs to fight each other in a dispute over their boundary; they had to be forcibly restrained as the boundary line in question ran close to the new cantonment at Razmak. The inhabitants then settled down to a life of road-making and lorry-driving in more or less peaceful surroundings, and the few minor disturbances that occurred were dealt with by the Scouts and occasional air action.

The Zhob district was restless for some years, but no actual rising occurred and the advent of the railway encouraged trade, a line (2 ft. 6 in. gauge) eventually joining Khanai to Fort Sandeman.

In 1925 a section of the 8th (Lahore) Battery, and again in 1926 a section of the 19th (Maymyo) Battery, went by rail with small columns to Dalbandin on the Zahidan railway in case of possible trouble on the Persian border, but the continued presence of troops was not found necessary.

ADMINISTRATIVE CHANGES

Most of the batteries were at this time suffering from frequent changes of British officers owing to demobilization, but the situation became easier after the reorganization of the Royal Artillery (A.O. 1 of 1924), when the distinction between R.H. and R.F.A. and R.G.A. ceased and one corps only, the Royal Artillery, was again constituted. Officers of Field and Mountain (Pack) became interchangeable, to the great advantage of the Service, their responsibilities and duties being similar. In actual fact, it had been found necessary during the First World War to relax the regulations and to post officers without regard to their branch of the Regiment. Fresh rules for appointment to Horse and Pack artillery were published in 1924.

By this date some re-designation of units had taken place. By I.A.O. 1279 of 1921 Pack artillery brigades became "Indian Pack Artillery Brigades" and the six existing brigades, 6th and 11th inclusive, received the numbers 20th to 25th. At the same time 80 was added to each battery number, thus 28th became 108th, and the distinction "(Frontier Force)" was omitted from the names of the former P.F.F. batteries. Territorial descriptions were restored: the 25th P.B. became the 105th (Bombay) P.B.; the 27th, the 107th (Gujarat) P.B.—all these descriptions being contained in brackets. The 106th retained the name "(Jacob's)" and the 37th became the 117th (Rawalpindi) P.B.

Alterations were again made by I.A.O. 515 of 1922, in accordance with which the "(Frontier Force)" was restored to the batteries formerly entitled to it, and the 107th (Gujarat) became the 107th (Bengal) P.B.; it had been formed as No. 1 Bengal in 1886.

From August, 1922, a list of the batteries reads as follows:

	Indian Pack* Brigade	Lieutenant-Colonel
101st Royal (Kohat) F.F.)	21st	F. W. Richey, D.S.O.
102nd (Derajat) (F.F.)	22nd	A. G. Haig, C.M.G., D.S.O.
103rd (Peshawar) (F.F.)	23rd	J. Hayes-Sadler
104th (Hazara) (F.F.)	22nd	
105th (Bombay)	24th	L. S. Bayley, D.S.O.
106th (Jacob's)	21st	
107th (Bengal)	25th	H. G. Carr, D.S.O.
108th (Lahore)	23rd	
109th (Murree)	20th	L. K. Stanbrough, D.S.O.
110th (Abbottabad)	22nd	
111th (Dehra Dun)	Unbrigaded (Maymyo)	
112th (Poonch)	20th	
113th (Dardoni)	25th	
114th (Rajputana)	21st	
115th (Jhelum)	25th	
116th (Zhob)	23rd	
117th (Rawalpindi)		
118th (Sohan)	24th	
119th (Maymyo)	20th	
120th (Ambala) ex-42 P.B.	Unbrigaded (Iraq)	
121st (Nowshera) ex-43 P.B.	24th	

* Each Indian Pack Artillery Brigade still consisted of one British Pack Battery and three Indian.

Batteries were moved from one brigade to another as required. The battery in Burma served a four-year tour of duty.

There existed also a Chitral Pack Artillery Section (Punjabi Mohammedan) at Qila Drosh, maintained by the P.A.T.C. since 1919. Officers and men were relieved after two years' duty.

The redundant batteries had nearly all been reduced, and the two remaining, the 120th (Ambala) and 121st (Nowshera), were amalgamated in 1925 as 117th (Nowshera) P.B., taking the place of the 117th (Rawalpindi) Battery, disbanded in 1923.

By A.O. 164 of May, 1924, the Indian Pack Brigades were ordered to be considered as belonging to the Royal Artillery and were shown as such in the Indian Army List. The Indian batteries, however, were not shown as R.A., and it took another A.O., 249 published in July, 1924, to bring this about. Batteries were then shown as: "102nd (Derajat) Pack Battery, R.A. (F.F.)," but the change seems to have been superficial because, for instance, their battle honours were not taken away in exchange for "Ubique," the motto of the Royal Artillery, and individual batteries were still shown in their former places in the Indian Army List, between Indian Cavalry and the Sappers and Miners. The Indian personnel remained under Indian Army regulations and no change was made in the conditions of service of British officers. Battery commanders were still shown as "Commandants."

The honour of belonging to a regiment of which the King-Emperor was Colonel-in-Chief was much appreciated by all ranks.

During the period of rearming the batteries with the 3.7-inch howitzer the suffix "How." was added to batteries which had received this weapon: in 1925 there were thirteen so marked.

In 1927, by Army Order 88, fresh changes of designation came about. Indian Pack batteries were to be known as Indian Mountain Batteries and their numerals were reduced by 100, the 1st to 12th batteries thus regaining their original numbers. The territorial names remained; as an example, the 103rd (Peshawar) Pack Battery, Royal Artillery, Frontier Force (How.) became 3rd (Peshawar) Indian Mountain Battery, Royal Artillery, Frontier Force (How.).

By an Indian Army Instruction of April, 1928, by dropping "Indian" throughout, this designation was changed to 3rd (Peshawar) Mountain Battery, R.A., F.F. (How.) and remained unaltered for several years; the other eighteen mountain batteries were simplified in the same manner.* For use in official correspondence "3rd Mountain Battery" was approved. The word "(How.)" was

---

* Note by the compiler. It is hard to see the benefits gained by the frequent changes of designation, except to provide examples of staff work.

omitted when all batteries were equipped with the 3.7-inch howitzer.
The British Pack batteries were renamed "Light" to keep in line with the Light batteries of the British Army and the word "Pack" disappeared.

In September, 1926, the Frontier Brigade, R.A., was broken up (see Appendix, page 434) and the personnel of the post groups absorbed in the Mountain Brigade in the area which then took over command and responsibility for the armament. These moves of personnel caused in many cases a dislocation of the class composition of the brigade which took some time to adjust.

After the war difficulty was experienced in obtaining the right class of recruit, and less than a dozen batteries were able to maintain their required numbers of half Punjabi Mussulmans and half Sikhs, recourse being had to other classes, such as Gaur Brahmins, Rajputana Jats, and Rajputs from the Eastern Punjab.

The 19th (Maymyo) Battery had always had a half-battery of Ahirs, a good class of fighting man from Rohtak (Delhi), and 5th (Bombay) maintained a half-battery of them from 1932.

Changes of class composition in the batteries were frequent in some cases. One battery, for instance, was ordered to change from equal numbers of Punjabi Mussulmans and Sikhs to half Punjabi Mussulmans, one-quarter Lobanas (who were re-classified as "Agricultural" by a stroke of the pen) and one-quarter combined Rajputs and Rajputs of the Punjab. A year afterwards a change was made to half Punjabi Mussulmans and half Punjabi Hindus. After six months, all Sikhs were withdrawn and the composition laid down was half cis-Jhelum Punjabi Mussulmans and half Rajputs from the Eastern Punjab. As none of the latter were forthcoming this half-battery was changed to Punjabi Brahmins, and a few months later to Punjabi Hindus. That is not to say that all batteries were so treated, but there is no doubt that great difficulties had to be overcome in this respect. The P.A.T.C. which undertook recruiting and enlisted for the "Corps of Mountain Artillery" gave up the struggle in 1923 and batteries enlisted their own recruits as they had been doing from the beginning. Recruiting was again centralized in 1926.

Enlistments were now made for six years' colour service for gunners and five years' for drivers, with reserve service to complete fifteen years altogether. The height standard of 5 feet 9 inches for gunners and 5 feet 4 inches for drivers, which had existed from the earliest days, was still being maintained. Proficiency pay was given with certain restrictions to men enlisting after June, 1926.

In 1925 reservists were reorganized into two classes: "A" at Rs7 a month included men up to the age of 40, after which they were transferred to "B" at Rs4 a month. When a man's colour and reserve service added up to fifteen years he was entitled to a Pension of Rs3 a month or a gratuity.

Some important changes brought in about this time may be noted here:

(*a*) In 1923 all second-line transport was taken away from batteries and became part of the train.

(*b*) Ammunition columns were ordered to be formed by brigades on mobilization from men surplus to batteries.

(*c*) Reliefs of units were, whenever possible, carried out by moving the personnel by train and the handing over of animals and equipment, which remained on the spot. This made it very difficult to retain any animal in a unit, and it was only after a very great deal of trouble that the 1st Royal (Kohat) Battery, on leaving Waziristan, obtained leave to retain a particularly fine mule, No. 115, which had won many prizes.

(*d*) All personnel were clothed as mounted men from 1923.

(*e*) The drivers' personal weapon was changed; the "sword, drummers" with which they were armed had the blade shortened several inches, and infantry bayonets were issued for use while swords were being cut down. This happened between 1921 and 1924. At the same time "pistols, Webley" were taken away from signallers and trumpeters.

(*f*) The status of regimental followers was improved by enlistment and attestation (of all except sweepers), and the grant of pay and furlough conditions as for fighting men. The Government's policy was to eliminate bhistis, replacing them by sepoys, but this could only be done in the case of piped water cantonments. It was decided that a bhisti was necessary as long as the mussack was used.

(*g*) Ceremonial dress was khaki jacket with R.A. buttons and badges, breeches with puttees and boots, and khaki pagris with red tasselled fringes. Working dress comprised shorts, grey shirts, jerseys, puttees, and boots. Badges of rank were worn by N.C.Os. on both sleeves, and saluting with the left hand was abolished.

(*h*) I.A.O. 203 of 1920 authorized the addition of one Indian officer in each section from the driver establishment. Thus a four-gun battery had two subadars and two jemadars, and no change was made until the early part of the Second World War, when the establishment was reduced by one subadar.

(*i*) Promotion of Indian officers was now made within the brigade, as were all promotions down to the rank of havildar. Promotion to naik was made in the battery.

TRAINING

An intensification of training began after the war to improve the intellectual and physical standards of the Indian soldier, and to enable the Indian artillerymen to keep pace with the many changes due to the war, and in particular to enable Indian officers and N.C.Os. to make the most of the more scientific forms of gunnery which had come into use.

A high standard of gunnery had become more important than ever; fire power had to be developed in the shortest possible time because the 3.7-inch ammunition was heavier than that used before and in consequence fewer rounds were carried. The many technical improvements introduced during the war had to be absorbed as second nature by hundreds of new personnel. This covered the use of meteor reports, survey, observation from the air, use of smoke and other novelties, and units were now trained to carry out the work of divisional artillery, in addition to the normal work of mountain artillery, which in practice was confined to the close support of infantry in difficult country. The artillery of two Indian divisions each included a mountain artillery brigade on mobilization.

In order to maintain the training of the artillery in India on the level of the units at home, the School of Artillery, India, was opened in April, 1923, by the first Commandant, Lieutenant-Colonel A. H. Moberly, who brought from Larkhill three officers (I.G.) and several assistant I.Gs. as instructors.

The School was first established in the mountain battery lines at Kakul and functioned only in the hot weather; the staff spent the rest of the year at practice camps or acting as umpires on manœuvres. The mountain batteries at Abbottabad benefited from the situation of the School as the batteries wanted for firing and demonstrations were taken from the brigade at Abbottabad, and an Indian officer and N.C.O. of mountain artillery were attached to the School.

Training throughout was on the lines of the current Field Artillery Training.

In 1923 the Major-General R.A. (Major-General E. H. Willis, C.B.) introduced an annual competition by Commands for all batteries, covering the following exercises:

  (i) Bearing picket shoot.
  (ii) Battle chart shoot.
  (iii) Tank shoot.
  (iv) Registering zero line.
  (v) G.F. targets including an advance.

In that year in the Northern Command three British medium

batteries took the highest places, and the next three places were taken by three mountain batteries—17th (Nowshera), commanded by Major R. G. Wordsworth, No. 6 British Pack Battery, and 2nd (Derajat) Battery, commanded by Major J. H. Knight, D.S.O.

Survey units (Indian Artillery) are described in App. (III) page 436. The Indian batteries were armed with 2.75-inch guns.*

Signallers had become very efficient with the telephone and lamp, and a headquarters section of two sub-sections was formed in each battery containing battery staff, signallers, and other specialists (with some followers), some of whom were mounted on the ten ponies available. A wireless (W/T) outfit for pack transport was in existence, and was first issued to mountain artillery during the Chitral reliefs 1922.

Although musketry in those days was not generally looked upon in the artillery as a matter of primary importance, there is no doubt that many batteries undertook this training in a very thorough and conscientious way.

The first "Manual of Educational Training" was published in 1925, but the lack of systematic instruction for Indian officers and other ranks had been felt for several years. The School of Education for the Indian Army was formed at Belgaum in 1921 to train instructors of all ranks who passed into the Indian Army Educational Corps. Roman Urdu was the basis of all instruction from the day of joining, and Special, First, Second, and Third Class Certificates were instituted to qualify for promotion to the relevant ranks. It was not until 1927 that trained schoolmasters (Educational Havildars) became available to all batteries. In 1933 Roman Urdu was replaced by English in Special Certificate examinations.

In addition to the regulation physical training, athletics, hockey and all possible games were pursued with great keenness. Competitions were held in all formations and units, and contested with enthusiasm. Motor transport made possible many visits to neighbouring stations, and assault-at-arms and horse shows were held regularly. Playing grounds were made everywhere.

The Mountain Artillery Hockey Cup generally provided a good finish, and there was also a P.F.F. hockey tournament in which the "Piffer" batteries took part.

---

* It is of interest that in December, 1922, the 16th (Zhob) and 18th (Sohan) Batteries each received 4 officers and 16 other ranks of the Tibetan artillery for a three months' course of gunnery, finishing up with elementary practice with the 10-pr. gun. The senior officer, Dipon (General) Duigja, was young (26) and keen and made a good impression. The party took four 10-prs. back to Tibet, and one at least existed in 1951.

Polo had increased in popularity and decreased in expense once the height standard had been altered, and there are many records of brigade and battery teams taking part in tournaments.

Many batteries held reunions to which pensioners and ex-soldiers were invited, and which gave a great deal of pleasure to all present. The father-to-son tradition* was very strong in the mountain artillery, and many sons were brought to be introduced to the battery.

Between 1920 and 1930 a great number of Indian officers with long service to their credit left the Army and others had to be selected and trained to replace them. The establishment had been increased by the appointment of Indian officers to brigade headquarters,† and the number of appointments to subadar-major was correspondingly increased.

It was now the policy of His Majesty's Government to provide places at Sandhurst and Woolwich for young Indians of a suitable stamp to be trained for a military career, and the successful ones were commissioned by His Majesty The King-Emperor to undertake the full responsibilities and duties of officers of the British Army. With this in view, the Royal Indian Military College was opened at Dehra Dun in 1922 to receive suitable candidates for preliminary training. No more were sent to Sandhurst after 1933, and the Indian Military College then provided the whole pre-commission training for K.C.I.Os., or I.C.Os. as they were then called.

Artillery candidates carried out in addition a gunnery course of four months, and attachment to a field battery for twelve months.

The existing type of Indian officer‡ continued to be promoted from the ranks (with few exceptions) and carried out his regimental duties as before, being known as a V.C.O. (Viceroy's Commissioned Officer).

The V.C.O. was entitled to salutes from Indian personnel only, whereas the K.C.I.O. was entitled to the same honours as a British officer.

Equipment

Notable changes of equipment were about to take place, both as regards the gun and the saddlery.

---

* This tradition was not confined to the Indian ranks: there were many cases of the sons of British officers following in their fathers' footsteps by joining the mountain artillery.

† See note at end of this chapter.

‡ A scheme for compulsory retirement at age limits had been introduced for these officers some years previously.

About this time the MacClellan type of pack-saddlery was issued. The method of transporting artillery loads in pack was, in the case of the heavier loads, to strap them on top of a saddle-tree which rested on two panniers stuffed with horsehair to fit the mule's back. The saddle-trees differed in construction according to the nature of the loads, all of which were dissimilar and required different fittings to receive them—*e.g.*, breech, muzzle, carriage, and so on. Ammunition and certain stores in boxes were loaded on to saddles of a simpler pattern with two hooks on each side on which the boxes were slung. There had been no change in the general principle for seventy-five years, but steel frames had replaced the original wooden saddle-trees.

The established principle was that each of the top load mules had a duplicate; *i.e.*, in a battery the existence of the "relief" line doubled the number of mules required for the gun and carriage, and as the saddles were all different a relief mule could only be used for one particular load. This was uneconomical and particularly so in the case of the 3.7-inch howitzers, which required eight mules to carry it as against six for the 2.75-inch gun.

With the new type of pack-saddle, invented by Lieutenant-Colonel G. P. MacClellan, except in the case of the "Pivot" saddle, alternative loads could be carried, thus reducing the number of relief mules by half (four instead of eight per gun). This system also reduced the number of drivers, and fourteen mules and drivers were saved in the battery. In the case of ammunition boxes it was a simple matter to fit hooks to several other types of saddle-trees.

The Peace Establishment for a 3.7-inch howitzer battery was now 149 mules; War Establishment, 120.

As has been explained, the 2.75-inch gun and 3.7-inch howitzers were used to supplement each other; the 20-lb. H.E. shell of the howitzer had a large radius of detonation and bolted the enemy from cover to run into shrapnel fire from the guns, producing very effective results nearly every time. Mountain gunners had hoped and waited for a super-efficient howitzer for many years, but the 3.7-inch was received rather coolly at first owing to the absence of shrapnel. After a year or two, shrapnel was provided, and although its range with the fifth charge was only 4,500 yards, it sufficed, and the mountain artillery could be proud of a first-class weapon of an unparalleled accuracy.

British mountain (now "light") batteries were the first to be rearmed, and afterwards, in 1930, orders were issued to complete the rearming of the Indian batteries. This was done within two years.

The Q.F. 3.7-inch howitzer is made in two portions, breech and chase, secured by a junction nut turned with a wrench. Both portions are of steel, consisting of an A-tube and jacket; the breech ring prevents any horizontal relative movement of these components of the breech part. The piece is 46 inches long when assembled and has a total weight of 4 cwt. The breech mechanism is of the single motion type, and firing is by percussion. The carriage has a "split" trail, consisting of two legs each hinged in the middle, to fold over when used with "short shaft" draught. These legs have a considerable splay when opened out, permitting a total traverse of 40 degrees. A shield is fitted on the axle-tree, and the 3-foot wheels are specially strengthened for draught, for which the normal arrangement consists of steel shafts joined to the trail by a draw-beam. Weight behind the team is 14 cwt. On firing, the gun slides back in a slipper on top of the cradle to a distance regulated by a hydraulic buffer, and is returned to the firing position by an air recuperator.

The gun is supplied with a No. 7 dial sight on a reciprocating bracket. A telescope sight is used for anti-tank shooting.

The cartridge consists of a brass case with a percussion primer and five ordinary charges, the full charge being the fifth. The charge is made up of a core of cordite M.D. round which fit rings which are detachable, making various weights of propellants from 3 oz. for the first charge to 9 oz. for the fifth. Some years later a super-charge was issued, giving a range of over 7,000 yards.

The ammunition consists of H.E., shrapnel, smoke, and star; the fuze for H.E. being 106 or 106E, and for shrapnel, T and P No. 80. The shell and cartridge are loaded separately.

At the end of 1929 the road from Sarwekai to Wana was completed, and the brigade group at Manzai (less one battalion) was moved permanently to headquarters at Wana, where the troops could now be supplied by motor transport. The 12th (Poonch) Battery and a post group for four 4.5-inch howitzers formed part of the garrison, and the reoccupation of the place was carried out without any incident to upset the system of civil administration which was being introduced into the district. Patrolling on a large scale—*e.g.*, brigade marches—was carried out frequently without opposition; the Tochi and South Waziristan Scouts moved freely in pursuance of their duties, and during the following years it seemed that civilizing influences had begun to take effect.

The risings about to be described in the Peshawar District had no repercussions in Waziristan.

Disturbances in the Peshawar District

The anti-British Campaign had been pursued without ceasing. This made little headway in the Frontier Province until 1929, when one Abdul Ghafar Khan, a landowner in the Charsadda sub-division, organized a Frontier Youth League with the avowed object of obtaining independence. After many revolutionary meetings up and down the Frontier, his followers took to wearing red uniforms and were known as "Red Shirts." The sons of the better-class Pathans had had by this time university education which had not increased their loyalty, and there existed a Pathan intelligentsia in the larger towns discontented with the limited constitutional reforms offered by the Government, outside emissaries exploited to the utmost any ill-feeling, and politics proved to be a most disturbing influence on the Frontier. The peasant class fell easy victims to promises of land.

A serious outbreak of rioting occurred in Peshawar city on 23rd April, 1930, on the occasion of the arrest of some agitators; an armoured car was burnt and troops were forced to fire on the mob at the request of the Inspector-General of Police. A strong brigade patrolled between Charsadda and Mardan, and unrest also broke out in Kóhat city. Normality was not restored for nearly a fortnight. The situation was restored at Kohat and Bannu by an early display of force, and although subversive agents worked hard amongst the Wazirs and Mahsuds, the Razmak Column, with the help of a few aeroplanes, restored order in Waziristan with little difficulty. The Redshirt movement was declared illegal in December, 1931, and thereafter faded away.

The Afridis were loath to miss an opportunity of taking advantage of a disturbed situation, and on 4th June a lashkar from Tirah joined a Zakkha Khel lashkar near Bara fort. Although the tribesmen showed a great advance in tactics and an improved administration, the lashkars still lacked cohesion and leadership. The following day a cavalry "drive" brought a good number of the enemy up against two small columns which dispersed them with machine-gun and artillery fire (from field howitzers), and by the following morning all had disappeared. The retreating parties on their way home provided bombing targets for the R.A.F.

During June the 16th (Zhob) Battery was with Fordham's Force, a temporary formation given the task of clearing up the situation round Shabkadar. In order to save time, when joining the force the left section guns were moved by lorry, the mules and the remainder of the battery following by road.

A more serious operation took place in August. A lashkar about 3,000 strong, carrying revolutionary standards instead of the usual tribal flags, arrived in the Bara valley with the intention of attacking Peshawar on the 7th or 8th.

For active defence the Nowshera Column [three battalions and 16th (Zhob) Battery], Fordham's Force [three battalions and 8th (Lahore) Battery], and a cavalry column were available. The 16th Battery was commanded by Major B. L. Marriner, D.S.O., the 8th by Major J. C. Meredith, D.S.O. The tactics which were successful in June failed on this occasion, and the lashkar closed in on the city from several directions, making a determined attack on "K" Supply Depot (petrol and oil) at 1630* hours on the 9th. The guard of the 4/11th Sikhs held off the attack until the arrival of armoured cars and infantry, on which the Afridis dispersed but remained in the vicinity in scattered parties.

The 8th (Lahore) Battery, which was armed with 2.75-inch guns, a field battery and a medium battery had some unsatisfactory targets, but the attack was not pressed. A fresh brigade was formed at Nowshera, and as the villages around Peshawar were assisting the enemy, martial law was proclaimed on 16th August. The Kohat garrison was increased by the 4th (Hazara) Battery from Abbottabad and a battalion.

Although the lashkar disappeared by degrees during the next few weeks, in order to prevent future incursions the Government decided to take over permanently the Khajuri and Aka Khel plains which lie on the north and south sides of the Bara river respectively. Bara fort is on the river seven miles from Peshawar. During October a camp at Miri Khel was occupied by the 9th (Jhansi) Infantry Brigade with 23rd Mountain Brigade Headquarters, 17th Light and 16th (Zhob) Batteries, and arrangements for water supply in the area were put in hand. The 2nd (Rawalpindi) and the Nowshera Infantry Brigades, with 58th Field Battery and the 8th (Lahore) Battery, arrived on the scene in November, and were joined by a section of 6-inch howitzers of the 15th Medium Battery. The 2nd Infantry Brigade camped at Karawal.

December was spent in road-making, reconnaissance for permanent camps and posts, and showing the flag all over the plains. The hills were entered for a visit to the Gandao Pass, where the road made in 1897 was found to be in good condition except for the bridges. An official survey of the whole area was made by the Survey of India, and the artillery laid out their own survey. Little

---

* This method of detailing times was introduced early in 1927.

opposition was met with and no action of importance took place, but the batteries were out nearly every day, and withdrawals were covered by leapfrogging batteries or sections.

The Mountain Brigade commander, Lieutenant-Colonel G. V. Dreyer, laid down that silent registration was to be carried out in order to avoid deliberate ranging on live targets, that fire was always to be opened without warning and in violent bursts of short duration, and that specially trained men were to be kept as lookouts. These methods produced very successful results, and the range-takers obtained much deserved kudos. The range-finder in use was the one-metre Barr and Stroud.

There was little sniping or interference except during withdrawals, and the batteries developed a high standard of snap-shooting; the 17th Light Battery reported that the 3.7-inch H.E. with fuze 106 was a good man-stopper as well as being very effective against towers. All the batteries acquired the habit of dropping a round of gunfire on the target without delay, and O.P. personnel became very efficient at spotting Afridis. The R.A.F. had little scope in observing on account of the fleeting nature of most of the targets.

The next month was spent in building posts and completing a network of roads to a M.T. standard so as to give control of the plains and connect with the roads to Kohat and Jamrud. Martial law was withdrawn in Peshawar District on 23rd January, 1931.

The Nowshera Brigade took over the whole area in March, with the 17th Light Battery in support, and on the 11th an operation was carried out on Spintigga in the foothills to destroy that village. An advanced column of three battalions started at 0200 hours and finished piqueting a two-mile gorge by 0430 hours; the next battalion passed through and ran into an Afridi outpost in the dark, driving it off, and the main body marched straight through to arrive at Spintigga (about twelve miles) at 0700 hours (daybreak) according to plan. Some sniping went on during the demolitions, but the village was destroyed and the troops withdrew with little hindrance. The brigade had no casualties.

Two battalions were left in the area as garrison, with some posts in charge of Frontier Constabulary, and the operations were considered as ended on the Afridis jirgahs signing in October, 1931, the peace terms imposed.

A bar, "N.W. Frontier 1930-31," to add to the Indian G.S. Medal (1908), was awarded to the troops present during the operations, and the medal was awarded to individuals not in possession of it.

The following year the North-West Frontier Province received full status as a Province (1st April), thereby acquiring a legislative assembly which, within a few years, was controlled by a majority of Congress members; Congress at the time being under the lead of Mr. Gandhi, a Hindu. The border tribes were now about to be further entangled in Indian politics.

The Governor of the Province was also Agent for the Governor-General in the five trans-border districts: Malakand, Khyber, Kurram, Tochi and Wana.

During the cold weather, 1932-3, General Sir George MacMunn, Representative Colonel Commandant of the Royal Artillery, paid a visit to artillery units in India, including, of course, the mountain batteries. He delivered a message from His Majesty the King-Emperor, as Colonel-in-Chief, to the mountain artillery and met many Indian officers and other ranks.

The next operation to be recorded was not connected with politics, but was a straightforward job of preventing the Mohmands from disturbing the peace by carrying on an inter-tribal war. The Upper Mohmands, who were neither under control of India nor of Afghanistan, resented the receipt of subsidies by the Lower Mohmands in our territory and attacked them, particularly the Halimzai tribe. This was in July, 1933. The troops which were mobilized under Brigadier C. J. E. Auchinleck, D.S.O., O.B.E.,* commanding Peshawar Brigade, contained no British units. No major operation took place. The 22nd Mountain Brigade, R.A. (Lieutenant-Colonel R. M. N. Forbes, M.C.), with its signal section and ammunition column, and the 4th (Hazara) and 10th (Abbottabad) Mountain Batteries, was with the leading troops, and the 2nd (Derajat) Battery was in the Force Reserve. As the Afghan Government withdrew its usual objection to our troops trespassing when operations led to a movement across the Frontier, the Upper Mohmands agreed to our peace terms, and the opportunity was taken to build a motor road up the Gandab valley to Yusuf Khel.

Our casualties were nine killed and nine wounded,† and the Haji of Turangzai, who was responsible for the disturbance, escaped scot-free, as did another anti-Government mullah, the Faqir of

---

* Later Field-Marshal Sir Claude Auchinleck, G.C.B., G.C.I.E., C.S.I., D.S.O., O.B.E.

† Lieutenant W. J. N. Norman-Walker, 10th (Abbottabad) Mountain Battery, was awarded the M.C.

Alingar in Bajaur. The latter spent the next twelve months in organizing a fresh campaign in the Malakand Agency; in this case the bone of contention was the country round Loe Agra, a salient just south of the junction between the Panjkora and Swat rivers, and a jumping-off place for Bajauris and others committing outrages in the Malakand and Peshawar Districts. The safety of the Swat canal, which irrigates large tracts of the Peshawar valley, was endangered so long as Loe Agra was not in our hands.

It lies in a cup in the mountains with precipitous approaches from all sides, except that there is an outlet to the Swat river which forms the northern and western boundaries of the area and flows in a deep valley whose slopes rise rapidly on both sides to a height of 4,000 feet. There was a motorable road from a point on the Malakand-Chakdara road, seven miles north of Malakand, to Kalangai on the Swat river, and a similar road from Dargai, seven miles south of Malakand, to Kot. Apart from these there were no tracks suitable for wheeled transport.

Operations in Yusufzai

In order to regularize the position at Loe Agra by establishing its dependence on the Malakand Agency, and to build and garrison a Levy Post there, the Government of India, on 18th February, 1935, ordered a force to be prepared to march from Kalangai through the Loe Agra area to Kot. Government's decision produced a fierce outcry from the Faqir of Alingar, who proclaimed that this move was a preliminary to the conquest of Bajaur, and called upon all Believers to resist the invader. By 18th February two lashkars of 200 or 300 men each had crossed the Swat river, making for Loe Agra and Kot.

The Nowshera Brigade, under Brigadier the Hon. H. R. L. G. Alexander, D.S.O., M.C.,* moved to Khar on the Chakdara road, arriving on the 22nd, having changed at Dargai from wheeled to pack transport.

The force consisted of one British and five Indian battalions, with the 3rd Light Battery (Major S. A. J. Grehan) and the 4th (Hazara) Mountain Battery (Brevet Lieutenant-Colonel H. M. M. Robertson) for support in the difficult country. Other artillery units were a section of the 66th Field Battery and the 15th Medium Battery. Air support was in strength; in fact, a demonstration of forty-five aircraft was made over the hostile localities on the 21st.

---

* Later to become Field-Marshal Earl Alexander of Tunis, K.G., G.C.B., G.C.M.G., C.S.I., D.S.O., M.C.

The establishment of permanent piquets on the route from Kalangai to Loe Agra was strongly opposed and took two days. On the 25th the column marched to Loe Agra, part of the way by a mountain track which was only fit for single file. Thirty mules (not all artillery) fell down the khud and were retrieved with difficulty. No further opposition was met and the force returned to Nowshera via Kot. Transport mules were left at Dargai, a precaution which turned out to have been a wise one.

The Faqir collected a bigger lashkar and was back in Loe Agra on 6th March. A mobile column was standing by in Nowshera, and reached Kot by 0700 hours that day by motor transport, changing there to pack. It contained a section of the 4th (Hazara) Battery and a section of medium guns, the latter being left at Kot when the column advanced to Bargholai later in the day.

There was very heavy sniping at this camp, and after the arrival of the rest of the Brigade on the 8th, the 3rd Bn. 2nd Punjab Regiment laid a very successful ambush for the snipers, killing three. Loe Agra was reoccupied and the Levy Post re-established, the troops leaving finally on the 16th. The 2nd Bn. The Duke of Wellington's Regiment was left with a section of the Hazara Battery at Bargholai; battery headquarters and the other section joined the medium guns at Kot as garrison with the 3rd Bn. 2nd Punjab Regiment.

The Faqir remained very persistent, having made up his mind that a permanent road through Bajaur was contemplated by the Government, and raised another lashkar in a few days, now being helped by the son of the Haji of Turangzai. A large party of the enemy was reported to have crossed the river, and a strong piquet of one company and a machine-gun platoon was established at Kila Hari to keep Loe Agra under fire if the tribesmen moved in. This piquet was named after Subadar Hari Singh, 3/2nd Punjab Regiment, who designed it, and included two platoons on top of a knoll and two more on a spur 300 feet lower. The approaches were so precipitous that the position was not wired. The piquet was attacked on the night of 5th/6th April from several directions under heavy covering fire. The lower post endured until midnight an almost continuous attack made with the greatest ferocity, the enemy getting close enough to grasp the machine guns, but the assaults all failed, although bombs and cartridges had to be rationed.

The attack on the summit was equally fierce, and at one time Subadar Sham Singh took a Lewis gun out into the open to enfilade an attack.

The F.O.O. of the section of the 4th (Hazara) Battery, Captain J. W. Palmer, who was in the piquet on the summit, directed the fire of the guns with great accuracy, putting his shell down within fifty yards of that piquet, a tribute to the confidence felt by the infantry after a long association with the battery. The guns fired 115 rounds, having to keep some ammunition in hand for the next day.

Subadar Sham Singh, 3/2nd Punjabis, was mortally wounded, one infantry N.C.O. afterwards died of wounds, one I.O.R. was killed and seven wounded, against twenty-eight of the enemy killed.

The Brigade Commander launched his attack on Loe Agra on the 11th April. The high ground to the south-west of the objective was cleared by two battalions, each supported by a section of the mountain battery. The attack was preceded by twenty minutes' intense fire from the mountain battery and the medium battery from Kot. The field and medium guns afterwards engaged targets in the enemy's rear to threaten his retirement. After considerable fighting, Loe Agra, under cover of well-directed machine-gun and artillery fire, was cleared, but in the process the Political Agent, Mr. Best, who had been taking an active part in the fighting with a company of levies, was killed. One I.O.R. was also killed in the course of the day's action. A few of the enemy were cleared out the next day from the northern hills, and this was the end of the fighting. The Faqir had become unpopular and was forced to leave the district.

It should be stated that the Air Force activities were hampered by the weather and by the great difficulty of distinguishing enemy groups in such country.

By 12th June all troops had been withdrawn and the area taken over by eight platoons of Frontier Constabulary. Battle casualties had been three killed and sixteen wounded: the official report noted that the standard of training of the troops was extremely high.

The Mohmand tribes had been very restless since the road to Yusufkhel was made in 1933, and there was no cessation of raids into administered territory. The making of motor roads was a sore point on the Frontier as all the tribesmen believed that it was the prelude to annexation and the loss of their independence. This was rarely the case, but no doubt the presence of a good road led to the capture of criminals and simplified the movement of troops if they were required. Open revolt was fostered by the Haji of Turangzai and his sons, and on 15th August, 1935, some 1,400 men began to destroy the road recently made, mostly at the southern end.

On that day the Peshawar Brigade Column, which included the 2nd (Derajat) Battery, F.F., moved out to Pir Kala at the edge of British administered territory, the infantry being carried in lorries. A section of armoured cars was also included.

An attempt was made at first to drive the tribesmen off the road by bombing from the air, for which work portions of No. 1 (Indian) and No. 2 (Indian) Wings were used, and after three or four days the inhabitants of the area had moved out, but there were no signs of submission.

By the 21st the Nowshera Brigade Column had arrived at Pir Kala and "Mohforce" came into being under Brigadier C. J. E. Auchinleck. It consisted of the Nowshera and Peshawar Brigade with force troops, amongst which were H.Q. 22nd Mountain Brigade, R.A., with the 2nd (Derajat) and 4th (Hazara) Batteries, reinforced a few days later by the 7th (Bengal) Battery, the 4th Field Brigade, R.A., and the 15th Medium Battery, R.A. A section of light tanks was also in the force, which was under the command of the Peshawar District. Orders were given that the force should visit the Gandab valley and open and repair the road.

The advance began on the 23rd, the objective being Dand, seven miles away. Close reconnaissance and artillery reconnaissance sorties were arranged with the R.A.F., and the force followed a very strong advanced guard once the line of the foothills was reached.

Strong opposition was met with from the hills on both flanks and both mountain batteries were in action, having to be reinforced by two field batteries before the infantry could get forward. The rear-guard was not in until after dark, some of the piquets having to be withdrawn by voice. Our casualties during the day were five killed and twenty-one wounded; the enemy had at least forty killed.

The next day the 4th (Hazara) Battery went with a battalion to reconnoitre a couple of miles along the road to Ghalanai, the objective for the following day, on which operations began with some good co-operation with No. 20 Squadron, who bombed a nala full of tribesmen who were caught by the mountain guns in the open on their way to shelter. Generally speaking, there was little opposition, and the Peshawar Brigade with attached troops camped at Ghalanai, the headquarters of the Nowshera Brigade remaining at Dand. The road was already sufficiently repaired for motor traffic.

A week's bombing brought in two of the smaller sections, but the Faqir of Alingar came to lend a hand, and the main lashkar increased considerably in numbers. Before our troops could advance, the security of the lines of communication, for which the Nowshera Brigade was responsible, had to be established. There were no dominating features which could be used and the road ran over many small hills intersected by many small nalas. On the west lay the Gandab valley, for the most part a narrow gorge coming out at Ghalanai. At the Karappa Pass were two permanent piquets, but elsewhere positions affording fields of fire and vision did not exist.

The problem was solved by the use of strong fighting patrols which searched the ground on both flanks daily. The patrols were supported by machine guns and where possible by artillery fire, and the system proved entirely successful.

The Peshawar Brigade, with the support of the field and mountain batteries, carried out several operations to search villages and to clear out nests of snipers, usually starting in the dark, and always met with opposition but not on a large scale. Two permanent piquets were established a few miles out along the road leading northward to Nahakki.

As the Haji and the Upper Mohmands showed no signs of surrender, the Government decided that "Mohforce" should advance over the Nahakki Pass and receive submission in the Halimzai country. Leaflets were dropped by aeroplane to this effect, and also to warn the enemy that a certain area of the Kamalai country would be heavily bombed on 16th September.

The force was strengthened by the addition of the 2nd Rawalpindi and 3rd Jhelum Infantry Brigades, and more tanks and artillery. Lieutenant-Colonel G. F. R. Wingate, O.B.E., O.C., 25th Mountain Brigade, R.A. was appointed C.R.A. "Mohforce." The force now came under Northern Command.

The Nowshera Brigade formed a camp at Katsai, half-way to the Nahakki Pass, in pursuance of orders that the force should establish itself at the northern foot of that pass and continue the road thereto.

On 18th September the advance was made on Nahakki by three brigades, starting in the dark, and that place was occupied with little resistance. The extension of the M.T. road over the Pass and the pipe-line were taken in hand at once, tank tracks over the Pass were made, and reconnaissances within a ten-mile radius were carried out. Major-General S. F. Muspratt assumed command of the force on the 24th. Daily expeditions in the vicinity found little opposition, and several sections of the Mohmands submitted, but there still remained in being a large lashkar three or four miles north of Nahakki. The camps of the forward brigades were heavily sniped every night until a successful ambush was carried out by the 1st Bn. 14th Punjab Regiment without any casualties on our side.

On 29th September the Peshawar Brigade, supported by 22nd Mountain Brigade, R.A., less one battery, and a section of light tanks, moved out to destroy a hostile village whose headman was a notorious enemy of Government. The left flank was protected by the Nowshera Brigade with 2nd Light Tank Company, less two sections, and the 3rd Light Battery (Major S. A. J. Grehan). The 3rd Jhelum Infantry Brigade with 7th Field and 13th (Dardoni)

(Major A. C. S. Kennedy) batteries was protecting the left of the Nowshera Brigade. The 4th and 66th Field and 15th Medium batteries under C.R.A. were supporting the Nowshera Brigade.

The 5th Bn. 10th Baluch Regiment (Jacob's Rifles) were in the objective by 0630 hours, and the village tower was blown up by the Sappers and Miners by 1000 hours.

The 5th Bn. 12th Frontier Force Regiment (The Guides) on the left of the Nowshera Brigade was reaching its objective as day dawned when a heavy and accurate fire was opened on the leading platoons from a large body of the enemy who had been occupying caves near by. Both artillery F.O.Os. with the battalion were wounded and communication with the guns asking for support failed. By 0800 hours the leading platoons were overwhelmed and the supporting company, under an incessant fire from the enemy now on the high ground above them, endeavoured to withdraw. All the covering fire possible was organized, and the battalion was later able to withdraw its forward elements, supported by artillery fire from field and medium guns which opened about 1000 hours.

The tribesmen were severely handled by the Guides and lost about fifty killed, but the casualties in the regiment amounted to 2 British Officers killed and 2 wounded, 27 I.O.Rs. killed and 37 wounded. Captain G. Meynell of the Guides was awarded a posthumous V.C. and Lieutenant J. N. D. Tyler, F.O.O. of the 3rd Light Battery, the M.C.

The troops returned to camp, any attempts to follow them up being easily checked by artillery fire. No further opposition was offered to any of the marches that were carried out, and the road was finished on 29th October, on which day the G.O.C.-in-C., Northern Command, motored through to Nahakki.

His Excellency the Governor of the N.W.F.P. held a jirga on 15th October, receiving signed acceptance of the Government's terms, which were the cessation of hostilities, an undertaking to maintain friendly relations and to prevent unlawful actions by outlaws, and a promise not to interfere with the road, which was to be left but not maintained. The jirga had nothing to say except to ask that unexploded R.A.F. bombs should be destroyed.

The withdrawal of the troops and pipe-line took place without incident, and the force ceased to exist from 3rd November. Total casualties were 45 killed, 115 wounded, all ranks.

The India G.S. Medal (1908) was awarded to those taking part in the campaigns last mentioned with clasps "Mohmand 1933", "North-West Frontier, 1935," or the clasps only to those already in possession of the medal.

Sino-Burmese Frontier

The farthest corner of the Frontier, the Sino-Burmese border, was still undemarcated in June, 1934, when a strong body of Yunnanese troops crossed the watershed which we regarded as the frontier into the Wa State. Burmese Military Police, supported by the Punjabi Mussulman section of the 10th (Abbottabad) Battery from Maymyo, moved forward from railhead at Lashio to cross the Salween at Kunlong ferry after an arduous march of eighty-five miles through the jungle during the monsoon. Some mules died of exhaustion on the way. The party camped on top of a mountain at Lufang and built huts as a base for expeditions to villages in the mountains, often using game tracks as the only access. The Chinese gave no trouble and withdrew, and most of the Was were friendly; the majority of them were armed with dahs and cross-bows with poisoned arrows, but a few muzzle-loading muskets were to be met with. The Police had some casualties during the ten months the expedition lasted, but the section was only involved in one brush with the enemy. The section was at first under the battery commander, Major E. L. Armitage, who was relieved later by Lieutenant W. S. N. Walker. The latter was awarded the M.B.E. and Major Armitage the O.B.E. Subadar Painda Khan, I.D.S.M., was also with the section.

The following year a League of Nations demarcation commission covered the same ground and demarcated the frontier after three months' hard marching with little opposition; this time Lieutenants J. G. Wilton and J. C. Edlmann each took one gun of the Sikh section with a column. On completion the Yunnanese troops of the escort disbanded and took to dacoity, which necessitated much marching and several minor actions before they were ejected.

In 1935 the Indian Regiment of Artillery was created as a new Corps. Its one unit was "A" Field Regiment of four 4-gun horsed batteries stationed at Bangalore; one battery each of Punjabi Mussulmans, Ranghars, Rajputs, and Madrassis. It was not part of the Royal Artillery as were the mountain artillery and survey section, and it adopted its own badge—"India" and a star over a gun, with the motto "Izzat o Iqbal".

The 16th (Zhob) Battery made an interesting march in May, 1935, through the Khojak Tunnel. After forming battery column, the animals marched down the centre of each track without incident. On the march back from Chaman the battery returned to Quetta from the Tunnel across country, covering seventy miles in forty hours over difficult ground which included a rock staircase 50 feet high.

On May 31st a serious earthquake, causing great damage and loss of life, occurred at Quetta. The cantonment was not much damaged —in fact, the troops pulled their charpoys into the open and went to sleep again after the first shock at 0300 hours. More shocks occurred, and all the troops undertook rescue work in the city, which was in flames and badly damaged. For five days the work of extinguishing fires and extricating persons from the ruins continued. The G.O.C., Lieutenant-General H. Karslake, formerly of the Royal Artillery, was also faced with an invasion of tribesmen in search of loot, but their hopes were disappointed. The estimated number of people killed was 26,000 in the city, and in the whole area there were 56,000 casualties. Training was suspended for the next few months while the troops were rebuilding their own accommodation which had suffered.

The following table shows the distribution of the Mountain Artillery at the end of 1935:

Mountain Brigade	Station	Batteries	Brigade Class Composition
20th	Kohat	H.Q. & 12th (Poonch) 5th (Bombay) 19th (Maymyo) 12th Light	P.Ms., Jat Sikhs and Ahirs
21st	Peshawar	H.Q. & 1st Royal (Kohat) 6th (Jacob's) 9th (Murree) 3rd Light	P.Ms., Jat Sikhs and Ahirs
22nd	Waziristan–Wana	H.Q. & 7th (Bengal) 2nd (Derajat) 4th (Hazara) 4th Light	P.Ms. and Jat Sikhs
23rd	Ambala–Dehra Dun	H.Q. & 3rd (Peshawar) 8th (Lahore) 17th (Nowshera) 7th Light	P.Ms. and Jat Sikhs
24th	Quetta	H.Q. 11th (Dehra Dun) 16th (Zhob) 18th (Sohan) 5th Light	P.Ms., Jat and Lobana Sikhs
25th	Abbottabad	H.Q. 13th (Dardoni) 14th (Rajputana) 15th (Jhelum) 17th Light	P.Ms., Jat Sikhs and Brahmans
—	Maymyo	10th (Abbottabad)	—

Note 1

There was usually one battery with brigade headquarters; the others were stationed singly in the area.

Note 2

Batteries were moved from one brigade to another as required.

NOTE TO CHAPTER VII

Establishment of an Indian Mountain Artillery Brigade Headquarters for 1 Light and 3 Indian Batteries. 16 3.7-inch howitzers.

British Officers	1 Lieutenant-Colonel, 1 Captain (Adjutant), 1 Subaltern.
Attached Officer	1 Doctor (I.M.S.).
V.C.O.	1 Subadar-Major.
Warrant Officers	1 R.S.M., 1 Fitter, 1 Artillery Clerk.
Sub. Asst. Veterinary Surgeon	1
Havildars	1 Battery Havildar-Major, 1 Battery Q.M. Havildar, 1 Pay Havildar, 1 Head Clerk.
Rank and File	1 Trumpet-Major, 2 Surveyors, 4 Gunners, 2 Clerks, 18 Drivers.
Followers	2 Cooks, 2 Water Carriers, 1 Saddler, 1 Sweeper.
Transport	20 Horses, 3 Ordnance Mules, 2 Bicycles.
Attached	
Mountain Brigade Signal Section	1 Subaltern, 1 Sergeant, 18 B.O.Rs., 1 Havildar, 16 I.O.Rs.
Mountain Brigade Ammunition Column	1 Subaltern and 50 I.O.Rs. (24 r.p.g.).

"The Old Woman's Nose," Kohat. A vision

CHAPTER VIII

North-West Frontier, 1936-1939

WAZIRISTAN HAD BEEN fairly peaceful for seven years, but those concerned were well aware that the youthful and turbulent elements in the tribes were bored with a quiet existence and that in the eyes of all the tribesmen the constitutional changes which had been made in India proved only the weakness of the Government. This reasoning was fostered by outside agents who went everywhere preaching sedition and found a ready welcome.

A very uncommon incident precipitated the next outbreak: a young Muslim kidnapped a Hindu girl and stated that he had converted her and then married her. Her parents sued him for her return and won their case; legally she was still a Hindu. An ecclesiastical firebrand, the Faqir of Ipi, seized this opportunity to raise a lashkar against the Government, which had just become involved in a military expedition to enforce an agreement made the previous year by the Tori Khels pledging themselves not to hinder roadmaking in the Khaisora valley. That section of the Utmanzai (Wazir) tribe was generally loyal, but on this occasion the Faqir built himself a house in the lower Khaisora valley and acquired considerable influence in that district.

He assumed the role of "Champion of Islam" in the Hindu-Muslim incident referred to and, after the usual manner of Frontier mullahs, promised his followers wonderful rewards which appealed to their credulity and superstition.

The Tori Khel were unable or unwilling to eject him and, in order to impress them, the Government ordered a demonstration of troops in the Khaisora valley. Accordingly, on 25th November the Razmak column (Razcol) started from Damdil and the Bannu column (Tocol) from Mir Ali, with orders to camp at Bicche Kashkai that night and to return to starting-points by the same route the next day. Resistance in strength was not expected: the distances were about twelve and fourteen miles respectively.

Razcol, comprising four battalions and the 22nd Mountain Brigade, R.A., of 3rd Light and 4th (Hazara) and 7th (Bengal) Mountain Batteries, met with considerable resistance and fought its way to the rendezvous, arriving at 1800 hours. The 3rd Light and 7th Batteries were in action supporting the advanced guard, which put out piquets to be collected by the rear-guard; the latter was closely followed up, and reached camp in the dark at 2015 hours.

Tocol, a column of two battalions and no guns, met with an even stronger resistance and was held up all day; ultimately the force continued its march during the night, but was brought to a standstill and camped where it stood.

Next morning the 7th Battery was sent with some infantry to support Tocol, but without this assistance the latter column arrived at its destination at 1230 hours. Ammunition was running short notwithstanding drops by the R.A.F., and the troops were rationed up to the 27th only, so it was decided that both columns should withdraw to Mir Ali on the following day. Casualties had been heavy, mostly in Tocol, though Razcol had two British officers killed. Altogether, of all ranks, 19 were killed and 102 wounded. Enemy strength was supposed to be about 2,000.*

The R.A.F., under O.C. No. 1 (Indian) Wing, provided one flight for reconnaissance, but this allowed only one machine in the air at a time for both columns and one flight for close support; on the 27th a second flight was allotted for close support, and six sorties were furnished that day.

The Government decided to punish the Tori Khel, in whose area hostilities had been initiated, and to demand the ejection of the Faqir. For this purpose the 2nd (Rawalpindi) Infantry Brigade was moved forward, and on 5th December "Wazir force" was formed under Major-General D. E. Robertson, C.B., D.S.O. Operations were controlled by advanced H.Q., Northern Command, at Bannu under General Sir John Coleridge.

More infantry and armoured cars joined the force and the 12th (Poonch) Battery was sent from Kohat to Tocol. No. 3 (Indian) Wing, R.A.F., under Wing Commander J. Slessor, M.C., with two flights of No. 5 Army Co-operation Squadron and No. 20 Army Co-operation Squadron less one flight, was placed under command of Wazir force with headquarters at Mir Ali.

With the Razmak Brigade was the 22nd Mountain Brigade, R.A., less one battery, and with the 2nd Infantry Brigade, the 25th Mountain Brigade, R.A., less two batteries.

General Coleridge's orders were to punish the tribal sections which had opposed the march of the two columns as related above, and to have a road constructed from Mir Ali to the Khaisora valley. Hence, for the first few weeks, the mountain batteries were

---

* During the advance a squadron of Probyn's Horse with Tocol had an opportunity to carry out a mounted attack and galloped a position to clear the front of a battalion. It had only two casualties.

occupied almost daily in covering the troops making the road, and although a good deal of ammunition was fired, no incident of importance took place until the 22nd December. On that day, whilst the 2nd Infantry Brigade was withdrawing to camp after destroying some towers, parties of tribesmen infiltrated behind a piquet, exposing the flank of an infantry company. The situation was righted with the help of the battery concerned, and two batteries then supported a counter-attack which was put in to recover the bodies of a British officer and some I.O.Rs. This was done without further casualties owing to accurate artillery fire and close support from the air.

In January, 1937, as only a few Tori Khels had submitted, various measures were tried to bring them over—leaflets from the air and pressure by political officers—but without effect. A section of 6-inch howitzers was then brought from Razmak and important targets were registered. The Faqir's prestige was on the increase, although he had to move his abode, and his new home at Arsalkot was thoroughly bombed without, however, damaging his person.

At the end of January Waziristan District was re-formed and the Razmak Brigade returned to Razmak, the additional air and land forces which had been sent up for the operations being withdrawn. The main roads were protected by the troops whilst work was being carried on, and by Scout and armoured patrols.

During the Khaisora valley operations the 12th (Poonch) Battery fired 28 shrapnel and 340 H.E. The battery returned to Kohat in February, but came back to Razmak in March and remained in Waziristan for the following two and a half years. Lieutenant A. G. Munn was awarded the M.C. and Captain J. Hills was mentioned in despatches for the Khaisora operations, and seven I.O.Rs. received the Force Commander's certificates.

During February two British officers were murdered and the situation deteriorated further; meantime the Faqir was collecting increased numbers of adherents. Preparation was made to renew operations and reinforcements were sent, including H.Q., 1st Indian Division; 1st (Abbottabad) Infantry Brigade; H.Q., 25th Mountain Brigade, R.A., with 13th (Dardoni) and 15th (Jhelum) Batteries; a battery of field howitzers, 2nd Light Battery, and more light tanks. Owing to interference from hostile gangs, traffic on the roads was considerably reduced; on the Manzai–Wana and Bannu–Razmak roads, traffic was run in convoys three times a week with infantry and armoured car escorts.

The troops were reorganized; 1st (Indian) Division (Major-

General E. de Burgh, C.B.) was allotted an operational area which took in practically the northern half of Waziristan, and the remaining troops and Scouts were under Waziristan District (Major-General Robertson). The latter was responsible for protecting and timing convoys.

Hostile activities were on the increase, bridges were damaged, camps were continually sniped, men kidnapped off lorries, etc., and a heavy attack was made on the troops of 1st Infantry Brigade when on road-protecting duties near Asad Khel on 29th March. The 13th (Dardoni) (Major A. C. S. Kennedy) and 15th (Jhelum) (Major L. A. Harris, M.C.) Mountain Batteries were in camp at Damdil with the 1st Infantry Brigade; one section of the former battery was in reserve in camp and the other section went with the 1st Bn. South Wales Borderers, who were responsible for protecting a length of road six miles northwards towards Mir Ali. The 1/6th Gurkhas and 2/6th Gurkhas, each supported by a section of 15th (Jhelum) Battery, moved out to guard the Razmak road, six miles south and west of Damdil.

The 1/6th Gurkhas were operating in very difficult and broken country covered with heavy scrub alongside the road, and their advanced guard was held up about two and a half miles out. It was attacked with great ferocity by tribesmen who poured in a heavy fire from close quarters and then attacked with knives. A section each of light tanks and armoured cars rushed at speed to the sound of the fighting, and obtained some good targets on the road. The 2/6th Gurkhas, also in rough ground, protected the right of the 1/6th Battalion and the section of 15th Battery found some good targets, but the 1/6th was pinned to its ground.

The convoy now arrived and was turned into Damdil camp while the reserve Battalion, the 2/5th Gurkhas, was brought up and made a turning movement from the north to drive the enemy out of the nullahs. This was successful, but the number of the enemy had increased during the day to about 1,000 and a heavy concentration of the batteries was required to cover the withdrawal.

Two British and two Gurkha officers were killed, and one of each wounded. Thirty Gurkha O.Rs. were killed and forty-one wounded. The enemy had about a hundred killed.

This affair was put down to the Faqir's account, and retaliation was made by bombing some villages, action being taken this time by No. 2 (Indian) Wing from Risalpur.

For the next outrage the Mahsuds, instigated by the Faqir, were responsible. On 9th April a M.T. convoy left Manzai for Wana at 0600 hours as usual; it consisted of forty-nine military and civilian lorries and two cars. No troops being available, road protection was provided by Scouts and Khassadars, and an escort of a V.C.O. and 51 I.O.Rs. of the 4/16th Punjab Regiment was with the convoy, as well as four armoured cars of No. 6 Armoured Company, Royal Tank Corps.

Vehicles were arranged in blocks of five; one armoured car led the convoy, one brought up the rear, and two were distributed down the column. The infantry escort was divided into three parties spaced down the column; a party of 72 O.Rs. returning from leave was just behind the centre party of the escort. There were also 14 officers on their way to Wana on duty, as well as some returning from leave.

On this particular morning the Scouts had not reconnoitred the Shahur Tangi, and at 0745 hours, when the head of the column was well clear of the defile and most of the convoy was inside it, intense and accurate fire was opened by the enemy along its whole length. There was ample concealment for direct and enfilade fire at very short range, and the petrol tank of the leading lorry was set on fire, blocking the road and preventing movement by the armoured cars. The escort, who bravely tried to climb out of the gorge to engage the enemy, were shot down. Scouts and light tanks were rushed from Sarwekai (eleven miles) and cleared some of the obstructions during the evening, and the 2/11th Sikhs arrived to restore communication with Jandola. The survivors were taken to Sarwekai; Major A. Paton, M.C., on his way to join 2nd (Derajat) Battery, who was in command of the convoy and had been wounded in the first burst of enemy fire, re-formed the convoy at Sarwekai to move to Wana the following morning.

The casualties were very heavy; 7 British officers killed, including Lieutenant M. Earle, 2nd (Derajat) Battery, and 5 wounded; 2 V.C.Os. wounded; 40 other ranks, drivers, etc., killed and 43 wounded. Major Paton was awarded the D.S.O. for gallant behaviour.

The authorities were perturbed at this disastrous affair and hastily closed the Manzai–Wana road except for lorries driven by Mahsuds who guaranteed the safe arrival of the heavy equipment and stores carried. When the 2nd (Derajat) was relieved by the 17th (Nowshera) Battery in the following November, an exchange of personnel was made by air.*

---

* Movement by air was becoming increasingly useful on the Frontier: in the same year the section at Qila Drosh was relieved by personnel and guns sent by aeroplane.

The success of the ambush encouraged the Mahsuds to greater activity; minor disturbances occurred almost daily, especially in the Razmak area, and gangs of men moved about the country looting and fomenting disorder. The 2nd Infantry Brigade was sent back to Waziristan from India, and General Coleridge was again invested with complete military, air and political control, with instructions to bring about the pacification of the area.

More operations took place in the Khaisora and Tochi areas during April, causing the enemy heavy casualties, but the general situation did not improve and it was quite clear that the Faqir of Ipi was the focus of all the trouble, and that he must either be kept under control or expelled from the country. There was also a road-making programme to be carried out, and the Mahsuds had to be punished.

The 9th (Jhansi) Infantry Brigade was sent up from India to Damdil, where it came under the 1st (Indian) Division about 6th May, and Wazirforce was reorganized to consist of 1st (Indian) Division and the Waziristan Division, the latter consisting of the Bannu Brigade, the 1st Infantry Brigade (temporarily), 9th Light Tank Company, and the Razmak Brigade (when the situation permitted). Advanced H.Q. was at Bannu and H.Q., No. 3 Wing, R.A.F., was now at Miranshah. Waziristan Division was commanded by Major-General A. F. Hartley, C.B., with H.Q. at Dosalli; Bannu, Manzai, and Wana became areas under Wazirforce, and the advanced base was located at Bannu.

The artillery of the force consisted of five batteries of field artillery, a section of 20/21st Medium Battery (6-inch howitzers) and 22nd, 23rd and 25th Mountain Brigades under Lieutenant-Colonels H. S. MacDonald, D.S.O., M.C., J. Penrose, M.C., and C. A. L. Brownlow, D.S.O., respectively. The three mountain Brigades included 2nd and 3rd Light Batteries and the following Mountain Batteries: 2nd (Derajat), F.F., 3rd (Peshawar), F.F.; 4th (Hazara), F.F.; 5th (Bombay); 7th (Bengal); 8th (Lahore); 12th (Poonch); 13th (Dardoni); 15th (Jhelum); 17th (Nowshera); 19th (Maymyo).

The Post Guns* were manned in their stations, Mir Ali, Wana and Manzai.

With a view to an advance on the Faqir's abode at Arsalkot, for which purpose a road or track had to be made, a preliminary operation was carried out by the Waziristan Division to clear the Sham Plain, on which about 4,000 tribesmen were reported to have gathered.

---

* Of the Frontier Garrison Artillery, an expansion of the Punjab Garrison battery at Kohat.

The 1st Infantry Brigade was ordered to march direct from the divisional camp at Dosalli, and the Bannu Brigade, which included the 7th (Bengal) and 19th (Maymyo) Batteries, was to make a night march converging on the plain from the eastward. Eight platoons of Tochi Scouts were to cover the advance, which started at 2100 hours on 11th May.

The route chosen over the Iblanke mountain presented more difficulty than had been expected and the going was very bad even for the mules. The column was strung out in single file, taking four hours to pass the starting-point, and the pace was extremely slow. By daylight the leading battery, the 7th (Bengal), was in action under Captain Streatfield, who took a section forward into a narrow, densely wooded col at the head of a nullah running down to the Sham Plain. The guns were almost wheel to wheel, and had some wonderful shooting at 300 yards; this flushed a large number of tribesmen who gave the R.A.F. its best targets of the day. The track was too narrow to bring any more guns into action at this spot, but the force worked down on to the plain, and after fifteen hours' climbing and fighting, Coronation Camp (it being Coronation Day) was marked out and occupied with a loss of only three killed and ten wounded. The 13th (Dardoni) Battery and three battalions were sent up for protection duty in rear of the Bannu Brigade, which advanced on 18th May to occupy a new camp on the Sham Plain, called Ghariom, as a jumping-off place for the attack on Arsalkot. This was to be carried out by the Bannu Brigade and the 1st Infantry Brigade, with the 2nd Infantry Brigade co-operating from the northeast.

The L. of C. from Bannu to the forward troops was now held by permanent piquets, and convoys were run at twenty-minute intervals without close escorts.

The Bannu Brigade left Ghariom at 0445 hours on 27th May, supported by the 7th and 19th Mountain Batteries, preceded by Tochi Scouts, the first day's objective being Pasal, which was reached by the transport at 1245 hours. The advance was opposed, at times in strength, but both brigades were in camp by 1800 hours, with total casualties seven killed and twenty wounded.

The 2nd Infantry Brigade left Mir Ali with great secrecy at 0345 hours on 27th May with no blankets or kits; its destination was Bichhe Kashkai on the Khaisora river, and it was organized in a mechanical column and a marching column; with the latter were the 3rd (Peshawar) and 8th (Lahore) Mountain Batteries. There was no opposition. As a shortage of water was feared, each unit carried a double echelon of water pakhals and each mule a chagal.

The 2nd Infantry Brigade moved before daylight on 28th to rendezvous at Arsalkot with the other column, but missed the direction owing to the difficult nature of the country, and camped for the night at 1400 hours at a point near the Shakhtu river, some seven miles on the map from its last camp. This was a very trying march over rough, steep going with no water for twenty-four hours; no transport or horses were allowed. It took the column six hours to reach Pasal the next day.

The Bannu Brigade that day moved to Arsalkot and the 1st Infantry Brigade passed through to complete the destruction of the village, which had been partly destroyed by air bombardment. The caves recently occupied by the Faqir were completely demolished, the Faqir having evacuated in good time. Both brigades were back at Pasal by 1900 hours, and all three brigades concentrated there the following night.

The first serious opposition occurred when the rear-guard of the Bannu Brigade, the 2nd Bn. The Argyll and Sutherland Highlanders, had difficulty in withdrawing a piquet, but the enemy's advance was checked by artillery fire; later in the day a similar incident occurred to a piquet of the 2/4th Gurkhas, but this time a barrage from ten 3.7-inch howitzers was put down between the piquet and the tribesmen, with immediate results.

The operation had been carried out successfully with very few casualties, and word came in that the Tori Khels were strongly in favour of submission.

Nevertheless, raids on a large scale, mostly by parties of Mahsuds, suddenly increased; one party about 400 strong even held up a train (the Heat Stroke Express*) in a cutting at Pezu, but the escort kept them engaged until the train drove clear. Mullah Sher Ali, the Faqir's lieutenant, collected a party and began to harass the troops at Wana, but retribution was postponed for the time being, and his effort then faded away.

There were many miles of road to construct, and ten Field Companies of the Sappers and Miners and four Road Construction Battalions were present to do the work, assisted by infantry working parties and hired labour. Road-making and road-protection duties went on incessantly for the next six months; the latter work monotonous except that it was carried out in the vicinity of eager guerilas who were always watching for a mistake on the part of the troops, of which they took every advantage and gave no second chance.

Mahsud country was visited by brigade columns, and in June the

---

* It was said that topees had to be worn *inside* the carriages to avoid sunstroke in the hot weather.

Razmak Brigade reconnoitred the vicinity of Ladha, but with little effect. Telegraph lines were cut as usual, roads damaged, and camps were generally sniped, and it was evident that many of the tribesmen were without any means of livelihood, and found it hard to live without looting. Another attempt was made to capture the Faqir, who had returned to the Lower Shaktu, and to disperse a lashkar which had collected there, but with disappointing results.

The Waziristan Division concentrated for operations about Torwam, during which Captain H. S. King, 3rd (Peshawar) Battery, and Lieutenant R. F. J. Anderson, Assistant Adjutant, were wounded. On 29th June the mountain guns with the Bannu Brigade had some good targets during an attack which brought a strong lashkar to bay and concluded with the destruction of Sher Ali's headquarters. The Faqir was declared a fugitive and kept on the move as much as possible.

The R.A.F. had taken part in all the moves and operations, but flying conditions had been adverse owing to the dust prevalent in the hot weather, and early in July General Sir John Coleridge sent one squadron back to India, retaining No. 20, consisting of H.Q. and three flights. Raids continued in the Mahsud areas, both on large and small scales; columns traversing the area were sometimes attacked and sometimes left alone, but sniping at camps and road protection troops seldom ceased. Nearly the whole of Waziristan was visited in force. There were several hotbeds of trouble, especially in an area west of Kaniguram which had never seen troops, but the opposition gradually grew less as the Faqir was kept on the move and pressed up against the Afghan frontier. Our casualties certainly increased steadily, but the tribesmen were losing many more men.

The mountain batteries used their opportunities of rest to keep up their technical training.

In October operations were carried out at Spinwam, fifteen miles south-west of Thal (Kurram) and in the Bhittanni country as well. Tribesmen in the latter area had suddenly become active in kidnapping Hindus and raiding, and a road was pushed out to Kot, preparatory to an advance. The 25th Mountain Brigade less one battery was attached to the 2nd Infantry Brigade for this operation. After some softening up by air action the Bhitannis submitted and work on the road was not molested further.

The 13th (Dardoni) Battery was with the 1st Infantry Brigade on a march from Bichhe Kashkai down the lower Shaktu valley on 18th November when it distinguished itself in support of a company of the 1st Bn. The South Wales Borderers forcing the eastern end of the Shaktu Tangi. The gap was only fifteen yards wide, and although the high ground on both flanks was occupied, the vanguard was held up by point-blank rifle fire which caused several casualties. The leading section of the battery was close behind and the acting battery commander, Captain G. C. Fawns, after making a personal reconnaissance, had his guns manhandled through the Tangi under fire and engaged the enemy over open sights. He then ran forward, still under heavy fire, and brought in a wounded man. Finding on a second trip forward that another casualty was dead, Captain Fawns returned to his guns in the open and controlled them until the position was cleared. Without this opportune artillery support many more casualties would have been incurred. Subadar Alam Khan, I.D.S.M., was with the leading gun and opened a quick and accurate fire with shrapnel at 200 yards; he then brought the other gun into action and remained fully exposed (a grand man, six feet five inches tall) along with Subadar Anant Ram until the enemy retreated. They set a magnificent example of steadiness to the detachments. For outstanding gallantry and leadership, Captain Fawns received an immediate award of the Military Cross, and Subadar Alam Khan was awarded the 2nd Class I.O.M.

This was the last operation on any scale, and as winter was coming on and most of the tribes agreed not to continue the war, fines and rifles were collected without trouble. The Faqir was still loose, but was unable to raise enthusiasm for his cause.

About 50,000 troops, including administrative services, had been engaged in this war. Fifteen mule and three camel transport companies were in use, animal transport being allotted to formations as necessary. The condition of the animals throughout was satisfactory.

Wazirforce ceased to exist on 15th December, 1937, and the G.O.C., Waziristan District, assumed control. The additional troops were withdrawn except for the 17th (Nowshera) Battery (at Wana), one light tank company, and one infantry brigade of six battalions.

Casualties had amounted to 245 killed, 685 wounded, and 73 deaths from disease; tribal casualties greatly exceeded these figures.

The road-making programme was not finished, although 114 miles of motor road had been constructed, and giving accessibility to most of the country was part of the policy of civilizing the inhabitants. The younger tribesmen were still restless, and the three brigades left in Waziristan—Bannu, Razmak, and Wana—had little rest from road protection and guard of their lines of communication.

In the latter part of 1937 the light batteries were turned into Indian mountain batteries by replacing the British gunner establishment by Indians drawn from the M.A.T.C. and other units. The new batteries were 20th to 25th, having been formed from Nos. 2,* 3,† 4,‡ 5,§ 7,‖ and 9¶ Light Batteries respectively. The 20th M.A. Brigade H.Q. moved to Quetta to take over the 22nd, 23rd, 24th, and 25th Indian Batteries; its class composition was now Punjabi Mohammedans, Lobana Sikhs, and Ahirs. The 20th and 21st Mountain Batteries replaced the light batteries in their own brigades. These new batteries were formed as "Mountain Batteries, R.A."

By Army Order 204 of 1938 the expression "Brigade" in the Artillery was replaced by "Regiment."

Amongst the honours awarded to Mountain Gunners for these operations was the C.B. to the C.R.A., Brigadier A. J. T. Farfan, D.S.O., O.B.E., who afterwards became Brigadier, R.A., Northern Command, India, and the C.B.E. to Brigadier C. D. Rawson, D.S.O., General Staff.

A number of awards of the D.S.O. were made:

Major E. W. Goodman, M.C.
Lieutenant-Colonel C. A. L. Brownlow (bar to D.S.O.).
Major L. A. Harris.

M.Cs. were awarded to Lieutenant C. W. B. Gilbert and to Captain N. R. Streatfield.

Naik Abdul Rasul (13th M.B.) was awarded the I.D.S.M.

Thirty-two British officers were mentioned in despatches, and the following V.C.Os. and N.C.Os. of batteries who were gazetted as "Indian Army, Royal Artillery":

Subadar Sher Singh, 12th (Poonch).
Havildar Ismail Khan, 13th (Dardoni).
Havildar Mahomed Alam, 8th (Lahore).
Havildar Abdal Haq, 15th (Jhelum).
Lance/Naik Khan Bahadur, 12th (Poonch).
Havildar Chanan Singh, 7th (Bengal).
Subadar Sher Mahomed, I.O.M., 3rd (Peshawar).

---

* No. 2 Light Battery had a long history, having been formed in 1749 as No. 1 Company, Bengal Artillery, and after losing its Commandant and 45 gunners in the tragedy of the "Black Hole of Calcutta" (1756), was reorganized in time to take part with distinction in the battle of Plassey (1757). The battery received the honour-title of "Plassey" in 1937.

† No. 3 Light Battery had been formed as a R.A. Company in 1759, had fought with distinction in the rear-guard at Corunna, and was awarded that honour-title in 1930.

‡ No. 4 Light Battery had been formed in 1770 as 5 Company, Bengal Artillery.

§ No. 5 Light Battery formed in 1771 as 2 Company, 4th Battalion, R.A.

‖ No. 7 Light Battery formed in 1794 as 3 Company, 5th Battalion, R.A.

¶ No. 9 Light Battery was formed in 1779 as No. 5 Company, 2nd Battalion Bengal Artillery, and in 1936 received the honour-title "Kabul 1842".

Subadar Anant Ram, 13th (Dardoni).
Havildar-Major Khan Gul, 4th (Hazara).
Naik Sirdar Ali, 7th (Bengal).
Havildar Sher Ram, 15th (Jhelum).
Lance-Naik Sher Jang Khan, 7th (Bengal).
Subadar Mahomed Sharif, 19th (Maymyo).
(The above includes some 1938 awards).

A new India General Service Medal (1936) was struck with clasp "North-West Frontier 1936-37" and awarded to individuals present during the campaign.

As the Guides Infantry marched into Damdil one day in October, 1937, the 4th (Hazara) Mountain Battery was marching out, and the occasion was seized for the presentation to the battery of a silver trumpet. Liaison between the units was very complete, having lasted for nearly five years: during the Mohmand and Loe Agra campaigns and the 1936-37 Waziristan operations. The battalion formed two sides of a square, the battery the third, and all the officers of both corps, British and Indian, the fourth. Lieutenant-Colonel Garrett of the Guides alluded to the admiration and affection his unit felt for the battery, and the trumpet was handed to Captain G. R. L. Hawkes, M.C., in temporary command of the battery. The Subadar-Major of the Guides called for three cheers.

The trumpet was inscribed with the badge of the battery and the words:

"Presented by Lieutenant-Colonel Grant and the British
and Indian officers of the Guides Infantry F.F. to the
4th (Hazara) Mountain Battery R.A. (F.F.)
In memory of many happy days spent together on
the Frontier in 1932, 1933, 1935-36-37 (Mohmand
and Waziristan)."

The battery returned this great compliment in 1947 by presenting a plaque showing the crests of the two corps and the engraved signatures of the officers of the battery with the inscription:

"1947
"Presented to the Guides Infantry by the 4th (Hazara)
Mountain Battery in memory of many years' service
together."

Damdil was the scene of another presentation in 1938 when the 1/3rd Gurkha Rifles presented the 18th (Sohan) Mountain Battery with a kukri to commemorate the comradeship and good feeling between the two units.

A unique ceremony took place in 1936 when the 5th (Bombay) Mountain Battery celebrated its centenary. A guardroom bell on a tripod which had been subscribed for by past and present officers was handed over to the battery by Brigadier A. J. T. Farfan, then B.R.A., Northern Command. On the bell were inscribed the R.A. crest and the dates "1836"—"1936", and round the top the inscription:

"Presented by Past and Present officers to commemorate One hundred years of Service."

When the evidence that the Battery was raised in 1827 was accepted by Army Headquarters, a plate was engraved and mounted on the tripod to record the fact.

During 1938 hostile activities never ceased. Kidnapping, mining of roads and railways, attacks on Khassadars, and sniping persisted everywhere during the spring. A novel form of nuisance was the contamination of water supplies. The tribes professed to be unable to capture the Faqir, but doubtless they could have done so if they had wished. Mullah Sher Ali was busy with a lashkar in South Waziristan; he attacked the Scout post at Splitoi, killed the British officer in charge, and would have cut up the garrison when it ran out of ammunition at dusk but for the gallantry of Flight-Lieutenant Jackson, R.A.F., who flew low and dropped S.A.A. on the Scouts. Datta Khel fort was besieged for a month and bravely held by the Scouts; during this time several night attacks were made and a tribal gun fired shot and shell—in fact, tribal artillery was now in frequent use.

The Wana and Razmak brigades were constantly on the move with results as indecisive as ever; it was expecting too much of the Army to ask it to round up extremely agile guerillas in bands of 200 to 500 in very difficult country. Hence, too, at the best it was impossible to inflict other than minor losses on the enemy. Six mountain batteries were left to carry out almost continuous operations.

The aeroplane, though of great value, did not solve the problem owing to restrictions under which the R.A.F. worked; for instance, a peculiar regulation forbade the bombing or machine-gunning of a tribal gathering unless the latter was firing at troops—or at the aeroplane. Planes were in demand for transporting troops and stores when, as often happened, the roads could not be kept open.

On 2nd June, 1938, Razcol, with which were H.Q. 23rd Mountain Regiment, 3rd (Peshawar) and 12th (Poonch) Batteries, and the 3rd Infantry Brigade, to which were attached 8th (Lahore) and 19th (Maymyo) Batteries, moved out from Razani and Gardai respectively to attack a lashkar which had burnt the Khassadar post at Datta Khel and was investing the Scout post. Stiff opposition was met at once and the 8th (Lahore) Battery came under fire from 200 yards. Five mules of one gun fell on a shale slope, and the other sub-section fired for twenty minutes as fast as ammunition could be got up to it. Once in action ranges were from 600 to 1,200 yards and a dust haze made observation difficult; this gave the Faqir of Ipi the opportunity to tell his men that he had brought it on by prayer. The battery lost a havildar killed and a naik wounded, and fired 84 rounds H.E., fuze 106E, and 70 shrapnel. The infantry attained their objective, and on advancing three days later found that much damage had been done which it took some days to clear up.

On the 15th the 8th (Lahore) Battery and the 19th (Maymyo) found themselves under fire from enemy artillery at about 1,900 yards and silenced it in fifteen minutes.

Disturbances grew more frequent and the two brigades were formed into a force christened "Wastrike." In July an expedition was made to Kharre on the Afghan border in an attempt to catch the Faqir: the advance had to be made over very difficult mountainous country against strong opposition, and although the Faqir evaded capture he was kept on the move.

His followers attacked the Scout post at Splitoi in South Waziristan with a tribal gun, but this gang was roughly handled. "Ipi's gun" turned out to be a breech-loader which fired 3.7-inch shrapnel cases which had already been used by us. A crater of two feet diameter and one foot depth was made when the shell exploded, which only happened on rare occasions with little ensuing damage. The striker was a metal pin protruding from the nose and intended to be driven by impact on to the base of a .303-inch blank cartridge in order to set off the charge. The metal of the striking pin was usually so soft that the pin bent and the blank cartridge did not explode.

The Ahmadzais who lived in the salient to the north of Bannu began to damage roads and started to raid in their district: they evaded our troops, and on the 23rd/24th July a gang of outlaws raided Bannu, causing £30,000's-worth of damage. A successful attack by Scouts supported by mountain guns was made on the Ahmadzais in September, and raiding on the Bannu–Kohat road ceased. It had been very prevalent during the hot weather, and a section of 20th Mountain Battery at Kohat had been employed with the column protecting this road.

In the intervals between offensives units were on road protection duties.

The Razmak–Wana road, which for several months had only been used on occasion, was declared open in September.

Occasional slight outbreaks of cholera amongst the men occurred, and anthrax amongst the mules, but generally speaking health was good. Camps were invariably sniped at night and the enemy had quantities of Mills grenades for close fighting.

There was little difference in the activities of the troops in the following year, 1939.

From the complimentary orders in battery records there is no doubt that batteries maintained the highest standard of efficiency and cheerfulness under very strenuous conditions of life. Night operations were now a commonplace.

A bar "North-West Frontier, 1937-39," was added to the India General Service Medal (1936) for operations carried out during those years.

During the frontier operations just described outside agitators had been giving the tribes every encouragement; the Pathan gleefully accepted aid from his foreign backers to accentuate his hatred of the British, and neither race looked ahead to an eventual settlement. At this time in India twenty-seven battalions of British infantry were detailed for internal security. Later the unrest in India subsided.

From 1st August, 1939, Indian Mountain Artillery ceased to belong to the Royal Regiment of Artillery, and again formed part of His Majesty's Indian Forces (A.H.Q. letter 347/R.A. of 18th December, 1939). The Corps of Mountain Artillery was transferred to the Indian Regiment of Artillery, later renamed Regiment of Indian Artillery. Some batteries recorded that the I.O.R. felt that it was a slight to have been moved out of a famous regiment of which His Majesty the King-Emperor was Colonel-in-Chief, and asked what they had done to lose "izzat." But these were the days of much talking amongst the politicians, of threats to obstruct all British measures. It is no wonder that the simple soldier was confused. As the Subadar said to his battery commander: "King's Commission we know, and Viceroy's Commission, but what is this Simon Commission?"

The "Simon" was one of the "commissions" sent by the British Cabinet to India to try to induce Hindus and Mussulmans to

---

Note by the Compiler. The I.O.Rs. would have had even more occasion to wonder if they realized that the authority for a large slice to be cut out of the Royal Artillery was an Army Council Instruction (554 of 1939). The Indian Mountain Batteries were not even given the formality of an Army Order, or thanks for their service.

combine peacefully in forming a constitution for a new Dominion, but no success was obtained. For some years it had been obvious that the two races would never unite, and the partition of the country had been advocated by the Muslim League. The professional politician was at the height of his glory; any proposal made by the British rulers for the benefit and safety of the peoples of India was met with obstruction and non-co-operation. This in no way disturbed the soldiers of the Indian Army; for several generations men of different races and religions had served happily in a regiment, bound together by loyalty to the Sirkar. The mountain batteries had always been mixed units.

It was a matter of common knowledge that another great war was imminent, and when it came the fighting races did not fail. An enormous army was raised for the King-Emperor's service, every man a volunteer. More than two million in all were eventually enlisted, and numbers were only limited by the equipment and training facilities available. Fortunately there were Indians with a sense of responsibility who spared no labour to assist the preparations for the war, the British Government having undertaken responsibility for the defence of India.

In September, 1939, at the outbreak of war, the distribution of the Indian Mountain Artillery was as follows:

Regiment	Commander and Batteries	Station
20th Regiment	Lieutenant-Colonel H. H. MacKenzie 22nd, 23rd, 24th, 25th M.Bs.	Quetta
21st Regiment	Lieutenant-Colonel F. C. A. Troup 1st Royal (Kohat) F.F., 6th (Bombay), 9th (Murree), 14th (Rajputana) M.Bs.	Kohat
22nd Regiment	Lieutenant-Colonel A. H. Peskett, M.C. 4th (Hazara) F.F., 7th (Bengal), 10th (Abbottabad), 21st M.Bs.	Malaya
23rd Regiment	Lieutenant-Colonel L. R. Stansfeld 3rd (Peshawar) F.F., 8th (Bengal), 17th (Nowshera), 12th (Poonch) M.Bs.	Abbottabad
24th Regiment	Lieutenant-Colonel G. H. Johnstone 11th (Dehra Dun), 16th (Zhob), 18th (Sohan), 20th M.Bs.	Peshawar
25th Regiment	Lieutenant-Colonel C. A. L. Brownlow 5th (Bombay), 13th (Dardoni), 15th (Jhelum), 19th (Maymyo) M.Bs.	Waziristan

The 2nd (Derajat) F.F. Battery was quartered in Maymyo, and there was an independent section in Chitral.

In December, 1939, Colonel R. V. M. Garry,* M.C., was appointed Colonel, Mountain Artillery, Northern Command, India—a new appointment. He was succeeded by Colonel J. W. English.

---

* Colonel Garry was afterwards killed in an air crash in Egypt.

The officer was in charge of Mountain Artillery, and artillery in Frontier operations.

During the early part of the Second World War there were disturbances on the North-West Frontier, but not on a large scale, and they can be described in a few words.

There was an exceptional number of outrages in the Bannu area in the latter part of 1939, for which gangs based on the Ahmedzai salient were again responsible. This feature juts out from Afghanistan into the area between Bannu and Thal and is, therefore, accessible from both the north and south sides.

After a British officer with one British and two Indian other ranks had been ambushed and killed within three miles of Bannu, operations were started to eliminate the gangs. The Kohat and 3rd Infantry Brigades under Brigadier A. E. Barstow, M.C., commanding the Kohat Brigade, assembled in February, 1940, to attack the south of the salient with the support of 21st Mountain Regiment. The 5th (Bombay) Battery had been sent from the Regiment at Razmak to replace the 1st Royal (Kohat) Battery temporarily, and with the 6th (Jacob's) Battery provided support for the 3rd Infantry Brigade; R.H.Q. with 9th (Murree) and 14th (Rajputana) Batteries was with the Kohat Brigade.

The 1st Battery went out from Damdil with a small column to assist the operations and a few days later joined a column from Bannu; it took the place of the 5th Battery on March 24th.

The 3rd (Peshawar) Battery went by train from Abbottabad to join Thalcol for these operations on the tribal border on the north of the salient, blocking the exits on that front. There was little opposition, and after an uneventful time the battery returned to Abbottabad at the end of May.

The 3rd Infantry Brigade found stiff opposition on entering the Gumatti Tangi, and the Kohat Brigade (Kohbde) had to undergo a great deal of sniping during its move up the Tangi Algad from Barganatu, but with the help of the guns the columns got through and concentrated at Gumatti on 22nd February. Resistance was met with, prisoners were taken and a few villages were burnt, and casualties were inflicted on the enemy. This strong display of force broke the back of the opposition and little more was met with during the stay of the force.

The troops were now turned on to road-making and road protection duties which lasted until the end of May. A useful road was completed from Bannu to Chappari via Gumatti, with other roads branching off, thus opening up a roadless country. The troops were withdrawn at the end of May, the only serious opposition having

Captain Ghulam Mohammed, Sirdar Bahadur

Was a sais in the Derajat Mountain Battery in Lord Roberts' march from Kabul to Kandahar. When old enough, he was enlisted as a driver, and having risen to the rank of havildar, his services were so much appreciated that he was commissioned as Jemadar in that battery. He was known as Ghulam Mohammed Dusra. His namesake was a gunner in the same battery in that celebrated march. He also retired with the honorary rank of Captain, having been Subadar-Major and Sirdar Bahadur in the Murree Mountain Battery.

Captain Kishen Singh, I.D.S.M.

Captain Kishen Singh enlisted as a driver in the 5th (Bombay) Mountain Battery in 1902. A man of strong personality, he rose rapidly to havildar. Was at the School of Artillery, Kakul, in 1923, where his outstanding intelligence was of great value in instructing N.Os. When the R.A. Survey Section, India, was formed, he was the key man. In 1927 he was selected as an Indian Orderly Officer to H.M. King George V.

Face page 261

been met in the Gumatti Tangi, where about 2,000 rounds had been fired by the artillery. The enemy confessed to nearly a hundred casualties.

Road protection duty went on during the hot weather and Razcol and Tocol were frequently called out to stop disturbances. The Indian Air Force was now taking a prominent part in maintaining peace in the tribal areas.

More outrages occurred the following year which were put down to the Faqir of Ipi, who was never far from the seat of trouble. Tappi, a village of the Lower Daurs, was its centre and a column was sent to Datta Khel, which was due for relief. There was scrapping on road protection duty almost daily in the Tochi valley during July and August, 1941. A story is recorded of Mirshahjan, a notorious outlaw, who was flushed out of his orchard by a shell and ran at great speed across the front of a battalion. In this sprint of 1,000 yards he ran the gauntlet of machine-gun, Lewis gun and rifle fire at about 1,200 yards range. He escaped untouched.

CHAPTER IX

Second World War

INDIA, 1939-1946

THE SECOND WORLD WAR broke out on 3rd September, 1939, when Great Britain and her Dominions and France declared war on Hitler's Germany. In June, 1940, when the French were about to capitulate, Italy joined Germany in the hope of an easy victory. Russia joined first one side and then the other, and the United States joined the Allies after Japan treacherously attacked Pearl Harbour.

Great Britain and her Dominions and India continued to carry on the war under Mr. Churchill's leadership.

In this chapter are recorded a number of facts as regards the formation of new regiments and batteries and the conditions of service.*

In December, 1939, Colonel A. J. T. Farfan, D.S.O., was appointed Colonel, Mountain Artillery, Northern Command, India.

In 1939 the 22nd Mountain Battery at Quetta formed two batteries, 22nd and 26th, the 22nd going in September to East Africa, where the 27th found itself in August, 1940, and the 18th (Sohan) arrived in 1941. The 27th Battery had been formed at Dehra Dun from details left behind when the 22nd Mountain Regiment went to Malaya, in 1939.

The 26th Mountain Regiment H.Q. was formed in Egypt to administer the batteries in Africa together with the 1st Jammu and Kashmir Battery which joined them. After its return to India in May, 1942, this H.Q. served on the North-West Frontier.

The 27th Mountain Regiment H.Q. (Lieutenant-Colonel W. G. Constable) was formed at Ambala in December, 1941, and sent to Rangoon to take over the batteries which had gone to Burma before the outbreak of war with Japan.

The 28th Mountain Regiment H.Q. (Lieutenant-Colonel W. H. Peskett, M.C.) mobilized with the 15th (Jhelum) and 28th Mountain Battery in January, 1942, for service in Burma. The 28th Battery was raised in Peshawar by 24th Mountain Regiment.

The first Light Mountain regiments were formed in the cold

---

* The overseas operations in which Indian Mountain Artillery units were involved will be found in Chapter X.

weather, 1942-3, for service in Burma and comprised two, and finally three, Light Mountain Batteries.*

The 21st R.H.Q. split during the last few months of 1942 to form 21st and 29th Light Mountain R.H.Q. The 21st Regiment (Lieutenant-Colonel W. J. Cooper) was composed of 1st Royal (Kohat) and 6th (Jacob's); the 29th Regiment (Lieutenant-Colonel G. Horsfield), 9th (Murree) and 14th (Rajputana), all now classed as Light Mountain Batteries. These two regiments joined 17 (Light) Division in Burma (page 264).

The 24th R.H.Q. from Peshawar became H.Q. of the 24th Light Mountain Regiment (Lieutenant-Colonel S. Picton), which comprised the 11th (Dehra Dun) and 20th Mountain Batteries in 26 Indian Division on the Arakan front in 1943. On the change of establishment the 2nd and 12th Batteries were added to complete it to a four-battery regiment.

The 27th Mountain R.H.Q., after returning from Burma in July, 1942, was mobilized as a Light Mountain regiment with 2nd (Derajat) and 12th (Poonch) as Light Mountain Batteries, and was sent to Ranchi in April, 1943, whence the two batteries were sent to 26 Indian Division on the Arakan front. R.H.Q. joined the batteries a few months later, but was amalgamated with 24th R.H.Q. on the discontinuation of the Light Mountain establishment towards the end of the year 1944.

Other regimental headquarters were formed from time to time when required, as will be seen from the following table, which shows moves and changes from 1943 to 1946.

SECOND WORLD WAR
MOVEMENTS OF REGIMENTS AND BATTERIES

Regiment	1939-40	1941	1942	1943	1944 Jap Offensive	1945	1946
20	Quetta 23, 24, 25, 26	Quetta 23, 24, 25, 26	Waziristan 24, 25, 26 1 Gwalior	Peshawar 24, 25, 26 1 Gwalior	Burma 24, 25, 26, 19 Div.	Burma 24, 25, 26 19 Div.	—

* This designation must not be confused with Light Batteries, which were the successors of the Mountain Batteries, R.G.A. (British gunners and Indian drivers). These batteries moved in draught, but had a minimum number of ordnance mules for use in pack as opportunity offered. The establishment of a Light Mountain Battery was 4 British officers, 3 V.C.Os., 221 I.O.Rs., and 6 followers. All tradesmen and followers (except sweepers) were taken on the strength and attested. The number of animals was 110 mules and 23 ponies: 72 rounds per gun were carried instead of 120.

MOVEMENTS OF REGIMENTS AND BATTERIES—*continued*

Regiment	1939-40	1941	1942	1943	1944	1945	1946
21	Kohat 1, 6, 9, 14	Kohat 1, 6, 9, 14	Burma 1, 6 17 Light Div.	Burma 1, 6, 37 17 Light Div.	Burma 1, 6, 37 17 Div.	Burma 1, 6, 37, 17 Div.	—
22	Malaya 4, 7, 10, 21	Malaya 4, 7, 10, 21	Malaya 4, 7, 10, 21 P.oW. Feb.	—	—	—	—
23	Abbottabad 3, 8, 12, 17	Abbottabad 3, 8, 17 2 J & K	Burma 3, 8, 17 2 J & K 14 Div.	Burma 3, 8, 17, 31 20 Div.	Burma 3, 8, 31 20 Div.	Burma 3, 8, 31 23 Div.	Saigon 20 Div. Malaya 7 Div.
24	Peshawar 11, 16, 20	Peshawar 11, 16, 20	Burma 23 Div. 11, 16, 20	Burma 2, 11, 12 20 5 Div.	Burma 2, 11, 20 5 Div.	Burma 2, 11, 20 5 Div.	Java 2, 11, 20 5 Div.
25	Waziristan 5, 13 15, 19	Waziristan 5, 13 15, 19	Quetta 13, 19 Bikanir	Burma 5, 19 23 Bik. 7 Div.	Burma 5, 23 Bikanir 7 Div.	Burma 5, 23 Bikanir 7 Div.	—
26	Africa not Regimented 18, 22, 27 1 J & K	Africa not Regimented 18, 22, 27 1 J & K	Peshawar 18, 22, 27 I J & K	Waziristan 18, 22, 30 1 Gwalior	Waziristan 18, 22, 30 1 Gwalior	Waziristan 18, 22, 30 1 Gwalior	—
27	—	Burma 2, 5, 12, 23 Bur. Div.	Burma 2, 5, 12, 23 Bur. Div.	Burma 2, 12, 26 Div.	R.H.Q. Amalgamated with 24 R.H.Q.	—	—
28	—	—	Burma 15, 28 17 Div.	Burma 13, 15, 16, 28 23 Div.	Burma 13, 15, 16, 28 23 Div.	Burma 13, 15, 16 23 Div.	—
29	—	—	Burma 9, 14 17 Light Div.	Burma 9, 14, 38 17 Light Div.	Burma 9, 14, 38 17 Div.	Peshawar 9, 14, 38 Baha'pur	—
30	—	—	Burma 32, 33, 34 26 Div.	Burma 32, 33, 34 26 Div.	Burma 27, 32, 33 26 & 81 (W.A.) Divs.	Burma 27, 32, 33 26 Div.	Bangkok 27, 32, 33 26 Div.
31	—	—	—	Kohat 27, 29, 35 2 Gwalior	Kohat 29, 35 2 Gwalior Patiala	Kohat 27, 29 2 Gwalior Patiala	Disbanded

MOVEMENTS OF REGIMENTS AND BATTERIES—*continued*

Regiment	1939-40	1941	1942	1943	1944	1945	1946
32	—	—	—	—	Burma 12, 17, 28 36 Brit. Div.	Burma 12, 17, 28 36 Brit. Div.	—
33	—	—	—	—	Burma 19, 34 25 Div.	Burma 19, 34 25 Div. Siam 19, 34, 35 7 Div.	Bangkok and Malaya 7 Div.

Of the batteries shown in the table which have not been mentioned earlier in this book:

29th was raised in Peshawar by 26th Mountain Regiment, 1942

30th (Jammu) and 31st (Jammu) were the designations given to the 1st and 2nd Jammu and Kashmir Batteries when taken over by the Indian Government from the Maharajah of Kashmir in 1942.

32nd, 33rd, and 34th were raised in Ambala to form 30th Mountain Regiment, 1942.

35th was raised in Campbellpur and joined 31st Mountain Regiment, 1943.

37th and 38th were raised in Ranchi as mortar batteries for 6th A.T. Regiment in July, 1942, and joined 21st and 29th Light Mountain Regiments repectively in Burma in August, 1943, as Mountain Batteries equipped with twelve 3-inch mortars. When the "Light" establishment was discontinued the mortars were exchanged for 3.7 howitzers and these batteries became standard mountain artillery units. The 38th Battery did not give up its mortars until May, 1944, and on arrival in Peshawar in August, 1945, received another issue which it retained as well as its howitzers.

36th Battery was never raised.

From 13th October, 1942, by Army Order 2403, the word "Indian" was added to the designation of Mountain Artillery units.

In the hot weather of 1942 the mules and drivers of the batteries of the 26th Mountain Regiment arrived in India via Basra. They had marched from Lajjun Camp (Palestine), where they picked up some first-class horses from the Warwickshire Yeomanry, along the Iraq pipe-line under Captain T. G. Chamberlain and Lieutenant Bumpus of the 27th Battery without the loss of an animal.

During the war mules became difficult to procure and most of the transport animals other than country breeds came from South Africa. Of the "ordnance" type, the finest American mule became more rare, but was still obtainable under Lease-Lend arrangements until the latter half of the war. From 1944 onwards, first-class equipment mules were issued to replace all except gun ammunition mules. Only 48 rounds per gun were carried in pack and the remainder was moved in M.T., perhaps another 80 rounds or as ordered. Refilling in pack was done by all the mules in the battery. The provision of a few jeeps and trucks was soon found to be essential for all batteries.

The outstanding change of mountain artillery equipment during this war was adoption of motor transport. This was by no means universal; certain units were mechanized and allotted to mechanized divisions, others were partly mechanized. Rubber tyres were a *sine qua non*; the first pattern issued was a standard motor tyre, but the axles could not stand up to the strain, and it was not until the end of 1944 that a suitable axle of nickel steel with ball-bearing hubs was provided, which was in every way satisfactory. These wheels were heavy and not easy to carry in pack, as sometimes had to be done, but a special fitting to an ammunition saddle was made for the purpose when they could not be put on a vehicle.

The gun carriage was slightly altered to permit the sides of the trail being hooked together when on the move. It was named Type IIP and carried a smaller shield.

Shrapnel was not issued after 1942; H.E., with No. 222 fuze was used instead.

Supercharges were issued consisting of a full charge V and Charge III. A range of 7,150 yards was obtained.

As explained in Appendix IV, in order to make possible an increase in the number of Indian batteries during the war, mountain batteries were "milked" of V.C.Os. and I.O.Rs. while they were in India, even those on the North-West Frontier. Drafts were frequently called for to form other than mountain artillery units, and batteries responded loyally to these calls though they lost trained V.C.Os. and men in so doing. This system, and the training of men below the standard, physically and educationally, made the officer's life a hard one, especially when it came to giving up trained N.C.Os. and specialists.

It was difficult to find enough Royal Artillery officers to fill the vacancies not only in mountain but also in other types of Indian artillery. An elementary test in Urdu was introduced during the war which had to be passed within twelve months of joining on pain of stoppage of leave and withdrawal of temporary rank. Before the war the Higher Standard was still compulsory, and an officer who failed to pass within two years was removed from mountain artillery.

Emergency commissions in the Indian artillery were given during the war after a course at Deolali to I.E.C.Os.

Compulsory retirement was brought in for subadars and jemadars on completion of 28 and 24 years' service respectively.

The honorary rank instituted as a reward for good service to V.C.Os. in addition to the honorary ranks of captain and lieutenant on retirement was often bestowed as a special award for distinguished service to V.C.Os. on the active list. This privilege was accompanied by the issue of double pay and the right to wear officers' uniform and badges.

In 1942 the universal web equipment with packs was issued to all ranks.

The driver's sword was finally withdrawn in 1939 and a generous issue of small arms as personal weapons was made. This had to be further increased during the war in Burma.

On return to India from overseas, personnel were issued with khaki trousers and cellular shirts, and a royal blue beret with a grenade badge as head-dress.

Pay and Allowances of a mountain gunner at the end of the war:
Basic pay everywhere, Rs18 per mensem.

Additional from date of enrolment:
Rs8 Batta, in areas detailed.
Rs7 Expatriation overseas and operational areas.
Rs4 Japanese campaign pay, in Burma or where ordered.

Additional after	12 *months' Service*	3 *years' Service*
War-time Proficiency Pay	Rs3/8	Rs3/8
Special non-tradesmen Proficiency Pay	Rs5	Rs5
War Service Increment ...		Rs6 increased by Rs2 each year.

Rations.—Pre-war in peace—atta, ghi, dal, etc. issued free with 10 annas a month for meat, milk, etc.

From 1943 Field Service Ration was issued free (to followers as well).

All tradesmen and followers (except sweepers) were taken on the strength and attested.

During 1944 all regiments except the two serving on the North-West Frontier were reduced to a strength of three batteries each.

The standard war establishment of a mountain regiment is shown at the end of this chapter. Batteries on the Frontier had 6 drivers and 12 mules extra. Ammunition was carried in M.T. except for 48 rounds which went in pack.

In August, 1945, His Majesty the King-Emperor granted to the Indian Artillery the right to be called "Royal Indian Artillery" in recognition of their good service. This privilege was very highly esteemed by all ranks.

The description "Royal" was discarded on the proclamation of India as a Republic in January, 1950.

The artillery of the Dominion of Pakistan was proud to retain the privilege.

The surrender of the Japanese armies in September, 1945, released a great number of units and individuals of the Indian Army to go back to India for demobilization, but several divisions were still required for policing the Asiatic countries which the Japanese had done their best to train and arm for subversive action against the Allies.

During the last months of the war, some of the King's Commissioned officers had been educating their jawans in politics, so that by the end of 1946 many of the rank and file of the Indian Army, now two and a half millions strong, were in favour of getting rid of the British, and any developments contrary to public opinion might have had serious consequences in the armed forces. Since the Cripps mission in 1942, the Indian ranks realized that partition, when it was brought about, would entail a struggle between Hindus and Mohammedans, and the troops began to smuggle grenades, etc., from Burma to India, so that after the end of the war there was no lack of lethal weapons in the villages.

In 1946 the Indian National Army* trickled back, or rather the survivors did, and it was found that its backbone was composed of renegade King's Commissioned officers; the principal offenders being the 1/14 Punjabis, an "Indianized" battalion of 11 Indian Division. When brought to trial for waging war against the King, those who were convicted received very mild punishment. This did not have a good effect on the Army.

In 1944 a start had been made to form one-class batteries; a simple affair in units with more or less equal personnel of either race. By exchanging sections with each other, the 1st Royal (Kohat) Battery became an all-Mussulman and the 9th (Murree) an all-Sikh battery.

---

* Composed of prisoners of war suborned by the Japanese.

Similarly 6th (Jacob's) became all-Mussulman and 14th (Rajputana) all-Sikh.

This was an early compliance with the order which turned all units of the Indian Army into one-class units, except those for disbandment. Changes in other Mountain Batteries were made in 1946:

    2nd (Derajat) F.F. and 25th became Sikh units.
    12th (Poonch) became a Sikh unit.
    5th (Bombay) became an Ahir unit.
    3rd (Peshawar) F.F., 8th (Lahore), 11th (Dehra Dun), 17th (Nowshera), 24th and 26th Batteries became Punjabi Mussulman units.

There was some confusion over selecting batteries for disbandment, but eventually ten remained in being as mountain batteries, six were put into "suspended animation" and the remainder, except nine which were converted into field batteries, disbanded. When going into suspended animation, funds, mess and battery property were handed over to the R.I.A. Centre, Ambala, and the unit still existed on paper.

Of the Regimental Headquarters, the 20th, 21st, the new 22nd, 26th to 33rd were disbanded: a new 21st was formed by changing the number of the 23rd, and another new 22nd from the 25th in the same way. The 24th remained as before.

The story of the disposal of the Indian States Artillery will be found in Appendix I.

In April three of the four batteries captured in Singapore were revived by transferring personnel from batteries which were not being kept up: the 19th (Maymyo) and 21st Batteries ceased to exist and the 4th (Hazara) (F.F.) and 7th (Bengal) came to life. The Left Section of the 33rd Battery joined the Right Section of the 34th Battery (both sections Ahirs) to form the 10th (Abbottabad) Battery. These two batteries (33rd and 34th) had seen service in the 2nd Arakan operation with 26 Indian Division, and the section of the 33rd Battery in the Kaladan valley in 1944 was the one in which Havildar Umrao Singh was serving when he was awarded the V.C. for gallantry in action—the only holder of the V.C. in mountain artillery (page 397). Jemadar Surat Singh was awarded the Military Cross at the same time.

The 21st Mountain Battery was not re-formed.

The 4th, 5th, and 10th Batteries under 22nd Mountain Regiment went to Peshawar in June, 1946, whence the 5th and 10th went to the last operation on the North-West Frontier to be chronicled in this book.

These expeditions end, as they began, in the Black Mountain country. In December the 5th (Bombay) and the 10th (Abbottabad) Batteries travelled to Hamsherian (twenty-five miles east of Abbottabad) by M.T. and thence marched to Oghi, where they spent three weeks in rain, mud and snow. At one time guns were in action in two feet of snow, at 9,500 feet. The presence of the troops was sufficient to create an atmosphere of peace, and they left Oghi on 25th January, 1947. On 20th February of that year the 10th Battery was put into suspended animation.

Victory Parades were held in London and Delhi to do honour to the troops. At the Delhi Victory Parade on 14th May, 1946, the mountain artillery was represented by a composite battery from 28th Mountain Regiment, commanded by Major J. G. Kidd, M.C., Commandant of 15th (Jhelum) Battery.

For the Victory Parade in London in 1946 a representative detachment was sent,* the senior artillery V.C.O. being Subadar-Major Sher Singh, who originally joined the 5th (Bombay) Battery as a gunner, leaving it as a Subadar.

During 1945 and 1946 His Majesty the King-Emperor approved the issue of Campaign Stars and Medals for the Second World War as affecting the campaigns mentioned:

> 1939-45 Star (Covering North-West Frontier,† India, Iraq, Syria, Persia, Malaya, China, Burma, in addition to the main theatres).
>
> Africa Star.
>
> Pacific Star (Malayan Campaign).
>
> Burma Star.
>
> War Medal (with Bronze Oak Leaf for "mention" if awarded).
>
> Defence Medal (after one year's service in non-operational areas outside their own countries).
>
> British General Service Medal, with clasp "South-East Asia 1945-46" (awarded for post-war operations in Indo-China, Java and Sumatra).
>
> India Service Medal 1939-45 (awarded for three years' non-operational service with the Indian Forces between September, 1939 and September, 1945).

---

* Sweeper Ram Sarup, I.D.S.M., of the 5th (Bombay) Battery was granted the honour of marching with his battery on this parade.

† Ahmedzai, February to May, 1940; Tochi Valley, June to August, 1941 (13, 14, 15 M.Bs.); Dalta Khel, July to August, 1942 (25, 26 M.Bs.); Tauda China, December, 1940 (13, 15 M.Bs. and in subsequent operations 6. 8, 17 M.Bs.).

Appendix to Chapter IX
ESTABLISHMENT

THE INDIAN MOUNTAIN REGIMENT, 1944

	R.H.Q.	3 Batteries each	Total	Notes
Officers				
Lieutenant-Colonel	1		1	
Majors	1*	1	4	*Regimental 2nd. i/c
Captains	2†	1	5	†Adjutant and Q.M.
Subalterns	1	3	10	
Total Officers	5	15	20	
Attached Officers				
Doctors	1	1	4	
Veterinary Officer	1		1	
Viceroy Commissioned Officers				
Subadar-Major	1		1	
Subadars	1*	1	4	*Survey Officer
Jemadars	2†	2	8	†Q.M. and Head Clerk
Total V.C.Os.	4	9	13	
Havildars				
Regimental Q.M.H.	1		1	
Battery Havildar-Major	1*	1	4	*Survey Havildar-Major
Battery Q.M.H.	1†	1	4	†Head Fitter
Trumpet-Major	1		1	
Cook Havildar	1		1	
Signal Havildar		1	3	
Gunner Havildars		4	12	
Driver Havildars		4	12	
Clerk Havildars‡	3	3	12	‡All clerks were Havildars during the war.
Total Havildars	8	18	62	
Rank and File				
Motor drivers	10	18	64	(including mechanics)
Fitters	1*	1	4	*Motor Fitter
Farriers		2	6	
Surveyors	5		5	
Specialist gunners		4	12	Survey
Signallers		22	66	
Blacksmiths		1	3	
Bootmakers		2	6	
Carpenters		2	6	
Saddlers	1	2	7	
Tailors		1	3	
Drivers, mule	11	107	332	
Gunners	8	56	176	
Cooks	2	6	20	
Trumpeters		2	6	
Total	38	226	716	

	R.H.Q.	3 Batteries each	Total	Notes
Followers				
Sweepers	1	5	16	

Attached Sub-units
   Mountain Regiment Signal Section: 1 subaltern, 1 havildar, 40 I.O.Rs.
   Light Motor Detachment Cl. 2: 1 E.M.E., 2 British Sergeants, 11 I.O.Rs.

	R.H.Q.	3 Batteries each	Total	Notes
Transport				
Horses	12	12	48	
Mules, Ordnance ...	3	94	285	
Mules, Equipment ...	14	11	47	
Attached Service Corps Mules	3	13	42	
Bicycles	2	2	8	
Motor Cycles	3	2	9	
Jeeps	4	9	31	
Trucks, 15-cwt.	3	2	9	
Tractors		2	6	
Water Trucks	1	1	4	
Trucks 3-ton	2	1	5	
Weapons				
3.7 Howitzers		4	12	
Light Machine Guns ...	2	6	20	
Pistols	18	13	57	
Rifles	17	78	251	
Carbines, Machine ...	18	78	252	
Grenades	60	120	420	
Ammunition per Weapon				
H.E.			144	⎫ 48 rounds on mule
Smoke			16	⎬ 124 rounds in motor
Anti-tank Shell			12	⎬ transport or on
Time Fuzes for H.E. ...			24	⎭ R.I.A.S.C. mules
Super-charge cartridge			32	
Pistol		18	18	
Rifle		100	100	
Carbines, Machine ...		200	200	
Light Machine Gun ...		1,250	1,250	

CHAPTER X

Second World War—Overseas Operations

A. EAST AFRICA AND ABYSSINIA, 1940-41

[Mountain artillery units are shown by ordinal numbers throughout the chapter. Formations and other units by official abbreviations.]

ITALY DECLARED WAR on Great Britain on 10th June, 1940, and at the beginning of July her East African armies started to move. In the north they quickly captured Kassala, Gallabat and Kurmuk, and in the south Moyale on the Kenya border. To the east, as soon as France was safely out of the way, they invaded British Somaliland, and by 18th August had captured Berbera and driven us out of the country. But having achieved so much, they halted and allowed us gradually to regain the initiative. Our patrols established complete ascendancy over the enemy, but until the arrival of reinforcements, consisting of 5 and later 4 Indian Divisions in the Sudan, and West African and South African brigades in the south, it was not possible to undertake a general offensive. This began in January, 1941, and within the short space of four months, except for mopping-up operations, the Italian East African forces had been completely liquidated.

In the north, General Platt's two divisions swept through Eritrea to the wall of Keren, 150 miles from the border. Here they were held for nearly two months of desperate fighting before the enemy decided he had had enough. Thereafter events moved rapidly. Asmara fell on 1st April, Massawa on the Red Sea on the 8th. The 4 Indian Division then went back to the desert, but 5 Indian Division turned south in pursuit of the enemy, to find him holding the formidable barriers of Wolchefit on the Gondar road and Amba Alagi on the road to Dessie and Addis Ababa. Leaving a detachment of the Sudan Defence Force at Wolchefit, General Mayne, commanding 5 Indian Division, pushed on to Amba Alagi. Here, within a week of the opening of the fighting, he had the enemy pinned on three sides; the fourth side to the south was closed by 1 South African Brigade moving up from Addis Ababa. As the troops prepared for the final assault, the Duke of Aosta, Viceroy and Commander-in-Chief, decided to capitulate.

In the south, Lieutenant-General A. G. Cunningham, himself a

Royal Artillery officer, had taken over command of the East Africa force on 1st November, 1940. Originally he meant to wait until after the winter rains before making any advance, but encouraged by the success of the El Wak raid on 15th December and by the victories of the desert army, he decided to move forward in January. The 11 (African) and 12 (African) Divisions* advanced into Jubaland in two parallel columns, and as a result of a neat turning movement, Kismayu was occupied almost without loss on 14th February. Stiff resistance was offered at the Juba river, but thereafter there was hardly a halt, except for administration to catch up, until Addis Ababa was reached on 6th April—a total advance of 1,725 miles in fifty-three days. Mogadishu, *en route*, fell on 25th February, and at Jijiga the force was joined by the brigade from Aden which had recaptured Berbera, which was adopted as a fresh base, shortening the L. of C. by 600 miles.

It should be mentioned that prior to the opening of General Cunningham's offensive towards Kismayu and partly as a diversion, 1 South African Division had advanced north at the end of January on either side of Lake Rudolph, 25 East African Brigade to the west, and 2 and 5 South African Brigades to the east.

With the capture of Addis Ababa and Amba Alagi, the remaining Italians were driven into two pockets: into the Lakes district to the south-west of Addis Ababa, and into Gondar to the north of Lake Tana in the north-west. Brigadier Fowkes with his 22 East African Brigade was quick off the mark in the Lakes area, his campaign resulting in the eventual capture of Gimma and the surrender of General Gazzera to the Belgian troops who had advanced across the Sudan frontier; but in the north the heavy rains held up attack until November. Here, however, as a result of combined pressure from the north, east and west, the Italians under General Nasi were forced to capitulate on 27th November, and the last resistance was over.

The 22nd Mountain Battery, 20th Mountain Regiment, stationed at Quetta, was the first Indian battery to go overseas, arriving at Mombasa on 10th September, 1939, less mules and drivers. The battery, under Major J. C. D'Arcy, M.C., was ordered to mechanize at once—with no restrictions, no delay, and with every possible help from the Kenya and Uganda Railway workshops in converting vehicles. The guns were carried on two-ton lorries converted to hold them with quick-release gear, ramps being used to run them off and on. Each gun had a similar lorry carrying 120 rounds per gun

---

* Mainly composed of East African and West African troops.

in pack transport ammunition boxes; the detachment was divided between the two lorries. This conversion took ten weeks.

Training for bush warfare began at once and the battery was ready for service* some months before it set out for the Wajir front in May, 1940, under the command of Major C. G. Fawns, M.C. (relieved in July by Major L. R. H. G. Leach).

By November the force was on a two-divisional front, 11 (African) Division on the right from Malindi to Bura (on the River Tana) and 12 (African) Division on the left; the battery was under 22 East African Brigade, the infantry of which consisted of three battalions of King's African Rifles. It remained with this brigade under Brigadier C. C. Fowkes during a great part of the campaign.

The front of the two African divisions was 650 miles as the crow flies; it was held by a chain of isolated localities where water existed, on tracks leading into Italian territory.

Much work was put in arranging convoys for water for use in a vast tract of waterless bush north of the Tana river—in fact, the great problem of this campaign was transport. As for water, the daily allowance of one gallon per man and half a gallon per radiator never failed even in the worst circumstances.

As a result of a successful raid on 15th December on El Wak in front of our position at Wajir, the enemy morale appeared low, and it seemed to fall lower after our success in driving back the Italian armies in the Western Desert. On 15th January, 1941, General Cunningham, after a fighter and bomber attack on enemy airfields the previous afternoon, loosed his two divisions, organized in five brigade groups fully motorized, with Kismayu as his objective.

The 1 South African Division to the north had been given a separate objective on both sides of Lake Rudolph. With 25 East African Brigade of this division was the newly-raised 27th Mountain Battery. After a bad monsoon voyage to, and delay at, Aden, this battery, commanded by Major J. H. H. Willans, which had left Dehra Dun on 6th August, 1940, arrived at Mombasa on 30th October, complete with mules. It had been fitted out portée, guns and mules, in order that there should be a mountain battery available for fighting in the highlands of Abyssinia; but eventually the mules were left at Kijabe, the School of Artillery near Nairobi.

The guns were put into lorries and the battery crossed the Abyssinian border under 25 East African Brigade Group (of which the

---

* The battery also found time to train on its guns the newly-raised 1st East African Light Battery.

infantry were King's African Rifles), and several forts along the Omo river, held by irregulars under Italian officers, were captured. The battery had a good day on 2nd February, 1941, engaging targets all day, and at one time stopping an enemy rush at 300 yards with shrapnel. Farther on there was no road fit for lorries, and in March the battery returned to Kijabe, having had to travel 1,200 miles in five days over bad roads.

The 27th Battery embarked at Mombasa in June and stayed three months near Suez, training for operations which were not carried out. From Suez it proceeded to Lajjun Camp, twenty miles south of Haifa.

To the south the rapid advance of 22 Brigade Group, leading 12 (African) Division over tracks which quickly became dustpans, was considered by the Commander-in-Chief to be instrumental in causing the enemy to evacuate Kismayu without fighting. Previously Afmadu had also been taken with little or no fighting. It was here that the 22nd Mountain Battery fired its first barrage on active service.

The battery then went on with the Gold Coast Brigade Group to capture Bulo Erillo. Sent with 1 Gold Coast Regiment to cut the road behind the Italian position, the battery's F.O.O. party, after a well-timed march, found itself in a leaguer of enemy armoured cars which went round and round in circles until put out of action. The next day, 14th February, Kismayu was occupied without opposition and the port was brought into use at once as a base.

Up to this period of the campaign all moves had been carried out at night, but, as the enemy had been driven from the air, this restriction was taken off. Three days later the battery supported an unopposed crossing of the River Juba; this entailed cutting a three-mile belt through tropical jungle. The battery then rejoined 22 Brigade Group for the encirclement of Gelib and reached the main tarmac road to Mogadishu. A halt was made at Merca while 11 (African) Division took up the pursuit. Rest and sea-bathing became the order of the day.

This went on for nearly a month while the pursuit continued, and Mogadishu was turned into the advanced base, being 800 miles from Kenya, to which road communications had to be kept up for use by M.T. convoys. So far enemy casualties numbered about 31,000.

Quantities of stores and some much-wanted petrol were captured in Mogadishu and an advance to Addis Ababa was ordered. The Italians continued to withdraw, and Jijiga was occupied on 17th March (744 miles).

The nearest port to Jijiga, Berbera (200 miles), had been in Italian hands since August, 1940. The Air Officer Commanding, Aden, now organized a force to capture Berbera consisting of two Indian battalions and attached troops, including the 18th (Sohan) Mountain Battery, commanded by Major R. T. Ashby, which had been sent there from Peshawar in October, 1940. It was armed with four 3.7 howitzers and had a "special portée" establishment which involved the carriage of guns and ammunition in Chevrolet trucks. Establishment: 4 British officers, 3 Indian officers, 129 Indian other ranks. (See note at end of chapter.)

The force had a rough sea passage, and after a preliminary bombardment by the Navy no opposition was made to the landing. Command of the sea thus gave us another base.

The East African Force made contact from Jijiga almost at once and the Brigadier, Royal Artillery, was an old mountain gunner, Brigadier E. H. Blaker, M.C. As a result, the 18th (Sohan) Mountain Battery was ordered to join the East African Force at Harar on 2nd April; this meant a march of 170 miles, the longest the battery made during the campaign in one day. Heavy kit was dumped and never seen again. The battery then joined 11 (African) Division at Miesso and was detached with a force called Fowcol, commanded by Brigadier C. C. Fowkes and composed of 22 East African Brigade with attached troops. Amongst these was the 22nd Mountain Battery, which had been hurried along from Merca at sixty to eighty miles a day to catch up, a rather boring experience combining dust and maintenance with little else, but no vehicle was left behind except one staff car which went over the khud. Full credit for this must be given to the British M.T. sergeants. The senior staff-sergeant was later commissioned into the Royal Artillery and commanded a battery in Burma.

The flat bush country now ended and hill fighting began, and the infantry had to fight on their feet.

After a brisk encounter at the River Awash, 22 Brigade Group with South African detachments entered Addis Ababa on 6th April, the 22nd Mountain Battery having the honour of being the first artillery unit to enter the capital.

To return to the northern front, General Platt's force, advancing on 18th January, found Kassala evacuated and started off in pursuit of the retreating Italians. This entailed an advance over difficult mountainous country with tracks barely fit for motor transport, and by 2nd February the force was held up at the fortified position at Keren. This is a sheer cliff barring the way, giving the enemy command of the approach and high ground for O.Ps.

The 1st Jammu and Kashmir Mountain Battery, which had been equipped with 3.7-inch howitzers in 1939, arrived in the Sudan in November, 1940, in the earlier stages of the campaign. After lending its mules for transporting supplies, the Force having very little pack transport at first, it supported, from a forward position under Pinnacle, 10 Indian Infantry Brigade of 5 Indian Division in the final attack on the Keren position on 25th March, 1941. After co-operating in a creeping barrage in front of 10 Indian Infantry Brigade's advance, fire was turned on to previously unlocated machine guns which were preventing our troops from debouching from a railway tunnel which was essential to our communications. The battery knocked out the machine guns with direct hits and the advance continued. The Italian troops were some of the best and fought determinedly from the first day of our investment, but the persistence of our attacks and the valour of the British and Indian infantry crushed his spirit, and when it became known to him that we were in a position to push our tanks through the gorge, his resistance collapsed. Keren was occupied on 27th March. The 1st Jammu and Kashmir Mountain Battery fired almost continuously from the morning of 25th March until the evening of the 27th, and was exposed throughout to a considerable amount of fire from enemy artillery and air. It was the only mountain battery present at the battle of Keren, a battle in which there was much scope for mountain artillery.

The battery, which retained its mules throughout the campaign, was part of the artillery which went forward with 29 Indian Infantry Brigade, the leading brigade of 5 Division, in the advance to Asmara. On 30th and 31st March the battery helped to support the attacks on the Ad Teclesan position—the last Italian position covering the capital. The lines to the O.P. were constantly cut by heavy enemy shell fire. Signaller Qabala Singh was awarded the I.D.S.M. for bravery on this occasion and two others were mentioned in despatches, as was a gunner who carried wounded men to safety with complete disregard for himself.

On the evening of 30th the battery was largely responsible for the repulse of a counter-attack from the left flank carried out by an Italian machine-gun battalion, and directed towards the area occupied by 29 Brigade H.Q.*

---

* The pivot gun of the battery was personally laid on to this counter-attack by the C.O. of 28 Field Regiment (the Field Regiment supporting the Brigade), who had run from Brigade H.Q. to the top of the hill overhanging the road, close to which Brigade H.Q. was established, to do this, since telephone communication to all batteries had been destroyed by shell fire. This was the nearest battery and no other method of dealing quickly and effectively with the situation

The port of Massawa on the Red Sea surrendered on 8th April, and the long, difficult line of communication from the Sudan was transferred. The 1st Jammu and Kashmir Battery left Eritrea on 3rd May and went on to Syria,* and was thus unable to take part in the final advance on Amba Alagi, which resulted after three weeks' fighting in the surrender of the Duke of Aosta and its garrison, who were granted the honours of war. This virtually ended the fighting in the north, which had resulted in the liquidation of six divisions and the capture of 50,000 prisoners. Only Gondar was left and that could wait.

To revert to the 18th Mountain Battery. In the highlands the weather was wet and, compared with Somaliland, cold, so the pursuit continued under less pleasant conditions, and communications were often difficult owing to roads and bridges being washed away by floods. Enemy morale was rapidly diminishing, and the duck and goose shooting was excellent. The 22 East African Brigade was at Adamitullo for some days, where the 18th (Sohan) Battery received an anti-tank gun with lorry and formed a detachment to man it. The Sikh section of this battery supported two companies of 1/5 K.A.R. in an attack on an enemy post at Fike, and had the satisfaction of destroying a 20-mm. gun by a direct hit.

The battery engaged tanks which were making a counter-attack on 11th May, but the enemy remained outside effective range.

The rains had begun and movement had become extremely difficult; the more so as the battery M.T. was in a poor state and breakdowns were frequent.

The 12th African Division arrived at Falla river at the end of May by the road from Kenya, making contact with 11 African Division to complete the pincer movement on Abyssinia. It had had many months of hard fighting and harder travelling.

The next enemy stronghold was Gimma on the far side of the Omo river; enemy guns had registered points on the approaches to the ford, and the range of the 3.7's was insufficient for counter-battery work, which was undertaken by the 18-prs. of South African batteries from a high escarpment in rear. Three platoons of 5 K.A.R. managed to get across and maintain their footing, and the 18th Battery then occupied a position nearer the river. More infantry crossed, and on 5th June, with good air support from the S.A. Air Force, the position was captured.

Another week elapsed while the Brigade crossed over on makeshift ferries; the battery crossed on the 12th and was supporting

appeared possible to him. The battery engaged this target over open sights, firing with excellent effect.

* See Appendix, p. 429.

5 K.A.R. on the Gimma perimeter on the 21st. This place fell after little opposition, and various minor operations were carried to the north with a view to the capture of Gondar.

The next obstacle was the Didessa river, which ran through a deep and narrow gorge. A desultory artillery duel was kept up for three days until the arrival of 6-inch howitzer shells produced a white flag from the enemy's side. The gorge was crossed by a platoon of K.A.R. in a bosun's chair, and a general and 650 men duly surrendered. A peculiar action fought by artillery only, in which the opposing infantry did not get within a mile of each other.

The 18th Battery returned to Gimma for rest and training until 8th August, when it left by road for Borama (686 miles) to join the blockade of French Somaliland, which was in Vichy French hands. The metre-gauge railway from Djibouti to Addis Ababa ran through this country, and the use of the railway would have reduced the work on our line of communications. Some training of men and refitting of transport was carried out during the stay at Borama. The battery returned to the Gondar area via Addis Ababa at the beginning of November, making a long roundabout trip over two 10,000-foot passes amidst most impressive scenery to arrive at Amba Giorghis (1,300 miles from Borama).

The battery had recently been issued with a makeshift supercharge which consisted of an extra charge III ring, giving an additional 700 yards range; this, together with the meteor effect of the high altitude, produced a range of well over 7,000 yards.

On 21st November the battery was in support of a column of 25 Brigade Group under Brigadier James when it was attacking a prominent feature named Kulkuber to the south-west of Gondar. This was very strongly held by the enemy, and at one time our infantry were held up. The situation was saved by the use of the battery No. 18 wireless sets, the K.A.R. having no battalion signalling arrangements, and a concentration for the final assault led to the capture of the objective.

The final assault on Gondar was carried out on 27th November with all available artillery support. By 1730 hours the Italians had capitulated and the campaign was over.

The attack on Gondar had set a difficult problem for the officer commanding the 22nd Mountain Battery. He was given twenty-one days to convert to pack, having neither mules nor saddlery within 1,500 miles. This change was necessary in order to get the guns to the position from which to support the attack. Captain D. J. Hartigan ransacked the countryside as far as Asmara and eventually a queer collection of mules and ponies were produced. Saddlery was improvised, and Abyssinian irregulars carried two rounds of ammunition apiece in nosebags. However, it worked. The guns descended a very steep escarpment and came into action in support of the attack as ordered.

Lieutenant R. M. Campbell went as F.O.O. with the left forward infantry company and was responsible for breaking up the only counter-attack; he continued observing after being wounded and controlled the fire of two field batteries as well as his own guns.

The F.O.Os. generally were noted for the offensive spirit they displayed, and their close liaison with local irregular forces led to the selection and accurate engagement of many important targets. The 22nd Battery often co-operated with Henfrey's Scouts, Irregulars under Captain Tom Henfrey, M.C., with the best results. Lieutenants Bruce Wilson and Lovatt Campbell were full of enterprise, appearing now and then behind or in the centre of the enemy's position, causing him dire disaster. The former was once seen riding a captured grey mule in the forefront of the battle looking for a good O.P. Lieutenant R. M. Campbell of the 22nd Battery and Second-Lieutenant P. B. Fox of the 18th were equally adventurous and straight-shooting, and won high praise from the infantry.

Battery records are very scathing on the subject of the M.T. issued. It was a mixed collection of part-worn vehicles out of which battery fitters had to get the best service they could, and their untiring efforts had much success though spare parts were generally non-existent, and use had to be made of serviceable Italian transport. Experience proved the vital necessity of a L.A.D.; the Divisional Workshop Company, though helpful, was seldom at hand.

Later on in the war a L.A.D. III* was mobilized with each mountain regiment.

When the Commander-in-Chief, Lieutenant-General Wetherall, inspected the troops at Gondar in December, his congratulatory message had to be read out in seven languages in addition to various Abyssinian dialects.

The 18th (Sohan) Battery had fired in all 2,179 rounds, of which 243 were super-charge.

The enemy artillery were greatly hampered by the use of bad ammunition and about 5 per cent. were "duds." Their guns were generally sited where the flashes gave away their positions.

Honours and Awards:
    18th (Sohan) Mountain Battery—Mentioned in despatches: Major R. T. Ashby, Captain L. H. Packard, Sig.-Havildar Sharam Singh, Naik Mohamed Sarwar.

---

* See Appendix, p. 453.

22nd Mountain Battery—Mentioned in despatches: Major L. R. H. G. Leach, Lieutenant R. M. Campbell, Lieutenant A. B. Wilson. Major Leach was awarded the Haile Selassie Military Medal. Signallers Inaiyat Ullah and Kartara Singh received the I.D.S.M.

Casualties: 22nd Mountain Battery—2 British officers and 2 I.O.Rs. wounded.

To the great sorrow of his battery, Captain Hartigan lost a leg by stepping on a mine and, on arrival in Ireland some time afterwards, his plane crashed and he was killed.

The Battery Commander, 22nd Mountain Battery, wrote: "A campaign of this nature was a gunner's dream. The battery was unbrigaded; we were always under command of one infantry brigade or another and thus were left to ourselves. The B.R.A., Brigadier Blaker, helped us in our administrative battles but otherwise observed only a friendly control except when a major action took place. Artillery was so scarce on the ground that any gunner got a royal welcome from the infantry, and we learned to know and appreciate the South Africans and the K.A.R., Gold Coast, and Nigerian battalions which we supported. Each brigade commander in turn took a personal interest in the unit, but especially Brigadier C. C. Fowkes who commanded 22 E.A. Infantry Brigade and who was for so long our staunchest friend and protector. There was also a lighter side to this war for, during the period 1st November, 1939 to 4th January, 1942, the four British officers in the battery killed by rod, gun or 3.7 howitzer 1,239 head of game. This large figure comprised most things from a buffalo to an Italian cow, also 463 trout, francolin, guinea fowl, geese, duck, snipe, and many of the species of East African deer."

The 18th (Sohan) Mountain Battery formed a close friendship with the 1st Battery, South African Field Artillery, while together in Fowcol. A hard-fought baseball tournament ended in two wins each and one drawn game; this result is not so surprising when it is realized that the Indian gunners had been taught the game in Waziristan by Captain L. H. Packard, the Canadian battery captain.

On the break-up of the force, the 18th (Sohan) and 22nd Mountain Batteries went off together to join the 26th Mountain Regiment at Lajjun Camp, near Haifa, and were readjusted to a pack basis. Entry in the 18th (Sohan) Battery History: "The loss of our M.T. and the return to pack was a very great disappointment to all ranks."

The 27th Mountain Battery also joined this regiment at Lajjun Camp.

NOTE

(i) *Special War Establishment for* 18*th Mountain Battery for service overseas on a portée basis*

Battery H.Q. and two sections each of two 3.7 howitzers.
Officers:
    British—1 major, 1 captain, 2 subalterns.
    Indian—1 subadar, 2 jemadars.
Indian O.R.

Battery havildar-major	1	Fitter havildar	...	1
Battery Q.M. havildar	1	Signal havildar	...	1
Havildars	4	I.O.A.C. fitters ...	...	2
Gunners	83	Driver mechanics	...	3
Drivers	30			

Total Indian ranks, 129

Non-Combatants (enrolled):

Workmen					
Blacksmith	...	1	Saddler	...	1
Bootmaker	...	1	Carpenters ...	...	2
Tailor ...	...	1			
Mess Servants	...	3			
Followers:					
Barber ...	...	1	Water carriers ...	...	5
Washerman ...	...	1	Sweepers ...	...	5
Cooks, I.T. ...	...	6			

Total, 27

Sub-Assistant Surgeon 1   (V.C.O. or I.W.O.)
Servant for above ... 1
Not included in above totals:
1 reinforcement   ... 1   Havildar
12 R. and F. (includes orderlies for B.Os.)

(ii) *Distribution by trades and duties*
    Tradesmen:

Motor mechanics	2
Driver mechanics	3
Total ...	5

Non-Tradesmen:

Gunners		Drivers	
B.C.'s Assistant ...	1	Clerks, 2nd grade ...	1
G.P.O.'s Assistant ...	1	Clerks, 3rd grade ...	1
Rangetakers ...	2	Drivers for vehicles ...	25
Signallers	16	Orderlies for V.C.Os. ...	3
L.M. Gunners ...	6		
*Sanitary duties ...	1		
*Water duties ...	1		
Storeman	1		
Trumpeters	2		
Gunners	52		
	83		30

* Trained in first aid.   Total Rank and File, 118

(iii) *Transport*

Motor cycles ... 3
Trucks (15 cwt.) ... 6
Lorries 30 cwt. ... 12
Lorries 2/3 ton ... 5
Trailers, water ... 1

(iv) *Weapons*

Pistols 12   for officers, V.C.Os., Battery H.M., motor cyclists and sub-asst. Surgeon.

Rifles 20
L.M.G. 2
A.T. Rifles 2
3.7 howitzer ammunition
   120 rounds p.g.

Notes by battery commander:
   (a) The motor cycles proved of little use.
   (b) The battery had to form its own L.A.D.

To face p. 284.

B. MALAYA

The Malay Peninsula was a natural objective for the Japanese, should they take an active part in the war, as the port of Singapore, standing at its southern end, dominated the sea routes to Australia and the Far East. Further, products of rubber and tin which made Malaya our most prosperous dependency would have been a great addition to the "Co-prosperity sphere for Greater Asia" which the Japanese said they aimed at establishing.

The peninsula is about 450 miles from north to south and varies in width from 60 to 200 miles. Down the centre runs a mountain ridge difficult to cross, and local traffic is mostly confined to the rivers; jungle of varying types, in some places a complete obstruction to the passage of men or animals and in others little or no obstruction, covers the whole country less a strip on both east and west sides between mountains and sea. A metre-gauge railway (built out of revenue) extends the whole length of the peninsula from Singapore to Padang Besar on the Thailand frontier near the west coast; it continues on to Bangkok. A branch which takes off at Gemas runs up the east side through Pahang and Kelantan and continues across the frontier to join the other line at Singora.

Malaya consisted of four federated states—Perak, Selangor, Negri Sembilan, and Pahang—under their own rulers with a British High Commissioner in control, and six unfederated states. There were also the Crown Colonies of Penang, Malacca, and Singapore, the latter containing the seat of government and a large dockyard, on an island at the extreme south of the peninsula. The Governor of the Colony was also High Commissioner for all the Malay States. The Commander-in-Chief, Far East, Air Chief Marshal Sir Robert Brooke-Popham, was responsible for operational control over military and air forces, the G.O.C., Malaya Command, being Major-General L. V. Bond.

The Malays are a pleasant and peaceful race, but had little experience of discipline,* and the protection of our possession was entrusted to a few Indian troops, a couple of Malay battalions, and the Malay States Volunteer Rifles, a fine body of British volunteers who were living in the country as planters, engineers, etc. There was also an all-British volunteer light battery (four 3.7-inch howitzers, mechanized).

At the end of 1940 and the beginning of 1941 11 and 9 Indian Divisions arrived in Malaya, as well as an Australian Division

---

* The Malay infantry "fought magnificently" on the Singapore beaches in February, 1942.

consisting of one Infantry Brigade Group. Artillery and administrative details were sent from the United Kingdom, and in May the H.Q., 3 Indian Corps, was formed at Kuala Lumpur. Lieutenant-General A. E. Percival became G.O.C., Malaya Command.

The 12 Indian Infantry Brigade Group, which included 22nd Mountain Regiment, was sent to the Command a few weeks before the Second World War broke out.

The 22nd Mountain Regiment (Lieutenant-Colonel A. H. Peskett, M.C.), comprising 10th (Abbottabad) and 21st Batteries from Ambala and the 4th (Hazara) F.F. and 7th (Bengal) Batteries from Dehra Dun, mobilized and entrained for Calcutta on 1st August. Drivers and mules were left behind; the drivers rejoined in Malaya and were trained as M.T. drivers, but the animals were never again seen by their batteries.

Commandants of batteries were: 4th, Major G. L. Hughes, M.C.; 7th, Major S. F. Fisken, M.C.; 10th, Captain D. C. G. Cowie; 21st, Major F. H. C. Rogers, M.C. The strength of each battery was: 4 B.Os., 3 V.C.Os., 103 I.O.Rs., with 14 public* and 4 private followers. Captain S. C. Hasan, I.M.S., was in medical charge.

The Brigade Group embarked without official knowledge of its destination, but this information was broadcast by the German wireless before the batteries left Dehra Dun.

On disembarkation at Singapore the Brigade Group found itself, as the only regular formation, responsible for the defence of the island, and the regiment, after a short period under canvas, spent some months in a hutted camp in the naval base. The 4th, 7th, and 10th Batteries were affiliated to the 2 Argyll and Sutherland Highlanders, 5/2 Punjab and 4/19 Hyderabad Regiments respectively for jungle training in Johore. A practice camp was held at Kuala Lumpur.

Soon after arrival the 4th (Hazara) Battery was rearmed with four old type 6-inch howitzers towed by Marmon-Harringtons (a F.W.D. type of American production), and its 3.7-inch equipment was divided between the 10th and 21st Batteries.

An order was received for the immediate mechanization of the batteries; this was not greeted with enthusiasm by the purists, but was loyally accepted and all ranks strove to make it a success. Pending the arrival of vehicles from the U.S.A., hired Chinese lorries were used with Chinese and R.I.A.S.C. drivers. The 3.7-inch howitzers were towed behind 3-ton lorries on locally made trailers

---

* Consisting of 2 saddlers, 1 smith, 3 water carriers, 1 tailor, 1 carpenter, 3 cooks and 3 sweepers.

similar to those of the Volunteer Light Battery. This system of transport gave excellent results.

The personnel of the batteries had to be trained in driving and maintenance as well as for jungle fighting, but after fifteen months' work they were in a high state of efficiency, due to Lieutenant-Colonel Peskett's drive and personality as a leader. A very good standard of gunnery, survey, and musketry had been attained; signallers were trained in wireless (which, as it happened, proved of no practical value), and officers, specialists, and senior N.C.Os. could ride motor-cycles. A war establishment for a mountain regiment (motorized) was issued in July, 1940. In this war establishment (issued by the War Office) it was overlooked that a section cannot be detached 200 miles from its battery (as in the case of 21st Battery) for a period and come into effective action without a "B.C. staff" of signallers and specialists extra to those required to fight the remainder of the battery. Fortunately, batteries had their "first reinforcements" with them.

In December, 1940, R.H.Q. with 7th and 10th Batteries moved to Ipoh to join 11 Indian Division, then beginning to arrive in Malaya. The other two batteries remained under 12 Indian Infantry Brigade at the Naval Base.

The following month (January, 1941) R.H.Q. with 7th and 10th Batteries moved forward to Jitra in Kedah, a few miles north of Alor Star and twenty miles south of the frontier, coming under command of 6 Indian Infantry Brigade of 11 Indian Division, whose role was the defence of the main road and rail communications with Thailand. The 7th Battery was affiliated to 2/16 Punjab Regiment and had a detached section at Padang Besar, and the 10th Battery was affiliated to 1/8 Punjab Regiment.

On the right of the 11 Division (H.Q., Sungei Patani) 9 Division (H.Q., Raub) was in position along the Thailand frontier to the east coast. Command was exercised by 3 Indian Corps, with H.Q. at Kuala Lumpur, commanded by Lieutenant-General Sir L. M. Heath.

C.R.A., 9 Division, was Brigadier E. W. Goodman, M.C., and of 11 Division, Brigadier A. E. Rusher, M.C.

In May, 1941, 21st Battery joined 9 Division at Kota Bharu, and two months later the 4th Battery was rearmed with four 3.7-inch howitzers on trailers and joined 11th Division in Kedah. This battery was affiliated to 3/16 Punjab Regiment at Kroh on the frontier.

On arrival at Kota Bharu the 21st Battery (four guns) went to Chongdong Camp, detaching the Punjabi Mussulman section to Kuantan (two guns). Major I. R. McIntosh commanded the battery and 2/Lieutenant F. C. Cross, the section. In June Major McIntosh was appointed Brigade Major, R.A., 11 Division, and Captain J. B. Sopper took over the battery as acting major.

The role of the battery was to support 8 Infantry Brigade in guarding the aerodrome (afterwards called "airfield") and preventing enemy landings. Reconnaissances had been made earlier in the year and gun positions, O.Ps. and other points surveyed. The section role was a similar one in support of 22 Infantry Brigade, also with surveys completed.

Training continued steadily, only broken in August by the visit of H.H. the Maharajah of Patiala, for whom a parade was held of all the Sikhs in Kelantan. His interest was much appreciated by them.

The Regiment found time to win the Command hockey tournament for the second time in 1941.

Practice camp was held in September under the C.R.A., 9 Division, and the shooting was found to be well up to standard. It was recorded that at the end of a long hot day seven people drank forty-five large bottles of beer in forty-five minutes.

In September R.H.Q. and 4th, 7th and 10th Batteries were concentrated at Jitra. The batteries were given additional equipment for anti-tank duties: 4th and 10th Batteries, two 2-pr. Breda guns each; 7th Battery, three 18-prs. Mk. I (these were "trophy" guns collected from police stations).

The Breda guns had been captured in North Africa. Personnel were provided for manning these extra guns, but not for control and administration. Each gun was issued with 300 rounds A.P., and practice was carried out immediately after receipt.

The latest war establishment (May, 1941) for a 3.7-inch howitzer battery (motorized) was as follows:

> 4 British Officers, 3 V.C.Os., 10 Havildars, 118 Indian other ranks, 6 workmen, 16 followers, 6 temporary personnel.
> Vehicles: 13 30-cwt. lorries (one with water-tank); 5 3-ton lorries [afterwards replaced by Marmon-Harrington (F.W.D.)].
> Ammunition (per gun): 90 H.E., fuze 106; 10 H.E., fuse 101; 20 Shrapnel. Some smoke shells were afterwards issued.

The 11 Indian Division had an offensive role of crossing the frontier to meet an invasion and an alternative defensive one of holding the uncompleted Jitra position to cover the Alor Star airfield. This line had been constructed mostly by military labour and consisted of an anti-tank ditch, weapon pits and a few pill-boxes, and was far from finished. There was a poor field of fire and a lack of O.Ps.

Training was continued during the year in all batteries, especially musketry and action against parachutists. Lewis guns had been replaced by V.B. guns.

At this time the officers of 22nd Mountain Regiment were as follows:

R.H.Q.:
    Lieutenant-Colonel G. L. Hughes, M.C.*
    Captain A. H. d'A. Willis, Adjutant.
    Subadar-Major Mumtaz Khan, I.O.
    Lieutenant A. E. Peters, R. Signals, Signals Officer.
    I. W. O. Fazal Ilahi, I.A.O.C.
    2/Lieutenant "Dizzy" Coleman (missing at Singapore, believed killed).
    Lieutenant Walker-Taylor, F. M. S. Volunteers, was attached to the Regiment during the campaign.

4th (Hazara) Battery:
    Major E. L. Sawyer.
    Captain A. Chevenix-Trench.
    Lieutenant R. M. Hare.
    Lieutenant E. R. V. Knox.
    2/Lieutenant Davindar Singh Bedi (afterwards missing, believed killed in action).
    Subadar Khan Gul.
    Jemadar Mir Zaman.
    Jemadar Sardar Ali.
    Jemadar Jogindar Singh.
    Jemadar Khuman Singh.

7th (Bengal) Battery:
    Major J. W. P. Scott (afterwards killed in action).
    Captain A. C. E. Long.
    2/Lieutenant H. P. James.
    2/Lieutenant Parshotam Das (from Subadar-Major, 22nd Mountain Regiment).
    Lieutenant W. S. Raw (with Sikh section at Padang Besar).
    Subadar Banta Singh (with Sikh section at Padang Besar).
    Jemadar Chanan Singh (with Sikh section at Padang Besar).
    Subadar Alla Ditta (afterwards missing).
    Jemadar Dur Khan.

10th (Abbottabad) Battery:
    Major D. G. C. Cowie (afterwards killed in action).

---

* Lieutenant-Colonel Hughes was also adviser to the G.O.C., Malaya, in all matters concerning mobile artillery in Northern Malaya.

Captain P. R. C. Standish.
Lieutenant T. S. Wright.
Lieutenant R. St. G. Wilcock (later 11th Division Ammunition Officer).
2/Lieutenant R. L. Roach (afterwards killed in action).
2/Lieutenant J. A. Drummond Black (died when prisoner of war).
Subadar Sher Mohamed.
Jemadar Fateh Khan (died when prisoner of war).
Subadar Khushall Singh (died when prisoner of war).
Subadar Nand Singh.
Jemadar Ghulam Mohamed.

21st Battery:
Major J. B. Sopper.
Captain R. Coleman.
Lieutenant F. C. Cross.
Lieutenant Elliott.
Lieutenant T. E. J. Murray.
2/Lieutenant C. J. K. Tombs.
Subadar Ali Akbar.
Subadar Khair Mohamed.
Jemadar Kartar Singh.

The international situation became worse in July owing to the fact that the Japanese had occupied French Indo-China by permission of the Vichy Government, and war seemed to be imminent. In November all units were placed in a state of readiness. Battle positions were ordered to be taken up on 6th December.

Taking first 9 Indian Division on the right:

21st Mountain Battery

On the evening of the 6th, Battery H.Q. and four guns were in action on the airfield at Kota Bharu with lines laid to two O.Ps. on the beach.

The information available was that a Japanese fleet with transports was approaching Singora (Thailand), and at 0230 hours on the 8th fire was opened by the battery on a ship at very long range, and an enemy ship was hit by a bomb and set alight. By daybreak it was found that a landing had been made on Sabak beach and the O.P. surrounded; but Lieutenant Tombs and the staff carried on as the line was not cut. The landing had been made in three-seater boats the whole length of the beach, the survivors being followed by armoured craft holding twenty to thirty men. Jemadar Gurmukh Singh in the other O.P. beat off an infantry attack and ran across the open to an infantry mortar position of which he directed the fire himself. His communications were cut, but he eventually got his entire party back to camp through the encircling infantry.

Notwithstanding a successful local counter-attack, and air attacks, many more Japanese were ashore by dark and the battery position was under musketry fire. While the R.A.A.F. squadron was evacuating the airfield, the battery fired concentrations with 73 Field Battery before withdrawing to the reserve line. Lieutenant Elliott brought back his O.P. party with their instruments along with the O.P. party of 73 Battery under fire in a Malay boat, crossing a 200-yard wide creek used as a covered approach by the Japs. His courage and resource saved both these parties.

The shooting this day had all been predicted, corrected by infantry reports, and the survey work proved to have been accurately carried out.

After some confusion in the early morning of the 9th, the battery was in action covering the building of a defensive line to be held by troops detraining at Krai. This new line was occupied, and an attack on it was beaten off on the 12th, but a further withdrawal had to be carried out.

The Japanese tactics of encirclement through the jungle and infiltration everywhere were now obvious. For the next day or two the battery was in close support of 2/10 Baluch Regiment, but on the 15th it moved to Krai to entrain.

On arrival at Kuala Lipis, orders were received from 9 Division to occupy two positions covering two approaches on the River Pahang. Infantry support at a later date was promised. This led to a week's rest in a comfortable rubber plantation in enjoyment of the hospitality of the planter, Mr. Maycock, which revived the tired battery. Its next move was to Kuantan, where the detached section rejoined and the battery came under 22 Infantry Brigade.

This section reported that a section of 5 Field Regiment, R.A. (4.5-inch howitzers), was in position and two troops of 25-prs. had arrived at Kuantan on 9th December, and after a short stay on the beach, firing seawards, the section took over airfield defence tasks. The airfield was bombed by twenty-seven aircraft the first morning, but it had been evacuated by the R.A.A.F. two days previously.

The 21st Battery moved to Gambang (fifteen miles west) on the night 27th/28th December, joining 2/12 F.F. Regiment. The enemy made a very heavy attack on Kuantan on the 28th, and a section under Captain Coleman was sent to occupy a position covering the river. Orders were received that the airfield perimeter was to be held to the last man. The attack continued and was effectively countered for two days. On 1st January, however, 2/12 was moved to the airfield, leaving two platoons with the four mountain guns in a position covering an approach from the north. The field of fire was poor and the gunners and drivers took to infantry work.

By the 3rd the situation on the west coast made it imperative for the Kuantan force to conform and a withdrawal was carried out, covered by 5/11 Sikhs and the battery from a position near Gambang. The 2/12 F.F. Regiment* fought a most gallant rear-guard action out of Kuantan, suffering very heavy casualties. One company was overrun and Lieutenant-Colonel Cummings, with the greatest gallantry and coolness, although twice wounded, extricated the rear-guard under severe attacks, being afterwards awarded the Victoria Cross.

Captain Coleman's section rejoined the battery without incident on the 5th, and the battery moved with the Kuantan column via Raub to Kuala Lumpur, where orders were received for the battery to rejoin 22nd Mountain Regiment which was with 11 Indian Division.

Front of 11 *Indian Division*

On the receipt of information on 6th December that Japanese transports had been sighted at sea, the mountain batteries were expecting to take part in the offensive role of the Division. They were then at their battle stations: the 4th Battery on the frontier astride the Alor Star–Singora road with the 1/14 Punjab Regiment under 15 Indian Infantry Brigade; 7th and 10th Batteries were farther south in the Jitra defences with 6 Indian Brigade, less the Sikh section of the 7th Battery at Padang Besar on the frontier with a detachment of 2/16 Punjab Regiment. A single gun of the 10th Battery was standing by to advance with the spearhead of two companies of 1/8 Punjab Regiment on the left. The only maps available were $\frac{1}{4}$-inch.

No orders to advance were received, and work was continued on the defences; at 0330 hours on the 8th information arrived that the Japanese had landed at Kota Bharu earlier that day.

The division had been keyed up for an offensive, but "political restrictions" prevented the order for this being given until it was too late. The change to the defensive certainly had a depressing effect on the troops.

The main Japanese advance with tanks was made on 8th December from Singora, following the railway across the peninsula and then south along the coast at Padang Besar. Troops also landed at Patani whence they moved across country to Kroh.

---

* Formerly 2nd Sikhs, P.F.F.

Krohcol and the 10th Mountain Battery

Krohcol (two battalions and a company of Sappers and Miners) was strengthened by the arrival of the 10th Battery from 6 Infantry Brigade on the 9th. Advanced parties of 3/16 Punjab Regiment met some opposition that day at a block a few miles across the frontier from some Thais, armed with Japanese rifles, and the battalion halted for the night at Betong. The next day an encounter battle developed and after heavy fighting the issue was decided by a surprise appearance of Japanese tanks. This action was continued on 11th and 12th.

The 5/14 Punjabi and the 10th Battery were preparing a defensive position near Kroh. After three days of continuous fighting, during which heavy losses had been incurred by the enemy, the 3/16 Punjabi had lost half their numbers, and the 5/14 and the battery advanced in front of Betong to extricate them. In a sharp action on the 13th the guns and infantry practically exterminated two companies of Japanese. Enemy tanks and an encirclement of the infantry led to the occupation of the new position about two miles west of Kroh.

The enemy were in contact all the 14th, and just before dusk on that day a brisk action opened; fire was suddenly received from the left, right, and right rear simultaneously. Much answering fire was forthcoming from our infantry, but the battery was inconveniently placed in the centre of the disturbance. No. 1 gun was firing at a target at 1,000 yards and in a short time all guns were loaded with shrapnel ready to stop a rush. However, the excitement died down and the guns were pulled out without casualties. The force halted that night at Baling.

The Kroh position covered a road running west to South Kedah, but there was also another road running south which was unmetalled for twenty miles and had not been considered seriously. The road came out at Grik, which was connected to the west coast highway by a good road, and this communication now became of great importance; so much so that the corps commander moved his advanced H.Q. to Bukit Mertajam, sending details of 12 Infantry Brigade to reinforce the Kroh front. These troops met the remains of the Kroh force at Baling, leaving the Grik road uncovered except by a very small detachment.

On the 13th the 10th Battery received news that the Jitra line had been broken and that the battery anti-tank detachment had been overrun by enemy infantry before seeing a tank. One Breda gun was saved, but had to be abandoned later. Casualties had been heavy: 1 killed, 3 wounded, 9 missing out of a total of 29.

It was known on the 15th that the Gurun position (page 296) had fallen, and Kroh force retired slowly during the next three days to the Salama–Taiping road. On the 18th the battery had some opportunities for harassing fire from a very good position, so seldom met with in this country, and caused very many casualties to the Japanese in the vicinity of Salama bridge.

4th (*Hazara*) Mountain Battery

On the 10th the 4th Battery was in action south of Changlun cross-roads on the Alor Star–Singora road covering 1/14 Punjabi in a position through which our forward elements withdrew. Next morning the position received a frontal attack which was repulsed, but the right flank was eventually turned and the battalion had to retire. During the withdrawal the rear-guard was surprised by a sudden attack of tanks and lorried infantry and the Japanese penetrated several miles, cutting in two both the battalion and the battery, of which the sections were widely separated. Two Breda anti-tank guns were lost, the casualties being one man killed, one V.C.O. and two gunners wounded.

That evening Major Sawyer, the battery commander, was making a reconnaissance with the O.C., 1/14 Punjab, when both officers had a narrow escape, their car being destroyed by a mortar bomb immediately they had left it. In the absence of Major Sawyer, who could not find his way back to the battery for some hours, the left (Sikh) section was surrounded in the jungle and captured with the loss of two wounded and twenty-three missing. Some lorries were also lost. The right section and details under Lieutenant Chenevix-Trench withdrew in the dark to Tanjong Pau, and were in action next morning under 155 Field Brigade supporting 2/9 Jats on the right of the Jitra line.

Notwithstanding stubborn resistance by the Jats and Leicesters, the line was penetrated that day (13th) and the battery joined R.H.Q. at Gurun, about thirty miles south. This position had only been reconnoitred on the 11th and no work had been done on it: it could not be held and was evacuated on the 15th. The two guns of the 4th Battery were in action that day under 137 Field Brigade covering the Kota ferry. On the 16th Jemadar Sardar Ali made a reconnaissance with three I.O.Rs. to get touch with Krocol, and was commended for a very prompt and useful report. The battery was at Ipoh on 20th, where it received one 3.7-inch howitzer and took up a position of readiness at the Kampar position until 26th. On that day the second howitzer arrived.

All the Breda troops in the Regiment were disbanded on the 21st.

The last Breda gun in the 4th Battery was lost at Jitra on the 13th; Lieutenant Bedi, a very promising officer, was reported "missing, believed killed."

7th Mountain Battery

The 6 Infantry Brigade, supported by 155 Field Regiment, had the task of stopping an advance along the railway and on two roads, one running through Changlun northward (page 294) and the other north-west from Jitra to Kodiang. The 7th Battery had been allotted to the support of 2/16 Punjab on the latter road.

At 1500 hours on 8th December the battery was ordered into action on the railway south of Padang Besar to cover the withdrawal of the troops from that place, including the other section of the battery. This was completed and demolitions carried out, and by the evening of the 10th the battery (four guns) was in action registering targets from a position near M.S. 22 on the Kodiang road. No contact with enemy ground troops had yet been made on the road. After repeated bombing, to which little reply was possible, Alor Star airfield, several miles in rear, was evacuated.

There was still no contact on the following day, but the troops withdrew a couple of miles in order to conform with the Changlun sector on the right which was being pushed back.

At about 1900 hours on this day (11th) the commander of 1/8 Punjab, on receipt of a report that the enemy had broken through in the sector on the right and that it was expected that the Kodiang road would shortly be cut, ordered an immediate withdrawal to Jitra. The order laid down that if M.T. could not get through, units were to make their way back as best they could.

Owing to the premature demolition of a series of culverts, traffic could not move along the road, and Captain Long, the senior officer with the battery, ordered the sights and breech-blocks to be thrown into the padi and the men to find their way back to R.H.Q. on foot.

It was soon dark and in the ensuing confusion a line of men from the battery and other units followed Captain Long through padi six feet high and water four feet deep, and on arrival at Jitra the report was found to be untrue—no break-through had occurred. Engineers were sent forward to repair the culverts with a view to the recovery of the guns, with which Havildar Ghulam Kadir had remained all night, having received no order to leave them.

What had happened was that some Japanese tanks had broken through on the right and been stopped on the Jitra position. A report that fire had been opened on the demolished culverts on the

Kodiang road was found to be correct; the battalion covering the road had mistaken the movement of water buffaloes for Japanese patrols.

As a result of this night march twenty-six officers and men were missing, but all rejoined during the next few days except Subadar Alla Ditta. Most of them went east to the railway and marched along it.

Next morning Captain Long took a party to manhandle the guns across the culverts and bring them in, but when he reached the battery position he was told that an officer had arrived earlier with transport and moved the guns to Pisang, a village a few miles west. This was confirmed by a V.C.O., but the road to Pisang had been cut, Pisang was in enemy hands and the guns were never seen again. Much equipment was also lost as well as all vehicles except eight "B" Echelon trucks which had been sent back beforehand. The battery now manned only two 18-pr. anti-tank guns, the third having been lent to the 4th Battery.

It was now evident that the Japanese had not only command of the air but command of the sea as well since the sinking of H.M.S. *Prince of Wales* and H.M.S. *Repulse* on 10th December; they were now able to land at any point on the peninsula.

About 1700 hours this day (12th) a report was spread that the Jitra line had been turned. Although there was no confirmation of this, a great deal of confusion was caused, and the details of the 7th Battery were ordered to march south without any definite destination. They halted at Gurun that night, but were moved on to Sungei Patani before dawn. Major Scott rejoined his battery from the 4th Battery, which he had been sent to command temporarily. The 18-pr. gun was now the only one left, but some equipment was obtained from Penang Ordnance Depot, now closing down.

The 15th Brigade disputed the crossing of the Kedah river and fell back to the position at Gurun. The troops by now had had no rest for a week, and the threat of an enemy advance from the frontier at Kroh was materializing. This would cut off the troops in Kedah and might bring about a major disaster.

At 0600 hours on the 15th the Japanese broke through the position at Gurun, capturing the 6 Infantry Brigade H.Q.

The 7th Battery moved to Bukit Mertajam, with R.H.Q., sending back their remaining vehicles to assist the withdrawal of 6 Infantry Brigade. The rest of the battery entrained for Ipoh, where it went into camp for a week to refit. Lieutenant W. S. Raw and seven signallers were lent to 4th Battery until the 18th, when 4th Battery rejoined the regiment. Four 3.7-inch howitzers were handed over by the Perak Volunteer Light Battery (which was rearmed with 4.5-inch howitzers). The M.T. was made up to strength and thirty rifles and two Lewis guns were obtained. At this time twenty gunners went sick with malaria and Lieutenant Parshotam Das had to be sent to hospital.

The Division concentrated in the Taiping area south of the River Krian, and after spending a night near a large petrol dump at Kamunting, the 10th Battery went with a force towards Kuala Kangsar to protect the threatened right flank. On starting, orders were received to detach a section to support 1/2 Gurkhas on the Trong road. Lieutenant Wright was detailed to take the Punjabi Mussulman section (guns, three trucks, and cook's lorry); he caught up with the battalion and came into action at dawn to cover a road junction. Captain Standish arrived the next morning (22nd) and took command of the section. No contact was made and a withdrawal was ordered to take place the next day. During the move some difficulty was experienced when crossing a narrow bridge with two sharp turns; the guns crossed successfully by a brilliant piece of driving. Before the other vehicles could cross an air attack was made with bombs and machine guns; in time, however, all were safely over and on their way to harbour at Ipoh, except "B" Sub-section lorry with the detachment. When the lorry was found some hours later it had just been pulled out of a ditch, but the whole detachment was missing, and was not seen for several days until it arrived at Ipoh on foot.

The 11 Indian Division had escaped the Japanese thrust to cut it off in Kedah, and it eventually came to light that the enemy rush down the road through Kroh to Grik for that purpose was their main strategic object. So toil, lack of sleep, and superhuman endurance of our troops had foiled the enemy. Fortunately throughout the operations transport was generally available to move the infantry, but the Division was now exhausted and needed rest and re-equipping, for which little time was available.

Practically no air support existed, nor were there tanks to counter the Japanese regiment of 150 tanks; a few armoured cars and un-armoured carriers fought through with great courage. So far the enemy made little use of artillery, in which arm we were superior, but it had small scope in close country. The enemy preferred to use mortars: however, our guns were responsible for many casualties. Our infantry were in most cases unequal to the Japanese owing to the superior training of the latter in jungle warfare, and on many occasions they moved quickly along the forest tracks on bicycles.

Neither Taiping nor Ipoh being suitable for defence, the Kampar area, some twenty miles south of Ipoh, was selected for preparation for a sustained defence.

The protection of airfields, which had been the primary object of 3 Corps deployment, now only involved the one at Kuantan; and the security of the naval base at Singapore had become of supreme importance.

Major-General Paris, from 12 Brigade, took over command of the 11 Division* and attached troops, and manned a hastily prepared position in depth from Kampar to Bidor, twenty miles south. It was a very good position in fairly open tin-mining country, permitting a field of fire of 1,000 yards in many places, with a steep limestone hill on the eastern flank providing ideal O.Ps. for the artillery. Its weakness was the possibility of an outflanking movement from the west where the port of Teluk Anson on the Perak river lay open to penetration by river and coastal craft.

4th and 7th Mountain Batteries

These two batteries with R.H.Q. moved to Kampar on the 22nd, leaving Ipoh a short time before a heavy air raid. On the way the axle of a trailer of the 7th Battery broke, and the gun had to be dismantled and put on a lorry.

7th Mountain Battery

This was in action three miles north of Kampar, east of the road and inside an all-round position with the British battalion of 6/15 Brigade (the East Surrey and Leicesters amalgamated). Christmas Day was celebrated in this position. On the 26th the enemy began intensive bombing operations from planes flying very low without hindrance, there being none of our aircraft to oppose them.

22nd Mountain Regiment

On the 27th the 10th Battery rejoined. On the 28th the regiment was sent back to Temoh into divisional reserve, on relief 88 Field Regiment. The 88 and 155 Field Regiments had inflicted heavy losses on the enemy during the retreat and were to continue their good shooting at Kampar where the battle opened on the night 28th/29th.

Early on the 30th, owing to a threatened landing at Teluk Anson behind the left flank, the 7th Battery was sent to support 8 Indian Brigade at that place. It was withdrawn to Temoh in twenty-four hours. On the return journey a fine piece of work was carried out by the M.T. havildar, Bachan Singh, who reset a spring of a Marmon-

---

* Now consisting of 6/15 combined Brigade and 28 Brigade.

Harrington which had been ditched—a difficult job at night, but he completed it in half an hour.

On 1st January Lieutenant-Colonel Hughes was admitted to hospital and Major Cowie, O.C. 10th Battery, took over the regiment.

The Japanese attacked the Kampar position very heavily for two days, their fiercest effort yet, which proved to be the culmination, being made on the 1st. Here the Gurkhas were marched against them in hilly scrub-covered country and proved their unquestioned superiority as fighters. The enemy losses were very heavy.

The next day a fierce fight went on all day, but strong enemy forces landed at Teluk Anson and Kampar was outflanked. The three mountain batteries were in action on the Kampar-Teluk Anson road, and were withdrawn to Temoh to support the evacuation of the Kampar position. The Japanese landed in strength at several points down the coast to the south, and the withdrawal had to be continued.

The 7th Battery was supporting 28 Infantry Brigade north of Temoh during the withdrawal down the road and railway, and was firing on D.F. tasks most of the night from 0230 hours onwards. Two signallers with Company H.Q. of the 5/14 Punjab disappeared during the night and were never seen again—they were probably victims of a Japanese patrol.

The next day, 3rd January, 7th and 4th Batteries were in action together in a rear-guard position supporting the 2/1 and 2/2 Gurkhas south of Tapah. Good targets were presented during the attack and many rounds of gun fire devoted to them, causing several hundred casualties. The two batteries withdrew in turn as the Gurkhas were getting clear. The 7th lost Havildar Mahomed Sadiq during an air raid; he was an outstanding specialist, and his loss was much regretted by the battery.

Taking every advantage of their control of the west coast, the Japanese made landings almost daily to cut the L. of C.

The arrival of reinforcements, untrained and in insufficient numbers, brought little relief to the exhausted troops of 3 Corps. The 45 Indian Infantry Brigade Group of 17 Indian Division arrived at Singapore on 3rd January, but had received a minimum of military training and was composed almost entirely of recruits. It had perforce to be sent up to the battle line, as had 53 Brigade Group of 18 British Division which arrived with two anti-aircraft regiments and more aircraft on the 13th.

The remains of 11 Indian Division endured another rough handling in a position on the Slim river on the 6th, enemy tanks having penetrated between brigades; General Wavell,* who was on a visit to the front, ordered its withdrawal for a rest: the whole battle front was to be withdrawn without delay to Johore, where fresh troops could form a new front.

The mountain batteries, now in corps reserve, moved to Kuala Lumpur; on the way, to everyone's regret, Lieutenant Roach of 10th Battery was killed in an air raid on divisional H.Q. where he was acting as liaison officer. He was buried at Sungkai.

An enemy force in considerable strength had, after landing, penetrated to Berjuntai, and the "British Battalion" with 3/17 Dogras was ordered to eject it. A barrage to be fired by the 7th and 10th Batteries was arranged in four lifts of 100 yards, with a concentration on the objective by 252 Field Battery. The barrage was accurate but owing to faulty information stopped short of the enemy's front line, and the infantry had to undertake some stiff hand-to-hand fighting to enable the objective to be gained.

Battalion H.Q. with Major Scott of 7th Battery and Captain Standish of 10th Battery moved forward up the road straight into the fire of an enemy machine gun which was hidden in the jungle close by waiting for a target. Major Scott was killed instantaneously. An outstanding leader and a very popular officer, he was a great loss to the Royal Artillery. He was buried at the gun position.

These events happened on the morning of 7th January: the retirement was not pressed by the enemy on this occasion. The regiment was in action at Labu covering the retirement from Kuala Lumpur through the Seremban Pass. It was then ordered into corps reserve at Kluang. It arrived after one of the most difficult night marches on record: headlights had to be dimmed, the rain was torrential, and convoys were moving on the road in both directions: vehicles ran out of petrol and drivers fell asleep at the wheel, and it took some hours of daylight on the 15th to re-form.

Some re-postings of officers were now necessary; Captain Standish was posted to command 7th Battery, and Captain Coleman joined 10th Battery; Lieutenant Parshotam Dass rejoined from hospital. Among others, Jemadars Gurmukh Singh and Khair Mahomed were promoted to Subadar.

The regiment now had a week to clean up and for rest and maintenance. Major-General Key paid the regiment a visit and heartened the V.C.Os. and men by telling them of the arrival of reinforcements.

---

* On 7th January, 1942, General Sir Archibald Wavell had assumed the appointment of Supreme Commander, S.W. Pacific Front, relieving the C.-in-C., Far East.

The regiment did not move until 22nd January, when the troops fell back fighting on to a new line Mersing-Kluang-Muar river, the withdrawal being considerably assisted by some minor offensives made by 27 Australian Brigade group, now in action for the first time near Gemas after its arrival in July. On its left rear, and on the left of the corps, 45 Indian Brigade, composed of unseasoned and untrained soldiers, failed to hold the Muar river line, and the left flanks had to fall back to Batu Pahat. This withdrawal exposed the communications of the troops holding Segamat on the railway in the centre of the peninsula, and although the front was maintained as long as possible by great efforts on the part of the Australian troops, by the 24th January it was back on the line indicated.

The new front covered about ninety miles, and the arrival of the main body of 18 British Division was anxiously awaited. The 44 Indian Brigade arrived, but was insufficiently trained for work in the front line.

On the corps right flank at Mersing, 22 Australian Brigade group had made strong defences. The Japanese now intensified their coastal landings on both flanks and at least four divisions were moving down the peninsula.

Air attacks on Singapore and the Naval Base were carried out at the rate of two or three a day from captured airfields on the peninsula.

The Mountain Regiment withdrew on 22nd January south to Skudai with orders to patrol the coast, and continued this work until the 28th, when it was ordered to cross the causeway to Singapore Island. By 0700 hours on the 31st the last unit, the Argyll and Sutherland Highlanders, were across and the causeway was blown. The Battle of Singapore had begun.

The Battle of Singapore

Singapore Island has an area of 200 square miles, and its greatest length from east to west is twenty-seven miles. It is separated from the Johore mainland by a strait varying in width from 600 to 2,000 yards. Its importance lay in the Naval Base, whose existence was vital to our fleets in Eastern waters.

The defences of the island were arranged to protect the Naval Base from seaward attack; no provision had been made against an attack from the peninsula in peace time because of the expense which would have been incurred in the construction of defences in Johore State on the mainland. Once the war had started some effort was made to prepare defences on the north side of Singapore Island, but this fell through owing to lack of labour, most of the coolies having disappeared when the bombing began.

The island was divided into three areas, each of which had a coastline to defend and a central reserve area. Except round the town in the southern area there were no beach defences—not even a strand of wire. The total coastline to be guarded was seventy miles. The Fortress Commander was Major-General Keith Simmons, who commanded the Southern Area also during the battle.

The open country is considerable, but covered with rubber and pineapple plantations, while the north and west coasts are difficult of access owing to mangrove swamps.

In January, 1942, the population was about double the normal, probably a million. There was food in abundance; the water supply was barely adequate, and hospital accommodation was short.

Of fighting troops there were now about 70,000, many of whom were much in need of rest, and in addition a large number of administrative troops. The 18 Division less 53 Brigade Group, which had already arrived, finished landing during the first few days of February, as did a light tank squadron from India.

The Japanese had at first three divisions and two tank regiments for the attack, no lack of aircraft, and ample artillery and landing-craft.

The few remaining Allied aircraft were driven out of the sky, and the bombardment by 75-mm. and 155-mm., returned by our artillery, began without delay.

On return to Singapore the 22nd Mountain Regiment was reorganized: the 4th Battery took over two 6-inch howitzers and shared its four 3.7's between the 7th and 10th Batteries. The three 3.7 batteries now had six guns each. A few days later each battery took over an 18-pr. for shore defence.

The divisional field artillery was weakened by losses in Malaya, and the value of the coast defence guns firing landwards was reduced by a shortage of H.E., of which the 9.2 guns had only 30 rounds each and the 15-inch none at all. Armour-piercing shell had to be used as an alternative, and it was believed that heavy casualties were inflicted on the enemy by these guns.

The Mountain Regiment, less 4th Battery, supported the 6/15 Indian Infantry Brigade, later relieved by 53 Infantry Brigade (Brigadier Duke) in its sector from Seletar Creek to Causeway (inclusive) on the northern shore. On 5th February 155 Field Regiment, R.A., came under command of 22nd Mountain Regiment.

On first arriving, the 21st Battery was detailed to the Naval Base which had been evacuated, and of which the oil tanks had been bombed and set on fire. The position ordered was not a good one, having no cover for flashes and an approach in the open. The battery, after being shelled out, was ordered to join the other two, which it did on 6th February. Much work had to be done digging and wiring the battery position and O.Ps. The 7th and 10th Batteries on the west of the Seletar river were linked, and registration was carried out, after which harassing and observed fire went on all day as well as D.F. fire at night. The range to the Johore mainland was about 4,200 yards. Star shell was issued to the 3.7 howitzer batteries for night work.

The 4th Battery was supporting 28 Infantry Brigade on the left of 53 Infantry Brigade from a position near Bukit Timah.

Lieutenant-Colonel Hughes returned from hospital on 4th February. Captain Coleman was now in command of the 10th Battery. On the 7th, Jemadar Aurang Zeb arrived from India with reinforcements and was posted to the 7th Battery. The 10th Battery had to move to a new position on the 8th after being heavily shelled.

Major D. G. C. Cowie was appointed Second-in-Command of the regiment on the 5th: he was killed by a shell splinter on the 7th. He was a very capable and resourceful commander and a great loss to the mountain artillery, in which he had served for many years.

Till now there had been no attack on the regiment's front, and after a heavy bombardment, the main attack was put in on the western sector held by the Australians. This attack, in great strength supported by tanks, was successful and the withdrawal from the western side necessitated a general shortening of the line to make a perimeter defence around the town. On 10th February a battle developed for the high ground at Bukit Timah, which fell into enemy hands. That night roving sections were sent out to carry out H.F. tasks from various positions, and on the 11th a concentration was fired on Seletar Island. That evening the 3.7 batteries harboured in a position near the town; the next afternoon the 7th Battery moved forward into a position from which it did not fire, and on the night of the 12th the complete regiment was concentrated in the Newton Road area on the outskirts of the town. On the way back an ammunition lorry broke down just inside the line of the rearguard; Naik Mahomed Naaz repaired the damage and brought in the ammunition.

Newton Road was packed with transport of every kind, and a most unpleasant night was spent under shell fire surrounded by infantry firing off their rifles. "B" Echelon, which included the followers, suffered several casualties. During the night Lieutenant Murray, Jemadar Kartar Singh, and three I.O.Rs. were fallen out and formed part of an official escape party; after adventures in Sumatra they reached India and afterwards fought in Burma.

On the morning of the 13th bombing attacks were continued, killing several men in the regiment, including Saddler Mem Raj. The troops assisted to rescue civilians from bombed buildings, while attempts were made to find battery positions in a congested town.

That night the three batteries occupied positions north of the Serangoon road in support of 53 Infantry Brigade (5 and 6 Norfolk and 2 Cambridgeshire), but did not fire: the front line was held and support was not called for. D.F. targets were registered during the day, and on enemy artillery opening a heavy fire the batteries retaliated, mostly firing at targets by means of the 1/25000 map. H.E. was getting short as some of the Ordnance dumps had been captured or bombed, and an order was received to ration it. The next day batteries had about 750 rounds left.

This day was the 15th February: the 53 Infantry Brigade fought on, making several local counter-attacks, and morale generally had improved since the retirements had ceased. However, there was no more petrol and the water supply could not last more than twenty-four hours; there was no alternative and the G.O.C. decided to surrender. Firing continued until orders reached the batteries about 1700 hours; the guns and instruments were then destroyed and the batteries marched to the Polo Ground. Major-General Key, Commanding 11 Indian Division visited the Regiment and congratulated the officers and men on the high state of morale and discipline they had maintained during the campaign.

The following day arms and equipment were handed over to the Japanese, and on the 17th the British officers were sent to Changi; with them went the Signal Officer, Lieutenant A. B. Peters, R.C.S., who had come out with the Regiment as a sergeant and remained on promotion. He was very efficient and well liked.

Lieutenant Elliott managed to escape. The Commanding Officer took the salute as the men of R.H.Q. and four batteries marched past him on their way to Farrer Park into captivity.

Thus ended the existence of these four mountain batteries; their names, however, were not struck out of the Army List.

The junior battery, 21st, well maintained the traditions of the mountain artillery in this its first campaign in that branch. Formed in 1759 as the 6th Company, 3rd Battalion, Royal Artillery, it had distinguished itself at Corunna with the rear-guard, and Sir John Moore's gunners would have been proud of their descendants.

The other three batteries had honourable records of many Frontier campaigns and of service in the First World War [the 4th (Hazara) Battery was the oldest of the Indian mountain batteries], but they had never taken part in a war with the handicaps met in Malaya.

At their own work as gunners they were acknowledged to have lived up to a very high standard. Their march discipline was favourably noticed by everybody; gun-pits and slit trenches were always made, however tired the men were; junior officers and N.C.Os. accepted responsibility without failure. Survey was prompt and accurate, and, best of all, the infantry, British and Indian welcomed them with open arms. Drivers, signallers, specialists—all received high praise from their officers.

The sufferings of British and Indian ranks during the slavery enforced by their savage enemy cannot be recorded here.

Much has been written of the disloyalty of the Indian ranks who joined, voluntarily or under pressure, the Japanese-sponsored Indian National Army. These men were mostly Sikhs; very few Mussulmans joined it—in fact, led by Second-Lieutenant Parshotam Das (7th Battery), Quartermaster-Havildar Mahomed Khan (21st Battery) and Havildar-Major Nur Khan of the Hazara Battery, they played a leading part in resisting pressure by the I.N.A. on an occasion when both sides suffered casualties. Nur Khan was the leader of a loyal body of Punjab Mussulmans numbering 350. Those V.C.Os. and N.C.Os. who retained their loyalty were a constant source of inspiration and encouragement to the men.

NOTE BY LIEUTENANT-COLONEL HUGHES

At the close of the campaign only four of the British officers—Lieutenant-Colonel Hughes, Major E. L. Sawyer, Major J. B. Sopper and Major P. Standish—also Lieutenant Peters (Royal Signals), who left India with the Regiment, were still with it. The remaining officers had joined the Regiment in 1939 and 1940. They came from all walks of life and included lawyers, stockbrokers, varsity students, insurance brokers, chartered accountants, bankers and tea planters. On joining the Regiment they lost no time in making themselves efficient Mountain Gunners, in learning the language and getting to know their men. During the campaign they all worked magnificently and rivalled the old hard faces who were left in the Regiment, not only in their loyalty to their batteries and to the Regiment, but also to the traditions of Mountain Artillery. One could not have wished for better officers, and they would have been a decided asset to any regiment in peace or war.

REWARDS GRANTED FOR DISTINGUISHED SERVICES
WHILE PRISONER OF WAR

M.B.E.: Major E. L. Sawyer.
B.E.M.: Havildar-Major Nur Khan.
Mentions: Lieutenant A. E. Peters, Royal Signals (attached); Lieutenant Parshotam Das, Indian Artillery; Jemadar Ghulam Mahomed; Havildar Bostan Khan, Havildar S'aif Ali, Havildar Mahomed Sarwar, Havildar Clerk Jalal Shah; Naik Mahomed Hanif; Lance-Naik Shah Wali; Driver Mahomed Ishaq.

C. BURMA, 1941-1945

1. FIRST BURMA CAMPAIGN

Fifty-one years after annexation Burma ceased to be a province of India and became a separate territory (1937). By this date communications had been improved beyond measure: the waterways were fully exploited and the railway had reached Myitkyina, with several branch lines, including one from Mandalay to Lashio. This latter place was railhead for the Burma Road, a lorry highway completed in 1939 running to Chungking, 610 miles away. It was the only method of supply to the Chinese capital except by air and the natural outcome of the Japanese encirclement of China, 1937.

The configuration of Burma has been described in Chapter III. It was cut off from Thailand (Siam) by an enormous massif in possession of the Shan States, a federation administered by its own rulers under the Government of Burma, difficult of access, although some branch railway lines ran to the foothills. On the west the great mountain barrier was pierced by the six-foot track from Tamu to Imphal which had been in existence for centuries, and was improved by British troops in 1886, but it had no value as a trade route and had been neglected ever since. There were several minor tracks but no road. On the north the Chinese mountain ranges were impassable, so that to all intents and purposes Burma was only accessible by sea or air.

The Bengal–Assam railway (single line, metre gauge), after a break to cross the Brahmaputra by boat, ran alongside that river to Dibrugarh, which it reached in 1903. A branch line was later taken on to Ledo, sixty miles to the east.

The Japanese had placed themselves in a very strong position in south-east Asia by entering French Indo-China some months before they made their treacherous attack on the United States fleet in Pearl Harbour on 8th December, 1941, and on the following day, after agreement with the Thais, they landed a strong force, including air units, in Thailand.

The Burmese had not been encouraged to defend their country until after the separation from India, when ten rifle battalions were formed. Battalions of the Burma Rifles had fought in Mesopotamia and Palestine during the First World War, but only one regiment (the 20th) was kept in existence afterwards. It enlisted Karens, Chins and Kachins, but few Burmans.

For operational purposes Burma was at first in the Far East Command, but a few days after the Pearl Harbour attack it was brought under the Commander-in-Chief, India. Defence arrangements had not been pressed forward owing to shortage of troops and other reasons, and the air forces were particularly weak. At the end of December, 1941, Burma was included in the A.B.D.A.* Command under General Wavell, whose headquarters were in Java. Lieutenant-General T. J. Hutton, C.B., M.C., an Artillery officer, was in command in Burma.

The 1 Burma Division (Burdiv) (Major-General J. G. Bruce-Scott, M.C.) consisted of 13 Indian Infantry Brigade and 1 and 2 Burma Infantry Brigades; it was deployed east of Mandalay guarding the approaches from the South Shan States, with several detachments.

The 17 Indian Division† (Major-General J. G. Smyth, V.C., M.C.) only started forming early in January and consisted of 16 and 46 Indian Infantry Brigades, there being in all one British and five Indian battalions and two battalions of Burma Rifles. It was completed on 7th February by the arrival of 48 Indian Infantry Brigade. Both divisions contained incompletely trained units and were well below strength.

There were several air squadrons in the country, also below strength, and the presence of an American Volunteer Group of fighters, a force manned by U.S. pilots for the defence of China, saved the situation during the defence of Rangoon.

The 27th Mountain Regiment H.Q. (Lieutenant-Colonel W. G. Constable) arrived at Rangoon in December, 1941, at the same time as the 5th (Bombay) Battery (Major W. H. H. Wilberforce) and took over the 2nd (Derajat) Battery (Major P. Hartley) and 23rd Battery (Major T. M. Witherow). The 2nd Battery had arrived in Maymyo

---

* American, British, Dutch, Australian.

† The Division had formed in Ahmednagar early in 1941, but two of its Brigades went to Malaya and only Divisional H.Q. and 46 Brigade to Burma, in January, 1942.

in relief in March, 1938. The 12th (Poonch) Battery, which had been in Moulmein since March, 1941, was also regimented with 27th Mountain Regiment. Lieutenant-Colonel Constable acted as C.R.A. to 1 Burma Division; his command also included one Anglo-Burman field battery (18-pr.), but he had neither Signal nor Survey section.

The 17th Divisional Artillery consisted at this time of an Anglo-Burman field battery and an anti-aircraft battery, but before operations began was strengthened by the addition of the 5th and 12th Mountain Batteries.

Defensive positions had been prepared to the east of Taunggyi covering the River Salween crossing and the road through the Shan States towards Lashio. Our Chinese allies sent troops to our assistance—the Chinese 5th and 6th Armies—by way of the Burma Road. They arrived early in March, 1942, under the American General J. Stilwell, and took over the left flank. Each army consisted of two divisions, under strength but battle-trained.

The Japanese were known to be assembling in strength near the Thai border, and on being attacked, Tavoy and Kawkareik were evacuated and the troops fell back on Moulmein, for the defence of which 2 Burma Brigade was responsible. The seven-mile perimeter was held by four battalions of the Burma Rifles with a fifth battalion in reserve; the only artillery support was provided by the four 3.7-inch howitzers of the 12th (Poonch) Battery, commanded by Major J. G. L. Hume. On 30th January the Japanese attacked in force and heavy fighting went on throughout the day. The battery was in action all day, the section supporting 8 Burma Rifles being thanked for its "excellent support," and the battery afterwards received a congratulatory message from Brigadier Bourke, commanding the force, for "magnificent work."

The attack was held for the time and the battery was sent to assist in the defence of the Kokine airfield, but the enemy's numbers told, and the whole front was forced to evacuate about 0800 hours on the 31st, the garrison withdrawing to Martaban.

The following morning Major Hume with a party went back through the enemy's lines, with an escort of 4/12 F.F. Regiment, to look for a section which had not reported. Both guns were successfully withdrawn.

At Martaban the battery wagon lines were bombed, causing a loss of six mules killed and five drivers wounded ; the men and guns were sent by train to Kyaikto, the mules following by road.

The 5th (Bombay) Battery had been in the Moulmein garrison, but did not take part in the fighting, having been withdrawn to Martaban early in the action. It crossed the Salween river and moved to Thaton, whence one section returned to Martaban in lorries and took part in the fighting. The other section (Punjabi Mussulman) moved in support of 7/10 Baluch to Paan ferry on the night of 11th/12th February to cover the river crossing and the battalion with the guns formed a perimeter camp, which was heavily attacked for forty-eight hours before the survivors of a very gallant regiment fought their way out to rejoin their brigade; though a new battalion, they had fought like veterans. The transport was outside the perimeter and the two guns had perforce to be abandoned.

The Martaban position was attacked for several days, air bombing was frequent, and attacks were nightly made on our all-round defences, accompanied by much noise of crackers and screaming. More Japanese were infiltrating through the jungle to cut the line of retreat of the force from the north, and a withdrawal was ordered to the Bilin river, where the next stand was to be made.

At Bilin the 28th Mountain Regiment H.Q. (Lieutenant-Colonel A. H. Peskett, M.C.), with the 15th (Jhelum) Battery (Major R. J. P. Lock) and 28th Battery (Major J. B. Chaplin), joined the division. They had arrived at Rangoon via Madras on 14th February and were sent up to the front immediately, owing to the serious situation.

The animals and details of both batteries under Captain J. R. Tysoe left Calcutta on the 15th, but the ship was turned back and the party went to Muzaffarpur, where they were issued with guns. At the end of their long fighting withdrawal through Burma the batteries found these guns waiting for them in action on the Shenam (Assam) position.

The strength of each battery on leaving Rangoon was 3 British and 2 V.C. officers, 100 I.O.Rs. and followers, four guns; transport, three jeeps and seven three-ton Chevrolet lorries. The lorry drivers were on loan from 2 Indian A/T. Regiment, but untrained, and the British officers had to undertake much of the driving. The batteries had twenty-four rifles each and only two bayonets for protection, with two Bren guns, a weapon they had never seen before. No wireless was available.

After a train journey to Kyaikto, where a day's work had to be put in on the lorries before they could move, the 15th and 28th Batteries went south to join in the action on the Bilin* position which had been going on for two days. After firing several concentrations in support of 1/9 R. Jats, whose departure was delayed

---

* Here the 5th Mountain Battery received two 3.7-inch howitzers (in grease and without lifters) to replace deficiencies.

by the enemy, the two batteries withdrew into the centre of 16 Brigade "box" at Kyaikto. During the night a party of Japanese drove into the box in an abandoned lorry, making a great turmoil shouting and firing off crackers, which drew a heavy fire from the area and some unnecessary movement. Order was restored in the battery by the accidental shooting by a British officer of a signaller who had been mistaken for an enemy soldier; he was not seriously hurt. None of the enemy was killed on this occasion.

On the same occasion Major Wilberforce was in the 5th Battery O.P. and found his O.P. party cut off. He organized a barrage, under cover of which the infantry were to restore communication, but the battery reported a shortage of ammunition. Forthwith, Subadar Sardara Singh, Tailor Umar Khan (who had served through the First World War) and a mochi loaded up 200 rounds and marched forward to the battery position; this allowed the barrage and attack to be carried through, and the infantry then linked up with the O.P.

The Kyaikto line was not a good one and the intention now was for 17 Division to form a strong line on the west bank of the River Sittang; the 7 Armoured Brigade (Brigadier J. H. Anstice), in the act of disembarking at Rangoon, was to come up to reinforce as soon as possible. It was realized that failure to halt the enemy on the Sittang must uncover Rangoon and lead to its eventual loss, but there was no alternative. The crossing of the river was by a railway bridge planked over for M.T., and, there being high ground both north and south of the bridge, the approaches to it were through cuttings. The river was nearly 800 yards wide, with a swift current.

During this retirement on 20th February the 28th Battery was in support of 2 Duke of Wellington's Regiment, which had crossed the river at Kyaikto when, owing to a mistake in liaison with the R.A.F., both these units were bombed and machine-gunned, suffering many casualties. A battery lorry was set on fire, but the gun and ammunition were saved at some risk by the detachment.

The 48 Infantry Brigade, which was leading, arrived at the bridgehead at Mokpalin on the evening of 21st; the motor transport of the division, 16 Brigade and 46 Brigade (rear-guard), halted together for the night on the unsurfaced track between the front and Kyaikto.

Soon after the advanced guard started to cross the bridge early on 22nd, a 3-ton lorry blocked the roadway and caused a delay of three hours. Only two battalions of Gurkhas had crossed when the Japanese 33rd Division began an attack on the bridgehead; it had moved rapidly from the eastern flank through dense jungle without transport to cut off 17 Division. The first attack was beaten off, and an attack at the same time on the stationary massed transport about a mile from the bridge, of which the 28th Mountain Regiment bore the brunt, including a bayonet attack which accounted for six unarmed followers, was also checked. An hour or so later the rear of the column was attacked from dense jungle five miles short of the village. Air bombing, small-arms and mortar fire, and later enemy artillery fire, added to the disorganization and confusion.

The Sikh section of the 12th (Poonch) Battery was the leading artillery unit, and Lieutenant J. O. S. Janson decided to cross as soon as he could. The bridge being blocked with transport, he unloaded the mules and loaded guns and ammunition on a steamer; this vessel was hit and set alight by enemy fire just as it reached the opposite bank, but the guns were saved by the detachments, who carried them up the beach and came into action, keeping up a steady fire to cover the crossing. The V.C.O., Subadar Jowala Singh, marched the mules over the bridge under fire later in the day. He and Naik Dulip Singh were afterwards awarded the I.O.M. The section lost one I.O.R. killed, fourteen wounded, and seven mules killed.

Captain J. W. Poole, 5th (Bombay) Battery, saw all his vehicles across the bridge and then returned to report, shooting on the way a Jap who had some valuable documents on him.

Meanwhile the artillery was in action near Mokpalin railway station, under 28th Mountain Regiment, all the troops being under continuous fire with little cover. Higher control had lapsed for the time being owing to lack of communication; there were not even Very pistols with the force. O.Ps. were established and the guns supported several infantry attacks by the remnants of 16 Infantry Brigade in an endeavour to break through to the bridgehead troops on the high ground, now isolated by the enemy who had interposed a strong block. The 28th Battery had some shooting at a pagoda full of Japanese at 450 yards over open sights, and a concentration of three batteries supported an attack by the 1/3 Gurkhas; the bridgehead was retaken once, but in the end numbers told and it remained in enemy hands. Fighting at the bridge went on all day and D.F. continued most of the night.

The rear brigades had also been fighting all day through and round Japanese blocks on their way to the front, suffering very heavy casualties. At Mokpalin a perimeter defence was established for the night and there was a good deal of firing, but enemy pressure went on increasing and the commander ordered the bridge to be blown at 0530 hours on the 23rd. This left most of his division on the east bank, including the survivors of the rear brigades, who cleared the enemy from the bridgehead about nine o'clock.

Orders were issued for a withdrawal and the evacuation of wounded, and a position was taken up on the beach to cover the operation. The Japanese renewed their efforts to wipe out our troops, but shrapnel, fuze 0, proved of devastating effect at short ranges. The batteries, having expended most of their ammunition against enemy artillery, were ordered to support the defence of the beach perimeter from the beach itself; eventually one gun was kept firing whilst the others were prepared for destruction. This was not fully carried out, but breech-blocks and sights were removed and thrown down wells or into the river.

The troops were told to get across the river as best they could, and many men accomplished a half-mile swim under fire. Lieutenant Gilmour of 5th Battery was missing and many casualties occurred from drowning; innumerable acts of great heroism took place helping to get the wounded across. Lieutenant Mackenzie of the 28th Battery helped two Gurkha officers to remove several wounded men across under fire, for which he was awarded the M.C.

Captain Poole had food ready for those who reached the other bank, and the survivors found their way to Pegu to entrain.

The havildar-major of 5th (Bombay) Battery, Wazir Khan, was captured at the river crossing, and escaped after a year as a prisoner. He made his way to Chungking, where he joined the U.S.A. forces.

The enemy did not follow up and the remnants of the division were reorganized at once as far as possible, but many men were found to have no rifles and some no clothes and had to be sent up-country to be re-equipped. The 46 Indian Infantry Brigade was broken up and units amalgamated or redistributed. There was no opportunity for rest, and part of the division was shortly afterwards fighting in Pegu with whatever transport and equipment could be obtained in a hurry. The 5th and the Punjabi Mussulman section of the 12th Mountain Batteries went to Mandalay to refit and were issued with 3.7-inch howitzers.

Major-General D. Cowan assumed command of 17 Division on 1st March, and on the 5th of that month General The Hon. Sir H. R. L. Alexander, K.C.B., C.S.I., D.S.O., M.C.,* took over the appointment of Commander-in-Chief, Burma. A.B.D.A.† Headquarters had closed down on 25th February, and control of operations in Burma fell to the Commander-in-Chief, India, an appointment reassumed by General Wavell.

Singapore had fallen on 15th February and strong Japanese reinforcements could now be brought round by sea unopposed.

---

* Later Field-Marshal The Earl Alexander of Tunis, G.C.B., G.C.M.G., C.S.I., D.S.O., M.C.

† See Appendix, p. 453.

General Alexander's primary task was the retention of Rangoon; the situation became worse during the 6th as a detachment was cut off in Pegu, and at midnight on the 6th the order for the evacuation of Rangoon went out. This was a disaster for the Allies as, apart from the destruction of the oil refineries there, the Japanese began to land reinforcements. The loss of the Rangoon aerodrome had very serious consequences for the air situation as well.

Reinforcements of aeroplanes had been arriving, including Hurricane fighters, and for a short period before the Sittang crossing the Allies had held their own in the air, but operational advantages were now with the enemy.

The Pegu detachment cut its way out* and during a lull in the operations a complete regrouping was carried out. The 1 Burma Division handed over the protection of the left flank on the line of the Salween river to Chinese troops and was moved by rail to the Irrawaddy front. During the weeks since the opening of the campaign the 27th Mountain Regiment with the 2nd (Derajat) Battery and the 23rd Battery had been carrying out local protection duties with the Burma Division, which entailed a great deal of marching and occasional minor engagements.

On 11th March the 2nd and 23rd Batteries supported an attack on a Japanese flank guard at Pyuntaza, but the attack failed through lack of reconnaissance and insufficiency of fire power. On this occasion the 2nd Battery was nearly overrun, but the attack was beaten off by fire and an orderly retirement became possible. The battery fired 200 rounds that morning. Lieutenant F. W. Graham went out to the left with an O.P. party and a company of Rajputs, but his line was cut and during an attempt to regain communication with the battery the party disappeared and was never seen again.

On 22nd March the division began to entrain north of Toungoo in rear of the newly arrived Chinese 200th Division. The 23rd Battery was allotted to the last train on the 24th, but its departure was delayed by an enemy attack and it went into action to support the Chinese, who put up a gallant fight. The battery stopped an infantry attack at close range in an indecisive artillery duel, during which it found that the enemy had cut it off from the train, ambushing the second-line lorries, which were set on fire, and the followers, Q.M. staff, etc. were burnt alive in them. The battery limbered up with speed and marched off through the jungle without an escort, rejoining the division a week later. There was little to eat and the pakhals were lost—they were not replaced for several weeks.

---

* As did also 17 Indian Division and H.Q. Burma Army at Hlegu on 8th March.

The Chinese 200th Division maintained a tenacious resistance on the flank at Toungoo for ten days of fierce fighting, while we occupied the Prome–Toungoo line.

The 1 Burcorps was formed at this time under Lieutenant-General W. J. Slim, M.C.,* to consist of 1 Burma Division, 17 Indian Division (which had been joined by 63 Infantry Brigade recently arrived from India) and 7 Armoured Brigade (in corps reserve).

The Allied Air Force had withdrawn fighter and bomber planes to Magwe aerodrome after the loss of Rangoon, and a serious reverse was suffered on 21st March when a large number of aircraft were destroyed on the ground. The nearest operational aerodrome was 400 miles farther north, and as the supplies of aeroplanes were very restricted owing to the number needed for the defence of India and Ceylon, it was decided that all R.A.F. units should be withdrawn from Burma.

Japanese encircling movements were accompanied by heavy bombing, which the few anti-aircraft guns with the force were unable to prevent. Marches in future, therefore, had to be carried out without any air cover; that is to say, the enemy could bomb columns of troops at his discretion, and six weeks' marching lay ahead of the troops. Marching was perforce carried out at night—an extremely tiring procedure for animals. Even when the guns and gunners were given lifts in M.T., which happened occasionally, the drivers and mules had many dreary marches at about one mile per hour between M.T. columns with many checks.

The Japanese were adepts at their own form of jungle fighting, which consisted of forming blocks to stop the head of a column and then attacking the rear and one or both flanks. Frequent checks led to congestion of transport, and although some of the infantry were carried in M.T., great numbers had to march.

The Japanese recommenced operations on 26th March in the Irrawaddy valley.

Three Japanese divisions and two tank brigades were now opposed to our reduced formations, and as British prestige decreased during the retreat, many Fifth Columnists and traitor Burmans joined the enemy.

The Sikh section of the 12th (Poonch) Battery never failed in its support of the infantry, occupying one defensive position after another; always in pack, its longest march was forty-one miles, followed as usual by digging in on arrival. No man fell out.

The section took up a defensive position at Prome on the 28th

---

* Later Field-Marshal Sir W. J. Slim, G.C.B., G.C.M.G., G.B.E., D.S.O., M.C.

March supporting 17th Dogras (63 Brigade) on the extreme right. It was soon discovered that some of the Japanese were already in Prome and the column was surrounded—so closely that one of the O.P. signallers felt a hand grabbing his equipment, which he hastily slipped out of and he then got away. Two days later the Japs surprised the gunners in the battery, but a joint counter-attack with a company of Dogras rescued the guns. The Sikh section moved off as soon as it was dark with little time to spare, and Jowala Singh (now Subadar) and his F.O.O. party had to fight their way back to rejoin. It was not long before Burcorps had to withdraw from its position: the Commander-in-Chief's next task was the preservation of the Yenangyaung oilfields, 150 miles north of Prome.

After the action at the Sittang river the 15th Battery, having refitted at Mandalay, took over fresh armament at Prome from 5 (Indian) Anti-Tank Battery. It consisted of seven Skoda 77-mm. guns, two jeeps, a 30-cwt. lorry, and seven Chevrolet four-wheel-drive 30-cwt. lorries, with four 101 wireless sets and operators. This peculiar outfit was supposed to be a two-troop field battery, and came into action many times in support of infantry, sometimes of 17 Division, sometimes of Burdiv. The 28th Battery, which was acting as infantry, acquired one 3.7-inch howitzer.

On 1st April 17 Division was forced to withdraw from Prome, and on the 3rd it moved back through Burdiv to the Kyaukpadaung area. By the 9th the front ran from Miahla to Taungdwinggi, and heavy fighting continued from the 12th onwards. Notwithstanding fierce resistance, a gap was made between the two divisions and there was now no alternative to the destruction of the oilfields: last of all, the power-house at Yenangyaung was blown a few minutes before the arrival of the Japanese on 16th April.

At Magwe on the night of 16th the 23rd Battery, finding itself unprotected and all but surrounded, prepared its guns for spiking, but the arrival of two tanks of 7 Hussars at dawn restored the situation. The 5th (Bombay) Battery and Punjabi Mussulman section of the 12th Battery, after rearming at Mandalay, went by boat to Yenangyaung and were fitted out with bullock-cart transport.

The 5th and the two Burdiv Batteries were surrounded along with the greater part of the division for two days at Yenangyaung. The Japanese came unexpectedly up the Irrawaddy river and the situation became critical, but the division and corps troops fought their way out. They were again surrounded on the night 19th/20th and fought a way through the Japanese blocks again. The division lost in these few days 20 per cent. of its personnel, four 25-prs., four 3.7-inch howitzers, two Bofors, most of its 3-inch mortars and nearly all of its M.T.

In this fighting the left section (Ahirs) of the 5th Battery was caught by enemy gun fire as it was coming into action, but Captain Magor opened fire at 600 yards with the section and, thanks to the gallantry of the two Nos. 1, Havildar Hari Singh and Naik Sheotaj Singh, who set the detachments a wonderful example of steadiness under a rapid fire, the guns continued firing. At the same time the right section came under fire, with the result that Havildar Ahmed Khan and another N.C.O. were killed and Lieutenant Harler and several men wounded. The wounded were extricated under fire by Subadar Hakim Khan and some of the men, and the gun was withdrawn. Subadar Hakim Khan, I.D.S.M., was killed here, later being awarded a posthumous I.O.M. for gallantry. Major Wilberforce, who had spotted the enemy gun, then engaged it with the left section and, although the O.P. was under small-arms fire at short range as well as artillery fire, he knocked it out in fifteen rounds. He then withdrew his O.P. party after the infantry had retired. Havildar Ali Bahadur was awarded the I.D.S.M. for gallantry under fire in this action, and Signaller Lance-Naik Sultan Singh was commended for repairing cut telephone lines under heavy fire. Captain Magor was wounded, and on the following day Havildar Hari Singh was killed in action.

The mules suffered badly from lack of water and never recovered entirely from the effects of two or three days without water. The lorries carrying the guns of the 5th Battery managed to reach Kyaukpadaung, where they tried to break out across country and stuck in the sand. They were then ordered to be burnt with the guns.

While the division was reorganizing at Popa and the mules had been watered, but not fed owing to dearth of grain and fodder, the 23rd Battery was given the fittest mules of the Derajat Battery so that it might support the Chinese 38th Division in an attempt to thrust back the leading elements of the enemy. This entailed a long march back the way the column had come, and the attack was not pushed home after all. On return to the place where it had left the division, the battery found that a further retirement had been made, lorries having become available for the infantry The starving mules had therefore to cover eighty-three miles in fifty-six hours to catch up, and the Derajat Battery received their mules back in very poor condition. The Regiment then had its first and only three days' rest. The animals suffered badly during the whole period of the retirement—marching was a shuffle at one mile per hour with infrequent opportunities for off-loading. Galls were not uncommon and, taken in all, what with starvation and thirst, the mules had a very bad time.

All this while the enemy was moving northwards through the Shan States with the object of enveloping the Allies' left flank and thus forcing a further withdrawal. On 20th April 7 Armoured Brigade was sent to Meiktila, and a few days later, owing to the enemy advance, was carrying out the duty of rear-guard to Burcorps on the line Meiktila–Mandalay with 17 Division and covering the withdrawal of the Chinese armies northwards.

The 48 Infantry Brigade, supported by tanks and artillery, fought a brilliant rear-guard action at Kyaukse to cover the passage of the Irrawaddy by the Ava bridge. The enemy's motorized infantry sustained about 500 casualties during an all-day battle. The Sikh section of the 12th (Poonch) Battery was still marching and fighting during its latest withdrawal; it recorded a march of eighty-seven miles by night and day with nothing more than tea for sustenance.

At 2350 hours on 30th April the Ava bridge was blown, and the Chinese were making their way north to try to leave for China by way of Lashio. The Japanese, however, arrived there first, via Loilem, and thus cut the Chinese line of retreat. General Stilwell was forced to move the remnants of his troops to India by a series of difficult mountain paths in the north of Burma.

General Alexander's plan now provided for the move of his main body to India via Kalewa, with two infantry brigades astride the Chindwin river to delay the enemy. A strong detachment was sent to the Myittha valley to hold an enemy force moving up that valley with the intention of cutting the Assam road at Kalemyo. A small detachment was attacked near Monywa on 30th April by a Japanese force which came up the Chindwin unexpectedly, and Monywa was occupied by the enemy until the following morning, when it was regained by a counter-attack. Tanks and infantry were sent to clear up the situation, as Monywa covered the approach up the Chindwin to the line of retirement of the troops from the Ava bridge.

On 1st May an enemy detachment reoccupied Monywa and attacked Burdiv H.Q., with which was 27th Mountain Regiment H.Q. Most of the personnel escaped in small groups once the defence company was overrun and the camp commandant killed. Later, a senior artillery officer insisted on returning to the bivouac to recover his false teeth and to collect some missing men, but enemy activity prevented this. The survivors walked half a day to join up with the infantry, being eventually picked up by a detachment which included a troop of 15th Battery which had been in action with its Skoda guns.

In the meantime the 2nd and 23rd Batteries were in action engaging the enemy with area bombardments and close support of the brigades to which they were attached, the 7 Armoured Brigade and the remainder of Burdiv having been sent to retake Monywa. However, the attack was not pressed home as the enemy gave way, and the force was able to move to Ye-u, on which 17 Division had been directed.

The batteries and the section of the 12th Battery recorded some more strenuous marching to reach Ye-u; forty-one miles of jungle in one day without a man falling out, following a long day in action after a march the previous night.

Although the enemy did his utmost to cut off Burcorps from the crossing, they were out-marched by our men—worn out, hungry, ragged, bootless in some cases, able to carry only their rifles and ammunition, but refusing to abandon their sick and wounded to a savage enemy. Still they went on.

On 5th May the 15th Battery was at Ye-u, where it received orders to dismantle guns and destroy ammunition and move across the Chindwin. Having done this (an officer wrote: "11 guns in $2\frac{1}{2}$ months!") it gave assistance to 2nd (Derajat) and 23rd Batteries on the move to the Chindwin.

The last thirty miles from Ye-u to Shwegyin along a sandy track was carried out at the usual crawl, with the remaining mules failing rapidly, and on arrival it was found that Japanese forward elements had come up the Chindwin river and were in position commanding the eastern terminus of the ferry. Having no ammunition left, the two batteries with 27th R.H.Q. marched upstream along a mountain path, losing six mules down the khud, and spent the night without food or water on the hillside. Next day they crossed at Kalewa, swimming the mules, and started the last lap to Imphal.

The 12th (Poonch) Battery was in action with 17 Division and contributed to the clearance of the Japanese and the safe crossing of the column. Both sections were now complete, the Punjabi Mussulman section having joined up with its guns. During the action, however, this section was again forced to destroy its guns, but the Sikhs followed through with the division and brought the last two mountain guns over the Chindwin. Of the twenty-five guns saved in the Corps, eleven were 3.7-inch howitzers.

On the morning of 10th May the enemy attacked the covering force at Shwegyin and fighting continued all day, the rear-guard, the 48 Brigade, driving off the Japanese in the evening. The 28th Battery took part in this action and finally moved their one and only gun to Imphal in an ambulance. Ferrying from Shwegyin became no longer practicable, and all the animal transport of the corps as well as 7 Armoured Brigade were halted at that place. The Corps Commander ordered motor vehicles and tanks to be destroyed, and personnel to move by a track to the ferry opposite Kalewa, where the animals were ferried across.

It was a sad day for 7 Armoured Brigade when it had to abandon tanks and vehicles which it had brought through Burma and which had played a great part in these difficult operations. In his despatch General Alexander especially stressed the high morale and great fighting capacity of this formation, which consisted of 7 Hussars, 2 R. Tanks and 414 Battery R.H.A., with a motorized regiment, the Cameronians, attached.

The 100 miles from Kalewa to Tamu was a nightmare march through hundreds of thousands of refugees of many different races, stricken with starvation and cholera, on their way to India. Seventy more miles had to be traversed before reaching Imphal where there was room to encamp and refit.

At 1800 hours on 20th May the rear-guard of Burcorps was placed under command of 4 Corps in Assam. The enemy did not follow up.

Many of the mules were unable to carry their loads up the steep tracks, and guns and gunners were glad to have M.T. provided. Even so, many mules without loads to carry died of exhaustion.

One battery commander wrote: "Within two marches of Imphal, when our drivers had marched and fought over 360 miles in seventeen days in tattered clothes and broken boots, and when rain, wind and mud made marching an agony and halting a misery, we sent for the now rested gunners to take the mules and so allow the drivers to finish in lorries. But of the drivers whose mules still lived, not one man would hand his animal over. We were not beaten."

The troops generally were worn out and most of the corps went to India for rest and recuperation.

The 28th Mountain Regiment, however, was allowed no rest for some months; it joined forthwith 23 Indian Division which was holding the front in Assam and remained on the Shenam position. Conditions for men and mules were extremely bad, as the monsoon broke at this time, but the jawans stuck it out and earned golden opinions from their new formation. As the Regimental Commander wrote, "All the men had malaria and all the mules surra, but they never let their tails go down."

The 2nd (Derajat) and 23rd Batteries marched out of Burma with their guns and most of their equipment (earning thereby the Corps Commander's congratulations), as did the Sikh section of the 12th (Poonch) Battery. These units were held in Imphal in reserve until September, the 2nd and 23rd Batteries forming a composite battery; the remainder of the 27th Mountain Regiment went to Ambala to refit.

The following received "mentions in despatches":
Lieutenant-Colonel J. W. Kaye.
Major R. J. P. Lock, 15th (Jhelum) Battery.
Major J. B. Chaplin, 28th Battery.
Major P. Hartley and Gnr. Lance-Naik Mahomed Khan, 2nd (Derajat) Battery.
Major J. G. L. Hume and Lieutenant J. O. S. Janson, 12th (Poonch) Battery.

Subadar Jawala Singh and Naik Dalip Singh of the 12th Battery each received the I.O.M., and Havildar Pratap Singh received a "Gallantry Card" signed by the Commander-in-Chief.

Subadar Hakim Khan and Jemadar Ali Bahadur of the 5th Battery were awarded the I.O.M. (posthumous) and I.D.S.M. respectively.

It is known that many recommendations for bravery were lost during these operations, otherwise a greater number of awards would have been obtained.

The mountain batteries received congratulations and thanks of the Commander-in-Chief for their good work.

FIRST BURMA CAMPAIGN
27TH MOUNTAIN REGIMENT

Headquarters

Commanding Officer ... ... Lieutenant-Colonel W. G. Constable
Adjutant ... ... Captain P. R. Brennan
   Captain J. Nettelfield
Ordnance Officer ... ... Lieutenant P. Warren
Subadar-Major ... ... Ahmed Khan

2nd (Derajat)
Mountain Battery F.F.
Major P. Hartley
Captain A. B. Howard
Lieutenant J. Nettelfield
Lieutenant F. W. Graham (missing)

23rd Mountain Battery
Major T. M. Witherow
Captain D. E. T. Jones
Lieutenant P. Carmichael
Lieutenant R. Challis (wounded, murdered by Japanese)

5th (Bombay)
Mountain Battery
Major W. H. H. Wilberforce
Captain Magor (wounded)
Captain J. W. Poole (killed in action)
Lieutenant Harker (killed in action)
Lieutenant Gilmour (missing, killed or drowned at Rittang)

12th (Poonch)
Mountain Battery
Major J. G. L. Hume
Captain G. N. Elsworth
Lieutenant M. C. Elton
Lieutenant J. O. S. Janson

28TH MOUNTAIN REGIMENT

Commanding Officer	Lieutenant-Colonel A. H. Peskett, M.C.
relieved by	Lieutenant-Colonel J. W. Kaye (March 1942)
Adjutant	Captain A. A. Lowson
Ordnance Officer	Lieutenant J. Kidd*
Subadar-Major	Fazal Khan

15th (Jhelum) Mountain Battery	28th Mountain Battery
Major R. W. P. Lock	Major J. B. Chaplin
Captain J. R. Tysoe*	Captain Wilson*
Lieutenant Heritage*	Lieutenant Willcocks*
Lieutenant Wasiud Din	Lieutenant Easton
	Lieutenant MacKenzie

* With the mule party to Assam via Calcutta

2. MAY, 1942, SITUATION

Burcorps slowly climbed from Tamu to the heights of the Imphal plain to find 23 Indian Division, which had been recently formed in Manipur, holding the Assam frontier. The 1 Indian Infantry Brigade was in the Shenam area; 47 Brigade at Palel; divisional headquarters and one battalion in reserve at Imphal, and 37 Brigade in the vicinity of Ukhrul. The 1 Seaforth Highlanders and 158 Field Regiment, R.A., were the only British units in the division, and the Indian troops had not completed their training. Fortunately, the Japanese did not follow up our retirement over the Chindwin.

The 23 Division transport was on a mixed M.T. and animal scale, as were other divisions formed later on, and the mule was to prove his indispensability in yet another campaign.

The 1 Burma Division reorganized at Shillong and became 39 Indian (Light) Division, whilst 17 Division also reorganized at Shillong, becoming 17 Indian (Light) Division, and sent a brigade to cover the road from Tiddim. A "light" division was equipped with less transport than a normal one and contained only two infantry brigades of four battalions each. The 17 and 23 Divisions formed 4 Corps under Lieutenant-General G. A. P. Scoones.

As already mentioned, the 28th Mountain Regiment joined 23 Indian Division; its strength, 15th (Jhelum) and 28th Batteries, was increased by the addition of the 16th (Zhob) Battery by the end of the year, and in the following April the 13th (Dardoni) Battery joined it.

The H.Q., 27th Mountain Regiment and the 5th (Bombay) Battery were joined at Ambala by the remainder of the Regiment when released from duty at Imphal.

The monsoon broke as the troops arrived at Imphal and the pause in operations provided an opportunity to improve the administration, which was in a poor state. The L. of C. was quite inadequate to deal with the troops at the front, and for many months most of the army had to accept short rations. The Bengal-Assam railway was not capable of carrying much traffic and roads were non-existent: for months the troops worked at road-making along with all the available coolie labour. No issues of forage or fodder were made for some months, and the animals were kept alive by grazing on the Imphal plain. The grass was long and alive with mosquitoes, and as the drivers had only shorts to wear the casualties from malaria, which brought a form of dysentery with it, were about 70 per cent. Once the daily mepacrin parade was in force, the number of unfit dropped at a startling rate, and during the 1943 monsoon malaria cases were far less common.

Training had to be carried on notwithstanding these difficulties, as most of the troops were young and untrained. The mountain batteries received drafts which took probably a shorter time to bring up to active service standard than those of the other arms.

The Chindwin front was continuously patrolled, but the Japanese were seldom encountered. During this period airfields had to be provided and every effort was being made to increase the strength of the Air Force; the full value of the increase was, of course, not felt until the following year.

When the Japanese main army started in pursuit of our forces in a north-westerly direction after the capture of Rangoon, it left only a small diversionary force to follow the coastline towards India. This force, of a total estimated strength of two battalions and eight guns, after spending the monsoon period at Akyab, came forward in October and held Maungdaw and Buthidaung. The barrier between the enemy and India was very thin, consisting of 14 Indian Division about Chittagong backed only by 26 Indian Division in front of Calcutta.

After his period in command of A.B.D.A., General Wavell was appointed Commander-in-Chief in India for the second time on 23rd February, 1942, and became responsible for the conduct of the war in Burma. His plan was by offensive action to keep the Japanese forces engaged and thereby prevent an enemy offensive into India at a time when India was unprepared.

His objectives were the capture of Akyab in Arakan; the strengthening of our position in the Chin Hills; and the establishment of forces on the Chindwin river between Kalewa and Sittaung with a view to an advance in Upper Burma. These operations were to be combined with those of the Chinese troops directed by General Stilwell, whose main purpose was to cover the construction of a road from Ledo via Myitkyina and Bhamo to join the Old Burma Road into China.

3. First Arakan Campaign (1943)

The capture of the airfield on Akyab island at the southern end of the Mayu peninsula had been originally planned as a sea-borne expedition, for which 6 British Brigade of 2 Division had been specially trained to form part of the landing force. The necessary resources for the landing operations and for ships and aircraft to cover it could not be made available at this time as they were required for more extensive operations in the Mediterranean. The Eastern Army (Lieutenant-General N. M. S. Irwin) was therefore ordered to capture Akyab by a rapid advance down the coast.

The 14 Indian Division (Major-General W. L. Lloyd) was detailed to carry out the operation. Once the division had taken Foul Point at the end of the peninsula, it was intended to launch a short-range assault on the island by the 6 Brigade. Speed was essential in order to forestall the arrival of Japanese reinforcements.

The divisional artillery at first consisted of 130 Field **Regimentt** R.A. (twenty-four 25-prs.), and the 23rd Indian Mountain* **Regimen,** (sixteen 3.7-inch howitzers).

Arakan consists of steep hills covered with thick jungle; there was a 1,500-foot range of almost impenetrable hills running down the centre of the peninsula, flanked by comparatively open strips on each side. The paddy-fields in the open ground were flooded at this time of the year, and there were a great number of water-cuts, mostly tidal, which had to be negotiated during every movement of troops; the mules soon learnt to swim well, even against the current, but the greatest difficulty was found at the edges, often mangrove swamp and always of soft mud. Further obstacles had been formed by channels cut in the open ground between the hills and the sea by the monsoon rains rushing from the high ground to the sea. The climate is particularly wet and unhealthy.

The only road across the range ran between the two small ports of Maungdaw and Buthidaung; it was a good metalled road and kept in excellent order by the Japanese who held the high ground covering it. It was originally made for a railway and ran through two tunnels, each about 200 yards long; defences had been erected at the outer ends of the tunnels. One or two mule tracks also existed.

The Japanese gun-park at Maungdaw was visited by a havildar of 3rd (Peshawar) Battery disguised as a Bengali in a dhoti and

---

* The word "Indian" was added to the names of all mountain artillery units from 13th October, 1942.

carrying an umbrella. He counted the guns and brought back much useful information to the battery.

In mid-December, 1942, 14 Division was about to attack Maungdaw and Buthidaung when the enemy withdrew southwards, and was followed up on a two-brigade front. The 47 Indian Brigade moved along the coast and 123 Indian Brigade down the east side of the Mayu river towards Rathedaung, arriving near that place on the 27th; by this date 47 Brigade had reached Indin. An unfortunate delay of ten days, due to administrative difficulties, now took place, and when the advance was resumed on 6th January, 1943, it was found that the enemy had constructed strong defences in our front.

For the first attacks of 47 Brigade on the Japanese position at Donbaik see page 329. This position was a very strong one, and a further attack with fresh troops and tanks also failed.

The 123 Brigade made several unsuccessful attacks on Rathedaung during January and February. Reinforcement and supply along a recently constructed road led to long delays, and supply by sea was hampered by a scarcity of craft.

A final attack on the Donbaik position by 6 British Brigade, supported by 71 Indian Brigade, was ordered for 18th March. More artillery was brought up, but it consisted only of two batteries of mechanized 3.7-inch howitzers (monobloc) and the vitally important 6-inch howitzers could not be procured. The earthwork already referred to having been converted into a fortress, this artillery support was inadequate; further, the proposal of the Brigade Commander and the C.R.A. not to open fire at the start of the attack in order to avoid putting the enemy on the alert was negatived by higher authority and the British battalions suffered terrible casualties, so although the attack was carried out with the greatest dash and determination, the result was again a failure.

Meanwhile a counter-offensive was being conducted by an enterprising Colonel Tanahashi, who moved his regiment through the jungle against our flank guard in the Kaladan valley. He dispersed a battalion of 123 Brigade acting as flank guard and nearly succeeded in trapping 55 Brigade outside Rathedaung, but the brigade got clear by withdrawing northwards. Tanahashi's force then straddled the Mayu range in order to cut off all the troops engaged to the south of him, causing a hasty retirement from the Donbaik front during which 6 Infantry Brigade H.Q. was overrun, the Brigadier captured, and the line of withdrawal completely blocked. Communications were not cleared without a very tough fight when the infantry and guns broke through Tanahashi's block. Covered by smoke and supported by fire from a battery south of

Kyaukpandu which had been called up by wireless, the column moved along the beach towards safety, dropping two 25-pr. troops of 130 Field Regiment, R.A., on the way by the water's edge, which were ordered to engage the enemy in full view on the hills over open sights. The guns continued to fire until all their ammunition was expended and the column had passed, and then with their R.W.F. escort in a carrier moved out at speed.

On the east side of the range 55 Infantry Brigade with two mountain batteries was pursued northwards to a position covering Buthidaung and besieged in a "box" for several days. Under further pressure the British evacuated Maungdaw, and early in May the line was more or less where it started from, *i.e.*, a position covering Bawli Bazaar.

23rd Indian Mountain Regiment, Arakan, 1942-3
(BY COLONEL B. C. BARFORD)

The 23rd Mountain Regiment, consisting of R.H.Q. and Signal Section, 3rd (Peshawar) (F.F.), 8th (Lahore), 17th (Nowshera), and 2nd Jammu and Kashmir Mountain Batteries from Kakul, joined 14 Indian Division, which had headquarters at Comilla, Eastern Bengal, in March, 1942. The batteries were armed with four 3.7-inch howitzers each.

Almost immediately 2nd Jammu and Kashmir Battery,* was sent off with 4 Indian Infantry Brigade to 4 Corps at Imphal. The departure of this brigade left 14 Division with one complete brigade (47 Indian) and other un-brigaded units, equivalent to about three battalions.

At this time it was anticipated that the Japanese would land at Chittagong, as they had command of sea, land and air and there was nothing to stop them. Chittagong had been almost entirely evacuated and dismantlement carried out in the docks, railway workshops and installations. The 47 Brigade, with 23rd R.H.Q., 8th and 17th Batteries and one battery of 130 Field Regiment, R.A., under command, held a position in three battalion "harbour" areas, between Feni and the Feni river. The 3rd Battery was in support of 1/17 Dogra Regiment at the railway junction of Laksham farther north, with Divisional H.Q. and Divisional Troops at Comilla.

In June, 123 Indian Infantry Brigade joined 14 Division. Chittagong was reoccupied by this Brigade with 23rd R.H.Q. from Feni,

---

* Later in the year (1st October) this battery was renumbered 31st (Jammu) Mountain Battery, and is hereafter referred to as 31st Battery.

3rd Battery from Laksham and 31st Battery, recently returned from Corps, in support.*

During all this period intensive training was carried out and much time was spent in teaching all ranks and all animals of the units to swim; the making of improvised rafts, for carrying equipment across streams, was concentrated upon, and means of keeping telephones, wireless sets and optical instruments dry during the monsoon period had to be evolved.

The wireless equipment with which the regiment had been equipped before leaving India proved to be quite useless under monsoon conditions. This was unfortunate, for not only could it not be used for operational purposes, but the Indian signallers of the units (it was their first introduction to wireless) were convinced that the use of wireless was beyond them, and it took considerable time to break down this prejudice and to restore a more rational outlook to wireless when the regiment was issued with more efficient equipment in 1943 (No. 18 set).

In October, 1942, 14 Indian Division began to move down to the Arakan coast. Previous to this the road from Dohazari (end of the railway line from Chittagong) to Cox's Bazaar had been improved, but it was fit for light M.T. only, and in the initial stages all stores and equipment had to be shipped from Chittagong to Cox's Bazaar by small steamers and then carried forward by coolie. At this time there were no Japanese north of Rathedaung, and the Arakan peninsula was held by "V force," formed of local irregulars, with British officers.

The 123 Brigade, supported by 23rd R.H.Q. with the 8th and 17th Batteries, led the advance, which on account of the administrative difficulties had to be carried out unit by unit, the 47 Brigade moving to Chittagong.

Two companies of 1/15 Punjab had worked their way down to Maungdaw, and had sent one platoon to Buthidaung, when a Japanese force, estimated at 400, landed at the latter place and more appeared south of Maungdaw. These two companies then had to fall back on to their battalion, which was in the area of Bawli Bazaar.

The night before the attacks went in, the Japanese withdrew. They blew up the bridges between Maungdaw and Buthidaung, but failed to cause any damage to the Tunnels. The main portion of the Jap force embarked in steam launches at Buthidaung and sailed south down the Mayu river.

8th Mountain Battery was the first unit to pass through the Tun-

---

* 123 Brigade consisted of 10 Lancashire Fusiliers, 8/10 Baluchis and 1/15 Punjabis.

nels and arrived in Buthidaung very shortly after 123 Brigade had entered it. This battery, a few days later, rejoined 47 Brigade in the Maungdaw area.

123 *Brigade*

South of Buthidaung there were no roads at all, and the objective of the 123 Brigade was Rathedaung. The main highway was the Mayu river. The Japs had taken away all the steam launches which in peace time used to ply up and down the river; nor was there any ferry across to the east bank of the river, which was fairly wide.

A few days were spent in collecting together as many country craft as possible, and eventually two companies of 10 Lancashire Fusiliers were ferried across the river to work down the east bank towards Rathedaung. No animals could be taken. In time, 3rd and 17th Batteries moved down the river by sections, in country boats, taking only their guns, gunners and the bare minimum of equipment. It was rather a hazardous undertaking as the country boats were manned by local Arakanese; progress depended on the tides and one never quite knew whether one was being taken in the right direction or not, as the boatmen often used subsidiary chaungs (rivers) rather than the main stream. The Jap still had command of the air and his steam launches on the main river. For a section to get into action it was necessary to run the boats into the bank, manhandle all the equipment ashore and come into action as near the bank as possible.

The two companies of 10 Lancashire Fusiliers entered Rathedaung, but were counter-attacked by the Japs and forced to retire from the village.

Exceptionally heavy autumn rains, which had made the local tracks impassable, had delayed the further move forward of 123 Brigade, which was still in the area of Cox's Bazaar and Ukhia.

In assessing the rate of advance in these operations it must be realized that so far as the leading units were concerned, there were no roads fit for M.T., units had to move on an all-pack basis, and in many cases supplies had to be brought along in small country boats, man-propelled; in fact the numerous rivers (mostly tidal) and creeks were the main highways. Bridges did not exist and the only ferries were made and operated by Sapper and Miner companies: in the majority of cases, animals had to swim the crossings, whilst the ferries were used for guns and stores.

However, by November, 123 Brigade (less 1/15 Punjab), now supported by R.H.Q. with 3rd and 17th Batteries, was in the area of Goppe Bazaar, on the east side of Mayu range. The pass over the range, the Goppe Pass, was mainly constructed by the personnel of 8th Battery, and was fit for pack only. The animals of the two batteries with 123 Brigade were used largely as additional pack transport for the maintenance of the brigade and "stock piling."

1/15 Punjab, supported by 8th Battery, moved down the west side of the Mayu range, well north of Maungdaw, whilst 47 Infantry Brigade with 31st Battery concentrated in the area of Bawli Bazaar. All troops on the west side of the range were put under command of 47 Brigade.

Further advance was again held up by bad weather, which made movement over the Goppe Pass impossible. By mid-December, however, the advance was begun.

47 Brigade was to capture Maungdaw, and then to work along the road to the Tunnels.

123 Brigade was to capture the Tunnel area and then turn west and capture Buthidaung.

During January two attempts were made by 123 Brigade, supported by 3rd and 17th Batteries, to capture Rathedaung, but both failed. Meanwhile 8/6 Rajputana Rifles had joined 123 Brigade, as 8/10 Baluch had been sent up to the Kaladan river to act as a left flank guard to the Brigade.

The animals of 3rd and 17th Batteries moved to the area of Rathedaung, from Buthidaung, by road shortly after their batteries had arrived there.

Regimental H.Q. did not move to Rathedaung with 123 Brigade, as it was ordered to join 47 Brigade at Maungdaw on 31st December, 1942.

47 Brigade

By 1st January, 1943, 47 Brigade, with 8th and 31st Batteries in support, had worked down to Indin on the west side of the Mayu peninsula. There was a fairly motorable track from Maungdaw to a point about five miles north of Indin. From this point southwards, in the early part of the operations, the sea-shore was the highway. Owing to the numerous deep tidal chaungs which ran into the sea between there and Foul Point, and which could be crossed only at low tide, traffic up and down the beach was limited to a period of two hours each side of low water.

On 2nd January 31st Battery crossed to west side of the Mayu range to support 1/7 Rajput, and a few days later 5/8 Punjab was also moved across. It was then thought that the whole of the Mayu peninsula was clear of Japs, as carriers had been as far south as Foul Point and a battalion had worked down the east side of the range of the low ground without encountering any enemy. On 6th January a patrol of Inniskillings, with a carrier escort, was fired on by the enemy from a position about one mile north of Donbaik village. A troop of a battery of 130 Field Regiment, which happened to be moving down the beach at the time, unlimbered and gave support to the patrol and the small force was extricated.

The terrain was a wide open beach, next a fairly flat plain about 1,000 yards wide, covered with thick scrub jungle and then the steeply rising thickly covered almost impenetrable Mayu range. The Jap position ran from the edge of the beach towards the Mayu ridge, with a tidal chaung in front of it. The position did not appear to be very wide.

The Inniskillings, with 23rd Mountain Regiment H.Q., 8th Mountain Battery and 494 Battery of 130 Field Regiment, were ordered to capture this position and then to advance to Donbaik. This attack failed, the infantry coming under very heavy fire as soon as the attack started, making a further advance impossible. One company, with a F.O.O. from 130 Field Regiment, worked round the left flank, along one of the lower ridges of the Mayu range and entered Donbaik village. This was a most strenuous effort; the actual distance was about three miles, and although no opposition was met it took the party nearly twenty-four hours to hack their way through the jungle. They found the village empty, but about half an hour later the Japs attacked and drove them out of the village on to the beach. From there this company started to work its way northwards along the beach to rejoin the battalion. When within sight of the battalion, the company came under heavy fire from the rear of the enemy defences, which were holding up the battalion. The casualties suffered by this battalion in the initial attack on the Donbaik defences and in the attempt to capture Donbaik village were very heavy.

The support given by the 8th Battery during this period earned the highest praise from the British battalion, and the promptness with which the battery answered SOS calls at night, and the accuracy of its close shooting, inspired the greatest confidence in the very depleted ranks of the Inniskillings. After these first unsuccessful attempts it was realized that Donbaik was too tough a nut for one battalion to crack. The whole of 130 Field Regiment was ordered forward to support a second attack on Donbaik by 47 Infantry Brigade. 8th Battery was placed under command of 130 Field Regiment and 23rd R.H.Q. rejoined 123 Infantry Brigade in the Rathedaung area.

A new attack by 55 Brigade failed, and heavy losses were suffered, particularly in the officer ranks of the 2/1 Punjab. Finally an attack by 6 British Brigade was put in against the Donbaik defences, but this also failed. This brigade had been trained and equipped for a sea-borne landing on Akyab and had been kept in reserve in the Maungdaw area. Owing to shortage of suitable craft and our failure to capture Foul Point at the southern end of the Mayu peninsula, the brigade had never been used in its proper role.

Lieutenant B. C. Kapur of 8th Battery, the only I.C.O. in the battery, distinguished himself as a brave and enterprising F.O.O. On one occasion, with a small infantry escort, he was able to get round the flank of the Donbaik position and make a sketch of its main features, which was of great assistance in planning one of the attacks and arranging its supporting fire plan.

The enemy was very active in the air. 8th Battery had its wagon lines in a well-concealed nullah some way back from the gun position. On one occasion this was bombed and 18 I.O.Rs. and 33 mules were killed.

Meanwhile 31st Battery remained on the west side of the Mayu range in support of 5/8th Punjab and, although not engaged in anything spectacular like Donbaik, it did a great deal of shooting.

In March 8th Battery left the Donbaik front and joined 123 Infantry Brigade. Major D. R. Corner, who had been commanding the battery, was posted to Staff College, Quetta, and Major L. H. Landon took over command.

123 *Brigade*

23rd R.H.Q. rejoined this brigade towards the end of January, 1943.

A further attempt, by all three battalions of the brigade (10 L.F., 8/6 Raj. Rif. and 1/15 Punjab), was made to capture Rathedaung. The attack was supported by 3rd and 17th Batteries and one battery (3.7-inch howitzers) of 99 (Royal Bucks) Field Regiment. The attack again failed and heavy losses were suffered, particularly by 8/6 Raj. Rif.

For their bravery in the attacks on Rathedaung, Major W. B. P. Milne and Lieutenant S. Kapilla, both of 17th Battery, were awarded the Military Cross.

3rd Battery H.Q. with the Punjabi Mussulman section was moved by the newly constructed track from Htizwe to the Kaladan river, in support of 8/10 Baluch Regiment. (Htizwe was rear H.Q. for 123 Brigade.) Soon after the arrival of the battery the enemy, who had been showing signs of increasing activity, attacked in force and three of the battalion's defended localities were overcome. Lieutenant

Brown, the section commander, was ordered to destroy his guns. One gun was safely destroyed, but the long lanyard on the other one broke. There was no time to repair it, as the enemy was already close to the gun position. Havildar Mahomed Khan, No. 1 of the gun, at very great personal risk and without hesitation blew up his gun, firing it by means of the short broken lanyard. For this act of bravery he was awarded the I.D.S.M. Havildar-Major Waris Khan was in charge at the wagon lines and led the drivers to beat off an attack; before abandoning the wagon lines he ordered all the animals to be shot to prevent their falling into enemy hands, and then with the drivers fought his way back to Battalion H.Q. The Kaladan position was completely overrun.

Lieutenant Brown then conducted the survivors of 3rd Battery across some extremely difficult country and after four days' journeying arrived back at Htizwe, where they were used in an infantry role. Major M. Heald, who was commanding the battery, also rejoined, having got away with his O.P. party and Baluch details.

For his bravery and leadership in the action on the Kaladan river and subsequent withdrawal to Htiswe, Lieutenant Brown was awarded the M.C.; Signaller Shamsher Singh was awarded the I.D.S.M.

Meanwhile the Japs had been pressing on all parts of the Arakan fronts and in consequence the Rathedaung position had been reorganized; forward troops were now slightly south of Taungdara, with Brigade H.Q. in Htizwe village. The left flank was guarded by 1/15 Punjab (later relieved by 2/1 Punjab), who occupied a position covering the newly constructed track from the Kaladan river.

On 7th March the Japs attacked in force at night and captured one of the forward areas held by 10 L.F. based on Thaungdara. Lieutenant M. Burrows (17th Battery), who was F.O.O. in this area, gallantly organized a counter-attack after the infantry officer had become a casualty, and led a party of infantry back to the position. For this he was awarded the M.C.

Jap pressure continued and further withdrawals were necessary. 8th Battery, which had recently arrived from the Donbaik battles, was in support of the centre battalion. The forward company, with which was a F.O.O. party of Jemadar Mohamed Hussein and signallers, withdrew without notifying the F.O.O. that telephone communication with the battery had been cut by the enemy. The Jemadar and party stayed there for a further twenty-four hours, withdrew at night, swam a chaung and arrived back with the majority of the O.P. equipment intact. He was awarded the I.D.S.M.

H.Q. 55 Brigade had just relieved H.Q. 123 Brigade, but no unit relief had taken place except for the relief of 1/15 Punjab by 2/1 Punjab.

The Htizwe position was by now becoming intolerable; Jap pressure had increased and battalions had suffered heavy losses. It was subjected to several very heavy attacks, supported by air bombing and shell fire; the latter was almost continuous.

On 11th March the Sikh section of 3rd Battery in support of 2/1 Punjab engaged Japs in the open. The surviving Japs who came on were charged with the bayonet with great effect by the Punjabis.

That evening 8th and 17th Batteries with the bare minimum of animals and equipment were ferried across the Htizwe chaung to take up positions to cover the withdrawal from the village. The capacity of the ferries, the state of the tide and hours of darkness were the deciding factors as to how much could be taken. Swimming of animals was ruled out on account of possible noise, which would have disclosed our intentions to the enemy. All animals, stores and equipment which could not be got over by ferry in the time allotted had to be abandoned.

R.H.Q. and 3rd Battery, which since the action on the Kaladan river had been reduced to one section of guns, stayed in Htizwe village. On the evening of 12th March the withdrawal of the remaining troops from Htizwe village began. All stores and equipment except those which could be carried by personnel had been destroyed during the day, and the crossing of the chaung was carried out in all the available craft.

Major M. Heald, commanding 3rd Battery, was ordered to destroy his remaining guns, but prevailed upon the commander of one of the Burma Navy launches to give them deck space and in due course the guns were landed at Buthidaung.

Fortunately the Japs did not follow up the withdrawal, although they had established a road-block across the Htizwe–Buthidaung road about ten miles north of Htizwe. This was successfully negotiated. The brigade then passed through 77 Brigade, which had been hurriedly dispatched south of Buthidaung to cover the withdrawal of 55 Brigade; on the third evening of the withdrawal 55 Brigade took up a fresh position north of 77 Brigade.

31st Battery was brought back from east of the Mayu range and with 8th Battery was put in support of 77 Brigade until relieved by 99 Field Regiment. 31st Battery then returned to its former area, while 8th Battery was again transferred to the Maungdaw side. The animals of 17th Battery were handed over to 8th and 31st Batteries in order to bring them up to strength and to keep two batteries of the regiment fully mobile.

R.H.Q. and 3rd Battery, which had lost the whole of its equipment, were ordered back to Buthidaung, where R.H.Q. was made responsible for the organization of Buthidaung area, under Mayforce, which took over control of all operations on the east and west banks of the Mayu river—*i.e.*, all troops on the east side of the Mayu range. Buthidaung was then the defended base and staging camp of Mayforce.

17th Mountain Battery was given enough M.T. to make it mobile and with a detachment of infantry was formed into Keecol, under Major R. E. T. Keelan, who had taken over command of the battery from Major Milne, for the defence of the Tunnels area between Buthidaung and Maungdaw.

In the withdrawal from Htizwe, Major Keelan had distributed his Imprest and Battery Fund money amongst personnel of his battery, collecting it later when the battery reassembled. On the check over he was about Rs150 deficient and this was duly reported to the Controller of Military Accounts, who demanded that Major Keelan should refund the money as he had disobeyed all rules and regulations regarding the handling and safe custody of public money. The correspondence was carried on with C.M.A. for nearly a year before the account was written off. 3rd Battery, on the Kaladan, had cast their treasure chest, containing over Rs2,000, into the river as it was too heavy to carry and the key was with the Battery Commander, who was not available to open it. This was reported to C.M.A., who agreed to a "write off" without a murmur.

Perhaps the greatest blow to the Regiment was the loss of all those fine horses and mules which had been left behind at Htizwe—animals of which the regiment was so proud and the drivers so fond. They had suffered great hardships during the campaign, but had always worked uncomplainingly, often in appalling conditions and on half rations. A sad heart-breaking farewell to great pals and comrades-in-arms.

After the withdrawal from Htizwe, 26 Indian Division relieved 14 Indian Division; the original infantry battalions of the latter were withdrawn to India for rest and re-equipment, but owing to shortage of artillery there was no relief for 23rd Mountain Regiment, which remained to serve under the new division.

The Japs continued pressing on all fronts; all positions on the east bank of the Mayu river were given up and the defence of the Buthidaung–Maungdaw line became the order of the day with the Japs occupying the ridge of the Mayu range, thus forming a wedge between the two flanks of the division.

8th Battery was brought back from the Maungdaw area and with

31st Battery placed in support of 55 Infantry Brigade at Kin Chaung, covering Buthidaung. For three weeks these two batteries in the brigade box fought off continuous attacks; additional artillery support was given by the two Field Regiments from the other side of the Mayu range, their fire being controlled from the box.

The services of an artillery co-operation squadron, R.A.F., were available, and the artillery defence as a whole was highly successful and was ably conducted by Major F. G. W. Walshe, M.C., who had taken over command of 8th Battery from Major Landon; the latter had been appointed to command 28th Mountain Regiment with 4 Corps.

Meanwhile Keecol was abolished and the M.T. was taken away from 17th Battery, which was sent to the river bank south of Maungdaw, where it was used in a "practice seawards" role. R.H.Q., 3rd and 17th Batteries, were eventually sent back to Chittagong, where they began the process of collecting fresh animals and equipment with a view to relieving the other two batteries of the regiment as soon as possible. The enemy, however, still continued his pressure; the Maungdaw–Buthidaung line was given up and the force at Kinchaung fought its way back via Buthidaung and the Ngakyedauk Pass to Bawli Bazaar, where the batteries arrived with very little ammunition. Animal casualties had been heavy; there had been no replacements and only about half echelon of ammunition could be carried.

At the end of May 8th (Lahore) and 31st (Jammu) Batteries were relieved by 2nd (Derajat) and 12th (Poonch) Batteries, which had been re-equipped at Ambala after their withdrawal from Burma the previous year.

8th and 31st Batteries then rejoined 23rd Mountain Regiment in Chittagong. A month later, while re-equipping was still in no way complete, 23rd Regiment was transferred to Ranchi to become the Mountain Regiment of the 20th Indian Division, then in the process of arriving from Ceylon.

Apart from the general good work done by 23rd Mountain Regiment in this campaign, special praise is due to the signallers of R.H.Q. and of all the batteries. Owing to the lack of efficient wireless all communication had to be done by telephone. This entailed the use of much cable through and over appalling jungle country. Normally there were two and often three lines from batteries to O.P. by different routes, which required a great deal of maintenance. At night these lines were often cut by enemy patrols, but maintenance parties invariably went out to repair them and several signallers were lost. The greatest credit is due to these I.O.Rs. who looked upon it as a point of honour that their lines should always "be through."

During this campaign, until they were relieved, 8th Battery had not more than three days' rest and 31st Battery only one.

A feature of all these operations was the necessity for close and accurate shooting, in support of our infantry, both by day and by night. The speed with which all batteries answered S O S calls at night was really amazing; and it was the proud record of the regiment that out of all the thousands of rounds fired, not a single round fell short to cause damage or harm to our own troops.

OFFICERS 23RD INDIAN MOUNTAIN REGIMENT
ARAKAN, 1942-43

Regimental H.Q.

Lieutenant-Colonel B. C. Barford
Captain Basil Humphrey, Adjutant
Lieutenant H. H. M. Ford, Assistant Adjutant
Captain Ghosh, I.M.S., Medical Officer
Lieutenant Goodyear, R. Signals, died December, 1942, of cholera
Lieutenant B. Singh, Indian Signals

3rd (Peshawar)
Mountain Battery F.F.
Major M. Heald
Captain B. J. Templeman
Lieutenant Brown, M.C.
Lieutenant C. A. Weston
Lieutenant Bharat Singh

17th (Nowshera)
Mountain Battery
Major W. B. P. Milne, M.C.
Captain R. L. D. Kelly
Lieutenant M. R. Burrows, M.C.
Lieutenant S. Kapilla, M.C.
Lieutenant Brockie
Major R. E. T. Keelan

8th (Lahore)
Mountain Battery
Major D. R. Corner
Major L. H. Landon
Major F. G. W. Walshe, M.C.
Lieutenant C. Whimster
Lieutenant B. C. Kapur
Lieutenant P. R. Geeke
Lieutenant F. E. Taylor

31st Mountain Battery
Major R. E. T. Keelan
Major J. P. Hollick
Captain J. Carver
Lieutenant L. E. Grose
Lieutenant S. Afzal

4. 1943 SITUATION (CENTRAL FRONT)

At the beginning of the year the Assam (central) front was held by 4 Corps with headquarters at Imphal, comprising 17 Indian (Light) Division, to which some levies in the Chin district were attached, and 23 Indian Division.

The 21st and 29th Indian Light Mountain Regiments joined 17 Division in December, 1942; each was composed of two four-gun 3.7-inch howitzer batteries, to which was added in August, 1943, one 3-in. mortar battery of twelve mortars, all in pack. The 21st Regiment comprised the 1st Royal (Kohat), 6th (Jacob's) and 37th Batteries, and the 29th Regiment, 9th (Murree), 14th (Rajputana), and 38th Batteries. The 37th and 38th were armed with mortars.

The 28th Indian Mountain Regiment was with 23 Division.

In the intervals of training, the units on this front were patrolling the Chindwin, retiring to the high ground to the westward during the monsoon (which this year brought 217 inches of rain). At first the enemy was seldom encountered, but after the monsoon aggressive patrols were met more often when our troops found themselves generally superior in action and their morale increased accordingly. The gunners took part in these patrols and acquired an aptitude for jungle life. Owing to a generous equipment of small arms, including six L.M.Gs., a battery was now capable of offensive and defensive action to a much greater extent than before and was able to protect itself. This was one of the lessons learnt in 1942.

Much progress had been made in wireless communication and efficient sets were available in good numbers. No. 19 set (M.T./A.T.) was used by R.H.Q. to higher levels, and within the regiment No. 18 man-pack set, replaced later by No. 48, was reliable, as was the M.T./A.T. No. 11 set, replaced later by No. 22. The M.T./A.T. sets could be carried anywhere by man-pack; one man carried the set, another the battery, with a third to assist.

In November, 1943, the enemy drove back the levies in the Haka area, and on the 11th pushed in some of our posts in the Fort White position, which was held by 1/16 Punjab with a section of the 13th (Dardoni) Battery from 23 Indian Division sent as a reinforcement.

The battle began early on 14th November at M.S. 52 from Kalewa, where the position, held by one company each of 1/16 Punjab and 1/3 Gurkhas, was attacked whilst the main position at Fort White was being heavily shelled. A counter-attack by a company of 1/10 G.R. became involved with the enemy in the dark, and the forward situation was not sufficiently clear for the guns to open fire before 0730 hours, when the registered targets were engaged and an enemy company debouched into the open and suffered heavy casualties. By 0930 hours, being surrounded by strong enemy forces, the commander received orders to withdraw and had no option but to move across country, always a difficult matter, and in this case no track possible for mules could be found.

The 1/16, after using up all their ammunition, withdrew from M.S. 54 to Kennedy Peak, whither the 1/10 also withdrew about 1130 hours.

The guns went on firing with open sights and by using smoke shell set fire to the jungle, covering the withdrawal along the ridge from M.S. 52 towards the gun position.

At about 1300 hours orders were received to abandon the guns, and the gunners, having buried* the guns, carriages and heavy parts of the equipment, carried away the instruments. All the mules were saved. The force moved in two columns along jungle tracks, and the section arrived at Tiddim about 1630 hours on the 16th, having marched with practically no food. There were no stragglers and the section came in fresh and in good spirits, led by Major Addison and Lieutenant Nazeer Ahmed.

During December, 1943, 17 Division was occupying the Kennedy Peak-Fort White position, and medium guns were in action at Kennedy Peak.

The 23 Division H.Q. was at Tamu, and after being on this front for eighteen months was relieved in December, 1943, by 20 Indian Division, which included the 23rd Indian Mountain Regiment, lately in Arakan with 14 Division. Its batteries were now on a new establishment, M.T. vehicles replacing half the ammunition mules and staff ponies. Continuous patrolling in the Kabaw valley, generally with a section of mountain guns attached, occupied the infantry for the next months.

During 1943 the Japanese forces in Burma had increased from 135,000 to 200,000—*i.e.*, to eight divisions and an independent brigade—and from items of intelligence obtained it seemed likely that an offensive was contemplated. The Japanese 55 Division with elements of another division and a detachment of renegades called "Japanese Inspired Fifth Column" (Jifs) formed part of a newly constituted Japanese Twenty-eighth Army. The "Jifs" and some units from Indian prisoner-of-war camps formed what the Japanese called the "Indian National Army." Only about a third of the prisoners of war had been coerced or persuaded to join the I.N.A. and their numbers rapidly diminished.

In May, 1943, the British and United States Governments had decided to organize the South-East Asia Command (S.E.A.C.) under a Supreme Commander who was to control all the naval, air and land forces in the area covered by Burma, Malaya, Sumatra,

---

* When the army advanced and recaptured Fort White in 1944 the guns were dug up by 24th Mountain Regiment and put into use (page 374).

Ceylon, Siam, and French Indo-China. Admiral Lord Louis Mountbatten, G.C.V.O., K.C.B., D.S.O., A.D.C., was appointed to the post in August, with Air Chief Marshal Sir Richard Peirse as Allied Air C.-in-C.

Lord Mountbatten visited the forward troops in Burma immediately after taking operational command on 15th November. By this date several offensive operations had been planned; those in which mountain artillery were concerned were an advance by 15 Corps on the Arakan front, and an advance by 4 Corps on the central front across the Chindwin with strong air support.

Supplementary operations were to be carried out by a Chinese force from Yunnan, by General Stilwell's Chinese Army in an advance from Ledo, and by Wingate's Special Force.

Brigadier O. C. Wingate, D.S.O., who had started his army career as an officer of the Royal Artillery, had had much experience of guerilla warfare in Palestine and Abyssinia before General Wavell ordered him to train a brigade for work within the area held by the Japanese. Intended to penetrate deep into enemy territory to operate against the Japanese L. of C., it was to be supplied and maintained from the air. Supplies and maintenance stores were to be dropped by aircraft and communication with the base was to be carried out by wireless.

In February, 1943, Wingate crossed the Chindwin with his brigade (77), which in June after a series of successful coups returned to India in small groups. This expedition established a new technique of supplying and maintaining forces by air which was of primary importance in jungle campaigns and a major factor in our eventual victory.

A special force of six brigades was put under training for operations to be carried out during 1944 by these "Long Range Penetration Groups."

The Supreme Commander laid down that operations were to be continued throughout the monsoon period, whatever the hardships: an enormous Allied Air Force was to be prepared, and pipe-lines were under construction from Chittagong to Imphal and on to Tamu as well as from Calcutta to Northern Assam to relieve the railways from carrying petrol.

The troops in Burma now formed the Fourteenth Army under Lieutenant-General Slim, composed of 4 and 15 Corps; the 4 Corps was making preparations to push forces across the Chindwin and to occupy the Kabaw valley early in 1944. This entailed heavy work for the troops who were put on to make roads and airfields.

5. SECOND ARAKAN CAMPAIGN, 1944

These operations were undertaken by 15 Corps. The 26 Indian Division held the line throughout the 1943 monsoon period, being joined by the 2nd (Derajat) and 12th (Poonch) Batteries (reorganized as "light" mountain batteries), which were sent to the front in May after a very short rest in India. These were the only two mountain batteries in the division at this time and they were continuously in action until November: there was little shooting, but O.Ps. were manned permanently; patrolling was routine, and battery positions were often attacked by enemy patrols. Units found it difficult to provide reliefs for four or five O.Ps. each.

These batteries, after being relieved at the end of September by 23rd Battery and Bijey Battery (Bikanir State Forces) of 25th Mountain Regiment, were sent to Chittagong for a short rest, returning in December to join 24th Indian Mountain Regiment, which had arrived from India with the 11th (Dehra Dun) and 20th Batteries on the "light" establishment. Headquarters of the 27th Mountain Regiment had returned to this front in October and was now amalgamated with 24th Regiment, the result being a new 24th Mountain Regiment (no longer "light") comprising the four batteries mentioned with survey and signal sections under Lieutenant-Colonel R. H. M. Hill. It was posted to 5 Indian Division, of which the C.R.A. was Brigadier E. C. R. Mansergh, who had been with the division from the beginning and was to command it later on. The 9, 123 and 161 Indian Infantry Brigades formed the infantry of the division.

The 25th Mountain Regiment joined 7 Division at Bawli Bazaar in October. It comprised the 5th (Bombay), 19th (Maymyo), 23rd and Bijey Mountain Batteries, and was commanded by Lieutenant-Colonel A. J. Booth, M.C. Lieutenant-Colonel Booth had held this command since December, 1942, but to the regret of the Regiment was killed by enemy artillery fire on 1st January, 1944. Lieutenant-Colonel L. H. O. Pugh took over the Regiment.

With a view to an eventual advance along the Arakan peninsula to seize the Maungdaw–Buthidaung road as a preliminary to the occupation of Akyab, Sir Philip Christison, the Corps Commander, planned the disposal of his formations as follows: 26 Indian Division was to be withdrawn into reserve at Chittagong, covering the road to India; 5 Indian Division (Major-General H. R. Briggs) to move to a position west of the Mayu range, and to share the ridge with 7 Indian Division (Major-General F. Messervy), holding the eastern flank.

Each of the 5 and 7 Divisions had a "Jungle Field Regiment" made up of one battery of sixteen 3-inch mortars carried in M.T. and two batteries each of eight 3.7-inch howitzers, monobloc pieces, towed by M.T. Divisions were now on a mixed M.T. and animal transport basis.

The mountain batteries were commanded by: 2nd (Derajat), Major P. Hartley; 5th (Bombay), Major Mohinder Singh; 11th (Dehra Dun), Major A. M. S. Fergie; 12th (Poonch), Major A. B. Howard; 19th (Maymyo), Major S. Clarke; 20th, Major T. H. Harrison; 23rd, Major G. A. Rowley-Conway*; Bikanir Bijey, Major Kishen Singh (Bikanir State Forces).

Some of the batteries had one or more I.C.Os. on the strength.

The left flank was to be protected by 81 (West African) Division (Major-General C. G. Woolner), which was due to concentrate at Chiringa by the end of December, and then to move down the Kaladan river. This division was very weak in artillery; its 3.7-inch howitzers and mortars were porter-borne, an awkward form of transport for the howitzers. Supply was to be carried out by transport aircraft of the newly formed Transport Carrier Command.

As already noted, movements on any scale on the Arakan peninsula could not be carried out until the communications were improved, and the Sapper and Miners of 7 Division undertook the laying of a M.T. track at Ngakyedauk (pronounced "Nukchidowk" and colloquially the "Okeydoke" Pass). By almost superhuman efforts, the track was carried through virgin jungle and over rocky hills to become fit eventually for tank movement. Preparations were made for an advance to begin as soon as this lateral road was ready.

By the end of October 7 Division had taken over the Mayu range from 26 Division. During the deployment of 5 and 7 Divisions in their respective areas, which was delayed by the bad state of the roads and tracks, the mountain batteries were distributed as required: the batteries of the 25th Indian Mountain Regiment were supporting 89 and 33 Indian Brigades of 7 Division on the west side, and the 20th Battery of the 24th Mountain Regiment was supporting the third brigade of 7 Division (the 114) on the east side of the range. At the beginning of December the 25th Regiment, less 19th (Maymyo) Battery, was supporting 33 Brigade on the range. The 19th Battery crossed to the east side of the Kalapanzin river, swimming its mules and making its own rafts to transport the equipment to support 114 Brigade. The two sections were employed independently, one with

---

* *Vice* Major P. R. Brennan, drowned swimming the Kalapanzin river on duty, 21st November, 1943.

4/5 Gurkhas and the other with 4/14 Punjab at some distance apart. The 20th Battery rejoined the 24th Regiment with 5 Division.

On completion of 5 Division's move, R.H.Q. and the three batteries of the 25th Mountain Regiment crossed the Ngakyedauk Pass, which was not yet passable for wheeled traffic, and joined 114 Brigade early in January, the complete Regiment being detailed to support an offensive to cut the Buthidaung–Rathedaung road.

The 19th Battery had already been in action in support of the 2 K.O.S.B. for the capture of Wabyin.

Lord Mountbatten, the Supreme Allied Commander, visited this front in December and his presence in the forward areas acted as a vigorous tonic to morale.

The 5 Division, whose objective was Maungdaw, was forced to clear the enemy from a strong position, Point 124, before the defences of Razabil at the west end of the Tunnels could be approached. An attack was made by 161 Brigade, supported by 24th Mountain Regiment less 12th Battery and a section of 2nd Battery, but only after several days of pressure did the enemy evacuate the height.

Maungdaw was taken on 7th January by 2 West Yorks of 9 Indian Brigade, supported by the 12th Battery, which with great skill put down several successive concentrations which chased the Japs from one rallying point to another and made a quick mopping-up possible. The remainder of 9 Brigade and of the mountain regiment were engaged at Razabil, the westernmost of the Tunnel defences. The batteries were in close support of the attacking battalions, 4 Rajputs and 1/1 Punjab, sending F.O.Os. with the leading companies. O.Ps. were established within grenade-throwing range of the enemy trenches, and the signallers' task in maintaining lines was particularly difficult and dangerous. Defensive fire stopped the frequent counter-attacks made throughout every night; in fact, D.F. became so much a drill that signallers were known to initiate it to soothe an agitated company commander sooner than wake a weary battery commander for the purpose.

Although our air strength had been greatly increased by squadrons of 224 Group, the Razabil bastion held out against dive-bombing and artillery owing to the depth of the dug-outs and the steepness of the hillsides, and tanks were required for an attack on the fortress area. On the other side of the range 7 Division was held up in its attack on Buthidaung, so, to strengthen a fresh bid for that objective, on 30th January Corps H.Q. sent from 5 to 7 Division the greater part of 25 Dragoons with 9 Brigade, a regiment of medium artillery and the 24th Mountain Regiment.

The reported arrival of strong Japanese reinforcements and an increase in enemy pressure led to the probability of an attack in the near future. The 89 Brigade and the tanks were withdrawn into divisional reserve and the 2nd and 20th Mountain Batteries were sent to join 26 Division in corps reserve at Briasco bridge. Formations and units were ordered to hold their ground and were promised supplies by air if they were cut off. The 7 Division administrative base was situated at the eastern foot of the Ngakyedauk Pass, near the corps forward maintenance centre at Sinzweya.

This base, or "Admin. Box" as it came to be called, was under command of Lieutenant-Colonel R. B. Cole, commanding 24 A.A./A.Tk. Regiment, R.A., and contained, in addition to that unit and some airmen, several hundred administrative personnel of various fighting and non-fighting units, which were joined on the evening of 5th February by two companies of the West Yorks. Defence positions round the box and round unit areas were completed and manned, and the same procedure was adopted in the positions occupied by 33 and 114 Brigades. Troops of a brigade group shared the protection of its boxes; other units were ordered to report to the Admin. Box. The 25th Mountain Regiment and its four batteries were with 114 Brigade.

While these preparations were being completed, Colonel Tanahashi with his 112 Regiment was making an encircling movement on a large scale in an endeavour to improve on his success of the previous year; this time he aimed at the complete destruction of 5 and 7 Divisions prior to the expulsion of all the British-Indian forces from Burma, and ultimately to the capture of India. The "March on Delhi" had begun. Tanahashi's column, moving clear of Buthidaung, cut in between 7 and 81 Divisions, arriving at Taung Bazaar at dawn on 4th February.

The positions of 114 Brigade were enveloped in thick mist during the night of 3rd/4th February, and considerable movement was heard in the narrow strips of paddy between the ridges on which were the defended positions of various units. The front was held by Battalion H.Q. and one company Somerset, H.Q. 114 Infantry Brigade, R.H.Q. and two mountain batteries of 25th Indian Mountain Regiment. The remainder of the brigade, less 4/5 R.G.R. and 4/14 Punjab, was deployed holding the right flank in the hills forward on the left.

During the night all telephone lines between R.H.Q. and the batteries were cut and spasmodic shooting broke out. Nothing could be seen in the thick mist. At first light Japanese were seen advancing along the paddy-fields and fire was opened at ranges from 100 to 600 yards by 19th and 23rd Mountain Batteries. At one moment 23rd Battery was engaging enemy over open sights with two guns firing forward at 600 yards and two guns firing directly to the rear at 300 yards.

As the sun rose, an enemy column appeared marching in formation past Brigade H.Q. like a crowd streaming away from a football match. Marching six abreast, with flags flying as a means of identification to their own aircraft flying low overhead, this column was just in rear of Brigade H.Q. when it came into view. Lieutenant-Colonel Pugh and his Intelligence Officer immediately established an O.P. on top of the Brigade Commander's O.P. and, traversing two guns of 23rd Battery (the only guns which could be brought to bear and were not otherwise engaged), brought fire to bear on the middle of the column. The enemy sought refuge in the bamboo-covered hills on either side, but suffered heavy casualties before they were able to dig in.

From Bawli Bazaar a Japanese subsidiary column (Kubo) of one battalion went on over the Goppe Pass and after crossing the range cut the coastal road, thus severing the communications of 5 Division. The main force swung round to cut the Ngakyedauk Pass and trap the 7 Division on the eastern side of the range. A holding force was to attack from the Buthidaung road, and the complete destruction of the two divisions was then expected. This offensive (Operation "Hago") was supported by the Japanese 55th Division, with elements of another division and detachments of the "Indian National Army."

The situation was resolved with little delay; H.Q. 7 Division was overrun at dawn on the 6th, the divisional commander narrowly escaping capture, and divisional H.Q. reopened later that day in Admin. Box, as did H.Q. R.A. R/T links were made forthwith to the 136 Field Regiment and all field and mountain batteries, 89 Infantry Brigade and 25 Dragoons. Brigadier G. Evans, commanding Brigade, arrived and took over command of the garrison, to which were now added two squadrons of 25 Dragoons and the 24th Mountain Regiment H.Q. with the 11th Battery and Punjabi Mussulman section of the 12th Battery. These guns were formed into a six-gun battery. The Sikh section of the 12th (Poonch) Battery fought its way through an ambush with great determination to reach the box, and had suffered some casualties before settling into a small box on the edge of the main Admin. Box occupied by "B" Echelon, 3/14 Punjab, and a mule company and a half. A platoon of the West Yorks joined them a little later.

The enemy cut the Ngakyedauk Pass on 7th February, thus separating the two divisions. The 4/8 Gurhkas (less two companies) of 89 Brigade was holding a ridge at the east end of the box on which was some commanding high ground. After suffering heavy losses, the Gurkhas were forced back; but the situation was restored by a counter-attack by "B" Company of the West Yorks supported by all the fire available; tanks, guns and mortars all firing point-blank. Five O.Ps. had been made available, and R/T communications permitted concentration and distribution of fire from field and mountain guns and tanks wherever it was required.

On the night of the 7th/8th the hospital at the Admin. Box was overrun by a strong party of Japanese who murdered doctors and patients alike. The next afternoon the box was steadily shelled and an ammunition dump was set on fire. The perimeter was too extended for continuous defence and the enemy could approach unseen from almost any direction. The Japanese made surprise attacks both by day and by night, and the mountain guns fired in many directions, mostly at point-blank range. Captain W. L. Worthington, adjutant of 24th Mountain Regiment, was killed on the 9th while collecting documents off dead Japs.

A message was passed to all units: "Supreme Commander promises strong and immediate reinforcements. It is essential that every man remains at his post and fights to the last."

The 7 Division was not completely encircled until the 10th, when the main enemy column made contact with the force on the Buthidaung road. Kubo Force was diverted from its attack on the Goppe Pass by the resistance of 18 Indian Mule Company, met with on the way, but dragged its guns over the range and did what damage it could on reaching the road on the west side.

On the 10th an all-night attack was beaten off; on the 11th the enemy captured a hill dominating the box, but a counter-attack after a terrific bombardment recaptured it within a few hours. It was of vital importance to the defence.

Supplies of every kind came in by air and their arrival had an extremely good moral effect on the troops, who went on fighting in the best spirit. Our air forces were in very good form; after several days' hard fighting, the Jap air force was mastered and air drops by Dakotas were carried out without difficulty, although it suited the air forces to do most of the dropping by night.

Casualties mounted up quickly, as it was hardly possible for a shell to burst in a box without hitting somebody. The mules presented a very vulnerable target, and the drivers, both artillery and transport, did great work dressing wounds. Forage was on a very short scale; about $2\frac{1}{2}$ lb., sometimes only $1\frac{1}{2}$ lb., of dry paddy stalks without any grain was all that was available.

The "B" Echelon box already mentioned had to undergo several severe attacks and held out bravely, causing the Japanese many casualties; the section of the 12th Battery was withdrawn under fire to rejoin the batteries in the Admin. Box after three days' fighting. Lieutenant Bagshawe and Jemadar Kartar Singh were awarded the M.C. for gallantry during this period. Driver-Havildar Mukand Singh of the 12th Battery was awarded the M.M. for outstanding leadership.

The 114 Brigade with the 25th Mountain Regiment covered the left flank east of the Kalapanzin river and had some heavy fighting of the same pattern, mostly point-blank fire, and stood firm, as did 33 Brigade which was positioned some distance to the south and had a very large number of animals to protect.

The 81 (West African) Division (less one brigade group) had been pushing south down the Kaladan river, but withdrew, closely followed up by the enemy, to cover the rear of 33 Brigade.

The pattern of the defence was much the same in all the boxes for the next fourteen days: there was very little cover; the enemy, who was under cover, could see into most of the positions; ammunition dumps were frequently hit and fires had to be fought. Suicide attacks happened on most nights, and most mornings found the wire festooned with dead Japanese. Casualties in the O.Ps. were numerous; but sorties and counter-attacks were always supported by the guns, which were never short of ammunition, which was dropped as required.

The 25 Dragoons evolved a successful method of dealing with Japanese bunkers which is of interest to describe: H.E. with instantaneous fuze was used to strip the jungle and expose the slits, which were then destroyed with H.E. with a D.A. fuze. Finally, solid A.P. shot was fired to support the infantry assault.

A gun of the 12th Battery received a direct hit by a 75-mm. shell, but was in action again the same day. A final attack from the south side on the night 21st/22nd was beaten back by anti-tank battery personnel, a mule company and the mountain guns.

Casualties sustained by 24th Mountain Regiment during the siege: 2 officers killed and 2 wounded; 14 I.O.Rs. killed and 26 wounded; 14 horses killed and 3 wounded; 15 mules killed and 34 wounded.

Notwithstanding a great effort by Japanese gunners who hauled their guns up steep cliffs and through the jungle of the Mayu range to stop movement on the west side, 5 Division was maintained from the sea, and both divisions were preparing to attack and force the enemy on to the reserves about to advance from the north.

No time had been lost in sending the 26 (Indian) Division from the north, and Taung Bazaar was recaptured on the 10th. The 27th Battery (Major J. G. Chamberlain) was sent forward to 71 Infantry Brigade in fifty 3-ton lorries, animals and all, on 7th February, and took part in the actions breaking up the Japanese attack. It was later joined by the 20th Battery. On the 12th General Briggs sent 123 Brigade to open the Ngakyedauk Pass from the west. This formation was unable to clear a hill, Point 1070, which commanded the centre of the pass, but the K.O.S.B. forced an entry at the eastern end for 89 Brigade, which had to sustain a fierce counter-attack on the 21st. The next day every known Japanese position on the range was pounded by bombs and artillery fire and the siege was at an end. The Japanese were everywhere on the run, having had 5,000 casualties.

The troops were justifiably proud of this splendid victory, and Lieutenant-General Slim, Fourteenth Army Commander, stated in a message to 15 Corps: "The Battle of Arakan was the first occasion in this war in which a British force had withstood the full weight of a major offensive—held it, broken it, smashed it into little pieces and pursued it. Anybody who was in 7th and 5th Indian Division and was there has something of which he can be very proud."

The morale of our men was never higher and the legend of Japanese invincibility in the jungle was broken for ever. Especially was it gratifying that Indian administrative troops had fought with courage and vigour alongside fighting units.

The 15 Corps and 224 Group R.A.F. with Troop Carrier Command had made a great success of the first experiment of air maintenance on a large scale; a system which was to have a great influence on our eventual victory.

There was a lot of mopping up to do and the troops made ready to continue the offensive.

Nothing is more descriptive of the fighting qualities of 15 Corps than the fact that the general offensive in Arakan was resumed five days after the Ngakyedauk Pass was opened. Buthidaung was captured by 7 Division with little difficulty, and 5 Division returned to the attack of the Razabil defences.

During this operation Major S. Clarke of the 19th (Maymyo) Battery was granted an immediate award of the M.C. for gallantry while supporting an attack by the 4/5 Gurkhas. The battalion afterwards made him an honorary Gurkha.

Several I.O.Rs. were granted awards for good work during this action: most noteworthy was the award of the M.M. to an O.P.

signaller who maintained communication throughout, though wounded three times carrying out his dangerous duties.

After bombing and bombardment had proved ineffective, a fresh attack by all three brigades was planned; 123 Brigade, supported by 24th Mountain Regiment, was to make a feint attack from the north; 9 Brigade was to protect the flanks and rear; and 161 Brigade, after a very long night march through the jungle in single file, was to attack from the south. In support of the attack a bombardment intense at this date in this war (200 guns) was carried out, in which all the mountain batteries took their share, and 4/7 Rajputs on going in to the attack found the position on the west flank evacuated. Other points, however, were strongly held, and further heavy pounding had to be undertaken; the 1/17 Dogras earned great distinction in several night attacks and eventually captured a strong position at its third attempt. The 161 Brigade continued the pressure along the Tunnels road: on one occasion a section of the 2nd (Derajat) Battery was sent forward along the road to shoot up difficult targets which could not be dealt with from battery positions and the F.O.O. found himself dug in on top of one of the tunnels.

During March 36 (British) Division took over from 5 Indian Division, and by the end of the month the Tunnels were in our hands, although the road itself was only partly ours. The 26 Division relieved 5 Division and the front was adjusted to a more convenient line by giving up Buthidaung; the east flank was protected by 81 (W.A.) Division from the vicinity of Kyawktaw.

Operations continued from March to June and were noteworthy in that infantry rode to the assault on tanks for the first time; also really intense artillery bombardments on limited areas in the jungle were carried out.

During this period the focus of trouble had shifted to the central front. Signs of an approaching offensive had been obvious for some weeks, and it turned out that the Arakan thrust was a subsidiary one and the main attack was to be made against our advanced base at Imphal. The 4 Corps was sorely pressed, and in addition to troops available from India, which were few in number, the 5 and 7 Divisions moved complete with guns and M.T. from Dohazari airfield to Imphal and Dimapur by air. All ranks became proficient very quickly in this new technique of movement, and, thanks to aircraft loading tables having been prepared beforehand, the move went off without a hitch in accordance with the time-table.

It took fourteen Commando planes to lift a mountain battery less animals: 1st load—holding group, Brens and defensive personnel; 2nd load—recce group, B.C., G.P.O., wireless and signals; 3rd load—G Group, G.P.O.A., one jeep, signal and specialist equipment; 4th to 7th loads—each gun complete with stores and 48 rounds; 8th to 11th loads—112 rounds per gun; 12th, 13th loads—admin. group, Q.M. stores, tradesmen, cooking, medical; 14th load—spare stores, tentage.

Personnel were divided up among the aircraft. The trip to Jorhat (339 miles) only took two hours, and all the batteries arrived during the first few days in April.

The mules of some batteries were sent by train. In the case of those sent by air, five mules were loaded in a plane, and gave no trouble in loading or on the journey.

In addition to the 27th Mountain Battery already mentioned, the 30th Mountain Regiment (Lieutenant-Colonel T. W. R. Hill) included the 32nd, 33rd, and 34th Batteries. As this regiment less 34th Mountain Battery moved forward to join 26 Division it met the 24th Mountain Regiment on 19th March on its way to the airfield to be flown to Jorhat. The 32nd Battery (Major B. E. M. Repton, later Major J. D. Olivier) fought with 71 Brigade on the Mayu range until May, when it crossed the Kalapanzin river to carry out an operation with 81 (W.A.) Division. The river crossing was very difficult, and a gun was damaged by a load which parted from its parachute. On returning to 71 Brigade a boat overturned during the crossing of a chaung and some men were drowned. The Battery rejoined its regiment in June after a successful operation.

The 33rd Battery (Major I. M. G. Williams) had its first action on 25th March, an unexpected proposition entailing open sights at 200 yards, and acquitted itself well. During further fighting on the 15th April, while in support of an attack by 4 Infantry Brigade, Lieutenant J. G. Downe was killed in action as F.O.O. to 33rd Battery, and Captain N. J. Deane, I.A., acting as F.O.O. to 32nd Battery, was also killed.

This attack was one of several to capture Point 551, a feature south of the Maungdaw–Buthidaung road in the Tunnels area, and the key to the Japanese position. After a softening by field and medium artillery concentrations and the destruction of many M.G. bunkers, it fell on the 3rd May to 4 Indian Infantry Brigade during a night attack without artillery support, but the Mountain Regiment during the following days fired a great number of rounds in close support; the gun range was 3,000 yards firing uphill. During the whole operation it fired 12,000 H.E.

The 26 Division was withdrawn to cover the flanks and rear during the monsoon, and 25 Division took over the front which ran from Godusara to Buthidaung (exclusive) on to Taung Bazaar. Maungdaw was the "keep" held by 74 Indian Brigade; the enemy relaxed pressure during the worst of the monsoon.

The 34th Indian Mountain Battery (Major Hadfield) had been working as an independent battery under 25 Division since March, and later joined that division permanently.

The 81 (W.A.) Division, which had done some splendid work building an air-strip and seventy-five miles of road through the jungle, was withdrawn to cover the left rear of the corps. In Arakan minor operations and small-scale offensives were continued throughout the monsoon, countered by the Japanese, who kept up continuous raiding. Further operations in Arakan form part of preparations for the main advance to drive the Japanese out of Burma.

6. The Invasion of Assam, 1944

During 1943, in addition to being engaged in the defence of the Indian frontier east and south of Manipur, 4 Corps was occupied in the preparation of an advanced base and of forward communications for a proposed advance against the Japanese. Meantime the troops had to be rested and trained, and reinforcements integrated into their units, and all this had to be done in a malaria-stricken country in which campaigning was particularly arduous. The "Monthly News-Letters" of the period—heart-to-heart talks on paper between regimental commanders and M.G.R.A. India—are very informative as to deficiencies of equipment and shortages of men and mules. Leave was of primary importance to the I.O.Rs., some of whom had had none for two years. Surra was common, and anthrax broke out from time to time amongst the animals. Drivers were being trained as M.T. drivers with a view to impending mechanization. To sum up, all ranks were most anxious to start operations against the Japs.

For 4 Corps operations in 1944 a small-scale offensive only could be undertaken owing to the diversion of resources to other operational theatres, and the corps plan was limited to advances down the Tiddim road and Kabaw valley with the object of occupying the Kalewa–Kalemyo area. Roads were also to be made for use in the eventual advance into Burma.

The enemy on his side was preparing for his main advance to conquer India, and although there was no close contact on this front, both sides were patrolling and gaining touch here and there.

In February, 1944, 4 Corps was deployed on a general south-north line as follows:

Levies with a stiffening of two regular battalions holding the Chin Hills and Lushai Hills.

17 (Light) Division (Major-General D. T. Cowan, D.S.O., M.C.) in the Tiddim area.

20 Division (Major-General D. D. Gracey, C.B.E., M.C.) on the Tamu road and in the Kabaw valley, where it had spent several months patrolling, during which the 8th (Lahore) and 31st (Jammu) Batteries had gained distinction under 32 Indian Brigade in an action at Kyawktaw.

23 Division (Major-General O. L. Roberts, C.B.E., D.S.O.), one brigade in the Ukhrul area, remainder south and south-east of Imphal.

50 Indian Parachute Brigade, Kohima.

From the main base at Dimapur Railhead—known as Manipur Road—ran a two-way road in good condition as far as Imphal, where it bifurcated, one branch going south to Tiddim and on to the crossing of the Chindwin at Kalewa, the other branch south-east via Palel to Tamu in the Kabaw valley. The Imphal–Tiddim section carried only one line of traffic at this time, but much work was being carried out to widen the road and improve the surface.

The only available maps were $\frac{1}{2}$-inch and showed simply the jungle road, form lines and spot heights adjacent. The milestones which provided definite locations of great value were numbered from Imphal 1 to 165 as far as Tiddim, and from Kalewa 1 to 72 as far as Tiddim; a system which led to confusion until a straightforward system was adopted later on.

The Commander, 4 Corps, ordered the withdrawal of 17 Division from Tiddim to Imphal, but left the date to the Divisional Commander.

The Commander, Fourteenth Army, was told that the security of the Imphal Plain was his primary task. He moved 5 Division from Arakan by air to the Imphal–Kohima area, beginning on 17th March: Divisional H.Q., 9 and 123 Brigades to Imphal and 161 to Dimapur by 27th and 31st March respectively.

By way of further reinforcement, 33 Corps H.Q. was flown from India to Dimapur, to which place 2 British Division was moved from Bombay by air and train and 7 Division travelled by the same means from Arakan. By the end of April the Corps comprised 2 British Division, 7 Division less one brigade, but including 161

Brigade of 5 Division, the equivalent of a regiment of tanks, and 23 L.R.P. Brigade. Five more L.R.P. brigades from India were moving, or about to move, into the Army area for their take-off for operations west of the Irrawaddy river. Later on a further reinforcement of 268 Indian Lorried Infantry Brigade arrived.

Chinese troops and levies co-operated on the north flank by guarding airfields and communications.

The Japanese moved three divisions west across the Chindwin into Assam, leaving as many more in Burma in support of the operation: 33 Division, of which one column reached the Tiddim road on 11th March and a second moved up the Kabaw valley; 15 Division, which crossed just north of Thaungdut on 15th/16th March with orders to capture Ukhrul and disrupt communications between that place and Imphal; and 31 Division, which crossed at Homalin for the purpose of capturing Kohima.

Kohima is the headquarters of a district of Assam, and consists of a village and the District Commissioner's offices on a ridge about a mile long over which, after a climb of forty-odd miles, runs the only road from Dimapur via Imphal down into Burma. The crest of the ridge is undulating and has no well-defined positional features, and the whole ridge is commanded from neighbouring heights. The enemy ignored the railhead at Dimapur, where enormous stocks of rations and military stores had been built up, but made a wide encircling movement to cut the road between that place and Kohima.

17 Division pulled out of Tiddim on 14th March and found the road to Imphal cut by a strong force of Japanese 33 Division from the Kabaw valley. The heavy fighting which took place during the 17 Division withdrawal to the Bishenpur area, about 134 miles, is described on pages 358-361.

20 Division was holding positions in depth along the Palel–Tamu road, pending a further withdrawal to Moreh.

23 Division was split up, 1 Indian Brigade forming the corps reserve at Imphal and the other brigades, 37 and 49 (less one battalion), were about to move down the road to Tiddim to extricate 17 Division.

At Ukhrul was the battalion of 4 Mahratta L.I. left behind by 49 Brigade, and two battalions of 50 Indian Parachute Brigade under Brigadier Hope-Thomson carrying out jungle training.

Action at Sangshak

Whilst the Japanese 33 Division attacked the communications of 17 Division on the right flank, part of the Japanese 31 Division was making for Ukhrul, a place of vital importance where several tracks converged, in order to turn the left flank. The defence of the district was a matter of extreme difficulty; movement was impossible except along the knife-edge ridges of the mountains which permitted the occupation of only very cramped positions; the valleys between the ridges were several thousand feet deep; thus, support of neighbouring units entailed slow and laborious climbing.

The attack opened on 19th March against the advanced posts covering the approaches to Ukhrul; these held off the Japanese during three days of fighting, and then withdrew to a defensive "box" position on more or less suitable ground at Sangshak about six miles south of Ukhrul. Here the mortar troop of 581st Field Battery, R.A., and the 15th (Jhelum) Mountain Battery (Major R. J. P. Lock) of the 28th Mountain Regiment, which had come forward from the advanced base at Litan, twelve miles to the south-west, were, by the night of the 21st, dug in awaiting the arrival of the infantry who were falling back. The mountain battery mules were left at Litan under Captain Hartly-Ayre. The other officers with the guns were Lieutenants J. G. Kidd and Malhotra.

Two O.Ps. were manned, one at the church and one in the 4 Mahratta lines; the guns and R.A. mortars were in action on a small feature about 100 yards by 50 yards on the highest part of the position, where there was no cover and very little elbow-room, as the area contained a mass of troops and trenches.

On the night of the 21st March, grenade and mortar bombing of the box was carried out by the enemy, who had followed up our rear troops and by midday of the 22nd had surrounded the position. The battery cooks (Punjabi Mussulman section) were killed and Naik Lall Chand was wounded at his gun. Some good shooting was made at enemy moving on the road to Litan. That night heavy attacks were made on the perimeter, especially on the position of No. 1 gun, which was more exposed than the others. The R.A. mortar troop provided splendid support, and, thanks to being well dug in, the 4 Mahratta had only five men wounded. The next day rations and ammunition were dropped from the air, and airstrikes were carried out as requested, on one occasion destroying an enemy gun. The force, however, was short of water. All day on the 23rd sniping continued and the Japanese tightened their hold. The O.P. at the church was attacked and a signaller wounded; in retaliation the O.P. party wounded and captured a Japanese officer. The guns inflicted much damage on a large party of the enemy in Sangjing village near by; targets were indicated to aeroplanes by smoke shell and the next day, too, very effective shoots were made on enemy concentrations. Lieutenant J. G. Kidd was sent to Brigade H.Q. as liaison officer during the periods of darkness.

On the 25th No. 2 gun under Major Lock had a duel over open sights at 3,000 yards with an enemy gun and silenced it. This gave intense pleasure to the infantry. That evening Major Lock was wounded in the face by a splinter or bullet, but returned to duty the following morning (26th) when the enemy penetrated into the box through the guns. A naik and a gunner were killed at No. 1 gun and eight more wounded, including Lieutenant Malhotra. A new perimeter was formed pivoted on No. 2 gun position, and a very strong resistance was put up by the gunners under Havildar Surwan Dass, aided by officers of 152nd Parachute Battalion and some gunners from No. 3 gun under Naik Ali Akbar. Gunners Gheba Khan and Ayub Khan fought a great fight with grenades and the new line was held, the men of the battery particularly responding to encouragement from Major Lock.

The 4 Mahratta mortars were very well fought in support of counter-attacks, but the enemy was firmly established. Eventually Major Lock and Major Smith (formerly a Mountain Gunner) made a gallant attempt to clear No. 1 gun position, and when the enemy was ejected later it was seen that Lock had bayoneted three Japs in the gun-pit and that he and Smith had been killed trying to clear a trench just beyond it.* At this time Brigade H.Q. sent an order to destroy the guns, and sights and junction nuts were sent back.

Attacks and rushes were continued, and Havildars Surwan Dass and Mohan Lal again and again went forward with grenades and a Bren. On one of these occasions Mohan Lal brought in a wounded British officer to the gun-pits.

Once during a counter-attack our infantry used the gun position as a rallying-point pending another advance supported by gunners with Brens and grenades. Havildar Mohan Lal brought back the sights of No. 1 gun and at the same time saved a gunner who had been left wounded in a gun-pit.

The Gurkhas then cleared the plateau and the mountain guns were put into action again. Owing to the shortening of the perimeter there was only room for two guns, and in fact No. 2 was the only one fired. At 1600 hours it fired 70 rounds on enemy guns near the village of Lingshang, which were reported as extremely effective, notwithstanding that the detachment was being sniped while firing; the Japanese guns certainly ceased firing.

A wireless message received at 1830 hours ordered the garrison to

---

* By Major Lock's death a brilliant Gunner was lost to the Regiment.

fight its way out. Unexpected by the enemy, the majority of the garrison marched over the southern edge of the box into the jungle without attracting attention—the rear-guard alone being attacked.

The guns were stripped of essential parts, which were carried away by the detachments after shells had been rammed down the barrels "fore and aft." Lieutenant Kidd concluded his report with the words: "2230 hours. The battery with its walking wounded marched out in a solid block behind 152 Battalion. The Nagas were very friendly and provided guides throughout the journey."

After some early straggling, Lieutenant Kidd and the two V.C.Os. with forty-three men plodded on through the jungle without food for four days and came out at Waithou on 30th March, joining other survivors there, all of whom were then withdrawn to Imphal.

The exploits of the 15th (Jhelum) Mountain Battery on this occasion are among the best recorded in the Mountain Artillery.

Casualties, 15th Battery:

Killed: Major R. P. J. Lock, Lance-Naik Mathra Das, Gunner Fida Hussain Shah, Gunner Gian Chand, three cooks.

Wounded, believed prisoners of war: 4 I.O.Rs.

Wounded and evacuated: 6 I.O.Rs.

Missing: 6 I.O.Rs.

Decorations: I.D.S.M., Havildar Surwan Dass; Havildar Mohan Lal.

The time gained by the gallant delaying action at Sangshak was of vital importance to the coming defence of the Assam front.

The 161 Brigade of 5 Division arrived at Dimapur by air from Arakan with very little time to spare to reinforce the garrison of Kohima. This consisted of 1 Assam Regiment, a Nepal regiment and a very large number of administrative personnel without military training. On 1st April the situation was: 4/7 Rajputana Rifles at Dimapur with 24th Mountain Regiment, less 20th Battery; 1/1 Punjabis at M.S. 16 between Dimapur and Kohima; the remainder of the brigade and 20th Battery (Major R. C. Yeo) in position four miles out of Dimapur. Lieutenant-Colonel R. H. M. Hill commanded the mountain regiment.

In the Kohima position, where Colonel H. V. Richards was in command, 4 Royal West Kent of 161 Brigade followed by 20th Battery in R.I.A.S.C. lorries joined the garrison on 5th April a few hours before the Japanese encircled it, the outposts having been drawn in after a stubborn resistance by 1 Assam Regiment. Brigade H.Q., 24th Mountain Regiment, less 12th and 20th Batteries, and 4/7 Raj. Rif. were two miles from Kohima in a defensive position which was extended towards Jatsoma on the arrival of 1/1 Punjab, and at once surrounded by the enemy.

Siege of Kohima

Thus began another siege of a box defended by our troops against hordes of Japanese outnumbering them by five to one and attacking with extreme fury, regardless of losses. And again after a stubborn resistance entailing many casualties the attacks failed. There was practically no cover in the box; in fact there was hardly even room for the troops, and no suitable position for 20th Battery's guns. The box was attacked without delay and the guns came into action, although there was no position that was not under enemy gun and rifle fire; several targets were engaged thereby, drawing retaliatory fire on our infantry, who asked the guns to stop firing. Artillery support was obtained from the guns of 2nd (Derajat) and 11th (Dehra Dun) Batteries in action in the Jatsoma box, as well as from Divisional Artillery units; instructions were sent by W/T from 20th Battery's F.O.O. in the Kohima box, and the Derajat Battery's F.O.O. party under Lieutenant J. S. Punia, R.I.A., which had slipped into Kohima before it was cut off. Covering and defensive fire were provided on demand all through the siege, and the infantry were never without this vital support. The wireless communication never failed as Lieutenant Dickenson fixed up an abandoned motor for charging the batteries.

The Japanese, urged to unwonted ferocity by propaganda and promises, attacked almost continuously for a fortnight. An enemy raid on the 9th led to fourteen casualties in the battery, and on the 10th Major Yeo and six I.O.Rs. were wounded. Sheer force of numbers gained the enemy a few yards from time to time, and counter-attacks were made to recover the ground; but the perimeter was slowly squeezed smaller and smaller. The British and Indian garrison clung to the battered ground, and reinforcements were not far away; 2 British Division was known to be arriving at Dimapur.

During the attack on the 10th the battery position was overrun. Two guns were hastily buried; the other two were moved to the top of Summerhouse Hill, where the D.C.'s bungalow and the hospital were situated. Several strong attacks were repulsed here; the new gun position was in the D.C.'s kitchen garden, but the guns were fired very little from there.

At the hospital the state of the wounded, who were all exposed in the open, was indescribable; but the medical officers did their utmost, and the courage of the wounded was beyond all praise. Mr. Pawley, the D.C., and Colonel Richards shared a bunker on Summerhouse Hill, where daily, almost hourly, actions were fought across the tennis court, one edge of which was held by each force. The enemy had by now brought up many 75-mm. guns and the ridge was exposed to fire from the east, south and north sides. Heavy concentrations preceded enemy attacks, but the Royal West Kent and Indian troops fought with the utmost gallantry.

The water pipe-line was cut early in the siege and the ration was reduced to half a mug per man a day, and had to be brought in from outside the perimeter. Supplies and ammunition were dropped from the air; and fortunately there was no shortage of shells as defensive fire had to be continued almost without ceasing. On the 15th water was dropped from the air, and on the 17th two gunners were killed by loads which parted from their parachutes.

During the siege the 11th Battery (Major Fergie), when not providing D.F. fire, was kept busy supporting the 4/7 Raj. Rif. making diversionary attacks from Jatsoma.

Notwithstanding the courage of the defenders, the enemy slowly gained ground until the 11th, when it was known that 2 British Division under Major-General John Grover was only ten miles off fighting its way from Dimapur. Relieving troops reached Jatsoma on the 13th along with the 12th (Poonch) Battery, and the 2 Divisional Artillery was at once put on the wireless net to the F.O.Os. in Kohima. The 18th was the last day of the siege: the 1/1 Punjab fought its way in on that day, and on the 20th the 1 Royal Berkshire of 6 (British) Infantry Brigade marched in and relieved the sorely tried Royal West Kent, whose losses in the siege were 16 killed, 13 missing and 125 wounded. The battery Havildar-Major, Mahomed Khan, was killed in action on the 18th.

On the 20th a final attack was made by the Japanese—an all-out effort which was frustrated, though our casualties were heavy; although tanks had now arrived, the battle lasted three days and nights before the enemy positions were captured. And this was by no means the finish. The Japanese were still occupying the high ground all round and had to be driven out of these positions. The 24th Mountain Regiment fired many thousands of rounds before the Kohima area was cleared about 2nd June.

The 20th Battery moved out with two guns on relief by 12th (Poonch) Battery, now commanded by Major T. H. Harrison (from second-in-command), *vice* A. B. Howard, wounded. Major Yeo became Second-in-Command of the regiment. Major Harrison was killed in his O.P. in Kohima a few days later. The batteries continued the support of the many actions in the vicinity of Kohima before the area was finally cleared. During this period 20th Battery was rejoined by its mules, which had been left behind in the Arakan under Lieutenant MacDonald. Officers of 20th Mountain Battery who went through the siege of Kohima were:

>Major R. C. Yeo (afterwards awarded the D.S.O.).
>Captain P. Kendall.
>Lieutenant A. B. Dickenson (awarded the M.C.).
>
>Casualties amongst I.O.Rs., 25.

Subadar Walidad, 11 (Dehra Dun) Battery, was awarded the M.C.

From 20*th Battery War Diary*:

" Apr. 5. Hav.-Maj. Amar Singh killed by a fall of stone during the move in to Kohima.
„ 6. Nk. Fateh Shah died of wounds, Lieut. Dickenson, 2 O.R. and 2 followers wounded.
„ 7. Moved gun positions.
„ 9. Heavy shelling all day—2 grs. killed in action; 9 O.R. wounded; 3 missing believed killed during an enemy inroad.
„ 10. Major Yeo and 6 O.R. wounded.
„ 14. Hurri-bombers arrived. Supplies now being dropped accurately.
„ 15. Water dropped from the air. Jemadar Sardara Singh wounded.
„ 17. 2 gunners killed by air-drop parachutes.
„ 18. Hav.-Maj. Mahomed Khan and 2 O.Rs. killed in action.
„ 20. 3 O.Rs. wounded. Battery rejoined regiment at Jatsoma."

The two guns buried in Kohima were unearthed by the battery and put into use, none the worse for the adventure. After the relief the battery was, for the first time, equipped with two pneumatic carriages.

The vacancies for battery commanders in the regiment were filled by the posting of P. Kendall as Major to the 20th Battery and J. Nettelfield to 12th (Poonch) Battery.

Whilst operations were in progress in Kohima, other formations of 4 Corps were taking up their positions for the defence of the Imphal Plain.

The Battle of the Imphal Plain

Imphal is the capital of Manipur State, and the Plain is a plateau in the heart of the mountains some sixty-four miles south of Kohima covering about 600 square miles. The road from Dimapur to Burma bifurcates at Imphal, one branch going south to Tiddim and on to the crossing of the Chindwin at Kalewa, the other south-east via Palel to Tamu in the Kabaw valley. These roads were metalled and in good condition after two years' strenuous work by the Engineers.

The Plain had been turned into a forward base containing the depots of all administrative services as well as airfields. It blocked the Japanese advance on India: the Japanese 15 Division which had captured Ukhrul had been directed to the east of Imphal with orders to sweep round to the north, whilst the Japanese 33 Division, after cutting off the troops at Tiddim, was to invest Imphal from the south.

Since December, 1942, the 17 (Light) Division had been guarding the right flank of the Corps in the Tiddim area, 2/5 R.G.R. keeping touch with the Lushai levies farther south (pages 335-336). Kennedy Peak (8,800 feet) was a dominating feature covering the tracks towards Imphal, 178 miles north. The 3.7-inch batteries were deployed, generally in separate sections, in support of the infantry holding what was a very extended position and protecting the troops working on the communications for a prospective advance. There being only two brigades in a light division, the 29th Light Mountain Regiment (Lieutenant-Colonel G. Horsfield) was supporting 63 Brigade and 21st Light Mountain Regiment (Lieutenant-Colonel P. E. R. Dawson) was supporting 48 Brigade. The Field Regiment was kept in the hands of the C.R.A., Brigadier J. H. de Robeck.

During January and February, 1944, enemy attacks increased both in strength and frequency, both by day and night, and were countered with great spirit by the troops of 17 Division. Patrolling was intensified and ambush parties very active: the 5.5-inch guns which were in action at M.S. 60 considerably strengthened the divisional artillery. Replacement of ammunition was a problem owing to long and difficult communications.

Lieutenant Webster and Subadar Mall Singh of 6th (Jacob's) Battery were killed by the explosion of a dud shell on 28th January.

The Supreme Commander, Lord Mountbatten, inspected representative parades on Kennedy Peak on 11th February, and addressed the jawans in Urdu.

During these operations 14th Mountain Battery turned out a mixed section of Punjabi Mussulmans and Sikhs for the Lethbridge Commission, which was sent out to determine the best type of artillery equipment for a given operation provided an ordinary field artillery unit could learn it quickly. The opportunity was taken to show up the inadequate equipment of the 3.7-inch batteries—*e.g.*, telescopes and open sights were not provided, gun rules were still in use; oil lamps were useless for night firing; canvas water tanks were a necessity: these amongst other improvements were suggested.

During February the Japanese artillery was reinforced and more skilfully handled; fire was nearly all predicted and very accurate. Much activity continued.

The Survey Subadar took his survey party to mark down targets from an O.P. near M.S. 53 and, owing to the absence of a milestone, walked on until a barrier was met across the road. This the party proceeded to dismantle, but hurriedly desisted and faded into the jungle on discovering that it was covered by a Jap L.M.G.

During a counter-attack the O.P. party of the Royal (Kohat) Battery covered the retirement of a party of infantry which was withdrawing past it; on another occasion an O.P. party of the same battery met a party of Japanese in a communication trench and fought it out with grenades and the bayonet. This action gained a Military Cross for Lieutenant J. Proctor, a Military Medal for Naik Bachan Singh and a Gallantry Certificate for the signaller.

When the Japanese offensive opened on 6th March their front was at Fort White—M.S. 52 on the Kalewa road—with advanced strong points flanking the Imphal-Tiddim road. Strong enemy forces were crossing the Chindwin, threatening Imphal and Kohima. Our defences at Tiddim had been strengthened and 63 Brigade was sent to reinforce the detachment at Tongzang whilst 48 Brigade was held as a striking force at Tiddim. The 3/10 Baluch and 4/12 F.F.R. with a field battery and 38th Battery in support held off strong attacks in the Tongzang area for several days. The Japanese cut the Imphal road at M.S. 100 and 17 Division was now spread out over eighty miles. On the 13th the Divisional Commander was ordered to retire towards Imphal at a time to be selected by himself.

The withdrawal commenced on 14th March, 63 Brigade protecting the right flank and 48 Brigade forming the rear-guard at area M.S. 146. The rearmost troops, 2/5 Gurkhas and 6th (Jacob's)

Battery, moved out with officers and men carrying on them what they could, everything else being destroyed. The column of 16,000 troops, 3,500 animals and 2,500 vehicles was collected from scattered positions in a remarkably short time and boxes were established at night for protection. M.T. was reserved for the carriage of rations and ammunition. Air-drops of supplies began without delay.

The Japanese by-passed our right flank and formed a strong road-block at M.S. 132 near Tuitum. This had to be blasted away by a divisional artillery concentration combined with a heavy air bombardment before it could be attacked and the road cleared (16th March). On the 17th 48 Brigade halted at M.S. 124 and the remainder of the division at M.S. 100 without interference by the enemy. A rear detachment held Tuitum, which was attacked for several nights by a large force which lost very heavily. About this time enemy radio reported that 17 Division had been completely destroyed.

Frequent attacks were made on the piquets covering the roads, and commandos were formed to work in jungle sweeps to harass and kill enemy parties.

A mountain battery commando was formed during the withdrawal under Lieutenant Evans and did some good work harassing the enemy. Lieutenant Joscelyne of 9th (Murree) Battery was killed leading an attack with small arms only against a very active enemy bunker.

Casualties quickly mounted up and all had to be carried along.

The mountain mortar batteries (of which the 37th Battery was commanded by Major D. J. Lloyd and the 38th by Major A. A. George) were in great demand and their fire was "most satisfactory and effective" according to the B.R.A. They could fire into hollows and on to reverse slopes and were ideal for local defence. It was usual for the battery officer to co-ordinate the fire of the infantry and artillery mortars, and fortunately mortar ammunition was plentiful.

The howitzer batteries had some opportunity targets; in particular Jacob's Battery at M.S. 108 ran forward on to the crest 1,600 yards from the enemy in full view and did great execution. This surprise was responsible for the successful capture of the position.

There was a stiff fight at M.S. 110 on 23rd and 24th March when the three battalions of 48 Brigade supported by two field batteries and 21st Mountain Regiment distinguished themselves by gallant attacks on a strongly defended position on high ground, where the enemy fought almost to annihilation.

On the night of 26th March the division resumed its retirement and the next night the Manipur river bridge was blown.

While the M.T. column moved along the main road, 48 Brigade with 21st Mountain Regiment used a mule track in the jungle to reach M.S. 92 on the road without enemy interference, and on 30th March the division concentrated at M.S. 82.

On 14th March 37 Brigade of 23 Division with a squadron of tanks and an Indian Field Battery left the Imphal Plain at short notice to assist the withdrawal of 17 Division, and at the end of a rush journey of 100 miles arrived at its objective, M.S. 82, only an hour or two before the enemy. After two days of fierce fighting 37 Brigade fought through to M.S. 96—another block. By this date (17th) 49 Brigade, less one battalion, with 28th Battery under command, had come up from the south of Imphal to help and formed a base at M.S. 82.

A dash through to M.S. 100 rescued a beleaguered detachment, but the "Battle of the Road-blocks" swung to and fro between M.S. 96 and M.S. 102 for some days. Air supply was now in good working order and air-strikes were supplied at short notice. Again the Air Force saved the situation.

The heliograph was taken into use on occasional days when the wireless batteries failed, and on the 21st a helio message came through to 37 Brigade from 17 Divisional Headquarters to the effect that the division had reached M.S. 109; but the enemy did not wait for a joint attack. When the division arrived at M.S. 82, 37 Brigade was covering it from M.S. 92, but by this time a new enemy block had been established at M.S. 72, north of 49 Brigade. This entailed more fighting, not very strenuous, but 17 Division reached Imphal on 5th April and the 37 and 49 Brigades rejoined their division soon after. The Supreme Commander recorded that he visited 17 Division on its arrival and "found them in great spirits."

The 63 Brigade was sent into action forthwith south of Kanglatombi, and cleared a troublesome party off a narrow ridge by a technique new to the brigade; the infantry followed two tanks and had little trouble. The use of tanks wherever possible against Japs dug in on a hill feature became a normal procedure.

Heavy fighting was now proceeding over a large area; the vicinity of Kohima was by no means free of Japanese and Imphal was completely surrounded. The 2 British Division was advancing south from Kohima through a mined area towards Kanglatombi, a large ordnance depot in the hands of the Japanese (ten miles north of Imphal), and 7 Indian Division was about to fight its way over very rough country towards Imphal from the east. The 20 Division (less one brigade) was holding the enemy in front of Palel, and 23 Division was covering the east flank which was open to the Japanese

31 Division operating from Ukhrul. The Japanese 33 Division made an attempt to cut the road between Bishenpur and Silchar, and on 14th April 17 Division was ordered to prevent any enemy attempts to push north of the Silchar road. Here, aided by 32 Brigade of 20 Division with 31st (Jammu) Battery, it resisted many fierce attacks. The Japanese 33 Division had been ordered to capture Imphal "even if the division is annihilated." The 4 Corps reported afterwards that it had done its best to bring about this result.

Meanwhile the Air Force, R.A.F., R.I.A.F., R.C.A.F., and U.S.A.A.F., operational and non-operational, under Air-Marshal Sir John Baldwin, were greatly strengthened, and notwithstanding a shortage of landing grounds (by June only the air-strip at Imphal could be used) our command of the air had a decisive effect on the battle; our fighter-bombers were used with telling effect; transport operations in the air were unhampered, and normal precautions against attacks from the air were not required.

During April and May Japanese attacks and our counter-attacks never ceased; the enemy certainly did his best to carry out his orders. His tanks were much in evidence, and 155-mm. guns took their toll. To capture Bishenpur (sixteen miles south-west of Imphal) was essential for the success of this plan, but this he never succeeded in doing. He further planned to block the Silchar track after the capture of Bishenpur and to pursue the British during their retreat to Imphal.

The mountain batteries were very fully occupied during these operations: the terrain was seldom easy especially in the Silchar area, where the slopes in front of the gun positions were often so steep that artillery and small-arms fire had limited opportunities, and the mortars came into their own again. Even so the howitzer batteries fired about 3,000 rounds a month. Both mountain regiments were heavily engaged; Captain J. H. Abbey, 38th Battery, was killed in his O.P. on 19th April, whereupon Havildar Sher Singh occupied the O.P. under intense fire and silenced three enemy machine guns. For this exploit he received an immediate award of the M.M. Another havildar of that battery was awarded the M.M. for gallantry in action; 120 bodies were counted in front of the battery. The same battery acquitted itself well at the end of the month at Potsangbam (twenty miles south of Bishenpur), which took five days of hard fighting to clear. The battery's work attracted a great deal of enemy mortar and artillery fire, and it had heavy casualties.

Major A. A. George and Subadar Fateh Khan were awarded the M.C. for gallantry in the Imphal area.

During April a sound-ranging troop of 43 Survey Battery, R.A., worked with the division with good effect.

Bishenpur was attacked continuously, and the Japanese 214 Regiment crossed to the north of the Silchar track on 22nd April; the Japanese 215 Regiment then moved east towards Bishenpur, which was bravely defended by 1/4 G.R. for three days. On the 29th attacks were made by 17 Division south of Bishenpur and from the west side of the Tiddim road, and enemy casualties were very heavy. The 3 Commando Brigade was acting from Silchar at the same time with good effect. At this time the enemy made another attack on Bishenpur, losing many men and five planes which were shot down by our A.A. fire. He also entered Potsangbam.

The 63 Infantry Brigade was now released from the operation in the north (8th May) and rejoined 17 Division. The 29th Mountain Regiment* was detailed to support the brigade. On 19th May the brigade captured Kha Aimol and established itself on the enemy's L. of C. A hill feature held by 7 Baluch and personnel of Divisional H.Q. sustained a very fierce attack on 20th/21st, and on the following day the enemy force was surrounded and wiped out with the help of tanks of 3rd D.G. and 7th Cavalry. Captain G. D. Badenoch, 29th Mountain Regiment, was killed in action here.

The enemy was now making a desperate bid to get through to Imphal and the mountain guns were close to the bed of a stream down which a large body of enemy troops moved during the night; the position was maintained until daylight, by which time the whole of 63 Brigade Group had concentrated in the Kha Aimol area. A strong party had entered 63 Brigade mule lines but were wiped out, and on the 29th the Japanese made a brave but futile attack on some of the guns.

On a very wet and dark night a picked party of the enemy charged and penetrated the perimeter wire at the 14th (Rajputana) Battery position. A fierce fight took place round the guns, clubbed rifles and bayonets being freely used. Dawn showed the battery's casualties to be six killed and thirteen wounded, but fourteen dead Japs were found and the guns remained undamaged. This incident resulted in the award of the M.M. and two Gallantry Certificates.

Tanks were used by the enemy in their frequent night attacks: on one occasion seven enemy lorries drove through the perimeter and left seventy-six dead inside and thirty outside.

The 48 Brigade formed a block of the Tiddim road at M.S. 33,

---

* 29th Mountain Regiment now commanded by Lieutenant-Colonel J. M. Hepper.

which was held by 2/5 R.G.R. and covered by 21st Mountain Regiment. It sustained a strong attack by infantry and tanks. Several tanks were destroyed and over 300 dead were counted. The 1st Kohat Battery maintained a good support under great difficulties, losing numbers of men and mules. Major E. D. Garnett, the Battery commander, was awarded the M.C. for his share in the action. The 48 Brigade then moved to Moirang, where a new block was established.

6th (Jacob's) Battery ran into a patch of ill-luck during this period of intensive activity. The battery with a section of 37th Battery was moving by night to Moirang when it lost its way and ran into an enemy ambush. In the ensuing stampede Jemadar Hakim Ali put up a fine resistance, bringing No. 3 gun into action and killing twelve Japanese. Lieutenants Taylor (6th) and Melvin (37th) made their way through the jungle and at daybreak some mules were found, but when reorganized the battery was short of thirty-two mules, and two guns which had sunk into a morass were out of action. Four I.O.Rs. were killed and eleven wounded. The next day all the gun parts were found except two chases. Jemadar Hakim Ali was awarded the M.C. and the battery tailor was awarded a Gallantry Certificate. The next night at Moirang one gun of the 6th Battery was forward in an anti-tank role and knocked out two tanks. Fighting was heavy and Lieutenant Taylor was killed. Early on 27th an attack was made on an advanced post which included a gun of 6th Battery and the infantry pulled out, leaving no time to get the gun away, notwithstanding covering fire from 37th Battery mortars. The counter-attack failed and the gun was not recovered. The remaining gun of 6th Battery was attached temporarily to 1st (Kohat) Battery, and two days later (31st) this battery had a gun knocked out. The 6th (Jacob's) Battery Commander recorded that his men were very wet and very tired, but stood up to it very well. The battery was issued with two monobloc guns shortly afterwards.

By 15th May 32 and 63 Brigades had cleared Potsangbam, capturing several mortars and three anti-tank guns. The 48 Brigade captured Moirang on 25th May, moving on 30th to Potsangbam.*

A new phase opened early in June when Japanese 33 Division (with a regiment of 53 Division attached) was to make a fresh attack to capture Imphal from the west. "On this one battle rests the fate of the Empire," the Japanese troops were told. The first phase was

---

* Lieutenant-Colonel J. B. Chaplin was now in command of 21st Mountain Regiment *vice* Lieutenant-Colonel Paul Dawson, who had gone on leave from Imphal in an aeroplane which was never again heard of.

to destroy our forces in the Bishenpur area, and in the second phase Imphal was to be attacked from the west.

Potsangbam was heavily attacked on 6th and 12th June with slight successes which were of little value, and our line was soon restored. Flamethrowers were used, but 1/3 G.R. fought back so bravely that Phase I of the Japanese attack was a failure. Phase II was modified: the enemy's numbers were so reduced by casualties that a withdrawal was essential. His food supply broke down and those who survived starvation and disease retired to the Chin Hills.

It took some weeks to clear the enemy out of the area, and the batteries had little rest. No praise is too high for the work of the F.O.Os. during these operations, which were carried on during the monsoon which broke early in June.

The 5 Indian Division had been carrying out a series of offensives against the communications of Japanese formations to the north of Imphal, gradually lessening the gap between Kohima and Imphal, which was the scene of very heavy fighting when the Japanese position on the Aradura Spur was stormed by 2 British Division. Kanglatombi was retaken on 6th June by 5 Division, which was fighting its way north and eventually made contact with 2 British Division on 22nd June at M.S. 109 on the Kohima–Imphal road, thus reopening the main L. of C. from Dimapur.

Convoys were ready to start and the supply situation improved at once; but notwithstanding the strenuous efforts of the Air Forces, many of the troops were on reduced rations for some time longer.

On 19th July 5 Division passed through 63 Brigade and continued the pursuit, 17 Division being withdrawn to India to refit.

As already narrated, 37 and 49 Brigades rejoined 23 Division after helping the retirement of 17 Division along the Tiddim road early in April, and found that 1 Brigade had been withdrawn from the Kabaw valley, coming into corps reserve.

The 20 Division had been holding strong attacks in front of Palel, and was sent to carry on the advance north to Ukhrul (pages 370-371) on being relieved by 23 Division on the Shenam–Shuganu front about 11th May. This was familiar ground to 23 Division, who had occupied it and fortified it in 1942.

Action at Shenam

The Shenam position guards the entrance of the Burma Road into the Imphal Plain, and on it 20 Division had stopped the advance of a strong Japanese column, Yamomoto Force, after much hard fighting during March and April. The position consists of a line of hills running south-east to north-west, rising 500 feet sheer above the line of the road. The tops were narrow ridges with little room for fighting, and all were 5,000 feet or more above the sea. From the Tamu direction towards Imphal they had been named Scraggy, Malta, Gibraltar and Recce Hill; on Recce Hill were 37 Indian Brigade H.Q. and 28th Mountain Regiment H.Q. The position had to be held at all costs and had been the scene of continuous fighting since the enemy advance began. Every day and often by night it was under gun fire, and many attempts to capture it had been made by the enemy. During daylight all positions were under observation of the Japs on adjacent hills to the east.

The two battalions forward were the 3/5 Gurkhas, holding Scraggy and Malta, and the 5/6 Rajputana Rifles on Gibraltar and Recce Hill. The 28th Battery was in action on Patiala Ridge, a little to the west, and the 13th (Dardoni) Battery on Assam Ridge, to the south. O.Ps. were on Recce Hill and Malta.

During the night of 23rd/24th May the 60th Regiment of the Japanese 15 Division overran Gibraltar, killed the garrison and consolidated under the flag of the Rising Sun. From morning light until about 0830 hours 28th Battery kept up a heavy H.E. fire on the hill—the left section controlled by the Malta O.P. on to the lower northern slopes, and the right section by Recce O.P. on the higher Jap positions. Many Japanese were hit as they were flushed out of the top bunkers and ran down the hill for safety. About 0830 hours the Rajputana Rifles put in a counter-attack, covered by the guns, but were stopped by fire from a 105-mm. gun and had to withdraw after a great fight.

Immediate preparations were made to recapture Gibraltar. Harassing fire was carried out by the mountain batteries and the field regiment's mortars until about 1400 hours: a strange duel because each side was in full view of the other. One enemy bunker looked straight into the Recce O.P., and for a period two Japanese came out into the open after each shell burst to show their unconcern. This habit ceased suddenly, a surprise shrapnel having been burst over them; it had to be fired with charge IV to clear the crest, but proved a winner.

After a five-minute artillery concentration, supported by a tank of 3 Dragoon Guards firing over open sights from Patiala Ridge, a company of 3/10 Gurkhas made a counter-attack. The first platoon reached the crest and was held up by a Japanese post and by artillery fire, but the second platoon passed through it and with a devastating blitz of grenades and small arms broke into the enemy position and overwhelmed it. The guns killed a great number who tried to run away down the hill.

The Gurkhas counted a splendid bag: 10 officers and 150 men dead on the field, 3 M.M.G., 8 L.M.G. and 200 rifles captured. Their own losses were 2 killed and 14 wounded.

In appreciation of the support it had given, the 28th Battery was presented by the Gurkhas with an officer's sword.

The monsoon broke a few days later, but fighting never ceased: the next serious operation was an attempt to capture Scraggy, but the front held firm.

The 1 Brigade on the left had several sharp actions in the hills to the north, supported by 16th Battery (Major G. T. Hull) in particularly difficult country, thereby relieving the pressure on 37 Brigade. On one occasion in a divisional artillery fire plan, 16th Battery was firing at 3,000 yards and the 15th Battery was firing a barrage with open sights starting at 600 yards. The enemy was given no rest, but he on his part did not cease offensive operations for several weeks.

On the eastern flank, early in June, as the monsoon broke, an endeavour was made to cut the communications of the Japanese 15 and 33 Divisions in the Jessami and Kharasom directions. For this purpose 114 Infantry Brigade of 7 Indian Division, with the 25th Mountain Regiment (less the Bikanir Bijey Battery), was sent to make an encircling movement in the Naga country to the east of Kohima. Japanese rear-guards were found to be in action covering a retirement from the Kohima area which was being carried out at speed. The going was extremely difficult, mostly against the grain of the valleys; but the drivers and mules lived up to their best traditions, climbing up and down mountain paths which slipped away under their feet. Fighting at heights up to 6,000 feet in mist and heavy rain against an enemy fighting to the bitter end was as strenuous a test as any yet experienced. It took three weeks to complete the movement.

During this operation two F.O.Os. of the regiment carried out their duties in support of the 2nd South Lancs with great bravery and efficiency. The forward platoons of the battalion were suddenly held up by the enemy concealed in bunkers which, owing to mist and heavy rain, could not be seen from a greater distance than forty yards. The F.O.Os., Captain R. H. Franks, 23rd Mountain Battery, and Lieutenant J. F. Kenyon, 5th (Bombay) Battery, who were with the leading infantry, brought down effective neutralizing fire from their guns, smothering the machine-gun, rifle, and grenade fire, thus giving the infantry time for reconnaissance and the preparation of a new plan of attack, in the making of which Captain Franks assisted and laid out a fire plan. The guns of the two batteries were then registered by the two F.O.Os. on points in the target area, the position of rounds which could not be observed being estimated by sound. The attack then went in, Captain Franks continuing to advise the infantry commander and Lieutenant Kenyon controlling the fire of the guns. Thanks to the consistent laying of the gunners and the steepness of the approach, an extremely accurate fire was kept up until the leading infantry were twenty or thirty yards from the bunkers. The position was then captured and the enemy destroyed, with few casualties on our side.

The two officers above mentioned were under continuous fire for nine hours during this action. Thanks to their coolness and promptitude, the lives of many infantrymen were saved and the success of the attack was ensured. Each was awarded the M.C. and Lance-Naik Mahomed Ajaib of the 5th Battery, who maintained communication by wireless with the guns throughout the action from an exposed position, was awarded the M.M.

The encirclement was only partly successful as the majority of the enemy slipped away through the jungle to the east and south.

The moves of the L.R.P. Brigades under Major-General Wingate* had begun in March: they were flown to air-strips behind the enemy lines in order to assist the Chinese-American forces in their advance south as well as to cause diversions during the attacks on the Assam front. The 23 L.R.P. Brigade, however, was not airborne and was employed by the Army Commander in the Naga hills, and afterwards at the recapture of Ukhrul.

Part of the 5th (Bombay) Battery had the experience, unique in the annals of the Mountain Artillery, of marching and fighting with this (23) Chindit Brigade, commanded by Brigadier L. E. C. M. Perowne. Captain G. F. A. Munns with Jemadar Khan Zaman, 45 battery drivers of the Punjabi Mussulman section, 34 artillery and 18 transport mules with two 3.7 howitzers, moved by M.T. from Kohima via Dimapur to Jorhat to join 23 L.R.P. Brigade. The guns were sent ahead in jeeps and the remainder of the party marched in pack to Phakekedzumi, where British gunners from 60 (North Midland) Field Regiment, R.A., took over the guns. These gunners, though full of keenness, were of insufficient physique to man the mountain guns, and the drill was, therefore, slowed down consider-

---

* Major-General Wingate was killed in an air crash at the end of March.

ably. The brigade-major of the column was a gunner, Major L. P. Cocks.

The Brigade began its advance on 22nd June, directed on Ukhrul with the intention of co-operating with 33 Indian Brigade of 7 Division, which started about the same date with orders to recapture Ukhrul. Several brushes took place with the retreating enemy and one is particularly noteworthy.

Jemadar Khan Zaman took a small party of drivers, to which Sweeper Ram Sarup (Jind State, Punjab) attached himself with his rifle, to reconnoitre a water point and found it was held by a strong party of the enemy. Battle was joined and the drivers were forced to withdraw with two men wounded and one killed, Driver Manawar Khan, whose body was left on the ground. The withdrawal was covered by Ram Sarup, who shot two Japanese, and when volunteers were called for to bring in the dead man in accordance with North-West Frontier traditions, Ram Sarup volunteered for the task, accompanied by two drivers, one of whom had recently been awarded the M.M. Under the covering fire of his companions, Ram Sarup dragged the body away inch by inch, but after a time the Japanese were all around them, so the body was hidden and the weapons removed. Next day the body was recovered as the result of Ram Sarup's directions, and he was awarded the I.D.S.M. for his courageous act—the first sweeper to be granted this distinction.

Lance-Naik Mir Akbar of the section was in charge of a ration party of R.I.A.S.C. drivers with mules on an occasion when it was attacked. He drove off the enemy single-handed and brought in all fourteen mules by himself. This led to his receiving the M.M.

On the arrival of 23 L.R.P. Brigade at Ukhrul, 33 Brigade and other troops were in position and the place was recaptured after a stiff fight (see page 370). The section then rejoined the 5th Battery there.

On return from the encircling movement in support of 114 Brigade, the 25th Mountain Regiment was hurriedly reorganized for its next operation, which was to support 33 Indian Brigade of 7 Indian Division on a flank attack over the mountains against Ukhrul. No replacements in men, mules or equipment were available, but the regiment was made up to the required strength, which included extra mules for replacing casualties, by using the Bikanir Bijey Battery and by borrowing mules and drivers from the 2nd (Derajat) and 20th Batteries of the 24th Mountain Regiment. The 5th (Bombay) Battery, which had detached a section with the 23 L.R.P. Brigade, was also made up to strength. The 33 Brigade was on an all-mule basis, and all supplies were dropped by air.

A jeep track from Ukhrul to the Chindwin was one of the main supply arteries of the Japanese; it was connected with Kohima and Imphal by other jeep tracks, but all the remaining communications in the area were jungle tracks. About the time the movement began the monsoon broke and almost incessant rain increased the difficulties of marching.

There were many rivers to cross, generally running between steep mountain sides and unbridged; the forest shut out light and air; the paths up and down the slopes were slippery with greasy mud, and they collapsed under the pressure of traffic. Many mules fell, some of which were never seen again, and to shorten the column the 23rd Battery was sent back after a few days. The mountain batteries solved their problem by making new tracks for themselves at the cost of considerable labour and fatigue: their officers were unanimous in giving high praise to the drivers for endurance and courage, and the transport mule drivers of the force, who each had three mules to look after, fully earned the same praise.

At the end of June the corps boundaries were rearranged: 4 Corps took Imphal and the areas of 5, 17 and 23 Divisions. The area between Imphal and Ukhrul inclusive was allotted to 33 Corps, which consisted of 2 British and 7 and 20 Divisions.

89 Indian Brigade rejoined its own division, 7 Indian, in exchange for 161 Brigade, which had been under command of 7 Division since it was flown in in April.

At this time formations were engaged as follows: 20 Division was fighting its way along the Imphal–Ukhrul road; 89 Brigade of 7 Division with the 1st Royal (Kohat) Battery was moving north of 20 Division to attack Ukhrul from the south-west; 33 Brigade, after crossing the mountains, was moving on Ukhrul from the north, and 23 L.R.P. Brigade was on its way to place stops to the east of the objective. Between these columns on jungle tracks were hordes of Japanese who lost cohesion as the days went by and moved in disorderly groups, many of the men, starving and sick, making their way to the Chindwin and escape; rear-guards were still ready to put up a fight, but the "Conquerors of India" were in full retreat.

Ukhrul was entered by enveloping attacks from three sides on 3rd July; it took a whole day to complete the operation by blowing up each bunker and building in turn by shell fire, often when no more than thirty yards from the leading infantry. The Japs then fled, 89 Brigade remaining until the 16th to clear up. 33 Brigade Group on 4th July had moved south-west to cut off an enemy force reported to be massing on the Imphal–Ukhrul road. This entailed some of the worst marching of the operation, and by this time the troops were tired out and incapable of their usual efforts. However, morale was at a high pitch and they responded when called upon; the pursuit was continued by a column made up of 4/1 Gurkhas and a composite six-gun battery.

The following description of the Japanese retreat was written by an officer of the 25th Mountain Regiment who was present:

"The Humine track presented a spectacle transcending any so far encountered. In the knee-deep mud and slime of the track floated the putrefying corpses of many Japanese, swollen and fly-blown, a mass of crawling maggots. Horses lay between the shafts of carts, worked to death in a last-minute attempt to escape the inevitable advance of our forces. Wrecked lorries lay in the jungle below the road which had in many cases collapsed beneath them. Their drivers sat dead at the wheel, victims of dysentery, typhus and mere starvation. Equipment lay everywhere, the untidy evidence of a rout. A tank was found embedded in the mud, a gun half-buried. From the north of Ukhrul, Naga tribesmen brought information of the deaths from sickness and starvation of thousands of Japanese, fugitives from Kohima, their only way of escape cut by our unexpected march on Ukhrul.

"Despite all this, fighting in the rain and mist continued with unabated bitterness on the 8,000-foot summit of the knife-edged ridges along which lay our advance. Day after day these small rear-guard actions were fought in the leafy twilight of the trees, in rain and in the mist which enveloped us for days at a time. They drained steadily our meagre reserves of health and strength.

"By mid-July it was decided that our task had been accomplished. The Japanese had withdrawn from the hills above Imphal."*

The tired column gladly marched to Imphal for a rest. The 25th Mountain Regiment distinguished itself in these operations in June and July, 1944, by its accurate fire and efficient support, and the award of the D.S.O. was made to Lieutenant-Colonel Pugh for his good handling of his regiment and for the courage and devotion to duty shown by him. Captain G. Neville, the Adjutant, was awarded the M.B.E.

Once the monsoon had broken the enemy main offensive ceased, but there was a lot of mopping up to do and therefore little rest for the troops. The Bishenpur area was full of very offensive Japanese, and when 17 Division came out of the line, 5 Indian Division (less

---

* Colonel Pugh's complete description of this operation may be read in the *Royal Artillery Journal* for July, 1946.

1 Brigade) and 11 East African Division kept the enemy on the run. Later, as will be seen, these two divisions took a leading part in the pursuit which began sooner than was expected by the troops.

Pursuit to the Chindwin

On 6th August 33 Corps was given the following tasks:
- (*a*) To pursue the enemy on the lines Imphal–Tiddim–Kalemyo–Kalewa, Tamu–Indainggyi–Kalewa, Tamu–Sittaung.
- (*b*) To occupy Sittaung.
- (*c*) To capture Kalewa and establish a bridgehead if opportunity offered.

There was thus no rest for the divisions which had been for many weeks fighting fierce and bloody battles to clear the Imphal Plain.

Certain adjustments were ordered: 4 Corps H.Q. was withdrawn to India to rest and 33 Corps took over the whole Assam front; 17 Light Division was to be withdrawn to refit, and 23 Indian Division was to pull out for rest, being relieved by 11 East African Division. Two brigades of 2 British Division were temporarily in the line; its 5 Brigade occupied Tamu on 4th August.

On the right, 17 Division, by the time it was halted, had pursued the enemy some twenty miles down the road to Tiddim. To 5 Indian Division was allotted the task of driving the enemy back on Tiddim, making contact on the way with the Lushai Irregulars, capturing the bastion of Kennedy Peak, and then to concentrate at Kalemyo, where 11 East African Division would arrive via the Kabaw valley on its way to form a bridgehead at Kalewa.

In the early days of August, 5 Division [less a section of 2nd (Derajat) Battery detached to 11 E.A. Division] passed through 17 Division, 9 Brigade leading, and met strong opposition at once. The brigade had under command 12th (Poonch) Battery (Major Howard) as well as 28th Field Regiment and a squadron of tanks. Day by day it approached a little nearer its objective, seldom without opposition by day and night, and the mountain guns were in great demand for engaging targets of opportunity. The daily downpour of rain continued, and the mud was knee deep, but the troops continued their attacks with the greatest tenacity. Malaria was always present, typhus soon showed itself, and the difficulties of evacuating sick and wounded were enormous.

The Lushai Brigade joined about M.S. 70, coming under command of 5 Division, and continuing the extremely useful work of harassing communications; M.S. 75 was on the Indian frontier, and at M.S. 83

the 161 Brigade with 20th Battery (Major P. Kendall) passed through to lead the advance. The 9 Brigade had covered two miles a day, with light battle casualties, but with heavy losses due to sickness.

The mountain battery with the forward brigade had to be made up to an all-pack basis, which entailed the use of drivers and mules from other batteries in the regiment, as well as from the 23rd Regiment. This was very hard on the drivers and mules, who in many cases had recently been out on an operation with their own batteries. The 161 Brigade with its supporting tanks found itself confronted with a mountain-side over which the only road spiralled up sharply 2,000 feet—the "Ladder"—a climb which only four-wheel-drive lorries could negotiate, and that with the greatest difficulty in the mud. The outside edge of the track slipped away under the wheels and landslides were common. Farther on, descents gave as much, or more, trouble, and this state of the road persisted until the end of September. As the L. of C. stretched out longer and longer, the division was put on air supply, although the available aircraft were only sufficient for a daily drop of 70 tons, less than half the normal daily supply for a division. The greatest economy had to be used; for example, if extra gun ammunition was ordered up, rations had to go short—but they sufficed and the troops won through. Dropping zones in the hills were few and far between and in every case dangerously small.

An opposed crossing was expected at the Manipur river (M.S. 126) and 123 Brigade, with which was the 11th Battery, was sent through the jungle on the eastern flank from Shuganu, and after much arduous marching with little opposition established a position near Tongzang, securing the crossing. Thanks to the energy and skill of the field companies, the crossing was made by 161 Brigade on rafts with few casualties notwithstanding spates and a very strong current.

Some of the services were sent back to Imphal to ease the administrative situation, now entirely dependent on the air; and it being now the end of September, 123 Brigade set out for Tiddim. The place was strongly held and the front was mined; the last seven miles of the road spiralled up in a series of some forty hairpin bends, a formidable obstacle known as the "Chocolate staircase." The 1/17 Dogras, supported by air-strikes and the mountain guns, established a roadblock near the top of the staircase, and after two days of terrific bombardment by the R.A.F. the troops pushed through and found Tiddim unoccupied. Kennedy Peak (8,800 feet) lay twelve miles ahead, dominating the countryside, and very difficult of access.

Ten miles east of Tiddim the 2/1 Punjab turned south off the

Imphal–Tiddim road, making for the Peak, but it was held up by Japanese positions on the only line of advance which lay along a knife-edge ridge. Here, under the worst possible conditions of terrain and weather, despite several attempts to get through which cost many casualties, the battalion was held up for three weeks. Even the air-drops often failed owing to rain and cloud, and the troops went short of rations.

The 3/2 Punjab moved across country from Tiddim and after some fighting discovered an almost vertical path which cut in between the foremost enemy position and the Peak: the 3/9 Jats then cut the road behind the main Japanese position on the Peak. On the next attack after heavy bombing the Japanese broke and 9 Brigade was hot in pursuit (3rd November). The Carabineers' tanks joined in, and all resistance was brushed aside; Fort White, or the rubbish heap which remained on the site, was overrun without resistance.

The monsoon had come to an end by now and the ground had begun to dry up.

Invigorated by success, the division pursued the enemy swiftly and relentlessly, making touch with 11 East African Division on 12th November. The 11th and 20th Batteries took part in all the actions from Tiddim to Kalemyo, where the division concentrated. The strain on the drivers and mules, already referred to, was considerable.

Kalewa was twenty-four miles ahead, and 11 East African Division met with stiff resistance before it captured the place. By the end of November the Japanese 33 Division was beyond the Chindwin in full retreat.

On relief by 20 Division, 5 Division was flown to Jorhat for a rest, except the animals, which had to march via Tamu. The division overcame all the difficulties encountered in over fourteen months' continuous fighting in Burma, during which time it had definitely killed 1,316 Japanese for a loss of 88 of their own officers and men.

The 11 East African Division (Major-General C. C. Fowkes), which had arrived in Burma in November, 1943, and had taken over from 23 Indian Division, left Tamu in July with orders to clear the Kabaw valley and join up with 5 Division at Kalemyo. Two brigades went through the valley, a particularly unhealthy area which was sprayed with D.D.T. to keep down malaria, and 25 E.A. Brigade with the 8th Battery crossed the Chindwin at Sittaung to work down the river on both banks. With the division was also the 17th (Nowshera) Battery, relieved by the 8th after the capture of

Mawlaik by 21 E.A. Brigade, and a section of the 2nd (Derajat) Battery under Lieutenant J. S. Punia, made up to full pack establishment by drawing on the drivers and mules of other batteries in the 24th Mountain Regiment.

Supply was entirely carried out from the air and Hurri-bombers gave most of the support. On 4th October Yazagyo was captured after being defended to the last man, and Kalemyo was entered on 15th November, a few days after meeting 5 Division. The division then moved on without delay to Kalewa by the Myitha Gorge, meeting strong opposition, in which our tanks were engaged. Kalewa was reached on 2nd December and a bridgehead formed after stubborn fighting. The two brigades sent forward to extend the bridgehead were very heavily attacked, but maintained their position. Indian Sappers here performed the noteworthy feat of throwing a 1,000 foot Bailey pontoon bridge across the Chindwin in thirty-six hours.

This is only one example of the magnificent work carried out without ceasing by the Indian Engineers. The mountain batteries maintained a warm admiration in peace and war alike for the corps, formerly Bengal, Bombay and Madras Sappers and Miners, whose work was indispensable to the success of the campaigns entered upon. The British officers of Artillery and Engineers had their first military experiences at "The Shop," the then Royal Military Academy, where cadets underwent similar training before selection for commissions in the Royal Artillery or Royal Engineers. Friendships formed during their early days proved of great value on many occasions when officers found themselves serving in the same formation during their military service.

The division,* after relief by 2 British Division which had been brought up from Kohima by the end of December, was then withdrawn. The 17th Battery had already returned to Imphal and joined the newly formed 32nd Mountain Regiment.

The 20 Indian Division was close behind 11 E.A. Division, and its 32 Brigade with the 31st Battery under command crossed the Chindwin thirty miles north of Kalewa on 12th December and swung south to attack an enemy rear-guard which was blocking the advance of 2 British Division, which had crossed at Kalewa. The 2 British Division captured Ye-u on 3rd January and made contact with 19 Indian Division on 8th January at Shwebo.

The 19 Division (Major-General W. T. Rees) was part of 4 Corps,

---

* The mountain gunners were firm friends with the King's African Rifles during the above operations.

now commanded by Lieutenant-General Messervy, of which Headquarters had returned to the front and was established at Tamu. This division was largely composed of pre-war regulars and had been training in India since 1941. Its mountain regiment was the 20th (Lieutenant-Colonel C. C. M. Macleod-Carey), comprising 24th, 25th and 26th Batteries, which joined the division for the first time at Imphal on 29th October, where it took over what was left of the 29th Mountain Regiment's equipment and animals, with some remounts, and was told to expect three months for re-equipping and training.

However, in less than a fortnight orders came for 62 Brigade to be made up to an all-pack basis and to cross the Chindwin at Sittaung, directed on Pinlebu, afterwards operating towards the railway near Wuntho. The 26th Battery was hastily organized for the purpose of accompanying this column at the expense of the other two batteries, including extra ammunition mules. These two batteries were then temporarily out of action.

The 26th Battery left Imphal on 12th November entirely in M.T., stopping on the way for calibration, during which a stray round dropped in an elephant camp, causing alarm and despondency to the official in charge. The river at Sittaung was 300 yards wide with steeply shelving banks, and various methods were used for taking the mules across; *e.g.*, hauling them over attached to an endless rope, buoyed by tins; tying five abreast to a bamboo pole towed by a boat, and carrying ten at a time on a two-boat raft. The last method finished with the fewest casualties.

The 62 Brigade with 26th Battery, all in pack and supplied by air-drop, arrived at Pinlebu on 16th December after some minor clashes with the enemy, having traversed some extremely difficult country. On the 18th a patrol from 64 Brigade made contact with 36 British Division at Rail Indaw.

The 19 Indian Division less 62 Brigade group was ordered to speed up the crossing of the Chindwin, and the divisional artillery (less 26th Battery) was detailed to reconstruct a road between two fords; so all available gunners set to work with a will. In addition to the mountain gunners, personnel of 115 Field Regiment, R.A., 4 Indian Field Regiment, I.A., and 33 Anti-tank Regiment, R.A., were thus employed, and provided a road capable of taking tractors with guns or loaded trailers eight days ahead of schedule. At Nantthanyit, the end of the road, a ferry was established over which the divisional artillery crossed without difficulty. It found going very difficult once across the river; petrol was not in too good supply and the remounts, which were not yet hardened to daily marches

3.7-inch Howitzer in Action in Burma in 1944-5

3.7-inch Howitzer towed by a Jeep: Burma, 1945

Bahut-i-Tagra—Reunion of Veterans: Ambala, 1933

Bikanir Camel Battery with 2.75-inch Mountain Gun

of twenty miles, began to show signs of exhaustion. Eventually 25th Battery was given all the sound mules of 24th Battery and the latter became a mechanized unit, towing its guns behind water trucks.

The country between Wuntho and Shwebo was cleared rapidly with little opposition: 25th Battery took heavy toll of a party escaping from a road-block five miles south of Shwebo. The division concentrated at Shwebo.

N.C.A.C.

The 36 British Division had been fighting its way south down the railway corridor since August against very stiff Japanese resistance in torrential rain and mud to join up with 4 Corps. Contact with this division was the beginning of a continuous front across northeastern Burma, of which the American General D. I. Sultan was now in command with Chinese and American troops and the 36 British Division. The Ledo road (opened 27th January) was carrying traffic to Northern Combat Area Command, as Sultan's armies were designated, and soon afterwards was able to take some of the British L. of C. work.

The 12th (Poonch), 17th (Nowshera) and 28th Indian Batteries formed the 32nd Indian Mountain Regiment of the 36 British Divisional Artillery.

Reorganization

Chain of Command: On 12th November all the allied troops were placed under the command of Lieutenant-General Sir Oliver Leese, with the new title of C.-in-C., Allied Land Forces, South-East Asia. His advanced headquarters were at Barrackpore. The Fourteenth Army under Lieutenant-General Sir William Slim consisted of 4 Indian Corps and 33 Indian Corps. 15 Indian Corps (Lieutenant-General Sir A. F. P. Christison) was directly under A.L.F.S.E.A. whilst engaged in operations in Arakan.

Adjustments had been found to be necessary in the establishments of certain formations and units: these changes were applied to all three corps during the last months of 1944.

A standard organization for an infantry division was adopted, and specialized formations, *e.g.* "Light Division," ceased to exist. The standard division consisted of three brigades of three infantry battalions each (one British and two Indian); a reconnaissance battalion; two regiments of twenty-four 25-prs. each; one 3.7-inch howitzer regiment of three mountain batteries (no longer "Light") and one anti-tank regiment equipped with 6-pr. A.T. guns and 3-inch mortars. The number of lorries was reduced and a large number of jeeps provided.

The East African and West African Divisions were not brought on to the "Standard" establishment.

The establishment of the standard mountain regiment is shown on page 271.

Other mountain regiments in Assam were re-formed to contain the following mountain batteries:

    24th (5 Division)—2nd (Derajat), 11th (Dehra Dun), 20th.
    23rd (20 Division)—3rd (Peshawar), 8th (Lahore), 31st (Jammu).
    25th (7 Division)—5th (Bombay), 23rd and Bikanir Bijey.
Each regiment had a signal section and an L.A.D. III.

At this period, too, began the formation of batteries into one-class units, involving changes which could not be carried out without disturbance.

Batteries of the 1st Indian Survey Regiment were now in the field. No. 1 Battery was attached to 2 British Division and No. 2 Battery to 11 E.A. Division.

7. Advance to and Crossing of the Irrawaddy, 1945

As already stated, early in January, 1945, Ye-u and Shwebo, which are both situated in the more open and flat country of the dry belt north of Mandalay, were occupied by 2 British and 19 Indian Divisions. Here our superiority over the enemy in armour and mobility would be bound to have effect, but it soon became clear that the Japanese intended to give up the dry belt and to take up a position south-west of Mandalay on both banks of the Irrawaddy river.

Lieutenant-General Slim's intention was to cross the river and to fight the major battle at the end of February in the plains around Mandalay and the low hills at Meiktila. He decided to make a crossing north of Mandalay to draw the bulk of the enemy's forces, whilst making his main crossing south of the enemy concentrations guarding the river below Mandalay.

The air transport situation was poor, and all available planes were likely to be required for the supply of the advancing troops.

The Fourteenth Army plan was to move 4 Corps from the left to the right flank by way of the Gangaw valley, seize a bridgehead on the Irrawaddy near Pakokku, and from there strike south-east with a mechanized and armoured force at Meiktila and Thazi. These were key points on the enemy road and rail line of communications from Mandalay to the south.

Before 4 Corps carried out its main attack on Meiktila, 33 Corps was to secure a bridgehead over the Irrawaddy to the north of Mandalay in order to mislead the enemy into thinking that this crossing was preparatory to our main advance coming from the north; whereas it was intended that the main blow should be made from the southwest of Mandalay at the same time as 4 Corps struck at Meiktila, farther south still. Both corps were then to exploit their success by moving quickly south.

The Fourteenth Army was regrouped on 26th December as follows:

33 Corps:
    2 British Division.
    19 Indian Division (from 4 Corps).
    20 Indian Division.
    168 Indian Inf. Brigade (from 4 Corps).
    254 Indian Tank Brigade.

4 Corps:
    7 Indian Division.
    17 Indian Division (to be available in February).
    Lushai Brigade (from 33 Corps).
    255 Indian Tank Brigade.
    11 Cavalry Regiment.
    28 E.A. Brigade.

Note.—5 Indian Division was in Army reserve at Jorhat. 5 and 17 Divisions were being reorganized; two brigade groups were motorized and one brigade group made air-transportable in the new establishment of these divisions. The mountain regiments of these divisions (24th and 21st) were trained to act on a fully mechanized basis or on an air basis (without any transport). Carriages with pneumatic tyres were issued to the batteries.

By January, 1945, the Japanese 15 Army had been pursued without respite since the end of June, and our Fourteenth Army was across the Chindwin in considerable strength.

The tasks allotted to 4 Corps were:
    (*a*) To capture Pakokku.
    (*b*) To seize a bridgehead across the Irrawaddy.
    (*c*) To capture Meiktila and adjoining airfields.
    (*d*) To be prepared to advance southwards.

The tasks allotted to 33 Corps were:

(a) To capture or construct airfields in the Ye-u–Shwebo areas.
(b) To capture Monywa.
(c) To capture Mandalay.
(d) To be prepared to advance on the axis Mandalay–Nyaunglebin.

Temporary air-strips were to be constructed every fifty miles. Formations were to move by march route.

The success of this plan could only be secured by the maintenance of complete secrecy, and by the provision of effective air cover over the area of the advance. Our administrative resources, however, would be strained to the utmost: petrol and ammunition had to be carried with the corps, and in the first place the 150 miles of road from Kalemyo to Pakokku had to be improved to allow two divisions and a tank brigade to pass down it.

19 Division, 33 Corps

From Shwebo 98 and 62 Brigades of 19 Indian Division fought their way eastwards towards the Irrawaddy, clearing up many pockets of the enemy on the way. Strong resistance was met at Kabwet, on the west bank of the river. Enemy aeroplanes were also active, but with little effect. The 4/6 G.R. with 26th Battery under command, after fighting all day on 9th January, captured late in the afternoon the forward enemy bunkers as the result of a fire plan prepared by Major Stocker of the mountain battery which included the infantry mortars. A fierce counter-attack ensued which was beaten off, and next morning the village was found unoccupied. Later on the enemy returned to the spot and caused a lot of trouble.

After sending reconnaissance patrols across the river, here 6C0 yards wide, a gap was found between two enemy formations opposite the village of Kyaukmyaung, forty-six miles north of Mandalay.

On 14th January the 1/15 Punjab made a surprise landing on the east bank and, followed by the 5/10 Baluch, established a bridgehead which was immediately extended. The enemy's reaction was quick and strong, with artillery concentrations and infantry attacks, but our troops refused to be dislodged and slowly widened the bridgehead. The country consisted of thick bamboo jungle which hindered movement, but a feature, christened Pear Hill from its shape, on the river bank two miles down-stream was quickly seized and provided good observation for the artillery. Another feature, Minban Taung, a ridge three miles inland, was denied to the enemy, and O.Ps. were established on both these vital positions.

The 19 Divisional Artillery had been considerably strengthened for the operation by the addition of a medium (5.5-inch) battery, a H.A.A. battery, a detachment of an Air O.P. squadron, a counter-battery team and 2 Battery of 1 Indian Survey Regiment. The 33 Anti-Tank Regiment dropped its 6-prs. and thereafter operated as three independent mortar batteries. The enemy artillery, at least fifty guns drawn from four divisions, continued to shell the bridge-head for days, causing heavy casualties. Once the sound ranging troop was in position, more success was achieved in fixing hostile batteries, and the flash spotters at some risk from exposed positions added to the numbers. Havildar Unwar Hussain of the Survey Battery showed great courage and a fine sense of duty by staying under heavy fire until a direct hit demolished his instrument and severely wounded him. Air photographs were soon available, and the close liaison which existed between the gunners and the air pilots restricted the Japanese artillery activities.

The divisional artillery manned twenty O.Ps., notwithstanding the difficulty of maintaining communications; *e.g.*, telephone cables lay on the river-bed and required frequent renewal, and wireless batteries could not be charged in forward positions. There was a C.R.A.'s representative permanently on Pear Hill as well as one with Infantry Brigade H.Q. Elaborate arrangements were made to concentrate when necessary the fire of the four groups of guns detailed for D.F., one group in each of the four defended localities. The mountain guns were ill-adapted to such procedure which entailed big switches, but when a determined attack was made on the night of the 30th, all went well and the attack was repulsed. Ammunition of the larger types of guns was now rationed.

Minban Taung was held for a fortnight by two companies of 1/6 Gurkha Rifles against repeated attacks, and on 3rd February a strong force moving in that direction had to undergo heavy shelling by the enemy. While the shelling was at its height, Lance-Naik Nur Hussain of the 25th Mountain Battery, a signaller in an O.P. party, helped the wounded lying in the open with utter disregard for his own safety, and made numerous trips across the open to take water to the wounded, adjusting their bandages in a very exposed place.

The maintenance of so many O.Ps. was a drain on all the artillery officers available, and several officers of 20th Mountain Regiment were noted for their good work. Major Kelly earned a large share of the credit for the defence of Pear Hill during the many attacks made on it by his energetic organization and control of the D.F. for that locality. By the end of the first week in February, enemy attacks lessened and preparations began for a break-out.

At Thaibeikkyin, twenty miles north of Kyaukmyaung, 98 Brigade had established a small bridgehead as a diversion. It was strongly opposed, but held on and endured a great deal of shelling. On the 24th a section of the 5.5-inch guns of the medium battery successfully engaged bunkers with open sights across the river (1,000 yards). During these operations the enemy suffered a great many casualties, and began to thin out, so that on 3rd February 98 Brigade, less the battalion at Thaibeikkyin, began to move towards the bridgehead at Kyaukmyaung as part of the preparations for a break-out. On the west bank Kabwet, which lay half-way between the two bridgeheads, contained a large pocket of Japs which took three days to reduce.

The 20th Mountain Regiment had been in action during the operations two miles west of Kyaukmyaung, where there was an opportunity to redistribute the mules, as a good many of the re-mounts were still soft. The 25th and 26th Batteries were, at the moment, able to move in pack with only a limited scale of ammunition, and the 24th in mule draught only. The regiment moved to Shwedaik, to which place the ferry was shifted, and joined in the advance, crossing the river on 12th February.

The advance opened with saturation bombing, and the division supported by tanks undertook a series of minor operations to clear the enemy away from the east bank. The mountain regiment later moved with 64 Brigade southwards along the bank of the Irrawaddy, after clearing Singu (page 385).

Major Kelly and Major Dowson were each awarded the M.C. for their good work in the operations at the bridgehead.

The passage of 19 Indian Division in two places in January, threatening Mandalay from the north, diverted the enemy's attention and kept him from reinforcing the troops guarding the main crossings: those of 33 Corps (20 Division) at Allagappa, west of Mandalay, and 4 Corps (7 Division) at Nyaungu, west of Pakokku, which were made almost simultaneously, 12th and 13th February.

20 Division, 33 Corps

After the passage of the Chindwin early in December, 20 Division moved over very difficult country and in January captured Budalin, an important Japanese communication centre. It continued its advance with three brigades up, and on 22nd January, after three days' fierce fighting, Monywa, an important river port, was captured by 32 Brigade, supported by 3rd (Peshawar) Battery.

In the centre 80 Brigade occupied Wadan, and Myinmu on the Irrawaddy fell to 100 Brigade after bitter hand-to-hand fighting.

Magnificent air support was a feature of this successful advance. The 23rd Mountain Regiment was in action here under regimental control for the first and only time.*

The crossing was made at Allagappa, where the river is 1,500 yards wide, by 100 Brigade by night, diversionary attacks being made by 32 Brigade. The operation was supported by a corps artillery concentration, one of the few attempted during the campaign. There was no hitch and within twenty-four hours a bridgehead six miles wide and two miles deep had been developed. However, the Japanese began a series of attacks which confined 20 Division to this bridgehead for some time; it was an all-out effort, but held by the division, which passed to the offensive on the 16th and linked up with the bridgehead of 2 British Division, ten miles east, on 2nd March.

This advance was strongly opposed and the division had to fight every inch of the way. Amongst many tough fights the following has been recorded: On the night 16th/17th February, near Mingyan, 8th and 31st Mountain Batteries with a troop of artillery mortars were supporting a British infantry battalion on the river bank, Captain C. J. S. Burne of 31st Battery being F.O.O. with the forward infantry elements. A suicide attack was launched at 0300 hours with accurate artillery support. It found the British Brens jammed with sand. Fortunately a M.M.G. manned by a detachment of 9 Jats remained in action on the left, but the front was forced back into trenches in rear of the command post. The enemy then set fire to the elephant grass, but the wind was wrong and D.F. went on till daybreak when the situation could be diagnosed. The left flank was open and plenty of Japs were still inside the original infantry perimeter, so Captain Burne made a quick decision and took charge of the affair. Thanks to his cool-headed gallantry, the line held and on the arrival of reinforcements at 0800 hours the original perimeter was made good. The garrison had ten killed and fifteen wounded, and Captain Burne received an immediate award of a "thoroughly well-earned D.S.O.," in the words of the divisional commander.

7 *Division*, 4 *Corps*

7 Indian Division selected three crossing-places at Nyaungu, south of Pakokku. 33 Indian Infantry Brigade was the brigade selected as the assault brigade. The first assault wave consisted of 2 South Lancashire, and the crossing entailed a two-mile paddle in

---

* From this time on the regiment was on a mechanized basis and the subadar-major followed in rear of the division with the animals. The 3rd and 8th Batteries went into pack when the monsoon broke in June.

the darkness. The leading company crossed successfully and consolidated their position on the crest of the cliffs on the opposite side of the Irrawaddy without a shot being fired. The remainder of the battalion was caught in mid-stream in daylight, due to the failure of outboard engines on the assault craft. Very severe casualties were sustained and the battalion was unable to reinforce the leading company, which was now under heavy attack.

4/15 Punjab were then ordered to cross and storm the town of Nyaungu. This operation was brilliantly carried out and Nyaungu captured without the heavy casualties expected. By midday the bridgehead on the eastern bank was secured, and the remainder of the division, with tanks, crossed in daylight practically unopposed. Pagan was captured by 33 Brigade on the 15th, and 114 Brigade cleared the west bank and entered Pakkoku on 18th February. Whilst 7 Division was holding off a Japanese attack on the south of the bridgehead, 17 Indian Division (less 99 Brigade) and 255 Indian Tank Brigade were crossing into the bridgehead, which they reached on the 20th (page 387).

On 28th February a small mixed force called "Puffcol" was formed under Lieutenant-Colonel Pugh, consisting of R.H.Q., 25th Mountain Regiment, two companies of infantry, a M.G. platoon, a troop of armoured cars and the Bikanir Bijey Battery*. Its orders were to locate and destroy the enemy, especially in the Popa area, and protect the flank of the division. For three weeks this force manœuvred over a very wide stretch of country, destroying and harassing the enemy, inflicting many casualties and gaining useful information. Lieutenant-Colonel Pugh gained great commendation for his energy, leadership and personal gallantry. The force was called "Kingcol" after Lieutenant-Colonel Pugh was promoted to command 33 Indian Infantry Brigade.

Major G. A. Rowley-Conway, from Second-in-Command, took over the 25th Mountain Regiment.

The 5th (Bombay) Battery was attached to a similar force—Westcol—during March.

4 *Corps*

The Lushai Brigade, with 5th (Bombay) Battery under command, captured Gangaw on 12th January after a month's serious fighting, with very strong support from the air. The brigade was then relieved by 28 East African Brigade, which had followed it down the Gangaw valley, and on 13th February this brigade captured Seikpu on the

---

* For this operation Bikanir Bijey Battery mechanized itself by carrying the guns in pieces in their vehicles.

west bank of the Irrawaddy, where its appearance was well timed to draw off strong enemy forces from the crossings.

A strong enemy counter-attack forced the brigade on to the defensive in the Letse box, but after reinforcements by a battalion of 7 Division and 23rd Indian Mountain Battery it fought its way out and contributed to the safety of the Nyaungu bridgehead. An assault on the actual bridgehead was easily driven off by 114 Brigade,* and 89 Indian Brigade routed an enemy force at Singu to the south of it. 7 Division had thus kept open the bridgehead for reinforcing troops to pass through; among them the animal party of 25th Mountain Regiment crossed on the 24th.

33 Corps

2 British Division crossed at Nguzun, ten miles east of Allagappa, on the night 24th/25th February. Here the moon was nearly full and the crossings were opposed, but the Camerons stormed up the steep bank under heavy fire and established a bridgehead. The division would not be denied, and by the 26th two brigades and a squadron of tanks were in possession of a bridgehead five miles deep. The third brigade crossed when 268 Indian Infantry Brigade arrived to fill the gap between the division and 20 Division. The latter division was the more heavily attacked, and after joining the two bridgeheads, 2 British Division began its break-out on 7th March.

By 17th March 5 Brigade captured Ava fort, liquidating a stubborn defence, and by the 21st the division had linked up with 19 Indian Division. The advance of both divisions continued, 2 British now moving to the south-west, and after clearing the area Myitnge–Myingyan linked up with 268 Infantry Brigade.

The Japanese armies had failed to hold the Fourteenth Army in the Irrawaddy valley. At the end of March the Burma Defence Army (page 407) turned against its masters, and on joining the Allies was renamed the Burma National Army.

The 2 British Division was selected to return to India, and after a stubborn fight at Mount Popa was flown back by 25th April.

20 Division, 33 Corps

On 12th February the mountain regiment and other artillery crossed the river and the division lost no time pushing out to the south and east. For some days the divisional artillery had to deal with a zone of 180°, and many minor operations took place before the division got clear of Singu (five miles south), to which place the

---
* The Bikanir Battery recorded a memorable direct hit on four boat-loads of Japanese troops in the act of landing, destroying the lot.

bridgehead was shifted. It was noted that a company commander of 2 R. Berks one day used the cardinal point method to put 26th Battery on to a Japanese bunker and a direct hit was obtained at the fifth round. The Air O.P. was of immense value passing up-to-date information to the C.R.A. and regiments; in thirty days' fighting the pilot, Captain McMath, was in the air for 120 hours.

The Japanese could not stand up against the division's pressure once the advance was well started, and they began to retreat in disorder, small parties of them being overrun everywhere. The speed and determination of the advance brooked no opposition from the Japanese 15th and 53rd Divisions, which completely failed to stop it.

19 Division had passed through Madaya before the enemy had time to occupy his defensive positions there, and on 9th March the division less 62 Brigade had closed up to the outskirts of Mandalay. On 7th March the Mountain Regiment had come under command of 62 Brigade, which was preparing an all-pack expedition to Maymyo; this place was occupied with little resistance on the 11th, cutting the enemy's communications between Mandalay and his forces facing N.C.A. Command.

The route selected was via Kyun-Bin to Taunggaung, from which place the column was to go over the hills to the east to enter Maymyo from the north-west: there was no track, the climb was 3,000 feet and the gradient in places was as much as a loaded mule could manage. Only 40 rounds could be carried for each mountain gun in pack, and the ration mules and drivers found their work laborious as the day's air supply drop was at the tail of the column. Some elephants were "entertained" to help with this problem. Wireless communication with the division failed while the column was in the hills, but an Air O.P. flew over and took a message.

The advanced guard, 4/6 Gurkhas with 24th Battery in support, moved half a day's march ahead of the column. This battalion, with great enthusiasm to reach Maymyo but forgetting the mules of the mountain battery, went ahead at a great pace and reached its destination at dawn on the 10th. The battery did its best to climb an unknown pathless hill in the dark to catch up with the battalion; this led to a good many casualties among the mules; but one section was in action in Maymyo by 0900 hours on the 10th. The Brigade column arrived the next morning, and the regiment came into action about 1,000 yards north of the Railway Quarters; but there was little opposition, and the troops camped near the Racecourse until the 17th, when a move was made to rejoin the division in completing the capture of Mandalay.

Later in the campaign the 4/6 Gurkhas presented the 24th Mountain Battery with a Japanese officer's sword in memory of Maymyo.

Capture of Meiktila and Mandalay, and clearance of Mandalay Plain

Meiktila was the advanced supply base for the Japanese forces in Burma and the site of their principal airfields.

17 *Division*, 4 *Corps*

On the 21st February a mechanized and armoured column composed of 48 Brigade, with tanks, broke out of the Nyaungu bridgehead, but was temporarily held up by deep nullahs after travelling fifteen miles to the east, where 63 Brigade and 255 Indian Tank Brigade joined it. The advance continued in two columns which reached Taungtha on the 24th after overcoming desperate resistance and clearing many minefields. By 0900 hours on the 26th Thabutkon airfield was captured intact, and the fly-in from Palel of the air-transportable brigade group began next morning. This consisted of 99 Infantry Brigade; 21st Mountain Regiment less animals; A/T Battery with mortars, and a Field Company. The Mountain Regiment (Lieutenant-Colonel J. B. Chaplin) arrived on 1st and 2nd March, requiring forty-eight aircraft.

Although taken by surprise, the enemy reacted very quickly and recaptured Taungtha, which commanded the road from Nyaungu to Meiktila.

Major-General Kasuya had been preparing Meiktila for defence for some time and had assembled 14,000 men in and around the town, ordered to fight to the last man. The approaches from the west and south were narrowed by large lakes, and thus easily covered by artillery, and the country in the vicinity was broken by nullahs and irrigation cuts, making the deployment of armour difficult.

At dawn on 28th February the attack went in from four directions and by nightfall the position was surrounded. It took three days and nights of savage hand-to-hand fighting to clear the town, which had to be done bunker by bunker and house by house. No quarter was given, and the Japanese afterwards acknowledged they had had 5,000 killed and 47 wounded prisoners taken in the battle. The few remaining Japanese jumped into a lake and were drowned or killed on the morning of 4th March. The 17 Division was on top of its form. Mobile columns of infantry, guns and armour spread out into the open country without delay to attack enemy reinforcements arriving too late to save the town.

Six enemy brigades with tanks and artillery had been collected for the seizure of our bridgehead at Nyaungu in order to cut our L. of C., but these formations were caught and defeated before a combined attack could develop and the bridgehead remained secure.

On 8th March 6th (Jacob's) Battery was with a mixed force under Lieutenant-Colonel Chaplin in the Pyawbwe direction which killed fifteen Japs; on the 11th the Kohat Battery (Major J. O. S. Janson) was in support of 9 Border Regiment at Yindaw when the position was rushed and overrun, but the enemy was quickly turned out with the bayonet, suffering many casualties. The attack went on all night and twenty-seven dead Japs were counted afterwards.

The mountain batteries had many opportunities during these minor operations and acquitted themselves well; varieties of M.T. were provided from what was available. The 37th Battery (Major N. Rawlins) went with a force against Thedaw using the following vehicles: one jeep (carrying 100 rounds a gun, two days' rations, water and petrol), seven F.A. tractors and four 15-cwt. trucks. Tank transporters were very popular when they could be obtained. The 17 Division was short of 1,000 "thin-skinned" vehicles owing to the road being blocked at Taungtha; the road was not cleared until the end of the month.

All the time that these clearing-up operations were going on the Japanese made many heavy attacks on Meiktila; for example, an attack on 48 Brigade perimeter on 22nd/23rd March lasted all night and 195 enemy dead were counted afterwards. The artillery and mortars were credited with a large proportion of these casualties, and 21st Mountain Regiment was specially mentioned by the division for its very accurate and effective defensive fire placed within fifty yards of our wire.

On 18th March Meiktila main airfield was recaptured by the enemy, and for some days stores had to be air-dropped; the airfield was occupied by day only, and that not without interruption. A F.O.O. (Lieutenant Spencer) was going out in a jeep to his usual O.P. on the parapet of a shelter in the dispersal area when he was engaged over open sights by an enemy infantry gun just below his O.P. Speed and evasive action down the runway got him clear.

The Meiktila operations were notable as being the first occasion on which our mechanized and armoured superiority was utilized on a large scale supported by heavy air attacks, and the result was devastating: the Japanese were completely bewildered and overwhelmed.

The "Cab Rank" method of air support was employed for the

first time in Burma, squadrons remaining over the operations area and being directed on to fleeting targets from ground control centres. These were known as Visual Control Posts (V.C.Ps.) at Brigade H.Q., and contained an Army and Air Force officer. Instantaneous air-strikes were thus provided during rapidly moving operations, and the system was a great success.

The napalm (jellied petrol) bomb was now in use on this front.

The next day the enemy captured the air-strip and it was only partly regained after a week's heavy fighting. A very heavy attack was made on the "Gunner" box on the 23rd, during which the 1/7 G.R. distinguished itself, 218 dead being counted on its front. Lieutenant Mallinson of 6th Battery was responsible for very accurate D.F. close in which caused many enemy casualties on this and the following days.

5 *Division*, 4 *Corps*

The 5 Indian Division had been sent to reinforce, and 9 Brigade (air transportable) was flown to Meiktila from Jorhat, completing its move on 17th March. The air-strip was under artillery fire when the brigade arrived, but the American pilots were undeterred and no sortie turned back.

The two mechanized brigades started on 5th March and covered the 700 miles from Jorhat to Nyaungu in ten days, experiencing excessive heat and dust on the way. The 24th Mountain Regiment, strength 19 officers, 9 V.C.Os., 565 other ranks, left Jorhat by road on 21st and arrived at Meiktila on 4th April. During this journey a gun axle broke; it was one fitted with roller bearings, a pattern afterwards replaced.

The brigades travelling by road could not get through to Meiktila until Taungtha had been recaptured. The 161 Brigade put in a joint attack on that position with 63 Brigade of 17 Division. It was successful, and 5 Division arrived complete in Meiktila on 31st March.

After a few days spent in mopping up, the advance to the south was continued, 17 Division leading.

During the first days of April, 21st Mountain Regiment supported 99 Infantry Brigade clearing villages in the vicinity of Meiktila and mopping up; the 3rd April was notable for much firing on a continuous stream of targets from O.Ps. and Air O.Ps. and in divisional concentrations. On the 6th Captain Hadfield's patrol ran into a party of Japs near 6th (Jacob's) gun position and was responsible for killing an officer in possession of operation orders, for which he received congratulations from divisional headquarters.

Strong opposition was met at Yindaw, and 99 Brigade was sent to by-pass the position by moving off the road eastwards. What might have been a quiet night in R.H.Q. on the 7th was disturbed by the presence of a cobra in one of the signallers' trenches.

The enemy was still holding out on the 8th when 5 Division, which was following down the road, took over the operation, wiping out the garrison and capturing three guns.

On the 8th 17 Division continued its advance, which included a sharp action during which the Royal (Kohat) Battery fought a duel with a Japanese mountain gun; the O.P. staff collected the trophy, which later found its way to the M.A.T.C.

On the 9th, 17 Division attacked Pyawbwe, twenty miles from Meiktila. With one of the columns the 21st Mountain Regiment was in support of 1 Sikh L.I. and 1/3 G.R., searching a large area of broken ground near point 733. Evicted parties of the enemy had to escape across the open plain—a gunner's dream of G.F. targets. This lasted until the following evening, when 99 Brigade attacked a strongly held position at the Waterworks, and the mountain guns and mortars were very effective in their support.

Capture of Mandalay

19 *Division*, 33 *Corps*

The division, less 62 Brigade and 20th Mountain Regiment, worked its way round the outskirts, meeting opposition everywhere which intensified on Mandalay Hill, a prominent feature dominating the city. The hill was captured after twenty-four hours of bitter hand-to-hand fighting, the enemy fighting to the end; and there were then three days of street fighting before the city was cleared.

Fort Dufferin was then invested; an ancient type of defence which withstood for some days modern and scientific forms of attack. It is enclosed by a 20-foot wall backed with an earth embankment 72 feet thick at the base and surrounded by an 80-yard wide moat. A gallant attempt by 98 Brigade to storm the fort failed, and the medium artillery (5.5-inch and 6-inch) continued to hammer away at the north and west walls. A low charge had to be used to burst the shell before it had gone right through the wall, and fuze 231 was used throughout. The gaps were covered by M.M.Gs. and L.M.Gs., and the rubble piled up in the gaps to make a considerable obstacle.

Escape routes all round were blocked as far as possible, but the enemy began to filter away. On the 18th, 62 Brigade arrived from Maymyo with the Mountain Regiment.

A white flag was shown on the 20th and our infantry, on entering, found the fort evacuated: an immense amount of military stores and eight tanks were left behind.

On the 21st at Tomokso, during the large-scale mopping up of the district, the mountain regiment and 4 Indian Field Regiment supported an attack by 2 R. Berks. on a defended position which did not meet with success, but a clearance of the whole area was in hand, and by the 24th the punishment was complete and there was no enemy left.

19 Division had a very short rest after its brilliant series of operations before taking up its new role, which developed into ceaseless mopping up, entailing much fighting.

20 *Division*, 33 *Corps*

The 20 Division's advance continued eastwards against steadily increasing resistance. By the 23rd March 80 and 32 Brigades were held up at Kyaukse, which took a week's fighting to capture. Its loss was a very severe blow to the enemy.

During this period 100 Brigade (less one battalion) and two armoured car regiments made a daring raid against enemy communications to the south. Moving with great speed, this column captured three important places in three days, and then turned north to rejoin the division. The enemy's system of command was disrupted over a wide area at a most inconvenient time to him.

By this time 20 Division had killed over 3,000 Japanese and captured 50 guns.

7 *Division*, 33 *Corps*

The 7 Division continued to operate on both banks of the Irrawaddy on the western flank of the Corps. At the end of March Lanywa on the west bank was occupied, the first oilfield to be recaptured. On the east bank steady progress was made southwards and eastwards; 33 Brigade with tank support forced an entry into Myingyan on 21st March, clearing the town by the 23rd. This gain opened the Chindwin as a supply route from Kalewa, and the railway to Meiktila could now be used.

N.C.A.C.

36 British Division (less 29 Brigade but including 26 Indian Infantry Brigade) was moving down the Railway Corridor on Mongmit during January and found the crossing of the Shweli river strongly opposed. A second attempt succeeded in getting the division across, and Myitson fell on 9th February, but the advance

encountered very stiff resistance and flamethrowers were used by the enemy in a counter-attack. A very spirited counter-attack by the brigade restored the situation at a time of stress, and Mongmit was captured on 9th March. 29 Brigade moved from Nabu to the westward on 18th February and co-operated. The division reached Mogok on 20th and moved forty-five miles south of that place to Kyaukme. Here it came under command of Fourteenth Army. 36 British Division's Mountain Regiment, the 32nd, comprised 12th (Poonch), 17th (Nowshera) and 28th Batteries, and had been formed at Imphal. The 12th Battery (Major A. B. Howard) left that place on 1st February and carried out a very rapid march of 415 miles to join its division, reaching the Shweli river on 7th March. The Chindwin was crossed on bamboo rafts and the Irrawaddy by motor ferry.

Its first action was at Mongmit in support of the 1/1 Gurkhas; 29 Brigade moved in from the west in a combined attack, and the enemy evacuated during the night. The next stop was at Mogok, famous for its ruby mines.

By now some of the mules were becoming footsore after their long march, as they had to move on hard roads from Mongmit and there had not been time to shoe them. The men's boots had in many cases worn through the soles, and some men had to be carried on officers' chargers.

N.C.A. Command operations now ceased on this front and 36 Division was directed on Kyaukme, making contact with the Chinese on the Burma Road, afterwards coming under Fourteenth Army. Its role was to control operations in the Maymyo–Mandalay–Ava area.

The 12th (Poonch) Battery went next to Maymyo and camped near the burnt-out club; the former battery lines were at this time a D.P. camp. Here the less fit battery mules were exchanged for fit mules from 28th Battery.

Minor mopping-up operations continued; the enemy had to be driven out of Kalaw, for which purpose 29 and 72 British Infantry Brigades attacked from different directions, 12th Battery in support of 72 Brigade. On the way an air-strike was asked for, and took place on time, but on to the battery position which fortunately was sheltered by a cliff. The doctor's bedding was set on fire, this being the only damage reported.

The Jap position was on a steep-sided rocky knob which dominated the approaches, and Charge 1 failed to reach the reverse slope. Jemadar Maula Dad was F.O.O. with the centre company and was engaging targets from a tree in the front line, the only possible O.P.

He was wounded three times by a sniper, but refused to leave his O.P. and continued shooting during the night. The battalion recommended him for a M.C., which was duly awarded. The enemy pulled out during the night.

An elephant was found near the battery position, but escaped, and when afterwards found refused to march.

The batteries camped at Meiktila and handed over mules to 24th Mountain Regiment pending their fly-out to Imphal, which took place early in May. The Regiment then moved by rail to Poona.

The narrative now returns to 15 Corps, which won the race to Rangoon.

8. Arakan to Rangoon, 1944-5

The disposition of 15 Corps during the 1944 monsoon was as follows:

- 25 Indian Division: In the Tunnels area covering the Maungdaw–Buthidaung road up to and including the East Tunnel.
- 26 Indian Division: One brigade in the Bawli–Goppe–Taung Bazaar area; one brigade at Taungbro and the third at Cox's Bazaar.
- 81 West African Division: Concentrated at Chiringa.

There were also some small detachments on the left flank.

During this period the 30th Indian Mountain Regiment comprised 27th, 32nd, 33rd and 34th Indian Batteries, and supported 25 Indian Division in their numerous activities, which consisted mainly of keeping the road in order and making offensive patrols to find and kill as many Japanese as possible. The welfare of the troops not at the actual front received due consideration; cinemas and reading rooms were established; sporting fixtures and competitions were encouraged, and most of the units were accommodated in bashas.

Instructions to the corps were to maintain an active defence on the general line Maungdaw–Tunnels area–Taung Bazaar and to prepare to capture Akyab by an advance starting early in the next dry season.

Moves on an important scale were not carried out until September, when 25 Division firmly established itself along the main spine of the Mayu range. Two commanding positions (named "Lion" and "Tiger") three or four miles south of the Tunnels road were captured after a stiff fight, previous to which the 34th Battery ran a single howitzer to the top of a high peak and pounded "Tiger" for several days over open sights with excellent results.

A plan for the recapture of Rangoon by combined sea-air operations had perforce to be cancelled owing to the shortage of landing-craft, which could not be spared from other theatres of war, and the intention of squeezing the enemy armies between a force from the south and the Fourteenth Army coming down from the north could not be implemented. The new general idea was that the Fourteenth Army would concentrate on driving the Japanese out of Burma, and that 15 Corps would operate in Arakan parallel with and in support of the Fourteenth Army by clearing Arakan and capturing Akyab.

At the end of September, therefore, 15 Corps was ordered to secure the Chittagong–Cox's Bazaar area to make sure of the landing grounds, and to make good the estuary of the Naf* river as a base for light coastal forces and landing-craft; also to carry out reconnaissance, bombardments and raids along the whole Arakan coast, and to exploit any withdrawal of the Japanese forces.

At this time the reorganization of formations and units was carried out as described for the Fourteenth Army (page 377), except that each Indian infantry brigade in 15 Corps possessed its own animal transport company (formerly these companies were pooled under corps control). This entailed training of mule drivers and the loss of some M.T. On being reduced to a three-battery regiment, the 30th Mountain Regiment shed the 34th Battery, and this battery with 19th (Maymyo), which had had much hard work in Assam, formed the 33rd Indian Mountain Regiment, commanded by Lieutenant-Colonel R. Ellis. The 33rd Regiment H.Q. was incomplete and the batteries were generally under command of infantry formations of 25 Indian Division, to which the regiment was allotted. The 34th Battery (Major A. Mackenzie) joined the division in September, and the 19th (Major S. T. Clarke, M.C.), after a long journey by road, rail and river, from 7 Division at Imphal, joined it two months later.

The 43rd Survey Battery of 2nd Survey Regiment, Royal Artillery, joined 15 Corps troops in October, followed by 44th Survey Battery in January, 1945. They were allotted to 25 and 26 Divisions respectively.

On 6th October a strong raid was made on Goppe Bazaar, but was beaten off by 26 Division with great slaughter of the enemy; 400 bodies were found. Major Chamberlain of the 27th Battery, under point-blank range from enemy small arms, fired infantry mortars from his O.P. and killed thirty Japanese. The same day he

---

* The Naf river is an arm of the sea to the west of the Mayu Peninsula with an average width of over a mile, and navigable for 6,000-ton steamers as far as Maungdaw (ten miles).

twice fired concentrations from his battery at a track junction from the map, and next day patrols found forty-seven dead. Lieutenant Lowe, 27th Battery (a Canadian officer), was killed while F.O.O. with the infantry.

On the 8th an attack was made on Taung Bazaar and 33rd Battery had an opportunity to engage infantry in the open. Lieutenant Charangit Singh, a young Sikh officer, was in the O.P. and fired his battery with great effect on the enemy caught in the paddy-fields, where seventy bodies and a flag were found the next day.

At the end of October the 27th Battery was ordered to join 26 Division for rest. At the same time the regiment, now R.H.Q., 32nd and 33rd Batteries, was ordered under command of 81 (W.A.) Division. This meant three weeks' marching to join the division in the Kaladan valley, where the enemy was showing considerable activity. By the end of October some fighting had led to the capture by the division of Mowdock, thus removing the threat to the airfields.

The division comprised two brigades only, and the 30th Mountain Regiment was the sole artillery support. The regiment (including signal section) marched at a strength of 10 B.Os., 6 V.C.Os., 436 I.O.Rs., 26 horses, 118 mules, with 187 A.T. mules attached, on a track cut for men on foot in single file. Gradients of 1 in 3 were common, and when up-gradients of 1 in $1\frac{1}{2}$ were met, loads had to be manhandled. On down-gradients loads were skidded down on bamboo sledges where possible. After the first three days supplies and forage were air-dropped, and the jawans agreed that they had never been better fed. It was noted that the powers of endurance of the men increased as the difficulties of the march increased, and as there was no hope of replacing animal casualties, animal management became of vital importance. Personal kits were reduced to 15 lb.

During November 15 Corps came under direct command of H.Q., Allied Land Forces, South-East Asia, and was about to be strengthened by the addition of 82 (W.A.) Division, 50 Indian Tank Brigade and 3 Commando Brigade. 22 (E.A.) Brigade was also on its way from Colombo. An advance was to be made as soon as possible down the Mayu peninsula and the Kalapanzin and Kaladan valleys to destroy or expel the Japanese within the area north of the line Foul Point–Kudaung Island–Minbya. An amphibious assault was to be carried out on Akyab island about 15th January, and the area north of Akyab–Minbya was to be firmly secured.

Tasks were allotted to divisions as follows:

(a) 81 (W.A.) to continue its drive in the Kaladan valley as far as Myohaung.

(b) 82 (W.A.) to cross the Kalapanzin, advance south to Htizwe, cross the Kaladan hills to Kansauk and take over from 81 (W.A.).

(c) 25 Indian to clear the Mayu peninsula and valley with flank protection from 82 (W.A.), with the object of seizing Foul Point and Kudaung Island.

(d) 26 Indian, with 3 Commando Brigade under command, to make a sea-borne assault to capture Akyab and advance north-east to Minbya.

15 Corps gave 12th December as a tentative date for the advance.

81 (*West African*) *Division*

The Kaladan river provided the enemy with a line of communication from which a stroke could be made against the rear of 15 Corps, and the Kyauktaw ferry, some forty miles south of Paletwa, where the river is three-quarters of a mile wide, was a vital point on the Japanese supply line.

The 30th Indian Mountain Regiment joined the division at Paletwa on 21st November and moved south with it a day or two later.

Moving down the valley with the grain of the country provided comparatively easy going, but necessitated more work in water, and marching behind African troops heavily burdened with head loads was a slow and weary business for men and loaded animals alike.

The division continued to advance down the valley during December, with frequent small-scale engagements. Formations were more accustomed to support from the air than artillery support, having had little experience of the latter.

The crossing of the Kaladan river had to be made on rafts provided by the African Engineers, and most of the chaungs had steep and muddy banks, but there was little opposition at first from the enemy. The horses and mules swam the half-mile stretch of water.

On the night of 15th/16th December a section of 33 Mountain Battery under Lieutenant V. N. Mathews, I.A., was posted in a forward company position of 8 Gold Coast Regiment which supplied the guns with local protection. The intention was to counter the shelling to which the divisional area was subjected nightly. However, the enemy put in a strong attack about 10 p.m. which

**Havildar Umrao Singh, V.C.
33 Mountain Battery**

continued for several hours. The radio link to R.H.Q. functioned badly, and the gun position was eventually overrun after a terrific struggle. The best description of the affair can be read in the citation which secured the award of the Victoria Cross to Havildar Umrao Singh of the 33rd Indian Mountain Battery.

Extract from I.A.O. No. 28/AP/45 of 10th July, 1945.

I.A.O. 28/AP/45. HONOURS AND AWARDS.

His Majesty The King has been graciously pleased to approve the award of the Victoria Cross to:

44928 Hav. UMRAO SINGH, Ind. Arty.
(Hindu Ahir—Palra, Jrajur, Rohtak, Punjab).

In the Kaladan Valley, Burma, on 15th/16th December, 1944, Havildar Umrao Singh was in charge of one gun in an advanced section of his battery, when it was subjected to heavy fire from 75-mm. guns and mortars for one and a half hours prior to being attacked by two companies of Japanese. When the attack came he so inspired his gun detachment with his personal example and encouragement to fight and defend the gun that they were able to beat off the attack with loss to the enemy. Though twice wounded by grenades in the first attack, he again held off a second enemy attack by skilful control of the detachment's small-arms fire and by manning the Bren gun himself, which he fired at Japs who had got to within five yards range. Again the enemy were beaten off with heavy loss; the third and fourth attacks were also beaten off in the same manner by the resolute action and great courage of Havildar Umrao Singh. By this time all the gun detachment had been killed or wounded with the exception of himself and two others. When the final attack came, the other gun having been overrun and all ammunition expended, he seized a gun bearer and closed with the enemy in furious hand-to-hand fighting. He was seen to strike down three Japanese in desperate efforts to save his gun, till he was overwhelmed and knocked senseless. Six hours later, when a counter-attack restored the position, he was found in an exhausted state beside his gun and almost unrecognizable with seven severe wounds and ten dead Japanese around him. By his personal example and magnificent bravery, Havildar Umrao Singh set a supreme example of gallantry and devotion to duty. When recovered, his gun was fit for firing and was in fact, in action again and firing later the same day.

He was the first and only Indian mountain gunner to achieve the Cross "For Valour," and was decorated by His Majesty King George VI at Buckingham Palace on 15th October, 1945.*

Jemadar Surat Singh of 33rd Battery was awarded the I.D.S.M. for courage in action on this occasion.

The advance continued, and the 30th Mountain Regiment continued to support 5 (W.A.) Brigade, but the enemy was well supplied with medium artillery and our light guns were outranged. Some success was obtained when the flash spotters of the survey battery arrived and several guns were silenced, but Major-General Loftus-Tottenham, the divisional commander, decided to take a "wide hook" through the hills to the east, and to attack with the maximum air support available. This was on a very large scale: from 29th to 31st December the Japanese concentration was attacked by 450 sorties from the air, in which 230 tons of bombs and 1,320 gallons of incendiary oil were dropped. The results were successful, and the division established a base near the Myohaung road; but not until 9th January, after stubborn fighting, was the area cleared.

On 10th January 4 Brigade of 82 (W.A.) Division arrived and came under command for the operation to capture Myohaung.

It was expected that this position would be strongly defended, and the operation was carefully timed in co-operation with 25 Division (pages 401-403) so that the combined attack would entrap as many Japanese as possible. On the 23rd it was discovered that the enemy was evacuating, and 1 and 2 Brigades of 82 (W.A.) Division were rushed to the spot. Features encircling the town were occupied, and it was entered on the 25th to find that the garrison had disintegrated.

On 20th January one gun of 33 Battery (now commanded by Major McGee, Major Williams having been posted to the Staff College) was ordered to come into action in a battalion-defended area well forward. Owing to a misunderstanding with the infantry guide, the gun, which was in draught, was moved on past the R.V.† through the area and deep into the Japanese lines. The sub-section was ambushed and, the mules having been shot in the first burst of fire, the enemy was able to capture the gun. It was found a few days later undamaged.

The 30th Indian Mountain Regiment then came under command of 82 (W.A.) Division. 81 Division, having completed its task, returned to Chiringa pending its final withdrawal.

---

* Havildar Umrao Singh was also the only other rank of the Royal Regiment awarded the V.C. in the 1939-45 war.

† Appendix, p. 453.

Lieutenant-Colonel T. W. R. Hill was awarded the O.B.E. and Major J. M. G. Williams the M.B.E. after these operations. Captain Pillar, quartermaster of the Regiment, was awarded the M.B.E. for his excellent work in organizing the supplies by air-drop.

The 30th Mountain Regiment's casualties since 1st November, 1944, now amounted to:

Killed in action	5 personnel, 13 animals.
Missing	1 personnel.
Wounded	23 personnel.
Evacuated sick	19 personnel.

82 (*West African*) Division

This division was detailed to guard the left flank of 25 Indian Division, whose task was to make a rapid move on Akyab along both sides of the Mayu range. Buthidaung was captured on "D" day (14th December), and the division moved swiftly south against little opposition through a country cut up by rivers and chaungs. The jeep-drawn 3.7-inch howitzers were left behind and field guns were run ashore from their rafts before coming into action.

Brigadier R. H. M. Hill was C.R.A. of the division, and on arrival at Htizwe in mid-January two mountain batteries (19th and 34th) of 25 Indian Division joined 82 Division for the operations against Myohaung. There was no very strenuous opposition, but a great deal of very bad ground to cover; three main river crossings, Kalapanzin, Kaladan and Lemro, and the Kan Zauk Pass, a very stiff climb, had to be negotiated. The batteries sent for their mules and started off in pack, and found it very hard work for man and mule. Myohaung was captured on 25th January, and the division, now under Major-General H. C. Stockwell, after relieving 81 (W.A.) Division, set off in pursuit of the Japanese, not without fighting on the way. On 9th February 2 (W.A.) Brigade, with 34th Battery in support, came under command of 25 Indian Division for the attack on Kangaw, this division having arrived by water. (For the battle of Kangaw see pages 402-403.)

The other two brigades of 82 Division, with the batteries of 30th Mountain Regiment in support, were pushing down from the north, directed on An, in order to cut the escape routes of the garrison of Kangaw, while 2 (W.A.) Brigade passed through the newly taken bridgehead at Ru-Ywa, where 34th Battery suffered considerable casualties, and moved on An from the south-west. Maintenance was by air, since the division was going through some of the thickest and most mountainous country in the whole of the Arakan, or, as officially expressed, "a country of great topographical difficulties."

Every yard of the path had to be cut out of the jungle. The battery commanders looked on it as "a three weeks' nightmare of wandering in awful jungle, short of rations and continuously attacked"—in fact, it was recorded as the most unpleasant part of the war. The I.O.Rs. kept up their spirits under these hardships, and the mules only suffered from lack of water occasionally. The lighter side of the picture was, as one officer wrote, the look of surprise on a Jap officer's face when his one remaining field piece received a direct hit. He had put it into action in a spot very convenient to No. 2 gun without any suspicion that a mountain battery was 300 yards away.

This encirclement, meant to entrap the Japanese 54 Division, had to be left incomplete owing to a sudden reduction in the air-drop, and 82 Division then took up the line An–Tamandu.

Near Tamandu a river had to be crossed by two brigades at the only ford, ninety-five yards across, which was dominated by an enemy bunker dug deep on our side of the river in the bank which fell twenty feet sheer to the river. After infantry attacks had failed, it was decided that the only effective way of destroying the bunker was for a gun to engage it at point-blank range from the far side of the river—obviously a job for a mountain gun. It entailed a very difficult approach through pathless jungle, up and down hills so steep that the loads had to be carried separately by the gunners, to a point upstream where the gun and ammunition could be ferried over. A double detachment was taken and willing helpers carried the ammunition boxes.

By good fortune a grove of banana trees grew opposite the target and certain trees in the rear of the river bank were easily cut down without noise. Noiselessly and with much crawling, a 3 foot 6 inch parapet was built up in the long grass of the undergrowth, with bags of grain and ammunition boxes filled with earth to protect the detachment. Shields were not fixed on account of the noise, and mortar discharges and desultory firing were carried out to distract the enemy's attention. The detachment was in some danger from splinters of our own mortar bombs.

Ten rounds H.E. with delay action fuzes were fired point-blank as quickly as possible, and when the smoke and dust had cleared away the target area was unrecognizable and the river bank had caved in and disappeared into the river. There was no answering shot or any sign of an enemy, so the area fifty yards round the bunker was destroyed with a mixture of delay action and direct action H.E. Many splinters came back over the gun, and cotton-wool in the ears was found essential.

This operation was carried out by the Regimental Commander of the 30th Mountain Regiment, Lieutenant-Colonel T. W. R. Hill, with a gun of 32nd Battery.

The enemy, however, continued to guard the ford by fire from the bunker, and it took a further attack and an airstrike to finally eject the last half-dozen Japanese from their position. For six days the division had been held up by small-arms fire at the crossing and it eventually crossed elsewhere after making a detour.

The 33rd Battery took part in the bombardments during this operation.

Close at Kyaukpyu the regiment bivouacked at Sanyin for a fortnight, and found that it was using the watering-place of a herd of wild elephants. They gave a lot of trouble for the first three nights and the mules were prevented with difficulty from stampeding. The nights were cold now and rugs made from parachutes were much appreciated by the animals.

On 26th March the regiment arrived on Ramree island, where 27th Battery was already camped, and remained there until sailing for Madras, where it arrived on 3rd June.

The 19th and 34th Mountain Batteries were sent to Akyab to rejoin their division.

82 (W.A.) Division remained in Arakan, clearing up the southern district and the ports, until June, when as part of 4 Corps it joined in the operations to round up the Japanese not yet dealt with in Burma.

25 *Indian Division*

On the Mayu front 25 Division was opposed by Japanese 55 Division Infantry Group, greatly under strength. The 74 Indian Brigade started two days before "D" day on the west flank of the range, keeping as close to the sea as possible with battalions leapfrogging by short bounds. After minor opposition the brigade reached Donbaik and closed up, then by rapid moves it seized Foul Point on 29th December, seventeen days in front of the time-table.

The 33rd Mountain Regiment [19th (Maymyo) and 34th Batteries] was under 53 Infantry Brigade, which had been trained for an amphibious assault on the north-west corner of Akyab island, to be followed by the capture of Akyab from the landward side. The brigade had first to clear Kudaung island, which lies to the north of Akyab. The Brigade Group was operating on a boat basis down the Kalapanzin river, and the mountain battery mules soon became a liability for feeding, and the ferrying over numerous chaungs which became tidal nearer the sea took up so much time that the Brigadier sent the mules back, and the howitzers and detachments continued the journey on very old rafts with outboard motors, coming into action on the bank when required. While crossing at Kwazu on 29th December, a raft or boat containing a sub-section of 34th Battery overturned and thirteen I.O.Rs. were drowned.

The brigade travelled downstream at speed, collecting prisoners here and there, and landed on Kudaung island on the 31st. Naval launches had now rounded Foul Point and joined the flotilla, and before dawn on 3rd January 4 R. Garhwal Rifles made a scramble landing on Akyab island, closely followed by a gun of 34 Battery. The town and harbour fell without opposition the following day, six weeks ahead of schedule.

The task of capturing Akyab had been allotted to 26 Division, but that division now by-passed it and carried on with the capture of Ramree.

The next task for 25 Division was an assault on Myebon. There was some sharp fighting when the Commando Brigade landed on Myebon Peninsula on 12th January after a heavy naval bombardment and air attack; 74 Brigade and Sherman tanks followed the next day. Stragglers had to be eliminated and naval craft cleared the channels, permitting divisional H.Q. to open at Myebon on the 18th.

Kangaw was on the supply line and line of retreat of the Japanese, now making a co-ordinated withdrawal, and, their water L. of C. being closed to them, their only escape route was the Myohaung-Tamandu road. The corps commander determined to cut this road at Kangaw where it leaves the plains and turns east into the hills.

The land approach was in the open and unfavourable, but after a naval reconnaissance of a twenty-mile route through some chaungs and mangrove swamps, 3 Commando Brigade landed a couple of miles from the position on 22nd January. The enemy was taken completely by surprise, but reacted quickly with intensive shelling and counter-attacks. However, the Commando Brigade gave no ground, and within forty-eight hours was reinforced by 51 Indian Brigade (an all-Indian formation) which landed under heavy fire and pushed through the beach-head. Enemy defences were found to be very strongly held and a considerable number of casualties were sustained. A very strong counter-attack was repulsed on 28th/29th, and early on 31st the Japanese launched the most desperate attack of the Arakan campaign, recoiling after receiving severe punishment.

Enemy shelling in this attack was the heaviest met with, and as it had only been possible to get small detachments of 43 Survey

Battery forward, counter-battery action was on a small scale. The flash-spotting post was knocked out by an unlucky round, though useful work was put in by a short base one manned later. The C.R.A. made use of a V.H.F. set and controlled C.B. work satisfactorily by this means.

The following day Kangaw was captured and the road cut. The enemy lost 2,000 killed and 16 guns. The trap was now closing from the north, whence 82 (W.A.) Division was arriving; and after clearing the road from Minbya, in the face of considerable opposition, this division passed under command of 25 Indian Division on 9th February.

25 Division then captured Tamandu while 82 Division was making its difficult march to An (pages 399-401); but the two batteries* of 33rd Mountain Regiment did not rejoin their division until it concentrated at Akyab. From Akyab 25 Division returned to India; the 34th Battery reached Calcutta on 11th April and 19th (Maymyo) Battery disembarked at Madras in May, where the 33rd Mountain Regiment was made up to strength by the addition of the 35th Indian Mountain Battery.

26 Indian Division

Major-General C. E. N. Lomax had been training the division for some months for a sea-borne assault to capture Akyab. During December information came in to the effect that the enemy was evacuating the island, and on 1st January Captain C. J. B. Jarrett, M.C., R.A., landed an aircraft of his Air O.P. Squadron on a strip prepared by the local inhabitants. The elaborate combined forces programme was, therefore, not required, and the divisional plan, which included 3 Commando Brigade and 27th Mountain Battery, was switched to Ramree island. This island—sixty miles long—contained a sheltered anchorage and plenty of room for airfields, and was a vital link in the enemy's L. of C. The operation was timed for 21st January, twenty-four hours before the landing at Kangaw and three days before Myohaung in the Kaladan valley was captured. A very heavy naval and air bombardment assisted to put 4 and 71 Indian Infantry Brigades ashore at Kyaukpyu,† and by the 24th, thirty miles of the west coast were ours. The 27th Battery embarked at Chittagong on 23rd January and on 26th landed on the beach-head at Kyaukpyu, joining in with 36 Indian Brigade on

---

* 34th Battery lost Lieutenant D. S. Nuttall, killed by a bomb, on 15th March.

† H.M.S. *Queen Elizabeth* and an aircraft carrier took part. The battleship had not fired her 15-inch guns in anger since the bombardment of the Dardanelles forts in 1915.

30th January in an assault landing on Sagu Kyun island, south of Ramree, which was supported by the fire of two destroyers and was successful. The battery went on in support of 8/13 F.F.R. for ten days in February, and on 15th February landed on the Kaladan Peninsula and was in action until the end of the month.

26 Division joined 82 (W.A.) Division in the operations in the An district, and on 14th April began to concentrate at Kyaukpyu for the return to India.

The Japanese had been driven out of Arakan and 54 and 55 Japanese Divisions practically destroyed.

The Fourteenth Army had driven the enemy southwards at a great pace, but the Supreme Allied Commander ordered a combined operation to be undertaken as early as possible with the object of the capture of Rangoon, should the Fourteenth Army not have arrived first. A parachute battalion was to be dropped at Elephant Point to destroy the defences there, and twenty-four miles of the Rangoon river had to be swept clear of mines. Landings were to be made on both banks by 26 Indian Division after heavy air attacks. The weather was bad, but the spirit of the combined force was magnificent and, against minor opposition, about 2200 hours on 3rd May 36 Indian Brigade landed in the dock area. Great numbers of prisoners of war and civilian internees were awaiting release. At this time 17 Indian Division of 4 Corps was still thirty-two miles to the north on the Pegu road.

This was the final operation carried out by the Arakan troops, and it only remained to redistribute the divisions.

On 15th May infantry of 26 Division linked up with 20 Division sixty miles north of Rangoon, and on 28th May 26 Indian Division began to embark for India to refit for the campaign in south-east Asia. The 30th Mountain Regiment disembarked at Madras on 1st June, where a ceremonial parade was held on 18th in honour of Havildar Umrao Singh, V.C.

In September 26 Indian Division, including 30th Mountain Regiment, sailed for Bangkok.

9. THE DRIVE SOUTH ON RANGOON, 1945

To return to the operations of the Fourteenth Army. On 18th March a Fourteenth Army Operation Instruction gave the Army Commander's intentions as follows:

(*a*) To capture Rangoon at all costs and as soon as possible before the monsoon.

(*b*) To capture Yenangyaung, Magwe and Prome.

(c) To secure the area Myingyan–Mandalay–Maymyo–Chauk and the road and railway axis Meiktila to Rangoon.

To implement this instruction the Fourteenth Army was regrouped early in April for the final thrust: 4 Corps, consisting of 5 and 17 Indian Divisions and 255 Tank Brigade from the Meiktila area, was to move south down the road and railway axis, and 33 Corps, comprising 2 British Division, 20 Indian Division and 268 Indian Infantry Brigade, was to join 7 Indian Division and move down the Irrawaddy axis. The 2 British Division, which was earmarked to return to India during April, was included in 33 Corps.

Fourteenth Army H.Q. was to control 19 Indian Division, now engaged in clearing the Meiktila area, which would be detailed to safeguard road and rail L. of C. to the south.

The Japanese had been ousted from the Mandalay Plain after suffering huge losses; the remnants of their 15 Army were being driven south of the Mandalay–Thazi road; their 33 and 28 Armies had had severe casualties and lost many guns. Our efforts were now centred on keeping the enemy on the move to prevent recovery and, equally important, to reach Rangoon ourselves before the monsoon burst in May. Enemy formations, greatly disorganized, were concentrating west of the Irrawaddy, in the Pegu Yomas between the Irrawaddy and Sittang rivers, in the area of Mawchi and to the north, and in the Sittang area covering Moulmein.

Advance down the Irrawaddy valley

A mixed force (Westcol) from 7 Indian Division fought its way down the west bank of the Irrawaddy; this column included the 5th (Bombay) Mountain Battery, which had passed some weeks with a Chin battalion protecting the right flank of the 28 (Independent) East African Brigade during its march south. The battery had taken part in repelling a serious attack at Kazumna in which area the column stayed six weeks clearing out many small parties of the enemy. A F.O.O. went out with infantry patrols, and much use was made of the Air O.P. After 114 Brigade relieved 28 E.A. Brigade the march was resumed, but the enemy continued in contact.

On the east bank 33 Indian Infantry Brigade, now commanded by Lieutenant-Colonel L. H. O. Pugh, R.A., was ordered to capture Kyaukpadaung, thirty miles south of Nyaungu. The brigade was strengthened with tanks and artillery, and after two night marches the objective was captured with very few casualties. A great deal of equipment and some guns were taken, and 33 Brigade Group advanced without delay to capture Chauk, causing more equipment and guns to be abandoned. By another rapid move the Brigade Group surprised the Japanese garrison of Yenangyaung, which put up a fierce resistance during three days' fighting, but this extensive oilfield area was completely cleared by 23rd April.

Colonel Pugh was awarded a bar to the D.S.O. for the skilful handling of his brigade in these actions, the successes of which were due to his "energy, personal example under fire and brilliant planning."

At the end of the month 114 Brigade had reached a point seventeen miles south-west of Seikpyu on the west bank, and 89 Brigade was preparing to cross over and join it.

From this time onward 7 Division, with 268 Indian Infantry Brigade under command, remained in control of the northern sector of the front from Prome to Shwedaung, and the southern sector was allotted to 20 Division. The two brigades of 7 Division on the west bank harried the Japanese cut off to the north of Magwe, forcing them to take to the jungle and cross where they could.

On 12th May, near Letpandaga, a platoon was caught in an ambush but was freed by the action of the F.O.O. from 5th Battery accompanying, who ranged by sound and brought down fire on the unseen enemy. While the battery supported 89 Brigade in mopping-up operations, an attacking enemy column was exterminated to the last man. The battery crossed the river at Minbu and rejoined the regiment on 27th May. Further minor operations continued throughout June.

From Kyaukse 20 Division was sent south-west to assist 2 British Division in the attack on Mount Popa, an extinct volcano which lent itself to defence. A Japanese force with artillery held out for a fortnight before it was eliminated. The vehicles of 2 British Division were reallotted to 20 Division when the former returned to India.

The division moved rapidly on Magwe, thereby cutting off a considerable number of enemy troops on the east bank retiring under pressure from 7 Division. These troops then crossed to join other bodies of Japanese on the west bank.

From Magwe 32 Infantry Brigade with 3rd (Peshawar) Battery under command (in pack) moved down the east bank to clear it as far as Allanmyo, which was the scene of some fighting. The 8th (Lahore) Battery formed part of the divisional rear-guard moving down the road to Prome, which was infested with small parties of Jiffs and Japs.

The capture of Prome on 2nd May cut the last escape route of the Japanese from Arakan, a strong force having to be dispersed before the district could be reported clear. The enemy made several ineffectual attempts to break across the river, and established for the purpose a bridgehead at Zalon, ten miles north of Prome, but were beaten back from there with very heavy losses and finally liquidated early in June. The Burma National Army, formerly the "Indian National Army," was now doing useful and loyal work as guerillas.

The division continued to guard the Prome-Rangoon road during the monsoon and to patrol and mop up parts of the Pegu Yomas, linking up with 26 Indian Division to the south.

The 31st Battery went with a force to capture Bassein, but found that the Royal Indian Navy had arrived before them. The 3rd and 8th Batteries returned to a pack basis.

The 23rd Mountain Regiment went into camp for training at Minhla and later at Hmawbi (thirty-five miles north of Rangoon).

Advance down the Road and Railway Axis

The 4 Corps, including the mountain batteries, was now completely motorized; 17 Division, headed by an armoured column, led the advance south from Meiktila.

The loss of Pyawbwe was a very costly defeat for the enemy; in fact, the Japanese 33 Army never recovered from the blow. During those actions the batteries of 21st Mountain Regiment distinguished themselves by the accurate and unfailing support provided; our infantry were so impressed that a Japanese sword was presented to the regiment.

On clearing up it was found that 2,200 Japanese had been killed and 28 guns, 6 tanks and 60 lorries captured by 17 Division. General Cowan congratulated the artillery on their good work. By dark on the 11th the surviving Japanese had disappeared and the whole area was cleared and occupied. During the next few days extensive patrolling was carried out, in which the mountain artillery took their share; a recorded patrol was one composed of men of 6th (Jacob's) and 37th Batteries, under Lieutenant Mallinson, which searched many villages.

The 5 Division, 123 Brigade leading, passed through 17 Division on the 11th and continued the advance to the south with great speed. The Japanese seemed to be bewildered by the rush and capable of only slight resistance by ambushes and road-blocks, but the defence stiffened on arrival at Yamethin, forty miles from Meiktila, and it took two days to capture and clear this place. After a whole night's harassing fire and a day's artillery and air concentration, the place fell with severe losses to the enemy.

On the 16th the armoured column with 161 Brigade took the lead and broke into Shwemyo while the R.E. were throwing a bridge over the near-by Sinthe chaung, but the brigade was unable to establish a bridgehead until the early hours of the 18th, aided by a flank attack by 123 Brigade and the presence of 9 Brigade at Takton, a few miles to the south. A very successful operation ensued, resulting in the clearance of the Shwemyo air-strip, and 123 Brigade handed over to 99 Brigade of 17 Division, which had come forward with the 21st Mountain Regiment. The 24th Mountain Regiment (less 11th Battery) had gone ahead with 9 Infantry Brigade on a jeep and light M.T. scale to take part in the action at Shwemyo, and came under command of 17 Division on the 21st.

Still in the lead, 5 Division with the armoured column cleared Pyinmana, took the Lewe airfield, and were then racing two enemy columns to arrive first in Toungoo. The tanks found the road difficult owing to mines and demolitions, but after great efforts Toungoo was entered on the 22nd, the leading tank running down the Japanese traffic policeman who gave the wrong signal in the centre of the town. The 20th Battery was well up in front with the leading brigade, 123, which went on with little opposition. The 19 Indian Division (62 and 98 Brigades) was close behind and took over Toungoo on April 26th, after meeting very strong opposition.

19 Indian Division

This division was responsible for securing the Mandalay-Meiktila-Thazi area and for safeguarding road and rail communications to the south: its further role was to clear up the area behind 4 Corps during its move on Rangoon.

The mopping-up of the Meiktila area entailed a great number of operations against parties of Japanese trying to make their way eastwards out of Burma. Kyaukse was captured by 20 Division before it left for the western flank; Wundwin and Thazi were captured by 64 Infantry Brigade (19 Division) with the mountain regiment's support; but the whole area was infested with groups of Japanese, the elimination of which took 19 Division several weeks' hard work to accomplish. The work was done thoroughly and methodically, and the troops stood the strain of continuous operations very well. Use was made of air-strikes and artillery bombardments on areas known to be harbouring enemy elements, but tanks and infantry had to go in to complete the work, and motor transport was short. The Mountain Regiment carried out its duties in pack, and water was not always available.

The enemy fought back hard and used his artillery very effectively. On 6th April a company of 2 Welch was pinned to the ground and surrounded south of Kume, being freed to advance only after Major Dowson, 24th Mountain Battery, had crossed over 200 yards of open plain under fire to find an O.P. from which he fired a strong concentration into the enemy's position.

The day before, 17 Indian Division had marched south towards Pyawbwe, followed by 5 Division, but the situation did not permit the advance of 19 Division until 17th April, when 62 and 98 Brigades followed down the Rangoon road.

The 64 Brigade was delayed at Meiktila to safeguard the area and later was ordered to clear the Thazi–Kalaw–Loilem road which ran eastward into the Shan States. This operation was successfully completed by the capture of Kalaw on 7th June, artillery support being supplied by medium and field artillery, no mountain artillery being available. The three batteries of the 20th Mountain Regiment joined 98 Infantry Brigade at Toungoo, where it had taken over from 123 Brigade of 5 Division on 26th April.

The 62 Infantry Brigade had been diverted to make a wide left hook to cut the Toungoo–Mawchi road, where the enemy was in considerable strength covering the escape road to Mawchi and Indo-China. This threat to our left flank was intensified by the enemy's possession of a strong position about three miles out of Toungoo on the Mawchi road which was hindering the operations of 98 Brigade. As 62 and 98 Brigades shared the elimination of the strong Japanese forces threatening the flank of the main advance to Rangoon, it is convenient to complete the story of this operation here.

By the time 20th Mountain Regiment reached Toungoo it had covered 215 miles on foot in seventeen days in very hot weather, the monsoon being about to break and the flooding of low-lying areas already beginning. There was strong opposition in and around Toungoo and the Air O.Ps. were very busy.

The Japanese 15 Division had been moving westwards in an attempt to reach Toungoo before 4 Corps arrived, but had been held up by Karen guerillas and was now protecting the flank of Japanese troops who were moving south on their way out.

Mawchi is sixty miles east of Toungoo; at M.S. 14 the road bifurcates, the northern branch leading to Thandaung, where the enemy was in position. His troops were being continually reinforced by groups which had escaped across country, and very aggressive warfare was carried on for some weeks.

The 25th and 26th Batteries marched to Nyaung Sakan, three

miles from Toungoo, and came into action on 6th May to support 3 Raj. Rif. and 4/6 G.R., but the attack was held up and the Brigade Commander and staff, which included Lieutenant-Colonel Kemmis-Betty as C.R.As. representative, and two F.O.O. parties, were ambushed on their way to the front. On the following day 4/6 G.R., with a section of 26th Battery, were to join up with 3 Raj. Rif., but the opposition was too strong and the infantry had many casualties. The guns were kept very busy and the Air O.P. put in valuable work, especially during the withdrawal, which was covered by the artillery.

That evening (8th May), to celebrate the German surrender, a victory *feu de joie* was fired by the artillery—one round troop fire one second, followed by a one round salvo (78 guns) at midnight.

On 9th May 62 Brigade plus 4/4 G.R. were allotted to the defence of Toungoo and its airfields as well as to the Mawchi road operations. The mountain regiment joined 98 Brigade in mopping-up operations south-east of Toungoo, meeting opposition everywhere, but less intense than that met by 62 Brigade on the Mawchi road. Every yard there had to be fought for, and it took seven days of close in-fighting to make good the next mile and a half.

On 19th May 20th Mountain Regiment (less 25th Battery) arrived at the Mawchi road front in relief, and an all-pack column was formed to move across country and cut the Mawchi road at M.S. 15. After a good start the column was furiously attacked without respite for forty-eight hours and compelled to withdraw. The enemy then occupied our recent position and gave us the opportunity to inflict enormous casualties.

The 98 Brigade took over on 24th May, and on the following day the mules of the 20th Mountain Regiment were sent back. An attack of surra began to run through the mules of the whole force, taking a heavy toll of every unit. Thereafter, the mountain batteries moved in M.T.

By the end of the month M.S. 14 was reached and the three batteries of 20th Mountain Regiment supported an attack on Thandaung. Vigorous patrolling continued, and the F.O.Os. with the patrols put in some very effective shoots. The front line on the Mawchi road had reached M.S. 17 when 62 Brigade came in again, and by this time the total of captured enemy guns was twenty.

On 7th June a further advance (Operation "Sunshine") of two separate columns, covered by all available guns, began. One of 26th Battery guns was hit the first night and some ammunition boxes set on fire. The direction of the advance led over the worst imaginable type of country—jungle with very thick undergrowth and so steep that the mules had to be sent back. At one place Captain Mahomed Adalat, the senior F.O.O., had to fire rounds of smoke in order to locate himself. This advance went on for five days unopposed, supplies being dropped from the air. The two columns put in their attack on the 12th, synchronizing with an attack by a battalion coming down from the north, and after two days' hard fighting the operation met with complete success. No more Japs were met, and the force made good M.S. 24, its ultimate objective. Captain Mahomed Adalat, who was F.O.O. with a forward company, almost continually received great praise for his brilliant work, bringing down fire wherever required and causing very heavy casualties to the enemy. On one occasion, when forward with a leading company, the company commander was killed and Mahomed Adalat joined the assault and encouraged the company to victory.

The Mawchi road did not quieten down for some time and 62 Brigade remained in contact. The 20th Mountain Regiment concentrated in monsoon quarters at Pyonchaung, and later on 26th Battery accompanied 22nd East African Brigade to Mawchi.

To return to the main thrust down the Rangoon Road (page 408). On 25th April, at a point 211 miles from Meiktila, 17 Division took the lead again, and against increasingly disorganized resistance 63 Brigade behind the armoured column worked its way through minefields and floods against obstacles under fire to reach the outskirts of Pegu. An armoured detachment cut the Pegu–Mokpalin road at Waw, fifteen miles north-east of Pegu. The Japanese situation was now critical as all the low-lying country was under flood.

The 17 Division had an old score to settle in remembrance of the enforced withdrawal three years before, and all ranks were straining every nerve to reach Rangoon before 15 Indian Corps from Arakan. The Pegu river was in full flood and violent tropical storms on the 28th and 29th made matters worse; movement off the road became impossible, and no aircraft could land or take off. On the 30th, 48 Brigade, after some work with the bayonet, seized the part of Pegu north of the river, and as a result of gallant work by infantry crawling over wrecked girders of blown-up railway bridges, a bridgehead was established on the west bank. By nightfall on 1st May the town was practically cleared of Japs and twelve guns had been captured by 99 Brigade. Air-strips were out of action and the troops had to be put on half-rations, but their efforts to reach Rangoon in spite of flood and demolitions were continued. Unfortunately the physical difficulties were too great, and 15 Corps entered the capital on 3rd May.* Contact with 4 Corps was made at Hlegu, twenty-five miles south-west of Pegu, on the 6th.

The 17 Division moved to the area Pyu–Pyinbongy to cut off enemy troops escaping eastwards, and 5 Division opened the road to Mokpalin and began to clear the area between Pegu and the south end of the Pegu Yomas. These two divisions spent a month in widespread patrolling in bad monsoon conditions, killing Japanese wherever met. There is very little detail in battery records concerning this period: everyone was occupied in a tireless pursuit of small parties of the enemy making for the Sittang river.

During May the Japanese forces west of the Irrawaddy, estimated to number about 18,000, began to cross the river under pressure from 82 West African Division advancing eastwards after the clearance of Arakan and from 7 Indian Division on the west bank. The enemy's aim was to join the other part of his forces which had been squeezed into the Pegu Yomas by our advance from Meiktila. He established a bridgehead at Zalon, but he was beaten back with heavy losses during ten days' fighting by 7 Division, and the Japanese who got away only managed to do so by crossing in small parties.

At the end of May, 33 Corps ceased to exist and Twelfth Army was formed under General Stopford: its formations were 4 Corps (5, 17 and 19 Indian Divisions), 7 and 20 Indian and 82 West African Divisions, 255 Indian Tank Brigade, 6 British and 268 Indian Infantry Brigades, with some Indians formerly in the enemy-controlled Burma Defence Army.

Operations in the Irrawaddy valley continued and 7 Division was relieved by 268 Indian Brigade and 22 East African Brigade to free it for taking over 5 Division positions when this division was pulled out for training in India. This relief coincided with a strong Japanese counter-attack across the Sittang from Mokpalin with a view to easing the escape of the Japanese troops concentrated in the Pegu Yomas. The 89 Indian Infantry Brigade bore the brunt of the fighting opposite the bridgehead at Mokpalin. The countryside was flooded and in many places impassable, part being a swamp mostly covered with coarse grass six feet high growing out of the water; ten feet or so above the water ran a single railway line on an embankment. On the night of 3rd July the Japanese attacked with great fury and after the failure of the assault started an investment. The Indian troops suffered many casualties from artillery fire, but splendid close support was provided by the R.A.F. and the Japanese eventually withdrew, so ending "the battle of the bend."

On 27th July a last display of offensive tactics occurred in this

---

* See the Army Commander's message to the Gunners, p. 422.

area a few miles east of Waw when a position in a bend of the river was heavily attacked and cost 1 Queen's comparatively heavy casualties before the enemy was cleared out.

Japanese break-out across the Pegu Yomas

By the end of June it became clear that the Japanese formations were preparing to break out from their hide-outs in the Yomas in an easterly direction towards Moulmein and Siam, and this was confirmed by an operation order captured on 4th July, and information given by an officer of the I.N.A. who turned against his Japanese masters.

The Pegu Yomas form a jungle-covered ridge of hills of an average height of 1,000 feet and extending for fifty or sixty miles parallel to the Rangoon road and railway and three to five miles from them. Movement was extremely difficult, but the lower ground was patrolled and it was known that there were many Japanese on the feature belonging to disorganized formations and cut off from all supplies.

By this time, reading from south to north, 4 Corps front was held by 7 Division in the Pegu-Sittang bend area, 17 Division in the centre between Pyu and Payagyi, and 19 Division in the northern sector. Of 19 Division one brigade was engaged on the Kalaw road from Meiktila, one brigade from Toungoo to Pyu (exclusive), and the third north of Toungoo.

The Corps was operating from prepared positions with armoured vehicles and artillery. During the operations the field artillery generally were engaged in observed shooting against the Japanese in the open, and the mountain batteries went out with infantry columns to clear up suspected areas. Until the enemy reached the Sittang river he attempted to fight back and his casualties were enormous. A high proportion of time H.E. was used and great value was obtained from the Air O.Ps.

From 9th May 37th Battery remained at Pyu under 99 Brigade. The remainder of the 21st Mountain Regiment provided officers' fighting patrols marking down parties of Japanese trying to cross the main road. In June the regiment, less 37th Battery, moved with 99 Brigade to Kalaw for the clearance of the Shan States. Few incidents occurred. Later, the whole regiment was training in Pegu, and after arrival in India in October, 1946, took up duty on the frontier.

From 19th July onwards bodies of 400 or 500 Japanese attempted to cross the main road at various times with little variety of tactics.

For instance, on 21st July a column of 5 Baluch, some tanks and 25th Battery moved out to attack a village seen to contain several hundred Japanese. The F.O.O. turned his guns on to the village and the tanks chased the enemy. The company commander then attacked without covering fire except from infantry weapons and the company was held up; at the same time an enemy bomb landed in the artillery O.P. Subadar Gulzar Khan, the F.O.O., then used his 48 wireless set to bring down a heavy concentration on the village, assisted by tanks and an air-strike. The result was a massacre.

The 24th and 26th Mountain Batteries had a busy day on the 22nd, and so the one-sided war continued; the Japanese showed great courage but little initiative, and those who managed to cross the road were faced with the crossing of the Sittang under fire.

As the days went on fewer and fewer Japanese were met with, but patrolling with occasional clashes continued into August, the enemy accepting unconditional surrender on the 14th. There were so many enemy units out of touch with their headquarters that the order for "Cease fire" took a long time to circulate, but operations ceased by the end of the month, and a preliminary peace agreement was signed on the 27th August.

The Japanese soldier had proved himself stubborn in defence and staunch in attack: the proportion of prisoners taken during the operations in Burma was the smallest on record.

Afterwards the mountain regiments went away with their divisions and found that police work in centres of unrest had become the order of the day: 5 Indian Division was sent to Malaya and Java, 7 Indian Division to Bangkok and Malaya (less 25th Mountain Regiment which stayed on in Burma under Twelfth Army), and 20 Indian Division to Saigon. More than a year elapsed before the last battery returned to India, and in the meantime a great number of changes of personnel had taken place.

Mountain regiments left their animals in Burma when they went out of the country, and the last regiments to leave (21st and 25th) acquired a magnificent collection of animals picked from units which had departed earlier. Even these, however, had to be discarded eventually.

A word is due here in praise of the ponies which survived the campaign. During the last few months of the war there was time for race meetings and mounted sports, and the ponies came into their own. In addition to regular gymkhanas, 19 Indian Division, while at Toungoo, put on a full-scale tattoo, with the Duke of Aosta's band playing at each performance. At Pegu on the racecourse built by Japanese prisoners, Lieutenant-Colonel Chaplin rode many a winner, and at Hmawbi Major Walsh, 8th (Lahore) Battery, organized popular mounted paper-chases.

During the Second World War the Indian Mountain Artillery maintained the good reputation it had had for close on a hundred years. The units were proud to support British infantry, and as proud to have served through the most strenuous war on record with their comrades-in-arms over many years in the Indian Army. The artilleryman's record was second to none—he was hard and tough, cheerful in hardship and not prone to grumble at the lack of amenities. He fought well, the result of the military traditions of a fighting race and the family spirit in the battery, and, last but not least, of his friendship and intimate contact with his British officers. It seems sad that the bond of friendship, grown so firm and strong through generations of soldiering together, should be ruthlessly broken a short time later.

A special tribute is due to the signallers, who carried out their difficult and dangerous work with unfailing courage and skill.

Of the other arms, to all of whom high praise was awarded by the artillery, too much cannot be said in favour of the Air Forces, British, Indian and U.S.A., whose help was absolutely vital to success. This war is notable as the first example in the East of air co-operation on a very large scale. Thanks to an early superiority in the air, the administrative problems of supply on wheels in a roadless country did not exist. Air supply was always available unless prevented by bad weather, and support by direct bombing on enemy defences or air-strikes was readily provided during a battle. The Army could not have achieved the success it did without the disruption of enemy communications occasioned, and the large number of casualties inflicted, by the Air Forces, and the evidence of air superiority kept the morale of our troops at its highest. This was especially noticeable with regard to the flying out of casualties and the accurate dropping of supplies. The Commander-in-Chief, 11th Army Group, wrote: "It is with gratitude and admiration that I acknowledge the immense debt which the Army owes to the Air."

The members of the Regimental Light Aid detachments have received little notice in this book, much less than their work merits. L.A.Ds. were small sections of the I.E.M.E.: originally formed of a British W.O. and a sergeant of R.E.M.E. with eight Indian I.O.Rs., in some regiments the personnel all came from I.E.M.E. They consisted of armament artificers, vehicle mechanics and electricians who carried out repairs to guns, small arms, motor engines and wireless sets. Without their technical assistance units would often have been immobile or incapable of offensive action. They had little rest as repairs often had to be carried out at night, and they deserve great praise for their skill and keenness to keep the machinery in first-class condition.

As an example, on 1st March a mountain regiment was suddenly ordered to mechanize and issued with 120 vehicles. The drivers handed in their mules and started learning to drive motors, and after three weeks' training successfully drove 900 miles in ten days over bad roads, losing only one vehicle on the way. The personnel of the L.A.D. spared no pains to increase the efficiency of the units they were attached to.

D. JAVA

After the reoccupation of Rangoon on 2nd May, 1945, some regrouping had taken place. The 15 Indian Corps was withdrawn to India and combined with a new 34 Indian Corps to form the Fourteenth Army, now commanded by Lieutenant-General Sir Miles Dempsey. This Army was to undergo special training for an elaborate combined operation for the invasion of Malaya and the capture of Singapore, called Operation "Zipper," in which the 5, 23, 25 and 26 Indian Divisions were to take part.

Owing to the Japanese capitulation, "Zipper" became an "occupation" rather than an "invasion," and the formal surrender of the Japanese forces to the Supreme Commander took place at Singapore on 12th September without incident. The 5 Indian Division was the first formation to reoccupy Singapore (5th September); it included only one mountain battery, the 2nd (Derajat) M.B., F.F., commanded by Major J. S. Wilson.

The boundaries of S.E.A.C. had been extended in August, 1945, to cover Sumatra, Java and the remaining Dutch possessions eastward as well as Siam and part of French Indo-China. These had been occupied by Japanese troops who had trained and equipped subversive elements in order to carry on a struggle against the Dutch and French Governments after the Japanese defeat.

The 23 Indian Division, leaving behind its 28th Mountain Regiment, R.I.A., had landed in Malaya at Port Dickson on 9th September as planned for "Zipper," and during October was redeployed in Java, pending the arrival of Netherlands troops. The 49 Indian Infantry Brigade under Brigadier A. W. Mallaby, C.I.E., landed in Soerabaya on 22nd October. Its task was to release all Dutch nationals interned by the Japanese and subsequently held under appalling conditions of hardship by the Indonesians, to collect Japanese forces now concentrated in Java, and to generally maintain

In Action with Fourteenth Army: Burma, 1945

3.7-inch Howitzer in Action at Grissee: Indonesia, 1946

law and order until the arrival of the Netherlands forces. On arrival the brigade found Soerabaya in a state of armed resistance, arms having been obtained from the Japanese due to their failure (doubtless voluntary) to safeguard their arms. The town and the port were seething with undisciplined mobs.

A Nationalist puppet government had been installed by the Japanese and an "Indonesian Republic" proclaimed. This was unable to establish law and order and many Dutch internees were ill-treated and murdered. Hostility to the British force was shown from the time of landing, and its movements restricted.

The Second-in-Command of the Brigade Group was Colonel L. H. O. Pugh, D.S.O., formerly commanding the 25th Indian Mountain Regiment of 7 Indian Division. He carried out negotiations with the local Government representatives and made a working arrangement for co-operation, which was later nullified by the dropping of leaflets from the air by order of higher authority offering the Indonesians terms which were unacceptable. The Government lost what little control it possessed and armed mobs attacked 49 Brigade on 28th October.

The Brigade Group was widely dispersed with Brigade H.Q. and one company of 4/6 Mahratta Light Infantry in some buildings in the centre of the town. The Indonesian armed forces, composed chiefly of Nationalists trained and organized by the Japanese, were everywhere in strength, supported by mobs amounting to some 75,000 men armed with rifles, swords, spears and other weapons. Colonel Pugh was on his way to visit 47 Indian Field Ambulance in the southern extremity of the town when he encountered roadblocks and came under fire from Indonesians on both sides of the road. Very shortly after his arrival at 47 Indian Field Ambulance an attack was made on that unit without any warning. He took charge, ordered in from a near-by position one company 6/5 Rajputana Rifles, personally sited defences and organized the few troops available. By his example of calm efficiency and disregard of his own danger under small-arms and mortar fire, he converted a collection of individuals of all arms into a strong and confident garrison.

Attacks continued without ceasing, and Brigadier Mallaby was murdered; many of his officers and men were killed in attempts to create order. On the 30th Colonel Pugh decided to cross the town (a five miles run) to Brigade H.Q. to take charge of the Group. He drove in a jeep with a small body-guard under fire from all sides, and by sheer audacity and determination achieved his purpose and took over command of his hard-pressed units, which were now suffering from a shortage of ammunition.

He reorganized the Brigade Group and conducted operations by W/T, and also carried on negotiations with his treacherous enemy. A truce was agreed to on 1st November, and the whole Brigade Group was ultimately concentrated within the Dock Area without further casualties. In addition to Brigadier Mallaby, 18 officers and 374 N.C.Os. and men had become casualties, mostly killed.

The troops remained in possession of the airfield, dock and harbour areas awaiting the arrival of reinforcements from Singapore. During this uneasy lull, punctuated by continuous sniping and minor actions, over 6,000 Dutch women and children were extricated under guard from the town and ultimately evacuated to Singapore, their first step home to Holland.

In the citation awarding Colonel Pugh a second bar to the Distinguished Service Order, it was stated: "Throughout the whole operation Colonel Pugh showed the highest qualities of leadership; his complete disregard of personal danger and his unruffled and cheerful efficiency at all times were an example and inspiration to all ranks."

Major-General Mansergh arrived by air in advance of his 5 Indian Division, sent to implement the instructions given to 49 Indian Brigade. The first troops to arrive were the personnel of the 2nd (Derajat) M.B., F.F., under Major J. Nettelfield in the destroyer *Caron* at 1130 hours on 1st November; as the guns were to follow later in a transport, the battery was detailed on landing for guards and patrols.

The battery's guns and lorries were landed on the 4th, the day on which the remainder of the division began to arrive. The 49 Brigade held a line to cover the landing, and 9 and 123 Indian Brigades* took up positions on the left and right, the latter being responsible for the defence of the airfield. At this time the 2nd (Derajat) Battery covered the whole perimeter, being the only artillery available until the 3rd and 5th Indian Field Regiments arrived. General Mansergh continued to negotiate with the Indonesian army, of which the young and irresponsible elements had control, but with little success. As the situation was becoming worse and the enemy more aggressive, an ultimatum was published that, failing the transfer of the remaining Dutch women and children, all men who had been imprisoned by the Indonesians, the return of prisoners and wounded, captured equipment and vehicles of 49 Brigade and Brigadier Mallaby's body by 6 a.m. on 10th November, the division would enter the town and release the internees by force. The 123 and 49 Brigades advanced

---

* The third brigade (161) of 5 Division had been sent to Batavia.

at that hour and were immediately fired on by the Indonesians, who used tanks, guns and mortars.

The opposition increased during the day and a five minutes' concentration was put down by artillery and the lighter naval guns on selected enemy positions. As little artillery fire as possible was used, the mountain guns having some quick targets to stop sniping, and Jemadar Pahlwan Khan was responsible for causing an enemy gun to cease firing. This gun was brought in that night by Lieutenant Langford and turned out to be an Austrian anti-tank gun. The jail was reached after a day's street fighting and some 3,000 internees were saved in the nick of time from being burnt to death by the Indonesians. There was a good deal of sniping during the night, which generally cleared after a round or two of D.F. fire.

A great loss to the Royal Artillery was caused by the death of the C.R.A., 5 Indian Division, Brigadier R. Loder-Symonds, in the crashing of an aircraft when taking off for a flight. He was an outstanding officer with much war experience.

During the next few days slow progress was made in clearing the city with the minimum damage and casualties; fire from artillery and tanks was restricted and the use of aircraft forbidden. On 12th December R.H.Q., 24th Indian Mountain Regiment, with 11th (Dehra Dun) and 20th Batteries, arrived in infantry landing-craft; the 20th was sent into action at once alongside the 2nd Battery, but the 11th Battery guns were kept in harbour as there was not sufficient personnel to man them until later.

Enemy resistance, especially mortaring, was particularly accurate and said to be directed by Japanese soldiers. Shelling was also plentiful, and the perpetual manning of O.Ps. and F.O.O. work began to tell on the batteries.

The occupation of Soerabaya was completed on 24th November after nineteen days' fighting. Casualties in the division had been heavy and fighting had to be continued to keep the enemy artillery outside gun-range. By mid-December conditions had stabilized and only a few marauding bands continued their activities, but continuous patrolling had to be carried on.

The 2nd Mountain Battery had had a variety of tasks since landing, being turned into an infantry company on several occasions and taking on infantry patrol work.

During January and February, 1946, 24th Mountain Regiment was made responsible for part of the perimeter round northern Soerabaya, and was deployed along the Grissee road. Usually, one or more batteries acted as infantry, supported by as many guns as could be conveniently manned, while the third battery would be resting or employed on internal defence duties. During this period very active patrolling was carried out in thick jungle, and a number of planned attacks on Indonesian strongholds were carried out, unfortunately not without casualties on our side. However, the enemy was held in check and many were killed, wounded and taken prisoner.

Early in March a Dutch brigade began to arrive and eventually took over from 5 Indian Division, the units of which returned to India by the end of April. Major Nettelfield was awarded the M.C. for services during these operations.

NOTE BY THE COMPILER

Readers cannot have failed to notice that the 2nd (Derajat) Mountain Battery, Frontier Force, had the good fortune to be sent on active service more often than most of the other mountain batteries, and on all these occasions it acquitted itself in the most admirable way; it never lost a gun and invariably drew praise for its soldier-like qualities, due to good discipline and the good leadership of its officers.

E. INDO-CHINA: SAIGON

During their occupation of Indo-China the Japanese had armed and trained the more violent "national" elements in the hope that the French would not be able to repossess themselves of their colony. Some of the French troops had been disarmed and the senior officers arrested, and the troops, which had retired into China, were held by the Chinese. After the Japanese surrender in Singapore the situation in Saigon became worse, and disorder increased until 12th September, when 20 Indian Division, completely mechanized, began to arrive by air from Burma with orders to police the country, enforce the surrender terms, and evacuate prisoners of war, pending the arrival of French troops.

The 23rd Indian Mountain Regiment (3rd, 8th and 31st Batteries) carried out guard and police duties until February, 1946, there being no fighting. While at Saigon the regiment met Major Abhe, 55th Mountain Regiment, Japanese Artillery, who had fought in Arakan, Manipur, and during the final days in Burma, and learnt from him that the 23rd was called the "Devil Regiment of Artillery" by the enemy.

The mules were left behind in Burma to be handed over to Remounts in March, 1946, and the drivers sent back to Ambala.

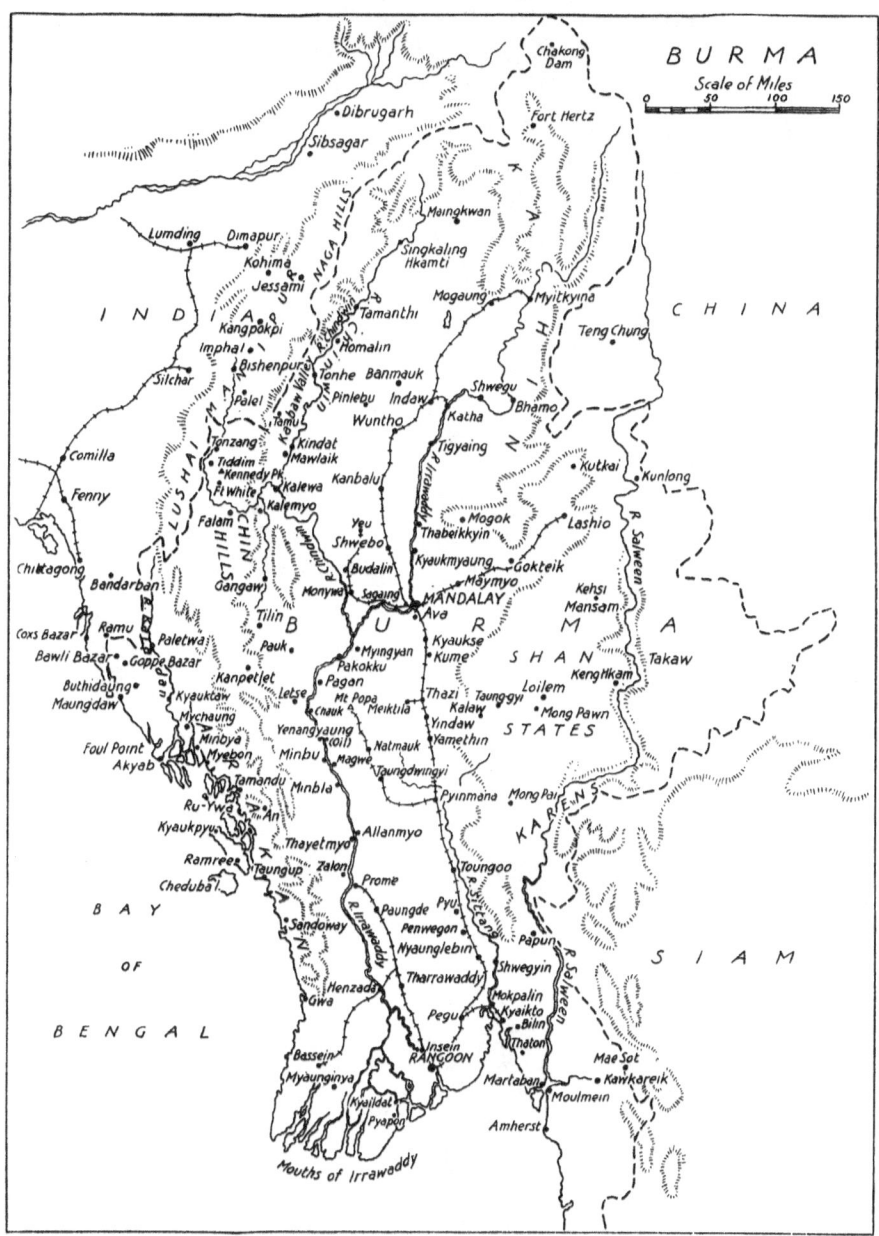

A Battery Commander wrote: "Of the mules which were on the handing-over parade, 40 per cent. had joined in Abbottabad between 1939-1942. Those which had been with the regiment from the time of leaving Kakul in April, 1942 until March, 1946 had travelled about 18,000 miles from place to place, of which 3,000 had been by rail or lorry. Their daily average was nearly eleven miles for the four years, and this figure does not include fatigues, etc."

On leaving Saigon the 23rd Indian Mountain Regiment did not return to India with 20 Division, but joined 7 Indian Division in Malaya and carried out police work again. It returned to India towards the end of 1946.

The 7 Indian Division began to leave Burma by air for Saigon in September, 1945, and after three months' work on watch and ward duties the tour concluded with an official surrender by senior Japanese admirals and generals. Afterwards a ceremonial parade in honour of the King of Siam was held by Admiral Lord Louis Mountbatten, and the division was flown to Malaya in February, 1946. It was joined there by 23rd Mountain Regiment.

The 33 Indian Mountain Regiment (less animals) was sent by sea from India and joined 7 Division at Bangkok, going to Malaya at Christmas, 1945. It was there broken up, Ahirs going to 25th Mountain Regiment and the Punjabi Mussulmans to 23rd Mountain Regiment.

GENERAL SLIM'S MESSAGE TO FOURTEENTH ARMY GUNNERS

"We regained Burma because we were a team, a team of many races, services and arms, in which each worked not only for his own show but for the whole side. In this team, the Gunners, British, Indian and African, played an outstanding part. They were in on everything.

"For artillery it was the most difficult theatre of all. The immense effort of moving guns through jungle, the problems of clearance, of an often meagre ammunition supply, the lack of visibility, and the constant threat of Japanese infiltration might have reduced the guns to comparative impotence. Yet all of these and a dozen other handicaps were overcome by brains, brawn and determination. Gunners developed new techniques of co-operation with infantry, tanks and air. They became adepts at close defence. They took on any job—road-making, lorry columns, air supply. They acted as infantry, and more than once artillery officers took command of infantry units which had lost all their own officers. They packed themselves and their equipment into aircraft as readily as they undertook a move by road. They mounted their guns in ships and manned them. Nor did three years in the jungle make them slow-moving or static-minded. When we broke out in the plains of Central Burma they, without hesitation, adapted themselves to almost desert tactics and mobility.

"They earned the admiration and gratitude of our own troops and of our allies for gallantry, efficiency and unselfish devotion in their support.

"I saw them come out of Burma in 1942, grimly covering the rear-guard; I saw them go back with the foremost troops in 1944 and 1945. For me, their spirit is typified by the gunner on the Toungoo Road, stripped to the waist, glistening with sweat, slapping shells into the breech of his gun, who, when I said to him, 'I'm sorry you've got to do all this on half rations,' replied, 'Never you mind about that, sir. Put us on quarter rations; give us the ammo., and we'll get you into Rangoon.'

"No wonder we got there."

A TRIBUTE TO THE MOUNTAIN ARTILLERY

by Brigadier G. de V. Welchman, C.B.E., D.S.O., C.R.A. 17 (Indian) Division, and C.C.R.A. 1 Burma Corps, 1942, B.R.A. Fourteenth Army, 1944-5 and B.R.A. ALFSEA, 1945.

"As one who, though never a Mountain Gunner, has seen much of the Mountain Artillery in Peace and War, including the Campaign in Mesopotamia in the First and those in Eritrea and Burma in the Second War, my admiration for them is unbounded.

"In Burma their support, selflessly given, helped to solve a number of problems and brought aid on many occasions to hard-pressed Infantry. They performed miracles with all manner of transport, from their traditional mule-pack to lorries and bullock carts, and more than maintained their great reputation.

"The batteries were well shot and well administered and that invaluable spirit of mutual trust between B.Os., V.C.Os. and men has at all times been evident.

"The debt of gratitude, owed to the Mountain Artillery, will never be forgotten by very many of us and particularly will it be remembered by me as B.R.A. Fourteenth Army, in 1944 and 1945."

CHAPTER XI
Partition

THE YEAR 1947 found an Interim Government carrying on, and the British Government still committed to handing over an undivided India to its new rulers; but public opinion energized by the politicians made it obvious that partition was inevitable. It was also apparent that the only factor capable of preventing chaos was the Indian Army, which was still in process of transformation into class units.

Lord Wavell gave up the Viceroyalty at the end of March, being relieved by Lord Louis Mountbatten. Communal and political riots had not ceased, and a solution was eagerly expected from the new Viceroy. Pandit Nehru and Mr. Jinnah were the leaders of the two sides destined later to become India and Pakistan respectively.

A pledge had been made that a decision would be given in June, and on the 3rd of that month the plan for the future of India was notified. This solution was based on partition; the new Mussulman state of Pakistan was to be cut out of India, and two separate Dominions formed. A plebiscite was held in the settled districts of the N.W.F.P., which voted to join Pakistan. The N.W.F.P. continued its old relationship with the trans-frontier tribes. The Indian Army had to be divided, and that in a very short time, as the 15th August was fixed for Independence day.

The Mountain Artillery had been prepared several months earlier for whatever might befall; many of the British officers had been replaced by Indians, and V.C.Os. and I.O.Rs. who were not to serve in the future armies were discharged or pensioned. Some mountain batteries had been put "in suspense," others had been or were about to be converted into field units or disbanded. Pakistan decided to keep up one mountain regiment of four batteries, and India two regiments of three batteries each. The Pakistani regiment was commanded for several years after Partition by Lieutenant-Colonel W. P. B. Milne, M.C., who may well be called the last Mountain Gunner of the Royal Artillery.

The final distribution of the Indian Mountain Artillery is shown in the table.

Thus ended a period of nearly a hundred years in the history of the Royal Artillery during which officers seconded for short period fought, worked and played with men of other races bound to them by ties of friendship, mutual respect and duty. The parting occasioned the greatest regret on both sides.

DISTRIBUTION AS ON 15TH AUGUST, 1947

ROYAL PAKISTAN ARTILLERY

21ST MOUNTAIN REGIMENT* (Razmak, Wana, Mir Ali).
    1st Royal (Kohat) Mountain Battery (Frontier Force).
    3rd (Peshawar) Mountain Battery (Frontier Force).
    6th (Jacob's) Mountain Battery.
    8th (Lahore) Mountain Battery.

The following became Field Batteries:
    17th (Nowshera) Mountain Battery.
    24th Mountain Battery.
    26th Mountain Battery.
    31st (Jammu) Mountain Battery.

ROYAL INDIAN ARTILLERY

22ND MOUNTAIN REGIMENT (PESHAWAR)
    4th (Hazara) Mountain Battery (Frontier Force).
    5th (Bombay) Mountain Battery.
    7th (Bengal) Mountain Battery.

24TH MOUNTAIN REGIMENT
    2nd (Derajat) Mountain Battery (Frontier Force).
    9th (Murree) Mountain Battery.
    12th (Poonch) Mountain Battery.

MOUNTAIN BATTERIES IN SUSPENSE
    10th (Abbottabad).   14th (Rajputana).
    11th (Dehra Dun).   15th (Jhelum).
    13th (Dardoni).   16th (Zhob).

The following became Field Batteries:
    18th (Sohan) Mountain Battery. 25th Mountain Battery.
    20th Mountain Battery. 30th (Jammu) Mountain
    22nd Mountain Battery. Battery.

---

* Present designation:
1ST MOUNTAIN REGIMENT
    1st (Jacob's) Mountain Battery.
    2nd (Kohat) Mountain Battery.
    4th (Lahore) Mountain Battery.

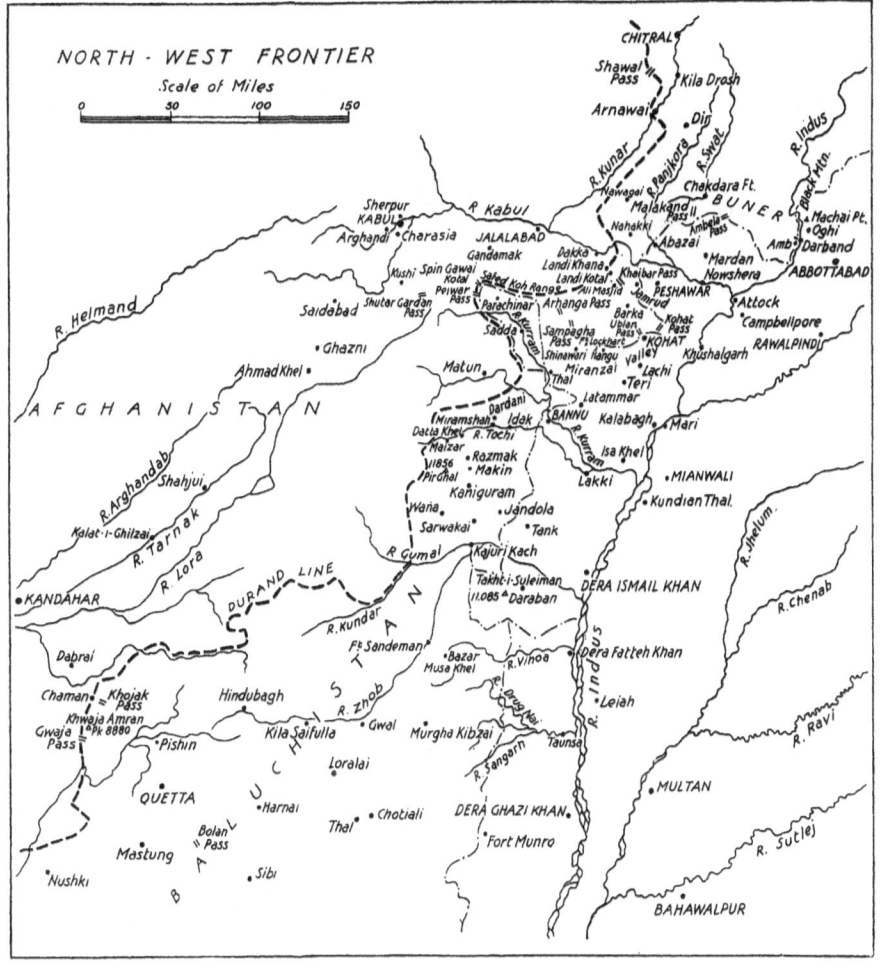

To face p. 424.

APPENDIX I

INDIAN STATES ARTILLERY

Jammu and Kashmir Mountain Artillery

THE KASHMIR ARTILLERY is a link with the old India when French military adventurers served in the armies of the Indian States in wars with each other and against the English. The Kashmir army was trained by French officers on a drill book of the *ancien régime*, and in the eighteen-nineties the older officers of the Jammu and Kashmir Army could still drill their men in the French language.

An Artillery unit existed in 1857 as the Bijli Topkhana, though an earlier mention of Kashmir mountain guns on service is found in Major James Abbott's report at the time of the Sikh rising which led to the Second Sikh War (1848). He raised the countryside against the Sikhs and invested the fort of Haripur with a scratch army supported by four guns lent by the Maharajah of Kashmir: "small guns about $1\frac{1}{2}$ to $2\frac{1}{2}$-prs. mounted on carriages with three wheels, and carried on mules" (No. 4 Hazara Mountain Battery History).

Colonel Mackeson, commanding the first Hassanzai expedition in 1852, mentioned the Dogra guns which supported the Dogra infantry in his left column as having been well handled, and reported that their pack equipment was better than the British.

In 1889 the Kashmir Artillery and infantry were amongst the first to become "Imperial Service" troops.

The Artillery was converted into No. 1 and No. 2 Kashmir Mountain Batteries in 1891 and 1892, armed each with four 7-pr. R.M.L. guns of 224 lb., with British equipment. They relieved each other in Gilgit, from which post two guns of No. 1 Battery had taken part in the Hunza-Nagar campaign under Commandant Hazara Singh in 1891. Lieutenant C. A. Molony was attached in charge (page 73). The India General Service Medal, 1854, with clasp "Hunza 1891," and the Kashmir bronze decoration were awarded to those taking part.

The bronze guns were replaced by 7-prs. of 200 lb. in 1894.

No. 1 *Kashmir Mountain Battery*

In July, 1894, No. 1 Kashmir Mountain Battery, with Lieutenant G. F. MacMunn, D.S.O., as Assistant Inspecting Officer, arrived at Rattu near Gilgit, having been presented with medals for the Hunza campaign by the Resident, Colonel Barr, at Srinagar on the way. After exchanging mules with the No. 2 Battery, the battery was complete to strength of 74 ordnance mules, 24 baggage mules and 7 ponies.

Officers: Hazara Singh, Commandant; Khajoor Singh, Assistant Commandant; Subadar Amar Singh; Jemadars Durga Singh and Alif Khan.

The battery moved to Nomal, eighteen miles north of Gilgit, for the winter; at this time Lieutenant C. G. Stewart was Assistant Inspecting Officer. In March, 1895, the garrison of Chitral was besieged in the fort by the adherents of the claimant to the mehtarship, assisted by several thousand Pathans led by Umra Khan of Jandol, an outlaw and soldier of fortune. Shut up in the fort were the British Agent and his escort and 300 men of the 4th Kashmir Rifles. On 22nd March Colonel J. G. Kelly, commanding at Gilgit, was informed of the situation and he at once set out for Chitral with 400 men of his own regiment, 32nd Punjab Pioneers, the Dogra section of No. 1 Kashmir Mountain Battery, and some Kashmir Engineers; this force was joined by levies from Hunza and Nagar. The guns were accompanied by Lieutenant C. G. Stewart.

Gilgit is some 5,000 feet above the sea, and the way to Chitral (220 miles) lies through the mountainous country of the Hindu Kush. There was a rough track fit for mules for the first 120 miles, and the real difficulties began on reaching the area of snow a few miles farther on. Across the narrow and slippery track in many places were deep drifts formed by avalanches, and ahead was the Shandur Pass (12,800 feet high) to be crossed: this involved thirty miles of snow, exposed to blizzards and without shelter. All available local labour was impressed to act as porters, and stores and baggage were cut down to an absolute minimum. Yaks were collected to trample down the snow on the track, and poles cut for coolie transport. The yaks proved a failure and the mules had to be left behind at the foot of the ascent of the pass. Snow goggles had not been issued and there were only half a dozen borrowed ones in the section. To add to these difficulties, the attitude of the tribesmen likely to be met was unreliable and opposition was expected.

There was no thought of being overcome by these difficulties, and the guns and ammunition were shouldered by carrying parties of infantry, gunners and coolies. The spirit of the troops, gunners and infantry alike, never wavered, and every effort was made to keep up with the advanced guard. Sledges were tried but constantly upset on the uneven track, and there was no alternative to the physical strain of shouldering the heavy loads—each gun weighed 200 lb.—and the advance was unable to make more than one mile an hour. The troops were not to be deterred, however, and after three days of severe exertion the guns were over the pass and ready to come into action. Some country ponies were now available for carrying ammunition and stores, considerably relieving the transport situation.

Ten miles on the far side of the pass, Umra Khan's followers held a strong position at Chakalwat. Here the guns came into action at 700 yards, hitting the sangars and bolting the men sheltering inside; the guns followed up the infantry front line and broke up more sangars, and the enemy fled. Casualties were few and the way lay open to Mastuj, where was a fort seventy miles from Chitral. At this place a halt was made, during which the ordnance saddles and equipment arrived after being brought over the pass, and the section continued the march on ponies.

Colonel Kelly's advance from Mastuj was blocked by a line of sangars at Nisa Gol on both sides of the track where it runs through a precipitous gorge. During the attack the guns were under a hot fire at close range and had seven casualties in a few minutes, but the detachments went on serving their guns steadily. Some friendly levies climbed the hills to turn the flank of the sangars, and when the enemy withdrew, the 7-prs. shelled them at ranges from 950 to 1,425 yards. Our force had nine other ranks killed and the enemy about sixty. The force went on to relieve Chitral on the 20th and gained touch with the relief force which was on its way from India.* This splendid achievement evoked from the Viceroy a

---

* Lieutenant C. G. Stewart's own story will be found in *Blackwood's Magazine* for November, 1926.

message of congratulation for the long and arduous advance, and Commandant Hazara Singh was created "Bahadur," and Havildars Bhalwan Singh and Dharam Singh received the Order of Merit (3rd Class). The Commandant also received a sannad from the Government of India. He shortly afterwards became Brigade Major at Gilgit, and was replaced by Khajur Singh. The India Medal, 1895, with clasp "Relief of Chitral," was awarded to all ranks who took part in this march, as well as the Kashmir lotus-shaped bronze medal. Lieutenant C. G. Stewart was awarded the D.S.O.

In October, 1897, the Government accepted the offer of the Kashmir Durbar of troops for service on the Frontier. From Malakand to the Tochi valley the Frontier flared up with no warning in July, and dire punishment had already been meted out to the Swatis and Mohmands concerned. By October the Tirah Expeditionary Force was ready to move against the Afridis and Orakzais in the Tirah area.

No. 1 Battery with 6 ponies, 65 ordnance mules and 72 baggage mules mobilized at Jammu and entrained on 8th October for Khushalgarh, with Lieutenant G. F. MacMunn, D.S.O., in command, to join the Line of Communication troops. One section was dropped at Usterzai under Commandant Khajur Singh, and Headquarters with the right section marched to Hangu, Kai and Shinawari, forty-one miles from Kohat.

Lieutenant J. B. Mackintosh took charge of the left section which moved to Kharappa on 1st December to join the remainder of the battery. From 6th December to 12th February, 1898, the battery was at Shinawari, thence H.Q. and the left section moved to Fort Lockhart and the right section to Gulistan: the weather was very bad with much snow.

The battery arrived in Kohat from the campaign on 16th April, marching for Khushalgarh on the 26th, and arrived back in Jammu on the 29th. Fourteen men and three followers were invalided: no other casualties occurred. Commandant Khajur Singh was thanked in despatches by Sir William Lockhart, and the services of the battery eulogized. The Commandant received the Order of British India (2nd Class), and the battery was granted permission to bear on its appointments, "PUNJAB FRONTIER". Clasps to the India Medal, 1895, for "Punjab Frontier" and "Tirah" were awarded to individuals present.

The battery moved to Gilgit in relief, arriving in July, 1899, receiving at Srinagar from the Commander-in-Chief, Rajah Sir Ram Singh, K.C.B., four sets of bagpipes as a reward for winning the competitive artillery practice for three years. The battery returned to Jammu in 1901, and in the following year was equipped with 2.5-inch screw guns. New establishment: 4 officers, 72 gunners, 110 drivers, 92 ordnance mules, 48 baggage mules, 6 ponies, 52 artificers and followers.

A depot was formed at Satwari, near Jammu, to which the first postings were Commandant Khajur Singh, Bahadur; Jemadar Balwant Singh; Havildar-Major Din Ram and Drill Naik Balder Singh. Subadar Anant Singh from No. 2 was promoted Major to command No. 1 Mountain Battery *vice* Jemadar Balwant Singh promoted to Subadar.

In November, 1902, the battery formed part of the Northern Army in the Delhi manœuvres, being brigaded with the Peshawar and Quetta Mountain Batteries under Lieutenant-Colonel A. Keene, D.S.O. The battery attended all the principal parades and ceremonies during the

Delhi Coronation Durbar, returning to Jammu at the end of January, 1903. His Highness the Maharajah commanded the battery when it marched past H.R.H. The Duke of Connaught on 1st January at the Durbar.

In August, 1903, the battery arrived in Gilgit on relief: the three worst winter months were spent in tents in Chilas, but in January, 1904, the battery went into new barracks at Bunji.

In August, 1905, No. 1 Battery was relieved by No. 2 and both batteries were inspected by Brigadier-General Coxhead, C.R.A., Northern Command, receiving a very good report.

On 25th October Lord Curzon, Viceroy of India, personally gave H.H. The Maharajah enhanced ruling powers at Jammu, and the battery fired royal salutes. In December the battery fired a royal salute for H.R.H. The Prince of Wales at Satwari, and was inspected by His Royal Highness.

In January, 1911, at the athletic meeting at Gwalior, the Kashmir Artillery won the championship; this was the first time any State other than Patiala had won.

On the occasion of the Coronation Durbar at Delhi, the Order of British India (2nd Class) was conferred on Commandant Balwant Singh, I.O.M.

In October, 1916, the battery was rearmed at Quetta with four 10-pr. B.L. guns for service in East Africa. Strength: 5 officers, 198 rank and file, 38 followers, 3 private followers, and 172 mules. It sailed from Karachi on 27th November and disembarked at Dar-es-Salaam on 7th December. Major A. F. Cole went as Special Service Officer; Major Dharam Singh, Bahadur, commanded the battery, and Jemadars Sarup Singh and Baldao Singh commanded sections. Sub-Assistant Surgeon Chandar Muni went with the battery.

For a report of the operations in East Africa see page 278. The battery returned to Satwari in February, 1918.

Major Dharam Singh went on pension 1st June, 1918, being replaced by Major Atta Mohammed from No. 2 Kashmir Mountain Battery.

The battery went to Bannu in June, and was expanded to a six-gun 10-pr. battery. It was at Quetta from October, 1918 to February, 1919, whence it was ordered to East Persia in June as part of a reinforcement to the East Persian Cordon, made necessary by the outbreak of the Third Afghan War. Major A. F. Cole went as Special Service Officer with the battery, which proceeded by rail to the new railhead at Duzdab, near Robat, where it was split up: two sections went to Seistan and one to Rui Khaf. The battery was reunited in October at Meshed, where it won the hockey tournament.

The Right Section was at Kuchan, north of Meshed, for a short time in 1920, and in October, 1920, the East Persia Force returned to India, the battery going back to Quetta, where it reverted to a four-gun establishment. In 1921 the battery relieved No. 2 Battery at Rattu in the Gilgit district in August. In June the Kashmir State Forces were reorganized on Indian Army lines; the ranks of Captain and Lieutenant were introduced, and Subadar Khushal Khan was promoted Major to command the battery. He received a brevet lieutenant-colonelcy in 1923.

By Indian Army Order 36 of January, 1922, the title "Indian State Forces" replaced "Imperial Service Troops." The new designation was

"Kashmir State Artillery," but the units remained as before, Nos. 1 and 2 Kashmir Mountain Batteries.

In 1923 and 1924 the batteries were rearmed with the 2.75-inch B.L. gun. Captain Rajour Singh was promoted Major to command No. 1 Battery *vice* Lieutenant-Colonel Khushal Singh, appointed Artillery Commander.

On 16th December, 1927, the battery was renamed "1st Jammu and Kashmir Mountain Battery."

In August, 1929, Major Rajour Singh went on pension, being replaced by Major Sher Baz Khan, who was promoted Lieutenant-Colonel in June, 1939, but remained in command of the battery.

In November, 1931, pensions of rank and file were increased by the Kashmir Government to:

	15 *years*	21 *years*	23 *years*
Sepoy	Rs4	Rs5	—
Naik	Rs4/8/-	Rs6/8/-	—
Havildar	Rs6/-/-	Rs9/-/-	Rs11/-/-

These rates were again raised in 1937. Tailors, blacksmiths, saddlers and carpenters, who hitherto had been graded as fighting men, were regraded as followers.

In December, 1938, both 1st and 2nd Batteries were reported as fit for active service. The 1st Battery moved to Secunderabad in September, 1939, for re-equipment with 3.7-inch howitzers, remaining there until September, 1940, when it proceeded to Eritrea. For a report of these operations see page 278.

After the operations at Keren, the battery moved to Lajjun Camp, south of Haifa; but after staying less than a week, left on 7th June, 1941, to take part in the Syrian campaign.

The Vichy French* Government of Syria opened Syrian airfields to German aircraft engaged in fostering the Iraq rebellion, and a force had to be sent in June, 1941, to prevent a German occupation of Syria. The 7 Australian Division moved from Palestine up the coast, and the Free French (six battalions, a battery, and some twenty tanks) with the 5th Indian Infantry Brigade of 4 Indian Division on the right along the Amman–Damascus railway, starting on 8th June. The right column captured Damascus on 21st June, but the Vichy French put up a very stout resistance owing to the great superiority in tanks. The 6 Division less one brigade was sent up to reinforce, and the 1st Jammu and Kashmir Mountain Battery was assigned for close support to 16 Infantry Brigade.

On 9th July the last remaining position of the Vichy French covering Beirut was assaulted against strong opposition. The 2 King's Own was the right forward battalion of 16 Infantry Brigade, and when touch was lost with one company the next night the battery sent out a F.O.O., Captain Madan Lal, who found the company in difficulties under heavy fire, and proceeded to establish its position by knocking out the enemy mortars and machine guns with his guns. Captain Madan Lal was awarded the M.C. for a fine piece of work. Firing was heavy on both sides all that day, 10th, and 2 King's Own had 40 per cent. casualties.

Early on the 11th the enemy's artillery found the battery wagon-

---

* The French Government under Maréchal Pétain, sitting at Vichy, had surrendered to the Germans and was under German control; the French, who under General de Gaulle were determined to continue the struggle, were known as the "Free French."

lines and kept them under heavy shell fire, killing 26 animals and wounding 52. The drivers behaved magnificently and let very few of the mules break loose; some animals were blown to pieces while actually being held by their drivers. Many acts of gallantry occurred: a typical case, only one of many, was that of Driver Devi Daval, who lost an arm but refused to let go of his horse. Casualties among the drivers were two killed and seven wounded.

Meantime the guns had been busy engaging many targets, including tanks and armoured cars, and Signaller Tarlok Nath gained a mention in despatches for keeping the line in repair under heavy shell fire. Great activity went on all day, but the enemy was surrounded when troops arrived from Iraq via Palmyra, and the coastal attack was supported by a naval bombardment. The cease fire was ordered at midnight, 11th/12th, and another operation in which the battery had distinguished itself supporting front-line troops at close ranges was over. The divisional commander visited the guns and gave the battery hearty congratulations and thanks for its good work.

After the end of the Syrian campaign, the battery rejoined 26th Mountain Regiment at Lajjun Camp in October, 1941, and returned with it to Peshawar in April, 1942. In July the Regiment took part in the Datta Khel operations and at the end of the war was in Wana.

The 1st Jammu and Kashmir Battery, equal to any Indian battery in courage in action and for years pre-eminent in sports and athletics, was unable to maintain the technical standards demanded by modern war without outside assistance, and so in October, 1942, it was handed over by H.H. The Maharajah Bahadur to the Indian Army and became 30th (Jammu) Mountain Battery, Indian Artillery, later Royal Indian Artillery. The States Officers were replaced by British Officers, Major H. G. Longstaff commanding; the V.C.Os. and men were compulsorily transferred. From Wana it went to Nowshera in November, 1945, where it stayed until disbanded by Captain G. Hussain on 30th June, 1946.

Dogra personnel of 30th (Jammu) and 31st (Jammu) Mountain Batteries were formed into a field battery of the R.I.A. The mules of 30th were taken over by the 5th (Bombay) Mountain Battery.

2nd Jammu and Kashmir Mountain Battery

This battery has been mentioned under the heading of "Jammu and Kashmir Mountain Artillery," and it would seem to have been raised at Satwari in 1872, and formed the "Artillery of the Bodyguard."

Another record states that it was raised in 1844 and armed with guns made in Jammu, in which case these may be the guns referred to by Major James Abbott (page 4).

The 2nd Battery did not have the same opportunities for active service as the 1st, being often used as a feeder to replace casualties in the latter. Its class composition was Mohammedan and Hindu Dogras, half and half. It took part in the Third Afghan War in 1919, being stationed at Gilgit.

It was taken over by the Indian Government in October, 1942, at the same time and under the same conditions as the 1st Battery, and soon began to make up for lost time as far as active service was concerned. After joining 23rd Mountain Regiment in replacement of the 12th (Poonch) Battery in 1941, it went with the Regiment to 14 Indian Division in Eastern Bengal, being detached for a short spell in Manipur under

14 Corps pending the reorganization of 17 Indian Division. In June, 1942, it returned to Chittagong, and on 1st October was renamed 31st (Jammu) Mountain Battery, Indian Artillery. It took part in the second Arakan operation and the defence of Assam, and went through the campaigns in Burma and Indo-China with 14 and 20 Indian Divisions, distinguishing itself at Dalet Chaung, in Arakan, 1944. (See Chapter X.)

On disbandment in 1946, the Mohammedans of 30th (Jammu) and 31st (Jammu) Mountain Batteries were formed into the 26th Field Battery, R.P.A. (S.P.)

Bahawalpur Mountain Battery

Raised in 1943 at Dera Nawab Sahib as an all-Mahommedan battery, it joined the 20th Mountain Regiment in Peshawar. In 1944, transferred to 29th Mountain Regiment, it remained in Peshawar until returned to the State in February, 1946.

Bikanir Bijey Mountain Battery

Bikanir State possessed artillery many years ago, as there is a record of artillery units serving in both the Sikh Wars and the Indian Mutiny. The artillery was modernized in 1906, and in 1924 a camel pack battery was raised armed with 2.75-inch guns manned by Rajputs. This battery was called Bijey after Sir Bijey Singh, the Maharajah of Bikanir. It moved at the trot: the loads were the same as for a mule battery, and each loaded camel was led by a driver on a riding camel with a gunner mounted behind him. The riding camels were interchanged with the loaded camels for relief, and the battery staff were mounted on camels. There was a slight delay on coming into action, as the driver had first to make the riding camel kneel and then the load camel. The battery was re-formed as a 3.7-inch howitzer mule battery in 1941 and trained at Quetta. It joined the 25th Mountain Regiment, which proceeded to Arakan to join 7 Indian Division. It saw service in Assam and Burma in 1944 and 1945, and returned to the State in 1946. For the operations, see page 339.

Gwalior Mountain Artillery

The Gwalior Artillery was formed at Morar about 1865, and consisted of one battery of Thakurs, Brahmins and Gujars. It was equipped with primitive muzzle-loading guns, but was reorganized as a mountain battery with 2.75-inch equipment in 1926. The mules were of a particularly good stamp. The second-line transport consisted of bullock-carts drawn by magnificent Malwa bullocks.

In October, 1940, the battery sent a section to Chitral in relief (it was flown from Risalpur), and was given six months to raise another section and prepare the battery for war. The battery, now No. 1 Gwalior Mountain Battery, joined the 20th Mountain Regiment in Quetta in April, 1941, and later that year moved with it to Wana, where it served for the remainder of the war. It was returned to Gwalior State in February, 1946.

No. 2 Mountain Battery was formed in Campbellpur by expanding the section from Chitral when the Chitral garrison was withdrawn, and it joined the 31st Mountain Regiment in Kohat and remained there for the rest of the war. In 1945 it was returned to Gwalior State and disbanded.

The Gwalior Artillery Training Centre was formed at Morar in 1941 to serve the Mountain Battery, the Field Battery, the Chitral Section and a ceremonial battery of muzzle-loaders.

Patiala Mountain Battery

This was originally a saluting battery at Patiala, but in December, 1942, was moved to Ambala to be turned into a mountain battery. It was for a time commanded by Major R. T. Ashby. After training, it joined the 31st Mountain Regiment in Kohat and stayed with it until returned to the state in February, 1946.

Note to Appendix I
Malay States Guides Mountain Battery

This battery had no connection with the Government of India, but was maintained by the Sultans of the Federated Malay States for Imperial Defence, along with a battalion of infantry, under the administration of the Colonial Office. It deserves a mention here as the Indian officers and men were Punjabis except for a few Pathans, many being ex-Indian Army soldiers, and the battery was formed and trained by R.A. officers on similar lines to an Indian Mountain Battery. One British officer only was allowed on the establishment.

It had existed for many years as a "Gun Company," armed with six 7-pr. R.M.L. guns without transport, until it was modernized in 1911 by Captain F. E. Spencer and rearmed with four 10-pr. guns as a pack battery, but the establishment of mules was insufficient to man more than one section, and some ammunition was carried on camels when the battery went on service. This shortage of mules was rectified later. The mules had been bought in China and were on the small side for top loads.

The battery under Captain W. Leslie, R.A., joined the Aden Defence Force from October, 1915, onwards, at a strength of 3 Indian officers, 54 gunners and 50 driver other ranks and 5 followers; also 2 ponies and 47 ordnance mules. This force was almost continually in contact with the Turks, had frequent engagements, and a great deal of marching under a very hot sun. Captain Leslie was killed in action in January, 1916, and his place was filled by other R.A. officers from time to time.

The Malay States Guides, Infantry and Artillery, were disbanded at the end of the First World War.

Appendix II

THE GARRISON BATTERY AND POST GUNS

AFTER Nos. 1, 2 AND 3 Horse Light Field Batteries of the Punjab Irregular Force had been raised, a fourth unit was formed at Bannu in 1851 by Lieutenant S. W. Stokes, Bengal Artillery, to include some horse artillerymen of the Sikh Army who were surplus to the requirements of the new field batteries. In 1852 it was named No. 4 or Garrison Company, P.I.F., and manned the guns for the forts at Bannu and Dera Ismail Khan. In 1859 it moved to Kohat, where headquarters remained for many years. It was called "Qila" (Fort) by the native ranks, and manned immobile to give artillery support to frontier posts.

The personnel were to a great extent interchangeable with those of the Mountain Trains and field batteries. For instance, in September, 1856, Sadut Khan of No. 4 Company was transferred to the Hazara Mountain Train as Subadar in exchange for an unwanted Jemadar. As time went on vacancies were filled from the mountain batteries of the Punjab Frontier Force, of which there were four in 1876. In that year the designation was changed from "Garrison Company" to "Garrison Battery," and in December of that year it became No. 5 Garrison Battery to prevent confusion. It was grouped with the four mountain batteries for promotion of Native officers, and one of the five Subadars was given the rank of Subadar-Major. One of the buglers was given the rank of bugle-major. Command was exercised by a subaltern, and for many years it was an understood thing that the Commandant of the "Blokes" (as the Garrison Battery was called), on promotion to captain, was the first on the list of officers to be posted to command a mountain battery. Later on, when subalterns were on the strength as such, they were appointed to mountain batteries after two years in the "Blokes."

The battery was renamed the Punjab Garrison Battery in 1889, and gunners were posted to it from all the eight native mountain batteries and from the drivers of British Mountain Batteries; they consisted of old soldiers and others who were not capable of the arduous work of a mountain battery. The men referred to the unit as the "boorhee" (old women's) battery. At headquarters in Kohat there were some 9-pr. R.M.L., 12-pr. R.B.L.* field guns and 6.3-inch R.M.L. howitzers as fort armament, and equally obsolescent types at Bannu. There was a British Park Sergeant at each fort.

In 1902 the unit was again reorganized ; it was termed the "Frontier Garrison Artillery," commanded by a captain, with two subalterns. By this year it had had twenty-three Commandants, each, no doubt, eagerly awaiting his posting to a mountain battery. The establishment of the unit was fixed to supply detachments to several outposts where there were one or more sections of guns: one subaltern was permanently at Malakand, for that post and Chakdara, and there were sections at Jamrud, Thal and Fort Lockhart (2.5-inch R.M.L.). A British Master-Gunner was stationed at each of the forts at Kohat, Peshawar and Bannu. The muzzle-loading and the R.B.L. guns were soon afterwards replaced by 15-pr. B.L. guns and the 2.5-inch by 10-prs.

* This was the earliest type of B.L. gun, firing a lead-coated shell.

When the mountain artillery was transferred to the Royal Artillery in 1924, the unit was renamed the Frontier Brigade, R.A. There had been an expansion in 1921 when it became a major's command, the number of the other officers being increased to two captains and five subalterns, with ten Indian officers. The Master-Gunners were still on the establishment. The number of posts varied according to the situation: in 1921 there were Malakand, Chakdara, Peshawar, Jamrud, Thal, Kohat, Fort Lockhart, Bannu, Saidgi, Idak and Dardoni, and in the Quetta area Chaman, Hindbagh and Fort Sandeman. Up-to-date guns were provided (4.5-inch howitzers and 18-pr. Q.F. guns) and every advantage was taken of the few opportunities that occurred for joining in field operations. As no transport was on the establishment, it had to be scraped together locally.

The Indian Army List showed in 1925 Major L. M. Davies as Commandant at Headquarters, Kohat, and fifteen detachments. They were:

(a) Malakand and Chakdara.
(b) Peshawar and Shagai (Khyber).
(c) Kohat, Fort Lockhart, Thal and Bannu (later Alizai).
(d) Saidgi, Idak, Razani, Damdil.
(e) Fort Sandeman, Hindubagh, Chaman.

In September, 1926, the Frontier Brigade was reduced, and to replace it groups of Frontier Posts were formed, each group being under command of a mountain artillery brigade, a reversion to the system of "Post Guns" in the Bombay Artillery many years earlier.

In addition to the advantage during operations of there being only one artillery commander for the O.C. Force to deal with, the Post Group System was more attractive to junior officers because they remained on the strength of their brigade during a tour of duty with the Post Group. The Frontier Brigade had never been a popular unit.

The original allotment of posts to Brigades was:

(a) 22nd Pack Brigade, H.Q. Abbottabad.
(b) 24th Pack Brigade, H.Q. Peshawar.
(c) 25th Pack Brigade, H.Q. Kohat.
(d) 23rd Pack Brigade, H.Q. Razmak.
(e) 20th Pack Brigade, H.Q. Quetta.

The situation of the posts was much the same as in the earlier table.

At the outset, personnel of the Frontier Brigade, R.A., were within the establishment of the mountain artillery brigades, but later the artillery brigade establishments were increased to permit the supply of a British officer, one Subadar, one Jemadar, and N.C.Os. and men to man the posts concerned.

After the Afridi operations in 1930-31, new posts on the Khajuri Plain were manned at Fort Salop, Fort Jhansi and Fort Milward. In 1940 the two latter posts ceased to be maintained and that at Fort Salop came under the Peshawar Group. About 1931 the Malakand Group came under the Peshawar Group until 1940, when it was taken over by the Gurkha Battalion at Malakand, 1/3rd Gurkha Rifles.*

---

* The Fort Armament at Drosh had for many years included mountain guns manned by the infantry battalion.

At this time the Frontier Posts still in existence were:

Under 21st Mountain Regiment, Peshawar ...	Landi Kotal, Shagai, Fort Salop.
Under 22nd Mountain Regiment, Ambala ...	Razmak, Arawali.
Under 24th Mountain Regiment, Kohat ...	Kohat, Fort Lockhart, Bannu.

In 1943 the Waziristan Frontier Post, Indian Artillery, was formed at Razmak; it consisted of an independent section of Rajputs.

Until the disbandment of the Frontier Brigade the Garrison Battery and its descendants always formed an integral part of the Indian Mountain Artillery.

APPENDIX III

SURVEY UNITS (INDIAN ARTILLERY)

SURVEY FOR FIELD ARTILLERY was introduced during the First World War, but some years elapsed before it was established in India: the delay was partly due to the fact that the co-ordinates on which the Survey of India was based were spherical, whereas R.A. Survey made use of rectangular co-ordinates.

On 4th August, 1924, the Survey Section was formed at the School of Artillery, Kakul, under Captain E. R. Culverwell, its establishment consisting of two British officers, several V.C.Os. including a Subadar-Major,* and I.O.Rs. from mountain batteries as well as volunteers from other arms who had passed an R.E. survey course at Roorki.

Rapid progress took place, and in a year or so the section took part in manœuvres as well as providing instructors for the Regimental Surveyors' Course at the School of Artillery. Yet more work was laid upon it, and it soon expanded to enable it to carry out the survey of all the artillery ranges in India and to provide data for the Post Guns in the North-West Frontier forts. It also undertook the survey of the Khyber Pass.

Captain Culverwell commanded the section for several years and was followed by Captains N. S. Sitwell, C. L. Ferrard, K. F. McK Lewis, W. J. Gyde and R. MacCaig.

In 1939 its strength included one Subadar, three Jemadars and about fifty I.O.Rs. of mixed classes (P.Ms., Sikhs and other Hindus), and twenty-four horses (twelve of which played polo). M.T. consisted of a truck and two lorries. In that year it began to provide meteor parties for regiments calibrating in all parts of India before going overseas as well as continuing to train surveyors. In February, 1940, a detachment took part in the Ahmedzai operations, surveying positions in support of the main attack.

In January, 1941, the section under Captain MacCaig became "A" Survey Troop, Indian Artillery, and was mechanized with a minimum of M.T. The troop moved to Campbellpur at the time of the School of Artillery move to Deolali, and was given an operational role in G.H.Q. reserve primarily for the North-West Frontier. Lieutenants J. H. C. Hunter and F. A. von Goldstein were its first subalterns. In April, 1941, parties went to Thal and Landi Kotal and fixed gun positions and O.Ps.

On Captain MacCaig's promotion to command an Indian field battery, Captain J. H. C. Hunter took command and Lieutenant S. A. Brighty joined as subaltern; he had had experience in the R.E. as Surveyor.

In January, 1942, the unit became the 1st Indian Survey Battery under Major J. H. C. Hunter, and shortly afterwards rejoined the School of Artillery at Deolali. By this time the strength had been increased by twelve officers, enabling a full scheme of technical training to be put into operation—*i.e.*, in addition to normal survey training, sound ranging, flash spotting and airburst ranging (with improvised equipment) were carried out, and an outdoor miniature range was in constant use.

In August, 1942, the 1st Battery and a new R.H.Q. were combined to form the 1st Indian Survey Regiment. The first Commanding Officer was

* Honorary Lieutenant Kishen Singh, one of the King's Indian Orderly officers.

Lieutenant-Colonel J. F. S. Rendall, with Major J. H. C. Hunter as Second-in-Command and Captain Matthews as Adjutant. Major S. A. Brighty commanded No. 1 Battery, which consisted of one flash spotting troop, one sound ranging and one survey troop. Schemes for training were carried out in conjunction with the School of Artillery. In November the Survey Troop carried out a survey of the Bombay anti-aircraft defences.

In June, 1943, No. 2 Battery was formed under Major F. A. von Goldstein on the same establishment as No. 1, but without a sound ranging troop.

Colonel Rendall, who left on promotion, was succeeded by Lieutenant-Colonel J. P. M. Haslam, who handed over to Lieutenant-Colonel J. H. C. Hunter when the Regiment proceeded to Bidadi (Bangalore area), where a sound ranging troop was formed for No. 2 Battery and each battery establishment was increased by a captain. The Regiment was now equipped with a L.A.D. and for the first time had non-Punjabi personnel posted. The personnel were mixed—flash spotters were P.Ms. and the other troops Sikhs and Hindus.

Each battery now had a battery commander, second-in-command and a subaltern on H.Q. Each of the three troops had a commander and two section commanders. The establishment was thus thirty British officers. From the twenty V.C.Os. were allotted a Subadar-Major to R.H.Q., a Subadar in each battery and eighteen Jemadars, of which each troop had two. The strength of each battery was about 300 and total regimental strength about 700, with 200 vehicles.

In November, 1943, the Regiment moved to Tarabanhatti in the same district and continued training with artillery regiments of 33 Corps and sent meteor parties to various regiments in North-East India. The work of training surveyors was greatly increased by the demand from many new units of Indian Artillery. The Regiment had the misfortune to lose Lieutenant-Colonel Hunter in March, 1944, when he was shot by a disgruntled Sikh. He was much regretted by all ranks. Major Brighty was appointed C.O. in his place.

In May, 1944, the Regiment went to Mysore for a month's intensive jungle training. "R" Troop, an extra survey troop, was formed at this time under Lieutenant R. Jebbs. Majors Slater and Todd were now battery commanders.

In July the Regiment moved by road to Ranchi and in August to the Imphal area, where it came under command of 33 Corps, which had begun the pursuit to the Chindwin River line.

The 11 East African Division, which had taken over from the 23 Indian Division at Tamu, was pressing down the Kabaw valley under conditions of great difficulty through seas of mud. It was joined in October by No. 2 Survey Battery (Major von Goldstein), which came under artillery fire near Honnaing on the day of arrival. A sound ranging base and flash spotting posts were deployed in this area, and Captain Todd, late of No. 2 Battery, being A.C.B.O. with the division, a very close co-operation resulted.

The Kabaw valley was one of the most unhealthy places in Burma, abounding in scrub typhus infection as well as having a high malarial risk. During the advance the road was sprayed with D.D.T. from the air and casualties were kept surprisingly low. The ground began to dry out when the monsoon stopped in the second half of October, and on 15th

November the division occupied Kalemyo. During this period 5 Indian Division had moved from Imphal to Tiddim, where the enemy put up a strong resistance, but by a vigorous attack 5 Division captured the position and went on to the capture of Kennedy Peak, which opened the road to Kalemyo from the east, and early in December 11 (E.A.) Division led the corps across the Chindwin at Kalewa. An extensive bridgehead was formed in spite of enemy opposition. The 11 (E.A.) Division was then taken out of action and No. 2 Survey Battery went into harbour at Kalewa.

The 2 British Division took over here, with R.H.Q. and No. 1 Battery (Major B. C. Slater) of the Indian Survey Regiment attached; Captain Todd was transferred to 2 Division as A.C.B.O. Sound ranging and flash spotting posts were deployed several times during the advance, at Ye-U and on the road to Shwebo, and No. 1 Battery then moved south to take part in the corps artillery concentration covering the crossing of the Irrawaddy river.

The 20 Division crossed at Allagappa on the night of 12th February, 1945, and formed a bridgehead six miles broad and two miles deep: a prolonged and bitter struggle went on for ten days, and enemy resistance was not finally overcome until 27th February. Rocket and fighter-bomber attacks played a great part in the battle: counter-battery work had to be limited owing to shortage of ammunition. The same factor hindered the best use of the guns when covering the crossing of the 2 Division on the 24th at Ngazun, but in both battles sound ranging and flash spotting bases were deployed with considerable success; in the case of the sound ranging bases the battery had to maintain over 100 miles of line.

After the crossings the survey battery joined 20 Division, but did little operational work until the link-up with No. 2 Battery after the fall of Mandalay.

No. 2 Survey Battery joined 19 Indian Division (transferred from 33 Corps to 4 Corps) for the northern crossings of the Irrawaddy, which took place in January. On the 14th two brigades secured footings at Thabeikkyin and another opposite Kyaukmyaung on the following day. The Japanese were taken by surprise, but launched a series of fierce counter-attacks which continued for some days. The battery was fully engaged and Captain Isserliss was awarded a M.C. for gallantry.

The 2nd Battery advanced with 19 Division to Mandalay and, when the main army continued the pursuit, the regiment was concentrated at Myingyan at the end of March. Orders had been issued that units not urgently required were to return to India, and on 13th May, 1945, the 1st Indian Survey Regiment was flown to Comilla. Lieutenant-Colonel H. G. Croly was now in command and repatriation had begun, and many changes of all ranks were taking place. The regiment eventually moved to Hyderabad (Sind) under Lieutenant-Colonel von Goldstein as C.O.

At the Partition the 1st Indian Survey Regiment became 20th Survey Regiment, R.I.A., under command of Lieutenant-Colonel Rajbahadur, having shed 2nd Survey Battery to become 2nd Survey Battery, R.P.A. (later 13th Survey Battery, R.P.A.)

During its lifetime more than eighty British officers served with the Regiment: at least four V.C.Os. and a havildar gained King's Commissions and returned to serve with the unit.

Members of the regiment were awarded one M.C., four M.Ms., a mention in despatches and three certificates of gallantry. Two officers were wounded and three I.O.Rs. killed.

APPENDIX IV

MOUNTAIN ARTILLERY TRAINING CENTRE

IT HAD LONG been the custom for mountain batteries to leave behind at their peace stations after mobilization a small depot of men and heavy baggage. In the early part of the First World War there were depots at Rawalpindi, Nowshera, Kohat, and Abbottabad, and some remained at these places until the end of 1919.

The Rawalpindi depot was responsible for the payment of allowances to the dependents in India of all Indian personnel of mountain artillery serving overseas. Later this depot moved to Dehra Dun, where it came under the supervision of the Mountain Artillery Brigade Commander (Lieutenant-Colonel R. P. Molesworth).

Many new batteries were formed during the war both in India and overseas, and the Mountain Artillery Training Centre was formed on 15th August, 1920, at Dehra Dun, combining the depot already there with all the scattered depots elsewhere. At this date the expression "Pack" was having its short life, and it was originally designated "Pack Artillery Training Centre."

The first Commandant was Colonel H. J. Cotter, most of whose career had been spent in Indian mountain artillery. He had seen active service in China, on the Indian Frontier, and in Mesopotamia.

In October, 1921, the Centre was moved to Lucknow,* which was a long way from the recruiting areas and from the majority of the battery stations. The I.O.Rs. were all renumbered right through and numbering by batteries discontinued. In 1928 it was moved to Ambala, where it remained until taken over by the Royal Pakistan Artillery.

Functions

(*a*) To recruit, approve, enrol, and train all recruits for Indian mountain artillery and the Indian drivers of British mountain artillery. The latter function came to an end when British batteries returned to the U.K. and Egypt.

(*b*) To keep and administer the Records of all Indian mountain artillery units and to be the official connecting link between Indian mountain personnel serving overseas (including the detachment, one section, in Chitral) and their dependants in India.

Chain of Command

Under M.G.R.A. in India for policy, training and posting of British officers.

Under the Adjutant-General in India (A.G.4a) for all Indian personnel. He decided which "Classes" were to be recruited; this in fact became almost a political question and had to be worked out with regiments having class compositions in the Indian Army.

Under the local Station Commander for administration and internal security.

---

* Whilst at Lucknow in December, 1921, a composite training battery from the Centre, under the command of Captain S. H. Wright, took part in the review of the garrison before H.R.H. The Prince of Wales.

Organization

The Training Centre was organized as a Headquarters and three Training Batteries. Establishment was roughly as follows:

Headquarters—British Officers:

Commandant	Lieutenant-Colonel.
Second-in-Command	Major.
Adjutant	Captain.
Orderly Officer	Subaltern.
Quartermaster	Subaltern.
Records Officer	Subaltern.
Accounts Officer	Subaltern.

Indian officers:
Subadar-Major.
Jemadar-Adjutant.
Jemadar-Quartermaster.

There were also some Indian other ranks and some attached Indian personnel from batteries overseas, *e.g.*, Persia and Aden.

Each Training Battery.—Commanded by a Captain with two subalterns, a Subadar, a Gunner Jemadar, and a Driver Jemadar, to assist him. There were about thirty Indian N.C.Os. per battery, of whom about twelve were Havildar Instructors, some sixty mules and a few ponies and, of course, mountain guns.

Each battery was designed to deal with a maximum complement of about 200 recruits. Each battery was divided into a Gunner, a Driver, and a Specialist section.

Recruiting

Mountain batteries in India sent out, and indeed were strongly encouraged to send out, their own recruiting parties, but all recruits had to be sent to the M.A.T.C. for approval by the Commandant and for enrolment and training. Recruits were normally earmarked for the battery which sent them. In addition, special recruiting parties were sent out from the M.A.T.C. from time to time under Indian officers and occasionally under a British officer. The M.A.T.C. took Punjabi Mussulmans, Jats, Jat Sikhs, other Sikhs, Ahirs and Gaur Brahmins, and there may have been other classes. The Ahirs (5 and 19 Mountain Batteries) turned out splendid material, and an Ahir was awarded the only Victoria Cross in Indian mountain artillery.

Training

The Training Course lasted six months. At the end of the course recruits were passed out by the Commandant and posted to batteries. Basic training included gun drill, rifle and marching drill, P.T., driving drill, care of animals, harness, equipment, and education. Some specialist training was also given. When the M.A.T.C. was first formed, training was on the 2.75-inch gun, but the 3.7-inch howitzer was added as soon as batteries were equipped with that weapon.

British and Indian officers from batteries were encouraged to visit the M.A.T.C., and officers and N.C.Os. represented their batteries in turn for tours of duty of from one to two years at the M.A.T.C. with regular reliefs.

The Second World War disclosed more difficulties than the previous one, inasmuch as the expansion (for which no previous plans had been made) was much greater owing to the number of mountain batteries having increased by thirteen, and anti-tank and anti-aircraft units being formed from the same classes. In 1939 the class composition of mountain batteries was 50 per cent. Punjabi Mussulmans, 38 per cent. Sikhs, 8 per cent. Ahirs, and 4 per cent. Punjabi Brahmans. The Punjab was over-recruited at the end of a few months, and men had to be obtained from other provinces; meanwhile the M.A.T.C. underwent a great strain providing V.C.Os. and N.C.Os. not only for mountain and survey units but also for other newly raised artillery units, there being at first no other source available.

The recruits themselves were of low educational and physical standards, and took longer than normal to train to the standard laid down for men ready to post to batteries; parades often began at 7 a.m. and finished at 9 p.m. Recruits were from mountain artillery classes, but were trained for three field regiments, three anti-tank regiments, three heavy, and two light anti-aircraft regiments and, for a time, the heavy batteries of the coast artillery. The Field Artillery Training Centre at Muttra assisted with the men for anti-tank and anti-aircraft artillery, but the drain of N.C.Os. was far greater than could be replaced. V.C.Os. and N.C.Os. were then taken away from mountain regiments to supply these new units. These transfers were made possible by the return of the mountain artillery to the Indian Army in 1939.

The class composition presented the grave drawback that for many months no N.C.Os. of a class, except the Punjabi Mussulmans and Sikhs, were sufficiently trained to act with their own class, and others, generally Sikhs, had to be appointed. This caused dissatisfaction about promotion in new batteries.

By the end of 1941 the situation was so far stabilized that the F.A.T.C. at Muttra administered the field and anti-tank; the M.A.T.C., mountain and survey; and A.A.T.C., the anti-aircraft units. All three Training Centres undertook to train specialists, a task previously carried out in the batteries.

It was difficult to find recruits with the intelligence required for signalling and other specialist tasks. Fitters and Drivers M.T. were trained at the F.A.T.C., but came on the scene rather late.

An N.C.Os.' training unit was formed at Deolali in 1941 to train all classes of all types of artillery to fit them as naiks, and this unit became of great value.

At one time it was proposed that infantry battalions on the Frontier should each have a section of 3.7-inch howitzers on their establishment, and large numbers of infantry N.C.Os. were trained at the M.A.T.C., but as this scheme did not materialize, a great deal of time must have been wasted.

During 1942 some recently raised infantry battalions were converted to anti-tank and anti-aircraft units. In the same year a scheme of enlistment of boys for field and mountain units was begun, whereby they received a long period of education, and a number of signallers and specialists were provided from them.

The difficulties imposed on the M.A.T.C. during the expansion—during the whole war, in fact—were enormous, but by hard work and *esprit de corps* the best possible results were obtained in the face of shortage of officers, of instructors, of equipment and, finally, of personnel.

During the following year the M.A.T.C. was reorganized into three regiments—a depot, a basic training, and an advanced and specialist unit. Its success during the war was owed to the energy and inspiration of Colonel J. W. English, who served in it in every rank, completing two tours of duty as Commandant, the final tour in the rank of Colonel. He was ably assisted by Subadar-Major (afterwards Lieutenant-Colonel) Nizam Din, O.B.I., formerly of 14th (Rajputana) Mountain Battery.

After the war the M.A.T.C. became the Royal Indian Artillery Centre (North), and at the Partition it became the Royal Pakistan Artillery Centre.

Appendix V

RANGE TABLES

ORDNANCE, BRASS, 12-PR. HOWITZER* (page 6)

The howitzer without the quoin stands at 32° nearly.
Common Shell: Bursting charge 5 oz.
Charge 8 oz.

Elevation	2°	4°	6°	8°	9°	10°	11°	Allow ¼" fuze per 100 yards.
Range	200	400	600	800	860	920	980	

Charge 4 oz.
 At 32° range = 1,000 yards : fuze 2.4"
Charge 2 oz.
 At 32° range = 515 yards : fuze 1.7"

Special Case Shot:
Charge 8 oz.

Yards	Elevation	Fuze
270–510	2¾°	.2"
365–595	3¾°	.3"
760–940	8°	.8"
904–1,070	9¾°	1.0"

Bursting Charge, 4½ oz.
Above is from M.S. "Regulations for the Service of the Mountain Battery, R.A. serving on the North Coast of Spain," by Lieutenant Hew G. Ross, 1839.

7-PR. R.M.L. OF 200-LB. (page 31)

Extract from Range Table (*Manual of Mountain Artillery*, 1882)

Charge 12 oz. F.G. powder. Common Shell.

T.E.		Range
°	′	Yards
1	31	500
3	12	1,000
7	45	2,000
14	45	3,000

Charge for double shell: 4 oz.

---

* Referred to as 4⅝ S.B. howitzer.

2.5-INCH R.M.L. STEEL GUN (page 57)

Extract from Range Table (Manual of Mountain Artillery, 1882)

Charge 1 lb. 10 oz. R.L.G.[4] M.V. 1,440 f.s.
Special for Star Shell: 6½ oz. R.L.G.[4]
Projectiles:

    Shell Ring, Cast Iron: 8 lb. 2 oz. with bursting charge 4¼ oz.
    Shrapnel, Steel: 7 lb. 6 oz.
    Star Shell.
    Case Shot.

T.E.		Range	50 per cent. should fall within	
			Length	Breadth
°	′	Yards	Yards	Yards
1	33	1,000	19	.6
4	9	2,000	18	1.3
7	19	3,000	18	2.6
11	7	4,000	20	4.4

10-Pr. B.L. JOINTED GUN (page 101)

Extract from official Range Tables, September, 1900

Projectile: Shrapnel, weight 10 lb.
Charge: 6 oz. 14 dr. Cordite, Mark 1 *or* 7 oz. 12 dr. Cordite, M.D. M.V. 1,289 f.s.

T.E.		Range	50 per cent. should fall within	
			Length	Breadth
°	′	Yards	Yards	Yards
1	27	1,000	20.8	0.5
2	44	1,500	24.5	1.0
4	7	2,000	28.3	1.5
5	36	2,500	32.1	2.0
7	16	3,000	37.0	2.7
9	8	3,500	42.7	3.3
11	12	4,000	49.0	3.9
13	28	4,500	56.1	4.6
15	49	5,000	63.5	5.5
18	16	5,500	71.2	6.3
20	47	6,000	79.0	7.2

A Range Table for Star Shell gives M.V. 991, charge 3 oz. 9 dr., Cordite Mark 1.

Note: This was the first Range Table to mention calibration and to explain a Meteor message.

2.75-INCH B.L. GUN MARK 1 (page 109)

Extract from official Range Tables

Projectile: Shrapnel, 12½ lb.
Charge: 7 oz. 9 dr. Cordite Mark 1 *or* 7 oz. 12 dr. Ballistite, *or* 8 oz. 12 dr. Cordite R.D.B.   M. V. 1,200 f.s.

FULL CHARGE   **HALF CHARGE**
H.E. 12½ lb. 4 oz. 6 dr.
Cordite R.D.B. M.V. 775 f.s.

T.E.		Range	50 per cent. should fall within		T.E.		Range
			Length	Breadth			
°	′	yards	yards	yards	°	′	yards
2	15	1,000	16	.8	4	58	1,000
3	32	1,500	19	.9	7	46	1,500
4	57	2,000	23	1.1	10	53	2,000
6	31	2,500	28	1.5	14	22	2,500
8	15	3,000	34	2.1	18	27	3,000
10	8	3,500	41	3.0	23	22	3,500
12	12	4,000	50	4.2			
14	35	4,500	59	5.8			
17	18	5,000	69	7.7			
20	20	5,500	79	9.8			
22	16	5,800					

Special Reduced Charge: 3 oz. 14 dr. Cordite M.D. H.E., 12½ lb. with fuze 101B. M.V. 836 f.s.

T.E.		Range
°	′	Yards
4	16	1,000
6	40	1,500
9	18	2,000
12	14	2,500
15	32	3,000
21	6	3,700

Q.F. 3.7-INCH HOWITZER MARK 1-1939 (page 154)

Extract from official Range Tables, Part I

Projectiles: H.E. : Shrapnel : Smoke : Star Shell : Weight 19¼ lb.
Charges: Cordite M.D. or R.D.B., size 2¼.

1st 2 oz. 15½ dr.
2nd 3 oz. 10½ dr.
3rd 5 oz. 0 dr.
4th 6 oz. 7½ dr.
5th 9 oz. 0 dr.
Special for Star Shell 8 oz. 11 dr.

1st Charge		2nd Charge		3rd Charge		4th Charge		5th Charge	
T.E.	Range	T.E.	Range	T.E.	Range	T.E.	Range	T.E.	Range
10° 49'	1,000	8° 3'	1,000	5° 23'	1,000	3° 51'	1,000	2° 19'	1,000
30° 2'	2,000	19° 16'	2,000	12° 52'	2,000	9° 23'	2,000	5° 56'	2,000
44° 10'	2,277	44° 10'	2,788	23° 33'	3,000	16° 16'	3,000	10° 14'	3,000
				44° 10'	3,641	26° 12'	4,000	15° 30'	4,000
						44° 10'	4,560	22° 47'	5,000
								41° —	6,000

APPENDIX VI

MOUNTAIN ARTILLERY STATIONS (1939)

BY LIEUTENANT-COLONEL C. E. C. BURTON, R.A.

ABBOTTABAD

This has always been one of the best Mountain Artillery stations, and the depots of the 5th and 6th Gurkha Rifles were situated here; also that of the 13th Frontier Force Rifles.

A mountain regiment, less one battery at Rawalpindi, was normally stationed in Abbottabad.

The climate was good and only a short period, mid-June to mid-September, was in any way unpleasant. Snow used to fall and lie for a short time in the cold weather, usually about Christmas.

Sports facilities were good and varied, and included two excellent polo grounds and a good golf-course. Good fishing was to be had in the Haro river, and a certain amount of rough shooting was obtainable in the hills around the cantonments.

A popular feature was its proximity to Kashmir.

AMBALA

A typical plains station, containing a mountain regiment less two batteries. The hot weather was long and very trying, although the monsoon brought a little relief, but with a great increase in humidity. The Mountain Artillery Training Centre was also situated at Ambala, having moved there from Lucknow in 1928.

There were certain compensations for those Gunners stationed in Ambala; good shooting of all kinds was obtainable and pig-sticking was a popular pastime, the country being suitable for beginners. There were polo grounds at Ambala and also reasonable sports grounds. Shortage of water was the ever-present problem in this station, and the perennial hot-weather droughts made life very difficult. The R.A. Station Mess was one of the oldest of the Gunner Station Messes in India, and maintained a very complete and interesting set of records.

BANNU

Although it ceased to be a permanent mountain battery station in the 1920's and became H.Q. of the Frontier Brigade, R.A., Bannu must be mentioned here owing to its long association with mountain artillery dating back to the very early days, and to the fact that all ranks going to or coming from North Waziristan, for which it was the railhead, were familiar with the place. It is sixty miles from the broad-gauge railway at Darya Khan. The fort, built by Ranjit Singh, housed the headquarters of the Bannu Brigade and one of its battalions, the others being quartered in the cantonment. The native city was the resort of criminals and murderers galore, and the cantonment was surrounded by a barbed wire entanglement.

The climate was hot from March to October, and the cold weather was subject to spells of snow and frost occasionally.

The amenities consisted of a club with swimming bath, tennis courts, polo, football and cricket grounds and a golf-course.

DEHRA DUN

Two batteries of the mountain regiment, with H.Q. at Ambala, were stationed at Dehra Dun.

Good shooting of all kinds was to be had near at hand. The usual facilities for games existed, including polo.

FORT DROSH, CHITRAL

The Chitral Mountain Artillery Section was very popular amongst subalterns. It was an independent unit, far from the beaten track, and the country offered unrivalled opportunities for shooting ibex, markhor and kindred game at very small cost.

Good winter sports were also to be had and a certain amount of small game shooting.

The officer establishment of the section was two, and the tour of duty was two years.

KOHAT

The H.Q. and one battery of a mountain regiment were stationed in Kohat, which was garrisoned by an Indian Cavalry regiment and an infantry brigade. The hot weather was very trying, being, if anything, worse than in Peshawar, but it was followed by an excellent cold weather.

Kohat was justly famed for the many colourful flower gardens in the cantonments, which were at their best in the cold weather at which season the two out-station batteries used to come in from Thal and Rawalpindi for regimental training. Sports grounds were good and included a polo ground and golf-course. A Gunner Mess was opened in Kohat a few years before the outbreak of war and was situated in an odd building which had been an elephant stable in the early days of Kohat.

The fourth battery was at Mir Ali.

LANDI KOTAL

A single-battery station, situated at the highest part of the Khyber Pass, and garrisoned by an infantry brigade. Its main advantage was that it was cooler than Peshawar in the hot weather. Restrictions on movement were irksome, and to move outside the perimeter of the camp and off the road required escorts of khassadars. Good sports grounds existed within the camp, as well as squash and tennis courts.

The Gunner Mess was famed for its all-concrete billiards table, built by the Sappers in the early 1930's, and which still functions well despite the earthquake shocks to which that area is prone.

MAYMYO, BURMA

This was a single-battery station, about 4,000 feet above mean sea-level and one independent mountain battery was stationed there. Buildings were reasonably good and the battery ran its own farm, producing barley and green fodder for its animals. The Mess was a pleasant two-storied building. There was an excellent club which catered for both the social and sporting activities of members. Reasonable polo was to be had for about six months of the year in the non-monsoon period. There was also a bi-weekly paper-chase. Plenty of big and small game shooting was obtainable within easy reach, and good fishing was to be had in the Northern Shan States. Mandalay was only forty miles distant.

MIRALI

This was a single-battery station after 1938 and consisted of a fort, garrisoned by part of an infantry brigade, situated some twenty miles from Bannu on the Razmak road. The garrison was confined to the fort except on "road-open" days, when it marched out and opened a sector of the Bannu–Razmak road.

This restriction on movement and the barren and rocky hills which flanked the fort did not popularize Mirali as a station. Normally, the mountain battery was relieved yearly.

NOWSHERA

This was a single-battery station, garrisoned by an infantry brigade and much resembling Peshawar, from which it is twenty-seven miles distant. Climate and amenities were the same as those of Peshawar, but on a smaller scale. There were two hunts near at hand, one in Nowshera and another in Risalpur, and also there were good polo grounds. Good shooting was handy.

PESHAWAR

The H.Q. and two batteries of a mountain regiment were stationed in Peshawar. This was a good station with a short and trying hot weather, followed by a long and, in the main, pleasant cold weather.

Amenities were good and included hunting with the Peshawar Vale Hunt, polo all the year round, and varied small game shooting within reasonable distance.

There were good sports grounds for all types of games in the cantonments. An excellent Gymkhana Club with grass tennis courts, squash courts, swimming-bath and golf-course was the principal social centre of the station.

Peshawar was noted for the profusion of its flowers, which were most attractive in the spring—particularly the roses. People took a pride in their gardens and the Cantonment authorities took a pride in the public gardens and the roadsides, and there was plenty of water at all times.

QUETTA

A mountain regiment, less one battery, was stationed at Quetta. Quetta is a large military station in Baluchistan and some 5,000 feet above mean sea-level. The climate was good and the hot weather not unreasonable. Facilities for all forms of sports were very good, including polo and hunting.

One battery of this regiment was stationed at Fort Sandeman, where some small game shooting was to be had. The fair sex was not allowed here.

RAWALPINDI

Two mountain batteries lived in the West Ridge Barracks at Rawalpindi during the hot weather, and moved to join their regiment at Kohat and Abbottabad respectively for training in the cold weather. As a hot weather station, Rawalpindi was not good; there were periods of intense heat broken by violent thunderstorms and followed by periods of much increased humidity and resultant discomfort. One advantage of Rawalpindi was its situation on the main route to Kashmir, it being only a one-day journey to Kashmir by car.

Razmak

Razmak was a large perimeter camp containing five infantry battalions and the H.Q. and two batteries of a mountain regiment, and a Medium Section, R.A. It was situated seventy-two miles from railhead at Bannu and some 6,500 feet above mean sea-level. It had a number of advantages and was a popular station despite the restrictions on movement outside the perimeter. The climate was excellent and hot-weather temperatures seldom exceeded 90° F. More or less active-service conditions always prevailed in Razmak. Amenities were good and sports grounds were plentiful—a zest was added to sport by sporadic sniping which was aimed at persons playing games, the only way to combat this being to put out piquets on playing fields. A good bazaar and cinema existed in the camp; also a roller-skating rink and an excellent club.

Thal

Thal consisted of a modern fort built to house an infantry battalion, mountain battery and ancillary units. It was situated some sixty miles from Kohat in the Kurram valley, and on the road to Parachinar and the Afghan border. It was an unpopular station for mountain artillery, being unhealthy and very restricted from a training point of view, and it was difficult to keep men and animals fit. A peculiarly virulent type of malaria was rife in Thal.

Wana

This was a two battery station in South Waziristan, just over sixty miles from railhead at Manzai and about 4,500 feet above mean sea-level. These two batteries were part of the mountain regiment with H.Q. at Razmak.

The garrison of Wana was an infantry brigade, and it was a somewhat similar station to Razmak, but much better built and laid out, and restrictions on movement were not quite so rigid.

As to climate, it was not as good as Razmak, but nevertheless better than many plain stations, and the hot weather was short, June to mid-September being hot and the season for violent dust storms. Barracks, messes and quarters were well-built stone buildings, and long baths were provided in officers' quarters. The Gunners lived in the R.A. and R.E. Mess, which was very comfortable and possessed of a fine fruit garden. Sports grounds were good and plentiful, and there was an excellent polo ground. Before the completion of the new aerodrome it had been a local rule on the original one that the ground had to be vacated by the players when aircraft came in sight. Piquets were put out to prevent sniping from a near-by village.

The Wana Drag Hunt used to meet twice a week and hunt over the Wana Plain, escorted by mounted Khassadars, and the jackal was occasionally hunted. There was chukor and duck shooting in season, under the eyes of an armed escort.

Appendix VII

THE REUNION OF VETERANS OF THE INDIAN MOUNTAIN ARTILLERY AT AMBALA IN MARCH, 1933

By Lieut.-General Sir George MacMunn, K.C.B., K.C.S.I., D.S.O.
Colonel Commandant, R.A.

It was my privilege in this March of 1933 to take part in one of the most interesting of occasions that I have ever seen in India—the first Reunion of Veterans of the Indian Mountain Artillery and Light Batteries. The Indian Mountain Artillery, which I joined in 1891, consisted then of 8 batteries, rose in the World War to 34 and now stands at 19. For some years it has had its own Training Centre, located at Dhra Dun for a while, at Lucknow, and since 1931 in its proper province of the Punjab at Ambala. The Mountain Artillery Centre is a Lieutenant-Colonel's Command, with a due proportion of all ranks and grades, and from what I saw of it a very efficient institution indeed. The large and long-famous station of Ambala, once the cantonment of a horse artillery and cavalry brigade, of infantry and pioneers, has fallen from its greatness, owing to the dying of the water supply, which involves also the fodder. This is believed to be due to the earthquake in the north of India some twenty-five years ago which was very severe near and in the hills. By it the water-bearing strata were injured and altered. Such a happening made the removal of the mounted troops imperative. Therefore the old glory has departed, though a new one has arisen, in that the station now holds three artillery regimental headquarters—vix., of a mountain artillery and a medium brigade as well as the Training Centre.

The result of this is that the old Artillery mess is once more a flourishing concern, at which many officers of the Regiment will rejoice. The officers of the Mountain Artillery have long planned this reunion, the first of its kind, and the move to a suitable centre in the Punjab in 1931 made it possible. Though it was known that there were perhaps 6,000 non-effectives of the Indian ranks of the Mountain Artillery, it was not till 1921 that a record office was established and their whereabouts centrally known. Even then many were not traceable, and eventually it was arranged that each of the six mountain artillery brigades should submit 200 names of men to be invited to a reunion, while further publicity was given in the *Fauji Akhbar*. Finally some 230 Indian officers and about 1,300 pensioners were invited. By no means all were well enough to come, but every facility by road and rail was offered and eventually there turned up some 152 Indian officers and 750 other ranks. Admirable arrangements were made by Colonel Little and his staff, a large camp was pitched and the young soldiers of the Centre organized to wait on and take care of the old. The Commander-in-Chief in India, Field-Marshal Sir Philip Chetwode, promised to come, and as many senior R.A. officers as could do so, with the commanders of all the Mountain Artillery Brigades, and any one else in important places of the Regiment.

I had arranged to visit India as the Representative Colonel Commandant for the year, and when His Majesty as Colonel-in-Chief of the Regiment heard that I was going he sent for me, bade me give his greetings to all ranks and all races, and especially to give his good wishes and appreciation to the gathering of veterans at Ambala.

The functions were to include sports, displays and spectacles while open-air cinemas had been provided. Information of the gathering had been sent to any old Mountain Gunner officers in England who could be traced, and the Commandant received hosts of messages—messages of great affection—from many old officers. From first to last all the arrangements worked admirably, and the gathering was a scene of romance and fidelity beyond description. I arrived myself on the day of assembly, or rather the day after, and I rode round with the Commandant to see the veterans in their camp, amid scenes of enthusiasm and at times of pathos. Assembled in a little clump as I rode in were the remnant of men who had been with me in No. 6 Mountain Battery (Jacob's), first among them Captain Muhammad Ismail Khan, of gallant memory. My own service in the Mountain Artillery has been far less than I could have wished, but in 5 for a short time and later in 6 I had passed some happy years and seen my *baptéme de feu*, under unusual circumstances.

The little clump of eight or ten were a gallant and somewhat pathetic remnant of good days . . . pathetic, for it is sad to see the best wrestler, or the man that would carry off a whole gun on his own back, among the feeble, in the sear and yellow leaf. "Creep home and take your place, then, the old and maim among." And then among them was that hearty embrace, breast to breast and hand over back after the way of the Punjab, and somewhere else. Among the veterans, and seemingly some of the youngest, were two Subadars of the same name, Captains Ghulam Muhammad, both of the Derajat Battery (No. 2), both of whom wore the star of Lord Roberts' March from Kabul to Kandahar when George Swinley commanded. I had the privilege of being photographed by their side.

Among the happy thoughts was to bring there 32 boys from the King George's Military Schools at Jhelum and Jullundur, all the sons of mountain artillery officers, a charming lot of nice-looking boys, lads of the old Punjab blood, who will form some of the material for the Indian Military Academy. It was specially desired that the old men should see what the Government was doing in this matter, and that more and more should aspire to see their sons there. The lads gave an excellent gymnastic display, and were, we will hope, equally impressed with the sight of the veterans and their "midals and sthars."

On 16th March, in the morning, the Chief arrived and with him the Quartermaster-General, Sir Alexander Wardrop, Colonel Commandant, R.A., Lieut.-General Kirwan, the Master-General of the Ordnance,* Major-General Newcome, the Inspector of Artillery, Brigadier A. H. Moberley, commanding the Artillery of the Northern Command, and Colonel Farfan, commanding the Artillery School at Kakul.

The Chief took immense trouble and walked down the long and eager line of veteran officers and men, talking to a great many, and asking the story of medals and decorations. Sir Philip told me that he had been greatly thrilled, that he had never seen so vast a gathering of India veterans, and that he had been astounded to see the medals and decorations and to think of the years of loyal, staunch service they must represent. He then received the veteran officers in a *shamianah*. The officers were all

---

* Now also Colonel Commandant.

in their uniforms (the other ranks in mufti), and he touched the hilt of each sword proffered in the old faithful Indian fashion. The Chief spoke to the pensioned officers as follows:

"I am an old soldier, and to you old soldiers I say how glad I am to meet you. Your medals show that you have a proud record, and have served in India, Burma, and in the Great War on many fronts. I even see some who marched with Lord Roberts from Kabul to Kandahar. Your services to the Sirkar are most honourable, and it should be an inspiration to your successors to keep up the great traditions of your Corps. I wish you all long life and prosperity."

Later in the day came the sports and display, which the Chief also attended, and the great feature of which was the turning out of a team carrying every one of the various guns issued to the mountain service during its history. Such were the 7-pr. S.B. and the 12-pr. howitzer of the period before the Mutiny; the 7-pr. R.M.L. of 200 lb., with its lighter model of 150 lb., used for coolie transport; the 7-pr. (2.5-inch), the original screw-gun; the 10-pr. B.L.; the 2.75-inch B.L., and the 3.7-inch howitzer Q.F., firing a high explosive or shrapnel shell of 20 lb. It is this powerful weapon with an effective short range shrapnel and long range high explosive that is being tried on a travelling carriage as a horse artillery gun in India.

The next day we had two special occasions, after much photographing. It had been arranged that I myself should preside at a formal Durbar of all the officers serving and pensioned, but before this there was a great assembly of all the other ranks and much talk and discussion to which I went and gave the King's message at some length. The King had said to me "Say to them the sort of things you know I should like to say to them." And this gave me room for a fairly ample talk in the vernacular. And then I sat while messages to old comrades were read out from old Mountaineer officers in England, after which it amused the men to call for cheers for various officers that they remembered, and I was interested to note that among many there was great veneration for *Percussion Sahib*, which, if you please, was Fergusson, just as in earlier days Broadfoot was Brasspot Sahib. But *Percussion Sahib* was the most famed among them, as well he might be.

The formal Officers' Durbar which followed was more like a frontier jirga than anything else. All were in uniform and swords; in fact, as the old jargon had it, "in full dress of their pay and rank,"

Lieut.-Colonel Little read out a telegram from the King, and from many who could not be there, and then I opened the Durbar formally, taking the occasion to give the King's message in more detail, with less Punjabi than to the rank and file, explaining how the King knew all that went on everywhere, and that his heart was very soft for his soldiers and how anxious he was that the various steps in Indianization should be a success, and that it was their sons who should go to the schools and the Academy and be pillars of state and of a Royal Army. Then stood up stout old Muhammad Ismail, number one of a gun when I knew him and immensely distinguished at the episode of Maizar, as had also been Uttam Chand who was with the other ranks. Gravely and elaborately did he on behalf of all present make exactly the right reply, one of much enthusiast and loyalty for the Crown and keen appreciation of all that was being done for them and all that the Crown and British direction stood for, and such-like and so forth, followed by one or two more of the veterans in the same strain, and when it was over the old feet crunched away, and I think we, their British officers and comrades, felt the glory and the pathos deep into our bones, as the Chief had done.

But I was to assure His Majesty that in one week they would clear out the whole of Delhi and all the *Ghandi-Shandis*, and the *babu-shabu*, and everyone else who talked too much and made *taklif*, if only the King and the Chief would give the word! Of such is the stout old yeomen peasantry and smallholder of the Punjab, and indeed of Hindustan. The Mountain Artillery is now drawing its men from the best stuff in Hindustan as well as from the Punjab—viz., Rajput, Moslem, Ahir and Jat—and some of these were there also. But the camp was deep in the slow drawl of the Punjab, the Prakrit like unto that of Sussex or Lancashire . . . the *aunnnda* the *jaaala*, long and deep and broad, as we have so often heard in our time.

And all the while the recruits, the strapping boys from the farms, the choice young men and goodly, were standing by agape, and we hope taking it all in. For, good as the old gunners and the old batteries were, from what I saw this year, of which I hope to tell later, the batteries are better than ever, and the boys in the depots like to be the same. Thus we talked it out with one another as old men should, saying:

"After me cometh a builder
Tell him I too have known."

To Lieut.-Colonel Little, who organized it all, with his officers, very many thanks of very many people are due, and it must have been a stirring finale to the close of his long and distinguished regimental career. The memory of his mountaineers, and his old brown mules, will be further stimulated when he thinks of the hundreds of veterans to whose lives the great gathering can have brought nothing but pleasure and gratification.

OUTSTANDING INDIAN VETERANS

Among the distinguished old soldiers of the batteries, both mountain and of the light batteries, the following names will interest those who knew them, as being alive and flourishing in the flesh—viz., Captain Muhammad Ismail, the hero of the Maizar episode, and Naik Uttam Chand. Other outstanding individuals at the reunion were: Hon. Captain Ghulam Muhammad of Dhulmial village, Jhelum, who enlisted in 1875 and was serving in the Derajat battery in Lord Roberts' march to Kandahar. Also Hon. Captain Ghulam Muhammad of Rawalpindi District, another Derajat battery and Kabul—Kandahar veteran; Hon. Captain Kishen Singh of Nawashahr, Jullundur, who was Orderly Officer to H.M. the King in 1927; and Hon. Captain Ude Singh of Nuthawal, Ludhiana.

Reprinted by kind permission from "The Journal of the Royal Artillery, October, 1933.

Glossary

atta	Flour.
bannia	Storekeeper.
basha (Burma)	A bamboo shelter.
bazar, bazaar	Permanent market or street of shops.
beehive (Burma)	Charge made up in conical form for blowing holes in roofs.
bhisti, bhistie	A water-carrier (enlisted follower).
box (Burma)	A perimeter camp of any size, wired if wire was available.
bunker (Burma)	A splinter-proof weapon pit.
chagal	Canvas water-bag.
chaudri	A native accountant.
china	Spring (water).
coolie	An unskilled labourer, often a burden-carrier.
dacoit	A robber belonging to an armed gang of five or more.
dah	Burmese knife.
dak	Transport by relays of men and animals.
dara	Pass.
darogha	A superintendent, generally used of an agent who buys rations and forage for troops.
diwan	Prime Minister of a native state.
dunderstick	A stick of which one end is fastened to a mule's head-collar and the other to the body roller to prevent him eating his blanket at night.
durbar	A levee. Durbar, the executive government of a native state.
ekka	Two-wheeled native cart drawn by one horse, used by Indians.
faqir	A religious mendicant (Mohammedan).
foxhole	A hole in the ground giving complete cover and permitting the use of a weapon.
ghar	Mountain peak.
ghazi	A Mohammedan fanatic.
Ghilzai	A large and important Afghan pastoral tribe.
gram	Pulse, used instead of oats.
harbour	A place safe from enemy interference.
havildar	An Indian non-commissioned officer, corresponding to sergeant.
havildar-major	An Indian non-commissioned officer, corresponding to sergeant-major.
jemadar	A junior Indian officer in an Indian unit.
jehad	Holy war of Mohammedans against the infidel.
jezail	Heavy firearm fired from a forked rest.
jezailchi	A man armed with a jezail.
jirgah	Meeting of tribal elders.
John Company	Personification of the Honorable East India Company.
kafila	Caravan.
kach	Alluvial flat on river bank.
kahar	A porter whose speciality is to carry a palanquin.
khan	A chief, properly of Pathan descent.
khwar (khor)	Ravine.
khud	Precipitous hillside.
kizilbash	(Red cap), a tribal policeman.
kotal	Mountain pass; col.
kot	Walled hamlet.
lakh	100,000.

lascar	Inferior class of artilleryman (gun-lascar); a sailor.
lashkar	Army.
Mahommedan	Also spelt Mussulman, Muslim, Mohammedan.
maidan	A plain.
mullah	A religous teacher.
moulvi	A teacher.
mistri	An artificer (enlisted follower).
malik	A headman.
mochi	A leather-worker (enlisted follower).
mutsuddy	A native accountant.
mussack	Leather water-bag (goatskin) carried by a bhisti.
naik	An Indian non-commissioned officer, corresponding to a corporal.
nalband	A shoeing-smith.
narai	Pass or col.
oba	Water.
paddy	Rice in the husk.
pagri	Turban. The soldier's pagri consisted of several yards of specially thin material.
pakhal	Leather water-bag, later a metal water container, carried one each side of a mule.
pakhali	Man who fills a pakhal and distributes water from it.
Pathan	Generic name for the Mohammedan tribes who live on both sides of the North-West Frontier of India.
Pir	Saint.
powindah	A nomad.
raj	Power or government.
ramzan	Fast month of Mohammedans.
raghza, rogha	Plateau on edge of valley.
sangar	Breastwork of large stones.
sannad	Robe of honour.
salutri	Indian farrier or horse-doctor.
sirkar	The State—the Government.
subadar later subedar	Senior Indian officer in an Indian unit.
subadar-major	A senior subadar.
sowar	A cavalry soldier.
syce, also sais	A groom.
surra	Fever affecting animals during the rainy season in the tropics.
tindal	Originally a corporal of lascars.
tor	Black.
tum-tum	Two-wheeled dog-cart drawn by one horse.
tonga	Substantial two-wheeled vehicle drawn by two horses.
viliayat (Turkish)	An administrative district.
wam	Same as kach.
yaboo	Large pony, generally applied to a useful type of animal bred in Afghanistan.
yak	Tibetan ox.
zam	River.

Abbreviations

A.A. & Q.M.G.	Assistant Adjutant and Quartermaster-General.
A.B.D.A.	American, British, Dutch, Australian.
A.L.F.S.E.A.	Allied Land Forces, South-East Asia.
B.L.	Breech-loading.
B.R.A.	Brigadier, Royal Artillery.
Brig.	Brigadier.
C.R.A.	Commander, R.A.
D.A.	Director of Artillery.
D.F.	Defensive Fire.
D.I.K.	Dera Ismail Khan.
Div.	Division.
E.F.	Expeditionary Force.
F.O.O.	Forward Observation Officer.
G.H.Q.	General Headquarters.
G.O.C.	General Officer Commanding.
G.S.	General Staff.
G.S.O.	General Staff Officer.
Hav.	Havildar.
H.E.	High explosive.
I.A.	Indian Army.
I.A.O.	India Army Order.
I.A.R.O.	Indian Army Reserve of Officers.
I.D.S.M.	Indian Distinguished Service Medal.
I.G.	Instructor of gunnery.
I.M.A.	Indian mountain artillery.
I.M.B.	Indian mountain battery.
I.O.R.	Indian other ranks.
L.A.D.	Light Aid Detachment.
L. of C.	Line of communications.
L.R.P.	Long Range Penetration.
M.A.	Mountain artillery.
M.A.T.C.	Mountain artillery training centre.
M.B.	Mountain battery.
M.C.	Military Cross.
M.E.	Martini-Enfield.
M.S.M.	Meritorious Service Medal.
M.V.	Muzzle velocity.
N.C.O.	Non-commissioned officer.
N.W.F.	North-West Frontier.
O.P.	Observation post.
P.A.	Pack artillery.
P.A.T.C.	Pack artillery training centre.
P.B.	Pack battery.
P.F.F.	Punjab Frontier Force.
Q.M.	Quartermaster.
R.A.	Royal Artillery.
R.E.	Royal Engineers.
R.F.A.	Royal Field Artillery.
R.G.A.	Royal Garrison Artillery.
R.I.A.	Royal Indian Artillery.
R.M.L.	Rifled muzzle loading.
R.V.	Rendezvous.
S.B.	Smooth bore.
T. and P.	Time and percussion.

Index

Abbott, Lieut.-General Sir J., 3, 4, 15, 35
Abbottabad, 15, 105, 447
Abbottabad mountain gun, 17
Abbottabad Mountain Battery (10th), 100, 117, 121, 158, 159, 161, 162, 165, 192, 199, 234, 241, 270, 286, 293.
Abbey, Capt. J. H., 362
Abdul Haq, 254
Abdul Latif, Quartermaster-Havildar, 196
Abdul Rased, Naik, 254
Addison, Major, 337
Addis Ababa, 273, 274, 277
Aden, 121
Admin. Box, 342, 345
Afghanistan, 1920, 203
Afghan War, Second, 41
Afghan War, Third, 203
Afmandu, 123
Africa General Service Medal, 123
Afridis, 7, 86
Agror valley, 32
Ahmed Khan, Havildar, 316
Ahwaz, 160, 182
Air command, 362
Air lift of mountain battery, 347, 348
Air O.P. squadron, 381, 386, 413
Air supply, 375, 415
Aitken, Lieut.-Colonel W., 84
Aka Khel, 12
Akbar Ali, Subadar-Major, 107
Akyab, 393, 394, 395, 399, 401, 402
Alaf Khan, Subadar, 149, 154
Alam Khan, Havildar, 217
Alam Khan, Subadar, 253
Alexander, Field-Marshal The Earl, 312
Ali Ahmed, Driver Naik, 133
Ali Akbar, Naik, 353
Ali Bahadur, Havildar, 316, 320
Ali Madat, Subadar-Major, 2, 8, 107
Ali musjil, 41, 113
Alla Ditta, Subadar, 296
Allenby, Field-Marshal Lord, 196
Allsop, Lieut. F. E., 46
Ambala, 447
Amman, 195, 196
Amanulla, 202
Amara, 159
Amb, Khan of, 33

Ambela, 28
Amir Singh, Jemadar, 14
Anaut Ram, Subadar, 253, 255
Anderson, Lieut. C. A., 52, 112
Anderson, Lieut. R. F., 252
Anzac, 128
Aosta, Duke of, 273, 279
Arab Rebellion, 188
Arakan, 322, 323, 339, 393, 404
Armitage, Major E. L., 241
Armstrong, R. B. L. gun, 26
Armstrong, Colonel R. A., ix, 126, 134
Armytage, Lieut., 134, 177
Arsal Kot, 250
Artillery schools, 201, 226
Ashby, Major R. T., x, 277, 281
Askaris, 141
Asmara, 273
Assam front, 1943, 335, 349
Atkins, Capt. P. L., x
Auchinleck, Field-Marshal Sir Claude, 234
Aurang Zeb, Lance-Naik, 155
Auraung Zeb, Jemadar, 303
Australians, 128, 285
Ava, 317, 385
Awdry, Lieut.-Colonel R. J., ix
Ayab Khan, Gunner, 353
Aylmer, Capt. F. J., 72, 73

Bachan Singh, Naik, 359
Backhouse, Lieut. J. B., 2, 3
Badenoch, Capt. G. D., 363
Baghdad, 157, 174, 189
Bagshawe, Lieut., 345
Bajour, 236
Baker, Brig.-General, 46
Baku, 176
Bala Hissar, 46
Baldwin, Lieut. J. G., 65
Baluchistan, 15, 119
Bannu, 219, 245, 260, 447
Bara Singh, Subadar, 192
Barford, Lieut.-Colonel B. C., x, 325
Barrington, Colonel J. F., ix, 122
Basra, 157
Baston, 2/Lieut. A., 149
Battle Honours, 215
Bayley, Capt. L. S., 121
Beachy Bill, 130
Bedi, Lieut., 295
Belgian Field Force, 144

Bengal Mountain Battery (7th), 56, 62, 63, 64, 66, 111, 118, 135, 138, 141, 142, 143, 145, 146, 151, 152, 153, 154, 156, 210, 212, 238, 244, 249, 286, 295
Bentley, Major P. R., x
Berbera, 122, 273, 277
Bhamo, 60, 64, 65
Bhanga Singh, Subadar-Major, 107
Bhutan War, 1
Biddulph, Major-General, 44
Bijey Battery, 339, 384
Bilot, 89
Birch, Lieut. A. H. C., 62, 66, 74, 82, 90
Birch, Capt. F. H. J., 76
Birbeck, Brig. J. H., ix
Birdwood, Lieut.-General Sir William, 128, 134
Bishanpur, 363
Black Mountains, 4, 5, 32, 270
Blackwood, G. F., 36
Blaker, Brig. E. H., 277, 282
Bohotle, 122
Boileau, Colonel, 7
Bolan Pass, 38, 44
Bombay Mountain Battery (5th), 20, 37, 51, 59, 60, 66, 88, 89, 91, 92, 94, 96, 97, 101, 178, 183, 185, 188, 192, 249, 256, 260, 269, 270, 307, 308, 312, 315, 321, 368, 384, 405
Boone, Lieut. H. G., 118
Booth, Lieut.-Colonel, A. J., 339
Bowering, Lieut. J. C., 150, 155
Bozdars, 15, 16
Brady, Lieut. R. E. M., 126, 206
Brake, Lieut. H. E. J., 77
Brigades, formation of, 104
Broadfoot, Capt. A., 45, 52
Brocklebank, Major G. R., x
Brougham, Capt. T., 6, 12
Brown, Lieut., 331
Browne, Lieut.-General Sir Sam, 41
Browne, Capt. J. F., 79, 80
Brownlow, Lieut.-Colonel C. A. L., 249, 254
Bruce, Major J. E. L., 128, 131, 132, 133
Bryant, Lieut.-Colonel, ix
Bryce, Lieut., 7
Buckland, Major G. N., 126
Budé, Capt. F. R. de, 23, 24, 25, 26, 28, 35
Bukoba, 140
Bumpas, Lieut. E. H., 265
Buner Field Force, 90, 91
Bunerwals, 27, 84, 198
Burma, 1941-45, 306

Burma, 1934, 241, 263
Burma Road, 306
Burmese, 307
Burmese War, Third, 59, 66
Burma Military Police, 61, 62, 241
Burne, Major C. J. S., x, 383
Burney, Lieut. A. E. C., 219
Burrows, Lieut. M., 331
Burton, Lieut.-Colonel C. E. C., x
Burzil, 72
Bushire, 179
Buthidaung, 333, 349, 399
Butt, Lieut. F. R., 23, 24, 25, 26

"Cab Rank" air support, 388
Campaign Stars and Medals, 270
Campbell, Major E. G., 202
Campbell, Lieut. Lovatt, 281
Campbell, Lieut. K. G., 123, 126, 131, 132
Campbell, Lieut. R. M., 280, 281
Campbell, Lieut. W. M., 55
Carew, Lieut.-Colonel R. L., ix
Carey, Colonel W., 59
Carrigan, Lieut. R. W., 150
Carwithen, Lieut. S., 112
Caspian Sea, 178
Caucasus, 128, 175
Cavagnari, Major Sir Louis, 44
"Cease fire," 414
Chadwick, Brigadier E. C., ix
Chakdara, 79, 82, 83, 198
Chamberlain, Field-Marshal Sir Neville, 12, 13, 23, 24, 26, 41
Chamberlain, Capt. T. G., 265, 346, 394
Chanan Singh, Trumpeter, 187, 254
Chanda, Subadar, 133
Chanda, Subadar-Major, 108
Chaplin, Lieut.-Colonel J. B., ix, 309, 320, 364, 387, 415
Chapman, Lieut. P. C., 129, 132
Charangit Singh, 395
Charles, Capt. J., 44
Chenevix-Trench, Lieut., 294
Chindits, 368
Chindwin River, 317, 318, 359, 374
Chinese, 308
Chins, 62, 63, 64
Chitral, 77, 79, 105, 202
Chittagong, 326, 393
"Chocolate staircase," 373
Chumbi valley, 116
Chunghing, 308
Chungli, 117
Chunuk Bair, 132
Clarke, Major S., 340, 346, 394
Cock, Capt. H. C. L., 158, 165
Cocks, Major L. P., 369

459

Coke, Major, 15
Cole, Major A. F., 149
Cole, Lieut.-Colonel R. B., 342
Coleman, Capt., 291, 300, 303
Colville, Lieut.-Colonel A. M., ix, 137, 140, 141, 415
Conquerors of India, 370
Constable, Lieut.-Colonel W. G., ix, 262, 308
Constantinople, 128
Cooper, Lieut.-Colonel W. J., ix, 263
Cope, Lieut. A. R., 142
Cordon, 179
Corner, Major D. R., 330
Coronation, 1902, 101
Corrie, Capt. G. G. W., 113
Cotter, Major H. L., 158, 170
Cotton, Major-General Sir S. J., 22
Cowie, Capt. D. C. G., 286, 299, 303
Crag piquet, 28
Crawford, Lieut. A. T., 89
Croly, Major H. G., x
Crowdy, Major C. R., 151
Crowe, Brig.-General J. H. V., 139
Cruikshank, Lieut. H. A., 79, 80
Ctesiphon, 165
Cunningham, Lieut.-General A. G., 273

Dacres, Major J. C., 78
Dalai Lama, 118
Damdil, 247
D'Arcy, Major J. C., 274
Dardanelles, 128
Dardoni Mountain Battery (13th), 205, 210, 239, 246, 247, 249, 252, 321, 366
Dar-es-Salaam, 135, 147
Dargai, 92
Darwesh Khel, 24
Daulat Singh, 133
Davies, Lieut.-Colonel L. M., x, 135, 141, 142, 143, 148, 149, 252, 321, 366
Dawaris, 24
Dawson, Lieut.-Colonel P. E. R., 358, 364
Deane, Lieut.-Colonel J. A. L., x
de Brett, Lieut. H. S., 80, 81, 94
De Butts, Capt. F. R. McC, 93
Dehra Dun, 448
Dehra Dun Mountain Battery (11th), 121, 174, 182, 192, 263, 269, 339, 343, 355, 373, 374, 419
de Latour, Capt., 36, 41, 75
Delhi Durbar, 1903, 101

Depot, Mountain Artillery, 198
Dera Ghazi Khan, 15, 202
Dera Ismail Khan, 115, 123, 211
Derajat Mountain Battery (2nd), 37, 42, 45, 47, 51, 55, 71, 74, 77, 78, 91, 94, 96, 97, 111, 112, 149, 150, 151, 152, 154, 156, 227, 237, 238, 249, 263, 269, 307, 313, 317, 319, 339, 355, 416, 418
de Robeck, Brigadier J. H., 358
De Sausmarez, Brig.-General C., ix, 112, 113
Devil Regiment of Artillery (23rd), 420
Dewan Singh, Gunner, 81
Dharam Singh, Major, 149, 154
Dickenson, Lieut., 355, 357
Dimapur, 347, 350
Distribution on Partition, 424
Dodd, Major, 200
Dodds, Lieut. B. W. P., 183, 184, 185, 186
Dodoma, 145
Dost Mahomed, 41
Dowell, Major G. C., 121
Downe, Lieut. J. G., 348
Dowson, Major, 382, 409
Doyle, Lieut. J. P., 149
Draper, Lieut., 134
Draught, 177
Dress, 107
Dreyer, Lieut.-Colonel G. V., x, 125, 150, 151, 233
Drivers, endurance of, 370, 373, 416
Drivers in Gallipoli, 131
Drosh Fort, Chitral, 448
Dulip Singh, Naik, 311
Dulla Khan, Jemadar, 81, 129
Dunsterville, Brig.-General L. C., 175
Dutch, 4, 16, 418, 420
Duthy, Lieut.-Colonel A. E., 86, 91
Dutton, Major R. M. L., 125, 137, 142, 180

Eagle's Nest piquet, 27
Earle, Lieut. M., 248
East Africa, 273
East, Lieut., 75, 97
Easton, Capt. F. A., 116
Eden, Lieut., 142, 148
Edlmann, Lieut. E. E., 93, 100, 101, 158, 162
Edlmann, Major J. C., x, 241
Edmond, Lieut.-Colonel J. H., x
Education, 227
Edwards, Sir H., 9
Egerton, General Sir Charles, 111, 122, 148

Elephants, 386
Elliott, Lieut., 291
Ellis, 2/Lieut., 151
Ellis, Lieut.-Colonel R., 394
Elsworth, Capt. G. N., x
Enfield rifle, 22
English, Brigadier J. W., ix, 179, 260

Farfan, Brigadier A. J. T., ix, 126, 135, 138, 141, 254, 262
Fata, Jemadar, 115
Fateh Ali, Gunner, 90
Fateh Khan, Subadar, 362
Fattoo, Subadar Bahadur, 108
Fazal Dad, Naik, 187
Fazal Ilahi, Gunner, 134
Fawns, Capt. G. C., 253, 275
Fergie, Major A. M. S., 340, 355
Fergusson, Colonel A. C., ix, 128, 132, 133, 207, 213
Fida Hussain Shah, 354
Field, Lieut. K. D., 118
Fiskin, Major S. F., 286
Flowers, Capt. C., 174
Followers, 108
Forbes, Capt. R. M. N., 160, 162, 234
Forrester-Walker, Major C. E., 137, 141
Fort Sandeman, 209
Foul Point, 402
Fourteenth Army plan, 379, 380
Fourteenth Army re-grouping, 379
Fourteenth Army re-grouping, 1945, 404, 405
Fox, Lieut. P. B., 281
Franks, Capt. R. H., 367
French, 420
French-Indo China, 306
Frith, Capt. I., 1
Frontier Brigade, 3, 224
Frontier Youth League, 231
Fuller, Brevet Lieut.-Colonel R. W., 113
Furney, Major J. E. L., x
Futeh Din, Subadar-Major, 215

Gaba Tepi, 129
Galanai, 115
Galkayu, 122
Gallipoli, 127
Gandamak, 42, 44
Garnett, Lieut.-Colonel, x, 364
Garratt, Lieut.-Colonel L. F., x
Garrett, Major R. C., 174
Garrison Battery and Post Guns, 433
Garrock, Major-General, 28
Garry, Capt. R. V., 192, 259
George, Major A. A., 360, 362

German East Africa, 135
Grasita Singh, Gunner, 28
Ghazan Khan, Havildar-Major, 155
Gheba Khan, Gunner, 353
Ghilzais, 46
Ghulam Mahomed, Jemadar, 151, 306
Ghulam Mahomed, Subadar-Major, 107
Gian Chand, Gunner, 354
Gibraltar, 366
Gilbert, Lieut. V. J., 209, 210, 254
Gilgit, 72
Gillies, Lieut. W. B., 27
Gilmour, Lieut., 312
Gimma, 279
Godley, Major-General, 131
Gomal, River, 15
Gondar, 280
Goodman, Brigadier E. W., ix, 254
Gordon, Lieut. L. C., 74
Gorton, Lieut. R. St. G., 72
Gould, Lieut.-Colonel H. C., x
Graham, Lieut. F. W., 313
Gray, Capt., 149
Green, Lieut., 3
Greene, Brevet Lieut.-Colonel, 126
Grier, Capt. H. D., 84, 158 165
Grissee road, 419
Guidedes, 255
Gul Ahmad, Gunner, 90
Gul, Naik, 45
Gulzar Khan, Subadar, 414
Gumatti, 111
Gumburu, 122
Gunner, Lieut.-Colonel E., 101
Guns
   3-pr. smooth-bore, 8
   4.2/5-inch howitzer, 8
   7-pr. R.M.L., 30, 31
   2.5-inch—The Screw Gun, 57, 58
   10-pr. B.L., 101
   2.75, 103, 109, 152
   3.7-inch howitzer, 154, 229, 230
Gurditt Singh, Havildar, 134, 151
Gurkha guns, 116
Gurmukh Singh, Jemadar, 290
Gurmukh Singh, Pay Havildar, 28
Gurun, 296
Gwalior Mountain Battery, 431
Gyantes, 116, 118

Habib Khan, Havildar, 182
Hadda Mullah, 85
Hadfield, Major, 349, 389
Hago, 343
Haider Khan, Subadar, 184, 187
Hakim Ali, Jemadar, 361

Hakim Khan, Subadar, 316, 320
Hamilton, General Sir Ian, 128
Hamilton, Lieut. C. de C., 63
Hammond, Lieut. H., 9
Handeni, 144
Hangu, 74
Hanza, 72
Hardett Singh, Subadar-Major, 107
Hardie, Lieut.-Colonel, x
Hardy, Major H. A., x
Hare, Lieut. R. M., x
Hari Singh, Havildar, 316
Haripur, 13
Harler, Lieut., 316
Harnam Singh, Jemadar, 186, 187
Harrington, Capt. E. C., 133
Harrison, Major T. H., 340, 356, 357
Harris, Major L. A., 247, 254
Hart, Lieut. E. G., 120
Hartley, Major P., 307, 320, 340
Hartley-Ayre, Capt., 352
Hartigan, Capt. D. J., 280, 282
Haskard, Lieut. D. D., 135, 146
Hassein Khan, Jemadar, 15
Hassels-Yates, Lieut.-Colonel G. A., x, 126, 174
Hawes, 2/Lieut., 149
Hawkes, Capt. G. R., 255
Hay, Lieut. W., 9
Hayes-Sadler, Major J. H., 125
Hazara Field Force, 70
Hazara Mountain Battery (4th), 32, 36, 42, 44, 49, 55, 59, 60, 66, 72, 74, 77, 78, 97, 119, 150, 153, 156, 232, 234, 235, 238, 244, 249, 255, 286, 294
Hazara Mountain Train, 4, 14, 23
Heald, Major M., 331, 332
Heaton-Ellis, Capt. J. S., 180
Hem Singh, Subadar, 134
Henderson, Lieut. H. E., 122
Hennersey, Capt. T. F., 202
Hepper, Lieut.-Colonel J. M., 363
Hickie, Lieut., 200
Higher Standard Urdu, 98
Hill, Brigadier T. W. R., ix, 348, 399, 401
Hill, Lieut.-Colonel R. H., x, 339, 354, 399
Hill, Lieut.-Colonel R. R., x
Hill 971, 131
Hill Q, 131
Hills, Lieut.-Colonel J., V.C., 36
Hills, Capt. J., 246
Hillak, 189
Himmat, Subadar, 108
Hindustani fanatics, 21, 26, 198
Hodgson, Brigadier J. S., 9

Hohinder Singh, 340
Honner, Lieut. W. J., 60, 72
Hong Kong-Singapore Mountain Battery, 193
Honorable East India Company, 20
Honorary King's Commissions, 215
Honorary rank, 267
Horsfield, Lieut. G., 263
Hoskyn, Capt. R., 131, 132, 133
Howard, Major A. B., 340, 357, 372, 392
Howitzers, 6-inch, 218, 246
Hughes, Major G. L., 286, 299, 303, 305
Hughes, Capt. T. E., 24, 26, 28
Hull, Major G. T., 367
Hume, Major J. G. L., 308, 320
Humine track, 371
Hunt, Capt. W. M., 160, 172, 173
Hussain Mahomed, Naik, 90
Hutton, Lieut.-General T. J., 307

Iles, Lieut. H. W., 66
Imam Din, Jemadar, 90
Imphal, 306, 321, 347, 350, 358, 359, 361, 365, 371
Inaiyat Ullah, Signaller, 281
Independent tribes, 10
Inder Singh, Driver Havildar, 134
Indian Distinguished Service Medal, 108
Indian General Service Medal:
  1854-95, 115
  1895, 97
  1908, 115
  1936-39, 255, 258
Indian Mountain Artillery Brigades, 201, 262, 263
Indian Mountain Artillery Brigade:
  2nd, 183, 184, 188
  4th, 141
  7th, 170
  10th, 194
  13th, 188
  1st, 158
Indian Mountain Batteries, 222, 223, 243, 254, 259, 262, 263, 269
Indian Officers, 228
Indian Regiment of Artillery, 241, 258
Indian Sappers, 375
Indo-China, 420
Indonesias, 416
Ipi, Faqir of, 244, 246
Ipis gun, 257
Iraq, 190
Iringa, 147, 148
Ironside, Field-Marshal, Lord, 182
Irrawaddy, 60, 317, 378, 405

Isher Singh, Jemadar, 90
Ismail Khan, Havildar, 254
Ismailia, 127
Italy, 275

Jacob, General J., 16, 38
Jacobabad, 16
Jacob's Mountain Battery (6th), 37, 50, 51, 63, 65, 127, 129, 130, 131, 132, 133, 135, 170, 173, 174, 176, 185, 187, 192, 219, 260, 263, 269, 360, 364, 388
Jagat Singh, Jemadar, 152
Jagat Singh, Naik, 187
Jaggat Singh, Havildar, 177
Jalal Shah, Havildar Clerk, 306
Jalalabad, 3, 41
Jalap La, 117
Jam Mahomed, Naik, 130
Jammu Mountain Battery (31st), 325, 328, 362, 383, 430
Jandola, 199
Jansen, Lieut. I. O. S., 311, 320, 388
Japanese, 285, 301, 308, 371, 414
Jarrett, Capt. C. J. B., 403
Jask, 121
Jatsoma Box, 355
Java, 307, 416
Jawala Singh, Gunner, 81
Jeffreys, Brig.-General, 89
Jerico, 194
Jerusalem, 195
Jervois, Lieut. R. N., 42
Jhelum Mountain Battery (15th), 180, 192, 210, 213, 217, 246, 247, 249, 309, 315, 317, 318, 321, 352, 354, 367
Jidbali, 123
Jiwan, Trumpeter, 90
Johnson, Colonel A., 51
Johnston, Lieut. M. R. W., 177
Jones, Lieut., 149
Joscelyn, Lieut., 360
Jowahir Khan, Subadar-Major, 14, 108
Jowakis, 38
Jowala Singh, Subadar, 129, 134, 311, 315, 320
Jubaland, 123
Juba river, 276
Jumrud, 41
Jungle warfare, 297

Kabul, 3, 41
Kabul Khel Waziris, 23, 34, 111
Kabul river, 42
Kachins, 65
Kahe, 142
Kajuri Kach, 55, 232
Kaka Singh Subadar, 28
Kakul, 201, 226
Kaladan, 324, 396
Kaladan river, 64
Kalat-i-Ghilzai, 44
Kalemyo, 372
Kalewa, 317, 372
Kamal Singh, Naik, 154
Kampar, 298
Kandahar, 38, 44, 51
Kangaw, 399, 402
Kanga mountains, 146
Kaniguram, 25, 213
Kantara, 127, 194
Kapila, Lieut., 330
Kapur, Lieut. B. C., 330
Karachi, 127
Karam Singh, Subadar, 182
Karbala, 189
Karenji, 155
Karm Singh, Lance-Naik, 130
Karoar, 186
Karslake, Lieut.-General, 242
Kartar Singh, Jemadar, 303
Kasala, 273
Kashmir Mountain Battery, 78, 91, 101, 149, 152, 153, 156, 179, 278, 325, 425
Kashi Ram, Hospital Assistant, 90
Katara Singh, Signaller, 281
Kaye, Brigadier J. W., ix, 320
Keam Khan, Havildar, 29
Keelan, Major R. E. T., 333
Keene, Lieut. A., 101
Kelatan, 285
Kelly, Major, 381, 382
Kelso, Capt. J. A., 39, 42, 43
Kemmis-Betty, Lieut.-Colonel M. F., x, 410
Kendall, Capt. P., 357, 358, 373
Kennedy, Major A. C. S., 240, 247
Kennedy Peak, 373
Kenya, 279
Kenyon, Lieut.-Colonel H. E., x, 121, 133
Kenyon, Major J. F., x, 367
Keren, 273, 277, 278, 409
Kermanshah, 176
Kestin, Lieut. G. A., 154
Kewal Salutri, 80, 81
Keyes, Lieut.-Colonel C. P., 34, 38
Khaisora valley, 245, 246
Khan Bahadur, Lance-Naik, 254
Khan of Kalat, 38, 119
Khan Gul, Havildar-Major, 255
Khan Zaman, Jemadar, 368, 369
Kharak Singh, Subadar-Major, 107

463

Khawki valley, 75
Khombala Pass, 118
Khojak Pass, 41, 44
Khushal Singh, Jemadar, 152
Khyber Force, 42
Khyber Pass, 41, 86
Khyber Rifles, 86
Kidd, Major J. G., 255, 352, 353, 354
Kigoma, 136
Kijabe, 276
Kilimanjaro, 136
Kilwa, 151
King, Capt. H. S., 252
King's African Rifles, 135, 140
Kirby, Lieut.-Colonel H. A., x, 129, 133, 134
Kirkpatrick, Colonel, 145
Kirkut, 176, 190
Kisaki, 146
Kishen Singh, Major, 340
Kishen Singh, Gunner, 177
Kismayu, 123
Kohat, 34, 41, 448
Kohat Pass, 38
Kohat Mountain Battery, Royal (1st), 37, 42, 45, 47, 52, 53, 55, 56, 57, 74, 76, 91, 92, 93, 94, 96, 97, 111, 115, 127, 129, 131, 133, 135, 170, 173, 174, 176, 177, 192, 219, 260, 263, 268, 364, 388
Kohima, 66, 351, 355, 365, 367, 370
Kohistanis, 47, 48
Kondoa Irangi, 143
Konisberg, 140
Knight, Major J. H., 227
Kuala Lumpur, 286, 300
Kung, 114
Kurdistan, 174, 184, 185, 186
Kurram, 205
Kurram Militia, 87
Kut al Amara, 157, 166, 171, 173
Kyaikto Box, 310
Kyaukmyaung, 382

"Ladder," The, 373
Ladha, 218
Lahore, 35, 63
Lahore Mountain Battery (8th), 64, 66, 76, 82, 84, 85, 88, 89, 90, 91, 97, 113, 114, 115, 122, 123, 137, 139, 141, 143, 145, 146, 148, 149, 156, 205, 206, 219, 232, 249, 256, 269, 325, 328, 374, 383, 406
Lake Victoria, 136
Lall Chand, Naik, 352
Lal Din, Subadar-Major, 215
Lamb, Lieut. G. R., 74
Landi Kotal, 45, 112, 113, 204, 448

Landon, Lieut.-Colonel L. H., x, 150, 330, 334
Landon, Lieut. R. P., 137
Langford, Lieut., 419
Langhorne, Lieut. A. P. Y., 112
Langhorne, Lieut. J. A. D., 111
Lashio, 308
Lawrence, Sir John, 19
Laws, Lieut.-Colonel M. D. S., x
Leach, Lieut.-Colonel L. R. H. G., x, 275, 281
Ledo, 306, 377
Lettow-Vorbeck, Von, Colonel, 136
Lewis, Major-General H. A., ix
Lhasa, 117
Lickman, Capt. H. S., 217
Liddell, Major D., x
Light Aid Detachments, 415
Light Batteries, 224
Light Field Batteries No. 6, 8, 20
Light Mountain Batteries, 263
Lindsay, Lieut. C. C., 42
Lindsay, Lieut. H. A., 42
Lindsay, Major W. D., 125, 194
Lister, Lieut.-Colonel F H., x
Liuta Hill, 152
Lloyd, Major D. J., 360
Lockhart, Sir William, 91
Loder-Symonds, Brigadier R., 419
Loe Agra, 235, 237
Long, Capt., 295
Long Range Penetration Groups, 338
Loralie, 55
Low, Major G. S., 217
Lowe, Lieut., 395
Luke, Lieut.-Colonel T. M., x, 116, 207
Lukigari river, 145
Lurio river, 155
Lushais, 35, 63
Lyons, Lieut.-Colonel R. N., x

MacClellan, Lieut.-Colonel G. P., x, 191, 192, 229
MacDonald, Lieut.-Colonel H. S., 249
Macgregor, Lieut.-Colonel A., x
Mackenzie, Lieut.-Colonel H. H., x, 126, 174
Mackenzie, Major A., 394
Mackenzie, Lieut., 312
Mackeson, Lieut.-Colonel, 5
Macleod-Carey, Lieut.-Colonel C. C. M., 376
MacMunn, Lieut.-General Sir G., ix, 65, 170, 184, 451
Macpherson, Brig.-General, 42
McCaig, Major R., x

McGee, Major, 398
McGowan, Major W. H., x, 179
McIntosh, Major I. R., 287
McLeod, Brigadier R. W., ix
McNeil, Lieut. D., 9
Mad Faqir, 83, 89
Mad Mullah, 122
Madras Artillery, 25
Magh Singh, Gunner, 90
Magor, Capt., 316
Mahenge, 151
Mahomed Adalat, Capt., 411
Mahomed Alam, Havildar, 254
Mahomed Ajaib, Lance-Naik, 368
Mahomed Baksh, Jemadar, 134
Mahomed Hanif, Naik, 306
Mahomed Hussain, Jemadar, 331
Mahomed Ishaq, Driver, 306
Mahomed Ismail, Subadar-Major, 195
Mahomed Khan, 331
Mahomed Khan, Havildar-Major, 356
Mahomed Khan, Lance-Naik, 320
Mahomed Khan, Q.M.-Havildar, 305
Mahomed Sadiq, Havildar, 299
Mahomed Sarwar, Naik, 281
Mahomed Sarwar, Havildar, 306
Mahomed Sharif, Subadar, 255
Mahsuds, 24, 110, 199, 200, 210, 247, 349, 357
Maister, Lieut. G., 16, 23, 24
Maizar, 79
Majhi Khan, Gunner, 155
Majors as battery commanders, 103
Makin, 219
Maktan, 139
Malakand, 77, 79, 81, 84
Malaya, 285
Malay States Guides Mountain Battery, 432
Malhotra, Lieut., 352, 353
Malka, 26
Mallaby, Brigadier, 417
Mallinson, Lieut., 389, 407
Mall Singh, Subadar, 358
Manawar Khan, Dirver, 369
Manawar Khan, Fitter-Havildar, 192
Mandalay, 59, 306, 379, 387, 390
Mangal Singh, Driver, 112
Manipur, 66
Manners-Smith, Lieut., V.C., 74
Manning, Brig.-General W. H., 122
Mansergh, Major-General E. C. R., 339, 418
Maranzai Field Force, 74
Mardan, 21, 71, 79
Marindin, Lieut. C. C., 118

Mariner, Major E. B. L., 232
Marrett, 30
Martaban, 308
Massawa, 273, 278
Mathra Dass, Lance-Naik, 354
Maula Dad, Jemadar, 392
Maymyo, 307, 386, 448
Maymyo Mountain Battery (19th), 194, 195, 197, 249, 256, 339, 394, 399, 401, 403
Mayu peninsula, 395
Mecham, Lieut. R., 16, 23
Mechanical Transport, 198, 236, 266, 281, 286, 337
Medals and bars, 215
Mehr Khan, Gunner, 140
Meiktila, 317, 378, 387, 408
Mekran, 119
Melvin, Lieut., 364
Mem Raj, Saddler, 304
Meredith, Major J. C., 232
Mesopotamia, 156
Militia, 208
Milne, Lieut.-Colonel, W. B., x, 330, 333, 423
Minto Elliot, Capt., 32
Mirali, 449
Miranshah, 198
Miranzai, 12, 13
Mit Singh, Subadar, 131, 133
Moberly, Brigadier A. H., ix, 201, 226
Mogok, 392
Mohammerah, 159
Mohan Lal, Havildar, 353
Mohmands, 12, 86, 113, 198, 234, 237, 239, 360
Molony, Lieut., 183, 187
Mortar Batteries, 73
Mombasa, 135, 137
Money, Lieut. A. W., 74, 112
Money, Colonel G. N., 45
Montanaro, Lieut. C. A., 42, 48
Morgan, Capt. H. R. L., 45, 47, 52
Moshi, 136, 141
Mosul, 183, 187
Moulmein, 307, 308, 405, 413
Mountain Artillery Stations, 447
Mountain Artillery Training Centre, 439
Mountain Battery:
  20th, 339, 355, 356, 373, 374, 408, 419
  21st, 286, 291
  22nd, 274, 277, 280
  23rd, 307, 317, 339, 383, 385
  24th, 386
  25th, 409, 413
  26th, 376, 409, 410

Mountain Battery—*continued*:
  28th, 309, 310, 313, 319, 321, 366, 367, 377, 392
  32nd, 348, 400, 401
  33rd, 348, 396, 397
  34th, 348, 394, 399, 401, 402
  38th, 362
  40th, 187
  41st, 197
  45th, 188, 189
  47th, 188
  49th, 185, 190
  50th, 185
Mountain Regiment:
  20th, 376, 382, 409, 410, 411
  21st, 387, 388, 407, 413
  22nd, 289
  23rd, 335, 337, 407
  24th, 356, 419
  25th, 369, 371
  27th, 320
  28th, 311
  29th, 363, 376
  30th, 348, 394, 395, 399, 404
  32nd, 375
  33rd, 394, 401, 421
Mountain Trains, 3, 19, 20
Mountain Warfare School, 202
Movement of regiments and batteries, 264, 265
Moyale, 273
Msiha river, 145
Mudros, 128
Mukand Singh, Driver-Havildar, 345
Mules, 104, 147, 148, 152, 154, 156, 182, 214, 266, 286, 316, 319, 333, 367, 373, 414, 421
Mullah Powindah, 75, 110, 199
Munn, Lieut. A. G., 246
Munns, Capt. G. F. A., 368
Munsha Singh, Havildar-Major, 182
Murdock, Colonel W. W., 77
Murdun Ali, Subadar-Major, 108
Murdun Ali Shah, Jemadar, 15, 24
Murray, Lieut., 303
Murree Mountain Battery (9th), 97, 120, 123, 194, 196, 197, 198, 199, 260
Mutiny, The, 19
Mwaika, 140
Myitkyina, 65, 306
Myohaung, 398

Nablus, 195
Nadir Ali, Naik, 187
Nadir Khan, 205, 206
Nahakki, 240
Napier, General Sir Charles, 1

Napier, Lord, of Magdala, 5
Narayan Singh, Naik, 155
Narian Singh, Driver, 130
Nairobi, 138
Nasiriya, 164
Natha Singh, Gunner, 186, 187
Nawab, Jemadar, 90
Nazar Khan, Subadar-Major, 108
Nazeer Ahmed, Lieut., 337
Nettelfield, Major J., x, 358, 418, 420
Neville, Capt. G., 371
New units, 125, 201
New Zealand Corps, 128
Nhama Curra, 155
Niani, 118
Nihala, Driver, 90
Nihal Singh, Havildar, 80, 81
Nizam Din, Jemadar, 187
Nodiz, 120
North West Frontier, 197
  1919-20, 217
  1936-39, 244
Nowshera, 81, 449
Nowshera Brigade Column, 238
Nowshera Mountain Battery (17th), 191, 219, 226, 249, 253, 269, 325, 327, 333, 374
Nur Alam, Subadar-Major, 108, 140, 149, 215
Nur Hussain, Lance-Naik, 381
Nur Khan, Havildar-Major, 305, 306
Nur Mahomed, Gunner, 90
Nuttall, Lieut. D., 403
Nyangao, 153
Nyaungu, 387
Nyasaland and Rhodesia Field Force, 144

Obbia, 122
Observation ladders, 168
Ogaden Somalis, 123
O'Leary, Lieut., 134
Olivier, Major J. D., 348
Orakzais, 33, 75, 86
Order of Battle (15th Corps), 1944, 339
Order of Battle, 4th Corps, 350, 370
Order of British India, 15

Packard, Major L. H., x, 281, 282
Pack Batteries, 190, 224
Padang Besar, 292
Pahang, 285
Pahlwan Khan, Jemadar, 419
Painda Khan, Lance-Naik, 151
Painda Khan, Subadar, 241
Paine, Lieut. J. H., 119, 120
Palestine, 193

Palmer, Capt. J. W., 236
Palosin, 24
Pare mountains, 136
Parker, Lieut.-Colonel J. L., 74, 77, 78, 87, 94, 104, 127, 132, 133
Parshotam Dass, Lieut., 300, 305, 306
Parsons, Lieut.-General L. W., 115
Partition, 423
Pasae, 251
Pasni, 119
Pathan, 11
Patiala Mountain Battery, 432
Paton, Major A., 249
Pay and allowances, 214
Pear Hill, 380, 381
Pearse, Lieut. G. G., 4
Pegu, 312, 411
Peiwar Kotal, 43, 45
Pemberton, Capt. A. L., 177
Pender-Smith, Lieut. O. R., 181
Penrose, Lieut.-Colonel J., 249
Percival, Lieut.-General 286
Perowne, Brigadier L. E. C. M., 368
Perry, Major S., 149, 174
Persian Gulf, 120, 128
Persuit, 372, 374
Peshawar, 10, 21, 34, 41, 231, 232, 449
Peshawar Mountain Battery (3rd), 32, 35, 37, 49, 53, 55, 74, 81, 87, 101, 113, 158, 160, 161, 165, 166, 168, 169, 172, 173, 179, 181, 192, 199, 202, 249, 256, 269, 325, 327, 382, 406
Peshawar Mountain Train, 6, 14, 21, 23
Peskett, Lieut.-Colonel W. H., 262, 286, 387, 309
P.F.F., 9, 10, 19, 29
Peters, Lieut., Royal Signals, 304, 306
Phillips, Lieut. F. R., 115
Picton, Capt., 399
Pipe line, 338
Pokokku, 379, 380, 384
Pollock, Sir George, 3
Poole, Capt. J. W., 311
Poonch Mountain Battery (12th), 121, 194, 196, 197, 245, 246, 249, 254, 263, 269, 307, 308, 310, 312, 314, 315, 317, 318, 339, 340, 343, 356, 372, 377, 392
Porters, 340
Portuguese East Africa, 153
Pot Sangbam, 365
Potter, 2/Lieut., 151
Pratab Singh, Havildar, 320
Procter, Lieut. J., 359

Prome, 406
Pugh, Brigadier L. C. O., ix, 339, 343, 371, 384, 405, 406, 417, 418
Pulman, Tyrwhitt, Lieut., 7
Punia, Lieut. J. S., 355, 375
Punjab Garrison Battery, 75
Punjab Light Field Battery, 12, 13, 15
Punjabi Mohammedans, 127
Purdy, Lieut.-Colonel, 91

Qabala Singh, Signaller, 278
Qizil Rabat, 175
Quetta, 38, 44, 242, 449

Rajputana Mountain Battery (14th), 183, 185, 186, 188, 192, 219, 260, 263, 269, 363
Ramree island, 403
Ram Sarup, Sweeper, 369
Range Tables, 443
Rangoon, 59, 309, 312, 393, 394, 404, 412
Ranjit Singh Maharaj, 3
Rathedaung, 324, 327
Rattan Singh, Subadar-Major, 108
Raw, Lieut. W. S., 296
Rawal Pindi, 449
Rawlins, Major, 388
Rawson, Brigadier C. D., ix, 130, 132, 133, 254
Razcol, 244, 256
Razmak, 218, 246, 450
"Red Shirts," 231
Reed, Colonel C., ix
Rendall, Colonel J. F. C., ix
Reorganization, Burma, 377, 378
Repton, Major B. E. M., 348
Reunion, Mountain Artillery Veterans, 234, 451
Richey, Capt. F. W., 135
Roach, Lieut., 300
Robat, 179
Robe, Lieut. W. L., 2
Roberts, Earl, 7, 41, 42, 43, 44, 45, 47
Robertson, Brevet Lieut.-Colonel H. M. M., 235
Robertson, Lieut. R. W., 51
Robertson-Glasgow, Lieut. N., 112
Robinson, Brig.-General C. T., 160
Ross, Brig.-General, 39
Ross, Capt. R. E., 177
Rossiter, Lieut. F. N. C., 129, 134, 151, 209
Rothney, Lieut.-Colonel, 32
Rothwell, Capt. R. S., 173, 179, 180, 181, 182

Rowley-Conway, Lieut.-Colonel G. A., x, 340, 384
Royal Artillery officers, 266
Royal, title of, 216
Royal Indian Artillery Centre, 269
Rufiji, 149
Rur Singh, Driver, 81
Russians, 41, 128
Russo-Japanese War, 103
Ruwu river, 143

Sa'at Ali, Subadar, 5
Sabak, 290
Sadon, 65
Sadulla Khan, Subadar-Major, 108
Sahib Singh, Shoeing Smith, 134
Saif Ali, Havildar, 306
Saigor, 420
Salween, 241
Salt, Capt. T. H., 28
Salaita, 141
Salamaniya, 185, 191
Salvin, Capt. H. C. J., 134
Samana, 74, 87
Sandeman, Sir Robert, 38
Santa Singh, Subadar-Major, 108
Santa Singh, Subadar, 154, 155
Santok Singh, Gunner, 155
Sapooran Singh, 45
Saraghari, 87
Sardara Singh, Subadar, 310
Sari Bair, 129, 131
Sarup Singh, Jemadar, 152
Sawyer, Major E. L., x, 294, 305, 306
Scott, Major, 296, 300
Screw guns, 57, 58
Searle, Major G. H., x
Senussi, 193
Shabkadar, 85, 231
Shahur Tangi, 248
Shaiba, 161
Sham Sher Singh, Signaller, 331
Sham Singh, Lance-Naik, 197
Shan States, 306, 307
Sharaf Ali, Naik, 80, 81
Sharam Singh, Signaller-Havildar, 281
Sharon, 194
Sharpe, Lieut.-Colonel J. Y. B., x
Sharqat, 184
Shaw, Lieut. D. H., 195
Sheik Mahmud, 191, 192
Sheik, Saad, 166, 167
Shenam, 365, 366
Sheotaj, Naik, 316
Sher Ali, Amir, 41
Sher Ali, Jemadar, 148, 215

Sher Jang Khan, Lance-Naik, 255
Sher Khan, Jemadar, 181, 182
Sher Mahomed, Subadar, 254
Sher Ram, Havildar, 255
Sher Singh, Subadar, 254
Sher Singh, Havildar, 362
Sher Singh, Jemadar, 62, 82, 90, 107
Sherpur, 48
Shields, 10-pr., 127
Shiranis, 56, 209
Shiraz, 179, 180, 181
Shires, Lieut. J. C., 42, 43, 45, 48, 52, 57, 78
Shrapnel, 131
Shutargardan Pass, 45
Shwebo, 375
Signallers, 227
Sikh Wars, 3
Silchar, 66
Sims, Colonel R. J., ix, 185, 186, 187
Sind Force Mountain Train, 16
Singapore, 285, 301
Sirdar Ali, Naik, 255
Sirdar Khan, Signaller, 180
Sitana, 22
Sittang, 370, 376, 412
Sittang river, 300, 312
Slim, Field-Marshal Sir W., 314, 346, 422
Small arms, 106
Smith, Major, 353
Smith, Lieut. E. A., 42, 62, 64
Smuts, Lieut.-General J. C., 141
Snowdon, Lieut.-Colonel H. S. K., x, 126, 219
Soerabaya, 416, 419
Sohan Mountain Battery (18th), 272, 279, 281, 282
Sokoji Rao, Jemadar, 65
Somaliland, 122
Somerville, Major J. A. H. B., 125, 194
Sopper, Major G. L., x, 305
South African Expeditionary Force, 141
South East Asia Command, 337
South Waziristan Field Force, 199
Spencer, Brigadier F. F., ix
Spencer, Lieut., 388
Spingawai Pass, 43
Spinwam, 205
Spragge, Lieut.-Colonel, 91
Stallard, Lieut. S., 7
Stallard, Colonel F. S., 168
Stanbridge, Major W. J., 190
Standish, Capt., 297, 300, 305
Stevenson, Major J. H. M., x, 150, 151, 154

468

Stewart, Lieut.-General Sir D., 41, 44
Stilwell, General J., 308
Stocker, Major, 380
Streatfield, Capt., 250, 254
Strover, Lieut.-Colonel M. R., x
Suez, 127
Sultan, General, American, 377
Sultan Singh, Signaller, Lance-Naik, 316
Sunnaiyat, 169
Surat Singh, Jemadar, 269
Surat Singh, 398
Surra, 410
Survey Indian Regiment, 378
Survey Units Indian Artillery, 436
Surwan Dass, Naik, 353, 354
Suvla Bay, 131, 132
Suwara, 185, 186
Swatis, 33, 78, 84
Swinley, Capt. G., 42, 47, 48, 52, 67

Takht-i-Suleimen mountains, 55
Tancock, Major O. K., 135, 139
Tanga, 135, 136, 137
Tanganyika Lake, 135
Tank, 24, 115, 200, 210
Tank Zam, 212
Taveta, 141
Tawney, Major A. E., x
Taylor, Lieut., 364
Thackeray, Lieut. F. R., 49, 52
Thailand, 290
Thais, 307
Thom, Capt., 130, 131, 132, 133
Thomas, Major F. G. S., x, 217
Tibet, 115
Tiddim, 337, 359, 372, 373
Tirah, 70, 85
Tochi, 81, 199
Tocol, 244
Todd, Major W., x
Tombs, Lieut., 290
Tori Khel, 244, 245
Toungoo, 408
Tragbal, 72
Training Centre, 224
Trenchard, Capt., 131, 132, 133
Trench warfare, 130
Triscott, Capt. C. P., 62
Troup, Major F. C. A., 194
Tsetze fly, 143
Tunnels, the, 326, 347, 393
Turbat, 119
Turks, 127, 128, 176, 184, 193
Turner, Lieut. W. M., 118
Twiss, Lieut. F. A., 82
Tyler, Lieut. L. B., 134
Tysoe, Capt. J. R., 309

Uganda, 138
Uganda railway, 136
Ukhrul, 352, 369
Uluguru mountains, 146
Utam Chand, Naik, 81
Utman Khel, 82, 84
Utman Zai Waziris, 244

Vaughan, Major J. L., 21
Victory Parade, London, 270

Wace, Lieut. E. C., 42, 44, 50, 54, 59, 60, 62
Walidad, Subadar, 357
Walker, Lieut. F. McF., 184
Walker, Lieut. W. S. N., 241
Walsh, Major, 415
Walshe, Major F. G. W., 334
Wana, 75, 199, 208, 217, 230, 450
Waris Khan, Havildar-Major, 331
Warren, Capt., x
Wa State, 241
Wavell, General Sir A., 300, 312, 423
Waziris, 11
Waziristan, 23, 253
Waziristan Field Force, 76
1919-29, 210
Wazir Khan, Havildar-Major, 312
Webster, Lieut., 358
Welchman, Brigadier G. de V., ix, 422
White settlers, 139
Whitting, Brigadier E. le G., ix, 134
Wilberforce, Lieut.-Colonel W. H., x, 307, 310, 316
Willans, Brigadier J. H., ix, 275
Willcocks, Major-General Sir J., 111, 113
Williams, Major I. M. G., 348, 399
Williamson-Oswald, Major O. C., 104, 121
Willis, Major-General E. H., 226
Willis, Capt. C. R., 125, 181, 182
Wilson Bruce, Lieut., 281
Wilson, Major E. R. C., 125, 137, 148, 149, 183, 187, 219
Wilson, Major J. S., 416
Wilton, Lieut. J. G., 241
Wingate, Lieut.-Colonel G. F. R., 239
Wingate, Brigadier O. C., 338, 368
Witherow, Major T. M., x, 307
Woodhouse, Brig.-General J. H., 84
Wordsworth, Major R. G., 227
Worthington, Capt. W. L., 344
Wright, Lieut., 297
Wyatt, Lieut., 95, 170
Wylde, Major-General Sir A. T., 32
Wynter, Lieut. F. A., 82, 89, 90

Yakh Dand, 114
Yaks, 117
Yakub Khan, 44, 47
Yeo, Major R. C., 354, 355, 357
Younghusband, Colonel F. E., 116
Yusufzais, 4, 26, 84, 235

Zakka Khel, 111
Zhob Mountain Battery (16th), 181, 192, 231, 241, 321, 367
Zhob valley, 55
"Zipper," Operation, 416

www.ingramcontent.com/pod-product-compliance
Lightning Source LLC
Chambersburg PA
CBHW031322230426
43670CB00006B/210